*Architects
and
Builders
in
North
Carolina*

Architects and Builders in North Carolina: A History of the Practice of Building

Catherine W. Bishir

Charlotte V. Brown

Carl R. Lounsbury

Ernest H. Wood III

Research Assistance by

J. Marshall Bullock and

William B. Bushong

THE UNIVERSITY OF NORTH CAROLINA PRESS
Chapel Hill and London

The paper in this book meets the guidelines for permanence
and durability of the Committee on Production Guidelines for Book
Longevity of the Council on Library Resources.

94 93 92 91 90   5 4 3 2 1

Library of Congress Cataloging-in-Publication Data

Architects and builders in North Carolina : a history of the practice
  of building / by Catherine W. Bishir . . . [et al.] : research
  assistance by J. Marshall Bullock and William B. Bushong.
      p.   cm.
  Includes bibliographical references.
  ISBN 0-8078-1898-4 (alk. paper)
      1. Architectural practice—North Carolina.   2. Building—Practice—
  North Carolina.   3. Construction industry—North Carolina.
  4. Vernacular architecture—North Carolina.   I. Bishir, Catherine
  W.   II. Bullock, J. Marshall.   III. Bushong, William.
NA1996.A68   1990
720'.9756—dc20   89-22521
                                                         CIP

The University of North Carolina Press gratefully acknowledges
the assistance of Richard H. Jenrette, the Kellenberger
Historical Foundation, and the late Fred W. Morrison in
the publication of this book.

FOR *Gene,*
Jonathan,
John,
Caroline,
Susan,
Emily,
and Laura

Contents

Preface

OUR IDEA of writing a history of the practice of building in North Carolina began in the late 1970s. We wanted to learn more about the people and practices that stood behind the architecture each of us had been studying. In 1980 we received a research grant from the National Endowment for the Humanities to support the project. We planned to prepare one volume comprising both a history of the practice of building in North Carolina and a biographical dictionary of architects and builders active in North Carolina. The authors, research assistants, and many contributing authors prepared biographical entries with lists of works for several hundred architects and builders; new research has discovered other practitioners requiring inclusion. During the several years of research, writing, and rewriting, the scope of the project expanded beyond our original concept. Because the richness of the material, the quantity of information, and the number of noteworthy architects and builders exceeded our expectations, we decided to publish the history of building practice in a first volume and the biographical dictionary in a second volume to follow.

It is a pleasure to remember and thank the many people and institutions that have helped us, from defining the initial idea through research and writing to publication. We have benefited from their generosity, knowledge, and support in far more ways than can be described here. To say that without their help this book would have been impossible is a great understatement.

The research and much of the writing were made possible by a grant from the National Endowment for the Humanities' State and Local History Program (Grant #1919-80). Early encouragement from several people was especially vital: Robert Burns, Malcolm Call, Will Corkern, John Ellington, Brent Glass, Betty Silver Howison, Claude McKinney, Keith Morgan, William Pierson, Bryan Shawcroft, Margaret Supplee Smith, Susan Stein, Larry Tise, and Peter Wood. Cary Carson, Louise Hall, H. G. Jones, and Sydney Nathans composed an invaluable advisory committee. Colonial Williamsburg, the Historic Preservation Foundation of North Carolina, North Carolina State University Division of Student Affairs, and the

State Historic Preservation Office of the North Carolina Division of Archives and History have been supportive in important ways.

In conducting our research in national, state, and local archives and libraries, we were continually aided by the knowledgeable and generous staffs of those institutions. Not only did they help us locate material but several of them sent us references they discovered in their collections over the years. These include the staffs of the American Institute of Architects Archives, the Archives and Records Section of the North Carolina Division of Archives and History, Avery Architectural Library of Columbia University, Duke Manuscript Collection, East Carolina Manuscript Collection, Library of Congress, Metropolitan Museum of Art, Museum of Early Southern Decorative Arts, New York Public Library, North Carolina Chapter of the American Institute of Architects, North Carolina Collection, North Carolina State University Archives, the Southern Historical Collection, and the Henry Francis du Pont Winterthur Museum Library. Special thanks go to John Bivins, Barbara Cain, Robert Cain, Bruce Cheeseman, Alice Cotten, William Erwin, Frank Horton, H. G. Jones, William King, Steve Massengill, Ford Peatross, Fay Phillips, George Stevenson, Maurice Toler, Carolyn Wallace, John White, Tony Wrenn, and Maurice York.

An important source of information on North Carolina architecture is the State Historic Preservation Office of the North Carolina Division of Archives and History. In addition to providing access to thousands of site files in the Survey and Planning Branch and the published local survey books, the staff has given us substantial help. We are especially grateful to David Brook, Claudia Roberts Brown, Al Honeycutt, Davyd Foard Hood, Peter Kaplan, John Little, Ruth Little, Peter Sandbeck, Michael Southern, Douglas Swaim, Mitch Wilds, and Drucilla York. Architectural consultants and surveyors who have shared with us their knowledge and insights include Allison Black, David Black, Tom Butchko, Tom Hanchett, Kate Ohno, Laura Phillips, Gwynne Stephens, Paul Touart, and Edward Turberg.

Historians who concentrate their research in particular communities have provided us with extraordinary assistance, among them Mary Boyer, James Brawley, Joe Elmore, Mary Claire Engstrom, Elizabeth V. Moore, Dan Morrill, Elizabeth Reid Murray, Bill Reaves, Edgar Thorne, and Ray Winslow. Historians studying individual architects, builders, or topics who have been generous with their help include Jane Davies, Lynda Vestal Herzog, Leland Roth, and Michael Tomlan. We learned a great deal from architects, contractors, and builders who shared their recollections in interviews or letters, including John N. Coffey, James A. Davidson, Archie Davis, Albert Haskins, Henry Kamphoefner, Marvin Johnson, Luther Lashmit, Anthony Lord, Jesse Page, Norman Pease, James Stenhouse, Conrad Wessel, and many others listed among the interviews in the bibliography.

For special assistance on present-day architectural practices, we are grateful to Nick DeMai, Russ Edmiston, Henry McGowan, Alastair Muirhead, Rob Strickland, and Lillian Woo. Jerry Cashion, Jeffrey Crow, and William S. Powell have helped us follow the complexities of North Carolina history. Marilyn Dutton, Jan Michaels, and Elizabeth M. Nashold provided assistance in research. Edward Chappell, Dan Chartier, Willie Graham, Myrick Howard, John Larson, Nicholas Pappas, Robert St. George, Janet Seapker, William Tishler, Edward Turberg, and Mark R. Wenger have given key insights, expertise, and support along the way. All those who have contributed biographies for the forthcoming volume have enriched our understanding of building practice as well as our sense of the numbers and variety of individuals at work. Particular thanks for assistance in obtaining illustrations go to Mary Beckner, Jerry Cotten, John Green, Roger Jones, Linda Kimbrough, Mills Lane, Joy Morris, Randall Page, Glen Petty, Neville Thompson, Maurice Toler, John Woodard, and, especially, Michael Southern.

We are greatly indebted to friends who have read sections of the manuscript at various stages. In addition to members of the advisory committee cited above, these include Paul Escott, Bernard Herman, Shane O'Dea, William S. Ward, Harry Watson, and Camille Wells. Gerald Allen, Edwin Hendricks, and Dell Upton gave us valuable readings of the entire manuscript, and Kate Hutchins greatly improved the text.

At the University of North Carolina Press, we thank Matt Hodgson, Iris Tillman Hill, and our fine editor David Perry for their patient and consistent support. For help in underwriting the publication we are grateful to Richard H. Jenrette and to the Kellenberger Historical Foundation, and to John Sanders and William S. Price for their assistance.

Central to the whole project were J. Marshall Bullock and William B. Bushong, resourceful and painstaking research assistants, and Sondra Ward, splendid typist and bookkeeper. No words can begin to acknowledge sufficiently the support we have had over the years from John Bishir, Eugene Brown, Susan Lounsbury, and Laura Wood.

Catherine W. Bishir
Raleigh

Charlotte V. Brown
Raleigh

Carl R. Lounsbury
Williamsburg

Ernest H. Wood III
Austin

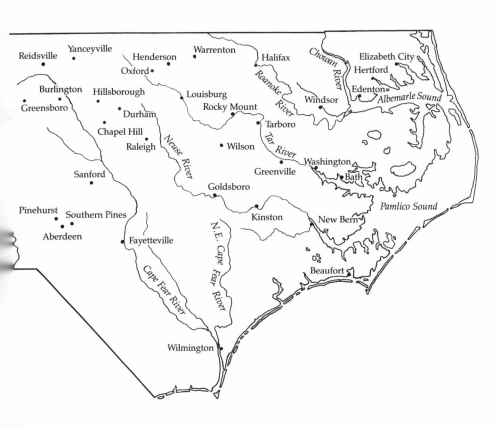

Reidsville
Yanceyville
Warrenton
Halifax
Chowan River
Elizabeth City
Henderson
Hertford
Oxford
Roanoke River
Edenton
Albemarle Sound
Burlington
Hillsborough
Louisburg
Windsor
Greensboro
Rocky Mount
Durham
Tarboro
Chapel Hill
Tar River
Raleigh
Wilson
Washington
Neuse River
Greenville
Bath
Sanford
Goldsboro
Pamlico Sound
Pinehurst
Southern Pines
Kinston
New Bern
Aberdeen
Fayetteville
N.E. Cape Fear River
Beaufort
Cape Fear River
Wilmington

*Architects
and
Builders
in
North
Carolina*

Introduction

THIS BOOK is about the people who built North Carolina's architecture. It describes how the practice of building changed from traditional craft to complex industry. Although there have been many studies of segments of the history of American building practice, this is the first work to look at the builders as a whole—artisan and architect, contractor and manufacturer, slave and free, rural and urban—and to trace the history of building practice from early settlement to the present. Rather than beginning with theory or pressing toward ultimate causes, in this study we seek mainly to tell a story in concrete and specific terms. It is a narrative that involves continuity as well as change, stability as well as conflict. And, although it suggests the outlines of the larger national picture of building practice, this is a story rooted in a single place—North Carolina—and a story that emerges directly from the personal sagas of hundreds of individuals laboring at thousands of building sites across this long-rural state.

The development of building practice in North Carolina parallels broader national and international patterns. In this state as throughout much of America and western Europe at the beginning of the nineteenth century, building, like other crafts, reflected technologies and work hierarchies that had been familiar for centuries. Construction was the domain of the independent artisan or the master artisan with a small shop of journeymen and apprentices. Whether a carpenter or a bricklayer, the artisan dominated construction from beginning to end: he worked directly with clients to plan buildings, he spent hundreds of hours of skilled labor fabricating building materials from timber or clay, and he assembled the parts he made into a finished building.

During the nineteenth century, roles and methods that had served for centuries changed forever. The development of steam-powered mass production and a network of rail lines revolutionized the production of building materials, reduced or eliminated the demand for skilled labor in fabricating building parts, and transformed the role of the artisan from maker to assembler of parts. Thus, if he lived a long and healthy life, a workman born about 1800 would have launched his career when master carpenters ruled the building industry, worked as a mature builder during

1

a time when new machines began to produce materials at astonishing speeds, and ended his working life in an age when contractors, manufacturers, and architects had assumed leadership of the building industry. Between 1800 and 1900, and especially in the half-century from 1840 to 1890, a series of sweeping and unprecedented developments—the expansion of industrial capitalism, the development of steam-powered mass production, the reorganization of workshops into employer-employee firms, the rise of large-scale contractors and manufacturers, and the separation of the professions from the trades—combined to reshape the practice of building and to redefine the role of every participant.

Various segments of the history of building practice have gained scholarly attention. There is a long, full tradition of British building history, which provides essential background for the study of American practice. M. S. Briggs's *Architect in History*, Frank Jenkins's *Architect and Patron*, and C. G. Powell's *An Economic History of the British Building Industry, 1815–1879* are among the many works that permit comparison between British and American developments. A still broader western European context is provided in Richard Goldthwaite's *Building of Renaissance Florence: An Economic and Social History*.[1] Several studies illuminate aspects of American building practice. Colonial carpenters and joiners of New England have received intensive study, best exemplified by Abbott Lowell Cummings's *Framed Houses of Massachusetts Bay, 1625–1725*. Henry Glassie's *Folk Housing in Middle Virginia* and others have analyzed the conceptual processes used by traditional builders. Ian Quimby's *Apprenticeship in Colonial Philadelphia* is one of several studies of traditional training adapted to American conditions.[2] Although seldom treating building workmen separately, many social and labor historians have examined the activities and situations of artisans and workingmen. Richard B. Morris's *Government and Labor in Early America* and Susan E. Hirsch's *Roots of the American Working Class: The Industrialization of Crafts in Newark, 1800–1860* are among the many analyses of American workmen in national or local settings.[3] Relatively few studies have focused specifically on the construction process in America. A historical perspective is begun by the essays in *Building Early America: Contributions toward the History of a Great Industry*, edited by Charles E. Peterson, while Tracy Kidder's *House* offers a microcosmic study of the dynamics among architect, client, and builder during a single late-twentieth-century project. Builders' efforts to control their status are discussed in such works as Louise M. Hall's "Artificer to Architect in America," Mark Erlich's *With Our Hands: The Story of Carpenters in Massachusetts*, Dell Upton's "Pattern Books and Professionalism," and Spiro Kostof's *The Architect: Chapters in the History of the Profession*. Yet each of these studies treats only one segment or period of American building history; none depicts the overall development of building practice.

From the outset of our research, we wanted to look at building and builders from a broad perspective. We hoped to learn how builders in North Carolina had made the gradual and profound transitions from individual craftsmen working at isolated colonial farmsteads to the huge construction industry and carefully self-regulated architectural profession of today. We believed that developments in technology, architectural style, social and economic status, training, and definition of work roles were not separate events but interwoven parts of a larger pattern. Likewise, we believed that artisans and architects, manufacturers and contractors were all participants in a single drama. Not only did they all contend with events that swept through the whole industry, and not only did the roles and actions of one group affect the other, but individuals in each type of practice knew each other, worked on the same buildings, competed with each other, faced common concerns or caused one another problems, negotiated with the same clients, and, in many cases, moved from one role to another.

We also believed that the story must be told in terms of particulars— of a particular place and particular people. For, though it has shared in broader patterns, building in North Carolina has also developed in ways that reflect the specific character of the state. From earliest settlement, geographical barriers limited the accumulation of wealth and the growth of cities. As an agrarian society evolved, the absence of metropolitan culture or lavish fortunes engendered a conservative, rural mentality, wary of change, local in outlook, and distrustful of extravagance. Even after the state became more prosperous and its towns grew into small cities, these values persisted, shaping the life and work of every North Carolina builder.

Our understanding of the interaction of the state's history and its building practice draws on several recent studies. *The Way We Lived in North Carolina*, a series edited by Sydney Nathans, illuminates the complexities of class and race, conservatism and progressivism from early settlement through the mid-twentieth century. Close attention is paid to the interplay of economic and social values in works on two eras: Roger Ekirch examines the impact of relative poverty on the formation of values in the colonial era in *"Poor Carolina,"* and Paul Escott explores nineteenth-century class conflict in *Many Excellent People*. These studies complement such enduring works as Guion Griffis Johnson's *Ante-Bellum North Carolina: A Social History*, H. Roy Merrens's *Colonial North Carolina in the Eighteenth Century*, and the state histories of William S. Powell and Hugh Talmage Lefler and Albert Ray Newsome.

In contrast to many states, however, the literature on North Carolina's labor history, economic history, and recent social history is sparse. We became acutely aware of the absence of any substantial labor history of the state outside of studies of the textile industry. Historically, workers in the building trades have constituted one of the most numerous occupation groups in the state. For example, in 1850, the first year that census figures listed occupations, the state's 2,474 free carpenters ranked third among occupations of the free male population, with only farmers and laborers being more numerous. In the next century, the pattern continued: by 1980, nearly 120,000 North Carolinians worked in construction, second only to textile manufacturing among non-farm workers.[4] Perhaps because builders are so mobile and their work sites are so dispersed, and because they span class groups from laborer to skilled artisan to white-collar professional and entrepreneur, members of the building industry have not gained the scholarly attention that has been focused on factory workers. We hope that this study will bring attention to a group that will be part of future labor histories of the state.

Local studies of North Carolina architecture, on the other hand, abound: especially valuable are the more than thirty architectural survey publications cited in the bibliography. These reflect the painstaking field-work and documentary research of architectural historians who have conducted historic sites surveys as part of the ongoing architectural survey directed by the North Carolina State Historic Preservation Office. They perform the crucial work of identifying and recording thousands of buildings and, in many cases, connecting a builder or architect to a specific work. Broader studies of the state's architecture include Frances Benjamin Johnston and Thomas Tileston Waterman's path-breaking volume, *The Early Architecture of North Carolina*, and *Carolina Dwelling*, edited by Douglas Swaim.

Along with being rooted in place, the history of building is the story of individual lives and personalities. Throughout our research, we found that however fragmentary and scattered the evidence of individuals' thoughts and actions and however elusive the links between given individuals and specific buildings, it was the powerful energy and eccentricities of individual human beings that surfaced again and again. Although they gave shape to and embodied the larger patterns of their times, these workers were not merely representative types but insistently real people. Competent and incompetent, rich and poor, black and white, slave and free, they were agreeable and grouchy, cautious and adventurous, drunk and sober, lazy and industrious, content with their lot and itching for change, lucky and unlucky. Moreover, the course of building practice and the character of buildings were influenced not only by overriding economic, technological, and stylistic developments, but also by such personal factors as family connections, friendships, personality conflicts, illness, and chance meetings, which brought builders jobs, created or ended partnerships, and stopped or started major projects. Thus, while tracing the outlines of large trends, we also hope to relate the history of building practice in terms that are faithful to the words and actions of these individuals.

Every individual who ever worked in building shared certain common ground. Whatever the changes through time, at the heart of every building project is the relationship between the builder or builders and the client. Whether that relationship be between the traditional house carpenter erecting a dwelling for a neighbor, the academically trained architect pushing a wealthy client toward more adventurous ideas, the twentieth-century developer creating suburbs for a market clientele, always the two parties must deal with one another on some terms, either face-to-face or through the vehicle of the market.

Within the builder-client relationship a few fundamental issues are always present: the process of conceptualizing and designing the building; the assignment of financial responsibility for construction; the making, transporting, and assembly of building materials; and the organization and supervision of workers. How these fundamental issues of design, money, materials, and labor are organized is central to the relationship between client and builder. Control over these issues defines the role of each participant in building.

Historically, two common arrangements have dominated construction. The most basic approach is for people to build their own buildings. The owner or user of the building decides and does everything, perhaps getting assistance from neighbors or hiring a helper. Client and builder are one. This approach reaches back for centuries beyond memory and persists today among farmers and do-it-yourselfers. Also rooted in the distant past is the two-party division of responsibility between client and artisan. The client engages in a direct relationship with individual carpenters, stonemasons, or bricklayers, usually hiring artisans separately to do the work of their trade and overseeing the project himself.

In the late eighteenth and early nineteenth centuries, two new modes of building developed that have come to dominate the industry in the twentieth century. In the contract mode of building, control within the two-party relationship is shifted to the builder who assumes full responsibility for producing a finished building for a set sum of money—either by agreement with a client or on speculation for a market clientele. In the professional mode, still another pattern appears when the client assigns authority over design to a third party—an architect or engineer. The resulting triangular relationship among client, architect, and builder creates its own questions of control and status within the building process.

Tensions and conflict are natural in every building project. The parties dicker over what each building is to be, how much it will cost, what each of them will do, and when the work will be done and paid for. Conflict intensifies when roles begin to change—when one party seizes opportunities to take greater control of the building process, thereby making a greater profit and assuming a new status within the industry, and when others see their roles, and hence their livelihoods, threatened. Thus the history of building practice is the story of how different members of the building industry have sought to control, expand, and defend their own roles. Each artisan, contractor, and architect knows that his place within this process ultimately shapes his role in society, grants him opportunities to succeed or fail, and defines the extent to which he shapes the architectural landscape of his time.

The relationship between builder and client; the handling of design, money, materials, and labor; and the tensions over control and status within the building process—these threads run through the three centuries of building practice encompassed in this study. The story is organized into seven chronologically arranged chapters. Chapter 1, "The Plague of Building," examines the transfer and adaptation of English building traditions to the new frontier of North Carolina's proprietary period (1650–1730). Although nearly all the buildings from this unsettled era have vanished, documents survive to demonstrate that the practices established in these years formed the basis for future development. The second chapter, "A Proper Good Nice and Workmanlike Manner," analyzes traditional artisan practice from 1730 to 1830, particularly the challenges faced by artisans in a rural slave society, and also touches on the first professional architects practicing in North Carolina. The third chapter, "A Spirit of Improvement," explores changes in practice from 1830 to 1860, the interrelated innovations in architectural style, the growth of the architectural profession, the rise of the large-scale contractor, and organized actions by building tradesmen who had begun to see their interests as separate from those of capital.

"The Wild Melody of Steam," Chapter 4, is a transitional chapter, reaching across periods to analyze a pivotal development—the nineteenth-century industrialization of building parts manufacture. Chapter 5, "The Advance in Industrial Enterprise," treats the post–Civil War era, when builders and architects renegotiated roles and relationships amid the turbulent, fast-moving changes of the industrializing, urbanizing New South. In the early twentieth century, as the sixth chapter, "The Day of the Great Cities," relates, North Carolina's first generation of professionally trained resident architects and a new breed of general contractors established themselves in the state. Throughout an era of boom, bust, and war, they sought new ways of controlling their place in the building process through organization, licensing, and education. The final chapter, "The Opportunities Are Unlimited," brings the story from 1945 to the present; it begins with the optimism and fierce stylistic debates of the postwar era and traces the far-reaching impact of the Agricultural Extension Department, the self-imposed exclusivity of the architectural profession, the rise of homebuilders and mobile home manufacturers, and the dizzying explosion of scale and diversity in the building industry as a whole.

Throughout the narrative, while we have necessarily emphasized patterns of change, we have also sought to stress the importance of continuity. In North Carolina as elsewhere, the aspects of building practice that resisted or withstood changing times are as significant as those that embraced innovation. While changes in building practice have come quickly in some locales or aspects of work, in other areas old ways have persisted. Building has responded differently than most industries to mechanization. Though most building materials today are standardized and mass-produced, construction itself remains site-specific and labor-intensive. With the exception of the factory-made mobile home, each building project draws a team of workmen to the construction site. Prefabricated steel beams and mass-produced roof trusses must still be put together. Thus, despite sweeping changes, an observer of the building industry in 1790 and one in 1990 would find continuities long lost in most American industries. From ranch house to skyscraper to nuclear reactor, every building site teems with workers—steelworkers, cement finishers, crane operators, plumbers, electricians, and sheetrockers; architects, contractors, and supervisors; and carpenters, bricklayers, stonemasons, and laborers. Familiar colleagues or strangers to one another, they come to a place to make a building; they work together for a long or short time in sequenced phases; and as their tasks are done they disperse to other sites. When their work is finished, a new building stands on the earth.

Change has also been uneven. Unlike many industries where new methods quickly supplant old ones, building continues along many different tracks at the same time. Where cities or rail lines created a sufficient market for mass-produced building materials, the industrial revolution quickly altered the way building materials were manufactured. Yet in remote communities and on farmsteads where cash was short and labor cheap, hand manufacture continued well into the twentieth century. Similarly, while professionally trained architects and engineers have taken charge of designing complex and sophisticated buildings for wealthy individuals and corporate clients, most citizens still look to builders—whether traditional artisans or the new breed of homebuilders—to design as well as construct their houses. And today, when large architectural firms and corporate construction firms dominate the fast-growing urban regions of the state, the independent carpenter still loads his tools in his pickup truck and winds along familiar country roads to meet the building needs of his neighbors. Yet, diverse as they are, all these builders share a common experience with one another and with generations past—that of trying to make a living at building, building in and for a state eternally ambivalent about change, a state intent on stability, evasive of conflict, and eager to make money yet wary of spending it. The practice of building in North Carolina continues to be, as it has been for over three centuries, part of the daily unspoken accommodation of paradox in a state "mighty proud of not being proud."

Carl R. Lounsbury

1

The Plague of
Building:
Construction
Practices on the
Frontier, 1650–1730

*I have been at great charges and trouble in
endeavoring to get my house fit to live in.*
—*Rev. John Urmston, 1711*

Introduction

THE PRACTICE of building in proprietary North Carolina was wrought from
a fusion of English custom and the needs of a thinly settled agrarian
society. The early settlers who immigrated to the Albemarle in the last half
of the seventeenth century inherited the terminology of English building
but often applied it to describe novel circumstances and methods that
were alien to English ways. The first carpenters, bricklayers, and glaziers
thought of themselves as English craftsmen, worked with English-made
tools, and trained their apprentices in a system whose form had developed in England's distant medieval past. The preparation of materials,
whether the molding of bricks or the shaping of timbers, varied little from
contemporary English practices.

Yet environmental, economic, and social conditions promoted experimentation and impermanent building methods. A heavily wooded landscape led to the use of timber almost to the exclusion of other materials.
The absence of lime deposits and stone narrowed the choice of building
materials and methods. A hot and humid climate fostered the development of open porches, breezeways, and detached kitchens. The many
streams and rivers, which cut through the forested terrain and provided
colonists with their principal transportation system, affected the placement and orientation of houses and outbuildings. The absence of large
towns coupled with the frontier conditions of this geographically isolated
and thinly populated colony made it difficult to sustain the practices of
highly skilled and specialized craftsmen. Many poor colonists could not
afford carpenters, joiners, and bricklayers while frontier settlers could

rarely secure their services. This encouraged the use of log construction and other methods that were less dependent on skilled builders. Trade and supply networks developed slowly, making it difficult to procure manufactured items. Faced with shortages and the high cost of items such as nails, hardware, and glass, builders developed alternative solutions that reduced their dependence on outside materials. Such forces as these transformed English ways of building into a new building tradition.

The Anglo-American practices of building reflected the level of material progress as the colony advanced from the dispersed frontier settlements of the 1660s to the beginnings of the more structured society with a diversified agrarian economy of the 1730s. Building practices during this seventy-five-year period varied to accommodate the diverse needs and capacities of a population of a few prosperous planters and merchants and a vast body of small farmers, landless laborers, indentured servants, and slaves. In some areas and among many inhabitants, building required only a few semiskilled laborers who, by using a few hand tools, could roughly fashion the primary building material, timber, into a structurally simple, unadorned building. The replacement of impermanent buildings with more permanent ones spurred the growth of specialized building trades. With well-framed houses came other signs of rising status and permanence such as brick chimneys, window glass, hardware, and planed, paneled, and molded woodwork. These features required the investment of money, the employment of trained artisans versatile in the use of specialized tools, and the organization of systems of supply that could furnish manufactured materials produced outside the immediate area or colony. Although building practices in most areas continued in the simplest mode, by the end of the proprietary period there was a tendency toward increasing sophistication and specialization in the fabrication of building materials as well as a growing division of labor on the building site in towns in the older Albemarle counties of the northeast.

Early Settlement

For much of their history, North Carolinians have struggled to overcome the geographic isolation imposed by a treacherous coastline. Finding no natural harbors or navigable rivers that flowed unencumbered into the ocean, early European explorers regarded the land lying between Cape Henry and Cape Fear as impenetrable. A narrow but shifting barrier of sand banks broken only by shallow inlets impeded access to the mainland by water. Since this coastal terrain hindered direct overseas immigration, the first colonial settlements of North Carolina consisted chiefly of people from the Chesapeake.

Between 1650 and 1675, the allure of fertile new lands, animal furs, and trade with the Indians attracted many Anglo-American adventurers

Settlement in eastern North Carolina at the end of the proprietary period. Edward Moseley map of 1733. From W. P. Cumming, *North Carolina in Maps* (Raleigh: State Department of Archives and History, 1966), plate 6. (Colonial Williamsburg Foundation.)

and settlers from the lower tidewater counties of Virginia to the southern frontier wilderness bordering the Albemarle Sound. These early settlements "to the Southward" represented the frontier expansion of a Chesapeake society dominated by the staple production of tobacco.[1] In 1663 Charles II issued a charter to eight of his supporters establishing the Albemarle and the unsettled territory further south as the proprietary colony of Carolina.[2] By 1675 perhaps four thousand people had settled in isolated farmsteads along the north shore of the Albemarle Sound and on both sides of the Chowan River.[3] At the beginning of the eighteenth century, settlement extended southward from the Albemarle into the Pamlico and Neuse river basins. After the defeat of the Tuscarora Indians in 1713, the lower coast and the vast Cape Fear Valley opened to settlement.[4]

Typical of many frontiers, the colony attracted a large number of settlers of small means who were drawn by the possibilities of cheap, new, fertile land. Many who had completed or escaped indentured service in Virginia or Maryland sought fresh opportunities in the Albemarle and later the Pamlico frontiers. Unable to purchase choice tracts of land along waterways, such men frequently squatted on unclaimed lands or settled in the inaccessible backwoods, establishing small farmsteads or living off the forest. Men of substance in the Chesapeake felt that Carolina, and particularly the fringes of settlement, was the province of "rude and desperate" men, the "sinke of America, the Refuge of our Renagadoes."[5]

Residents also acknowledged the relative poverty of the colony. The vestry of St. Paul's Parish in Chowan Precinct—the principal parish in North Carolina in 1714—reported that "we have a large parish with many poor inhabitants and those seated at a great distance from each other."[6] Such individuals either eked out a living on their small plots or hired themselves out to the few large tobacco planters as field laborers. When laborer George Branch died in 1695, he left little more than a ragged suit of clothes and a few debts—an estate valued at less than three pounds.[7] Similarly, in 1728 when William Byrd and a party of surveyors visited the farm of Cornelius Keith "who liv'd rather in a Penn than a House, with his Wife and 6 Children," Byrd recorded, "I never beheld such a scene of Poverty . . . the Hovel they lay in had no Roofe to cover those wretches from the Injurys of the Weather: but when it rain'd, or was colder than Ordinary, the whole Family took refuge in a Fodder Stack . . . the man can read & write very well . . . yet is poorer than any Highland-Scot, or Bog-trotting Irishman."[8] This account of the Keith family dwelling illustrates the primitive living conditions of the colony's poor and the impermanent nature of much of North Carolina's first generations of architecture. Such poverty, however, was not confined to the Albemarle but existed in the Chesapeake as well, for people throughout the southern colonies who did not establish their own households and farm their own land accumulated little wealth even after long years of labor.[9]

Despite the introduction of the production of tobacco by the first settlers, the colony never developed an overweening dependence upon a single cash crop. Instead, there emerged an economy of small subsistence farms coupled with the modest export of forest products. Tobacco required the possession of slave or indentured labor and good shipping outlets. North Carolina's sand barriers limited the direct supply of laborers from England or the Caribbean, reduced the importation of essential commodities that had sustained the growth of the Chesapeake economy, and retarded direct export of the crop from most plantations.[10] Some Albemarle planters paid high freight rates to transport tobacco to Virginia ports, but in 1679 the Virginia assembly sought to suppress even this outlet by forbidding the shipping of tobacco from Carolina through Virginia ports.[11] In the meantime, few Carolina planters could compete with the main tobacco-growing regions in the Chesapeake, and fewer still grew wealthy solely from the cultivation of the staple. Thus, despite the region's fertility, settlers found that "for want of Navigation and Commerce, the best Estate affords little more than a coarse Subsistence."[12] Instead of becoming a society dominated by a few wealthy tobacco planters controlling an indentured or slave labor force, proprietary Carolina developed into a society of small landowning farmers and poor, landless laborers.[13]

A patchwork of deciduous and pine forests, tidal marshes, cypress and juniper swamps, and fertile river valleys, interspersed with clearings of arable land planted with corn and tobacco, formed the landscape of the early Albemarle settlement. The small farmstead, lying along any one of the numerous creeks and rivers that flowed into the Albemarle Sound, remained the predominant agricultural unit through the proprietary period, which ended in 1729 when most of the colony reverted to the Crown. More than two-thirds of these small farms were tended by family members without the aid of slave or servant labor.[14] On no more than a few hundred acres, the Albemarle farmer mixed subsistence farming with a money crop such as tobacco, corn, or wheat and supplemented his family's diet and income by raising cattle and hogs.

Thomas Luten's plantation at Sandy Point in Chowan Precinct probably typified many Albemarle farmsteads. In the early 1720s it consisted of "one manor house, one kitchen, one barne, one stable, one garden, one orchard, thirty acres of arable plow land, seventeen acres of meadow land, seventy acres of pasture land, and 320 acres of woodland amounting to 440 acres."[15] The relatively small acreage under plow was not unusual. The labor demands of tobacco and corn limited cultivation to a few acres per hand. Because of this, woodland comprised a substantial part of a plantation even in long-settled areas. Many of these woodlands supplied farmers with an added source of income through the production of naval stores and the manufacture of shingles and barrel staves.

Surrounded by forests, the isolated farms often presented an unkempt appearance to travelers such as William Byrd of Westover who found few "Tokens of Husbandry or Improvement" among the plantations of the Carolina backwoods.[16] Settlers allowed their livestock to forage freely in the woods, so that fences were few, serving to enclose crops and domestic yards. In clearing their fields, farmers left tree stumps to decay on their own. Because most early settlers invested their time and labor in tending their crops, they generally expended little effort on the construction and maintenance of their houses and farm buildings. Repeatedly, writers of the time praised the natural fertility of the soil but condemned the lack of productivity of the colony, which they attributed to the indolence of the inhabitants. North Carolinians were "such improvident People, who take no thought for the Morrow," William Byrd argued, that they "save themselves the Trouble to make Improvements that will not pay them for several Years to come."[17] Anglican minister William Gordon believed the colony fully "capable of better things were it not overrun with sloth and poverty."[18] Such comments typified many observers of North Carolina's economic development who saw little value in the "coarse subsistence" the fertile colony provided to so many and bemoaned the slow development of major cash crops and commerce.

Buildings

The early architecture of North Carolina followed the patterns established by an English vernacular building tradition modified by the conditions of proprietary society. Given the frontier character of the colony for its first seventy-five years of settlement and the difficulties of accumulating wealth, it is not surprising that so few buildings survive from that era. Indeed, very little material evidence remains of the society that emerged in the late seventeenth century in northeastern North Carolina. Modern roads occasionally trace the routes of old trading paths and some property lines follow the boundaries of ancient farmsteads, but the buildings from the first two generations of settlement have long since disappeared. This absence of early buildings contrasts with the earlier settled regions in New England and the Delaware Valley but repeats patterns seen in the Chesapeake colonies of Virginia and Maryland where fewer than a handful of late-seventeenth-century buildings remain.[19]

Scattered about the eastern part of the state are barely a handful of brick and frame buildings that may date from the 1720s and 1730s. Buildings such as the small, Flemish-bond, brick Newbold-White House in Perquimans County or the two-story, framed Cupola House in Edenton represent the highest achievement in building of the period but are far from typical of the dwellings most inhabitants built.[20] Until systematic archaeological work is undertaken at settlement sites in the Albemarle, contemporary written sources and archaeological evidence from the nearby Chesapeake will remain the principal sources for the study of early building practices in the area.

Seventeenth- and eighteenth-century archaeological sites in Virginia and Maryland have revealed a variety of ways in which English colonists adapted old building traditions to New World conditions. Like their contemporaries in New England and the Delaware Valley, Chesapeake settlers drew on a wide range of techniques and forms common to English and continental builders and chose those which suited the climate, materials, and way of life in their particular place. Southern colonists commonly erected "earthfast" wooden buildings—whose lower framing members

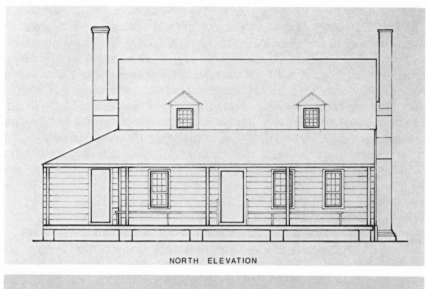

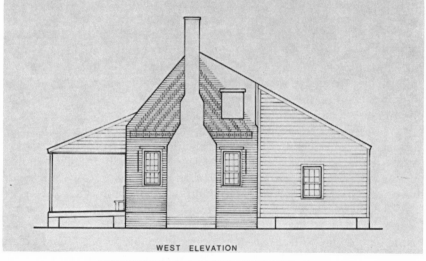

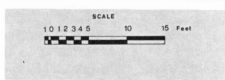

Sutton-Newby House, Perquimans County, second quarter of the eighteenth century with nineteenth-century additions. (Drawing, author, 1976.)

either sat directly on the ground or were embedded in post holes or shallow trenches.[21] Many of these earthfast structures were constructed with their posts, the principal vertical framing members, anchored three or four feet in the ground and secured at the eaves by wall plates. Above the plates and structurally independent of the wall frame rested a roof frame composed of a series of common rafters. A covering of four- or five-foot-long riven clapboards provided structural rigidity for the wall and roof frames. This relatively light and simplified structural system contrasted with the English (and New England) tradition of building a complex, heavy, box frame and roofing system, which required no exterior cladding for structural support.

By the late seventeenth century, this simplified framing system had become the predominant construction method in the Chesapeake. Such a building differed so markedly from any contemporary English type that it became known among the colonists as a "Virginia house."[22] It required less carpentry since it reduced or eliminated many of the complicated joints that secured a traditional English box frame. Chesapeake builders eschewed many standard English practices such as tying the principal rafter trusses into the wall posts and mortising those posts into raised sills.[23] Rather than spend long hours sawing lumber, these carpenters adopted less precise but much faster methods of fabrication. They rived logs into shingles and clapboards and hewed principal framing members into smaller-than-customary English sizes. The omission of sills in many buildings also eliminated the need for wooden floors and further reduced the amount of time artisans labored on a site.

With these cheaper methods of construction, however, colonial settlers sacrificed durability. Earthfast structures—subject to dry rot and insects—fell into disrepair and decay faster than solidly framed buildings resting on masonry foundations. Though patching and repairing might have prolonged their usefulness, few survived longer than a few decades.

This simple and economical framing system that minimized joinery suited the needs of the Chesapeake economy and, presumably, the Albemarle frontier far better than demanding techniques that offered greater permanence. Abundant timber made wood extremely cheap, but labor costs were high due to the scarcity of carpenters, joiners, and sawyers. In 1687, Virginia merchant and planter William Fitzhugh of Stafford County summarized the experience of many by advising an English friend contemplating settlement in the Chesapeake to "build an ordinary Virginia house" and warned him not "to build either a great, or English framed house, for labour is to intolerably deer, & workmen so idle & negligent that the building of a good house, to you there will seem insupportable." Fitzhugh had found that labor was so costly that "when I built my own house & agreed as cheap as I could with workmen, & as carefully & as diligently took care that they followed their work notwithstanding we

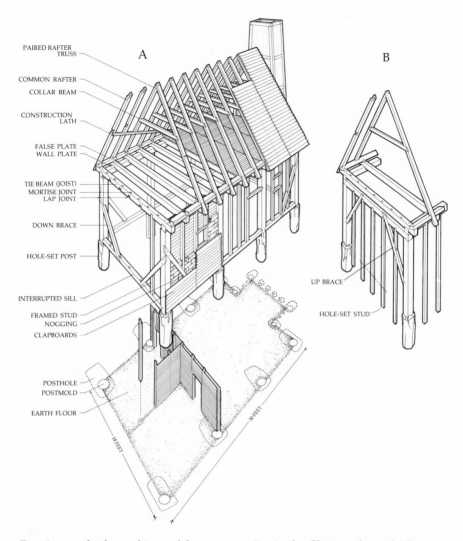

Framing methods used in earthfast construction in the Chesapeake and Albemarle in the seventeenth and eighteenth centuries. A: posts in the ground with interrupted sills. B: posts and studs in the ground, no sills. (Drawing, Cary Carson and Chinh Hoang, from *Winterthur Portfolio* 16, nos. 2/3 [summer/autumn 1981]: 143.)

have timber for nothing but felling & getting timber in place, the frame of my house stood me in more money . . . than a frame of the same Dimensions would cost in London, by a third at least where every thing is bought, & near three times as long preparing."[24]

Although Chesapeake immigrants like Fitzhugh recognized the inferiority of post construction, they also acknowledged that it was generally beyond "our ability . . . to build stronger" than "a house after the forme of a Virginia house."[25] What they settled for was a one-story, clapboard-covered, earthfast building with gable-end chimneys and either a one-room (hall) or two-room (hall and parlor) plan. It was this house type that the seventeenth-century settlers brought south with them into the Albemarle frontier. In terms of plan configuration, use of materials, and framing methods, the Virginia house became the source from which later house types developed in the eastern part of the colony.

Complementing the archaeological evidence, the fragmentary records of the period offer a tenuous guide to building practices and housing standards. An alternative to frame construction was log building—the stacking of logs or sawn planks on top of one another. By the end of the proprietary period, it had become popular in the poorer settlements of the backwoods since it was an expedient and cheap form of building. Although not a traditional English building method, log construction appeared in the Chesapeake colonies by the 1650s and the Albemarle by the 1670s probably as a natural response to the abundance of timber and the ease by which noncraftsmen in a labor-starved society could master its techniques.[26] As in frame construction, the degree of workmanship and permanence in log building varied greatly. If a degree of strength and security was required for a building such as a prison or storehouse, logs were carefully shaped to fit tightly. In the 1680s a carpenter spent more than a month constructing a log structure, later described in 1709 as built in the manner "such as the Swedes in America . . . make, and are [sic] very strong," for use as a storehouse on Governor Sothel's plantation.[27] Log buildings also appealed to those who wanted to erect a simple shelter since a structure of unhewn logs, roughly notched at the ends, could be fashioned with only a few tools or skills. The prevalence of log building in eastern North Carolina during the proprietary period is difficult to judge, but it appears to have been fairly common in remote regions where few craftsmen plied their trade. In the sparsely settled land along the Virginia border, William Byrd noted that "most of the Houses in this part of the Country are Log-houses, covered with Pine or Cypress shingles." When he visited one of these log houses a few years later he observed that it was so poorly built that it afforded "a very free passage of the air through every part of it."[28]

The difficulty of building in a remote and poor colony, where a few thousand settlers were dispersed over several hundred miles, ensured that the scale of architecture in proprietary North Carolina would remain modest. The earliest houses were small, seldom larger than two rooms and a loft. Most were one room and measured between twelve and twenty feet in width and from fifteen to forty feet in length. In the mid-1650s, the colony's first known settler, Indian trader Nathaniel Batts, lived near the Roanoke River in a house "20 foote square with a lodging chamber, and a Buttery, and a chimney."[29] At the other end of the Albemarle Sound, Peter Carteret found on his arrival at Colleton Island in 1665 "a 20 foot dwelling howse" of simple frame construction.[30] Within small houses such as these, resembling contemporary buildings in the Chesapeake, inhabitants cooked and ate their meals, performed domestic chores, entertained their friends and neighbors, and slept.

The one-room house remained the predominant type of dwelling built by North Carolinians through the eighteenth century, especially on the expanding frontier, where travelers regularly complained of primitive housing conditions. In a survey of the North Carolina–Virginia border in 1710, for example, commissioner Philip Ludwell objected to spending a night in "a wretched kennell of a loghouse where one could hardly have our length and breadth."[31] Two decades later, on another border survey, Col. William Byrd's party lodged at the "castel" of a Captain Embry that consisted of "one Dirty Room, with a dragging Door to it that will neither Open nor Shut." In this room, where Embry and his guests cooked, ate, exchanged news, and slept, Byrd was "oblig'd to Lodge very Sociably in the Same Apartment with the Family, where, reckoning Women and Children, we muster'd in all no less than Nine Persons, who all pigg'd loveingly together."[32]

Crudely worked framed and log buildings offered a relatively inexpensive solution to the housing needs of many colonists. Those planters who had capital to spend on erecting more permanent buildings often chose to invest it on additional labor rather than on housing. Those who did not own the land on which they lived had even fewer incentives to build well. In the late 1680s Stephen Hancock refused to build a better house for his family "on land that was none his owne."[33] Planters who rented farms to tenants frequently placed the onus of improvement upon the renters, many of whom could ill afford the outlay.[34]

However, a few planters did choose to erect more spacious houses. Thomas Bray of Chowan Precinct wanted to build in 1715 a house "twenty foot long and fifteen foot wide with a shade or lean too of eight foot wide"—the shed providing more storage and sleeping room.[35] One house built in the 1670s measured "forty foot Long 20 foot wide; with a shade on the back side; and a porch on the front."[36] A dwelling of these proportions would have had two principal rooms downstairs, perhaps both of them heated by gable-end chimneys, with smaller unheated storage and sleeping chambers in the attic and in the back shed extension. Houses with two principal ground-floor rooms (usually a hall and a parlor or chamber) not only provided more space but allowed household activities to be divided between rooms. In the late 1720s, merchant Isaac Ottwell of Bath lived in a house consisting of a hall, closet, parlor, cellar, and at least two rooms above stairs. His family prepared and ate their meals in the hall. They kept pots, gridirons, and frying pans by the fireplace and ate from wooden bowls, earthenware dishes, and pewter plates at a large table. The presence in the parlor of several chairs, a few books, a map, spectacles, an assortment of cloth, glass tumblers, wine flasks, a sugar box, and a teapot and cups on a bureau suggests its use as a sitting room, while a feather bed and a trundle bed indicate that this smaller room, like the loft, served as a sleeping chamber as well.[37] Ottwell ranked among the wealthiest members of early colonial society, yet even he adhered to the common usage of rooms as semipublic, multipurpose spaces. In contrast to present-day notions of privacy and space, few families had a private bedchamber or rooms set aside for the exclusive use of the family or for specific functions such as dining or entertaining. Only later in the eighteenth century did the desire for privacy within the family and between neighbors begin to affect the plan and size of colonial houses.

Material success in proprietary Carolina was not necessarily manifested by the building of a large house but by the construction of one that had "workmanlike" attributes of solidity and refinement. Only a small minority could afford houses with brick chimneys and foundations, sawn frames, joined woodwork, planed floorboards, plastered walls, and glazed windows, and such refinements were regarded as important accomplishments.

Some colonists sought to provide better dwellings for their families after their deaths by stipulating in their wills that new houses were to be erected or improvements made to existing structures out of money from their estates. Planter George Durant of Perquimans Precinct made a special provision in his will in 1730 that stipulated the addition of a new brick chimney to his daughter's house.[38] Similarly, Patrick Maule of Bath County directed his executors to build a new house "twenty foot long & Sixteen foot wide" for his wife.[39]

Even in the seventeenth century when resources to build well were severely restricted, there were those few such as merchant Francis Godfrey of Perquimans Precinct who chose to invest in more durable buildings. Although unfinished at his death in 1675, Godfrey's 40-by-20-foot house consisted of a frame of "all sawed worke" which surpassed most contemporary structures in the quality of workmanship. The frame alone was appraised at a value of nearly eight pounds, a sum far greater than the few hundred pounds of tobacco at which other buildings were valued in the seventeenth century.[40] One of the most expensive building projects undertaken in the first quarter-century of settlement must have been on

Theophilus White House, Perquimans County, perhaps second quarter of the eighteenth century. (Photo, 1940, Thomas Waterman, HABS Collection, Library of Congress.)

Powells Point in Currituck Precinct. In 1673 Peter Carteret spent nearly forty-five pounds to build a dwelling and quartering house there.[41]

Building with brick was an expensive proposition throughout the proprietary period. Because of the labor and cost involved in the manufacture of bricks and lime as well as the scarcity of trained brickmakers throughout much of the colony, brick buildings remained uncommon. Even the use of brick for chimneys, hearths, firebacks, underpinnings, and floors was far from widespread. From initial settlement in the seventeenth century, brick was regularly manufactured in the colony but it remained a fairly expensive material that few could afford. For the construction of a single brick chimney, bricklayer Andrew Lathinghouse charged one client in 1717 ten pounds, a price that probably exceeded the value of many dwellings at that time.[42] With his usual acerbity and perhaps some exaggeration, William Byrd noted in 1728 that in Edenton "a Citizen is considered Extravagant, if he has Ambition enough to aspire to a Brick-chimney."[43] Brick chimneys along with brick underpinnings achieved a status that symbolized permanence and prestige.[44] Gradually, for those who chose to invest in this expensive but durable material, brick replaced wood foundations, chimneys, and walls. Edenton physician John Brickell observed in 1737 that the "most substantial planters generally use Brick and Lime" in their houses.[45] A few early-eighteenth-century buildings were substantial structures of brick such as the Isaac Gregory House in Camden County, the Newbold-White House in Perquimans County, and St. Thomas Church in Bath.

Refined and embellished woodwork accompanied the construction of permanent buildings. Some of the best houses of the proprietary period had well-crafted ornamental details on the exterior and the interior. Wood and plaster moldings, wall and door paneling, and vigorously carved mantels, balusters, and handrails became important decorative elements inside many of the better houses like the Cupola House in Edenton, the Customs House (now destroyed) in Nixonton, and the Old Brick House near Elizabeth City.[46] But the sense of fashion, of building well with an eye toward what was architecturally "correct," was scarcely a pervasive notion in the young colony. The knowledge of an academically correct building grammar may have circulated among a small elite, but such men faced many difficulties in carrying out their ideas in what was a remote and poor colony. Except for a log jail here and there, no public buildings appeared in North Carolina until the eighteenth century. The late-seventeenth-century inhabitants of the Albemarle were too few in number, too dispersed geographically, and too divided politically to demand or support construction of centralized church and government buildings.[47] By 1729, however, most of the established counties had erected courthouses and jails, and Anglican, Quaker, and Baptist congregations had built a few chapels and churches. Acknowledging the same frontier conditions that faced farmers and merchants in building their houses and agricultural buildings, church vestries found it unsuitable or impossible to embark on costly building programs. The vestry of St. Thomas Parish in the village of Bath decided to build a 30-by-52-foot brick church in 1734 but quickly acknowledged that "our abilities will be far short of completing and adorning the same."[48] Church members struggled for many years before they were able to finish the ambitious project.

Other colonists settled for small, cheaper buildings. Most of these first public buildings repeated the size and scale of contemporary domestic structures. On the 1728 border survey, William Byrd was unimpressed with the public buildings he saw in North Carolina: a Quaker meetinghouse had "an Awkward Ornament on the West End of it, that seem'd to Ape a Steeple," while the courthouse in Edenton appeared to have "much the Air of a Common Tobacco-House."[49]

The Practice of Building

Rudimentary Building

In proprietary Carolina as in most frontier settlements and traditional rural societies, much building was accomplished by those who intended

St. Thomas Parish Church, Bath, begun 1734. (Photo, 1977, Michael Southern, North Carolina Division of Archives and History.)

to use the structures, as men erected hovels, pens, sheds, and other primitive buildings to house themselves, their goods, and their animals. The pioneer, laborer, farmer, and hunter constructed simple dwellings and outbuildings in a manner that reduced labor and limited the preparation of native materials to a few simple operations. With rarely more than the local materials he gathered, purchased, or made himself, the builder may have worked alone or relied upon other members of the community. Whether a bower covered with bark or a hut of crudely fashioned logs, these ephemeral structures were capable of being built without the assistance of a skilled craftsman such as a carpenter. Their shape and appearance owed little to the emerging vernacular building tradition but depended more upon the rudimentary abilities of the maker and the qualities of materials near at hand.

Because it generated no drawings or accounts of payments for skilled labor or manufactured materials, this most basic mode of building left little documentary evidence. Hence it is difficult to discern how pervasive it was during the proprietary period. The notion of the pioneer family, carving a farmstead out of the wilderness with little more than a few simple tools and their own labor, has permeated literature on early colonial settlement. An eighteenth-century visitor to the southern colonies saw "many small, separate, badly kept cabins of wood, without glass in the windows, of the structure and solidity of a house of cards" and ascribed them to necessity:

> In the settlement of a new plantation there is concern for only the most indispensable buildings, and a hastily built blockhouse is all that is needed at first; but by degrees, the family increasing and more land brought into cultivation, greater convenience becomes an item. And thus are built gradually a good many small houses and cabins, commonly without the assistance of carpenters, patched together by the people themselves or their negroes. This being an easier method than to put together a large house all at once, one often sees such little houses growing up where there is neither material nor capital for bringing them together in one solid house.[50]

Not only the exigencies of frontier life but also the shortage of labor prolonged the use of simple building methods. John Urmston reported in 1711 that "workmen are dear and scarce" in the Albemarle and that in order to compensate for the paucity of craftsmen, an enterprising planter was forced to learn as many skills of "carpenters, joiner, wheelwrights, and coopers" as possible. Urmston warned that if the prospective settler "cannot do all of these things, or have slaves that can," then he "will have a bad time of it."[51] For many jobs where it was not worth the money or effort to obtain an artisan, the relative scarcity of trained builders forced many farmers to rely upon their own skills and resources.

Artisans in the Colony

The task of building more substantial structures demanded the skills of artisans trained in the construction trades. Few though they were, building craftsmen appeared in North Carolina from initial settlement. In fact, they occasionally preceded permanent settlement, for planters of means sometimes sent out carpenters and other laborers to new lands to clear fields and build temporary structures in preparation for settlement. Indeed the first structure known to have been built by white settlers in North Carolina was erected by such a craftsman, when in 1654 Col. Francis Yeardley of Norfolk County, Virginia, hired carpenter Robert Bodnam to build a frame house "to the Southward for [Nathaniel] Batts to live in and trade with the Indians."[52] When another Norfolk County man, George Catchmaid, determined to move southward, he employed Richard Watredge and three other men in 1662 "to settle and seat" his new plantation lands on the north shore of the Albemarle Sound. Watredge and his fellow laborers probably erected some sort of temporary dwelling since Catchmaid and his household soon followed them.[53] Although carpenters Bodnam and Watredge returned to Virginia after their work in the Albemarle, other craftsmen had taken up residency in the colony by the early 1660s.[54]

Evidence before 1680 is too scarce to follow the immigration of other artisans into the colony, but records from the next half-century reveal a number of carpenters, joiners, bricklayers, glaziers, and sawyers practicing their trades for the tobacco planters and farmers of the Albemarle. From the 1680s through the 1720s nearly a hundred carpenters are known to have worked in the coastal settlements. Because of the difficulty of identifying colonists by trade and the paucity of records in some regions, this figure probably represents only a small portion of the actual number of carpenters in the colony. Members of other building trades also appear during the proprietary period though fewer in number than carpenters.

Woodworkers

The conditions of early Carolina society blurred the divisions found in the English building trades. Traditionally, woodworking was separated into two principal crafts, carpentry and joinery. The main task of the carpenter was the framing, enclosing, and covering of a building; the joiner finished the building with doors, windows, mantels, and wainscoting. In the early eighteenth century, English writer Richard Neve defined "the Art of a Joiner" as "a Business requiring great Ingenuity, being the nicer and more delicate Part of wood-work; as Carpentry is the larger and rougher." Neve believed joinery to be a more accomplished craft since "a good Joiner may more easily supply the Place of a Carpenter, than a Carpenter can do the fine Work of a Joiner."[55] Another English commentator on the building trades described joinery as a skilled art "whereby several Pieces of Wood are so fitted and join'd together by straight-line, squares, miters, or any Bevel, that they shall seem one entire Piece."[56] Components such as rails, stiles, panels, and muntins had to be worked to a degree of accuracy and finish in order for doors, sash, and paneling to fit securely together.

In practice the distinction between the work done by the carpenter and that done by the joiner in the provincial towns and countryside of England was less rigid; joiners often supervised the framing and enclosing of buildings, and carpenters occasionally made interior trim, sash, and doors. In America, particularly in a poor and isolated frontier such as North Carolina, the distinction between joiner and carpenter was often in name only. The versatility of some woodworkers is readily apparent in building documents from the proprietary period. In 1683, for example, carpenter Nicholas Gent spent a month building a log house on Governor Sothel's plantation, and also made a ladder, two latches, two drays, and a pair of cart wheels—thus doing the work of a turner and a wheelwright as well as a carpenter.[57] Similar versatility can be found in the account of work that Thomas and William Stephenson did for Joseph Comander in the winter of 1697:

covering the dwelling
building the Mill house
building a Hen house
making a Cart
finishing the house
making a table leafe
underpining the house
mending the Canoe.[58]

In an age when so many household and agricultural objects were fashioned out of wood, it was not unusual for the early Albemarle woodworkers to spend much of their time away from building engaged in making such items as cradles, coffins, and hogsheads. Only toward the end of the proprietary period, with the development of towns such as Edenton, Bath, New Bern, and Brunswick, did there appear to be some specialization in the woodworking trades. In Edenton in the 1720s, several craftsmen practiced the type of work traditionally associated with joiners—the making of furniture and the fabrication of doors, windows, and interior woodwork. There, the concentration of merchants and government officials along with a growing desire for more permanent and refined buildings provided joiners such as Patrick Ogleby with a steady demand for well-crafted woodwork. The volume of work that he commanded warranted the full-time maintenance of a shop. When he died in 1727, Ogleby had outstanding accounts from nearly fifty customers, many of whom were the leading merchants of the town.[59]

Until the end of the proprietary period, when the fashion for planed finishes, paneled doors, wainscoting, and sash windows became important elements in more substantial houses, there was scant demand for the work of the joiner in house construction. Through the proprietary period carpenters outnumbered joiners nine to one, a ratio which roughly corresponds to figures in other colonies. In seventeenth-century Massachusetts Bay, there were seven carpenters for every joiner, and in apprenticeship indentures recorded in Tidewater Virginia in the first quarter of the eighteenth century, the ratio was nearly the same.[60]

In transforming timbers into planks, posts, and clapboards, a carpenter required only a small number of woodworking tools. At his death in 1719, carpenter Francis Beasley of Chowan Precinct owned a "broad axe, club axe, broad hatchet, rabit plain, finale bead plain, 6 carpenter's chizels, 3 mortising chizels, 1 broad chizel, a small whip saw, 2 small files, a large drawing knife, 7 augers, 2 ads, vice, froe, 2 handsaws, 4 gouges, a crosscut saw, jointer stocks, a felling axe, and two wimbles."[61] Such a brief list exemplifies the tools needed by a rural carpenter in Carolina in the early eighteenth century and probably varied little from those employed by contemporary English craftsmen. In constructing a frame building, Beasley used his broad axe to dress the faces of framing timbers which had been cut out and roughly scored with a felling axe. He removed irregularities on the timbers with the long-handled, broad-bladed adz, a tool designed to smooth large framing surfaces. To cut mortise and tenon joints that would secure the different framing members together, he drilled holes in one piece with an auger and in the other squared the mortise with various mortising chisels and gouges. On corner posts and ceiling joists, he could use a "finale bead plain" to apply a narrowly channeled, decorative bead.

After cutting the framing members and fitting them together, the carpenter then supervised the tricky and laborious task of rearing the frame. For a building of considerable size, many laborers were needed to guide the ropes and pulleys which coaxed the heavy wall frames into place. It was during this assembly process that the special skills of a carpenter such as Beasley became readily apparent. Under his guidance, the workmen reared different parts of the frame—the wall plates, joists, and rafter pairs—in a specific sequence so that the various members would lock together properly and thus secure the frame's structural stability.

Once the frame was up, the carpenter then completed the building with protective weatherboarding and shingles on the outside and some interior woodwork, perhaps sheathing, stairs, doors, and windows. He split clapboards, plaster laths, and shingles by pounding an iron-bladed froe with a wooden mallet or maul along the grain of a log. Using his drawing knife—an especially valuable surfacing tool—the carpenter rough-sized the edges of floorboards and tapered the sides of shingles. Finally, he used his hammer, an essential tool for driving hundreds of nails.

The plane was probably the most important and specialized smoothing and shaping tool in a carpenter's tool chest. A carpenter like Beasley used only a few basic planes. Indeed, for crudely finished houses typical of the late seventeenth and early eighteenth centuries, there was no need for a builder to own a large collection of planes. Carpenters employed planes to smooth surfaces, make tongue-and-groove joints, straighten edges of boards, and fashion decorative molding trim. Beasley owned a rabbet plane which he used to groove the edges of boards so that they would lap into one another. As in England and other colonies, carpenters who included the intricacies of joinery in their trade usually acquired more planes, chisels, and gouges, which allowed them to perform more specialized and elaborate work. Thomas Robinson, a carpenter from Little River in Perquimans Precinct, owned fifteen chisels, six gouges, and twelve small molding planes, suggesting that he did more finishing or joinery work than his neighbor Francis Beasley with his two planes.[62]

Part of the colonial carpenter's expertise lay in his ability to recognize which types of trees were most suitable for certain uses in building. Virginia craftsmen who moved southward to Carolina in the late seventeenth century were familiar with the peculiar qualities of the native oak,

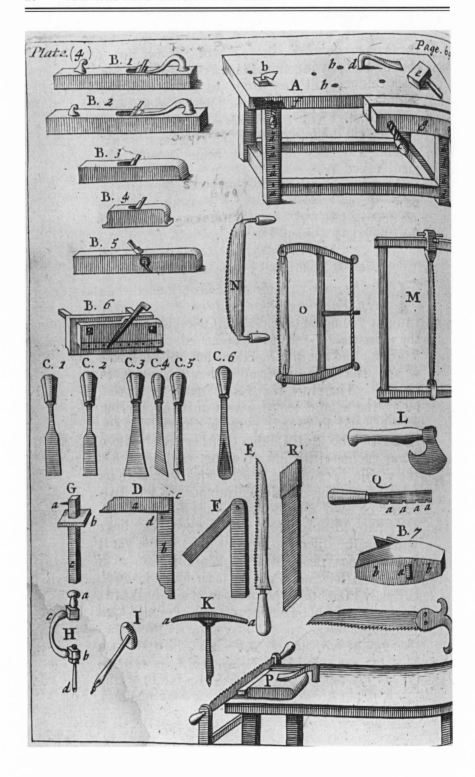

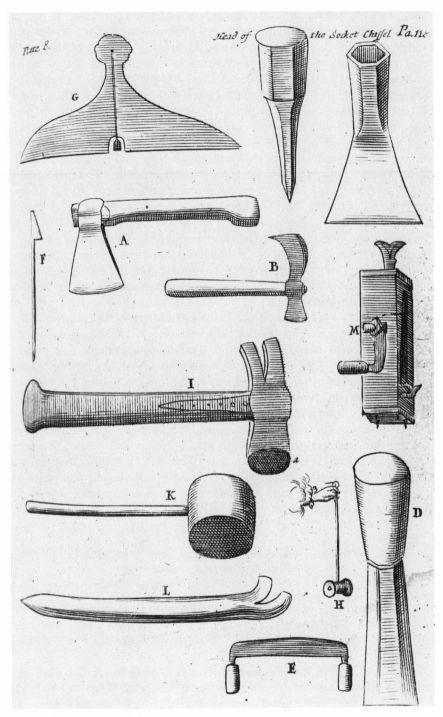

(Caption on following page)

pine, poplar, cypress, and cedar. Each species had its particular merits, as surveyor John Lawson noted in 1709. The chestnut oak yielded "the fairest plank," while the red oak made "good Clap boards." The live oak was "the most durable oak" of extraordinary hardness. Lawson believed that "there are some few [oak] trees, that would allow a stock of twelve Foot, but the firmness & great weight thereof, freightens our Sawyers from the Fatigue that attends the cutting of this timber. A Nail once driven therein 'tis next to an Impossibility to draw out." White oak was recommended for principal framing members such as sills, posts, and plates, as was locust which was considered essential for earthfast construction. Red cedar was another durable wood, "much used in Posts for Houses and Sills." The softer white and yellow pine were plentiful and easily worked into floorboards, doors, stair treads, paneling, and framing members. Poplar made "very pretty wainscot, Shingles for Houses, and Planks for several uses."[63] White cedar, cypress, and pine were the most popular woods for shingles.[64]

Before the construction of sawmills in the second quarter of the eighteenth century, building demanded arduous hours of sawing large timbers into planks and boards by hand. Some carpenters such as Beasley preferred to purchase planks and boards fabricated by a small band of professional sawyers who appeared in the colony by the last quarter of the seventeenth century. The time and labor involved in sawing boards with pit and whip saws made sawn lumber a relatively expensive commodity. In the inventory of Col. John Lear, for example, appraisers in 1700 valued 1,800 feet of sawn poplar plank at three farthings per foot, a price which must have seemed prohibitively expensive for most Carolinians.[65] Riven clapboards and hewn framing pieces, produced with less labor, provided a cheaper alternative. At the same time, the absence of a large body of sawyers and water-powered sawmills forced those Carolina colonists who could afford it to import sawn lumber from other colonies. In 1721, for example, merchant Thomas Pollock ordered five thousand feet of plank for his son's new house from Boston, one of the early centers for traffic in building materials.[66]

On preceding pages:

Joiner's tools from Moxon's *Mechanick Exercises*. A: workbench (b: hook, d: hold fast, e: mallet, g: bench vice); B1: fore-plane; B2: jointer; B3: strike-block; B4: smoothing-plane; B5: rabbet-plane; B6: plow; B7: underside of a plane (a: mouth, b: sole); C1: former; C2: pairing chisel; C3: former; C4: skew-former; C5: mortise chisel; C6: gauge; D: square; E: compass saw; F: bevel; G: gage; H: piercer; I: gimblet; K: auger; L: hatchet; M: pit-saw; N: whipsaw; O: tennon saw; P: whetting block; Q: hand saw; R: mitre square. (Colonial Williamsburg Foundation.)

Carpenter's tools from Moxon's *Mechanick Exercises*. A: axe; B: adz; C: socket chisel; D: ripping chisel; E: drawknife; F: hook pin; G: level; H: plumb-line; I: hammer; K: commander (mallet); L: crow. (Colonial Williamsburg Foundation.)

Construction site. This eighteenth-century French illustration shows the variety of skills and labor organization necessary for the erection of large buildings. From Denis Diderot, *Encyclopédie* (Paris: Briansson, 1751–65), vol. 2, plate 1. (Colonial Williamsburg Foundation.)

Many early settlers saw the need for sawmills in the timber-rich colony. Believing that a sawmill would turn a handsome profit, Swiss Baron von Graffenried, the founder of New Bern, erected one at his new town on the Neuse River in 1710. Since "they saw every thing, in England as well as here by hand," Graffenried contended that "planks are incredibly dear. For one plank I will, at a saw mill, get 6, yes indeed 10 [pence]. An Englishman has offered me the yearly revenue of the saw mill, fifty pounds sterling; but if the city progresses . . . it is worth 100 £ yearly."[67] The Tuscarora War of 1711–13 devastated the town and destroyed the baron's hopes for profits from a sawmill. Other early attempts to establish water-powered sawmills soon appeared in the northern sections of Albemarle County. There were water-powered gristmills in Perquimans, Chowan, and Pasquotank precincts by 1730, but if any of these mills included a saw, the output remained small and inconsequential.[68] Not until the middle of the eighteenth century, with the rise of a sawmilling industry in the Cape Fear Valley, did power-sawn lumber become an important part of the building process.

The production of shingles, like that of sawn lumber, became a specialized industry. Large stands of durable cypress and cedar grew along

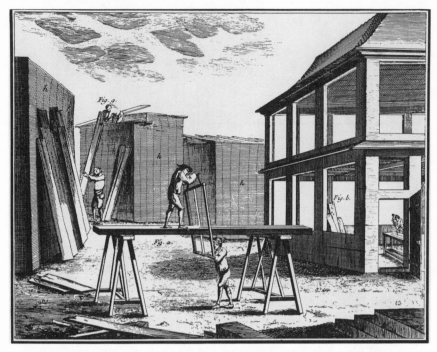

Pit sawing timbers into planks and boards. From Denis Diderot, *Encyclopédie* (Paris: Briansson, 1751–65), vol. 7, plate 1. (Colonial Williamsburg Foundation.)

the river bottomlands and on the edge of the swamps in many areas along the coast. The Albemarle developed a local and export trade in shingles and barrel staves by the 1690s. Dozens of ships yearly cleared the port of Roanoke with loads of shingles bound for South Carolina, the West Indies, and the northern colonies.[69] Thousands of shingles were produced for export and the local building trades by slave-owning planters who set their workers to making shingles and tar during the winter season. By the 1720s planters regularly delivered shingles to Edenton for sale to craftsmen and merchants.[70]

Bricklayers

The responsibility for forming and firing clay bricks belonged to a handful of bricklayers who appeared in North Carolina by the late seventeenth century. As in rural England, the bricklayers in the proprietary colony did far more than make and lay bricks.[71] In the absence of craftsmen specializing in making lime and applying plaster, bricklayers assumed these tasks as well. Because of the local nature of production and the difficulty of transporting bulky bricks over any distance, early bricklayers established brickmaking operations over broad areas. In the 1690s, Chowan bricklayer

George Chambers traveled to William Duckenfield's plantation on Salmon Creek in Bertie County, where he fired "three kilns of Bricks" and burned "300 bushells of oaster shells."[72] When Thomas Pollock employed Edenton brickmaker Thomas Cooke to work on his son's house on the south shore of the Albemarle Sound in 1722, the merchant allowed Cooke "what lands are necessary for him for Burning the . . . Bricks" that were to be used for laying the chimneys, cellar, and underpinnings of the house.[73]

Apprenticeships

In every trade, artisans passed their knowledge of their craft on to a younger generation through an apprenticeship system which promoted training through practical experience. The custom of master workmen taking young boys into their shops to teach them all aspects of their trade had flourished in England and Europe several hundred years before American settlement. As in other colonies, the apprentice system that developed in North Carolina in the late seventeenth and early eighteenth centuries reflected English practices modified to suit local circumstances. Very few laws were passed in North Carolina during the proprietary period governing the apprentice system; English precedents and colonial experience regulated apprenticeships.

Compulsory indentures were the most commonly recorded form of apprenticeship. The high mortality rate in early Carolina society frequently disrupted the voluntary pattern of training and left many children without parents or other means of support. In order to prevent poor orphans from becoming burdens to the parish, magistrates bound young boys to craftsmen. The established custom of binding orphans to artisans became a law in 1715 when the General Assembly specified that an "Orphan shall be bound Apprentice to some Handycraft Trade" until he reached the age of majority.[74] The promise of the apprentice's work as a competent young adult made it worth the master's while to support him as a child. Thus many young orphans found themselves obliged to learn one of the building trades through no choice of their own. In 1712 the Craven Precinct court bound Joseph Simson, an eleven-year-old orphan, to Alexander Goodgroom.[75] In 1703, after the death of her husband, Thomas, Mary Hancock bound two of her children to Gabriel Newby of Perquimans Precinct, who contracted to teach one of them "the trade of a wheelwright."[76] The apprenticeships were subject to alteration by parent or master. In 1711 the Chowan Precinct court ordered that Edward Titman, who had been apprenticed to carpenter William Branch, be returned to his mother after she proved to the court that she and her new husband could care for him.[77]

When an apprentice entered into the service of a master craftsman, an indenture was usually drawn up which specified the obligations of each party. The term of service varied with the age of the apprentice. A boy

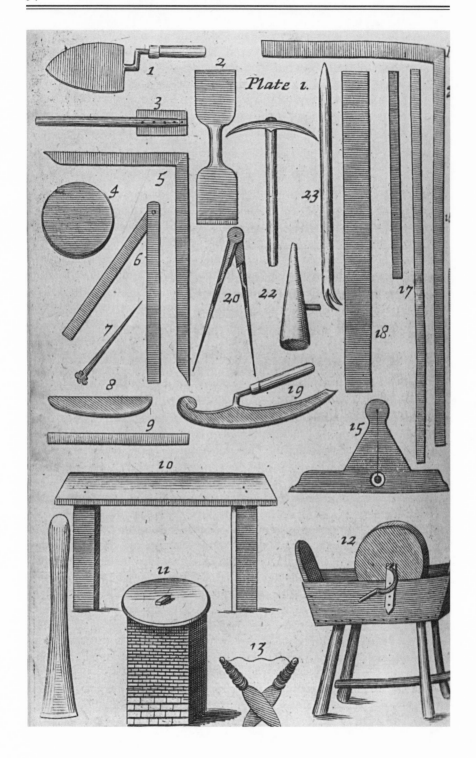

apprenticed at an early age usually remained under the tutelage of his master until he reached his twenty-first birthday. On occasion orphans or poor children as young as three years old were put into the service of a craftsman, but more commonly apprentices were boys in their teens who served from two to seven years. As in England and the other colonies, the contract between master and apprentice strictly circumscribed an apprentice's activities. The apprentice could not absent "himself from his masters service day or night without leave . . . from his master." Neither could he "contract Matrimony nor use . . . unlawful gaming as cards or dice" for the length of his service. Most servants—as apprentices were categorized legally—were forbidden to frequent alehouses. They could not lend or sell their masters' goods, or make and sell their own. Some contracts simply referred to practices in the homeland and stipulated that "to behave him Selfe as an Apprentice by the Law of England is Required."[78]

The master agreed to provide food, clothing, and lodging for his apprentice and to teach him reading, writing, and the "full art and mystery" of his trade. Thus an apprentice carpenter learned from the experienced craftsman the properties of the different timbers he would use, how to select and fell the proper trees, how to shape a particular timber through riving, hewing, or sawing, and how to finish or embellish different members through planing and turning. A master instructed his apprentice in the measurement and estimation of materials as well as the intricate and customary methods of framing and erecting a building, from the cutting of mortise and tenon joints to the sequential assembly and rearing of the timber frame. Added to the "mystery" of the craft were the many long hours spent at dull and repetitive tasks such as planing planks and boards.

At the expiration of his indenture, an apprentice received freedom dues, often money, clothing, or tools, from his master. Some indenture contracts specifically stipulated the amount or type of goods. One master promised to give his apprentice all the "tools that he might need" at the end of his term, while another was to provide his apprentice with a horse at the expiration of three years' service and "a sett of Cooper Tooles Useful for this Compty . . . at the Expyration of the time," along with "two new Suits of Apperell."[79]

Apprentices fled from their service for various reasons. Some complained to the courts of bad treatment, as did Stephen Scott of Perquimans Precinct. The court, however, ordered him to return and continue his

Opposite:

Bricklayer's tools from Moxon's *Mechanick Exercises*. 1: brick trowel; 2: brick axe; 3: saw; 4: rubstone; 5: small square; 6: bevel; 7: iron treenail; 8: float stone; 9: ruler; 10: banker; 11: brickpier to lay rubbing stone in; 12: grinding stone; 13: line pins; 14: plumb rule; 15: level; 16: large square; 17: ten-foot and five-foot rod; 18: jointing rule; 19: jointer; 20: compass; 21: hammer; 22: rammer; 23: crow. (Colonial Williamsburg Foundation.)

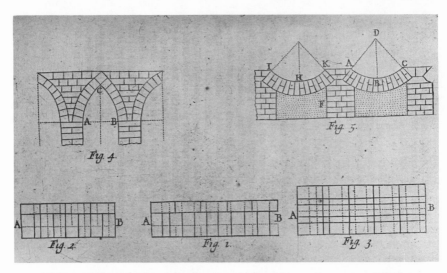

Geometric procedure for constructing brick arches from Moxon's *Mechanick Exercises*. (Colonial Williamsburg Foundation.)

training in "ye trade and mistery of a Carpenter & house joiner" and admonished his master, Quaker Thomas Robinson, to "not Imoderately correct or abuse ye sd Scott dureing ye said Service."[80] On occasion apprentices complained that their masters were not living up to the terms of their contracts, as, for example, when craftsmen found it more profitable to work their apprentices as agricultural laborers on tobacco plantations rather than in the building trades.[81] Others simply left service and headed to the frontier or another colony. Runaway apprentices and servants from Virginia continually filled the ranks of craftsmen in Carolina, a practice that annoyed Virginia officials. It was not unknown for farmers and merchants to entice apprentices away from their masters with promises of paid employment, as did Cary Godby of Chowan Precinct, who, "intending to profitt and advantage himselfe by the Labour and usefullness" of shipwright's apprentice John Fox, lured him away from his master for several months. As in most instances, the court directed that the runaway be returned to his master.[82] Such decisions failed to soothe ill feelings between master and apprentice.

Besides apprenticeships, the skills of a trade were often transmitted more informally from father to son. Lemuel Taylor, a carpenter and glazier from Perquimans Precinct, instructed his son in the mastery of his craft. Young Lemuel Taylor inherited his father's carpenter's, turner's, and glazier's tools in 1720 and continued his father's business.[83] Familial trade connections also extended to brothers, cousins, and more distant relations. Carteret County carpenter Joseph Bell taught the two sons of his

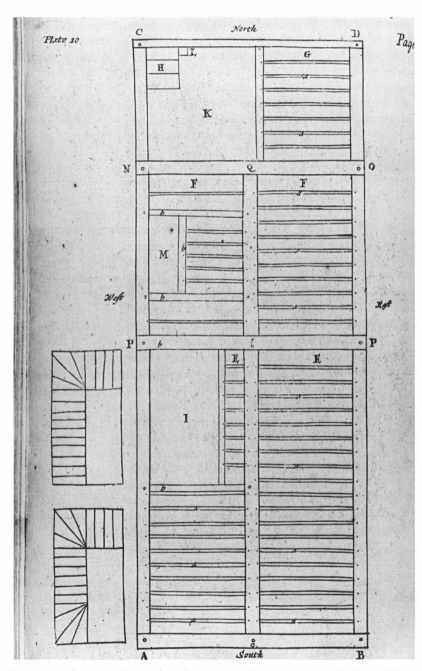

Foundation framing scheme from Moxon's *Mechanick Exercises*. (Colonial Williamsburg Foundation.)

brother the "Mistery of Building houses," and carpenter John Dicks of Chowan Precinct trained his son-in-law and left him all his carpenter's and joiner's tools.[84] Artisans sometimes bound their children to other craftsmen to learn a different trade, as did Thomas Houghton, a tailor from Perquimans Precinct, who indentured his son to a carpenter and cooper.[85] Thus, through familial connections or more formal legal indentures, young men learned the practical lessons of craftsmanship in a manner that had been only slightly modified from traditional English practices.

Artisan Building

The arrangements between an artisan and a client for a simple earthfast structure or more finely finished and well-crafted buildings followed patterns well known in English practice and common throughout the other colonies. When an artisan was employed to work on a building, various arrangements were possible. Some craftsmen were hired by clients for their skilled labor and nothing more, while others were responsible for an entire building project and the coordination of the various aspects of construction. Contracts between builders and their employers typically outlined the obligations of the two parties and the nature of the project by stipulating the size of the building, the framing system, the type and quality of materials, methods of construction, and payment schedules.[86]

On some projects a craftsman supplied both the materials and the labor. In other cases clients sought to reduce the cost of building by gathering their own raw materials and limiting the work of the craftsman to that which the client could not do himself. Often the client and builder shared the task of felling trees, transporting them to the site, and sawing them into boards. Such an arrangement was made between carpenter Stephen Manwaring and his client Robert Beasley of Perquimans Precinct in 1694 whereby both parties jointly undertook to saw 5,500 feet of plank for Beasley's dwelling.[87] By contrast, planter Thomas Bartlett of Chowan Precinct in 1721 decided "to gett or cause to be gott all the Frame, shingles, weatherboards, etc. in the proper place for building the said house" and hired carpenter William Davis to supervise the assembly of the frame and enclose it with weatherboards and shingles.[88]

Clients and builders were careful to note in their contractual arrangements who was responsible for the manufactured materials, and generally the procurement of imported materials was left to the party with the best access to local merchants since difficulty in securing sufficient amounts of glass, lead, paint, hardware, and nails often delayed building activities. Because such items were not manufactured in North Carolina but had to be imported from England or other colonies, they were scarce and thus fairly valuable commodities. Indeed, so desperate were the Albemarle inhabitants in the 1670s for nails that they would burn houses, fences, or unattended or abandoned farmsteads in order to recover the used nails.[89] More than fifty years later the relative scarcity and cost of nails still plagued backwoods and poor builders. William Byrd ran across one man who "had rais'd a kind of House but for want of nails it remain'd uncover'd."[90]

Carpenters and clients obtained nails through merchants who purchased them from outside the colony. There is no evidence that nails were manufactured on a commercial basis in the colony during the proprietary period. Massachusetts was the principal source of supply for nails and hardware. Merchant Joshua Lamb of Roxbury, for example, shipped dozens of casks of nails to the Albemarle throughout the last quarter of the seventeenth century—in 1684, he sold a Perquimans planter 10,000 eightpenny nails.[91] Thomas Pollock, an Edenton merchant active in trade with Massachusetts in the first decades of the eighteenth century, ordered "12 good spring locks, 12 pair of crossd Garnett hinges" from a Boston supplier in 1716.[92]

Responsibility for supplying labor, like materials, was divided variously between client and artisan. Since most craftsmen worked on their own, perhaps with the assistance of apprentices or unskilled laborers or slaves, the planter often provided workmen—servants, slaves, or hired men—to help the carpenter saw timber, rear the frame, and attach clapboards and shingles. Edward Moseley's slaves dug the foundation for a new house at Rocky Point on the Cape Fear River, while farmer William Long of Perquimans Precinct hired a laborer to help carpenter Thomas Love in building Long's house.[93]

The dispersed nature of settlement and shortage of artisans forced many craftsmen to travel great distances from one building site to another, an occupational pattern that would continue well into the nineteenth century. Clients often provided builders with housing during construction. A contract might specify the use of a servant's quarters on a plantation and allow for space for the artisan to grow his own food or simply assure him of "sufficient Diet & lodging."[94] The provision of food and shelter was not so much a kindness on the part of the client as an incentive for the craftsman to remain on the job. Some contracts had a clause specifically restraining the carpenter from departing or neglecting his work for some other job until it was completely finished. This was vital, for if a craftsman left prematurely, it was often months, even years, before a client could find someone else to finish the work.

Compared with later building documents, contracts drafted between an individual client and a craftsman during the proprietary period generally revealed little about the character of a building beyond its basic dimensions, materials, and quality of workmanship. The primary purpose of many such contracts was not to spell out the precise design of the building but to state the obligations of both parties. Matters of design could be worked out face-to-face at the building site, but the difficulties of finding manufactured materials, skilled labor, and means of transportation, the logistical problems involved in getting the proper men and materials to some isolated farm at the right time and in an orderly sequence, loomed as far more crucial issues that had to be resolved at the signing of a contract. In a society where building was difficult even in the most favorable circumstances, a misunderstanding between client and craftsman on an issue of logistics could lead to long delays, aborted building projects, and many bitter lawsuits. Contracts were as concerned with the process of building as with the product.

Public Building

Although public building projects involved the same construction techniques and logistical problems as did private buildings, their legal and financial arrangements were often more complex. Governed by corporate decisions and funded with public money, the construction of courthouses and churches tended to be more complicated and therefore also generated more written records than did private buildings.

Responsibility for planning and overseeing construction of public buildings rested in the hands of building committees appointed by court or church officials.[95] After deciding to erect a new courthouse, for example, county magistrates selected three or four of its members and perhaps one or two men from the community to form a committee authorized to raise and dispense funds, enter into contracts with workmen, and direct the construction of the building. The magistrates themselves frequently decided the location, dimensions, materials, plan, and general specifications for the building, leaving the building committee to work out specific details with the craftsmen. The Currituck Precinct justices in 1723 directed their commissioners to contract with the necessary workmen to build a frame courthouse "thirty feet in length eighteen feet in width with a fashionable over Jet" and went on to outline the arrangement of the justices' platform, clerk's table, attorneys' bar, and other courtroom fittings.[96]

The task of directing the construction of public buildings belonged to "undertakers," men who acted as general contractors or clerks of the work. Undertakers assumed full responsibility for the hiring of skilled and unskilled workmen and the purchase of materials. Since the practice of letting the contract to the lowest bidder had not yet gained currency, most undertakers of public buildings tended to be local planters or merchants, many of whom sat as members of the same parish vestry or county court that had initiated the project. Some of these undertakers saw the work as a way to make money and lobbied hard to obtain the contract. By posting a security bond, they assumed all financial liabilities until the buildings were officially accepted by the governing authorities, but they also stood to profit handsomely from satisfactorily completed works. In 1719, for example, the Chowan Precinct court let the construction of the first court-house in Edenton to Col. Edward Moseley, no craftsman himself, but a planter with sufficient capital and labor to undertake the job. Moseley obtained nails from Boston merchants and lumber, oyster shells, and shingles from neighboring planters and then hired carpenters to frame, erect, and enclose the building. When the courthouse was completed to the satisfaction of the magistrates, Moseley submitted a bill of mate-rials and was reimbursed for his expenses out of taxes levied on county residents.[97]

Only a man with capital or credit could extend himself so far and reap such profits. Not many artisans in the proprietary period had the capital, labor, and materials required to take on major public building projects. One of the few who had the financial wherewithal to do so was carpenter William Davis who assumed the role of undertaker when he contracted to erect the Carteret County courthouse in the 1720s.[98]

The construction of the first Anglican church in Chowan Precinct illustrates many of the problems encountered in early public building projects. In December 1701, the vestry of St. Paul's Parish decided to build a church on a peninsula southeast of the present town of Edenton on the Albemarle Sound. The church wardens appointed to oversee the project were to "agree with a workman for building a Church 25 feet long. Posts in the ground and held to the Collar beams, and find all manner of Iron work, vizt. Nails and Locks, etc.; with full power to contract and agree with the said Workman as to their Discretion shall seem neet and convenient."[99]

The church wardens contracted with John Porter to build the church. Porter had immigrated to the colony from Pennsylvania in the 1690s, bringing with him thirteen black slaves. As a merchant and landowner with slave labor, Porter possessed the necessary materials and manpower to undertake such a project. His slaves probably cut the timber for the posts, sawed the clapboards and interior sheathing, and assembled, reared, and covered the frame. The church wardens made separate ar-rangements with Edward Smithwick to clear the building site and with an unidentified joiner to build windows, benches, and a communion table. In October 1702, the church stood near completion. The vestry paid Porter twenty-five pounds for the carpentry work, three pounds to Smithwick for his work, and six pounds to the joiner.[100]

But, as the undertaker was finishing the chapel, the members of the building committee became disenchanted with the quality of Porter's work, particularly the disfigured boards that sheathed the interior. To mediate the dispute between builder and committee, the vestry proposed

Edward Moseley's account for the construction of the Chowan County Courthouse in 1719. (Chowan County Loose Papers, Chowan County Courthouse, photo, Willie Graham, Colonial Williamsburg Foundation.)

to "choose one indifferent man that is skilled in building and Mr. John Porter shall choose another who shall meet at the Chapel . . . to give their judgment whether the boards be fit for ceiling such an House." Such means of arbitrating building disputes reflected English custom: the monitoring of the work of one artisan by other craftsmen was a means of upholding and regulating "workmanlike" standards in the building trades. The differences were resolved when Porter accepted the decision of the referees and whitewashed the interior of the building. On December 12, 1702, one year after the proposal to build a church had been adopted, the vestry received "the house and keys" from the builder.[101]

Even though the building had been accepted by the vestry, parishioners worshiped in a church that had no floor, windows without glass, and a pulpit unfinished "for want of nails and Boards." Minister John Urmston described the church as having "neither floor nor seats only a few loose benches upon the sand; the Key being lost the door stood open . . . all the Hoggs & Cattle flee thither for shade in the summer and warmth in the Winter; the first dig Holes & bury themselves, these with the rest make a loathsome place with their dung and nastiness which is the peoples regard to churches." Recognizing "the many and great inconveniences which attend the Chappell . . . both in respect of its ill situation, smallness, and rough and unfit workmanship," the vestry in 1708 resolved to build a larger church in another location. Plans for a 40-by-24-foot building were drawn up, but funds were not forthcoming and parishioners waited another thirty years before a new church was begun.[102]

Craftsmen in an Agrarian Society

Craftsmen who came to Carolina in the proprietary period faced a paradoxical situation: the colony was in desperate need of skilled builders, yet because of its dispersed settlement and rudimentary economy, it could not offer them constant employment. A population of a few thousand inhabitants, thinly spread across miles of difficult terrain, offered the builder an unappealing market. Farmers and merchants needed houses and agricultural buildings, but the jobs were few and far between. In May 1721, Thomas Pollock informed a firm of merchants in Boston that he was "ingaged in the plague of Building For my sons" and asked them to send him any carpenters that might be available in Boston since he considered the few craftsmen in North Carolina to be "verry indefferent, lasy, and slow."[103]

To supplement their livelihood, craftsmen often combined their trade with farming. Many did so out of necessity, as one Virginia report explained, because "a Tradesman having no Opportunity of a Market where he can buy Meat, Milk, Corn, and all other things, must either make Corn, keep Cows, and raise Stocks, himself, or must ride about the County to buy Meat and Corn where he can find it."[104] The absence of commercial markets forced many craftsmen, if they had the resources, to buy or rent land so that they could raise crops and keep animals for domestic consumption. Thomas Robinson, a carpenter who lived in the Quaker community of Little River in Pasquotank Precinct in the early eighteenth century, raised corn, sheep, and hogs on his small farm.[105] In neighboring Perquimans Precinct, carpenter and glazier Lemuel Taylor kept chickens, cattle, and hogs and cultivated a vegetable garden.[106]

Some artisans who turned to farming to augment their incomes found it so lucrative compared to the instability of the building trades that they quit practicing their craft when money crops such as tobacco, wheat, or corn commanded high prices. John Brothers, a carpenter by training, probably spent more time in the fields of his plantation in Pasquotank Precinct than in building. Before his death in the early 1730s, he raised corn, tobacco, and livestock with the aid of eight slaves.[107] If few artisans farmed to the extent of Brothers, nevertheless in the absence of a specialized food market and a less than buoyant economy it was common, as John Urmston observed, for "tradesmen [to] turn planters."[108]

North Carolina attracted many craftsmen from the older colonies who hoped to get ahead in the expanding settlements of the frontier and the fledgling coastal towns where there was no entrenched hierarchy of tradesmen. Dozens of young carpenters and bricklayers who had completed apprenticeships in the Chesapeake journeyed southward to Carolina. Carpenters from Virginia were among the first to purchase lots in the new village of Edenton in the 1710s and 1720s. This small provincial center held the promise of steady labor for some of them in building the wharves, warehouses, and dwellings of merchants and government officials who began to congregate there.[109]

The attraction to the colony was not without its difficulties. After completing their apprenticeships, young carpenters and bricklayers often possessed only a set of tools and some clothing—no basis for establishing their own households. Hence, like many agricultural laborers, artisans often contracted to work for planters in exchange for food and lodging. Bricklayer William Tomson emigrated from James City County, Virginia, to the village of Bath on the Pamlico frontier, where in 1701 he agreed to work on Nicholas Jones's plantation in exchange for lodging and a one-half share of the harvested tobacco and corn crop. Carpenter Tomson was to oversee the work of four agricultural servants as well as to clear land, erect fences, and repair houses and outbuildings.[110] Mrs. Sarah Durant provided carpenter William Lyon with his meals but charged five pounds "for his accomandation for one yeare." In return, Lyon built a milkhouse and repaired Mrs. Durant's dwelling.[111] Although men like Tomson and Lyon played an important part in the building process on plantations, they seldom established their own shops or practices. Many of these landless carpenters and bricklayers died leaving little. One carpenter's inventory consisted of only a few clothes, a gun, a trowel, and three brick molds, while another's estate included four old axes, a handsaw, a parcel of nails, clothing, a chest, a bed, and some tobacco, with a total value of £12.15.6.[112]

Yet other craftsmen with more luck or enterprise prospered, acquiring land, servants, and modest material comforts. Those who managed to purchase land and establish an independent household generally obtained a modest level of social status and personal wealth that at times surpassed the self-sufficient farmers in Carolina society in the first decades of the eighteenth century. Of 88 surviving probated inventories returned between 1712 and 1726, 16 can be identified as those of carpenters. The average value of their inventories totalled more than £168, whereas the assets of the 62 probated inventories belonging to land-owning planters amounted to an average of £75.[113]

Because of the paucity of records, it is difficult to determine what proportion of craftsmen managed to reach this level of economic success. They may have been only a few score out of the many men who practiced the building trades. Some owned little more than the general average wealth of all recorded inventories. Francis Beasley, one of the first native-trained North Carolina carpenters, died in 1719 with an estate appraised at nearly £70, mostly household goods and carpenter's tools, for he owned no livestock or slaves.[114] In contrast, William Davis of Pasquotank Precinct, who became one of the few carpenters to move into the entrepreneurial role of an undertaker, left an estate in 1728 valued at more than £350, carpenter's and joiner's tools worth £18, and three slaves valued at £190, a sum that suggests that they were skilled laborers, perhaps trained in one of the building trades.[115] Few craftsmen achieved the wealth attained by Davis; more could match the modest success of Beasley.

Successful artisans also assumed leadership in local affairs—a role usually closed to poorer members of their trades. As provincial government gradually became the preserve of wealthy tobacco planters and merchants, tradesmen sought positions of power in local and county affairs. Capt. James Coles, one of the most prominent carpenters in Perquimans Precinct in the first decade of the eighteenth century, served as "her Majesties [justice] of the peace" for the precinct. During this time, the court frequently met at his house.[116] James Beasley, a Carolina-trained artisan, became a justice in neighboring Chowan Precinct in 1718.[117] The local reputation and social standing of both men must have been high for them to have been appointed to the self-sustaining oligarchies that ruled local governments.

The quarterly sessions of the precinct courts played an important part in the craftsman's life. Landowning artisans were called upon to participate in the judicial process by arguing cases, serving on juries, and filling minor offices such as constable or overseer of the roads. Local courts entrusted artisans with the management of many services essential to the welfare of the community. They were often asked to appraise estates, especially those of other tradesmen since they were familiar with the value of building tools and materials.[118] Artisans also assumed guardianship of young orphans and managed their estates until they came of age.

It was not only public responsibility that drew artisans to court. Sometimes the need to settle claims with recalcitrant clients forced builders to go to court. Appearing at court also helped builders find work. In a colony where literacy was low, local newspapers nonexistent, and settlement dispersed, meetings of the court provided craftsmen and farmers with the opportunity to exchange news, purchase supplies, and promote business. Not only were public building jobs and repairs awarded at the courthouse on court days, but private building projects were often initiated and settled during court sessions. At the August 1715 meeting of Chowan Precinct court, Thomas Bray hired Edward Jackson, a millwright and carpenter from Perquimans, to build him a small frame house on his plantation in Chowan.[119] William Davis, an active participant in courthouse affairs in several precincts, agreed during the 1721 winter term of the Chowan court to build a house for Thomas Bartlett the following summer.[120]

The pattern of public activity among the more prominent artisans can clearly be seen in the career of carpenter Anthony Dawson. Born in 1643, Dawson spent his early years in Dorchester County, Maryland, where he eventually inherited a plantation from his father. The year before he emigrated to the Albemarle in 1687, he had overseen construction of a 20-by-40-foot frame courthouse in Dorchester County.[121] Three years after he settled in Perquimans Precinct, Dawson purchased and farmed part of several hundred acres of land, an essential step in his subsequent rise to provincial power. The following year, 1691, court records referred to him as Capt. Anthony Dawson, which suggests that he had already obtained a rank of courtesy sometimes associated with the militia and a certain level of social prominence. In the early 1690s, the precinct court held many of its meetings at Dawson's house with the captain taking part in many local affairs. As an important landowning member of the community, he served on various commissions and juries, inventoried estates, and argued cases for his neighbors as an attorney of fact before the magistrates. As one of the leading craftsmen in Perquimans, Dawson arbitrated building disputes and took under his care a number of apprentices. As his wealth and prestige grew, he presumably took on more building contracts and taught a new generation of Carolina carpenters the techniques and methods used by Chesapeake builders that he had learned more than thirty years earlier. From 1694 to 1696 Dawson achieved the height of his power and influence: he served as an assistant justice on the provincial court. Dawson's influence in provincial politics, however, was short-lived. In March 1698, the same provincial court on which he had served found him guilty of "pillaging and destroying" a ship that had run aground in the Albemarle Sound. Granted an alternative to the death sentence, the carpenter chose banishment to the province of New Jersey, where he spent the remaining twenty years of his life.[122]

Few craftsmen managed to match Dawson's political eminence. In later years, as planters and merchants of eastern North Carolina consolidated their political power, skilled craftsmen found high offices of government difficult to achieve, and what power and status they may have attained in local affairs gradually slipped away.[123] In the unsettled conditions of early proprietary society, however, a handful of craftsmen with force and determination, like Dawson, could still gain access to positions of authority.

Conclusion

The demands of the Carolina frontier transformed many of the traditional English ways of building that had been inherited by craftsmen. Following patterns established in the Chesapeake in the mid-seventeenth century, building forms and construction techniques gradually changed to suit local conditions. The modest nature of nearly all the buildings needed by proprietary society worked against the development of a highly organized system of skilled labor or the establishment of workshops and businesses solely concerned with the manufacture and supply of building materials. Artisans in early Carolina employed Chesapeake framing methods and log construction for the simple wooden buildings favored by proprietary settlers. Some of these craftsmen knew the sophisticated joinery techniques involved in the construction of solid "English framed houses," but they were seldom called upon to make elaborately framed, turned, carved, or molded woodwork. Only in the last years of proprietary government, when some merchants and members of the gentry began to erect substantial buildings, did carpenters, joiners, and bricklayers have the opportunity to exercise the full range of their skills.

Proprietary society built for the moment rather than for the future. Most of the settlers set aside any aspirations for well-built dwellings and erected expedient, often impermanent, buildings. "The plague of building" was fraught with so many pitfalls—the scarcity of skilled craftsmen, the difficulty of finding and transporting materials, and the long and drawn-out construction process—that individuals who wished to improve their dwellings and farm buildings were deterred at nearly every step.[124] Despite the impediments, these early Carolina settlers and craftsmen established a distinctive regional building practice that would be followed for more than a century.

Catherine W. Bishir

2

A Proper Good Nice
and Workmanlike
Manner:
A Century of
Traditional Building
Practice, 1730–1830

*The County being Remote from Navigation there is
no trade in it, the general and Individual Wealth in it
Rises from the Production of their lands and labour of
their Negroes, none are very Rich. . . . The first
Inhabitants . . . built and lived in log Cabbins, and
as they became more Wealthy, some of them Built
framed Clapboard Houses with Clay Chimneys, at
Present there are many good Houses, well
Constructed, with Brick Chimneys, and Glass lights,
there are no Stone or Brick walled Houses, nor any
that can be called Edifices in the County.—The
greatest Number of the Citizens yet build in the old
Stile.*

—William Dickson to Thomas Henderson, November
24, 1810

Introduction

THE TRANSITION from settlers' cabins to well-crafted houses, described in
this 1810 account of Duplin County, occurred again and again across
North Carolina.[1] As the society developed from a new frontier to a populous agricultural state, carpenters and bricklayers erected the new buildings that transformed the architectural landscape—an accomplishment
seen at the time as a major achievement. Traditional artisan practice grew
and flourished, dominating construction and occupying a central place in
the pre-industrial economy.

Like the pioneer artisans who built for the rough settlements of the
proprietary period, builders of the late colonial and early national eras
continued to adapt ancient craft traditions to the circumstances of the
rural South. They confronted issues that sprang from the dispersed rural
character of settlement, from the growing institution of slavery, and from
the increasingly entrenched conservatism of North Carolina's frugal elite.
And, by the 1810s and 1820s, they faced changes in taste, expectations,
and work roles that challenged the long-standing dominance of traditional
practice.

Settlement and Growth in "A Good Poor Man's Country"

North Carolina's growth in the eighteenth century was phenomenal. The
population rose from about 35,000 in 1730 to about 200,000 in 1775, as
settlement by people of British and African stock continued in the coastal
region and a new stream of British and German immigrants from the mid-
Atlantic colonies poured into the piedmont backcountry. After the Revolu-

tion, Indian lands beyond the Blue Ridge Mountains were opened to settlers. By 1800 continued immigration and natural increase brought the population to 478,103, more than double the 1775 figure. Thus the transition from new frontier to settled agrarian community repeated itself in one region after another. In 1800, towns and farms in the Albemarle and Cape Fear regions were three or four generations old, while in the mountains, pioneers were felling virgin trees to get their first crops in and temporary houses built. Growth became less dramatic in the new century and leveled off in the 1810s and 1820s as westward expansion diverted the direction of immigration and drew off thousands of North Carolinians to new opportunities.[2]

New or old, small family farms were the basic economic and social unit, for North Carolina was almost exclusively rural, and most of its farmers owned small landholdings and raised crops mainly for their own sustenance. Those who participated in the market economy raised such provisions as corn, beans, peas, and pork; planters along the Virginia border produced some tobacco, and those near South Carolina raised small amounts of rice. North Carolina's main export, however, came from its great virgin forests in the form of timber, shingles, and the pine rosin products—"naval stores"—essential to maintaining wooden ships.

Yet despite North Carolina's temperate climate and fertile land, the absence of good ports and the difficulties of transportation limited the development of trade and plantation profits. In contrast to the neighboring colonies of Virginia and South Carolina, few North Carolinians accrued great landholdings or large numbers of slaves. Many who hoped to make fortunes as merchants or planters found their ambitions thwarted because, as one planter phrased the common complaint, "the badness of our Navigation makes our Land and Slaves of very little profit to us." At the same time, the small farmer thrived, for the fruitful forests, cheap and fertile land, and long growing season enabled thousands to achieve lives of ample subsistence and quiet independence. By the mid-eighteenth century, North Carolina had earned a lasting reputation at home and abroad as "a good poor man's country" and, more specifically, "a fine Country for poor people, but not for the rich."[3]

The same conditions also kept towns small. There was no superior port, for the principal rivers from the hinterlands led to harbors in Virginia and South Carolina. Only the Cape Fear River drained a wide region and led directly to the sea, but the shoals surrounding its outlet hindered oceangoing trade. Edenton, located on the Albemarle Sound, became the first town of any consequence, with sixty houses in the 1730s and twice that number by the 1770s. Wilmington, near the mouth of the Cape Fear River, and New Bern, at the confluence of the Trent and Neuse rivers midway up the coast, emerged as competitors by the mid-eighteenth century.

After the American Revolution, New Bern, chosen as the colonial capital in the 1760s, became the largest town in the new state and maintained its position as leading port even after a new capital, Raleigh, was established in the Piedmont in 1792. As towns in other seaboard states grew into cities, North Carolina's communities remained small. The 1790 federal census-taker claimed that there were no urban areas worth listing, and as late as 1820, in a total population of 638,829, fewer than 15,000 North Carolinians lived in towns of 1,000 or more. About half these urban residents were slaves. New Bern had 3,663 people, Fayetteville 3,532, and Raleigh and Wilmington about 2,600 each; Edenton and Washington were the only other towns with populations over 1,000.[4]

Under these conditions, North Carolina's social structure and values assumed a character that, once established, prevailed over the years. The general configuration of the class structure followed patterns familiar in eighteenth- and early-nineteenth-century America. There was the usual division of the white population into upper, middling, and lower segments, a small number of free blacks, and a bottom tier of slaves. Over time, North Carolinians also participated in a general trend away from the relative equality of frontier life toward a greater concentration and stratification of wealth, property, and political power. By the mid-eighteenth century a small oligarchy of lawyers, planters, and merchants controlled local and colonial politics, and in the early nineteenth century, distances between classes were growing more pronounced.

Yet, in contrast to neighboring colonies, members of North Carolina's eighteenth-century gentry were neither as rich nor as numerous as their counterparts along the James River or in the South Carolina rice country. Most of the social and political leaders in the colony were relative newcomers, and many were first-generation settlers. Further, in this "good poor man's country," the proportion of middling and poor whites was unusually large for a southern colony: over two-thirds of free North Carolina families owned no slaves, and more than half of the slaveholders owned fewer than five slaves.[5]

The combination of a small, newly arrived elite with a large population of small farmers created its own set of accommodations, which distinguished North Carolina society, politics, and architecture well into the twentieth century. Visitors consistently remarked on the informality of the gentry's style of life and the "excesses of freedom and familiarity" the common folk displayed toward them.[6] But this apparent egalitarianism was not as simple as it seemed. It masked a complex system that "allowed functioning patterns of lower-class autonomy and upper-class control to operate simultaneously."[7] The elite maintained their tenuous position by two complementary strategies. On the one hand they enacted rigid, self-protective property laws and kept a tight grip on local and provincial government posts. On the other hand, aware that their hold on privilege and oligarchic government depended on the compliance of the yeoman class, they accommodated the independence of the small farmer and, particularly important in the development of architectural patterns, made gestures toward shared values with lesser folk. In contrast to elites who maintain power and social distance by displaying it, North Carolina's wary gentry retained rank by downplaying it, eschewing ostentation and avoiding burdensome taxes for public ventures that might test the patience of the yeoman class. This strategy tended to emphasize stability and to discourage innovation, and thus reinforced the conservatism already present in such a rural state.

After the Revolution, intense debate emerged over the proper direction for North Carolina's development, as different factions promoted different ways to assure social stability and promote prosperity.[8] At one extreme stood those who sought to keep the state and its residents independent, self-sufficient, and agrarian, and who believed in keeping taxes down and government at a minimum. Challenging this view were advocates of public investment in internal improvements, education, and trade, who pushed the state toward greater participation in commercial agriculture and the national market economy. The reformers gained ground briefly when a flurry of enthusiasm after the War of 1812 generated some ambitious public works schemes and unprecedented public investment in patriotic works of art, most notably a nationally renowned sculpture of George Washington in Roman garb, the work of Italian sculptor Antonio Canova.[9] But soon, lack of money exacerbated by the panic of 1819 curtailed public and private investment and left to the next generation the changes envisioned by early-nineteenth-century reformers. The economy remained sluggish, out-migration to the promising western territories sapped energy and leadership, and North Carolina gained such nicknames as "the Rip van Winkle state" and "the Ireland of America." Well into the 1830s, life in North Carolina continued "in the old Stile."

In the century from 1730 to 1830, North Carolinians had laid the foundations for a way of life that would persist through another century. The absence of focal urban centers; the uneasy dominance of a minor planter-merchant group in a large, scattered population of small farmers; geographic isolation that encouraged east-west frictions; and a stubborn and pragmatic unpretentiousness shared by rich and poor alike—all emerged as patterns during this period, and all shaped Carolina's architecture as well as her social development for decades to come.

Architectural Patterns: Building for "The Meridian of Carolina"

As the 1810 account of Duplin County indicated, building in this period was generally unpretentious, practical, and conservative. The architecture shared in a broad tradition that extended throughout the American seaboard, and individual buildings were conceived and their construction arranged in familiar ways, in which artisans and clients chose among known forms and combined old and new elements to suit their situations.

Many North Carolinians continued to rely on methods that permitted them to build quickly and cheaply from locally available materials. As had been the case during the proprietary era, such choices made sense where wood and clay were plentiful but currency and labor were scarce and transportation of imported materials was difficult and expensive. As settlers poured into North Carolina, the demand for housing was tremendous: if a household averaged 5 to 7 persons, the population increase from 35,000 to nearly 500,000 between 1730 and 1800 required construction of 60,000 to 100,000 new houses in seventy years. Thousands of families lived in small log or frame structures "built for a day's shelter or a year's convenience," while others built sturdier but still modest dwellings of frame or log.[10] A visitor to the coastal plain in 1745 found that the "Common peoples houses" were small wooden dwellings, tarred instead of painted, and heated by wooden chimneys. And in 1780 a traveler found still typical "Virginia cabins, built of unhewn logs and without windows. Kitchen, living room, bed room and hall are all in one open room into which one enters when the house door opens. The Chimney is built at the gable end, of unhewn logs looking like trees, or it is omitted altogether."[11]

Public buildings followed similar patterns. Congregations erected their first churches—often of log—with whatever labor and materials their members could donate. Newly established county seats required courthouses and jails in order to set about the business of administering laws and confining criminals. Keeping taxes to a minimum, magistrates erected frame or log structures that were appropriately cheap, quickly built, and sufficient to last fifteen or twenty years. Courthouses erected in such coastal plain counties as Craven (1730), Onslow (1734), and Johnston (1760) required replacement within twenty years, and those built in backcountry counties such as Rowan and Orange in the 1750s were by the 1770s "ruinous" and too far gone in decay for use. The repairs or replacements of the second phase, too, lasted only a few years or decades, and new buildings were needed again in the early years of the nineteenth century.[12]

Increasingly, however, other North Carolinians erected more substantial and better-finished buildings. The century after 1730 produced the first generations of permanent, well-crafted structures that survive to the present. Residents of the coastal plain began to erect substantial and well-finished courthouses, churches, and dwellings by the mid-eighteenth century. Similar steps came later in the century in the piedmont and still later in the mountains. In nearly every locale across the state, there is a period of a few decades after initial settlement from which practically no buildings survive, or at most a tiny number—three or four in a several-county

McCurdy House, Cabarrus County, late eighteenth century. Log building dominated throughout the backcountry during the eighteenth and nineteenth centuries. (Photo, North Carolina Division of Archives and History.)

region, perhaps—that were obviously extraordinary accomplishments for
their time. After about thirty years of settlement, a scattering of buildings
typically survives, and after a fifty-year interval, the number of surviving
buildings rises sharply to become noticeable in the landscape. Whatever
the variations generated by local differences and by wars and depressions,
the sequences are regular enough to suggest trends in building practice
over the decades. This pattern parallels another: although building artisans were among the first settlers in most communities, there is typically a
lag of twenty or thirty years between initial settlement in a county and the
first regular appearance of apprenticeship bonds for carpenters, joiners,
and bricklayers in the county's records. A few more decades pass before
apprenticeship bonds become common enough to suggest a fully developed artisan practice. Taken as a whole, the large pattern is of an erratic
but ultimately steady emergence of a demand for well-crafted buildings
and of an artisan practice required to create them.[13]

Most of the achievements in building appeared, as in the 1810 account of Duplin County, in the form of unpretentious, solid structures of
log, frame, and occasionally brick or stone. The Duplin report was one of
several written by local leaders in response to a survey of the state conducted by the editor of the Raleigh *Star* in 1810. Item six in the question-

naire included the topic, "Remarkable edifices; general style of building." The respondents who addressed this matter told remarkably similar stories of the transition to good buildings and evaluated them in remarkably similar terms from the piedmont to the coastal plain. In Rockingham County, the buildings were "Generally of wood, some Framed but the greater part of hewn logs, covered with Shingles with Brick and Stone Chimneys, which render them more warm and comfortable than elegant," while in Franklin County the buildings were "comfortable, snug, and neat." In the coastal area, "plain and cheap" summed up Edgecombe County's buildings, while in Greene County, "the inhabitance Generally live in framed houses with chimneys of brick which are comfortable but seldom eligant." In Wayne County, the reporter noted that the houses were generally one-story wooden structures, but "There are However some Handsome two Story houses and the taste for Building seems to improve." In Moore County, "the Major part of our buildens are Log Houses—but . . . a taste for improvements in this way is becoming universal."[14]

As these reports suggest, and standing buildings confirm, one-story buildings of log or frame were the norm, their gable roofs covered with wood shingles and their walls protected by weatherboards or clapboards. Most houses had one or two main rooms, and the hall-parlor plan continued in common use in all but the grandest dwellings. Only a few houses before 1830 had more than three main rooms, and still fewer boasted a central passageway. Two-story houses were rare throughout the eighteenth century but became more common among prosperous citizens after the Revolution—a development considered a major step toward improvement, as the Wayne County observer acknowledged. Brick and stone dwellings or public buildings were symbols of the highest status, and brick and stone chimneys were marks of good quality structures.

From region to region there was considerable diversity. Building along the coast reflected patterns of trade and immigration with Virginia and with the Caribbean islands, particularly in the use of the long piazza or porch which was ubiquitous from Wilmington to Edenton. The house plans, barn types, joinery techniques, and brickwork patterns of the backcountry bore the stamp of traditions evolved among German and British builders in the mid-Atlantic region and carried south along the Great Wagon Road through Virginia and into the Carolina hills. Cultural diversity was most marked in the first generations of permanent buildings, for as the years passed, Carolinians melded their separate traditions into forms and methods that suited local conditions.

A recognized range of craftsmanship and finish served to differentiate status among buildings and their residents. As had been true among proprietary-period buildings, quality was defined by such elements as well-made weatherboards, the kinds of wood used, the thickness of fram-

Clear Springs Plantation House, Craven County, ca. 1760. Broad piazzas characterized eastern North Carolina houses from the mid-eighteenth century onward. (Photo, North Carolina Division of Archives and History.)

ing members, and the presence of glass windows or interior woodwork. Within the sway of English tradition, the most costly work had moldings, paneling, and hardware of good quality, whose forms exemplified the broad influence of the English Georgian version of international classicism throughout the Atlantic seaboard. Around the turn of the century, changes in taste toward the lighter, neoclassical architecture of the Adamesque style had begun to appear in North Carolina towns, and the motifs introduced by pattern books of the federal period—sunbursts, garlands, decorative gougework, and ever more delicate forms and moldings— appeared in most locales in the 1810s and 1820s.

Few "edifices" were erected, and those that were took a heavy toll in effort and money. Construction of Anglican parish churches dragged on for years as funds ran low and parish leaders died. St. Paul's Church in Edenton was begun in 1736 and not covered in until 1748, St. Philip's in Brunswick was begun in 1751 and not completed until after 1770, and Christ Church in New Bern took from 1741 to 1752 to build.[15] The monuments of the late colonial era—Gov. William Tryon's residence and capital at New Bern and the great Germanic communal buildings in the Moravian

Alexander Long House, Rowan County, 1790s. The paired chimneys display patterned glazed header brickwork seen in the mid-Atlantic region and the North Carolina Piedmont. (Photo, Randall Page, North Carolina Division of Archives and History.)

community of Salem—were magnificent, hard-won accomplishments. Frederick William Marshall, who guided the creation of Salem, observed, "The present building of Salem is an extraordinary affair, which I would not have undertaken had the Saviour Himself not ordered it. I verily believe that the rich city of London could not do that which we must accomplish."[16] The first public buildings erected for the new state in the 1790s—the university buildings in Chapel Hill and the State House in Raleigh—were plain, conservative brick structures. During the early nineteenth century, however, substantial public buildings, including handsomely finished brick courthouses, began to appear as part of the gradual rebuilding throughout the state. These, like even the finest dwellings, remained relatively modest in scale and conservative in form. Most Carolinians, as one resident put it, "appear to affect what may be called a Snug, rather than a Splendid way of living."[17]

Probably the most pervasive—and for some the most puzzling—aspect of North Carolina's emerging architecture was the widespread satisfaction with unpretentious building. Visitor after visitor observed that even the wealthiest built more simply than their counterparts elsewhere.

Typical were the comments of Janet Schaw, a Scotswoman who visited relatives near Wilmington in the 1770s. She praised the most substantial buildings and those that bore an identifiably British stamp, and she scorned those that represented other values. Schaw complained that her own brother's estate would have twice its value if only he had "followed the style of an East Lothian farmer" instead of "adhering to the prejudices of this part of the world." She looked askance at a wealthy Cape Fear planter who boasted an "excellent library with fine globes and Mathematical instruments of all kinds, also a set of noble telescopes," but who lived in a house "little better than one of his Negro huts, and it appeared droll enough to eat out of China and be served in plate in such a parlour." Similarly, in 1825 a traveler in western North Carolina marveled at a farmer who resided in a log house, though he had 1,400 acres of first-rate land and produced 3,000 to 4,000 bushels of grain a year: "The House Mr. Jones now lives in, which he built ten years ago, is not as commodious as might be expected for a man of his standing, would be contented with, yet it is considered here a good house." Strangers often attributed such choices to laziness or heat exhaustion, but a local explanation was that "the prevalent ambition seems not to run this way [toward building], but more to the Spirit of accumulation."[18]

The preference for simplicity also carried subtler implications related to the elite's strategy for maintaining their position. The grandeur, as well as the cost, of William Tryon's "palace" in New Bern was one of the issues that offended the backcountry Regulators: "We want no such house, nor will we pay for it," wrote one spokesman. After the completion of the palace, a political opponent of Tryon, writing as "Atticus" in 1771, put the politics of architecture into explicit terms. Atticus emphasized that Tryon's efforts at English elegance had been not only inappropriate but reprehensible in a poor colony where "publick Profusion should have been carefully avoided." By "chang[ing] the Plan of a Province House for that of a Palace, worthy the Residence of a Prince of the Blood," the governor, according to Atticus, had betrayed the public trust to "gratify your Vanity" by "leaving an elegant Monument of your taste in Building behind you."[19] These criticisms, however partisan, expressed prevailing values about the appropriate scale and place of architecture—values which Tryon had violated.

Similar views obtained in private undertakings. In 1817, planter James C. Johnston (son of Samuel Johnston, a prominent lawyer and governor of the state), stated matters plainly when he asked his New York agent to select furniture for his new plantation house near Edenton: "It is unnecessary for me to say that I wish them of the plainest and neatest kind and not in the extreme of the fashion but what would suit a moderate liver in New York." He explained, "A man by appearing very different from his neighbours is more apt to excite their ridicule and perhaps envy than their esteem & respect—you know very well what will suit the meridian of Carolina and I don't wish to be much out of the latitude—I trust altogether to your judgmt only I wished you to have [an] eye to the latitude & longitude of the place for which they are intended."[20] That such a statement of republican simplicity was made by a man who had just completed the most stylish private residence in the state suggests the complexity involved in the elite's avoidance of the appearance of opulence.

Other leaders shared Johnston's understanding of architectural politics. Federalist leader William R. Davie teased his friend John Steele on the completion of a new plantation house that it was "ornamented too with no little taste, enough I am afraid to mark you soon as an Aristocrat."[21] At the opposite extreme of the political spectrum, the archconservative leader Nathaniel Macon epitomized his own philosophy—"why depart from the good old way, which has kept us in quiet, peace and harmony—every one living under his own vine and fig tree, and none to make him afraid?"—by living frugally in a tiny dwelling in the midst of his vast plantation.[22] For the cautious Carolina elite, a reasonably spacious, well-finished dwelling was a sufficient assertion of wealth and status. The owner's continued position and support in his local community was more likely to be bolstered by a statement of shared values with a stubbornly republican populace than by a display of pretension and distance. Thus practical and symbolic concerns meshed: decent construction without extravagance assumed the status of an acceptable standard, and grandeur was viewed with skepticism. Throughout North Carolina architecture ran a strain far deeper than the often-cited indolence: a focus on practicality and profit, a distrust of unnecessary expenditure or pretension, and even a stubborn pride in the lack of ostentation—values that would prevail even when more money was available.

Yet this viewpoint did not go unchallenged. Particularly after about 1800, dissatisfaction with traditional attitudes about architecture began to be voiced, often in concert with urgings for change in other aspects of the state's life, such as internal improvements and public investment in education and the arts. Some writers saw the old-fashioned character of North Carolina architecture as a visible symbol of backwardness, and they espoused the new, the nonlocal, the tasteful, and, particularly, the "elegant" as proper models.

"Elegance" implied a degree of taste and even grandeur beyond mere adequacy or even permanence. The term had been in common use for many years but it gained increasing emphasis in the early national period. When the State House was erected in Raleigh in the 1790s, the building committee was given a low budget that produced a conservative brick building that was quickly condemned as "devoid of any taste or elegance." Advertisements for buildings for sale used the term frequently: an estate was listed for sale in 1803 as an "elegant and highly improved Villa" with

Hayes, Chowan County, 1814–17, William Nichols, architect. (Photo, C. O. Greene, Library of Congress.)

pleasure grounds "disposed with much taste," a Wilmington dwelling was advertised in 1816 as having a double piazza with two "elegant flights of stairs," and in 1818 a brick house in Fayetteville was to be "finished in the first style of elegance."[23]

For some, sufficient elegance could be achieved by grafting motifs from architectural books onto familiar building forms. For others, however, the achievement of elegance required rejection of traditional and local models in favor of new national or international fashions.

Calvin Jones, a Massachusetts-born civic leader in Raleigh, typified the latter point of view. This energetic proponent of internal improvements and scientific methods continually sought to bring the state and its public architecture into the national mainstream. In 1810 his newspaper, the Raleigh *Star*, commented that a new building in town promised to be "a handsome specimen of the chaste, elegant and correct style of building," which, the writer hoped, would "contribute somewhat to eradicate the Vandalism that so generally pervades our architecture." In 1814, Jones persuaded the state to model a new governor's residence after the stylishly neoclassical Wickham Mansion in Richmond, Virginia. In 1816, probably in anticipation of building a new church in Raleigh, Jones consulted a Virginia friend who shared his views. The Virginian responded, "We are as much at a loss here, as you can be south of us for models and improved plans in Architecture." He advised Jones to consult his congressman in Washington, where the best craftsmen were at work, in order to obtain from a builder there a design "upon the most modern improved plans."[24]

Such efforts to modernize the state and its architecture found little success in early-nineteenth-century North Carolina, where they represented a minority view. Not until the mid-nineteenth century did these ideas gain headway and bring about widespread change. The proponents of change always operated in tension with the insistent conservatism of a cautious elite. This tension shaped not only the direction of the society and its architecture but also the development of the practice of building in North Carolina.

The Heyday of Traditional Building Practice

In the century from 1730 to 1830, traditional building practice flourished in North Carolina. Although the challenges of new architectural ideas and new work roles and the rejection of traditional models began to appear in the early nineteenth century, their real impact remained small.

Much construction during this period was done by the people who would use the buildings. Gov. William Tryon repeated in 1765 a familiar story of settlers arriving with "not more than a sufficiency to erect a Log House for their families and procure a few Tools to get a little Corn into the ground," but self-reliant building was by no means limited to the first years of settlement. Farmers' equipment commonly included a set of carpenter's tools, and farmers typically considered basic carpentry skills a necessary area of competence. "If my daddy wanted a barn," recalled a later-generation farm resident, "he would just build it." But this continuing bedrock of rural building practice seldom appears in the written record, so that only local and family traditions and occasional travelers' reports suggest the thousands of unrecorded times when farmers built their own houses and barns, or neighbors joined to erect a structure together.[25]

Hence, the principal picture of building practice in this century is of full-fledged artisan work. As communities matured beyond the frontier stage into small towns and country neighborhoods, more specialized divisions of work emerged among all the trades, among carpenters and masons as well as potters, coopers, silversmiths, and cabinetmakers. In the process, artisans' roles, duties, and relationships with others took on more of the configuration of traditional, pre-industrial artisan practice prevalent throughout the eastern seaboard and in Europe. While drawing on precedents known from time immemorial, they encountered problems and opportunities peculiar to the southern, rural colony and state.

The Traditional Design Process

At the heart of traditional building practice lay the face-to-face relationship between artisan and client and their shared expectations about every aspect of building. The concept for each individual building emerged as the participants drew on a common tradition of building and, from its possibilities, recombined familiar forms and room arrangements and a few standard construction and finishing components. Any novelties in layout or finish could be suggested by either the owner or the artisan. The most complete record of private building appears in the papers of planters, merchants, and lawyers who invested in substantial construction projects. Their records reveal a variety of approaches, for in planning a building, the client might work out a scheme alone, confer closely with his carpenter or mason, or offer only general suggestions and leave most of the decisions in the hands of the craftsman.[26]

Many owners had some competence in planning and judging construction, a fact well understood by a drawing teacher in New Bern who advertised lessons in drawing plans for buildings not only for "Architects" and "Mechanics" but also for "the Husbandman" and "the Gentleman." The client's and builder's shared role in design was implicit in carpenter J. H. Smith's letter to Duncan Cameron concerning a house Cameron was planning to build:

> I have sent you a plan (to the best of my knowledge it has something Like what I understand you). If it suits you and you want any further explanation I shall be at home in Abought five weeks, I mentioned in the plan that you must have the wall five inches thick the wing to be the same pitch as the front on account of the Stares going out of the passage in the Wing and Landing in the Front. . . . This was the only plan I could think of that would answer a good purpose, I should wish for you not to have the weatherboarding sawed for the front untill you see or here from me, the Plan I have sent you I have made allowance for a good porch in front, if wanted.[27]

Either the client or the owner might turn to architectural books for information and inspiration. Although a few artisans owned several architectural books, the typical builder was unlikely to own more than one or two.[28] Carolina lawyers, planters, and merchants also occasionally purchased architectural treatises and placed them alongside their law books, dictionaries, farming manuals, Roman classics, English novels, Bibles, and Books of Common Prayer. Relatively few Carolinians owned large, expensive classical architectural treatises with their gorgeous renditions of Roman or Greek orders and their plates of elegant classical buildings. Gov. Arthur Dobbs's library was a rarity, for among his eight hundred books were several architectural tomes—works by Renaissance architects Palladio and Scamozzi, two volumes of *Vitruvius Britannicus*, "LeClerk's Architecture," "Architecture by Monsieur Bell," and a practical little "Builder's Dictionary."[29]

More commonly, clients and artisans bought the smaller, cheaper, practical builders' guides. Aimed at provincial builders, these little vol-

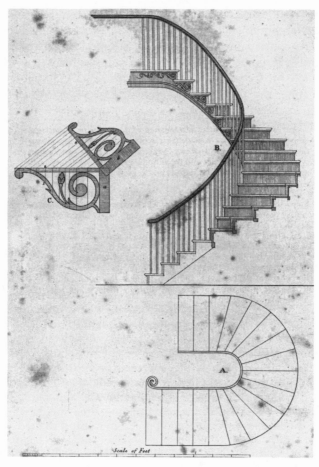

Design for stair, Owen Biddle, *The Young Carpenter's Assistant* (Philadelphia: Benjamin Johnson, 1805), plate 31. (Courtesy of Henry Francis du Pont Winterthur Museum Library, Collection of Printed Books.)

umes not only illustrated examples of buildings and classical orders, but also supplied simple drawings and explanations of structural problems such as roof trusses and staircases. They showed dozens of examples of mantelpieces and moldings of all sorts, explained and illustrated in simple terms the geometric formulae involved in "proportioning" classical orders, and gave instructions and mathematical charts for figuring quantities and sizes of materials. The most popular books went through many editions and were used for several decades. Among these were such English books as William Pain's *Practical House Carpenter* and Batty Langley's *Builder's Jewel*. Englishman Peter Nicholson's books had the best treatment of the difficult problem of circular stairs, and both American and

Stair at Moore House, Caswell County, early nineteenth century. The delicate detailing of the stair is based on Biddle's widely popular plate. (Photo, North Carolina Division of Archives and History.)

English authors repeated his examples. After 1800, Americans began to publish books aimed specifically at an American market, such as Owen Biddle's *Young Carpenter's Assistant* and Asher Benjamin's *American Builder's Companion.*[30]

Working from such volumes or from experience, it was not unusual for a planter to lay out a framing scheme for his barn, figure up a bill of timber or plastering, lay out a floor plan for his house, and supervise construction with a critical eye. The successful planter, like the yeoman farmer, required a range of practical and mechanical knowledge to manage his operation, and construction was part of that knowledge. Planter Ebenezer Pettigrew, for example, sketched the framing for a barn, estimated amounts of materials and their costs, and superintended construction. At various times, planter Duncan Cameron wrote up contracts and bills for plastering, carpentry, and other construction work. Such agriculturalists were little different in this respect from their counterparts in town. A merchant such as James McKinlay of New Bern was consulted by his acquaintances on technicalities of brickwork because in his business he "built much in brick."[31]

Suggestive of countless unrecorded planning sessions between client and artisan is the series of floor plans sketched for William Lenoir's frame house in 1788. Probably working with his carpenter, Thomas Fields, Lenoir sketched at least three ways of arranging the rooms in his two-story frame house before settling on a plan 40 by 28 feet with four different-sized rooms. On the back of the sketch they figured up the quantities and costs of materials and workmanship.[32] Working together, client and builder planned a building to meet the client's needs and fall within the capabilities of the artisan.

Contracts, Drawings, and Specifications

With a basic scheme established, craftsman and client could embark on the project with a verbal agreement and perhaps a handshake. In many cases the two individuals were known to one another and so embedded in the community that they could rely on a verbal bargain. One nineteenth-century artisan, millwright Berry Davidson, recalling a career that had spanned most of the century, stated proudly that "looking back over the years, I am safe in saying, I never found a man that asked me to sign a written contract for the undertaking of any job, nor did I have an unsatisfactory settlement."[33]

Sometimes, however, the parties found it appropriate to sign a written agreement—in the case of a complicated or unfamiliar type of building or potentially difficult financial concerns. Thus, in a time of uncertain currency in 1786, carpenter Gilbert Leigh of Chowan County agreed to build a plantation house in nearby Bertie County for £115, and an agreement was written to specify that "if the money should grow worse," the client would "make it as good as Dollars at 10 sh. & five Gallons West India Rum." In other cases, personal character was the issue, as a planter commented when he hired a brickmaker, "he seems to be a slippery fellow and I determined to write out the contract & have it witnessed."[34] In still other cases, it may have been habitual for one party or the other to prefer written agreements.

In their agreements and in the drawings that occasionally accompa-

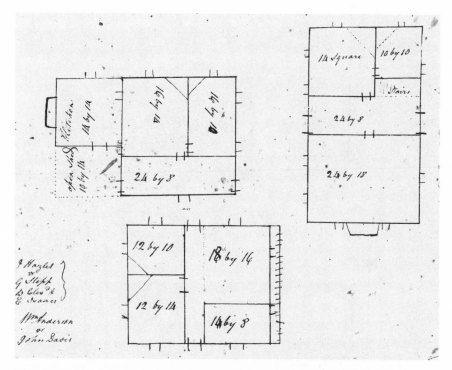

Plan drawings and estimates for the construction of Fort Defiance, Caldwell County, 1788. To plan his house, William Lenoir and his carpenter Thomas Fields sketched plans and on the back of the page estimated materials. (Southern Historical Collection, University of North Carolina Library, Chapel Hill.)

nied them, the planter and the artisan recorded mutual intentions in terms that followed age-old patterns, both in the topics they covered and the language they used. Traditional language carried from England to the colony continued to serve as architecture became more complex and more varied. Agreements specified only what was necessary to assure that both parties understood what was wanted, how much it would cost, and how it would be executed. If the project required any drawings, usually a simple floor plan or a depiction of special features sufficed. Elevation drawings were employed occasionally, sometimes with lines sketched in to show relationships or proportions. Perspective drawings, sections, and intricate detail drawings were rare. Such simplicity did not indicate naïveté but sufficiency: given traditional expectations and limited choices, a sketched plan showed both parties all that needed to be shown.[35]

A striking characteristic of traditional specifications is the gap between what the two parties found necessary to state in writing and what the present-day reader requires to envision the intended building. Following standard legal conventions similar to those common in deeds, wills,

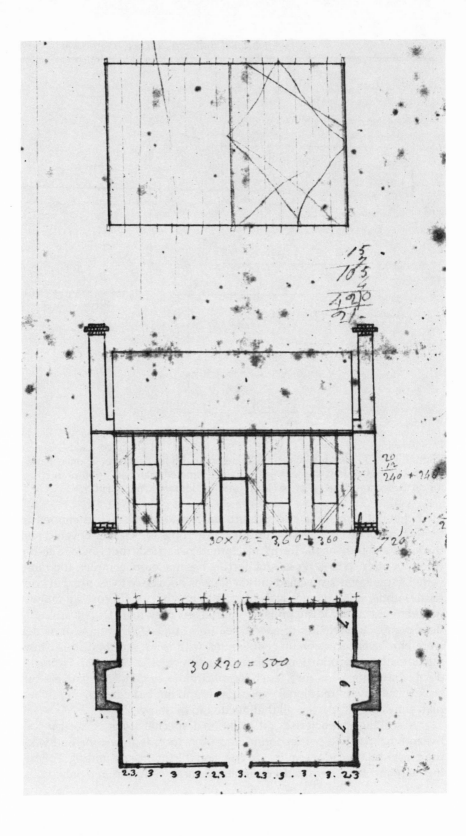

and other kinds of contracts, a building agreement typically began by identifying the parties involved and citing the size and materials of the building. It included such essentials as the financial terms, projected time of completion, and customary legal phrases. Beyond these standard clauses, the two parties defined some particulars of workmanship and materials precisely, while treating others quite summarily or omitting them altogether. As a rule, the elements that had to be specified were those that would affect cost or might be subject to debate. Especially significant are the kinds of issues that the client and artisan saw no need to mention—those they could assume as part of the customary way of doing things, those that could be left to the discretion of the artisan, and those that the parties could work out as needed. For many critical aspects of the building, they turned to time-honored, serviceable phrases: "good," "decent," "neat," "plain," and occasionally "elegant," and more commonly "necessary," "suitable," and "workmanlike." The client and the artisan counted on these seemingly vague terms to define their expectations, terms whose power and usefulness depended upon a common understanding of their meaning.

The essence of such a contract appears in a 1774 agreement between Macon Whitfield and carpenters Richard Gill and Benjamin Ward for a house in the village of Windsor in the northeastern coastal plain:

> The said Gill & Ward have by these presents agreed with the sd Whitfield, to build him a fraimed house Sixteen feet Square, with the body of the House to be Ten feet pitch between Joints, the Shead 8 feet between Joints in the Town of Windsor Where the said Whitfield shall direct—one six pannel door Thirty Lights of sash a pr of Stairs & the other doors to be Batten doors—& all to be finished & Compleated the whole House in a workmanlike manner by the first day of may next, in Consideration the said Whitfield shall pay unto the sd Gill & Ward the Sum of Nineteen Pounds Eleven Shillings proc. money & The Sd Gill & Ward do bond themselves and their Heirs &c for the perfomance aforesd in the Penal Sum of forty Pounds Proc. money if they should fail on their part & the Said Whitfield Bindeth himself in Like Maner to them in case he should fail. In witness whereof the parties to these presents have hereunto set their Hands & Seals this 14 Febr 1774.[36]

Here, as in many similar cases, the two parties wrote a binding legal document in which they relied heavily on implicitly understood mutual knowledge that permitted them to leave many critical elements about the building unstated. They defined only the basics—size and use of frame construction and a few details—and left all other features to be inferred

Opposite:

Plan and elevation drawings, Preparatory School, University of North Carolina, Chapel Hill, 1795. (North Carolina Collection, University of North Carolina Library, Chapel Hill.)

from them. The thirty lights of window sash suggest two windows with fifteen lights each. The six-panel door might well be the front door, and the other batten doors, however many, rear or side ones. The sixteen-foot-square dimension suggests a single-room plan or perhaps a room and a narrow passage, and the presence of stairs indicates an upper chamber.

Elements not mentioned in the agreement probably followed common precedent. Thus the roof would likely be a gabled one formed of common rafters and covered with shingles or boards. The walls would doubtless be covered with clapboards or weatherboards. For the foundation and chimney, if any, Whitfield probably hired a bricklayer separately, unless he relied upon the carpenters to set the building on wooden blocks and erect a wooden chimney lined with clay, which was not an unlikely possibility. The location of doors or windows, the pitch of the roof, the finish of the interior, the character and placement of the stairs, and most of the quality of the building were left to customary "workmanlike" standards. Such brevity did not necessarily imply a lack of concern about the quality of the building but rather sufficient knowledge to assure performance. Thus, also in Bertie County, another planter could contract with a reputable artisan, Gilbert Leigh, specifying only that he finish the work in "a good workmanlike manner what belongs to a carpenter & joiner," and receive a substantial and carefully crafted house.[37]

In some cases, however, the parties deemed it necessary to define their expectations of performance in greater detail. In 1788, when planter William Lenoir replaced his log dwelling with one of the first well-finished large houses in his neighborhood in the western foothills, he wrote a detailed contract with carpenter Thomas Fields to define both parties' responsibilities and the quality of workmanship expected. Fields was to

> frame said house with proper Girders and every thing that [is] necessary thereto—To lay all the lower Floors in the first & second stories with Plank Tongued & Gruved—To do all the weather-Boarding Plain'd Jointed & Beeded &c—To sheat the Roof with square edged Plank, and to get good thick shingles from the Stump, Joint them to a Guage, round them and nail them on, cornish said house with Mondilions &c—make sixteen 18 light window Frames worked out of the solid wood & folding shutters of six pannels to each window the sashes &c—make Ten 8 light windows & shutters of Two pannels Each & sashes &c.—make nine 6 pannel Doors & Frames &c—run up one pair of Stairs well Bannistered & a small pair cased up &c.— put Wash Boards and chair-Boards in the nicest manner Round all the Rooms and hang all the Doors and windows—Which is all to be Done in a proper good nice and work-man-like-manner.[38]

This sequence of tasks defined a house of first-quality craftsmanship. Each element treated in detail was one for which the regional craft tradition offered alternatives significantly different in quality and cost. Lenoir wanted each task to be done in the best fashion. He specified tongue-and-grooved plank, which required more work and fit more neatly than square-edged plank or, worse, random boards. Planed, jointed, and beaded weatherboards were better than irregularly cut or square-edged ones. Shingles could be of sap wood or have irregular edges or squared-off lower ends, but Fields was to make them of long-lasting stump wood and finish them with handsome, split-resistant rounded ends. Window frames might be made up of plain boards or a series of applied moldings, but Lenoir wanted the best and most demanding craftsmanship to be used in creating the molded form out of one solid element of wood. Yet, with all this stated so carefully, definition of other elements, such as the method of framing and the finishing of stairs and chair rails, was subsumed in such old phrases as "proper," "every thing . . . necessary thereto," "well Bannistered," and "in the nicest manner." And, if any room for doubt remained, all other matters were placed under the powerful ancient rubric that culminated the agreement—"all to be Done in a proper good nice and work-man-like-manner."

Both in its balance of explicit and implicit elements and in the actual elements described this agreement typifies many others written throughout the eighteenth century and much of the nineteenth century. A carefully crafted, traditional frame building of 1790 or even 1840 was described, understood, and built in the same fashion as one of 1750. And, even when building techniques and materials began to change, patterns of thought and expression remained much the same.

By contrast, when an occasional client sought a radical departure from the local vernacular, he had to take a different approach, for in such cases he could not rely on the efficacy of "good" and "workmanlike" standards alone. A case in point occurred when John Steele, a Federalist politician, piedmont planter, and head of the United States Treasury, decided to build a new house on his Rowan County plantation according to Philadelphia tastes. He knew he must take painstaking steps to get what he wanted. In contracting with a local carpenter, Elam Sharpe, to erect and partly finish his house, Steele left nothing to custom or to Sharpe's judgment; instead, he drew up a plan of the house and surrounded it with rows of precise notes, and the building agreement spelled out countless details that would normally have been left unsaid. Unlike the exterior end chimneys common in the region, Steele wanted his chimneys to "run up in the center of the partition that Divides the two parlours." He wanted "the front and rear of the house to be exactly alike in every respect," and his roof was to have a pitch "rather flatter than the common run of the Buildings in or near Salisbury."[39]

As Steele's house began to rise, its unfamiliar form attracted notice. Maxwell Chambers, Steele's farm manager, wrote urgently to him in 1799, "I wish you could be here before your chimneys are built. Perhaps you

Steele House (Lombardy), Rowan County, 1799–1800, Elam Sharpe and John Langdon, carpenters. (Photo, Randall Page, North Carolina Division of Archives and History.)

would alter your plan as to them. If the building was mine I would make two outside chimneys, it would make your parlours much more roomy, and the House as to the outward appearance would look much better to my notion; However, dont let my opinion operate against your own Inclination, for in our free country every man ought to please himself."[40] Steele did precisely that; as he explained to his wife, who like many women was managing aspects of the day-to-day construction work in his absence, "I am not so much concerned for the price of the work as that it sh'd be properly done."[41] To finish up his house in elegant fashion, Steele contracted separately with Philadelphia joiner John Langdon. Despite his intentional departure from local norms, however, Steele typified the traditional involvement of the client in his building process, directing the work in a stream of letters to his wife and his manager as the building moved slowly to completion.

Bargains and Payment

The records of many planters, merchants, and lawyers indicate that for substantial private projects before the mid-nineteenth century, most clients served as their own contractors, hiring a series of individual artisans to do the work of the different trades—a carpenter and a mason, perhaps a joiner or a specialized plasterer—and obtaining some or all of their own materials. Except for small jobs that involved only the work of one trade, it was relatively rare for a private client to contract with a single artisan to complete a whole project.

The artisan was paid for his work according to several standard methods of payment. English architect Christopher Wren summarized in 1681 the three principal "ways of working"—"by the Day, by Measure, by Great."[42] Working by the day was common, and pay was set at a lower rate if the owner supplied food and lodging and higher if the workman paid his own expenses—"found" himself was the usual expression.

Working "by Measure" involved an ancient system of pricing work by physical units and by the type and quality of the work—7 shillings a square for laying a barn floor, 3 shillings a square for framing, and so on. Carpenters' work of framing, roofing, and flooring was measured by the square—10 by 10 feet—or subdivisions in feet. Plastering and joinery work were figured by the yard, brickwork by the square rod, and stonework by the perch (a cubic measure usually equal to 24¾ cubic feet).[43] Many practical builders' guides contained tables for measuring work in the various trades. Either workmanship alone or workmanship and materials could be figured in this manner. Measuring was also the standard method of judging proper payments in cases of litigation.

Working "by Great"—contracting for the whole building—was, as has been noted, relatively rare in private jobs in this period. However, it was common for a carpenter to contract for the whole work of his trade, or the brickmason to give a price for the full masonry job. A common variation of working "by Great" was payment by the piece. Bertie County workman William Freeman's 1768 account with Mary Harrell was typical:

To Work on her House agreed on	£10.6.0
To Building an Outside Chimney	1.1.6
To work on the Meeting House	10.
To making her Coffin	7.6[44]

In a single building project, the owner might pay artisans by different methods—by the piece, the whole, the day, or the yard. Individual artisans were equally flexible, so that most charged according to whichever system was appropriate to the circumstances.

Payment was often made in kind rather than cash—"country pay," as some called it. Barter was central to the economy, especially in rural communities. Mary Harrell's credits with William Freeman ran thus:

By 1 Maire	£1.10. –
By 2 Cows and Calves @	2.10. –
By Cash @	1.10. –
By 1 Bushel of Corn & 1 Do Meal @	3. –
Bringing my wife to Bed	5. –

This account typifies the ongoing, face-to-face exchange of goods and services that enabled communities to function without a great deal of cash. The builder, like his neighbors, continually performed services for others, accepted goods and services from them, and kept close account of their value. Accounts might be settled immediately or run on for years. This intricate, personalized system of exchange, which one scholar has called the "social economy," recorded on the pages of account books the mutual interdependence of community members who, like Harrell and Freeman, served one another's needs from birth to death.[45]

Barter was also customary when individuals contracted for single large projects. In 1788 carpenter Thomas Fields agreed to build William Lenoir's house in exchange for a barrel of corn in the spring, 500 pounds of beef the next fall, five barrels of corn and 500 pounds of pork the next winter, plus the use of "the fort field to tend in Corn next year," provided that the carpenter would "take good care of all the fruit Trees & Return said Plantation at the year's end in as good order as he receives it." Payment through the use of land made sense if the artisan expected to work on the site for many months, as a house like Lenoir's would require; moreover, it probably helped guarantee that the workman would stick with the job. Lenoir also bargained with his bricklayer in "country pay." On March 22, 1790, Olivo Roberts agreed to build two chimneys for Lenoir and underpin the house at the rate of twelve shillings per thousand bricks; in exchange, Lenoir gave him a gray horse valued at twelve pounds and promised him on completion of the work "a middling good Cow & Calf" worth four pounds. Similarly, when Lenoir ordered manufactured goods such as glass and nails, he commonly paid his Fayetteville factor not in cash but in tobacco.[46]

The question of whether the artisan or the client would supply materials was resolved in every possible way. A carpenter might supply only his workmanship, workmanship plus timber, or, less often, workmanship plus all materials required to complete the carpentry work. When Raleigh carpenter William Jones proposed to build a 30-by-20-foot frame house in 1810, he included in his estimate of £327 the heart-pine timber, hardware, and glass but commented, "observe that I do not make pillars or do any underpinning or painting." Similarly, a bricklayer might lay brick supplied by the owner, he might make brick from the client's clay and with the help of the client's workmen, or he might furnish everything himself. A single workman might strike different bargains in different projects, depending on circumstances. Typically, though, an owner found it advantageous or necessary to provide most or all of the raw materials—either from his own land or through bargains he could arrange to his own best interests—and to hire artisans mainly to fabricate and assemble components.[47]

By serving as his own contractor, the client could retain the greatest degree of control over his project. The trade-off came, however, in the continual demands on his time and the need, even in a relatively simple project, to strike bargains with as many as a dozen different workmen and suppliers and make sure that each bargain was met as work progressed.[48] The account kept by planter-merchant Richard Bennehan during construction of a frame store building in 1787 suggests the multitude of bargains involved in completing even a simple construction project.

Martin Palmer for Building Storehouse	109
Ditto for Building Lumberhouse	58/10
John Waller for Plank & Scantling	30/2
William Ausley for ditto	13/10
Isaac Forrest for 11 M [thousand] shingles	11
Sampson Wood for Plank	1/18
Henry Hargrave for Brickwork &C	22
Cash pd for 50 Bus. Shells & Hawling	10
Anthony Ricket for underpining	10
Cash pd for 3 Barrels Tarr	2/10
Stephen Smith for Staples, hooks &c.	2/5
Martin Palmer for Building Shed to the Lumberhouse	19/10
Edward Wood for hewing & Sawing Scantling &c.	7/10
Stephen Forrest for 2 M Shingles for Ditto	2
Anthony Ricket for underpinning Lumberhouse cellar &c	8
Isaac Forrest for Making 2 Large Gates & 2 small ditto 200 feet Pailing, Horse Racks &c.	12/5
	——
	£420
Merchandise for Sundries [10 items of nails, hinges, latches, locks, plus white lead, 4 gal. linseed oil, 50 panes glass]	55
	——
	£475
Add 50 pct on £420 being Customary Allowance for Accommodations Hawling &c.	210
	——
	£685

£685 currency of No. Carolina equal to £342 Virginia Money rating dollars at 6/ The 15 November 1787

Richard Bennehan opened Store at Stagville.
(Bennehan Account Book, Cameron Family Papers,
Southern Historical Collection)

Getting Building Materials

The owner or the artisan was well advised to begin acquiring construction materials as soon as he had a good idea of the size of the building and the materials needed. The narrow, familiar range of components made it relatively easy to estimate the kind and quantity required—so much timber for a building of a given size, so many thousand shingles, so many bricks for a chimney of a certain height and mass, and so on. Window glass came in a few sizes, with 8-by-10-inch panes a standard size. Thus as soon as the owner knew the number of windows and their configurations—twelve, fifteen, and eighteen lights were common for normal-sized windows—he could place orders with local merchants or distant suppliers.

The owner or carpenter began, as had been the case for time immemorial, by making out the bill of timber, a document that set forth all the members and their sizes, both for scantling (pieces of wood measured in three dimensions, such as 24 feet by 4 by 8 inches) and for the plank (measured in standard thicknesses between 1 and 2 inches, then by length and width). Using standard mathematical formulae and relying on standard framing systems, the builder could determine how many board feet were needed for a building of a certain size, how many board feet of timber could be gotten from variously shaped timbers, how long rafters must be to form a roof of a certain pitch, and so on.[49]

If estimating amounts of materials was simple, obtaining the materials themselves was troublesome. The problems clients continued to face in obtaining construction materials is a critical part of the story of building practice in this period, as it had been earlier and would continue to be. The planter who possessed high-quality woodlands could cut building timber from his own lands; others purchased standing timber; and still others obtained timber from a sawmill operator.[50] If he used standing timber, the owner must employ workmen to cut down the trees, and then he must either haul the timber to the mill and then to the building site or have it sawn by hand into usable members. When planter James C. Johnston began his large frame plantation house, Hayes, near Edenton in 1814, he bought standing timber from land several miles away. Deciding not to have it sawed at a mill, he hired two teams of slave sawyers to come from Virginia to saw his scantling and plank and hew the large timbers, which required over six months of work.[51]

Even when the owner used a sawmill, the process was still complicated, for he surrendered a degree of control over his project into the hands of the miller. In building John Steele's house in 1799, his manager

Maxwell Chambers reported: "Plank will be somewhat difficult to get. The mills in the vicinity of [Salisbury] are so indifferent and their owners such trifling animals that there is no dependance in any engagement they make, and untill you have the Scantling they agree to deliver you are not sure of it. Stokes' mill is best of any in the neighborhood, But the dam of it is very lakey and it will go in the first [freshet?] that comes And he himself is going to the assembly." Two months later, Chambers found a reliable source of sawn planks, but they still had to be hauled and kiln-dried by local handymen, the Houcks. Again, there were complications, typified by one entry: "making the kilns, hauling wood, attendance of Billy 15 days, making up the kiln that fell down, and all the other work in drying the plank—20 [days]." At one point, Chambers worried, "I have been obliged to let the Houcks have 20 Bushels of corn from your place to feed their teams, or they could not have done the haulling; and it is difficult getting teams this busy season of the year, I was very unwilling to let them have it, but I saw if I did not they could not do the work."[52]

The ease of obtaining brick or stone for chimneys and foundation, or in rare cases for masonry walls, varied greatly with the locale. Clay suitable for brickmaking could be found throughout most of the state, being most plentiful in the piedmont. Brickmakers either dug clay from their own pits or often dug it right at the building site. Building stone was scarce in the east, but in the piedmont and west there were a number of good deposits of granite and other building stone. Although conditions varied from place to place, when local stone was available it was likely to be cheaper than making and firing brick. An estimate for masonry work for a piedmont frame house in 1799 compared the costs of stone and brick for the same project.[53]

Difference in the Expense of Brick & Stone Work

Stone	
24 perches at 1.00	$24
Laying Stone .50	12
Pointing with lime	3
Lime for the whole	4
Clay for do	4
Making mortar	4
	$51

Same of brick	
10 M [thousand] Bricks at 6.00	$60
Lime for the whole	8
Laying bricks 2.50 pr. M	25
Mortar, sand, water, &c	4
	$97

Along the coast, however, where there was little or no good building stone, the occasional stone trim for lintels, sills, or steps was usually brought by ship from New York or other northern sources. Moreover, while coastal builders normally used locally made bricks, for the most costly buildings it was not uncommon to invest in superior-quality bricks sent by ship from northern manufacturers. Philadelphia brick in particular had such a reputation for excellence that some clients preferred it despite the expense. In 1821, an order of about 100,000 Philadelphia bricks for a jail in New Bern cost six dollars per thousand for the bricks themselves, plus three dollars per thousand for shipping—nearly twice the cost of locally made bricks at five dollars per thousand. Use of imported brick and stone was evidently restricted to coastal communities and did not occur inland.[54]

Coastal clients also had an advantage in getting lime needed for masonry, for it could be burned from locally gathered oyster shells or from shells brought as ballast, and casks of lime arrived as ships' cargo. Away from the coast, as Moravian Bishop Spangenburg noted in the mid-eighteenth century, "There is stone which can be used for building, and also sand, but no limestone, which is very rare in North Carolina. . . . That is the reason for the poorly built wooden houses one finds everywhere."[55] The backcountry mason might use local freshwater shellfish to make lime or use clay mortar, while others paid the cost of hauling shells or lime from distant ports or limestone deposits.[56] But generally, as Spangenburg observed, the difficulty of obtaining lime limited masonry construction and the use of plastered walls to the finest buildings well into the nineteenth century.

The client who envisioned a handsomely finished house also knew the high cost of obtaining manufactured materials—glass, paint, decorative elements—that were not produced locally. Merchants and planters typically relied on trade networks that were part of their market connections. They ordered from Philadelphia or New York suppliers luxury building materials, such as fanlights, decorative plaster and ironwork, and even turned columns for porches, that were sent by ship to New Bern, Wilmington, or Edenton, or, for piedmont customers, to Charleston, Petersburg, or Fayetteville, and hauled from the wharf by wagon to the building site. For his Rowan County piedmont plantation house, John Steele had crates of goods sent from Philadelphia: nails, glass, paint, screws, doorknobs, and a carton packed with elegant composition figures—festoons, roses, classical maidens—manufactured by the Wellford firm in Philadelphia.[57] More typically, individuals relied on local merchants for erratic supplies of glass and paint or obtained hardware from local blacksmiths or nail manufacturers.[58]

Not only were manufactured and imported goods expensive, but their availability was unpredictable. North Carolinians struggled to get paint and nails and often simply took anything they could get when they needed it. When state treasurer John Haywood of Raleigh sought pigment

Portico, Donnell House, New Bern, 1815–19. The stone steps, iron railing, and portico columns came by ship from New York in 1818. (Photo, Frances Benjamin Johnston, Library of Congress and North Carolina Collection, University of North Carolina Library, Chapel Hill.)

Mantel, Steele House (Lombardy), Rowan County, 1799–1800. The composition ornaments came from Philadelphia manufacturer Zane Chapman and Wellford in 1800. (Photo, Frances Benjamin Johnston, Library of Congress and North Carolina Collection, University of North Carolina Library, Chapel Hill.)

and oil to paint his house in 1805, his Fayetteville factor informed him that the firm had on hand only white lead (13 shillings a keg), yellow ochre (10 shillings 6 pence a keg), and Spanish brown (6 shillings a keg). (All prices were at sterling, "on which we will charge 55 percent.") Further, oil was in short supply in Fayetteville. One local man reportedly had two barrels "coming up the River" costing about 17 shillings 6 pence a gallon, but the merchant recommended that his client try Salem, North Carolina, for oil "if a conveyance could be had, as it can generally be got as cheap there as in New York."[59] The problems and costs involved in getting materials from outside a locale meant that only a few ambitious clients and those determined to produce buildings of a certain character were likely to invest the time, money, and effort to obtain them. Most North Carolinians, having less money and other priorities, used local materials entirely and bought only a minimum of supplies for construction. The result was that well into the nineteenth century many carefully built houses still had clay mortared

Leary-Stroud House, near Pink Hill, Lenoir County, early nineteenth century. Such unpainted, unglazed houses were common in many North Carolina rural communities well into the twentieth century. (Photo, North Carolina Division of Archives and History.)

chimneys and interiors finished entirely with wood, and window glass and paint were considered signs of unusual prosperity and effort.

On the Building Site

With bargains struck and arrangements made for obtaining materials, the building process proceeded in a sequence that was both predictable in general outline and unpredictable in the multitude of problems that could occur. Traditionally, the most dramatic task was making and raising the heavy framed "carcass," a job the carpenter directed, with workmen assembled from throughout the neighborhood. Custom demanded that the owner supply food and drink to all hands; "2 galls. whiskey at the raising of the new house, $1.80," and "Dinners for the people at the raising, abt. 15 people, $4.00," were part of one construction account.[60]

Once the frame was up, the masons could build the chimneys and carpenters could roof and weatherboard the building. Thereafter continued a schedule of work that depended on a carefully ordered sequence of trades. The construction of the Edenton Academy in 1800, a modest frame building, typified the pattern. Mason Joe Welcome and other slave workmen alternated with carpenters and painters over several months. From July 18 to 23, Welcome and his co-workers cut and laid the stone foundation. On July 24 and 25, the masons joined with the carpenters in raising the frame. During August and September, carpenters completed the outside carpentry work. In October, Welcome and his cohorts carried the bricks by boat from the brickmaker, made mortar, and built the brick chimneys while the carpenters worked on the interior. In November and December, Welcome and his crew lathed and plastered the interior and the porch ceiling, fitting their work around the woodwork installed by the carpenters.[61]

To assure that work proceeded apace, the client had to recruit workmen to arrive when needed and complete their tasks so that the next phase could begin. This was a continuing problem. Often it took several inquiries and much negotiation before the client could locate and hire an available workman; as was true during the earliest years of settlement, skilled workmen were hard to find. Thus, when planter Ebenezer Pettigrew sought a bricklayer, he heard from a friend acting on his behalf, "Been to see Mr. Skinner concerning his bricklayer, he says that the Boy is a good plasterer, but he is at work for Mr. Charles W. Skinner at present and from thence he is to go to Mr. Benj. Skinner, but if he should get done in time for you that you can have him to do your work."[62]

Even if workmen promised to come, often competing projects, weather, and illness could prevent their arrival and delay the whole job. In December 1814, planter James Johnston began to scout the region for brickmasons and negotiated with Marshall Park to build his chimneys the next year. But, when the time came in October 1815 to begin the job, Park reported that his work on a Norfolk building had been delayed by gales and he could not come until November: "If your Frame is ready to put up I am afraid it would not be advisable to wait until next month."[63] Maxwell Chambers reported similar problems in managing construction at John Steele's house:

> The Houck's will not be able to perform their Contract with respect to the Bricks for your Chimney, they begun and made a few thousand, and were all three taken sick, one after an other, and have been so ever since July . . . it is therefore out of their power to have them made this fall. If you wish to have the Chimneys up, at all events, I believe I could get as many Brick from Mr. Long as would do with what the Houcks have made: But if you would think it better to put off the building to the spring, the Houck's would made the quantity that would be wanted.

Moreover, Chambers informed Steele, "Mr. Sharpe [the carpenter] is gone to South Carolina I am told, there is therefore no expectation of getting him to finish your House, I have been Casting about for a good workman ever since I heard he was gone, but have not yet heard of any that I should like to employ." By spring, construction had begun again, raising new questions about the schedule of work. Chambers wrote, "Henry Houck is employed in quarrying and hauling the Stone for underpinning the fraim as Mr. Langdon [the new carpenter] says he don't wish to lay the floors until that is done. You have said nothing about lime or the plasters Work, or do you mean to defer that untill you come, perhaps it may be as well, as the joiners work will not be completed until you arrive."[64]

Throughout the entire building process, artisans and clients dealt with one another on a personal, direct basis. In building Hayes, planter James C. Johnston kept a watchful eye on his workers' progress, keeping records by name and by day of each workman, whether free or slave, who worked on his house. His accounts for his building project include amounts due "Cato for Making Doors, Dave for laying floors, Jack for painting house, Joe Welcome for himself and boys," and notes such as "Brady and Macky commenced work 27th May, Macky lost 8 days by cutting his leg," and so on.[65] If the owner could get workmen to arrive on time and stay to completion, and if all the materials arrived as planned— seldom a reasonable expectation—construction of a substantial house usually required the better part of a year, and the largest buildings commonly took two to three years. It was little wonder that when James Johnston neared completion of his building campaign, his friend Ebenezer Pettigrew congratulated him in sympathetic tones, "I am satisfied you have had severe survitude to house building but I am glad to know that your labours are nearly at an end."[66]

Public Building Projects

As had been the case in the earliest construction projects in the colony, the important differences between public and private building projects were mainly procedural, for public buildings were similar in form and materials to private ones. And, while the buildings they were charged with producing became increasingly substantial and complex as communities matured—as handsome brick and frame courthouses and churches joined or replaced small log and frame structures—the essential role and duties of building committees changed little. Acting as corporate clients for the community, citizens applied to the task of public building the same expertise they used in private building projects. As in their own projects, they expected to work directly with builders to plan buildings and oversee construction. A frame tobacco warehouse in Perquimans County in 1755 was to be built in a manner "agreeable to the Directions the said Nathan

Newby shall receive from Joseph White or other persons the court shall appoint," and many other projects repeated similar phrases.[67]

Commissioners appointed to erect a brick courthouse in Roxboro in 1824 reported on their work in unusual detail. After developing a general plan and advertising the project in newspapers, the committee members attended on the day of bidding. There, once the contract was let by public crier to the lowest bidder, the commissioners and builders finished up the plan and specifications and the committee accepted bond from the undertakers for the "faithful and due performance of the work according to the plan & specifications." Then, "during the performance of the work [they] attended to the materials of which the house was composed to see that no green or unsound timbers were used." In the process, they found that "one or two specifications in the plan of the building had been omitted which it was important to add to promote the convenience and comfort of the building," and thus they continued to refine the design as construction proceeded. With work satisfactorily done, they "received" the building and authorized payment to the contractors.[68]

Planning the Public Building

Building committees typically settled on the kind of building they wanted before contracting with undertakers. They found various means of devising a suitable scheme. Occasionally a building committee established only a general idea of the intended building and asked bidders to provide plans as well as bids for construction.[69] Others commissioned someone to provide a scheme for them.[70] Still others invited local builders to "partake in their consultation."[71] A few committees pled inexperience in building or insisted that they were "indifferent draftsmen . . . possessing no architectural skill."[72] Most often, however, building committees relied on their own resources and knowledge of local building norms. Thus the committee for building an academy in Lincolnton in 1824 knew the general type of building they needed and simply voted on questions: "Should the house be long or square?" "Should it have a portico?"[73]

Many committees used a nearby building as a model for new construction. When planning a courthouse in Onslow County in 1755, the committee was instructed to "confine themselves to the design of the former Co't House at Johnston." A tobacco warehouse to be built in Tarboro in 1772 was to be of the same size and plan as one just completed in nearby Halifax.[74] Commissioners building a jail in Richmond County in 1813 recorded how this tried-and-true method operated. At first stymied in their efforts to plan a suitable jail, they requested more time before submitting their report. They agreed that their best approach was to seek out "the Plans of several of the best Joals in any of the adjoining or neighboring counties." Having "compared them together and duly reflected on the Different plans, Different expenses and usefulness and convenience of the several Houses," they decided to copy—"with one or two small alterations"—the jail in neighboring Anson County.[75]

Reference to existing models as a method of planning was rooted in medieval building agreements, and it became more common as communities matured.[76] In the early years of settlement, when the first buildings were erected in a newly cleared land, there were few nearby examples of satisfactory construction on which to rely. But as growth and rebuilding continued, the landscape offered examples of a wide range of types and qualities of buildings. Thus, in the late eighteenth and early nineteenth centuries, this ancient approach to design became more common in the workings of building committees. One committee after another advertised for bids on a structure to be "not inferior to" or "at least equal to" one in a nearby community.[77] This approach not only communicated expectations clearly but also assured by concrete example that the model was a workable one. Moreover, it put into written form the adherence of traditional architecture to the familiar, the time-tested, and the local as the main source of knowledge.

Once they had arrived at a suitable plan or at least a concept for their building, a committee chose among several means of providing potential bidders with the information they needed to make knowledgeable bids. These choices doubtless represented many considerations, both logistical and political. A few committees published detailed verbal descriptions in their advertisements, allowing full public knowledge of their expectations. For early federal government projects, such as lighthouses, advertisements for bidders usually contained detailed specifications to inform potential bidders from distant places.[78] Often, however, local committees chose to narrow and thus control the process. It was common to deposit a description and perhaps a plan in an accessible place. The vestry seeking bidders for an Anglican church in Hillsborough in 1768 explained: "As it is too tedious to recite the particular manner in which the [church] will be required to be done, any person inclinable to become a bidder, is desired to apply at the Clerk's office in Hillsborough, where he may be more particularly informed."[79] Other committees promised to describe the building personally to interested builders "upon application" to one of the members.[80] Still other committees, such as the trustees to build the courthouse in Edenton in 1767, gave a general description of the building—a brick courthouse, 68 by 45 feet—and announced that they would "attend with a plan of the house" on the day of bidding. Similarly, the committee for the Beaufort County Courthouse in 1819 sought bids for a two-story brick building, 32 by 37 feet, and promised that "the mode and style of finishing, and other minute particulars, will be known at the time."[81]

Elevation and plan of Anglican church in Hillsborough, 1768. These were evidently the plans available for inspection by bidders. (Southern Historical Collection, University of North Carolina Library, Chapel Hill.)

Contracts and Specifications

Contract specifications for public buildings were likely to be considerably more detailed than those for private works. The first public buildings for newly formed Johnston County, authorized in 1759, were modest examples of standard construction—a 30-by-20-foot framed courthouse and a 12-by-16-foot log prison. Yet the court gave explicit instructions to assure that the contractor produced decent if not fine workmanship and materials: heart-pine shingles, feather-edged weatherboards, and framing members of specified dimensions for the courthouse. As was typical in planning sturdy log jails, the security requirements of the prison gained special attention. The specifications required that the logs be hewn or sawn four inches thick and dovetailed, the floorboards be four inches thick, and so on. Other matters such as the placement of windows and the character of furniture could be described merely as "sufficient."[82]

More elaborate public buildings were defined at a correspondingly

Beaufort County Courthouse, Washington. The building committee advertised in 1819 for bidders on a brick courthouse 32 by 37 feet and offered further details at the time of bidding. (Photo, North Carolina Division of Archives and History.)

higher level of detail. The 1771 specifications for Nutbush Church in Granville Parish (now St. John's Episcopal Church, Williamsboro) describe a building within the same craft tradition as the agreement for William Lenoir's 1788 frame house at Fort Defiance, yet the document is a far more explicit definition of best-quality work.[83]

For the handsome frame church, 60 by 34 feet with walls 18 feet high, the contract explained element after element with great precision, from the brick foundation—3 feet above ground, 18 inches below—to the massively framed principal rafter roof supporting the concave ceiling. The workmanship of window frames (made out of the solid wood again), weatherboards, and shingles was specified. Nail sizes, finish of weatherboards, paint colors (stone color outside, Spanish brown roof, cream color and whitewash inside) were all given. Characteristic of many public specifications, the sizes of framing members (an index to sturdiness and cost) were listed, including the great 12-by-14-inch sills and 14-by-22-inch corner posts cut out in an L shape "so as to make flush walls with the other framing." Yet, also characteristically, many elements even in this detailed document were categorized in familiar terms—girders were to be "sufficient" in number and as "necessary in framing a House of these Dimentions so as to make it strong & substantial," and the whole was to be "framed in a strong proper manner agreeable to the Rules of Architecture." Aesthetic matters were treated similarly; the contract stipulated "elegant" turned posts to support the balcony, a "genteel" pulpit, "good" panel doors to the pews, a "neatly" bannistered communion rail, and a "good" table. In these and scores of similar documents, building committees and the artisans with whom they worked put into the most explicit terms their understanding of the rules and variations available within their building tradition yet left much to the larger definition of craft standards.

Such relatively explicit specifications were needed for public building projects both because of the public responsibility involved and because of the greater reliance on contracting by the whole in public projects. In contrast to the day-to-day control over materials and workmanship maintained by the private individual who managed his own project, by contracting for the whole work the building committee turned much responsibility over to the undertaker. Therefore, the agreement they signed was the committee's principal means of controlling the end product. Despite the lack of control, however, the practice of awarding contracts had obvious advantages from the point of view of the committee and the institution it represented: it meant that the cost of the project was known from the outset, and it reduced the daily responsibilities of the committee members.

Some building committees chose not to let contracts but to arrange the project item-by-item, hiring workmen individually and obtaining various materials, as was often done in private undertakings. Sponsors of St. Paul's Church in Edenton in 1737 paid separately for materials, hauling, labor, and bricklaying.[84] Construction of a jail in New Bern in the 1820s was handled similarly and required constant attention from the committee chairman, who ordered and paid for all the brick, stone, lime, wood, slate, and glass from New Bern, Philadelphia, and New York, and hired and supervised brickmasons, plasterers, and carpenters from New Bern and slaters from New York.[85]

In general, however, as public building projects became more frequent and more complex during the late eighteenth and early nineteenth centuries, building committees preferred to let contracts for the work. This approach, which followed patterns adapted from English precedent and

St. John's Episcopal Church, Williamsboro, 1771–73, John Linch, carpenter; framing exposed during restoration. (Photo, North Carolina Division of Archives and History.)

used in the earliest public buildings in the colony, would in the nineteenth century give rise to full-fledged contracting practice.[86]

One of the most remarkable aspects of public contracting in the late eighteenth and early nineteenth centuries was the range of possible ways of arranging contracts. Building committees, like private clients and artisans, approached their tasks with pragmatic flexibility. Far more often than in private jobs, public committees awarded lump-sum contracts for a whole building to a single bidder. Others, however, let small contracts for each trade's work and each type of material, and many had bricks made locally, then announced that they would let a contract for the rest of the job.[87] Some committees expressed a firm preference for one method of contracting, while others were willing to make whatever arrangements "shall best comport with the public interest" or would "comport with the convenience of the contractor."[88] Builders could be equally pragmatic in their bidding, such as one man who bid on a church project, putting in one bid of $6,300 for carpentry workmanship alone and another of $18,700 for the whole job.[89]

Whatever the particulars of the contract, customary English terms used since the earliest building projects in the colony required the undertaker to post bond to assure performance, sometimes in the amount of the contract price, sometimes up to twice that sum. The contract might provide for a single lump-sum payment upon completion of the building—typical in small projects requiring little financial investment.[90] For bigger jobs, a series of payments enabled the builder to buy materials and pay workmen as the project proceeded. Often payment was keyed to stages of construction: a start-up payment or a payment when materials were on the ground, another when the building was raised or covered in, and the last when it was completed.[91] The terms of such contracts, from the posting of bond to the manner of payment, were established practices when used for the first public buildings recorded in North Carolina and have continued to serve with some amendment to the present.

As in early years, too, the undertaker might be either an artisan or a local landowner who organized workmen and materials. If an artisan did not have the necessary property to post as bond, he might enlist propertied citizens to cosign his contract as his securities. In some cases, too, a planter and an artisan joined forces to take on a public contract. Planter Ebenezer Pettigrew and carpenter J. D. Carraway, for example, joined together to build a bridge and jail in Tyrrell County in 1821, the former providing materials and slave workmen, the latter his workmanship and additional men. The contract was let for $1,294.90, the two men's expenses totaled $763.86, and, as agreed, they divided equally the profit of $531.04.[92]

Large Contract Projects

The increasingly ambitious state and local building projects of the early national period offered new opportunities for large-scale contracts. In these years, the taking of contracts for the whole work of large, costly buildings was a perilous new venture, though such jobs would become more common later in the nineteenth century. The major public works of the 1790s—the construction of a state house and a university for the new state—illustrate the problems. The public coffers were low after the ravages of war and inflation, and the legislature sought to avoid any accusations of extravagance, so the budgets for these projects were extremely tight. Commissioners showed a preference for awarding lump-sum contracts, but they found it difficult to attract bidders and to assure satisfactory completion.

For the first university building of 1793 (Old East), the committee planned a plain brick building and awarded a contract to a local man, James Patterson. He completed the work for about two thousand pounds with the help of slave workmen belonging to him and two partners in the project.[93] In 1796, the institution's sponsors set their sights a little higher and envisioned a somewhat more elaborate main building (present South Building). It soon became obvious to university leaders that "such a house as we want" would cost more than the institution could afford, and even advertisements in northern papers failed to attract suitable bidders. The commissioners resorted to separate contracts for work and materials.[94] This approach had its own problems. For example, in the fall of 1799, Samuel Hopkins, who had agreed to lay the brick but had no responsibility for delivery of materials, reported that the supply of oyster shells hauled from Fayetteville to Chapel Hill was insufficient to finish the outside walls as he had intended. Therefore, Hopkins announced, "as the time of our bricklaying was too short to make it worth while to send Waggons to Fayettev expressly for more oyster shells, we have quit the Brick work for this season."[95]

For the State House, by contrast, the commissioners were determined to let a contract for the whole. Here too financial limits had a controlling role. The committee appointed in 1792 was given a budget so small they had found it necessary to threaten the legislature with the embarrassing prospect of a frame State House to get an appropriation of even ten thousand pounds. In June 1792, the committee produced the best design they could devise for the money available—an essentially domestic brick building enlarged to a scale of 52 by 110 feet. The prospect of the big lump-sum project drew prospective bidders from as far as Virginia and Wilmington. But when the gathered builders compared the plans with the money, they all agreed on the impossibility of completing the project within the budget. One bidder vanished, another proposed an alternate scheme, and none would make a bid. The committee finally had to settle on the contractor who would agree to get the most done for the price. Rhodham Atkins, a local carpenter of Massachusetts origins, contracted for ten thousand pounds to erect and partly finish the structure within two and a half years from July 20, 1792.[96]

Atkins had committed himself to a daunting task, which, as he knew, his colleagues had turned down. Not only was the State House the largest building erected under a single contract thus far in the state, but as contractor he had to find, haul, and work all the necessary materials and hire and superintend workmen—all in a brand new, essentially unpopulated town whose first streets were to be cleared as he cut the timber. Neverthe-

South Building, University of North Carolina, Chapel Hill, 1798–1814. (Photo, ca. 1890, North Carolina Collection, University of North Carolina Library, Chapel Hill.)

less, by August 1793, Atkins had six brickyards operating and an abundance of shells on hand for lime, timber was being cut in the public lots, and carpenters and a master brickmason were directing a force of free and slave workmen. The walls rose about ten feet high, and the doors and windows of the first story were installed.[97] As work proceeded, Atkins weathered complaints from competing political factions, only to find himself facing potential financial disaster near the end of the job. He had ordered window glass to be imported by Fayetteville merchant Robert Donaldson and Company, but in August 1794 he learned that "there was reason to believe that some accident had happened to the vessel in which [the glass] was shipped." Desperate to meet his schedule, Atkins ordered a whole new shipment of glass from a Philadelphia supplier, only to learn that the first shipment had in fact survived. Atkins found himself responsible for paying for two full sets of expensive glass. Only the legislature's concession to take the extra glass off his hands saved him from a severe loss.[98]

Despite its perils, the taking of large lump-sum contracts increased in early-nineteenth-century North Carolina as the potential for profit attracted ambitious artisans to make bids and then to organize work forces, obtain credit, and get materials to meet their commitments. Many succeeded without incident, while others got in over their heads: their plight

State House, Raleigh, 1793–95, Rhodham Atkins, contractor. Watercolor by J. S. Glennie, 1811. (Princeton University Library.)

was memorialized by the bankrupt but undaunted contractor for the State Bank in Raleigh, Lewis Nicholson. He gave notice in the Raleigh newspaper to more than two dozen creditors involved in the project: "Having built, completed and finished the State Bank buildings, I am as poor as a church mouse" and about to take the oath of insolvent debtors at the jail house door. He assured them all, "If I was cashier instead of builder of the Bank, all of the above should be paid. . . . All the world knows I am as industrious as I have been unfortunate, and it is reasonable to hope luck will change."[99]

Artisans at Work

The central figure in large jobs and small, public works and private projects, was the artisan—the carpenter, the bricklayer, the joiner, the plasterer. From start to finish, from initial planning with the client to the transformation of clay, wood, and stone into building materials and the assembly of materials into a completed building, the knowledge, skill, and labor of artisans shaped the character of architecture. The distinction of the best traditional buildings rose not from grandeur or innovation but from the proportions and skillful execution of basic elements—the shape of a chimney and the precision in laying bricks and stone, the placement of windows and the swelling curves of their molded sills, the crisp carving of a mantelpiece, and the harmonious relationship of all parts to the whole.

In some ways, North Carolina builders participated in patterns of work and in social and trade roles similar to those of the artisan class throughout pre-industrial America and England. Artisans were, by and large, independent workmen or masters of small shops. They grounded their identity in their possession of specialized skills essential to the society. They possessed knowledge, tools, and training for a trade, combined with personal characteristics of industry, reliability, and sobriety. The pre-industrial artisan class, ideally at least, had a sense of broad unity in which the ranks of apprentice, journeyman, and master were not opposing or permanent social divisions but stages of potential development.[100]

Yet, while sharing roles and duties with artisans throughout the country, North Carolina artisans also had to adapt to the specific conditions of their locale. Two factors had an especially powerful influence on building practice: the dispersed rural settlement patterns and the institution of slavery. So great was the impact of these conditions on artisan practice, in fact, that the one community in North Carolina that sought to replicate European craft traditions—the Moravians in Salem—found it necessary to enforce an urban concentration of tradesmen and to prohibit slaves from working as artisans.

Many aspects of North Carolina artisan practice are familiar within the broader national picture. The leading towns, though small, supported development of trades along lines similar to other cities. The Census of Manufactures for Raleigh in 1820—the most complete record of its type for the period—suggests the distribution of town artisans, though it probably lists an atypically large number of artisans in the building trades due to renovations to the State House at the time. In a city of 2,674 people, 163 individuals were counted in various handicraft trades, with 60 house carpenters being the most numerous among them. Eleven men were listed as bricklayers, plasterers, and stonecutters. Among the county population of about 20,000, there were only a few more artisans than in town, including 68 house carpenters and 16 workers in masonry trades.[101] The concentration of artisans in town and the proportion of carpenters to masons parallels patterns elsewhere in the nation and is probably indicative of other Carolina communities as well.

New Bern, the largest town in North Carolina from the mid-eighteenth to the early nineteenth century, exemplifies traditional urban practice on a small scale. Well-equipped artisans were working there by the 1750s. Benjamin Soane, a carpenter who died in 1753, possessed a large collection of architectural books and building tools. He owned not only the hammers, planes, and saws required for general carpentry but also the specialized planes for quarter-round, ogee, bolection, and astragal moldings, cornices, and bed molds necessary for fine finish work. Such luxuries as silver, sixteen books, black velvet breeches, and, sure sign of gentility, three wigs, reveal Soane's place in New Bern's social hierarchy.[102] In the late 1760s, construction of Tryon Palace evidently brought to the community a number of specialized Philadelphia craftsmen, some of whom may have stayed to expand local practice. A construction boom that began in the 1790s and continued through the 1810s supported a group of expert artisans who crafted the community's handsome federal-style townhouses and public buildings.

Building in New Bern during these years was dominated by a small group of artisans whose careers spanned two or three generations.[103] Some of the oldest may have been immigrants, but the younger men were trained in New Bern within the close-knit community of mechanics. Carpenter John Dewey, for example, took sixteen-year-old Benjamin Good as his apprentice in 1796; Good by 1804 apprenticed fourteen-year-old Uriah Sandy, who by age twenty-nine could take on the job of head carpenter for the First Presbyterian Church (1819–22), where he worked with his own "grandfather" in carpentry, John Dewey.[104] These men operated primarily as independent masters, each with a small shop of apprentices and slaves; every major building project involved a recombination of familiar names. The work is remarkably unified: for example, in the Masonic Building (1799–1806) credited to Dewey and the Smallwood and Donnell houses (ca. 1810 and 1816–19) attributed to carpenter Asa King, the woodwork is nearly identical, and all three bear strong resemblances to other contemporary work and to earlier buildings.[105]

New Bern's builders occupied positions of some prominence in the community and displayed the customary ranking of status within trades. In the procession to lay the cornerstone for the large brick Christ Church in 1821, near the front strode carpenters Martin Stevenson and Thomas Gooding, identified for the day as "the architects"—probably indicative of a leadership role in designing and building the church; behind them marched Wallace Moore and Bennett Flanner, described as "master masons." Such public events provided recognition of the importance of these artisans to community life and acknowledged the status of "master" among the tradesmen who had erected the town's principal buildings.[106]

Apprentice, Journeyman, Master

In New Bern and elsewhere, the sequence of artisan training from apprentice to journeyman to master continued along the informal lines established in the early eighteenth century and typical of other labor-short communities. With the exception of the Moravian settlement, North Carolina had no legal regulation of either length or quality of training. Nowhere was the traditional European seven years' apprenticeship adhered to or even implied. An orphan or bastard child bound by the court faced a period of indenture until he reached his majority, a period that could run as long as fifteen years or as little as one year, depending on his age. For the youth who entered apprenticeship solely to learn a trade, two to four

First Presbyterian Church, New Bern, 1819–22, Uriah Sandy, John Dewey, and Martin Stevenson, builders. (Photo, North Carolina Division of Archives and History.)

First-floor mantel, Smallwood House, New Bern, ca. 1810–12, Asa King, carpenter. Similar carved work appears in other federal-era buildings in New Bern. (Photo, Bayard Wootten, North Carolina Division of Archives and History.)

years ordinarily sufficed. The few amendments to apprentice law in the eighteenth and nineteenth centuries addressed social rather than trade concerns; mainly they regulated and expanded the involuntary apprenticeship of indigent and illegitimate children and gave special attention to free black children. Furthermore, in contrast to some American cities, no craft organizations emerged to regulate training or admittance to a profession. Thus North Carolina artisans gained their training and maintained

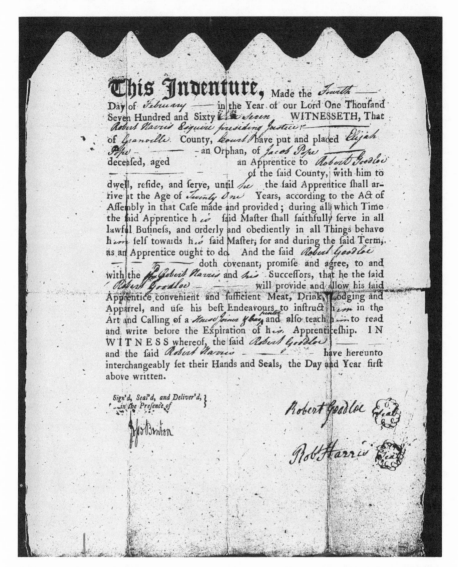

Indenture, Granville County, 1767. In the mid-eighteenth century, printed indentures began to replace handwritten ones, especially for the growing number of court-ordered apprenticeships. As for handwritten indentures, two copies were made and their tops were cut or indented in identical fashion. In this one, Robert Goodloe agreed to train Elijah Pope, orphan, in the "Art and Calling of a House Joiner & Carpenter." (North Carolina Division of Archives and History.)

their identities without the aegis of law or trade organizations, guided only by the force of custom.[107]

Nonetheless, the old terms of status within a trade, like distinctions between trades, remained strong. The status of journeyman was commonly observed, though not in the traditional European sense of one who takes a journey after apprenticeship to gain wider knowledge before being admitted to the status of a master. In America, a journeyman was usually considered to be a workman who had (presumably) completed an apprenticeship and who usually worked for others rather than operating an independent shop. Undertakers who had contracted for large projects frequently advertised for journeyman carpenters or masons.[108] Journeyman artisans often cited their training as an attraction to potential employers, and foreign-trained men especially prided themselves on being "regular bred" to their trades. At the same time, master tradesmen sometimes boasted that their journeymen, especially if trained elsewhere, were "regular brought up to the business."[109]

The move from journeyman to independent master was not regulated in any way. Rather, the artisan who possessed the skill, connections, and money to take on projects alone did so. It was not unusual for a carpenter to begin taking apprentices within a year or two of completing his own apprenticeship. Nearly every town and county had a few men in each of the building trades who, like New Bern's leading builders, gained positions of responsibility and a degree of success. Typically such men owned property including a few slaves, they took apprentices and hired journeymen, and they occupied a status within the community's middling class. Usually these men regularly worked on the largest building projects in their communities and had ongoing relationships with community leaders.

Thomas Bragg was an artisan who worked hard and took risks to attain the status of master builder. Born near New Bern to a family of sailors and navigators, Bragg learned his trade and then left home. He went first to Raleigh, the new capital, but by 1802 he had settled in Warrenton, center of a prosperous plantation region. Often relying on credit, he began to invest in land and slaves: he bought Harry for $377 and Kingston for £137 in 1812, Wilson for $700 in 1816, John for $900 in 1817, Claiborn for $800 and Will for $1,024.50 in 1818, and others. From time to time he advertised for journeymen and apprentices. Like many artisans, Bragg employed both black and white workmen. His shop built a number of elaborately finished houses and most of the local public buildings, and his growing reputation brought him jobs from as far away as Raleigh and Jackson, North Carolina. When a building committee called him in for consultation, they referred to him as "Major" Bragg, an "eminent architect and undertaker." The reference to carpenter Bragg as "architect" was not unusual; it was commonly applied to master builders, as it had been when New Bern's master carpenters marched in procession toward Christ

Church. Thus when carpenter William Jones completed a cupola on the State House in Raleigh, the local paper accorded "much credit to the talents of Capt. William Jones, who was its architect." Where planning and executing a building were part of an integral process, the distinction between architect and builder carried little meaning; the term referred not so much to a professional status as to the broader idea of the conceiver and maker—"the architect of the universe" or "the architect of the constitution" are apt parallels.[110]

Pay and Working Conditions

The workaday lives of North Carolina artisans shared much with those of their contemporaries throughout the young nation. The workday ran from daylight to sunset, so that a man worked several hours longer in summer than in winter. The workweek was considered to be six days long, with an occasional holiday. Typical of the pre-industrial era—and in contrast to later work ethics—eighteenth- and early-nineteenth-century artisans considered a ration of rum standard fare; many accounts for building projects included small sums supplying quarts or drams of rum or brandy to the workers. Nevertheless, moderation was expected if not always attained, and excessive drinking was the problem most commonly cited among builders by both their employers and other builders. Similarly, sobriety and industriousness were the two characteristics most commonly demanded by builders in hiring or recommending employees. Thomas Bragg made his priorities clear when he advertised for journeyman carpenters in 1825; he wanted "steady, sober men who are good carpenters."[111]

North Carolina building artisans earned pay at rates comparable to their fellows elsewhere, though their earnings usually ranked toward the low end of the scale. The value of money shifted too often to make hard and fast statements, but the colonial builder's pay conformed generally with Gov. Arthur Dobbs's observation that North Carolina's artisans received 3 to 6 shillings a day—a rate he considered excessively high. In 1752 a rural Albemarle area carpenter charged 2 shillings 6 pence for a day's work, while another got 5 shillings a day in the 1770s, a bricklayer made 6 shillings 8 pence a day in 1764, and a piedmont carpenter received 3 shillings 8 pence a day in the 1760s and 1770s.[112]

The standard of living such wages supported is difficult to ascertain, but if an artisan relied solely on an erratic 3 or 4 shillings a day, he was unlikely to achieve any degree of prosperity, particularly if he had a family to support. At face value North Carolina artisans' wages were comparable to those paid in other colonies, where housewrights were paid an average of 3 to 4 shillings sterling a day by the end of the colonial period, and where a man needed 25 pounds sterling a year to survive, 40 pounds to support a family, and at least 100 pounds to enjoy a life of modest comforts. If a workman made 3 shillings a day for 300 days a year—assuming he found that much work—he earned about 45 pounds a year, theoretically enough to maintain a family at survival level. But North Carolina artisans were typically paid in proclamation money, which was worth half or less the value of sterling, a situation that greatly reduced the artisan's buying power. Although its value fluctuated, Carolina currency was usually valued quite low. In 1745, for example, when a traveler from Pennsylvania bought a horse in North Carolina for 50 pounds, he reckoned the sum equal to about 8 pounds in Philadelphia money.[113]

In the 1790s the American dollar came into use, though pounds and shillings continued to be recorded in many accounts. Artisans' pay rates remained low, though they rose somewhat in the 1810s and 1820s. About $1.00 a day for a journeyman carpenter compared to 50 or 60 cents a day for an apprentice or laborer and from $1.25 to $2.50 a day for a master artisan represented the common range.[114] Town and rural rates, too, were similar: a master carpenter in remote coastal Tyrrell County earned as much as $2.50 a day in the 1820s, equaling New Bern's master builders and workmen on Raleigh's public buildings.[115] While commentators such as Dobbs complained that North Carolina artisans charged too much for their work, even an artisan who worked regularly at normal rates of pay was living hand to mouth and had little chance of accumulating wealth or property. A large proportion of artisans in the building trades continued to be poor. Many remained essentially permanent journeymen, working for a day's pay and never owning more than a few personal items and a tool kit, often the workman's most valuable possession.

Slave and Free Black Artisans

Critical to every aspect of building practice in North Carolina, as throughout the South, were the hundreds of artisans who, as slaves, had little hope of profiting from their work. As early as 1711, John Urmston observed that European settlers had "a bad time" unless they were among those who had "great numbers of slaves who understand most handycrafts," and in the 1730s John Brickell reported near Edenton "several Blacks born here that can Read and Write, others that are bred to Trades, and prove good Artists in most of them." By the late eighteenth century, reliance on slave artisans and laborers was so widespread that visitors to the Moravian settlement in 1773 viewed the productive community with "wonder and pleasure" and, upon learning that there were only two blacks in the community, "were the more surprised to find that white people had done so much work." An early-nineteenth-century politician commented that in every branch of the mechanic arts, blacks were "distinguished for their skill and ingenuity" and "in every place we see them equalling the best white mechanics."[116] Slave artisans worked in all the building trades, practicing as sawyers, carpenters, joiners, plasterers, house movers, bricklayers, and painters. Some combined several skills, such as ship and house carpenter and joiner Larry in Wilmington, and carpenter and shoemaker Robin of Halifax County, whose combination of trades was a common one. Sam, trained originally as a cabinetmaker, switched to carpentry, and Stephen, a carpenter in Wake County, also understood the millwright's business.[117]

Though some slaves learned trades informally from other slave artisans, many were apprenticed to black or white masters by owners who hoped to increase their value for sale or hire. Five young black men were sent to Charleston to learn the carpentry and bricklaying trades and, upon their return to Wilmington, were advertised for sale by their owner. Around 1810, six slaves owned by Raleigh banker William Polk were apprenticed to local artisans to learn the carpentry trade. When Willis, also owned by Polk, finished training under carpenter William Jones in 1815, his owner advertised the workman's availability and included a testimonial from Jones that Willis was "brisk, active, obedient, and very healthy" and "capable of doing very good work." Another Raleigh carpenter specifically sought young slaves to train and assured their owners that "any gentlemen who may think proper to put their boys under my care may expect the greatest attention will be paid both to their usage and learning."[118]

The popular image of slave artisans focuses on those who worked on their owners' plantations, and certainly this did occur. Other slave artisans worked for owners who were also artisans. Many of the leading builders, like Thomas Bragg and the New Bern builders, owned slave workmen. However, the number of slave artisans owned by other artisans represented but a fraction of the total number of slaves active in the building trades. The key to the work of slaves in building was the practice of slave hiring, a system that allowed free North Carolinians to use slave builders when and where they needed them.

Slave artisans were hired by the day, the month, or the year. Widows and children who inherited slaves; planters, lawyers, or merchants who did not need their slave artisans' services at the moment; and men who bought or trained slave craftsmen simply as investments all profited from the wages earned by slave artisans. Because both the hire and the provisioning of slave artisans was usually lower than that of free workmen, contractors and clients found it cheaper to hire slaves than to employ free workers.[119] In many communities, slave-hiring day took place at a public site, a market or courthouse, about the first of January, and often the bidding for hiring occurred along with the sale of slaves.

Hiring slaves had benefits and risks on both sides. The owner could profit from the slave's work, the client or builder who employed him had a workman who could not leave, and the slave artisan had an opportunity for more freedom of action than the field hand or house servant. At the same time, however, the hiring out of a slave presented risks. An employer, without a long-term investment in the slave's welfare, might abuse or neglect the slave; slaves working away from owners often used the opportunity to run away. As one observer commented, "A negro is capital, put out at a very high interest, but because of elopement and death certainly very unstable."[120] Nevertheless, because it permitted such efficient allocation of the labor supply and consistently benefited slave owners, the practice of slave hiring persisted.

Sometimes the artisan's owner received money directly from the client, as when Edenton merchant and planter Josiah Collins hired out his brickmasons Joe Welcome and Jim Millen for a dollar a day to work for planters Ebenezer Pettigrew and James C. Johnston. Similarly, during the remodeling of the State House in Raleigh, the state paid local slave owners for their artisans' work: "Peter the carpenter" earned $19.45 a month for his owner and John Haywood's slave carpenters Jacob and Mumford and laborers Jim and Russell drew $118 for two months' work.[121]

In other cases, slave craftsmen were hired by other artisans. The cost of a skilled slave artisan—perhaps $500 to $1,000—meant that few artisans could afford to own many, but it was feasible to hire slaves at rates that ranged from about $80 to $200 a year. The hirer, not the owner, usually fed and clothed the worker—an annual cost that one slave owner estimated in 1817 at $17.00 for clothing and $27.50 for food.[122] The conditions of employment of one slave artisan appear in records kept by New Bern lawyer and slave owner John Donnell in the 1820s. Ben, a carpenter who had been owned by New Bern carpenter John Oliver, was sold to Donnell on July 1, 1823, for $615. Donnell also bought Ben a set of used tools—an adz, compasses, axes, planes, a square, and chisels. In 1824 Ben was hired out to Mr. Stevenson (probably leading carpenter Martin Stevenson), at the rate of $18 for a 26-day workmonth. Donnell noted that "of this I allow [Stevenson] to pay Ben 1.50 per week provided Ben has lost no time & not misbehaved during the week (out of this 1.50 Ben is to board and clothe himself)," while Donnell received $12 per month. At a possible rate of $144 per year, Ben's work would enable Donnell to recoup his purchase price in a little over four years and thereafter take a profit on Ben's time.[123]

In a few communities, slave owners permitted their slaves great autonomy and allowed them to make their own arrangements with employers, live on their own, draw their own pay, and simply return a portion of their earnings to their owners. This practice, by which slaves "hired their own time," was forbidden by state law, but many slave owners openly flouted the law. In Wilmington and Fayetteville, in fact, the practice was so common and so interwoven into the economic system of the communities that slave owners gained local exemptions from state proscriptions. Owners registered their slaves and purchased pewter badges for them to wear when working on their own in the community.[124]

Carpenters and masons were numerous among the slaves who sought to escape their bondage. Building artisans, who were practiced in dealing with white society, accustomed to a degree of autonomy, and often sent to sites far from their owners, were among the slaves who found it easiest to take on identities as free men. Many of them could read and write, which also facilitated their escape. Working alongside men with equal skills who were free, slave artisans heard of opportunities in distant places where they could disappear among a busy work force. Owners of runaway artisans often surmised that their slaves had gone to northern cities or were attempting to pass as free men in southern states; in 1815 and 1816, several artisans along the Virginia border ran away to Petersburg, their owners believed, in hopes of finding work amid "the high wages given there in consequence of the destructive fire."[125]

A small but significant number of artisans in this era were free blacks. Some had been born free, some had been manumitted by their owners, some had earned enough at their trades to purchase their own freedom, and others had had their freedom bought by a parent or other benefactor. James Sampson, a Wilmington carpenter, is said to have been the son and slave of a planter, who freed him and established him in his trade in 1819.[126] Brickmaker and plasterer Donum Montfort in New Bern and cabinetmaker Thomas Day in Milton were among the free black artisans most successful in the building trades, and both of them owned and hired slave artisans themselves.[127] Most free black artisans, however, remained among the ranks of the hundreds of carpenters and masons who worked by the day or piece.

Relationships between black and white artisans, and especially between slave and free workers, were complex and contradictory. For the client and the master builder, slave artisans represented a source of reliable, relatively cheap labor. The journeyman, however, perceived slave artisans as threatening competition because of underpricing—a viewpoint held in many communities and trades. There was a paradoxical and self-perpetuating dichotomy of scarcity and competition: even when clients sought to hire white workmen for a job, they often found them so scarce that they turned to hiring slave artisans from their neighbors; yet white artisans insisted that it was the clients' reliance on blacks and the resulting low pay and lack of opportunity that kept more whites from working in the trades. As we will see, competition between black and white workmen constituted one of the major complaints of artisans' organizations.

The Rural Artisan: Versatility and Mobility

Most North Carolina carpenters and bricklayers, whether free or slave, were country workmen. Over 95 percent of the population was rural, and few towns were large enough to support exclusively urban practices. Even New Bern's artisans had to turn to rural jobs occasionally, and the heyday of that town's artisanry was relatively short-lived, waning rapidly after

1825 when West Indies trade declined. By 1839, when the architect of the Capitol in Raleigh wrote to New Bern carpenter Hardy B. Lane in search of eight first-class joiners, Lane reported that he doubted one such man could be found in New Bern.[128]

Rural artisans needed to be versatile. If an artisan, perhaps with a small crew, could undertake a wide range of tasks, he could complete all the masonry or carpentry work on a given building. He could get many different kinds of jobs, and thus find frequent employment among a scattered clientele. Rural carpenters completed frame buildings from framing to roofing to interior finish, and country masons were equally versatile. During construction of the Edenton Academy in 1800, Joe Welcome had cut stone, laid brick, and applied plaster. Similarly, Robert Warren advertised in Murfreesboro his skills as bricklayer, plasterer, painter, and glazier.[129] Thomas Trotter, an especially versatile mechanic working in the Albemarle and Pamlico regions, reported to client Ebenezer Pettigrew from Washington, North Carolina, in 1810: "I am as the old saying is up to my B. side in bussness, I cannot have sawing done to go about my house &c. and have engadged to finish the Iron work of a new Ship, and also expects to do the Cabbin work &c., these things are all new to me, but I must be doing something, it is as the saying is a Cash Job, my Negroe men will clear me one dollar pr. day, . . . I have cut 3600 lb. of Nails and they begin to be saleable."[130]

The rural setting also required the country workman to be mobile. In addition to the linear mobility common among building artisans, who often moved their places of residence several times in a career, even the most stable rural artisan operated in a pattern of circular mobility. North Carolina examples of this period suggest that builders commonly worked over a range of two or three counties around a home base, with occasional ventures to distant communities if a big project appeared. When bricklayer Francis Owen died in Chatham County in 1805, for example, it was reported that he had been "long . . . known in this county, in Cumberland and Moore." Many other artisans followed similar patterns.[131]

The rural artisan counted himself successful if he owned land and maintained a degree of independence by combining his trade with farming. In 1764 Gov. Arthur Dobbs complained that it was the warm climate and the ease of making a living from farming that encouraged artisans to abandon their trades for agriculture; this pattern, he said, created a scarcity of artisans that permitted them to work less and charge higher rates than their European counterparts. If this situation galled the cost-conscious client, it satisfied the artisan who hoped for a degree of economic stability and independence. Visiting Philadelphia in 1817, a Carolina landowner commented on the urban-rural contrast: "In the country, a man by tilling the ground gains a subsistance and feels that proudest sensation an independance of his neighbour; not so here the shoemaker, the tailor and the whole host of mechanics together with the merchant looks to the rich for patronage which if with-drawn they must starv[e]."[132] The combination of a trade with farming was not peculiar to the building trades. Millers, blacksmiths, and cabinetmakers, like lawyers or physicians, knew that a farm would enable them to raise their own food and give them stability in a world where opportunities for specialized work were scattered and unpredictable. Beyond that, landownership was the basis of financial independence, status, and political participation.[133]

Accounts of several individuals suggest the character of traditional rural practice—the basis of most building in the rural state and nation. Farmer and carpenter John Allen was born in Chester County in southeast Pennsylvania and migrated as a youth to the rolling Carolina piedmont, where he settled in the Cane Creek section of Orange County on a tract granted to his father in 1756. There he engaged in the life of a multiskilled yeoman farmer, continually participating in the social economy of his neighborhood. He farmed his own land, taught school, supported a family, and accumulated a good estate in land, household possessions, farming implements, and carpenter's tools. In addition to his own farm tasks, he did farming and carpentry work for others, which he exchanged for work done for him or goods received. His account book of the 1770s shows that during June he often worked for other farmers to reap and bind their wheat, and throughout the summer he worked an occasional day for others reaping wheat or oats or pulling flax. At intervals throughout the year, he employed his woodworking skills for his neighbors: he turned spindles and spoked cart wheels, sawed and rived boards, and made coffins and cupboards. He often took on small construction jobs, making doors, building partitions, shingling roofs, "fixing" mantelpieces, laying floors in springhouses and barns, and an endless variety of tasks needed in a rural community.[134]

Our most complete picture of a traditional rural builder in North Carolina appears in the career of Chowan County carpenter William Luten, whose account book from 1764 to 1786 provides an unusually detailed view of tasks, rewards, and problems typical of many such artisans over the years. He was part of a close-knit family of craftsmen and had been trained by his father, a carpenter and farmer. When William died in 1787, he left a modest estate valued at thirty pounds, in which his tool chest worth 12 pounds 5 shillings was counted as his most valuable possession.[135]

Luten displayed the usual versatility in his trade, making furniture as well as constructing buildings.[136] For John Vail in 1765 he framed a house, put in a partition, turned stairs, and installed a door and two window shutters. The next year he made a coffin for Nancy Curtis. In 1767 he made a chest "with feet to it" as well as a wooling wheel. For Joshua Bodley in 1770–71 he made a cupboard, mended a cider wheel, worked on an apple

mill, and built a "house over the mill." In 1776 he made for Richard
Hoskins a "candel stan to set candle stick on." Two years later he framed
a house for William Roberts, weatherboarded and shingled it, laid the
underfloor, made two doors, and "ran up the stairs."

The buildings Luten erected were typical of the region, being small
framed dwellings and outbuildings. John Vail's house had only one partition, a set of stairs, a door, and two window shutters. A building for
Joseph Blount measured 16 by 13 feet with a pitch of eight feet. William
Roberts's slightly more ambitious house had two doors and stairs to upper
rooms. For Richard Humphreys, Luten framed a "dayray" (dairy) and also
framed, raised, weatherboarded, and shingled a house and made the
"chimley." The house had two doors and two windows, a wooden floor,
and at least one clay chimney. This was a chimney built of logs or sticks
and plastered inside and out with clay, a cheap and ancient construction
typical of eighteenth- and nineteenth-century North Carolina. Luten
made no record of finishing interiors beyond "running up" and turning
stairs and installing partitions and window sash. Possibly he adhered to
the traditional role of the house carpenter—framing and covering the
house, installing partitions, putting in doors and perhaps windows and
stairs—and left the finer work of wainscoting, sheathing, paneling, and
mantels to one of Edenton's joiners. The other possibility is that these
houses, like so many others, remained unfinished, without benefit of
plaster or paneling.[137]

Luten both worked alone and occasionally hired other workers to
help him. In building for Humphreys in 1772, he employed several men,
for whose time he charged only 2 shillings 8 pence a day. He also charged
an additional penny a day for board for himself "and the rest of them that
work with him" and sometimes resided at a farm for several days while
working there, in both respects following practices common among artisans working at a distance from home.

Luten charged for his work by all the standard methods: by the day at
5 shillings—"3 days work on your barn," or "1 day work on your peasor"
(piazza); by the item—10 shillings 8 pence for making a gate and pales, 15
shillings for making a clay chimney; and by the measure—framing a house
at 3 shillings 6 pence a square, 19½ squares. Occasionally he took in cash,
usually proclamation money, but he also accepted all sorts of goods and
services: corn, rum, hauling of materials, the use of a cart, building materials—"a pasel of old plank and old scantling"—bushels of lime, chickens,
and pickled shad. He often had trouble collecting what was owed him, in
much the same fashion as the rural Virginia tradesman of the early eighteenth century who was described as roaming the countryside for his corn
and meat.[138] After he worked for Joshua Bodley in the summer of 1770,
Luten entered a charge of 3 shillings 4 pence for a trip to Bodley's place for
"stoping my tuls that I was fost to come another time for them." And for

yet another fruitless trip he charged Bodley the same sum, complaining that, "I did come for corn and you did Disappoint me."

Itinerant Specialists

Within an overall picture of versatility, there were some opportunities for trade specialization. Yet because chances for specialized work were limited to a few expensive and elaborately finished buildings, most specialty craftsmen combined two or three lines of work or lived an itinerant life. Thus a furniture maker such as Lewis Layssard in Halifax had equipment and skills for turning, which enabled him to make such building parts as columns, newel posts, balusters, drops, corner blocks, and rosettes for sale to clients or builders. A traveling group of artisans advertised a stay in Fayetteville in 1790 to do fancy carpentry, joinery, cabinetmaking, and turning.[139] Itinerant decorative painters left an array of vivid work in a community or region, then moved on to another. George Ladner came from New York to Edenton in 1788 to produce "Mahogany-Graining to its Perfection; also Marbling after the Italian method," while Henry Spencer from Philadelphia appeared in Washington in 1823, Salisbury in 1828, Lincolnton in 1830, and Charlotte in 1831, ever ready to paint pictures, furniture, carriages, and houses in the towns and adjoining counties.[140] Occasionally tinners and slaters appeared for specific jobs, but few found permanent work in their specialty at a time and place where wood shingle roofs were ubiquitous.[141]

Specialized subdivision of trades occurred on some projects—usually repeating customary distinctions between the rough construction work of the carpenter and the finish work of the joiner or between the tasks of the bricklayer and the plasterer and painter. Again mobility came into the picture, for a client might hire a town craftsman to finish a building erected by a country builder. When Duncan Cameron built his plantation house Fairntosh in piedmont Orange County, he employed the Fort family of carpenters from Wake County to erect his house and farm buildings, while for the final touches of the main house he recruited joiner Elhannon Nutt and carpenter John J. Briggs to come from Raleigh to execute the elaborate mantels and stairs. Similarly, he hired a local brickmason to erect his chimneys but turned to a Raleigh man, Henry Gorman, for the plastering.[142]

Opportunities for specialization were limited not only by the general simplicity of building but also, it seems, by the frugality of even the richest clients. A telling commentary appears in Rowan County planter John Steele's dealings with John Langdon, the Philadelphia house carpenter he hired to finish up his plantation house in elegant fashion. Before Langdon ventured to Rowan County in 1800, Steele had agreed to pay him according to Philadelphia rates, as listed in the carpenter's rate book—washboard with molding, 7 cents a foot; wainscot with molding on panels,

Fairntosh, Durham County, 1810–11, Elias and John Fort, carpenters. (Photo, Charles Clark, North Carolina Division of Archives and History.)

$1.10 a yard; open newel stair, plain brackets, kneed rails, $2.13 per riser; and so on. The rates were to apply to the agreed-upon work and to any additional work. But soon after the artisan arrived, Steele sought to reduce the payment for new work: "The prices which he showed me in his Book of rates appear excessively high considering the low price of bread, meat, wood, house rent &c [here]. He is I think a man of very fair intentions, and will no doubt see the reasonableness of conforming his Philadelphia prices for coarse work which common carpenters can do, to the change of place and circumstance."[143] (Langdon soon departed Rowan County for Fayetteville and then disappeared from record.) Such tightfistedness even among the style-conscious elite indicates at least one reason why there was little to encourage talented itinerants to stay or local artisans to develop specialized skills.

The mobility characteristic of both itinerant specialists and established local artisans had complex effects on architecture. Rather than each locality having a stable team of artisans working within a definite stylistic idiom, there was instead a changing, mobile multitude of individual artisans, all working within a general framework of traditional form and craftsmanship, but each operating independently among a scattered clien-

tele. This situation, combined with the common practice of hiring different artisans individually to perform the work of various trades, meant that
even within a short time period and a small region, each major building
was more likely to be erected by a different combination of artisans than by
a single shop that took on one project after another. Not surprisingly, the
buildings in a given neighborhood or community were seldom identical;
but instead they exhibited myriad combinations of forms and techniques
within a widely accepted standard vocabulary of craftsmanship. Even
where the regional repetition of a distinctive vocabulary of finish woodwork suggests the prominence of a particular craftsman, it is the individual components of buildings—woodwork, brickwork, a way of treating
a roofline or a window—rather than whole buildings that typically exhibit
the personality of the artisan; buildings are related chiefly as part of a
broader tradition.[144]

Artisan Protests

As North Carolina artisans sought to profit from their trades, they repeatedly encountered problems rooted in the broader society. One of the most
troublesome was the curious duality on the part of their clients. On the
one hand, community leaders sought to keep pay rates low—Governor
Dobbs in 1764 complained about paying local artisans 3 to 6 shillings a day
which he claimed exceeded European rates; planter John Steele objected
to paying Philadelphia rates for ordinary Rowan County work; the legislature put public building budgets so low as to scare off all but the bravest
local contractor; and so on. Yet, at the same time, when elite clients—
private or public—desired grand and elegant buildings, they snubbed
local workmen and sought to draw in specialists from distant cities. William R. Davie, Federalist political leader and devoted sponsor of the university, complained bitterly about having to rely on local builders and in
1795 placed an advertisement for contractors in Philadelphia papers. Similarly, in 1814, when the state set out to erect a governor's mansion, local
bidders were rejected by the building committee, which held bidding
open in hopes of attracting bids from "Architects at a distance."[145]

It was in this context that early-nineteenth-century North Carolina
artisans, like their fellows elsewhere in the nation, began to organize to
assert their status and improve or protect their working conditions. Their
efforts reflected not only the rising self-consciousness of the workingman
and questions about the artisan in the economy but also a response to
changes in expectations about building itself. With the increasing demand
for complex, large-scale buildings, as well as new ideas about elegance,
old traditions were beginning to show a few cracks. Artisans began to test
the waters from their own side. If their traditional skills were not considered sufficient to suit clients' heightened tastes and get the best jobs, why
should they remain content in their customary positions and pay rates?

Mantel, Wilkinson-Dozier House, Edgecombe County. Such patterned reeding appears in several federal-era houses in Edgecombe and nearby counties, which compose one of many regional groupings of distinctive workmanship. (Photo, Randall Page, North Carolina Division of Archives and History.)

North Carolina's small towns and rural communities did not foster the concentration of workmen that typically created trade or working-men's organizations. Yet, North Carolina artisans displayed signs of a collective consciousness of their identity as tradesmen, engaging in activities whose spirit shared much with that of their urban contemporaries. Although they organized only on an ad hoc, usually local, basis and addressed seemingly different issues, all shared common threads—the fear of erosion of their traditional status in both social and economic terms, and, increasingly, resentment toward a political system that gave more and more advantages to slave and property owners and prevented the workingman from making a living wage. Their efforts were aimed not at changing the social order but only at protecting and assuring their own fair treatment within that order.

One small, highly localized effort was an attempt to establish predictable pay rates—an effort oft repeated across other states where there were no guilds to assure standard rates. In 1816, Elias Fort (a house carpenter employed by Duncan Cameron at Fairntosh) called together the carpenters and house joiners in Orange County "for the purpose of consulting and forming uniform RULES whereby the measurement and prices of work may in future be regulated." Fort argued that different ways of measuring work and different prices charged for the same kind of work by different men had produced "disagreement and strife" and "many lawsuits" between employer and undertaker. Claiming that "many brother mechanics" had encouraged him to raise the issue, he sought to impose a unified code that would shield the employer from "exorbitant extractions" and protect the artisan from having his earnings withheld unjustly. The group met at least once and placed advertisements locally against the practices of two Orange County builders who had evidently caused the difficulties in the first place.[146] Though the outcome of their efforts is not known, such attempts to regulate prices among competing artisans of equivalent rank had deep roots among workmen, American and European.

Another source of artisan discontent lay in the emerging gulf between the journeyman and the master builder or employer. The increase in these years of large public-contracting jobs paralleled a general national movement away from small independent masters in all trades toward contractors and manufacturers who employed large numbers of workmen. The interests of master and journeyman under such circumstances became more and more divergent, as indicated by a notice placed by "a Tradesman" in 1815. In "A BONE For Journeymen Carpenters and Joiners to pick," he presented a series of complaints that typify the emerging problems of workmen in the period. He began by asking, "Is it not exceeding strange that men, who have served a regular apprenticeship to a trade should then work for the prices that common day-laborers do?"—echoing the continuing demand of artisans for proper recognition of their status. He believed that journeymen's problems arose from working for contractors. For years, he recalled, he had worked for the low pay of fifteen dollars a month so "that my employer might make as much as I did on my work, for his trouble of undertaking." Little traveled, he had been unaware of prices and customs in other cities, but, recently—probably during the War of 1812 when many journeymen found new work opportunities—he had learned that in some communities, "any man who has the most ordinary use of tools, may there get his dollar per day, and very often a much larger sum." But the tradesman's complaint went beyond pay rates: "Some of the gentlemen who undertake extensive business in the carpenter's line, are not calculators sufficient to make out accurate estimates of the work to be done. Hence, very often, journeymen are not paid, although they work cheap. It is well known that in large contracts, chiefly for public work, the unddertakers have to meet men of the first rate talents—keen calculators, who are selected for known economy, and who can split the utmost fraction of a single cent." If a bid was too low, "the man is ruined and his hands lose their wages." The writer urged his "brethren," "Let us firmly agree no longer to labor at their prices," but to work by the day and demand eight to ten dollars more a month.[147]

Much bitterer were the protests of white mechanics against black ones, though again the underlying issues were fair wages and the perceived abuses of workingmen within the dominant economic system. In 1802 a group of Wilmington artisans, including some of the town's leading builders, organized as "the Mechanical Society." They presented a petition to the General Assembly that indicated the complexity of their problems. They stated that, despite laws against it, many of the city's slave owners allowed their slaves to hire their own time and to undertake work on their own at half the rate that a "regular bred white Mechanic could afford to do it." Moreover, the slaves then hired other slaves to work under them and also took apprentices, flouting state law. As a result, the petitioners claimed, white mechanics found themselves "underworked and deprived of bread," and many had been "obliged to relinquish the tasks they were regularly brought up to, and follow other occupations to procure sustenance for themselves and their families." Further, the mechanics suggested, the practice threatened the stability of the community at large, for the "gangs" of unsupervised blacks "consort daily and nightly together," possibly plotting against the citizenry. The mechanics believed that the blacks, "circumstanced as they are," were "the irreconcilable enemies of the Whites," and that for the white artisans to survive, the assembly must find a means of preventing continued abuses of law by Wilmington slave owners.[148] These artisans were not objecting to slavery per se, nor even to the practice of slave hiring, but rather to Wilmington slaveholders' open disobedience of existing laws. They wanted the legislature to assure that the law of the land would be obeyed. Their efforts were in vain, however, for Wilmington slave owners continued to profit from their slaves' independent work and free artisans continued to protest.

Although their accomplishments were few, the protests of North Carolina workingmen were no less significant than those of their more successful brethren in northern cities. Their gatherings and advertisements alone indicate builders' growing sense of a trade or workingmen's identity and their need to protect their status in a changing economic system. They addressed problems that were at least as complex as those of artisans in big cities, and they did so amidst a system that was growing daily more entrenched and resistant to challenge. The issues raised in the early years of the nineteenth century would intensify during the decades to come.[149]

Moravian Building Practice:
Old World Traditions on the Southern Frontier

A telling contrast to the general character of artisan practice in North Carolina appears in the Moravian communities at Bethabara and Salem. Here, in the 1750s and 1760s, a highly disciplined communal religious society transplanted European craft traditions to the backcountry frontier, a process that telescoped within a few years the usually long transition from pioneer and rural versatility to specialized artisanry and professionalism. The buildings they erected were among the most substantial in the colony, and the reputation of their crafts was so formidable that when North Carolina's provincial congress sponsored premiums for home manufacturing in 1775, one member "wanted to bar the Moravians, for they would win all the premiums."[150] In the late eighteenth and early nineteenth centuries, the Moravians protected and nurtured their craft traditions by creating and enforcing an environment intentionally different from the southern rural society around them—insisting on an urban concentration of crafts and industries, regulating in guildlike fashion the stages of training from apprentice to journeyman and master, protecting the exclusive status of master craftsmen, determining pay rates, and, finally, prohibiting the use of slaves as artisans.

The Moravians were a Protestant, German-speaking group who had been persecuted for centuries before finding a haven in the early eighteenth century on the estate of Saxon nobleman Count Zinzendorf. Here they established the community of Herrnhut, from which they sent missionaries to the New World where by 1740 they established Bethlehem, Pennsylvania, as their chief colonial town. A reputation for industry and stability gained the Moravians an invitation from Lord Carteret, Earl Granville, to settle on his North Carolina lands, and in 1752 they obtained a tract of 98,985 acres in the frontier lands of the western piedmont. They named the tract Wachovia or Wachau after Zinzendorf's ancestral home in Austria. The Herrnhut leadership planned several stages of development for the community: an initial pioneer settlement supported by a communal way of life called the "oeconomie," establishment of farming and industries, and, finally, the creation of a central town as the location of trades, government, and commerce.

Moravian communities were closed societies intended to "safeguard the faith and protect the faithful." Their way of life was "grounded on a simple 'heart' religion in which the making of shoes, the grinding of corn, and the playing of a musical instrument served the cause of the Lord no less directly than ministering to the heathen." Excellence in craftsmanship and the hard work of all citizens were central to community life. Discipline was tight, for every member's material as well as spiritual life was closely monitored and directed by congregational councils, and those who found the system onerous were invited to leave. Thus, unlike most of the thousands of individual families and family groups across the piedmont, the Moravians had a long-range plan, reliable sponsorship, and a strong government that directed individual efforts toward well-defined common goals.[151]

During their first year in Wachovia the Moravians dealt with the universal challenges of making a new life in the wilderness. The fifteen men who went south from Bethlehem in the fall of 1753 were chosen for the versatility demanded of pioneers and included two who were millwrights and carpenters. Finding an abandoned log cabin on the Moravian property, they moved into it for the winter and made it the beginning of a settlement which they called Bethabara, "house of passage."[152] Everyone worked at clearing and planting and, when possible, building. Even this sturdy crew of young men, without the burden of families to feed, found frontier life daunting. Intending to build a house to replace their leaky cabin, on January 7, 1754 they selected a site, staked it off, and the next day began to fell trees. But in the evening of January 12, the men "conferred together and decided not to build the new house yet, as there was so much work to be done in preparing the land for corn. Meanwhile we will content ourselves in the little cabin."[153] This decision to put off improved construction doubtless echoed choices made by thousands of other settlers across the frontier. Thus for their first year the brethren relied on expedient log construction to erect buildings in a day or two: On January 3, 1754, "Several Brethren built a stable"; February 8, "We began to build a cabin for strangers"; February 9, "By evening our lodging place for strangers was finished. It is built of wide rails laid up like logs"; August 17, "Built a stable for the calves"; August 27, "Built two corn cribs near our cabin"; August 31, "We thatched the fodder huts built . . . yesterday"; September 9, "Built the third corn-crib."[154]

At the end of the first year, with land cleared, a crop made, and a shelter up, the brethren could embark on sturdier buildings, beginning with a two-story Brothers' House of squared logs. This move toward substantial building was made possible both by the efficiency of the oeconomie and by the arrival of new settlers including artisans. Seventeen brethren took time out from farming from November through May to cut the timber, saw the boards, split the shingles, raise the frame, and lay the floors. In 1755 they began a large log meetinghouse and a saw and gristmill of half-timber or "fachwerk" construction—projects that went slowly for lack of time.[155] By building the mill of fachwerk—heavy timber framing infilled with clay wattle and daub—the brethren erected a structure that replicated a traditional building technique in Germany and northern and central Europe. Fachwerk, filled with wattle and daub or with brick and

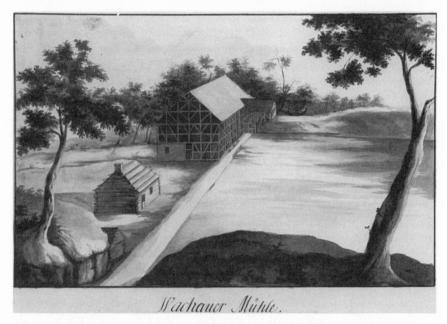

Wachauer Mühle.

Drawing of Bethabara, ca. 1759–60, by Christian Gottlieb Reuter. These first log and fachwerk buildings in Bethabara have all been lost. (Courtesy of Old Salem Restoration, Winston-Salem, and Moravian Church Archives, Herrnhut, East Germany.)

clay, was also appropriate because it made use of shorter timbers than did large log structures, and unlike stone construction it could be built without lime, which was scarce in Wachovia.[156]

By the end of Bethabara's second year, full-fledged operation of the building trades had begun. In the fall of 1755 new immigrants arrived after a six-week journey from Bethlehem, including European-trained specialists who defined Wachovia's building trades for a full generation: master carpenter Christian Triebel; brickmaker and plasterer Christoph Schmid; master mason Melchior Rasp, trained in Germany and celebrated as builder of Nazareth Hall in Bethlehem; and potter Gottfried Aust. They swiftly completed the meetinghouse and sawmill and set about to replace frontier expediencies with traditional German and Pennsylvania techniques. In October 1756, Aust the potter burned his first roof tiles for the saw and gristmill, which, as the Moravian diarist commented, had "so far been roofed in North Carolina fashion"—with wooden shingles. In November Aust made his first stove tiles and set up tile stoves in the Gemein Haus and Brothers' House, which the diarist observed were "probably the first in Carolina."[157] Although the settlement developed more slowly than leaders had hoped, new arrivals continued and farms and industries were established, so that by 1762 the community had 148 people. By 1768 Wachovia had "at least in a small way . . . all the really necessary businesses and handicrafts, which are greatly missed in other localities here" —the grist and sawmill, distillery, apothecary shop, pottery, tanyard, saddlery, and bakery, and the shops of a shoemaker, a tailor, carpenters, joiners, and masons.[158]

In the mid-1760s planning began for the congregation's main town— the "Gemein Ort"—long intended as the trade and government center of Wachovia.[159] Some residents of Bethabara resisted the idea, preferring to retain the status quo, but in 1765 the Herrnhut board announced that "it was determined by lot that we are to let our Brethren and Sisters in America know that the saviour wills that Salem is to be the place in Wachovia for commerce and the professions, and they are to be moved thither from Bethabara."[160] From 1766 to 1772 the citizens of Wachovia devoted their efforts to the task of town building, with all the building artisans, plus outside workmen hired for the occasion, turning their hands to its construction, while Bethabara's industries and the farms supplied materials and provisions.

The planning, construction, and ultimately the operation of Salem carried building practice in Wachovia into a new stage of complexity. To plan the new town and its buildings, Herrnhut leaders drew upon professionally trained European specialists. Christian Reuter, an accomplished German-trained surveyor who had laid out the town of Lititz, Pennsylvania, was sent to Wachovia in 1758 to survey and map the Moravian lands. Like many surveyors, he was also competent in town planning and architectural drawing. Functioning as one of the first resident professionals in the colony, in 1765 Reuter drew up the plan for Salem, and as work proceeded he mapped out the square and streets, surveyed each lot as buildings were planned, drew plans for new buildings, and staked out their sites for the builders.[161] Frederic William Marshall, assigned to administer the creation of the new town, also possessed architectural and planning skills. He not only advised on technical matters of construction and town planning but, after moving to Wachovia in 1768, functioned essentially as community architect, designing its buildings as well as administering its business, drawing up plans, and superintending construction of all the major buildings until his death in 1802.[162] Both Reuter and Marshall brought to Salem specialized European training and both operated in professional capacities as planners and designers.

The building trades, too, expanded to meet the new demands. Despite recurrent labor shortages and anxieties over nearby Regulator conflicts, the master mason Rasp and carpenter Triebel directed the construction of buildings of traditional Germanic form and finish.[163] A dramatic moment in their long labors came on a hot day in May 1769, when the biggest frame yet seen in the colony, that of the half-timbered Single

Brothers' House, was raised. The diarist reported, "The heat today was oppressive, but by four o'clock the framing of the first story of the Salem Brothers House was raised, with the help of Brethren from Bethabara, Bethania, and beyond the Eno [River]. Next day the rest of the framing was put up, though a piece of timber fell." The great timber took with it a wall not yet secured and "might have swept a number of Brethren from the second story to the ground, or have crushed others as it fell, but the angels guarded them, and no one was hurt." When the frame was up, "the musicians played their trumpets from the top of the house."[164]

In 1772 Salem began its life as a carefully regulated trade center. To prevent competition with the new town, Bethabara became a secondary farming village. The individuals "destined for Salem, moved thither from time to time." The "common housekeeping" of the oeconomie was abandoned in favor of a new system of administrative units and individual leases and businesses guided by a board of overseers. In October 1772 the tools held communally by the "building account" of the oeconomie during construction of Salem were parceled out among the artisans.[165] The operation of the new town was as carefully designed to assure its success as a trading center as the oeconomie had been to begin a settlement in the wilderness. Building trades, like other enterprises, operated in a system modeled after European guilds, with the overseers' board and masters' conference taking the place of the guild in setting standards and disciplining artisans. Here alone in North Carolina did government provide any official vestige of the trade organization and training requirements that had characterized the practice of the urban European artisan.[166]

The Moravians followed customary patterns of apprenticeship but added their own requirements. Informal apprenticeships had operated in the early days in Bethabara, but after some problems occurred, the first formal apprenticeship contracts were made in 1769. The indenture contained the customary provisions that the master would feed, clothe, and train his apprentice at his trade. In addition, a performance bond stated that the master could not remove the boy from Wachovia or transfer his indenture without the administrator's consent; the master agreed also to lodge and board the boy at the Single Brothers' House, where all apprentices were obliged to reside, whether bound to a single or married brother.[167]

Salem's board of overseers and masters' conference monitored every aspect of training, including assignment of boys to masters, discipline of problem apprentices, transitions to the status of journeyman, and attainment of the status of master. Thus, for example, in 1773 several youths who had completed their apprenticeships in masonry and other trades were formally interviewed by the board in the presence of their masters, and "the duties of journeymen explained to them, and they were urged to be faithful and industrious in their work and obedient to their masters."[168]

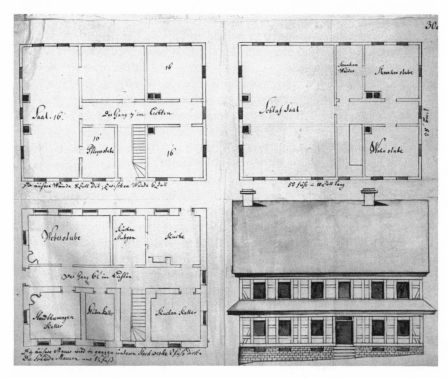

Plan and elevation, Single Brothers' House, 1769. The large fachwerk building still stands in Old Salem. (Courtesy of Old Salem Restoration, Winston-Salem, and Moravian Church Archives, Herrnhut, East Germany.)

The masters' conference lamented in 1789 the "tendency for liberty and impudence among the boys" and four years later there were problems when apprentices complained about working during the evenings. On the other side, the congregational council also had to step in when masters took advantage of their apprentices by discharging them when they became eligible for journeymen's pay.[169]

Salem's rules also defined and protected the duties and status of master craftsmen: "No one can start a business, open a store, or begin a profession, until the Congregation has recognized him as a Master-work-man. If a business, store, or profession is already being carried on in the town all other Brethren who wish to work in it, whether they come from Europe or Pennsylvania or grow up here, shall be considered as journeymen under the Master-workman, and shall be personally responsible to him."[170] Only a master tradesman could operate an independent shop; all others were tied into the Single Brothers' Shop, though married men were allowed to maintain separate households. The status of master required specific action by the congregational council. In 1784 Johann Gottlob

Krause, born and trained as a potter and mason in Wachovia, was given the status of master mason when old Melchior Rasp became too feeble and sick to work. Krause had just completed construction of the Salem Tavern, the first of several large brick buildings erected in Salem after the Revolution. Before granting him the new status, the council considered his qualifications carefully and observed, "Not everyone who can build a good wall has the judgment which is needed, and which can be expected of a good supervisor." Krause was also given new authority: "That he may have more weight with his journeymen he shall get his own and their wages from the Vorsteher, and shall himself pay them."[171]

Krause was "strictly enjoined to follow the rules laid down . . . for building inspection," for masters in building trades had special responsibility for regulating Salem's architecture as well as building it. This role was incorporated into a building code enacted in 1788 to ensure that all building in Salem would meet orderly standards of appearance, safety, convenience, sanitation, privacy, affordability, and fire prevention. Anyone intending to build in Salem had to follow the community rules, including the requirement to draw up plans and present them to the congregational council, who would then recommend any appropriate changes before approving construction. Before beginning a project, an individual also had to consult the community's master building artisan, who was responsible for making sure that all building projects adhered to the rules. Thus the masters took on a doubly powerful role in defining the nature of the community's architecture.[172]

Every aspect of a workman's day, whether master or journeyman, was monitored by congregational councils to assure efficiency, quality, and order. On March 31, 1784, for example, the council decided that "the bell shall be rung at 7 a.m., as is usual in the summer, and those of our Brethren who are engaged with the building shall breakfast at the same time, otherwise there is much delay." On the same day the council observed, "In the wood which has been cut for building there is much that is rotten or full of cracks. [Carpenters] Triebel and Strehle shall be spoken with about this."[173] The congregational councils also regulated pay rates, adjusting them as necessary and deciding whether charges presented by workmen should be paid. In 1775 the handworks conference decided to pay laborers 2 shilling 8 pence a day in winter and 3 shillings a day in summer, journeymen 16 shillings a week, and master masons, joiners, and carpenters 4 shillings a day in winter and 6 pence more in summer because of the longer workdays. In 1784 journeymen were authorized to receive 4 shillings a day in summer and 3 shillings 6 pence a day in winter.[174] In 1778, amidst the political and economic turbulence of the American Revolution, eleven or twelve young journeymen working at the Single Brothers' House went on strike over pay issues but matters were soon resolved by the council.[175] When local labor shortages required the employment of "stranger" artisans, the councils insisted that their tenure and behavior be watched closely "to see to it that no evil influences creep in through them."[176]

To maintain control over building projects, Moravian leaders preferred to hire workmen by the day rather than let contracts for the whole. In rejecting a lump-sum bid for building the Salem Tavern in 1784, they explained that in contracts "it is easy to agree to too little or too much, and too often the workmen are led to do poor work in their private interest. If the work is paid for each day all can be seen clearly, honorably, and in an orderly manner, and can be handled to the satisfaction of both sides." In later years, however, the community did award partial contracts. To build Home Church (1797–1800), a large and beautiful brick building designed by Frederic William Marshall, the council gave a contract to outside artisans for the workmanship of stonework and carpentry, but retained control of paying for materials, laborers and assistants, and board and lodging.[177]

One of the most pressing issues that Salem's community leaders faced in nurturing the trades was that of slavery. Although early rules forbade slave ownership, Moravians sometimes hired slave workers; as time passed, exceptions were made and Moravians began to own slaves, though there was always a degree of ambivalence about the situation.[178] In 1814, responding to growing interest in using slave workmen in labor-short trades, the overseers' board stated their "conviction that trades and handwork in Salem ought to be continued by residents of the town. Experience in other places in this country has proved that even if at first the introduction of slaves into trades and handicrafts seems profitable, in the end it led to their ruin."[179] But the problem continued. In 1820, confronted by increasing numbers of blacks in the community and a growing tolerance by community members for slavery, the board reiterated that experience demonstrated that whatever the initial advantages, "Negro slaves entering the professions and trades" invariably brought "the ruin of the whole trade and community, since the industriousness and ingenuity of the whites, mainly that of the younger folk, on which the wealth of a place finally rests, will come to an end."[180] The board laid down rules that, while allowing slaves in domestic and manual labor, stated that "in no trade or profession whatever under any circumstances whatsoever shall any slave be acquired or admitted for the learning or management of the same." This injunction was reaffirmed in 1845 as essential to the practice of trades by citizens of Salem.[181]

With time, change penetrated even Wachovia. The pressure to employ slaves was only one of many challenges to Moravian traditions in the 1820s and 1830s. No longer an isolated town in a remote frontier, Salem absorbed outside influences, and the old discipline gradually loosened. In 1823 the Single Brothers' Diacony ended as did the protected status of master artisan. By the 1830s various brothers joined together in businesses, taking apprentices and competing freely with one another as did their fellow artisans across the state.[182]

For eighty years, however, the Moravians had perpetuated trade traditions whose survival they knew depended on maintaining an environment quite different from the world around them. Salem's rules enforced an urban concentration of craftsmen, protected exclusive master status, assured adequate training and pay, and prevented competition from slave workmen. In this way, the realities of the rural southern economy were held at bay, so that here alone in North Carolina a traditional European model of artisan practice flourished.

The Beginnings of Professionalism

The concept of architectural professionalism, like the Moravians' vision of traditional artisan practice, appeared in North Carolina not through gradual evolution but by direct transfer from the Old World. As was true in nearly every colony and in the young nation, it was principally European-trained immigrants—surveyors, engineers, and architects—who established the first professional practices. A few native-born men became competent land surveyors, but more often such specialists were immigrants such as Moravian surveyor Christian Reuter, the Frenchman Claude Joseph Sauthier, and Swiss military engineer and surveyor Abraham Collet.[183] The pattern continued in the early nineteenth century, as European-trained professionals arrived in hopes of finding work in a growing country.

The distinction between artisan and architect was relatively new, having begun to appear in English practice in the mid-eighteenth century. This was part of the wider development of professionalism in the eighteenth and nineteenth centuries in Western countries. Men in various lines of work sought to carve out through education and specialized knowledge a status superior to the artisan. The new definition of the professional architect put him in charge of design and supervision, asserted his responsibility to the client's interest in the project, and separated him from the contractor, builder, or artisan whose work he directed. The architect might be paid by the day, by a monthly or yearly salary, or by a percentage of the estimated cost. His identity as the client's representative, his liberal education, his specialized conceptual and design expertise, and his differentiation from the artisan or contractor were the keys to his professional standing.[184]

In North Carolina, where traditional building practice persisted throughout much of the nineteenth century, the architectural profession remained small until the twentieth century, and architects continually struggled to assert their claim to professional status and pay. Yet, few as they were, professional architects appeared as early in North Carolina as

Frontispiece, J. Leadbeater, *The Gentleman and Tradesman's Compleat Assistant* (London: A. Wesley, 1770). This is an English depiction of the late-eighteenth-century construction site with architect, clients, and workmen. (Courtesy of Henry Francis du Pont Winterthur Museum Library, Collection of Printed Books.)

anywhere in America; their roles and duties illustrated fully the emergence and development of the profession nationally.

Probably the first professional architect in America by today's definition was John Hawks, architect of Tryon Palace in New Bern. Trained in England, he came to North Carolina in 1764 and from 1766 to 1770 was employed by Gov. William Tryon to design and superintend construction of the Palladian-style brick palace. His role was unique in the colonies. Elsewhere, to be sure, gentlemen such as Peter Harrison of Rhode Island provided handsome architectural designs, artisans such as William Buckland of Virginia and Maryland combined their trades with sophisticated design work, and advertisements occasionally appeared in colonial newspapers for men who described themselves as architects. Hawks, however, was apparently the first man in the colonies not only to be identified as an architect (and, in keeping with the times, occasionally as surveyor and master builder) but also to make his living by earning a professional salary as architect, with specific and exclusive responsibility for design and superintendence.[185]

The tools of the architect's trade, as Hawks's estate inventory showed, were not hammers and planes but pens and pencils and camel hair brushes, ivory rules, T-squares and mathematical instruments, and a set of architectural books. Furthermore, as a well-connected professional, Hawks occupied a social status above the middling rank usually held by the successful artisan. He associated with the gentry and possessed such gentlemanly luxuries as mahogany furniture, a good supply of silver plate, and a large library that included English novels and Roman classics. His wardrobe included eleven waistcoats, a black silk dressing gown, jeweled gold rings and earrings, and silver knee and shoe buckles.[186] That Hawks embodied so many aspects of emerging professionalism owes to his being an English architect working for an English patron, notwithstanding their colonial setting.

In January 1767, Hawks and Tryon signed an agreement that defined Hawks's duties and, in the process, epitomized current English understanding of the architect's role and his relationship with his client. First, Tryon asserted his own authority as governor and client to have a residence built under his "sole direction and management, or such other person as he shall appoint." To this end he required "the constant inspection superintendence and industry of a person acquainted with the value of work, qualified to adapt the proportions, experienced to direct the quality and choice of materials, and of ability to judge the performance of the several artificers and tradesmen to be employed in the said Building"—in short, an architect. These qualities, together with "skill and integrity," were what Hawks promised to supply. Rather than working by the day, Hawks was to be paid a salary of three hundred pounds a year proclamation money for three years. This was no small sum in North

Carolina: at nearly a pound a workday Hawks was making about four times the four to six shillings a good carpenter might earn, and his total salary for the project exceeded the entire cost of building the substantial St. John's Church in Granville County. The articles of agreement outlined the architect's duties in detail, both the design and provision of drawings and, in the usual English role of clerk of the works, his management of the project and keeping of accounts.[187]

First, Hawks was to "prepare and deliver" to the workmen and managers "all necessary designs, plans, Elevations, proportions, drawing or directions, for carrying on the said Building and Offices, with all suitable elegance, and Strength." The drawings he produced at the outset of the project survive as probably the fullest set of architectural drawings for a colonial American building. During the winter of 1766–67, Hawks and Tryon had worked through at least four stages of planning during which, evidently at Tryon's behest, the design progressed from a simple town house to a grand three-part complex of a type familiar in English country houses and architectural books. Typifying standard architectural drawing techniques of the period, Hawks used clean, thin lines to depict the ground plans and elevations for the various stages, as well as drawings of the roof framing, plumbing and draining systems, and a section showing door and window moldings and other finish. These drawings were but the beginning, for Hawks prepared working drawings as required during construction, including full-scale details for the workmen to use directly on the materials as models and then discard—a standard practice Hawks continued in later work.[188]

Hawks was also to hire and pay "all necessary Workmen, Artificers, Labourers, or others." He began immediately by traveling to Philadelphia in February to recruit workmen, since Tryon believed "this province affords none capable of such an Undertaking." As the artisans proceeded, Hawks was "continually [to] superintend, and as often as necessary Survey, Examine, and Measure every part of the said work, and oblige the several Workmen to execute and perform their several undertakings, according to the plan, and in a proper and workmanlike manner." He was also to inspect all building materials. Brick and wood were apparently obtained locally; other materials came from Philadelphia or England.[189] Finally, Hawks was to give Tryon a regular account of materials, wages, and all other money expended on the building, and to keep accounts ready for inspection at any time.[190]

Hawks pushed the work ahead efficiently. The first brick was laid on August 26, 1767; by March 1768, the brick walls had been "carried up to the plates"; by January 1769, the buildings were roofed with wooden shingles, a metalworker from London had installed gutters and downspouts, and joiners were at work on the interior. By mid-1770, Tryon and his family were able to move in. Upon the completion of the palace, Tryon

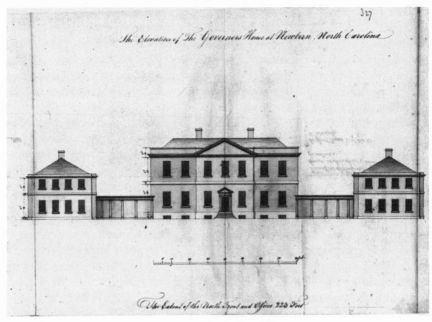

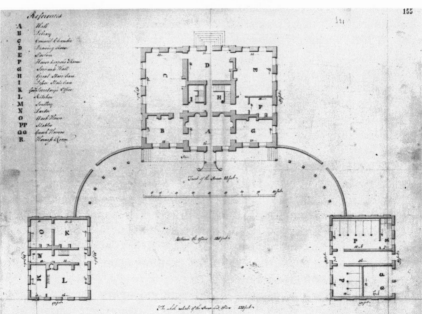

Elevation and plan drawings, 1767, Tryon Palace, New Bern, by John Hawks, architect. These drawings, which were sent to England in February 1767, represent the design from which the palace was built; they were used in the 1950s reconstruction of the palace. (North Carolina Division of Archives and History, from British Public Record Office.)

publicly acknowledged his satisfaction not only with the building as "a Credit to the Colony, . . . an Honor to British America," but also with the "Integrity, Diligence, and Ability, of the Architect."[191]

Although Hawks remained in New Bern until his death in 1790, executing a few additional designs and taking a prominent role in political life, his example did not generate a wave of professionalism in North Carolina but remained an isolated case.[192] The development of the architectural profession came slowly in the state as it did nationally. It was another British immigrant, Benjamin H. Latrobe, who became America's "father of professionalism" by introducing to postrevolutionary Philadelphia and Washington new concepts of design and technology and by pressing for professional ethics and methods of payment; he saw himself as the man who would "break the ice" for his successors.[193]

In early-nineteenth-century North Carolina, opportunities for professional architects and engineers increased amid the enthusiasm for large public improvements projects in the wake of the War of 1812 and the growing impatience with traditional building. American-trained engineer and architect Ithiel Town of New York and Connecticut tapped the desire for modern improvements when he erected two large bridges in North Carolina. His Clarendon Bridge across the Cape Fear River, erected in 1819 amid a burst of improvement in Fayetteville, was the wonder of the state and among the first examples in the nation of his patented Town truss bridge. Soon after this, Town's 200-foot span built across the Yadkin River near Salisbury in 1824–25 was hailed as a symbol of long-awaited progress. Salisbury's newspaper praised Town as a heroic example of native American genius, and Samuel Lemly, the local builder of the bridge, named his son Ithiel Town Lemly.[194]

Similarly, the public improvements initiated by the legislature of 1815 created a demand for professional services. The legislature's internal improvements committee sought a well-trained engineer to survey the state and plan and execute public works. They offered the job first to Benjamin Baldwin of Massachusetts and then to Latrobe, but both turned it down. A French émigré engineer initially accepted the post but returned to France when its political climate changed.[195] Finally, the committee sent one of their number to England and eventually recruited engineer Hamilton Fulton, who had worked for prominent British engineers Rennie and Telford. Fulton commanded a fabulously high salary—£1,200 sterling a year. In 1819 he arrived with his assistant, Robert Brazier, to begin surveying, drawing maps, and planning impressive improvements to the state's inadequate waterways. But Fulton found himself embroiled in financial problems and political conflicts; the legislature refused to fund anything like what he recommended. Finally he sold his books, his slaves, his surveying and drawing instruments, and his houseful of elegant furniture and left the state in 1826. His associate Brazier continued an increasingly unsuccessful private surveying practice until his death in 1837.[196]

The plans envisioned by engineers and internal improvements committees too often ran far ahead of the money the legislature was willing to expend. This conflict created frustration on both sides. Even such a devoted advocate of progress as university president Joseph Caldwell warned the public against the plans proposed by some architects and engineers. He believed that too many of them acted "upon the principle that people ought not to be informed at first of all the amount of expense, and all the difficulties of a public undertaking, lest they be deferred by an apprehension that they are insurmountable." These men, he claimed, gave underestimations knowingly, so that the "people being once induced to commence" would continue until the work was well advanced, and then be forced to find additional money for the rest, "that what has been already expended may not be wholly lost. This differs little, if any thing, from absolute knavery."[197]

Yet such "knavery" seemed to be the only way to open the state's coffers sufficiently to accomplish any ambitious projects. The professional who cut the broadest swath in North Carolina in the first quarter of the century was a past master at persuading his clients to build what they dreamt of, not what they could afford. English engineer and architect William Nichols may well have been the very "knave" who piqued Caldwell's ire. More than once he led the state—including Caldwell's university—into a project that vastly exceeded his original budget. But despite and perhaps because of this propensity, he functioned effectively in appealing to a clientele accustomed to conservatism yet eager for elegance. This Bath-trained architect offered the latest in taste, not only suave versions of the Adamesque style but also the novel Grecian and even Gothic fashions. Men such as Calvin Jones or William R. Davie had complained about the limitations of local models and local builders. Nichols gave Carolina's leaders what they wanted and more, and he made them pay for it.

Nichols came to North Carolina in 1800 in his early twenties. He worked as surveyor, engineer, house carpenter, and architect in New Bern, then Edenton, Fayetteville, Raleigh, and Chapel Hill. He became official state architect before leaving in 1827 for Alabama and Mississippi. Initially Nichols combined carpentry and architecture, but as he gained patronage, he took on more of the role of architect. He commanded considerably higher pay than local artisans, whether paid by the day or job, and as state architect he drew a professional salary of four hundred dollars per quarter or the standard 5 percent professional fee.[198] Yet in contrast to Latrobe's strict insistence on professional distinctions between architect and builder, Nichols combined architectural services with contracting. His ability to encompass all aspects of elegant building was a novel and powerful drawing card. As Nichols began a house for the Mordecai family in Raleigh, a family member marveled, "He will have the *whole* trouble of the building and deliver up the house ready for painting."[199]

Like Hawks, Nichols enjoyed a relationship with his merchant and planter clientele different from that of the artisan. If not socially, at least in terms of taste, he was his clients' equal or superior. During an 1817 trip to New York to find materials to finish James Johnston's plantation house, Hayes, Nichols informed Johnston that he found the city's resources barely adequate. He had found suitable undertakers for stone and iron-work, but he was "not so well satisfied as to the marble work," the mantelpieces being "devoid of taste for which they have the impudence to ask $300—so that I have struck that article from the list being satisfied that with the assistance of a few composition articles I can make one of wood that will answer the purpose much better." He added that "their taste in furnishing the interior of the Houses in New York is greatly improved, particularly in plaster cornices," and he insisted that "cornices are indispensable in two best rooms & the passage."[200]

Nichols's taste, and his own effective promotion of it, fueled his success. These talents had appeared during his renovation of old St. Paul's Church in Edenton in 1806–9. He proposed a program of neoclassical interior woodwork, plus a spire flanked by urns to finish the ancient tower. His price for workmanship alone, not including materials or masonry repairs, was $3,300. The startled building committee urged a cheaper and plainer scheme. But Nichols refused any such "abridgement of the work," for, as he explained with remarkable candor, "it would procure me no credit which is an object with me." A compromise contract of $2,150 omitted steeple and vases. But by the time he finished, he had his spire and vases, plus other refinements, to a total of $522 extra.[201]

The next decade brought Nichols the "credit" he sought. He was neatly placed to catch the state in the midst of postwar zeal and to set about remaking the old public buildings so long considered a disgrace. His skill in prodding his clients' ambitions appears in the reports of the committee appointed to install the Canova statue of George Washington. The group, formed in 1819 to determine where to put this celebrated and costly icon of the state's rising cultural ambitions, immediately turned to state architect Nichols for "professional assistance." He rapidly expanded their vision. In an impressive salvo of architectural erudition, he reviewed the possible locations for the statue: "Had it been equestrian a space in centre of the west front would have been suitable, or had it been pedestrian, then a kind of Monopteros Temple or Canopy supported by twelve collumns and open all round might have been a sufficient appendage and protection. But from its being formed in a sitting posture an enclosed building either a circular or parallelogram with a dome & portico would be proper."[202] Dismissing the notion of a separate small structure, Nichols proposed a complete remodeling of the old State House to create a suitable space for the statue and, in the process, supply additional space for the legislature and "give the house a respectable appearance worthy of the capitol of the State of North Carolina, keeping economy directly in view"—all for $20,000 to $25,000.[203] He had hit all the right chords. The committee's "undivided approbation" of his plan carried to the legislature. After the architect presented his plan, the assembly authorized spending up to $25,000 on the remodeling. Nichols was to superintend. Nichols remade the old Georgian brick box into a domed, porticoed monument enriched with the latest in Grecian detail. The senate and commons chambers became circular and semi-elliptical spaces with galleries and columns in the "Greek Ionic order," and a central rotunda beneath a dome received the celebrated statue.

By the time it was finished, the building had cost $65,000, some three times the price Nichols had given the legislature. But it also did precisely what Nichols promised it would. In 1822, Gov. Gabriel Holmes praised "the talents of the Architect" evident in "such an elegant specimen" and expressed his satisfaction at "giving encouragement to genius and attainment in one of the fine arts, which has hitherto been so little known, or properly estimated, among us."[204]

Even after his departure in 1827, Nichols's impact remained remarkably strong among those eager to modernize the state and its architecture. At his death more than thirty years later he was remembered as having "made the public greatly his debtor for a decided impulse given to architectural improvements throughout the State, in private as well as public edifices."[205] During a quarter-century in North Carolina, Nichols had, as his admirers recognized then and later, done much to change the state's concept of the role of architecture and architectural practice. He brought new emphasis on the most correct and stylish taste, and he pressed successfully for greater investment in impressive buildings. He both whetted and satisfied the appetites of those eager to abandon old building patterns and to attain "elegant specimens" that suggested a new direction in the state's life. In the process he presented to political leaders and tastemakers the image of the professional architect as a newly vital element in the state's building practice.

Between 1730 and 1830, North Carolina building practice achieved a diversity and complexity commensurate with the state's varied conditions and needs. Throughout most of the state, versatile rural artisans accommodated English customs to the requirements of a dispersed and frugal clientele. Slaves, free blacks, and white journeymen confronted the complexities and limitations of a social structure where the dominance of property pitted one class of artisans against another and kept wages low. In the most prosperous communities, a few builders found the where-

State House, Raleigh, remodeled 1820–22 by William Nichols. (Drawing, W. Goodacre, North Carolina Division of Archives and History.)

withal to develop large shops, to specialize in their trades, and to take on big, risky projects. In the same towns that supported the most developed artisan practice, major building projects and European-trained immigrants created early models of architectural professionalism.

In 1830 North Carolina artisans held preeminence in architecture as they had done for a century and more. The traditional relationship between artisan and client and the artisan's ancient role in designing and executing buildings persisted. Yet times had begun to change. In terms of numbers alone, contractors and architects were few indeed amid the hundreds of carpenters, joiners, masons, and plasterers at work in the 1820s. Yet, as both Nichols's successes and journeymen's complaints suggest, the new roles of architect and contractor had begun to shift the balance of power. The developments of the 1810s and 1820s presaged events that were soon to reshape building and builders' roles forever.

3

A Spirit of
Improvement:
Changes in
Building Practice,
1830–1860

*Time was when every North Carolinian in travelling from
Wilmington to Weldon was certain to have his feelings
wounded at the sneering remarks of "scoffers" and "wit-
lings" as they defamed the old North State for her poverty
of soil and primeval style of log cabin buildings. . . . Since
that time a spirit of improvement has been abroad. Pine
barrens have become fruitful, wild weeds have given place
to cereal grains, esculent herbs and luscious fruits, and the
modern neatly painted mansions have long since supplanted
the "log cabins" of the early pioneers. Sixteen years ago I
passed over the [Wilmington and Weldon Railroad] and as
I heard the carping, captious remarks of travelers from the
sunny South and frozen North, I blushed, and dared not
vindicate our State fame, so great were the odds against
her. [Recently] in passing over the same route, my State
pride was exalted in listening to encomiums on the style of
buildings, and crops of grain and fruits and grass that met
the eye, as the Steam horse sped along its iron track.*

—*"B" from Baltimore*, Fayetteville Observer,
September 1, 1856

Introduction

THE RAILROAD, the steam engine, fruitful farming, renewed state pride,
and modern, stylish buildings—these, along with invocation of the "spirit
of improvement," represented a vision that had appeared in the early
national period but gained new power in the antebellum years. The vision
had its shadow side, too: a persistent defensiveness about the poverty and
slow development of the state, especially when compared with the rapid
progress promoted by the national popular press. The ideology of improvement specifically tied progress and prosperity to the achievement of
"modern" architecture to replace "primeval" local traditions, as the construction of rail lines and greater access to capital and credit underwrote a
statewide rebuilding boom in the 1840s and 1850s.

In the building industry, these changes combined with the shift toward industrial organization of work and the growth of professionalism to
bring new roles for builders. Antebellum North Carolina saw the rise of
the state's first generation of large-scale contractors and the first widespread employment of professional architects. Though their numbers
were still relatively small, contractors and architects assumed increasing
influence and dominated nearly all the major building projects. This chap-

ter focuses on these changes, on the men who stepped into these new roles, and on the impact of such changes on builders throughout the state.

Rip van Winkle Awakes

Between 1830 and 1860, North Carolina moved toward fuller participation in the determined modernization and optimistic materialism that were reshaping the nation. If long-standing conservatism and obstacles of geography slowed the process, political realignments nevertheless combined with the transportation revolution and a sense of progress to make North Carolina in the 1850s a very different place from that of the 1820s or 1830s. [1]

The old debate continued between two opposing philosophies—characterized by one satirist as "Squire Oldway" and "Jack Steamer." The former wanted to maintain agrarian independence of government involvement, of entanglement in credit and debt, and of taxation for internal improvements. [2] Proponents of this view attacked expenditures like that for the work of state engineer Hamilton Fulton, who, they stated, had been paid five thousand dollars a year "to run about the country, up one creek and down another, to find places to spend more." They predicted that "millions may and will be thrown away, if this double game of taxing and squandering, inflicted on us by . . . internal improvement men, continues." [3]

The "internal improvement men"—the "Jack Steamers"—promoted public and private investment in canals and railroads to facilitate the transportation of the state's produce to national and world markets. They sought thereby to expand North Carolina's participation in the market economy, credit systems, industrial development, and slavery-based commercial plantation agriculture to supplant old-fashioned subsistence farming. Such measures offered the Carolina gentry the opportunities for commercial wealth that had eluded them for so long. Only through these improvements, reformers insisted, could North Carolina maintain economic and social stability and regain parity with her sister states. Conservative and progressive labels applied only to economic philosophies, not to social ideologies, for leaders of both groups were planters and slave owners determined to defend the existing social structure and slavery in particular. [4]

In the 1830s, North Carolina continued under the conditions that had earned it such nicknames as the "Ireland" or "Nazareth" of America and "the Rip van Winkle state." Out-migration mounted and population growth sank to 2 percent in the decade between 1830 and 1840. Property values and morale sagged, and disaster struck key cities. In May 1831, most of Fayetteville went up in flames. The next month fire consumed William Nichols's glamorous State House in Raleigh and destroyed the Canova statue of Washington—"our pride and glory." Two more fires ravaged Raleigh's business district the following year. For a time there was thought of abandoning Raleigh as the capital.[5] A typically dreary newspaper account reported in 1834 that "our commercial towns present decayed wharves, dilapidated warehouses and untenanted dwellings; while in the country, may everywhere be found deserted plantations and abandoned settlements. Our roads are thronged with emigrants to a more favored country; who have been forced unwillingly to forsake the homes of their fathers." The building industry suffered from the hard times, made more difficult by the panic of 1837. In 1840 private construction seemed almost at a standstill: in a state of more than 750,000 people, the federal census of 1840 recorded that in the previous year only 1,822 wooden houses and 38 brick ones had been built. Their total value of about $410,000, an average of about $200 per house, put North Carolina's investment in housing at about 54 cents per capita, one of the lowest rates in the nation.[6]

In the 1830s, amid the worst out-migration—and taking advantage of it as an issue—economic progressives gained the upper hand in politics and the popular press. A new constitution was approved in 1835 which, while conservative in terms of property requirements for political participation, gave greater representation to the piedmont and western counties and, by putting the election of the governor to the vote of male white taxpayers rather than the legislature, encouraged political parties to appeal more directly to the people. From 1836 to 1860, Whigs and subsequently Democrats were elected on programs of internal improvement and public education.[7]

A symbolic turning point came in June 1840 when for three days North Carolinians gathered to celebrate at "The Great Festival gotten up by the citizens of Raleigh, in honor of those two Magnificent Public Works, our NEW CAPITOL and the RALEIGH AND GASTON RAIL ROAD." During the difficult years of the 1830s, two ideals of the progressive leaders had been realized: a proud modern building to claim the state's position in the nation and a railroad to carry agricultural products to distant markets. Speeches, balls, train rides, parades, and tours of the Capitol marked the state's pride in what it had done and what these hard-won accomplishments symbolized for the future. "To the Good Old North State," went one of the many toasts, "It has been said she slept a Rip Van Winkle sleep. If it be so, it must be plain to all who now visit her, that she has awoke from her slumber, 'like a giant refreshed.' "[8]

And change had begun. More railroads were built: the Wilmington and Weldon Railroad (1834–40) ran north from the port of Wilmington to the Virginia border. The North Carolina Railroad (1849–56) began at the Wilmington and Weldon junction at Goldsboro and reached west via Raleigh, Greensboro, Salisbury and Concord to Charlotte. By 1860 extensions to the North Carolina Railroad led east to New Bern and west almost to Morganton, at last linking the piedmont to North Carolina ports. Other lines radiated out from Wilmington. A feeder system of plank roads—"the farmer's railroad"—was built at the same time. The road from Fayetteville to Salem, called the "Appian Way of North Carolina," was the longest plank road in the world.[9]

The effects of the new roads were dramatic. Wilmington boomed as a rail and steamboat center to bypass New Bern and Fayetteville as the state's largest city, growing from about 4,700 to nearly 10,000 people between 1840 and 1860. Other towns reported that the mere prospect of the railroad brought "new and beautiful" buildings and infused a new life into the people "who talk of nothing now but the railroad." Arrival of tracks raised land values from five dollars to as much as fifty dollars an acre and encouraged factory construction.[10]

Railroads, as their proponents had claimed, enabled planters to get crops to market for a lower cost and at greater profit. This new potential in turn encouraged many agriculturalists to expand their production, buying more land and slaves and turning their attention to scientific farming methods and agricultural societies. Crop prices increased as did staple crop production, and the cotton gin encouraged the cultivation of the profitable fiber. Between 1850 and 1860 the value of North Carolina crops sold rose from approximately $23 million to $33 million a year.[11] The impact on industrial production was less dramatic, for agriculture still ruled the economy. Although better transportation encouraged the growth of textile factories, sawmills, and foundries and the occasional investment in steam-powered machinery, it also brought greater dependence on northern-made goods and discouraged home manufacturing and local industries.

Politicians displayed a new, if still grudging, willingness to raise and use tax money for public purposes. The state established a school for the deaf and blind and a hospital for the insane and expanded the public school system. The University of North Carolina began a building campaign, while private colleges and academies proliferated and grew. Newspapers, libraries, churches, theaters, and cultural societies multiplied, and the number of merchants and the variety of their goods increased. As conditions changed, the tide of out-migration slowed. After 1840 the rate of population growth returned to previous levels of about 15 percent per decade, increasing the total from 737,987 in 1830 to nearly a million by 1860. There was even immigration—significant not so much in numbers as in the renewal of energy and ideas—as merchants, artisans, teachers, architects, industrialists, mechanics, and others from the North and from foreign lands made their way to North Carolina's newly promising railroad towns and country villages.[12]

Such a sweeping description of change, however, reveals only a small part of the picture. These hard-won accomplishments came so slowly and fell so short of national developments that some progressives feared that "old Rip" was in danger of dozing off again.[13] Much of the state remained poor and resistant to change, and life outside the cities and rail corridors scarcely changed at all. Despite public schools, illiteracy continued. Despite promotion of new farming techniques to increase production, most farmers distrusted "book" farming and continued old soil-depleting ways. And despite improvements in communication and the growth of trade and cities, rural isolation, provincialism, and poverty persisted. Thus even in the 1850s spokesmen repeated the old refrain that perhaps, after "years of disappointment and inactivity . . . North Carolina will yet rise superior to the obstacles which grew out of her inhospitable coast and her inconvenient geography, and march side by side with her sisters in the course of improvement."[14]

Nor did the new improvements benefit all equally. Most measures served to bolster the political and economic power of the planter class. The constitution had the most conservative property requirements in the South and the legislature contained one of the region's highest proportions of planters and lawyers. The costly internal improvements tended to entrench and expand the plantation system, while taxes to pay for them fell heavily on the small farmer and the workingman, whose pay rates were among the lowest in the nation. And, as commercial agriculture gained sway in an ever-larger area, the status and power of the subsistence farmer shrank.[15]

Yet there was change, long-lasting if not universal. More important perhaps than the miles of road or the numbers of new buildings and steam factories was the sense that a "spirit of improvement" was abroad, that Rip van Winkle was awake, and that Jack Steamer was the man of the day. Great faith was placed in the new wonders of science and technology, the nationwide networks of steamboats, telegraphs, and railroads, and the perfectibility of man by education and betterment of his surroundings. It was a time when it appeared to many that "the application of steam to machinery [had] almost annihilated space," and "Morse [had] accomplished what perhaps Prometheus attempted."[16]

"A More Modern and Pleasing Style of Architecture"

Demands for modern and stylish architecture as an essential part of overall progress had been voiced early in the century, but they swelled to a chorus amid the mid-nineteenth-century quest for improvement. Replication of national architectural models was part of a package that usually incorporated railroad and industrial growth, temperance, genteel domestic life, public education, and scientific farming as the means to prosperity and pride.

The theme was sounded repeatedly in North Carolina's popular press and public deliberations. "There are now few things in which we are more deficient than in Architecture," claimed one dissatisfied resident, while a taste-conscious clergyman observed, "We have such villainous barns called houses that anyone who will set the example of the contrary style of building will be a benefactor to the community." Some condemned the prevalence of "old revolutionary, barn-like Court Houses" and objected to farmhouses that were "huge squares and parallelograms of painted weatherboards" and immense chimneys that made houses resemble bake ovens—indications that their occupants had not "improved on the examples of their ancestors." The symbolic importance of handsome building gained new attention. "The respected standing of Caswell [County] would seem to require of the court if not a splendid at least a respectable House," commented the county's building committee in 1831. The rhetoric spiraled higher by 1858, when the "beautiful and magnificent Temple of Justice" under construction in Lexington inspired a Greensboro newspaper writer to comment, "There will always be croakers to cry out extravagance, but let us have something on which we can look with pride and delight, something of which we can boast, something grand, noble, and sublime, which will cause the hearts of our children as they gaze upon the wonderful works of art, to swell with emotions of pleasure and pride, which will endear them to their native soil."[17]

But there was more than status and appearance at stake in the popular mid-nineteenth-century view of architecture. Many architectural improvers attached moral values to the type of architecture they promoted.[18] Construction of masonry public buildings, one public body asserted in 1831, not only served the cause of durability and fire safety but promoted the community's wealth, enterprise, and "lastly, tho' not least, the great improvement in the morals of our people." Proponents of neat and picturesque housing claimed that "perfect sanity of mind and morals is almost impossible without a suitable habitation."[19]

Such were the ideas abroad as North Carolina began in the 1830s a rebuilding campaign that increased rapidly in the late 1840s and crested in the 1850s. Old dwellings were made into wings or outbuildings for new, larger houses. Courthouses of log or frame gave way to bigger frame or brick ones. Frame commercial districts burned regularly and were replaced in growing towns by masonry buildings.[20] This was a period of such effective and widespread rebuilding that from these years, as from none before, buildings have endured by the hundreds to the present day.

New construction embodied the tenacity of old patterns as well as the advent of dramatically new ones. If "Squire Oldway" had lost ground in the popular press, he was alive and well at the building site. Not only the subsistence farmer but also the planter and the public building committee continued to choose log and simple frame buildings for many purposes. Committees working with tight local budgets depended on familiar methods of cheap, sturdy construction as they contracted for a "good & complete log house" for a school, a "good" dirt chimney for a poor house, or a "sufficient" log jail. So, too, planters and industrialists erected rows and clusters of little frame or log dwellings to house the slaves on cotton and tobacco plantations and to accommodate workers at new textile mills.[21]

More substantial buildings—brick or frame churches, courthouses, mills, stores, residences, and farm buildings—often repeated customary construction methods, forms, and plans. Notwithstanding the introduction of mass-produced balloon framing of light scantling in some northern cities in the 1830s, North Carolina frame buildings of any quality continued to employ heavy mortised-and-tenoned framing.[22] In brick building, common-bond and running-bond brickwork became popular, but Flemish bond persisted as a hallmark of quality construction, sometimes appearing only on the front facade while the other walls were executed in common bond.[23] Most dwellings repeated the combination of gable roof and rectangular form, though now executed in broader, more horizontal proportions than in previous decades. The two-room plan continued in use, and the central-passage plan with one or occasionally two rooms on either side became increasingly common. Exterior end chimneys of brick or stone and simple finish still predominated. The broad piazza retained its popularity in the coastal plain and mountain valleys. Taken as a whole, buildings retained familiar forms and materials and accommodated stylish novelties to the mold of simplicity and practicality.

It was, predictably, in the growing towns, on plantations, and along the rail lines that new architectural ideals found their principal outlets. Wilmington's building boom epitomized the transformation. As late as 1837 a visitor found that "with a few exceptions the houses seemed to me to have been built in purgatory and used there till no longer fit for use then sent up to this place to moulder and decay." But even as he wrote, the new railroad north was under construction, and by 1846 another visitor observed: "Formerly the town had a rather shabby appearance, and reminded one of a certain yankee town, in which it was said, the people build old homes. But it has been almost destroyed by the numerous fires that have occurred here within the last thirty years, and the buildings erected during that period, and particularly within the last seven years, are of a much better character than those that have passed away; and many of them in fact are elegant." The story repeated itself across the state. Like proud "B" from Baltimore traveling along the Wilmington and Weldon line, a reporter from *Harper's* observed, "As you approach the line of the railroad, . . . signs of life and improvement begin to be manifest . . . the old dwellings are in better repair, there are many new ones of a more modern and pleasing style of architecture."[24]

The new architecture took many forms. Moving away from the essentially domestic forms shared by most earlier buildings, some new buildings followed specialized—typically northern and urban—models that dictated specific shapes for specific purposes. The Insane Asylum at Raleigh had a central core and long flanking wings patterned on the latest models

Market Street, Wilmington, 1850s. (North Carolina Collection, University of North Carolina Library, Chapel Hill.)

for the care for the insane. Hotels began to follow newly complex plans to allow for ventilation in their many rooms.[25] Textile mills employed clerestory roofs and towers copied from northern mills. Courthouses and churches often took the form of a temple rather than a house.

Replacement of "ephemeral" wood buildings and "unsightly wooden shanties" with masonry structures was considered an especially significant accomplishment in a town's effort to gain a "City like appearance."[26] Most of the new urban masonry buildings were of brick, decorated in corbeled patterns or stuccoed and scored to resemble stone blocks.[27] Towns took special pride in construction of stone buildings. Raleigh's Capitol (1833–40), erected of locally quarried gneiss, was the prime example. Doubtless it inspired construction of the city's "Granite Block" of commercial buildings in 1833 on Fayetteville Street; the block was described as being "in the fashionable style of the New York stores, viz. the entire front of the first stories composed of granite pillars, and doors and windows," with "an air of lightness and beauty to the Stores which will make Raleigh again, one of the handsomest towns in the Southern country." Other "granite rows" of the type prevalent in New England appeared in Wilmington's, Charlotte's, and Salisbury's commercial districts in the 1850s.[28] Buildings in Raleigh, Yanceyville, and Tarboro boasted brownstone trim from newly discovered piedmont quarries, while Wilmington prided itself on its brownstone, granite, and even marble buildings of imported stone.[29] Cast-iron storefronts were announced as hallmarks of architectural modernization in Wilmington in 1851, Raleigh in 1856, and

Charlotte in 1860.[30] In the 1840s and 1850s, structural and decorative ironwork became more popular.[31] The advent of such amenities as indoor plumbing, gaslights, and steam heating gained proud notice in the local press.[32]

Perhaps the most obvious sense of modernity, however, rose from innovation in the use of architectural styles. It no longer sufficed for buildings to be permanent, handsome, or even elegant. No longer did one prevalent mode of classicism shape most ambitious architecture. Instead, by midcentury the client or builder could choose among several styles, each with its own appropriate usages and aesthetic and moral attributes, which were described and promoted in newly self-conscious literature on architecture.[33]

In North Carolina as nationally, the associative and aesthetic appeal of ancient Rome and Greece, the Middle Ages, or the Italian countryside went hand in hand with a powerful and optimistic faith in modernization and material improvement. The neoclassical styles gained the most universal use and required the least deviation from familiar forms. The Capitol was the principal monument of the new ideal, but scores of North Carolina churches and courthouses were built in temple form with columned porticoes. Houses, by contrast, adhered to standard forms and plans and attained a classical demeanor from columned porches, broad moldings, and pilastered mantels and entrances. These elements were often drawn from popular architectural books by American architects, including Asher Benjamin and Minard Lafever. Especially popular in North Carolina was Asher Benjamin's *Practical House Carpenter* (1830) with its plain, bold decorative motifs and clearly explained Grecian orders geared to the provincial builder. A Fayetteville drawing teacher offered instruction to those who desired "to become acquainted with the orders of Architect [*sic*], both Grecian and Roman, each example being fashioned according to the style and practice of the present day, taken from A. Benjamin's latest edition." (As earlier, the instructor expected to appeal not only to carpenters but to laymen, especially "all enterprising men who may be called upon as a committee to superintend public buildings.")[34]

The Gothic revival exerted a more specialized appeal. It appeared in the 1830s and 1840s in Episcopal churches whose clergy were influenced by English high-church liturgists, but it was considered a difficult and expensive style to build; furthermore, its symbolism engendered distrust among low churchmen. Gradually, however, the style lost its "popish" aura and by the 1850s had gained popularity among urban congregations of other denominations.[35] The Italianate style, redolent of the wealth of Italy's merchant princes and pastoral agriculturalists yet relatively inexpensive to build, held particular appeal for North Carolina's mercantile elite, whether planter, merchant, or railroad man. The Italian-villa style with its bracketed roofline and occasional tower, like its cousin the pictur-

Poteat House, Caswell County, ca. 1855. The columned portico, broad forms, and shallow roof typify many North Carolina versions of the Greek revival style. (Photo, JoAnn Sieburg-Baker, North Carolina Division of Archives and History.)

esque Gothic cottage, appeared mainly in Wilmington, along railroad routes, on big plantations, and in the homes and public projects of leading modernizers.[36]

As new styles made their appearance in North Carolina communities, they attracted immediate notice. There was seldom any hint of southern chauvinism against new styles as northern. Rather, the popular press expressed delight and pride in having—and recognizing—the latest fashion. In the early 1830s a Fayetteville newspaper admired the town's new Gothic revival–style St. John's Church as "a singularly happy effort, and the more so, as it introduces into our Southern Country a style of architecture to which we have been hitherto unaccustomed." In 1850 a Raleigh paper praised the city's new Yarborough House hotel as "the Italian modern style of architecture" and claimed that a new towered villa was "the handsomest private residence we have ever seen" and "entirely on a new style." Occasionally a touch of irony appeared, but it was good-humored, as when a reporter for a Raleigh paper noted that a new "Cottage" was "of a new style of Architecture for this region; but though somewhat odd and singular in its appearance, it strikes the eye most agreeably, nestled as it is among lofty oaks, and reminding one of the banks of the Hudson—which, by the way, we have never seen."[37]

A host of new architectural books appeared to promote the new ideals. Beginning with the influential works of landscape designer An-

Mantel, Bracebridge Hall, Edgecombe County, 1840s. The mantel with Greek key design repeats a popular plate in Asher Benjamin's *Practical House Carpenter*. (Photo, Tony Vaughn, North Carolina Division of Archives and History.)

St. James Church, Wilmington, 1837–40, Thomas U. Walter, architect, John Norris, builder. This building was the state's first full-blown example of the Gothic revival style. (Photo, Frances Benjamin Johnston, Library of Congress.)

drew Jackson Downing, volumes such as his *Architecture of Country Houses*, his associate Calvert Vaux's *Villas and Cottages*, and Philadelphian Samuel Sloan's *Model Architect* took a different tack from earlier builders' guides. Rather than offering means for carpenters to add new items to their repertoires, the new books presented ensembles—building details, landscaping, furniture, even colors—intended to be replicated in toto. The picturesque cottages and villas were promoted as the models for modern life, which would benefit not only the taste and convenience of the resident but also his health, morality, and family happiness.[38]

The values and models espoused by Downing and his successors gained wide exposure in national agricultural journals and found their way into the North Carolina press. Such progressive periodicals as the *Farmers Journal*, the *Arator*, and the *Carolina Cultivator* ran plates and texts from Downing's books, and the *Weekly Post* (Raleigh) carried several columns promoting Downing's "rural architecture" and "the cottage style" as the means of bettering the state's "comfort, health and morality."[39] Planters and politicians raised the same theme. In 1854 Paul Cameron, railroad and scientific farming advocate and probably the richest planter in the state, urged the members of his local agricultural society to enhance Orange County's farmsteads with "the rural embellishments of the gifted and lamented Downing." In 1859 Congressman Daniel Barringer advised a Charlotte gathering of agriculturalists to "embellish our rural homes" to make the North Carolina farmhouse "a sacred spot full of opportunity, for high moral, religious, and mental culture," to stabilize society, and to encourage "noble deeds of patriotic duties and Christian charity."[40]

For most North Carolinians, the impact of such messages was far greater in popular propaganda than in actual rural building. Examples of the cottage style were rare in the antebellum period, as was farmers' use of scientific agriculture.[41] Yet the effect of the new architectural ideal was far broader than the adoption of this style or that one: the important theme was the belief that the spirit of improvement required its devotees to abandon local custom as the source of building ideas and to turn instead to the pages of books published in distant cities.

Continuity and Change in Building Practice

The new ideas about architecture affected the practice of building as much as they did the character of buildings themselves. Changes in style, technology, and work roles were inextricably interwoven. The new architectural ideals placed emphasis on the achievement of a recognizably stylish image rather than on the display of laborious and skilled craftsmanship as the chief indicator of architectural status.

This shift in emphasis was apparent in the finish work of the new buildings, as the new styles omitted the very elements that had been

"A Bracketed Cottage, with Verandah," from *Carolina Cultivator*, May 1855. This plate from A. J. Downing's *Cottage Residences* was one of the several designs for rural residences inserted in the Raleigh agricultural journal. The editor hoped that his readers might "derive some valuable hints, if they do not adopt the plans in detail." (North Carolina Collection, University of North Carolina Library, Chapel Hill.)

the hallmarks of the best workmanship in traditional buildings. Beaded weatherboards and molded windowsills and frames gave way to plain squared ones; laboriously molded chair rails and paneled wainscot disappeared; massive exterior chimneys were supplanted by narrower chimneys, by interior stacks, or even by stoves and stovepipes. The broad, flat moldings and bulls-eye corner blocks typical of Greek-revival woodwork, like the ornate brackets and latticework of the Italianate style, could be made by steam-powered machinery or semiskilled workers and attached to surfaces with machine-produced nails. Moreover, where an image conceived by an architect or taken from a book became the controlling aesthetic, the task of the artisan was to execute that image in literal and workmanlike fashion. If the parts could be made by machine or by a semiskilled workman, the artisan's role was further compressed into an assembler of parts. Although full-scale industrialization came later in the century, the transformation began in the antebellum period.

But it was not only new styles and technology that threatened traditional methods. The traditional client-artisan model of building, the reliance on local models, and the customary role of the artisan became the specific targets of attacks by architectural modernizers. A. J. Downing led the assault. Along with promoting new architectural designs, he urged his readers not to hire a "country carpenter or mason" who too often altered the concept of buildings as he proceeded. Nor should an individual try to plan his own house, unless he wanted a mere "fac-simile of his neighbor's, so that the builder has only to copy what he has already done." The essence of traditional building was thus anathema. Instead, Downing stated, a client should employ the best "professional" expert—an architect, if possible—and should insist on getting a plan of "originality" and "character," "composed by a man of talent, taste, and experience," plus a full set of plans and specifications for the workmen to follow.[42]

North Carolina clients and artisans could absorb this message not only through Downing's popular books and those of other writers of similar persuasion but through their local press. Both the *Carolina Cultivator* and the *Southern Weekly Post* ran one such article in 1855:

> Generally, now when a farmer wishes to build a house, he just goes and consults the "builder," commonly a house carpenter mechanic. . . . Then if he concludes to build, the plan and "architecture" of the house is left to the "builder to determine," which in most cases will be a mere "copy" after some dozens of others. Now the farmer should know something of style and architecture himself. Then he should consult the best works on that subject and not depend on the house-carpenter for this service. The farmer will find that it will cost him no more to build his house in tasteful style, than to build it in violation of all the forms of good taste and of the rules of architecture.[43]

Continuity and Survival of Traditional Practice

Before examining changes in antebellum building practice, it is important to recall that the vast majority of building projects continued along familiar lines unaffected by the new notions. The very intensity of the modernizers' attacks on traditional building methods suggests the strength and tenacity of the customs they sought to eradicate. Farmers and laborers went about the normal business of self-reliant building—cutting, rolling, and hewing their own timber, hauling their own stone, and devoting their labor to their own and their neighbors' building projects. Thousands of carpenters and masons worked directly with their clients, planning their buildings together and making slight adjustments to form and finish in response to new ideas. Individuals and building committees still set their sights with an eye to the capabilities of local materials and artisans, and they still used familiar terms to describe their expectations—defining a pulpit in a new church, for example, to be made "after manner and form of the one in the methodist church in Wadesboro, but entirely plain and of good hart plank." Clients still expected to take the usual direct and active role in their building projects, obtaining materials and hiring a series of individual workmen, both for small structures built for ten or twenty dollars and for plantation houses that cost thousands.[44]

Such undertakings differed little from those of past decades. It was in the dimension of technology, of manufacturing and transportation, that change was most evident. For example, in 1838 during construction work on his Franklin County plantation house, a conservative frame building with Greek-revival detail, planter Nicholas Massenburg supplied his own timber, used his own slave workmen, and hired local black and white masons and carpenters job by job. Yet, even as the house rose, the Raleigh and Gaston Railroad pressed southward bringing shipments of materials ever nearer. A few years earlier lime or iron might have been brought at great cost by wagon the hundred miles or more from Petersburg to Louisburg—if they were obtained at all. In April 1838 Massenburg sent his slave Lewis to drive the plantation wagon a mere fifty miles to the Gaston depot to deliver cotton and pick up roofing iron; in September, he got lime from the new Warrenton depot only thirty miles distant; and in October, when the wagon set off to cover the twenty miles to Henderson, Massenburg noted, "This is the 1st trip to that depot." As railroads cut the cost of shipping in half, increasing numbers of buildings across the landlocked state could be erected from materials that were manufactured hundreds of miles away.[45]

Massenburg's management of his building project and the dispersal of work among individual artisans was as typical of the nineteenth century as it had been of the eighteenth. In the 1840s and 1850s, however, this approach met with increasing competition. In one advertisement "To house builders" in 1859, the owner wanted a summer residence built but "not being able to give his personal attention to it, he will let it out on contract."[46]

The Contract Mode of Building

Paralleling developments that had occurred earlier in London, New York, and other cities, contracting and contractors gained new importance in North Carolina in the 1840s and 1850s. Several factors interlocked to support this change. New prosperity and rising hopes generated a record number of big, potentially profitable construction projects—brick courthouses, colleges and academies, state institutional buildings, handsome churches—which expanded the opportunities for taking public contracts. At the same time, the growing desire for unfamiliar types and styles of buildings and the construction of larger houses and stores put many private projects beyond the capability or willingness of the client to man-

Massenburg Plantation House, Franklin County, expanded 1838, William Jones, carpenter. (Photo, North Carolina Division of Archives and History.)

age. Other changes in the local and national economy were critical as well: the general shift toward larger shops rather than small individual ones and from master craftsman to manager of employees in various industries; the construction of railroad lines which permitted builders to supply several dispersed projects at once; and the expanding market economy that encouraged greater investment in construction and gave both client and builder greater access to money and credit. In many respects, it was the contractor who brought industrial capitalism into building practice.[47]

In the contract project, the builder agreed to complete a product—a finished building—for an agreed-upon price, and it fell to him, not the client, to organize and manage the labor force and to obtain and assemble all materials. Delays from weather, labor shortages, lack of materials, and rising costs were his problems, not the client's. This was the method promoted by popular literature of the period. Downing regarded "the contract mode of building" as unquestionably the "most economical mode of building in the United States," for it replaced the artisan system with the industrial organization of work. He stated that costs were cheaper than in the "days-work system" because in contrast to the artisan hired by the day, the contractor was likely to assign much unimportant work to apprentices "at a cheap rate." Further, Downing believed that "a great deal more judgment and proper economy will always be exercised in the purchase of materials, etc., by a master-builder for himself, than for the proprietor."[48]

Such an approach was by no means a new development; as we have seen in previous chapters, working "by Great" had been a common practice for public projects for many years. Nor did contractors suddenly take over the building business and reduce carpenters and masons to hirelings. Only a few individuals established large building operations in the antebellum period—thirteen men were listed as contractors in the 1850 census and twenty-two in 1860. Even taking into consideration others who were listed as carpenters, mechanics, or masons but who actually functioned as contractors, such men represented a tiny fraction of the building trade population of over four thousand free carpenters and masons.[49] The significant change was that builders emerged in the 1840s and flourished in the 1850s who took on contracts regularly and in quantity and for the first time advertised themselves specifically as "contractors." This new breed of builders promoted their ability to "take contracts for building . . . in a master-like fashion and in the shortest time possible," their capacity as "contractor for public and private buildings of every style of architecture," and their readiness to "take contracts in any part of the state."[50]

The operations of such men suited the changing times perfectly: they seemed to be the "Jack Steamers" of the building industry. They had begun as artisans and retained the traditional artisan's personal touch and practicality as well as a knowledge of local men and materials. Yet they took on new, larger roles that expanded their responsibilities, workshops, and geographic range, and they gained the abilities and confidence to create up-to-date architectural images, to take advantage of new technology, and to organize large and efficient work forces.

North Carolina Contractors

The careers of a few of the state's most prominent builders suggest the character of such contractors' origins, methods, problems, and achievements. Typically they came from out of state to North Carolina communities newly served by rail lines, where they found work among merchants or planters hungry for stylish new buildings. The same rail lines also expanded their potential scope of operations. Virginian Dabney Cosby moved to Raleigh at age sixty in 1839, just before the completion of the Raleigh and Gaston Railroad to the city. His practice extended north to Virginia, east to Greenville, and west to Pittsboro and Salem. Jacob Holt, a Virginia-born carpenter, came to Warrenton soon after the Raleigh and Gaston line crossed Warren County and soon developed a business that reached across a nine-county region from southern Virginia to Raleigh and from Chapel Hill east to Northampton County. Carpenter James F. Post of New Jersey and brick builders Robert and John Wood of Nantucket came

Dabney Cosby, daguerreotype, ca. 1845. (Private collection of John C. Cosby.)

to Wilmington at about the same time as the Wilmington and Weldon line and became the city's leading contractors. Brick builder John Berry, by contrast, was one who succeeded in his home community, for he was born in Orange County, learned his trade locally, and established a shop in Hillsborough from which he served several nearby piedmont counties.[51]

Pragmatic to a man, they took jobs of any scale, from a chimney to a courthouse. They would bargain for payment by the measure or day as well as for contracts for the whole job or part, and they regularly executed construction of major architect-designed projects. But their special forte lay in contract projects in which they undertook the entire process of design and construction to yield a finished product.

By taking responsibility for the design, the expenditure of money, the manufacture of goods, and the use of workmen, the antebellum contractor assumed a role in the building process seldom rivaled before or since.

Contractors as Designers

The contractor's role as designer gave him direct control over the process of building and, equally important, offered an attractive drawing card to clients. From a builder who had already mastered a vocabulary of stylish possibilities, the aspiring client could expect better results than he might obtain by showing unfamiliar pattern-book plates to local carpenters and masons. Such builders thus promoted their stylistic versatility—some advertising in newspapers their competence in "every style of architecture," for which they could furnish plans if necessary. Others, such as Cosby and Holt, built their own houses—dramatically new towered villas in both cases—as showcases of their abilities to work in locally unfamiliar current styles.[52] In a national context, perhaps, builders such as Post, Cosby, Berry, and Holt were not trendsetters, but on the local scene they often stood in the forefront of taste. A few towns boasted stylish monuments by nationally active architects, but for the most part it was the practical builder who translated national styles into widespread reality.

Antebellum contractors drew upon current architectural books and their knowledge of local conditions to create a few prototypes that they knew they could build successfully and that would appeal to their clients. John Berry of Hillsborough explained early in his long career the method that served him well: "I have procured a number of books on the science of Buildings and have made it my study for a number of years back, and I flatter myself at this time from the experience I have had both in practice and theory that I can have their building executed in good stile and as substantially as any person in this section of the country."[53] From Owen Biddle's *Young Carpenter's Assistant*, Berry adopted federal-style motifs including a delicate stair bracket, and from Asher Benjamin's *American Builder's Companion* and *Practical House Carpenter* and Minard Lafever's *Young Builder's General Instructor*, he selected several Greek-revival designs. He continued to use these elements from the 1820s and 1830s throughout the 1840s and 1850s to give his conservative, well-crafted brick and frame buildings a suitable degree of correctness and style.[54] Dabney Cosby favored a vocabulary of traditional Virginia forms and neoclassicism learned—as he frequently mentioned—during his work under Thomas Jefferson at the University of Virginia. For some projects, however, Cosby drew on current books or the talents of his son John to create more modish Gothic and Italianate compositions.[55]

James Post and his frequent associates, brick builders Robert and John Wood, used current pattern books such as those of Downing, Sloan, and Calvert Vaux to create stylish town houses for Wilmington merchants. Sometimes their buildings copied specific plates, but more often they melded the books' cubical-dwelling and Italianate window-and-porch forms with classical elements to create the city's own domestic style.[56]

John Berry and his wife, Elizabeth Vincent, daguerreotype, before 1870. (Photo, North Carolina Collection, University of North Carolina Library, Chapel Hill.)

Warrenton builder Jacob Holt combined old builders' guides and the new pattern books to create an idiosyncratic style tailored to a rural elite. He began like Berry with Greek-revival elements from Biddle, Benjamin, and Lafever, which he applied boldly to a standard two-story square-house form. In the 1850s he updated his work with motifs from William Ranlett, Downing, and Sloan. Like his Wilmington contemporaries, he sometimes replicated published plates of fashionable villas, cottages, and churches, but more often he picked out Italianate or Gothic details such as brackets, arches, lattices, and quatrefoils, which he exaggerated or simplified to suit his shop technology and then lavished on his standard prototype.[57]

Some contractors employed architects to translate new design ideas into workable reality. Cosby had his son John, a competent draftsman and sometime "architect," to provide designs for the family firm's major buildings.[58] When construction boomed in Wilmington, builder James Post

Orange County Courthouse, Hillsborough, 1844–45, John Berry, builder. Berry's courthouse included elements from the books of Owen Biddle, Asher Benjamin, and Minard Lafever. (Photo, Tony Rumple, North Carolina Division of Archives and History.)

wrote to a friend in Jersey City, New Jersey, and "asked him to find him some architect to come to Wilmington." The young draftsman, Rufus Bunnell, arrived by train on May 7, 1859. Post put him to work at two dollars a day making drawings while Post ran the business. Bunnell recalled that in developing designs, the builder gave him "some merely general direction, so leaving me a pretty independant swing. But I found him to have a considerable direction for classic designs." When Post did not need Bunnell's work on a specific project, he set him to "making some

Bellamy Mansion, Wilmington, 1859–60 (at left). Contractor-architect James Post hired architect Rufus Bunnell to draw details for his buildings, including the Bellamy Mansion. (Photo, North Carolina Division of Archives and History.)

designs for ornamental house entrances to stock up with." Post possessed a good collection of architectural books, Bunnell recalled, from which the younger man sometimes "found it necessary to do some *sly studying . . .* to help out my knowledge of what I might be supposed to know."[59]

While using new images as inspiration, these builders still followed old methods of working out designs with their clients. Contract specifications commonly expressed the client and builder's mutual understanding of the building in familiar terms. An example of how the design process worked in such projects appears in records of the construction of Eureka, a plantation house erected by Warrenton builder Holt in Mecklenburg County, Virginia, in the late 1850s.

Holt's 1857 agreement with his client Robert Baskerville called for a house to be erected "agreeable to the following specifications and to be 31st plate 19th Volume 2nd Ranlets Architect (Except) in length of Veranda which is to be 40 ft long and not to extend on the ends to have in the rear of the Building a piazza 8 by 12 feet inplace of kitchen Bedrooms &c as described on Ground plan drawn by J. W. Holt. . . . The style and finish of the work is to be like Col. W. R. Baskervilles or not inferior." A small ground-plan sketch showed the agreed-upon modifications to the pattern-book plan, including the characteristic southern placement of the kitchen in a separate structure.[60]

The project thus began with a pattern book and proceeded to create a new design. The reference to Holt's recent work for his client's father as model assured that the builder would apply his finest finish including ornate brackets, elaborately made doors and windows, and marbleizing, details that were not part of the Ranlett design for an "Italian Villa" of relatively simple cast. It also indicated which version of his established set of possibilities the contractor would produce. When a builder made an estimate for a project, he might employ similar terms: a proposal for a plantation house in Warren County described a two-story building 40 by 52 feet, with a "Plan like Mr. J. B. Williams," which included "2 Stair ways like Mr. Williams (back one) if Circled they will cost more."[61] Despite similarities with earlier agreements, such references to existing models suggest a change from traditional methods; where once negotiations to define a version of a prototype centered around commonly held vernacular traditions, now the builder offered the client a variation on models he himself had developed with reference to current books. The builder's own design standards took on new importance relative to local tradition and the taste of the owner.

As construction on Eureka progressed, the concept continued to change. Bills for "extra work on dwelling house" included adding two side piazzas and expanding the rear piazza. The most dramatic change, denoted by a bill for "changing roof and building Tower difference," came when Holt or Baskerville decided to recast Ranlett's horizontal design by adding a central tower to emulate a more vertical "Italian Villa" pictured in Samuel Sloan's *Model Architect*. Neither Holt nor Baskerville found any problem in beginning with one idea and changing it as they saw fit.[62]

Money, Materials, and Labor

Once they had agreed upon an initial design, client and builder set forth in their contract the terms of executing the building. Holt's agreement for Eureka typifies such bargains:

> J. W. Holt on his part agrees to execute in a good & workmanlike manner the aforesaid Building and defray every expense necessary to completion of the work and to have the building finished by about the 15th of August 1858, Dr. R. D. Baskerville on his part agrees to pay the above mentioned sum of $4885 for the said work and im-

Design for a villa, design 31, from Ranlett, *The Architect*, vol. 2, plate 19. (Courtesy of Henry Francis du Pont Winterthur Museum Library, Collection of Printed Books.)

provements in the following manner—one third when the work is commenced to pay for materials, one third when the house is covered in and underpinning done, the remaining third to be paid on the completion of the house.[63]

Although such terms had been common in public building contracts, they represented a change in private building practice. The client now had only the responsibility of making payments; the builder took on everything else. This type of contract defined the roles of contractor and client in a multitude of projects. If other agreements varied in their particulars, all followed this basic pattern and assured a single or staged payment tied to completion of the building.[64]

The client's end of the bargain—payment of a set sum—could be met in a surprising variety of ways. Although cash was the usual medium of exchange, builders still accepted payment in goods and services. For installing shelving and a "strip in store for hanging up Boots" in a store in Wilmington, James Post received $9.35 worth of "shoes for self, Boys, wife, children." Planters, often short on cash, continued the old practice of feeding the builder's crew and putting their slaves to work on their own building jobs, and some went further, making substantial payments in

Eureka, Mecklenburg County, Virginia, 1857–60, Jacob W. Holt, builder. (Photo, Catherine W. Bishir, North Carolina Division of Archives and History.)

kind. A descendant of one of Holt's Warren County clients recalled that her great-grandfather, planter J. E. Boyd, "supplied him with timber & labor for other homes he was working on at the same time. When J. Holt & my great-grandfather settled up, Holt told J. E. Boyd that he [Holt] owed him 25 cents & said he would make him a ladder to go into the attic. We have the ladder here."[65]

The contractor often manufactured many of his materials in his own shop—following the precedent of the carpenter who made his own moldings, doors, and mantels or the brickmason who made as well as laid bricks. Wilmington's Wood brothers, Cosby of Raleigh, and Berry of Hillsborough all operated their own brickyards, both in their home communities and at their scattered building sites. Holt cut timber at building sites, but he also maintained a carpentry shop and lumber and brick kiln on his lot in Warrenton where he produced in quantity the elaborate decorations that distinguished his buildings.[66]

Such builders, who had enough business to benefit from mass production of building parts, were among the first entrepreneurs to invest in steam-powered, large-scale manufacture of finished components as well as sawn lumber. It was a house carpenter, Alonzo Willis of New Bern, who established the state's earliest known steam-powered sash and blind factory as an adjunct to his building business in the 1840s. In the 1850s, as will be discussed in the next chapter, other builders joined the industrial revolution, including William Murdoch in Salisbury, Ephraim Clayton in

Asheville, and Thomas Briggs in Raleigh, who along with others saw what steam-powered factories could do to boost profits and expand the capabilities of their building firms. If they produced such materials to their own specifications, builders could produce distinctively finished buildings at a greater rate and potentially at a higher profit than ever before.[67]

The contractor also offered a ready market for the new manufactures. A brick builder who contracted for a whole building had to obtain and install the woodwork. Some hired or subcontracted with carpenters, but where a building parts manufacturer was accessible, a brick builder could purchase goods direct—a strategy Dabney Cosby employed in Raleigh.[68] Even the carpenter-builder benefited from new manufacturing methods, as did Albert Gamaliel Jones who contracted to build a frame house in 1854, then subcontracted with a nearby steam-powered mill to make his doors, sash, flooring, moldings, cornice, and pilasters. An observer pointed out to Jones's client the advantages: "It will be better by considerable than if done by hand, & besides he will select & throw out all that does not pass inspection if there be any defective which is a considerable advantage in your favor, & will expedite the work greatly as he will have nothing to do but to go right off to framing, & as soon as the house is raised he will have nothing to do but to go to putting up work & finishing off instead of spending so much time in getting out & dressing up timber sticking moldings &c &c."[69]

However large and self-sufficient a builder's shop, the challenge of obtaining certain manufactured items remained unpredictable. The age-old problems of acquiring materials often evaded the builder's control. Factories were few and often short-lived, and most building projects lay far beyond the reach of rail lines. Builders often saw their expenses soar when drayage cost more than expected, or, like Atkins at the State House half a century earlier, waited nervously to see if shipments of glass arrived in time and intact. As Eureka neared completion, builder Holt reported to his client his most recent problems:

> I received yours by Mr. Wyatt, but not until last Friday, and I found that I could get the sash weights by today and now send the tin and sash weights and I hope the delay which I could not prevent owing to the fact that I have lost all my horses (but one) with distemper and could get no way to send sooner, the sash locks I will get in Petersburg this week and the S.S. I will carry with me when I come over which I expect to do next week.
> Aug. 9, 1859
>
> 11 Aug./59
> P. S. On going with the waggon to get the weights I found there were 10 or 12 lacking (Altho I was told repeatedly that they were all ready) is the reason the wagon did not come over tuesday.

Aug. 29, 1859.
I will attend to the matter mentioned as soon as possible it will require 8 or 10 days to get the weights cast here as they only cast 6 or 7
at a time. I will try and come over this week anyhow.[70]

Not until after the Civil War did the railroad and the factory completely
transform the process of getting materials to the building site.

The Contractor as Manager

Probably the most demanding responsibility the contractor took over from
the client was recruiting and managing a labor force. Though still often
calling himself carpenter, mason, or mechanic, he had taken the same
step as many others throughout the nation's changing economy and had
moved into the ranks of employer as separate from the workman. Whether he used his own crew, hired or subcontracted with other workmen, or
combined the three, once he took a contract, he had to make sure that
enough men with sufficient skills were on the job throughout the full
sequence of tasks. The artisans in his employ no longer worked for the
client in their own versions of the local vernacular but for the builder
according to his design and construction standards.

Antebellum builders found various methods of organizing their work
forces. Nearly all of them, like the planters and merchants for whom they
built, relied on slave laborers and artisans as well as free journeymen. A
few, such as John Berry, maintained self-sufficient shops that encompassed a full range of trades. Berry had begun his career in partnership
with a carpenter, John A. Faucett, and he owned not only slave masons
and brickmakers but also a carpenter, Joe Nichols, and a tinner, Ned
Haughawout, so that he could easily take contracts for both brick and
frame buildings. When Berry undertook a big project far from Hillsborough, he moved his workmen and even his family to the site. Once
established, he took on other jobs nearby, assigning teams of two or three
black and two or three white workmen to each one while dividing his own
time among projects to supervise and confer with clients. As Berry family
tradition relates, "When he found his men had put up brick or plank in a
way that did not come up to his standard . . . Captain Berry quietly took a
big hammer and knocked the brick and plank down, then walked off
without a word. His men knew that they must do a better job." When the
job was completed, "The Captain took his family, his men, tools, equipment, wagons and teams and either went back home or to another job."[71]

Many builders shared in the practice of joining forces to assemble a
work force sufficient to meet contracts. In some cases two builders formed
a partnership in order to take on a specific contract, while in others a
builder of one trade contracted for a whole building project and subcontracted the work outside his trade. When contractor Ephraim Clayton of

Asheville, a carpenter by trade, joined with brick builder George Shackleford to build the Polk County Courthouse, the two agreed that each should do "that part of the work belonging to his trade or calling."[72]

Raleigh brick builder Dabney Cosby maintained a work force composed principally of masons, plasterers, and laborers and seldom took contracts for anything but brick buildings. When necessary he subcontracted with a carpenter or bought manufactured woodwork. His workshop included two slaves, brothers Albert and Osborne, whose expertise as plasterers gained the Cosby shop a regional reputation. Cosby sent his workmen to distant building sites and returned from time to time to check on their progress. Addressing university president David L. Swain, Cosby explained, "Albert comes to help his Bro. do the Plaisterin in the halls. I have told him to Examine the sand to be used . . . and to procure such as in the Judgment of him and Osborne will make the best work. You may rely on what he tells you."[73]

Although Cosby owned a core work force, he and his sons augmented their shop by hiring slaves. This practice, well established in previous decades, was critical to the contractor's ability to take on large jobs, yet it involved a degree of risk, as Cosby observed to his son: "You doubt the propriety of Hiring for another year because you have no prospects for imployment. Now I cannot but believe . . . sometime shortly some will be turning up that will alter the present state of business, there is to much public improvement going on not to make a stur in other ways and after the regular Hiring time not a hand can be let your wants be what they may—those you can get upon *fair* terms take."[74]

Jacob Holt's shop in Warrenton, the largest in the state, included both free and slave workmen. He attracted as many as nineteen journeyman carpenters from many different communities in North Carolina and Virginia, but he also employed nearly forty male slaves of working age in his household, including at least one bricklayer, Corbin Boyd, whose expertise in chimney building earned him an outstanding local reputation.[75] Holt evidently hired rather than owned most of these workmen, either paying their owner by the year or allowing their owners to provide their labor as payment for building. Like Berry, Holt commonly sent two or three slaves and two or three whites to each of several building sites, where they worked for weeks or months at a time. He sometimes delegated superintendence of distant projects to his brother Thomas or trusted employees. In some instances, Holt subcontracted with independent masons and plasterers to complete elements of his contracts.[76]

James Post operated his urban building business in Wilmington along somewhat different lines from his rural and small-town compatriots. For one thing the city was large enough and business brisk enough that he could oversee several projects concurrently within a single community. He contracted for some buildings, provided designs for others, and supervised still others. He often took carpentry subcontracts on masonry build-ings contracted by brick builders Robert and John Wood. Although Post did not own slaves, he followed common Wilmington precedent of hiring slaves for projects as needed.[77]

The recollections of Rufus Bunnell, the young draftsman who came from New Jersey to work for Post in 1859–60, give a rare and vivid picture of the operation of a builder-architect's office in an antebellum southern city. Post occupied a two-room wooden office opposite the courthouse, with the drafting table in the rear room. The young northerner urged Post to find a more pleasant office site, for he objected to the "disagreeable scenes of punishment and auction sales of negroes at the Court House opposite" and the flies, fleas, noise, and smells associated with a nearby livery stable. But Post insisted that the busy central location was best for his business. Typical of the community, Post employed a slave, Jim, as a servant in his office during 1858 and 1859 to lay the fire, wash color dishes, clean up, and run errands. However, when Bunnell and Post attended the traditional first of the year hiring day, a cold Monday, January 2, 1860, Bunnell recalled, "Hundreds of negro slaves [were] huddled about the Market House . . . sitting or standing in the keen atmosphere waiting their separate turns or in lots, to be auctioned off by sales on the spot, or to be let or hired out to any successful bidder for their labor for the year 1860. . . . Mr. Post let 'Jim' go to some other person," for he decided he did not want him around the office for another year.[78]

Post's entire building business involved continual interaction with both slave and free workmen. The northern draftsman commented, "I found the negro mechanics quite docile and I took pleasure in showing the foremen how to carry out my drawings; it however seemed quite strange to ever keep in mind, that almost to a man those mechanics (however seemingly intelligent) were nothing but slaves, and capable as they might be, all the earnings that came from their work, was regularly paid over to their masters or mistresses." On payday, the builder and his assistant engaged in the weekly ritual of payment to the city's builders:

> Saturdays were busy days for me in the Post office, even tho I hap-pened to have a slackness in drawing; for I had to calculate with Mr. P. the quantities of work done on the buildings during the week, set-ting the prices to it and writing orders for the money for all the white mechanics and for their masters to draw their money for the labor of their slave mechanics. In the latter part of Saturday after-noons, they all white and black, flocked into the outer office for their pay for working on the various buildings, or "jobs," that Mr. P. had under his charge.[79]

Challenges and Risks in Contracting

However the contractor organized his work, expansion of a shop beyond the traditional master and a few journeymen, apprentices, or slaves was a complicated business. To support a shop large enough to take on big projects and to assure continued work, particularly if he employed both brickmasons and carpenters, the builder needed to work on more than one project at a time, yet getting and coordinating multiple projects put still more demands on the builder.

The challenges of a big contracting shop were complex enough for urban builders but loomed even greater for the builder whose jobs—and future prospects—were dispersed across a wide region. In a letter to his son, Dabney Cosby described his far-flung activities in 1845. He was aboard a steamboat to Smithfield, Virginia, where he was accompanying his slave workman, Albert, to "set him to build" a church. Cosby reported that a courthouse and jail he had built in Pittsboro, North Carolina, were just finished. Two buildings in Petersburg were nearing completion and were likely to rent for seven hundred dollars a year. He had undertaken a contract for brickwork and plastering for two buildings at the University of North Carolina at Chapel Hill. Looking ahead, "I have in prospect the church in Greensboro & a clerk's office . . . Jail is to be built at Raleigh this summer which I shall put in for, if the [Charlotte] Mint rebuilt I shall [bid on] it. . . . I have not had time to clear my head enough to write you."[80]

The contractor's most serious problem lay in the ever-present danger that he would not be paid. Whereas an artisan whose client failed him faced primarily the loss of his own wages for a day's or a month's work, the contractor stood to lose not only his own wages and profit, but potentially thousands of dollars in materials and wages already paid out. Sometimes the builder found it wiser to settle for short payment than none: "I knew I was in their power," wrote one frustrated contractor, "I was obliged to have my pay if but little, & to put off in order to dispute the matter I could not. . . . I contracted last spring, the wheat and tobacco crops both destroyed since had made a gap in their means. . . . So I had to do the best I could."[81]

The boom in big academy buildings sponsored by private or denominational groups seems to have been an especially high risk area for contractors. The expensive new brick buildings offered tempting opportunities for big profits, but because fund-raising often fell short, builders found themselves carrying costs without receiving payments. In such circumstances, they took various more or less desperate actions. When Ephraim Clayton and George Shackleford discovered that commissioners for building a school in western North Carolina lacked funds to meet their contract, the two took matters into their own hands, seized a commissioner's slave workman, and held him in jail until they got their money.[82]

When John Berry and Jacob Holt completed big masonry and carpentry contracts of more than $11,000 each for a Masonic school at Oxford, they found that the sponsors were short some $13,000. Berry took a mortgage on the property and waited until 1868 to collect final payment.[83]

For some contractors, nonpayment meant disaster. It was not unusual for a builder to borrow money or obtain materials on credit to complete a job, expecting to pay his creditors when he himself received payment. Carpenter and contractor Albert Gamaliel Jones of Warren County contracted to build three big brick academy buildings and several houses in Louisburg and Murfreesboro. When one of the institutions defaulted, Jones, who had given substantial securities and obtained credit to finance his undertakings, was unable to absorb the shortfall. He had to sell and mortgage his potential profits and the materials and hands involved in active projects, as well as his slaves, livestock, land, household goods and furnishings, three wood shops, and all his property in Hertford County "excepting his working tools." He could not even complete jobs for which he might have gained payment. To a client in Louisburg he wrote that "in consequence of my situation it is impossible for me to finish your job though it is a source of great mortification to me not to do so." He proposed that the client "take all the work & materials that is not worked in the Job and let 2 disinterrested workmen and one farmer value the Intier work done and then you can get some other person to finish you job if you do not agree to this some of my friends will come out and attend to it in some way but I think you had better accept my proposition."[84]

Few antebellum North Carolina builders ventured into the riskiest arena of building—speculative construction for the market rather than custom work for a known client. This full-blown capitalist approach offered the greatest potential for profit or ruin. In the 1850s Edgecombe County builder George Lipscombe entered this market for a time, offering for sale a few houses he had built in Tarboro; but he seems not to have thrived, for he was soon forced to mortgage or sell his property for debts.[85] Dabney Cosby was one of the few North Carolina builders in this era who used his men and materials to build for investment on a large scale. He built houses for sale or rent in Petersburg and Raleigh, but his most spectacular venture was Raleigh's Yarborough House, the elegant Italianate-style hotel designed by his son John Wayt Cosby and built by Cosby and other investors. When his hotel was ready to open in 1850, the elder Cosby exulted, "The Yarborough House is filled with the best custom, all the Big Fish are with us and a good many Ladies also and if as big again would have been filled up. I did just get the inside prepared we are yet on the outside and will be for a week or so yet but it will be a Beautiful Building."[86] Though common in northern cities by this time, builders' speculative investments remained rare in North Carolina until after the Civil War.

Yarborough House, Raleigh, 1850, Dabney Cosby, builder. (North Carolina Division of Archives and History.)

"Far Fetched and Dear Bought": The Growth of the Architectural Profession

North Carolina's growing architectural ambitions fed upon and fed the development of the architectural profession in America. In 1830 the ranks of American architects were thin, with a tiny number of European and native-born architects concentrated in New York and Philadelphia. Despite Latrobe's efforts, the American architect's professional status was by no means well established. Architects did not share common training or professional standards of work or payment, and they had not yet established a public professional identity separate from builders. There was no licensing requirement or nationwide organization to delineate the architect's position. Each man had to define his own status with client and community.[87] Between 1830 and 1860 the profession grew as European-trained architects continued to arrive and as American men, many of whom had begun as carpenters or masons, took on the duties and title of architect. By 1850 the United States census enumerated 591 individuals identified as architects. In 1857, the fledgling American Institute of Architects was organized in New York, successor to the short-lived American Institution of Architects formed in 1837.[88] Architects promoted their professional status by appealing to those who wanted to share in the national mainstream of "correct" and "modern" architecture and suggesting that they as architects possessed the requisite knowledge to accomplish these goals. North Carolinians eager for architectural improvement expressed the same views. As one clergyman wrote in 1859, "I want a *Church*, not a meeting house or a barn & therefore I want to engage an *architect*."[89]

Architects working in antebellum North Carolina fell into three main categories: American- and British-trained professionals who maintained offices in major cities—principally New York and Philadelphia, with a few in Boston and Baltimore—but also served a national clientele by mail and occasional visits; British immigrant architects who came to America in hopes of finding work and settled for a time in North Carolina, a continuation of the patterns set by John Hawks and William Nichols; and, by the end of the period, the first generation of local men who had started work as artisans and now took on the new and promising status of architect.

Architects, of course, were not new to North Carolina, but in the antebellum period both architects and high-style buildings became more numerous and assumed a more prominent role in the state's building campaigns. By the end of the antebellum period, employment of an architect became standard practice for most large state works, and urban building committees and a few private individuals also sought architects' services. In such endeavors, the old two-party relationship of client and builder-artisan was replaced by a triangular division of authority. The new professional projects confronted all three parties with unfamiliar challenges as they worked out issues over the definition of the architect as a professional, the services he provided, and the new roles and relationships among client, architect, and builder.

Issues of Professional Status

New definitions of professionalism surfaced on a large scale during construction of the Capitol (1833–40)—a complex and demanding project that brought North Carolina face-to-face with issues of an American architectural profession still in its infancy. The project was seen from the outset as having great symbolic importance in bolstering the state's self-image and its status among its sister states. The building committee, instructed by the legislature to copy the cruciform plan of Nichols's former State House, but bigger and in stone, took the view that they were building for the ages and sought a building of national rather than local stature. A Fayetteville visitor voiced a common theme: "Whilst we are erecting an edifice for such a purpose let it be one that will do honor to the State—one that will last as long as her liberties are preserved. We believe that if the work is completed in the style in which it has been commenced, it will be excelled by no legislative building in the Union, the Capitol at Washington excepted." As work progressed, the building committee became increasingly aware that they were operating in a national rather than local arena this time, not only in the building they envisioned but in the money, materials, and men it required.[90]

The building committee began along familiar lines by hiring William Nichols, Jr., to draw up plans for a larger, stone version of his father's State House, probably with help from the elder Nichols. After the Nichols cruciform plan was accepted, Nichols, Jr., was paid $350 and dismissed in the summer of 1833; the commissioners, with plans in hand, anticipated needing no further architectural services.[91] After deciding against letting a contract for the job—the uncertainty of costs recommended against it—they hired a superintendent of construction, one William Drummond, but retained the role of contractor and kept their own records as had many building committees before them.[92]

In August of 1833, with the Capitol's foundation laid, a new man appeared on the scene: Ithiel Town of the firm of Town and Davis, which was considered by some the only truly professional architectural firm in New York at the time. An earlier plan by the firm had been rejected, but now Town was able, probably through Fayetteville connections, to gain the commission.[93] Town thus became the first of many urban American architects to take a major long-distance commission in North Carolina. Although the cruciform plan was too far along to change, he altered other aspects of Nichols's scheme to recast the building in the firm's own brand of modern Grecian style. He added porticoes east and west and substituted square-headed windows for Nichols's arches in the lower story which he believed "violated true architectural taste."[94]

In 1834, superintendent Drummond left the project, and Town replaced him with a young Edinburgh architect, David Paton, who had worked in London under the old neoclassicist Sir John Soane and had come to New York in search of work. Town assured Paton that the job was an opportunity the like of which "does not . . . occur to a beginner in this Country once in thirty years." In Raleigh in September 1834, Paton found himself in charge not only of superintending the stonework, as he had expected, but also managing the budget and workmen and executing working drawings from Town's directions.[95]

In 1835 tensions arose between the two architects, focusing on the critical issues of design and relations with the client. Town accused Paton of attempting to "impair the confidence of the Commission in me & place it in your self as the Architect" and of placing "your experience in the science & practice of building, on a par with mine." He threatened to have Paton fired, but in fact the commissioners severed connections with Town and in March 1835 gave Paton full responsibility.[96] Thus the project changed from a long-distance arrangement with authority delegated to a superintendent to one with an on-site architect in charge.

Paton began to put his own stamp on the building. Using Edinburgh

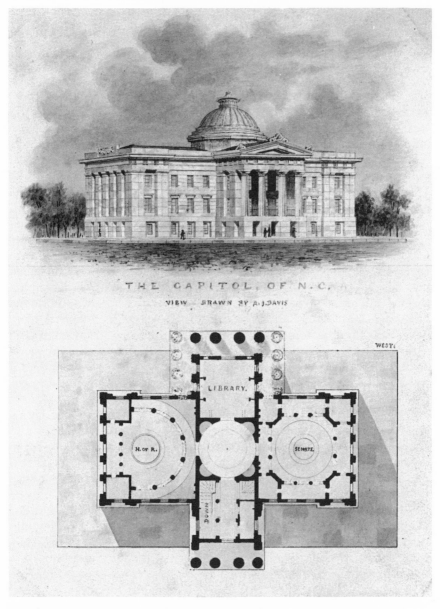

THE CAPITOL, OF N.C.

VIEW DRAWN BY A.J.DAVIS

Perspective and plan, ca. 1833, Capitol, Raleigh, 1833–40, by Alexander Jackson Davis. (The Metropolitan Museum of Art, Harris Brisbane Dick Fund, 1924 [24.66.1401 (23)].)

techniques of cantilevering, he opened up the rotunda to create a great dramatic space from ground level to skylight, and he brought a touch of Soane's abstract neoclassicism to the vaulted rooms, great domed and columned chambers, and smaller third-floor vestibules with their top-lighted elliptical domes.[97] He completed working drawings—229 of them —as work proceeded and explained the complex structural and finish work to the boss artisans. The essence of the architect's role appears in a local legend: After the last stone was placed in the cantilevered balcony around the rotunda, Paton ordered the workmen to remove the scaffolding, but they refused, "declaring that nobody but a fool would dare pull the supporting structure from beneath the unsupported stonework." Then Paton, so the story goes, told the men to stand aside, took off his coat, and, working alone while they watched, removed the timbers until he "stood beneath his achievement unafraid."[98]

Despite his obvious expertise, however, Paton's professional status remained uncertain. When disagreements arose between him and the commissioners over proper ways of executing various classical details, they turned to yet another architect, William Strickland of Philadelphia, for advice. The latter confirmed Paton's ideas with a series of authoritative judgments on matters classical, ending with a rejection of the notion of a balustrade atop the dome as "Roman and inadmissable."[99] More troublesome, however, and more indicative of the uncertainty of professional status at the time, were conflicts over Paton's pay. He insisted that though he had arrived and been first paid as superintendent of masonry at $3.00 a day, his duties as manager, maker of drawings, and thus of architect, entitled him to more money; belated raises to $3.50 and $5.00 a day fell short of what he believed to be his due, the $7.50 a day paid to his "brother Architect" in Washington, D.C. Paton left the project a few months before its completion; for years afterward he sent the legislature appeals for back pay, elaborate memorials with explanations of his professional qualifications and testimonials from other architects, but to no avail.[100]

In the 1830s, urban architects like Town and Strickland had achieved a degree of authority, but in general the architect's struggle to carve out a clear professional and economic status had only begun. Paton had come from Britain with his own idea of professionalism but found himself on uncertain ground in a nation where the profession was still young. For a time the only architect in North Carolina, he had no firm basis from which to claim the status or pay he believed he merited as a "thorough-bred architect." Paton, like Latrobe earlier, was still "breaking the ice."

Architectural patronage expanded in North Carolina over the next several years. Federal construction projects in the state brought some early professional commissions. In 1835 the director of the United States Mint commissioned Philadelphia architect William Strickland to design a mint in Charlotte. The United States Army sent Scotsman William Bell (at

David Paton memorial, Capitol, Raleigh, 1833–40. The lithograph was made in Edinburgh by J. Sutcliffe; it was probably from a drawing provided by Paton and, if so, depicts the only known example of Paton's drawings. It served as the cover for one of Paton's many appeals to the legislature for additional payment. (North Carolina Division of Archives and History.)

David Paton's recommendation) to serve as architect of the Federal Arsenal in Fayetteville. The United States Treasury Department commissioned two big projects in the port city of Wilmington: in 1843 New York architect John Norris was awarded the job of designing and superintending the Federal Custom House, and in 1858–60 John Walker of Washington, D.C., and Petersburg, Virginia, contracted to erect a Marine Hospital designed by Treasury architect Ammi B. Young.[101] Local initiatives to employ nationally active architects also multiplied in the 1840s and 1850s. Ambitious citizens, especially in Wilmington, commissioned institutional and private work from a variety of northern architects. The vestry of St. James's Church began the trend in Wilmington by employing Thomas U. Walter of Philadelphia to design their handsome Gothic-revival church in 1837; other major projects soon followed suit. Some congregations even sent committees to Baltimore and New York to recruit architects.[102] Episcopal clerics desirous of bringing their country flocks into the denomination's architectural mainstream turned to Richard Upjohn, Frank Wills, and other New York proponents of the Gothic revival.[103] During the same period, the progressive "internal improvement men" of the piedmont, led by Gov. John Motley Morehead, commissioned New Yorker Alexander Jackson Davis to provide neoclassical and Tuscan designs for schools, a state insane asylum, and their own villas.[104]

Whatever the enthusiasm of outward-looking clients, out-of-state architects met with skepticism from some North Carolinians. When Davis, for example, first arrived in Raleigh en route to Chapel Hill, one citizen—calling himself "Macon"—wrote to a Raleigh paper to register his objections to hiring an "Architect, who had come all the way from the City of New York" to redesign two buildings at the university. Recalling longstanding problems, the writer asserted that it was typical of state leaders to hire northerners without giving southerners a chance—to "underrate our own citizens" and to engage in the old "passion for the far fetched and dear bought" that discouraged native proficiency. It was especially galling that the state's own university should employ such an outsider, which amounted to an "acknowledgement of inferiority" of "Carolina talent." The newspaper editor defended Davis's involvement by claiming that he had accepted a commission for specialized landscape planning and only incidentally for architectural services.[105] But "Macon" was right; Davis won the job over a local contender, beginning a long patronage in the state for himself and other northern architects.

Even those who regularly employed architects expressed a familiar note of caution. In 1857 a Fayetteville newspaper dredged up the thirty-year-old observations of former university president Joseph Caldwell about the "knavery" of architects and engineers who planned beyond the limits of budgets, and in 1859, William H. Battle, a member of the University of North Carolina building committee, commented to fellow committee member William A. Graham during William Percival's work at the university, "Contractors and architects require to be looked after as well as other persons, and it may not be amiss that those in our employ should learn at once that we shall hold them to proper accountability."[106]

Moreover, local considerations sometimes aborted ambitious projects, as familiar themes of frugality and the desire to accommodate local standards exerted a strong pull. More than one Episcopal priest obtained a Gothic-revival church plan from Upjohn but eventually gave up on raising money and returned the drawings to their author. Lawyer William Gaston of New Bern obtained an elaborate Gothic church design for his Catholic parish from A. J. Davis but finally relinquished the idea in 1839 after his bishop, John England, advised: "Unless we give up the impossible for the possible neither you nor I will ever see [a church] in New Bern." England recommended that they "erect the best Church that our means would allow, and leave to others a better when they have better means" and urged a "handsome plain framed building of ordinary materials . . . which will not involve us in debt or difficulties."[107] Former governor William A. Graham obtained from Davis elegant Italian and Gothic proposals for an expansion of his house near Hillsborough but eventually concluded, after consulting his builders, that a simpler scheme would be easier and cheaper and would comport better with the "exceeding plainness of the buildings of our town."[108]

Nevertheless, professional projects continued to multiply, and North Carolina clients took pride in their familiarity with the progress of the profession nationally. An English story about an architect's testimony that the Tower of Babel had fallen because no architect had been involved in its design made the rounds among North Carolinians who enjoyed the benefits of professionalism.[109] Big city architects like Town and Strickland had achieved respect for their professional status. Davis, who came from New York with the panache of the nationally established professional and perhaps the artiste, enjoyed not only professional pay rates but also many perquisites during his visits to North Carolina where he socialized with and met as equals the state's political and social elite—dining with the governor, traveling in his coach, and making the acquaintance of progressive leaders. At the same time, in these nascent years of the American architectural profession, men such as Ithiel Town, A. J. Davis, and Richard Upjohn worked hard to attract and maintain patrons. They responded quickly and courteously to inquiries from distant communities, ordered goods for their clients from New York suppliers, and provided designs and instructions to meet the needs of the far-flung clients so essential to their business.[110]

In the same period, men working on the local scene began to establish themselves as architects. In 1850 North Carolina had five men who identified themselves as architects and by 1860, six. Some had begun as builders and then taken on the role of architect: Thomas J. Holt, for example, was working as a builder with his brother Jacob in Warrenton in 1850, but he became architect of the Raleigh and Gaston Railroad in the 1850s and was listed in the 1860 census as architect. William Bogart advertised as a builder in eastern North Carolina in 1856 and four years later as an architect. James F. Post of Wilmington likewise was listed in the 1850 census as carpenter and in 1860 as architect; he reflected his transition in his account book as he continued to take building contracts but increasingly focused his time on supplying drawings and specifications and serving as superintending architect on big projects—following a path traced by many in this fluid era.[111]

Other men arrived in North Carolina in hopes that their foreign professional training would gain them opportunities among a provincial clientele. Prominent among these was William Percival, who, like William Nichols a generation before, combined British training, knowledge of stylish designs suitable to a local market, and a certain dash and talent for self-promotion. He produced attention-getting work in Gothic and Italianate styles for clients in Raleigh, Tarboro, and Chapel Hill and took advantage of local newspapers and antitraditional attitudes to acquaint the public with the architect's special virtues. He entered into public events, won prizes for architectural drawings at state fairs, and attracted reporters to cover his projects, recounting to a convenient newspaperman the "peculiar qualifications" necessary for an architect: he must be an educated man who possessed not only knowledge of mathematics, practical philosophy, and the basics of all the building trades, but especially "the genius and feelings of a true artist."[112] It was on the public's acceptance of these qualities, Percival knew, that the architect's claim to professional status depended.

Professional Architectural Services

The antebellum architect's attraction for clients lay in his ability to give them modern buildings conceived from international and national rather than local models, works of originality rather than outworn custom. To accomplish this, the architect's task was not only to create designs but also to provide services sufficient to translate his concept into reality: drawings, specifications, and, in some cases, superintendence.

Changes in the nature of drawings and specifications exemplify the deeper changes in the building process. In the professional project, sheet after sheet of drawings replaced the traditional project's simple ground-plan sketch. So, too, the traditional specification with its informal order and reliance on tacit assumptions gave way to systematic, highly explicit specifications that detailed every element of the building. They usually proceeded from ground to roof, outside to inside, or trade by trade. These

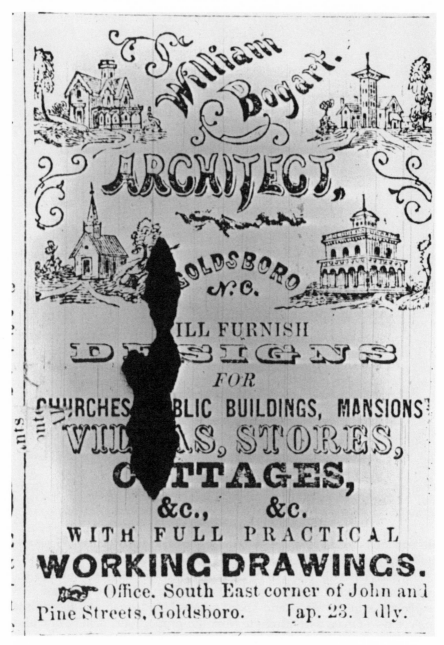

William Bogart advertisement as architect, *Goldsboro Daily Rough Notes*, February 25, 1861. (North Carolina Division of Archives and History.)

Perspective drawing, 1860, Calvary Episcopal Church, Tarboro, by William Percival. This is the only Percival drawing known to survive. (North Carolina Division of Archives and History.)

instructions could require five, ten, or twenty pages for a fairly simple building and were often keyed to an accompanying set of drawings.[113]

It was not only the unfamiliar complexity of buildings but also the rejection of the old client-artisan division of control that demanded new explicitness in drawings and specifications. No longer was the artisan expected—or even permitted—to work out proportions, details, or craftsmanship according to customary or personal rules of thumb. Moreover, the professional project involved different relationships on the building site itself. Instead of the client and artisan's continuing face-to-face negotiation of the building process, in a professional project, conceivably the cast of characters included a client who had turned full design authority over to the architect; an architect who might not ever appear at the building site; a contractor who might manage work without laying a hand to plane or trowel; and finally, an artisan charged with executing unfamiliar work he had had no part in conceptualizing. In such circumstances, drawings and specifications assumed a new purpose and took on a new and more explicit form.

The Philadelphia or New York architect who designed stylish Gothic or Greek-revival buildings for distant clients had to produce documents adequate to assure the faithful execution of his scheme. For Raleigh's Christ Church, New York architect Richard Upjohn provided for five hundred dollars drawings and specifications. The drawings included ten plans, elevations, and sections drawn at ¼ inch to the foot; a roof section at ½ inch to the foot; sixteen sections and details at 1 inch to the foot; and twenty-eight details drawn full size. A model of the roof showed the unfamiliar Gothic roof-truss system. Upjohn advised his client to "examine the plan of the roof . . . and you will see how to put [the model] together. One side shews the timbers finished and its connection with the wall. . . . The other side shews the mode of putting the different timbers forming the principal rafters together and the pencil lines shew where the bolts are to be applied. I believe you cannot fail in understanding the models and the plans." With Upjohn's package in hand, the congregation could contract with builders and require them simply to "conform in every particular to the plans & specifications furnished by Richard Upjohn of the City of New York . . . which are hereby agreed & declared to form a part of this agreement."[114]

The emerging national definition of professional standards was demonstrated by New York architect A. J. Davis. Davis's practices, like his leadership in founding the American Institution of Architects in 1836–37, embodied his continuing effort to advance the status of his profession in America.[115] He followed fee schedules that would eventually become standard, basing his payment on percentages of the cost of the building: 5 percent for "full professional services" including superintendence, 3 percent for design services without supervision, and 1 percent for drawings and sufficient specifications to obtain an estimate. He also supplied single drawings, at prices that started at fifteen dollars for a principal floor plan for a "medium class of building." Adhering to standard practice, Davis made most of his plans and elevations at the scale of ¼ inch to the foot. Other drawings ranged from full-scale (usually for moldings) to ⅛ inch to the foot. Davis supplied principal drawings at the beginning of the project, then working drawings as the project proceeded.[116] For such a major project as the Insane Asylum in Raleigh in 1850, Davis's design services included visits to other hospitals, an on-site inspection with the commis-

Elevation drawing, 1846, Christ Church, Raleigh, by Richard Upjohn. (Avery Library, Columbia University.)

sioners, several weeks of drawing back at his office to produce sheafs of drawings, the first batch costing three hundred dollars, then revisions after additional visits.[117]

In his work on the Insane Asylum, Davis also made use of the printed, standardized architectural specification form, which he had introduced into American practice a few years earlier. Instead of laborious handwritten instructions for each job, Davis's printed specification form defined every component, trade by trade, in a set order from ground up according to standard criteria of materials and workmanship and included a list of ten standard plans, elevations, and sections usually provided for

SPECIFICATION OF THE MATERIALS AND WORKS REQUIRED FOR BUILDING A DWELLING HOUSE *and*

N. C. State Hospital for the Insane.

in the vicinity of Raleigh, the capital.

ACCORDING TO THE ACCOMPANYING DRAWINGS, AND THE CONDITIONS SUBJOINED. *Alex'r J. Davis Arch't*

The writing and figuring on all the drawings are to be considered as part and parcel of this specification; and this specification, and the drawings are to be considered as reciprocally illustrative of each other. In many of these drawings, if, to save the labor of repetitions, some parts are shown complete, and others omitted or left incomplete; in all such cases, the drawings are, nevertheless, to be understood as if they had each been distinctly and severally shown complete in every respect. The parts colored gray or blue, indicate stone; those colored red are intended for brick; and the yellow for wood.

THE SEVERAL DRAWINGS referred to by this specification are in Number and consist of as follows:

NUMBER I. Basement or foundations. *Scale 8 ft to one inch.*

B. II. Plan of the Principal floor.

C. III. Plan of the Second story, *or Physician's apart'mt.*

D. IV. Attic and Roof. *Dome ceiling and tanks.*

E. V. Elevation of Principal front. *N.E. by East towards R.*

F. VI. Elevation of *the South side of central building*

G. VII. Elevation of the *fascade under the Arcade*

H. VIII. Longitudinal Section, *front to rear, centre building.*

I. IX. Transverse Section, *thro' the east wing. 2 sections.*

K. X. Common Windows, *shewing general construction.*

D *Is also the Third floor of centre. §8 or highest of wing*

E *Is also Attic and tanks.*

Printed specification, North Carolina Insane Asylum, Raleigh, 1850–56, Alexander Jackson Davis, architect. (North Carolina Division of Archives and History.)

each building. The form also provided space for additional customized descriptions and drawings required for a particular building. Besides its obvious convenience, the printed specification form also had the effect of promoting national standardization of the concept of quality—in the minds of builders and suppliers who bid on projects and in the actual execution.[118]

"Considerable Patience and a Great Deal of Labor": Executing the Work

Once the architect had provided the requisite drawings and specifications, the client had to find ways of getting the work executed. Wilmingtonians found that good results came from hiring a superintending architect. As early as 1839, John Norris of New York had come to Wilmington to supervise construction of Thomas U. Walter's Gothic-style St. James Church, and in later years Samuel Sloan of Philadelphia sent associate Addison Hutton to superintend his First Baptist Church. Wilmington clients also employed resident builders as superintendents. James Walker, brother of the contractor for the Marine Hospital, supervised Sloan's First Presbyterian Church in Wilmington, and James F. Post was paid four dollars a day for over three years as superintending architect of the principal civic building, City Hall-Thalian Hall, from designs supplied by New York theater architect J. M. Trimble. In the latter project, changes in the design were made by local men, but to the satisfaction of the client.[119]

But Wilmington, as a sizable port city, possessed a better supply of urban-trained men, and its citizens were more willing to spend money on architectural services than were most individuals and small-town building committees. Many North Carolinians who obtained designs from distant architects undertook construction by employing artisans or builders in the usual fashion. Some let a single contract for the whole work, some gave separate contracts to different trades, and others took the architect's drawings and specifications in hand, bought materials and hired local workmen, and hoped for the best.[120] There was always a strong possibility that, however clear the architect's drawings and instructions, the design would change in the translation—as John Morehead acknowledged when he invited A. J. Davis to visit the villa he had designed for him and "see if Blandwood is erected according to the plans."[121]

For most clients, the best laid plans and specifications represented but the beginning of an undertaking that was made doubly demanding by the architect's designs. Execution of buildings that would have been taken for granted in New York or Philadelphia was still difficult in North Carolina, and the very qualities that clients sought in nationally prominent architects made execution of their designs even harder. The traditional artisan based his buildings on precedent, his own capabilities, and the nature of local materials, but now the reverse was true: the urban architect based his plans on Greek, Gothic, or Italian models and modern functional ideals. Even if he knew something of local conditions—not always the case—neither regional traditions nor local materials were the sources of his ideas. It fell to the clients to contend with the differences between national style and local capabilities. What is remarkable in this era is that so many of these ambitious clients did precisely that. They wanted recognizably modern buildings, and they were willing to spend money and take the trouble to get them.

Wise clients informed their architects about local conditions and materials. Early in Davis's work for the University of North Carolina, his friend and patron Robert Donaldson warned, "You must take into consideration the materials & mechanics there" and suggested he use stuccoed brick rather than stone.[122] Similarly, a priest in a rural coastal parish informed Upjohn, "As respects stone for foundation—we use brick here altogether—Stone must be imported & costs very high. As regards the use of hemlock, spruce & white pine—we have not such wood & we have just as good without importing . . . cypress backed by our common yellow Carolina pine will certainly make a very good church for any country."[123] Without such local knowledge, projects could run into real trouble, as John Walker of Virginia learned when he took the contract with the United States government to build the Marine Hospital in Wilmington. He had submitted his bid on the assumption that local stone could be found to meet Treasury Office specifications, but learned on arriving in Wilmington that there was no good local building stone. He was forced to stop work and head north to Virginia, where he reopened a quarry and spent months quarrying stone and arranging for shipment to Wilmington.[124]

It was common practice for urban architects to order and send to their clients the specialized finish items essential for completion of their designs—stained glass, lighting fixtures, decorative moldings, first-class hardware, even furniture and artwork. Some items were specially commissioned, as when Davis found a New York firm to carve capitals of corn and wheat foliage he had designed, then had them boxed up and sent to Chapel Hill for builder John Berry to install on Smith Hall's classic portico.[125] Baltimore architect E. G. Lind sent almost all the building materials—slate mantels, lumber, brackets, fancy furniture and carpets, gas lamps, and lightning rods—as well as specialized workmen to fulfill his designs for Coolmore, a villa near Tarboro.[126]

The Professional Triangle: Client, Architect, Builder

The greatest source of tension in professional projects arose from the triangular relationship that put design authority in the hands of the architect. Problems sprang both from the specific character of new designs themselves and also from the process that required men to build from unfamiliar rather than familiar models. Some clients, especially those who had come from the North, were highly critical of local artisans' capabilities. A Raleigh cleric advised Richard Upjohn, "Our workmen are not well skilled in the mysteries of architectural rules and phrases" and asked the architect to send "such drawings as will be intelligible to a *rural* carpenter, and such verbal directions as will prevent the possibility of a mistake."

Rufus Tucker Villa, Raleigh, 1858–59, William Percival, architect, Thomas Briggs and James Dodd, builders. (Photo, North Carolina Division of Archives and History.)

Another asked the architect to make out the bill of timber for a small frame church, for "carpenters here know little about such plans & I am afraid to trust them to do it, if I can do better—I believe that I might take one of our best carpenters & study it out *pretty well*, but this wd not suit so well."[127] Clients who understood the challenges of the new work counted themselves fortunate when their builders rose to the occasion. When Raleigh contractors Thomas Briggs and James Dodd completed a complex and extravagant villa designed for merchant R. S. Tucker by William Percival, complete with hot and cold running water, hot air heat, and acetylene gas lighting, Tucker gratefully acknowledged their accomplishment: "The style of the House being new to our Mechanics and the work tedious and difficult—Must have required considerable patience and a great deal of labor but you have shown in its successful completion (according to the designs of the Architect) that you are Master Builders."[128]

It was not unusual for clients to find themselves caught between the architect's vision and the builder's practical concerns—a perpetual source of conflict, exacerbated when the architect operated from a distance. The builders who took the big contracts were usually men of established reputation and skill, held in high esteem by their clients and well grounded in their firm understanding of building and materials. They were not cowed by architects' reputations and often took a sharper look at plans than did the admiring client. When Dabney Cosby, the 66-year-old brick builder, began to execute A. J. Davis's remodeling of university buildings in 1845, he challenged the architect on several technical points and on one occasion refused to dig out the cellars as specified, commenting: "The short time Mr. Davis was there would not enable him to percive the rottenness of the foundation work." Soon after, while executing Davis's neoclassical temple, Smith Hall, in 1850–51, Hillsborough builder John Berry presented the architect with a politely phrased series of technical questions, including one query that epitomized the distance between their architectural experience: "Governor Swain shewed me your letter touching the stile you desire the collums to be finished, our workmen are not famillier with the stile you give your prefernce to but if you would send me out a plan of the collum representing the [?] and also particular instructions perhaps I can have them exicuted to your notion but in the event we adopt the plan of fluting laid down in the books shall we use the Doric or Ionic flutes?"[129]

Two divergent views of the architect's role met when Charles Phillips, idealistic professor of mathematics, civil engineering, and classics at the university, was assigned to superintend construction of Davis's Tuscanstyle Presbyterian church in Chapel Hill. The task thrilled Phillips, who was undertaking his "first essay in minutely scanning the plans & designs for a building *in futuro*." He hoped one day to meet Davis to "learn by personal intercourse how to enter into the deeper mysteries of . . . [the] glorious art . . . of the Architect" and added, "We who plod along among Greek roots and Mathematical equations Must be thankful for the dust that flies from the heels of Pegasus." Phillips apologized for his need to get clearer instructions on practical details, and, suggesting something of the flavor of negotiating between his admiration of Davis's ideas and the crusty pragmatism of the builder—Dabney Cosby again—Phillips put another question: "You specify that the front, and I suppose the whole of the outside of the Church is to be a *lilac grey*. Now it has been so long since the last spring that our mason has forgotten the colour of the lilacs—nor does he know how to imitate it. Will you be pleased to help him, & us."[130]

For the builder, however, working from an architect's designs presented more fundamental questions than those of taste or construction details—questions of power within the building process and, ultimately, of the builder's control over his economic fate. This was the case whether the architect was a New Yorker or a local man. Two small-town projects illustrate builders' awareness of their situations.

In 1848 Benjamin Gardner of Wilmington served as architect for a Greek revival–style courthouse for Wayne County, producing drawings keyed to five pages of itemized specifications. The county's agreement with the builder specified how any conflicts over the contractor's execution

Presbyterian Church, Chapel Hill, 1847–48, Alexander Jackson Davis, architect, Dabney Cosby, builder. (Photo, 1892, North Carolina Collection, University of North Carolina Library, Chapel Hill.)

of the design were to be resolved: the architect was to be the judge. But the builder, John Becton, countered with a codicil that changed the division of power; it removed sole authority from the architect and specified that in case of a disagreement between builder and committee, Hillsborough builder John Berry was to consult with the architect and the two would render a decision. Moreover, if these two were unable to agree, then Raleigh builder Dabney Cosby was to serve as "umpire." Becton's codicil suggests the complexity and anxiety involved when a new actor, the architect, assumed unfamiliar new power in the building process. The builder, who would in previous years have dealt directly with the building committee without any architect as third party, felt it necessary to take exclusive authority over his economic fate out of the hands of the architect and share it with his own brethren, the established builders of the state.[131]

At worst, unresolved tensions among the client, architect, and builder could result in the complete breakdown of a project. This occurred in the town of Greenville shortly before the Civil War. After the Pitt County courthouse burned in 1858, a building committee was appointed to adopt a plan for a new courthouse and to contract with a builder. The committee procured from an architect identified as Mr. Holt the plans and specifications for a towered, buttressed, Gothic-style building of smooth oil-stock brick. Then they advertised for proposals to build it for $12,000 or less.[132]

Builder Dabney Cosby, now nearing 80, arrived in Greenville, inspected the plans, and, shades of the State House bidders, concluded that the building as designed could not be constructed for the sum. Then, as Cosby later recalled the events, "Inasmuch as Holt the architect who had drawn the plan and specifications was not in Greeneville he concluded to make a proposition to the Commissioners to make some alterations and modifications in the plan & finish of the building to enable [him] to bid for the contract." Cosby met with committee member George Singletary, and the two agreed on certain changes and recorded them on the plans: "The Buttresses are to be reduced to four inch projections. The turrets and other Gothic work to be dispensed with and the front finished with a heavy portico similar to that of the Court House of Wake County, and instad of outside finish oil stock brick it is to be finished with a complete rough cast concrete imitation." These changes were all money-saving moves, including the use of cheaper brick covered with rough-cast plaster, a specialty of Cosby's workshop. Cosby entered a bid, got the job, and began work. At commissioner Singletary's request, Cosby's son John drew up plans, which were approved by a majority of the committee.

As the soft brick walls began to rise, committee members began to realize how radically the building differed from the design their architect had provided. When Cosby refused the demand of one member that he give bond that his work would conform to Holt's original plan, the committee halted the project and took Cosby to court. He defended himself vigorously, ticking off each of the differences they cited and explaining that each had been approved by them or, in several cases, proceeded from the approved changes. Thus, "As to the charge that the dimensions are not the same he answers that the dimensions of the main building are the same and that the Turrets in which the stairway was to be being dispensed with and the stairway necessarily put inside the building the rooms were necessarily thereby diminished by the space which became necessary for the stairway." He similarly defended the changes in chimneys, vaults, and so forth. Cosby "denied that he got angry with the commissioners or any of them or forbade any of them from visiting the work," insisted that he had in fact invited them to inspect his work, and assured them that the building when completed would be "a pleasant and convenient courthouse . . . not unworthy of the County of Pitt." Such was never to occur. Cosby lost his case and was dismissed from the job. The following year a new man was given a contract to build from new designs, and his first task was that "the present walls are to be taken entirely down . . . and the building begun from the foundation."

For each party—client, architect, and builder—the triangular division of authority offered new possibilities—for architecture reflecting a modern image, for professional status, and for profitable jobs. Yet, as each learned through experience, this arrangement also presented new risks and uncertainty for all, requiring each to establish a new degree of control over his own place in the building process and thus in the world.

Artisans in Antebellum Society

While the newly important professionals and contractors were struggling to assert their roles in the upper strata of the building industry, the carpenters and masons upon whom building finally depended were facing their own problems. The new emphasis on professionalism and the growth of large workshops were part of broader changes in North Carolina and the nation, as the economy changed and old work roles began to split apart. These changes interacted with other strains in the social fabric, as the midcentury brought conflicts over the future of the slave system, the role of the workingman, and the relationships among various classes and members of society. Three patterns predominate among the state's antebellum carpenters and masons: general continuity in the makeup of the building trades, especially in small towns and rural areas; the creation of new situations for artisans who worked on big urban projects; and workmen's rising anxiety and willingness to organize in defense of their economic status.

The broad picture of the artisan population, quantified for the first time by the United States censuses of 1850 and 1860, had in many ways changed little from earlier eras.[133] Because mass production was only beginning to affect building technology, hand labor was still needed to shape as well as to assemble materials. Carpenters, masons, joiners, and plasterers still undertook familiar tasks and trained in an apprenticeship system that was essentially unaltered.[134] The proportions of men in various trades also remained constant. The 1850 census of free workmen listed 2,474 carpenters, who outnumbered the 498 stonemasons, brickmasons, and bricklayers by about five to one—a ratio comparable to earlier estimates; in 1860 the figures had risen to 3,217 carpenters and 594 masons and bricklayers. Carpenters constituted the largest male occupational group after farmers and laborers.[135] Free black artisans, as earlier, composed a small but important part of the building trades. In 1860, although free blacks represented only about 4 percent of the total population, they composed about 10 percent of the free men in the building trades, and the proportion of free blacks in trowel trades was greater than that of whites, with 257 free black carpenters, 120 masons, 24 plasterers, 66 painters, and 2 brickmakers.[136]

The spectrum of occasional specialization and widespread versatility also persisted. There were a few specialists in tinwork, decorative painting, or stuccoing, but many more workmen traded on multiple skills.[137] A Warren County mason advertised his competence in stonework, underpinning, whitewashing, plastering, and bridge building; a Washington cabinetmaker offered to make furniture and serve as undertaker furnishing coffins, while continuing in the business of ship and house joinery. Most workshops remained small operations run by independent artisans who might employ one to twelve journeymen, apprentices, and laborers.[138]

Pay was still reckoned by the customary measure, piece, and day methods. Flexibility in arranging bargains and computing pay continued as well. A Hillsborough bricklayer offered various rates per thousand bricks: for making and laying bricks ($8.50), making and delivering bricks to the kiln ($4.50), laying bricks and supplying laborers and board ($2.75), and laying bricks if laborers and board were furnished ($1.25). Pay rates fluctuated with the economy but overall there was little real improvement in artisans' incomes. In 1832, an artisan wrote to a potential client who had not hired him,

> thinking your objection were my prices (as I can think of no other for I execute my work with neatness and dispatch) I have taken the liberty to write you informing you my prices. Six or seven years ago I had for lathing and plastering 20 cents pr yard which might be called high now But I have been gradually falling ever since last summer I got down to 12 ½ cents for lathing and plastering. . . . I am willing to come Lower as the times are hard I will do plastering this summer at 11 ½ cents . . . and if the job can be made worth $200 I will doe it at 10 cents.[139]

In 1860, North Carolina carpenters' average wage of $1.50 a day put them among the lowest paid carpenters in the nation; such rates kept building artisans at the lower and middle rungs of the economic ladder.[140] Less than a third of North Carolina's free carpenters owned real estate in 1850; the proportion ranged from as little as 15 or 20 percent in counties where there were large towns or where the plantation system dominated the economy to well over 50 percent in yeoman farmer counties of the piedmont and mountains.[141] As earlier, of course, the most successful carpenters and masons were able to acquire real estate and sometimes slaves. Carpenter John A. Waddell was one of many men who worked his way up in the business. In 1850 the 24-year-old journeyman was employed in Jacob Holt's shop in Warrenton. In the mid-1850s he worked in Chapel Hill, married the daughter of a minister—despite objections from the father who considered the carpenter "a little rough"—and returned to Warren County where he built a number of elaborate plantation houses. By 1860 he owned some seven thousand dollars in real and personal property, and in the late 1860s he and a partner established a successful lumber and building business.[142]

Yet, however competent and successful the artisan might be, a social gulf lay between him and the local gentry. Whatever the American ideal of equality might assert, in practice social distinctions and sometimes tensions remained. This situation was acutely obvious to builders themselves. The story was told in New Bern that Hardy Lane, the town's leading antebellum builder, was once approached by a "gentleman" who remarked that his son was studying to become a doctor, but if the boy failed, he would send him to Lane to become a carpenter. Lane retorted, "I want you to understand right here in your tracks it does not take the biggest fool you ever saw in your life to make a carpenter."[143]

The artisan's pattern of circular mobility from a home base continued as workmen typically advertised for work within a three- or four-county range, such as Charles Foose and Oliver Davies, plasterers and bricklayers, who sought jobs in Wayne, Wilson, Greene, and Edgecombe counties, and David McDuffie, who was willing to plaster or lay brick anywhere within one hundred miles of Fayetteville.[144]

At the same time, the big building projects of the period provided new opportunities for work and expanded old patterns of mobility. Each big project was like a magnet that pulled men from the local hinterland as well as many British and other European immigrants who had come to America in search of work. The Capitol project employed more than three hundred artisans and laborers at the height of construction, while other public projects required dozens of workmen. The new building campaigns brought Raleigh small armies of men with unfamiliar Scotch burrs and Irish lilts and filled little towns like Tarboro and Yanceyville with northern and foreign strangers.[145] Some artisans were itinerant by choice, but many sought to put down roots eventually. John Campbell, a young Scotsman, came to America and found work on the Capitol in Raleigh, but his real hope, as he wrote to his brother who was engaged in construction at Harpers Ferry, was that if both worked hard and spent little, "between us we can buy a pretty good farm" in Illinois or the West.[146]

Wilmington with its many big building projects exemplifies the period's remarkable mobility among artisans. As the number of free men in building trades in that city rose from 120 in 1850 to 171 in 1860, their makeup changed so thoroughly that only 12 of those listed in 1850 reappeared a decade later. Roughly half of Wilmington's free building artisans were native North Carolina whites, a quarter were native free blacks and mulattoes, and another quarter were whites from other states or from northern Europe.[147] New arrivals in Wilmington assured potential employers that their experience in "the North" guaranteed their "correct knowledge of Modern Architecture, as practiced in the large cities," while departing workmen had their eyes on still better prospects, some of them joining the shiploads of "California adventurers" lured by gold rush country reports of builders' wages of twelve to sixteen dollars a day.[148]

Each of the hundreds of artisans on the move followed his own path from project to project, but many traveled on a scale larger than the local artisan's familiar circuit. Another Scotsman, stonecutter William Murdoch, came to Raleigh to work on the Capitol in 1834, left to work on the arsenal at Fayetteville, then worked at Fort Sumter. By the 1850s he was building railroad bridges, a job that took him to Salisbury, where he settled down as a manufacturer with a lumber mill and foundry. James Boon, a free black carpenter, completed his apprenticeship in 1829 and began working on planters' houses in Franklin and nearby Halifax counties. But in 1848 he joined his brother who had found employment amid Wilmington's bustling growth, and the next year went to Raleigh to work for contractor Dabney Cosby on construction of the Yarborough House hotel. Stewart Ellison, a slave trained near Washington, North Carolina, also came to work in Raleigh's building boom, where he was sent by his owner to Raleigh to join the workmen constructing A. J. Davis's huge Insane Asylum.[149]

Ellison was one of many slave artisans involved in the antebellum building boom. Busy construction sites brought white and black, northern and native, free and slave artisans and laborers together. When the scaffolding collapsed during one Wilmington project, three whites, two slaves, and a free black carpenter tumbled to the ground.[150] Although some studies have suggested that slave artisans were "stripped of their skills" in antebellum years, this does not seem to have been the case in North Carolina's building trades.[151] Individual clients and artisans used their slaves on building projects as regularly as ever, and slave owners continued to allow their slave artisans to arrange work on their own. Stonecutter Allen Lane of Raleigh, for example, belonged to the daughters of a former secretary of state, lived with his wife and children who belonged to Gov. Charles Manly, and worked independently, returning a portion of his wages to his owners.[152]

The increase in the scale of projects and the expansion of contractors' shops, nearly all of whom employed slave workmen, served to expand the practice of slave hiring.[153] Slave hiring was also encouraged in the 1850s as the cost of purchasing a slave artisan—as much as two thousand dollars—rose faster than the cost of hiring.[154] Certainly many of the biggest and most elaborate projects of the era involved the work of slave artisans, including such urban landmarks as Wilmington's massive, richly finished City Hall-Thalian Hall. A former slave recalled in later years:

Haywood Dixon, daguerreotype, ca. 1854. Dixon was a slave carpenter in Greene County; the daguerreotype depicts him with his carpenter's square. (Private collection, courtesy of William L. Murphy, Jr.)

I remember all the bricklayers, they was all colored. The man that plastered the City Hall was named George Price, he plastered it inside. The men that plastered the City Hall outside and put those colum's up in the front, their names was Robert Finey and William Finey, they both was colored. Jim Artis now was a contractor an' builder. He done a lot of work 'round Wilmington. Yes'm, they was slaves, mos' all the fine work 'round Wilmington was done by slaves. They called 'em artisans. None of 'em could read, but give 'em any plan an' they could foller it to the las' line.[155]

The Artisan as Workingman: Complaints and Collective Action

The members of the building trades who voiced the greatest concern over their social and economic status were white journeymen. Despite new opportunities for work, the problems journeymen had complained of in previous years intensified, and the contrast between their status and that of others in the building trades became more troublesome. White carpenters were squeezed between the competition from slaves and free blacks who underpriced them and the contractors who seemed to profit immeasurably from their labor. Their frustration mounted as they saw workingmen in other states gain economic and political power, while North Carolina's power structure seemed to ignore the needs of local journeymen. Carpenters and masons joined with workmen in other trades to express their collective ambitions and frustrations.[156]

The first effective organized protests among builders took place during construction of the Capitol. This was not surprising, given the unusually large work force, the longevity of the project, and the interaction between local carpenters and the mostly Irish, Scotch, and English stonecutters recruited from New York and Philadelphia. The stonecutters' display of their status was impressive, as they marched in full artisan regalia in civic parades, flying banners with such mottoes as "Industry, the sure source of Independence," topped by an American eagle. This was strong stuff for Raleigh citizens, including the local artisans who were accustomed to a society that attached "a strange dislike to the name of mechanic in this country." Besides such symbolic actions, the stonecutters also demanded a ten-hour workday, insisted on more pay "according to the northern rates," sought different summer and winter pay scales, and were willing to strike or leave their jobs if they did not get what they wanted. Their attitudes spread to the carpenters, many of them local men, who struck for higher wages in 1839 and, protesting insults to their character in 1840, collectively signed their petition to the commissioners, "the State Capitol Carpenters."[157] The commissioners, mindful of the desperate financial state of a project that had far outstripped all cost estimates, conceded some measures but used firings, demotions, and threats of hiring black workers to control the restive work force.

It is no coincidence that the Raleigh Mechanics Association organized during the project and gained its charter the month after the Capitol was completed in 1840. The group, whose officers included the lead carpenter, a stonemason, and the blacksmith from the Capitol project, was one of several organized in the state in the 1840s to promote workmen's mutual improvement and assistance. In 1842, the organization gained recognition for having "done more towards placing the Mechanic on a level with, and even above, the purse-proud aristocrat, than you are aware of."[158]

Yet the mechanic's status remained curiously ambiguous, as an 1842 address to the Raleigh association indicated. Newspaper editor and self-declared proponent of workingmen W. W. Holden spoke in uplifting tones, citing the popular myths on the marvels of the modern age, the nobility of labor, and the importance of the workingman to the community, and encouraged the mechanics to better themselves by learning the scientific principles upon which their trades depended and by improving their status over that of their fathers. But at the same time, he warned his audience to avoid the "trappings and garniture of high life," to abjure the current "cry of the poor against the rich" as the work of demagogues, and, above all, to remember that "labor and capital are inseparable."[159]

This was the consistent message North Carolina artisans received from the press and political leaders—to improve their skills but not to push above their allotted place in society.[160] The message grew stronger whenever mechanics suggested that their own interests diverged from those of capital.

Again and again, in short-lived and scattered bursts of bitter energy, North Carolina artisans rallied against perceived threats to their economic status. About 1850 white mechanics held rallies across the state to object to competition from northern workmen and underpricing from local free blacks. They petitioned the legislature to bind all free black mechanics to white masters for life—essentially enslaving them—or to encourage them to leave the state. This measure was not enacted, but ten years later another law passed that forbade free blacks to hire, apprentice, or own slaves; this measure, while not retroactive, aimed a potentially fatal blow at the leading free black builders, who depended on—and often nurtured—slave artisans.[161]

White artisans more often leveled complaints at competition from slaves. Like the early-nineteenth-century Wilmington mechanics, they attributed their problems not to the slaves themselves but to the slave-owning classes. In Wilmington, where old patterns continued, resentment toward slave competition resurfaced, this time in violent form. On a hot summer midnight in 1857, a group of men vandalized a building under construction and left a notice that "a similar course would be pursued, in all cases against all buildings to be erected by Negro contractors or carpenters." The action was attributed to an "organized association" of 250 or more workmen. Wilmington white artisans reiterated their claim that blacks who were "cared for by their master's, were at trifling expense for living, and were thereby enabled to underbid them in contracts." They insisted that this system "cheapened labor to such a degree that they the white mechanics could not live, and would be compelled to abandon their occupations or to leave the place." The establishment's point of view became clear when, at a public meeting generated by the event, a speaker for the local elite condemned the artisans' lawless action, urged more peaceful means of stating complaints, and chastised what he saw as "the arraying of one class of the community against another." He suggested, moreover, that "if under the present situation of things as regards slave competition in labor" and "if the present business did not justify them in remaining here, they were at liberty to leave the place and seek a living elsewhere."[162]

Repeatedly in the 1850s artisans sought protection against what they perceived as the dominant interests of capital and property. The issue took many forms. In 1854 mechanics found common cause with builders, ship builders, and architects in petitioning the legislature for a mechanics' lien law. Such laws had been enacted elsewhere to protect workmen by permitting a builder to take a lien on the property on which an owner had failed to meet the terms of a construction contract. The initiative began among Wilmington's artisans but spread to other areas. The "laboring classes," the petitions stated, had "long felt the want of protection of law" when they invested labor and materials in a contract. Without such a law, the mechanic who must "live by the daily sweat of his brow" had little recourse if a client died, could not comply with his contract, or sold or disclaimed title to the property. Despite support from several communities, the measure died in committee.[163]

A few years later, taxes became the issue. Raleigh workingmen rallied to fight a new revenue law that expanded the state's income tax from professional salaries to workers' wages—a tax increase intended, ironically, to pay off debts for internal improvements.[164] In October 1859, "Justice" protested in a Raleigh paper the injustice of taxing "me as a carpenter, five dollars on my wages of five hundred dollars, and not tax[ing] my neighbor's two negro carpenters working at the same bench with me *one cent*, although they are making for him as much as I make." The carpenter also objected to big employers getting rich from the labor of journeymen without paying tax on their profits. He believed that the new tax amounted to "odious and oppressive discrimination against the industry, energy, and property of a large majority of the population." Within a few days, when the annual state fair brought crowds of workers to Raleigh, the Wake County Workingmen's Association organized to combat the tax. "Justice"'s letter, reprinted in Salisbury and Greensboro newspapers with a somewhat admiring comparison to the Regulator movement, disturbed some readers. One objected that it was "intended to array the poor against the rich" and that the views were "monstrous—agrarian—leveling down in their tendency, and calculated to disturb the quiet relations of social life," and, bringing the threat of outside violence into the picture, "akin to the motive that excited the recent mob at Harper's Ferry."[165]

The next year, the Wake County Workingmen's Association took on another tax issue; this time they supported a proposal to tax slaves on an ad valorem basis—as property taxed "at value" rather than as polls or individuals. Another attempt to pay off internal improvement debts, this proposal would have increased the tax paid on slaves and thus hurt slave owners and help those who competed with slave workers. This was a hot issue in the gubernatorial election of 1860, and the workingmen's association urged fellow mechanics and workingmen to "look to their own rights and interests, and to insist on that political equality and that participation in public affairs to which they as free men are entitled." A Raleigh newspaper editor found it necessary to defend the right of workers to unite in the cause of "protecting & advancing the interests of labor," as being as "well founded as the right guaranteed by the Legislature to capitalists . . . to protect and advance the interests of capital." The Democrats and the slave-owning faction narrowly won the election and prevented change in the tax law.[166]

The End of an Era: Building Trades at the State Fair

It was ironically appropriate that the Wake County Workingmen's Association scheduled its organizational meeting to coincide with the State Fair, an event designed to celebrate and symbolize the popular progressive ideal. The fair promoted the causes of betterment in agriculture and the mechanical arts, lauded internal improvement and public education, and boosted "North Carolina patriotism" by bringing citizens together to celebrate the state's accomplishments. Begun in 1853 by the state Agricultural Society, the fair enjoyed statewide press coverage and mounting interest. Attendance soared in the late 1850s. Crowds came from distances unthinkable before the railroad to meet their fellow citizens from across the state for the first time, to listen to addresses by political and Agricultural Society leaders, to watch planters' thoroughbreds race, and to view prize-winning displays of Grecian paintings, steam-powered machinery, efficient plows, Carolina-manufactured textiles, and outstanding grain, tobacco, and vegetables.[167]

Among the competitions were displays of architectural drawings: first prize went to Salisbury architect A. B. Hendren in 1857, William Percival in 1858 and 1859, and railroad architect Thomas J. Holt in 1860. In another category, builder-manufacturer William Murdoch of Salisbury won a premium for window sash and blinds one year, succeeded by Raleigh contractors and factory owners Thomas Briggs and James Dodd who won prizes for a sliding door architrave, a veranda column, circular sash and blinds, rolling slat blinds, and a circular-headed window.[168] Architecture thus

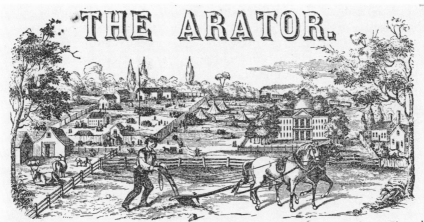

Arator masthead, 1850s. The masthead depicts the progressive ideals of the late antebellum era: a farmer, a state fair, the Capitol, and the railroad. (North Carolina Collection, University of North Carolina Library, Chapel Hill.)

took its place among prize pigs and Alamance plaids as evidence of North Carolina progress.

In its every detail, the State Fair promoted a specific point of view— that of the "Jack Steamer" planters, industrialists, and railroad men who were the leaders of the Agricultural Society, and who, not incidentally, propagated the progressive ideal in architecture. The Agricultural Society leaders, principal speakers, and judges for awards were the same men who, by presenting Downing's views in public forums and patronizing architects A. J. Davis, William Percival, and E. G. Lind, had done much to introduce national models of modern architecture into North Carolina communities. Percival also served on premium committees.[169] The prizes focused attention on the very products of builder-manufacturers' steam-powered factories that would fit out buildings in the latest national fashions. And Percival's architectural drawings at the fair promoted the virtues of professionalism and modernity so eloquently that a newspaper reporter was inspired to repeat the familiar theme, "We are very deficient in Architectural taste, and it is a source of pleasure to see a new spirit spring up. We hope Mr. Percival may be instrumental in awakening every corner of the State on the subject."[170]

The crowds arriving by rail car, the pride in accomplishments, the optimistic hopes for the future (carried in newspapers alongside predictions of war) symbolized for many observers the realization of the "spirit of improvement" evoked in the June 1840 celebration of the completion of the Capitol and the railroad. Not only political leaders but builders such as the prize-winning Thomas Briggs and William Murdoch—who had begun their North Carolina careers as carpenter and stonecutter on the Capitol—could look back on some twenty years of accomplishment.[171] The fair also summed up critical changes in building practice as it celebrated the progress of the architect's creation of new images and the builder and manufacturer's efficient execution of modern components. It was the artisan, once the kingpin of building, who found it necessary to unite with his fellow workers during the fair in an effort to protect his status in the economy. Wandering through the halls of exhibits, the carpenter or mason looked in vain for recognition of his handiwork but saw only the products of the architect's pencil and the manufacturer's machine—the forces that had begun to transform the building industry.

The Civil War halted construction nearly everywhere in North Carolina, stopping work on some buildings before they were finished and aborting plans for others. When building began again after long years of war, trends that had barely begun before the war took off rapidly. The men who revived the building trades included many familiar faces. Though Dabney Cosby and John Berry died and Jacob Holt left the state within a few years of the end of the war, William Murdoch and Thomas Briggs entered quickly into postwar construction booms. William Percival vanished in 1860, and in New York, A. J. Davis became isolated from postwar architectural trends, but Samuel Sloan of Philadelphia used his prewar connections to acquire commissions for the state's massive postwar institutional buildings, and James F. Post revitalized his business as Wilmington's leading architect. Stewart Ellison, who had come to Raleigh as a slave carpenter in the 1850s, settled in the capital and became a prominent contractor and political figure in a new age.

Carl R. Lounsbury

4

The Wild Melody
of Steam:
The Mechanization
of the Manufacture
of Building Materials,
1850–1890

And ask you whence that smoky cloud,
Whose volumes half the sky enshroud?
'Tis the "wild melody" of steam:
Rear'd in the centre of the flood,
The greedy saw-mill grinds its food.

—*Stephen Chester,* New Bern Carolina Centinel,
October 17, 1818

Introduction

INNOVATION in the manufacture and distribution of building materials in the second half of the nineteenth century transformed the way North Carolinians built their houses, factories, barns, and public buildings. As Horace Greeley stressed in his 1872 study of American industries, "With . . . new methods of transportation, the use of steam, and the application of machinery to lessening the expenditure of labor, domestic architecture has partaken fully of the new spirit of the age. . . . Our methods of construction, like our means of transportation, have passed into the railroad phase of development."[1] At midcentury the work of a carpenter or bricklayer in North Carolina was essentially the same as it had been in the colonial and federal periods, yet within a few decades the woodworking and brickmaking trades were fundamentally altered by machine technology. Steam machinery replaced man and beast as the principal source of power and became the agent that propelled North Carolina and the nation into the modern industrial age. By 1900, the use of efficient, labor-saving machinery and methods of mass production penetrated even the most remote areas of the state, unifying the appearance of the man-made landscape and rendering many traditional building practices obsolete.

The Civil War disrupted North Carolina's economy, but by the 1870s and 1880s industrial expansion and the rapid growth of cities and towns had generated a new demand for industrial, commercial, and domestic structures, straining the capacities of suppliers and contractors. Old craft methods of specialized piecework fabrication proved too laborious and slow. Faced with an overwhelming demand for new construction and a chronic shortage of skilled labor, builders organized factory methods to mass-produce building materials and developed new construction techniques that steadily reduced the reliance upon skilled craftsmen.[2] Both carpentry shops and brickyards acquired machinery that replaced work done by hand. Improved transportation systems reduced much of the state's old dependence upon local materials, linked manufacturing establishments with the sources of raw materials in the forests, clay pits, and quarries elsewhere in the state, and expanded the use of new materials such as pressed brick, cast iron, and plate glass.

The change in the production of materials turned skilled custom handcraft operations into standardized mechanical ones, increased specialization in the building trades, and reduced the importance of master craftsmen. The prefabrication of materials in woodworking factories and brickyards and the introduction of simpler wood-framing techniques usurped many of the skilled operations formerly the province of the master carpenter, joiner, or brickmaker. By the first years of the twentieth century, machine-worked joinery and moldings produced in shops known as sash and blind factories so permeated the construction industry that handcraft methods of production had all but disappeared.

This transformation of the manufacture of building materials from traditional handcraft methods to industrialized mass production was not an abrupt episode created solely by some new technological development as it may first appear, but emerged over several decades in the middle of the nineteenth century. Although the scarcity and cost of skilled labor and the consequent willingness of contractors to employ machinery encouraged the organization of factory systems in many parts of the nation, the building trades in North Carolina at midcentury showed few signs of impending change. Several factors retarded industrialized manufacturing in the state. Capital was scarce and those individuals who had it were reluctant to put it into anything other than land and slaves. The state also had no major cities which might have spurred local demand. Perhaps the greatest impediment to industrial manufacturing, however, was the absence of reliable and inexpensive transportation capable of carrying bulky materials over extended distances. The few navigable water routes were confined to the coastal plain and mainly directed trade out of the state. Before the 1850s, the overland shipment of raw materials such as timber or processed products such as bricks proved extremely difficult and costly.

As a result, builders often found it more economical to manufacture many items such as framing members and bricks on or near the building site. Since they were restricted to site construction and to local shop fabrication, most contractors and builders had few incentives to change their handcraft methods. Faced with such a limited market for their products, they recognized that the initial capital expenditure for an assortment of power-driven machinery was not worth the benefits that might be realized in either the saving of time and labor or the increase in productive capacity. Thus what prompted industrial development more than the introduction of new machinery or methods of production was the lowering of transportation costs.[3] The emergence of a statewide system of plank roads and railroads in the third quarter of the nineteenth century provided the impetus and prospect of larger markets for North Carolina manufacturers of building materials and made the mechanization of the building trades feasible. Some mechanics and builders began to experiment with new methods of production and distribution but the nascent antebellum transportation systems had yet to open broad markets. Following the disruption of the Civil War, the rapid growth of cities and towns with their unprecedented demands for houses and commercial buildings in the last quarter of the century made the factory production of building materials both essential and feasible.

Old Patterns of Production

The high cost and erratic methods employed to produce and distribute building materials plagued early builders in North Carolina. Early sawmills often proved unreliable, producing nearly as much sawdust as sawn lumber and frequently standing idle for long periods when the stream feeding the mill was too low to power the machinery. Brickmaking depended on the weather and good luck as much as skill. Rainstorms or a mishap in the firing of a kiln of bricks might ruin the entire batch, leaving nothing to show for several days of hard labor.

The basic raw materials, wood and clay, were plentiful and fairly cheap, but the time and labor employed in the production of "neat" and "elegant" craftsmanship was costly. This assured that elaborately finished materials were affordable by only a small minority. Every molding added to a window frame or every hour spent planing a surface meant that the finished product would be just that much more expensive. What the colonial and antebellum client paid for when he specified the best materials was actually the time and labor of a skilled craftsman.

Even experienced workmen could not always ensure an untroubled supply of materials. As has been illustrated in previous chapters, one of the most frustrating tasks of colonial and antebellum builders was coordinating the manufacture and supply of materials. Building plans often went awry when materials failed to appear when needed or proved to be of such inferior quality that they could not be used by reputable craftsmen. Since most materials were fabricated for a particular job rather than for a local market, any delays in their manufacture or supply brought building activities to a halt. The more ambitious the project, the more difficult it became to coordinate the orderly production and supply of materials.

Sawmills

The first systematic application of power-driven machinery to the fabrication of building materials in North Carolina occurred in the eighteenth century when millwrights began to erect water-powered sawmills that could cut logs into planks, boards, and scantling. Before that time and long afterward in many areas, people depended upon skilled hand sawyers who worked long and arduously to saw the lumber used in building.[4]

By the end of the American Revolution, water-powered sawmills had become increasingly common in the eastern coastal plain and even appeared in the backwoods of the piedmont. From this period until the middle of the nineteenth century when steam machinery, improved saws, and new means of transportation transformed the sawmilling trade, the mechanical sawing of lumber fell into two distinct categories. The first was commercial sawing that manufactured lumber for a largely out-of-state and overseas market. The second was composed of mills cutting lumber for local or small regional markets.

Commercial sawmills concentrated along the coast, principally near Wilmington and New Bern, where they took advantage of port facilities and sizable rivers that furnished abundant waterpower and timber. Steam-powered mills capable of producing several million feet of boards flourished there by the 1820s. Some of this sawn lumber went to markets in adjacent coastal towns but most, such as the more than three million board feet produced by the Cape Fear Steam Sawmill near Wilmington in 1820, was exported to Caribbean islands and northern cities.[5]

The second type of operation, which consisted of sawmills catering to sporadic local needs throughout the state, was far more important to the practice of building in North Carolina. These small mills were situated wherever there was adequate waterpower, ample timber, and sufficient demand to warrant their construction. Streams that twisted through the rolling hills of the piedmont offered many good sites though they were not always convenient to populous agricultural communities or towns. In contrast to the coastal plain, only a few rivers in the piedmont could be used to transport raw materials and manufactured items, and the difficulty and cost of hauling sawn lumber by wagon limited a sawmill's market to a relatively small area. As a result nearly every piedmont county had at least one or two local sawmills while a few thickly populated and prosperous counties blessed with good rivers had many more. In 1850, a dozen sawmills served the people of prosperous Rowan County, but more typical was Alamance County, where small farmsteads and a population of about 12,000 supported eight mills.[6]

Although incomplete records preclude an exact count of sawmills in operation in mid-nineteenth-century North Carolina, there were probably between three and four hundred.[7] Of this number, only the large commer-

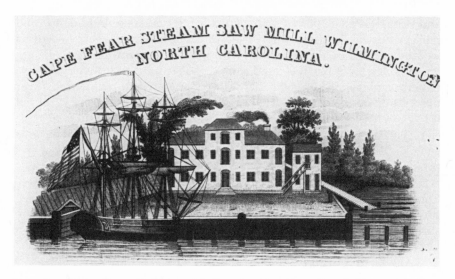

Cape Fear Steam Sawmill, Brunswick County, 1820. From Fourth Census of the United States, 1820, Brunswick Co. Manufacturing Schedule. (North Carolina Division of Archives and History.)

cial mills along the coast produced lumber exclusively. Local mills typically functioned in tandem with a gristmill or with some other industry such as a cotton mill or wagon factory. In fact, for most local mills, sawing logs was only a sideline. At the Lambeth Mill in Alamance County in 1850, for example, the miller ground 500 bushels of flour valued at $7,000 and 5,000 bushels of cornmeal valued at $3,500, while he cut 70,000 feet of lumber valued at only $525.[8] The manufacture of lumber was important to the community miller but not as profitable as the steady business of grinding wheat and corn.

The operation of local sawmills required far less capital investment in machinery, labor, and raw materials than commercial mills. In the middle of the nineteenth century, the owner of a small mill rarely had more than two or three thousand dollars invested in his business. In contrast, capital necessary for a commercial mill ranged from about four to eighty thousand dollars, with the average being about eight to ten thousand dollars. In both types of mills, the physical plant—the building and its machinery—accounted for a sizable portion of the investment. Smaller mills usually had one or two water-powered up-and-down sash saws. A simple reciprocating sash saw that was connected by wooden gears and a crankshaft to a waterwheel cost no more than a few hundred dollars. By contrast the larger steam-powered multiple saws used in commercial mills in the coastal plain cost several thousand dollars to install and maintain.

Because of the relatively inexpensive machinery, small labor force, and negligible stock of materials necessary to operate a community sawmill, ownership of these enterprises varied. Many mills were owned as well as operated by a miller, a man with some mechanical skill who gained the greater part of his livelihood from grinding meal and sawing lumber. Others were owned by substantial planters or merchants who turned over the daily operation of the mill to one of their employees or slaves or rented it to a professional miller. Some mills were run by partnerships of merchants or mechanics who also provided other services on or near the mills such as blacksmithing, carpentry, or the selling of dry goods. In many rural areas the local mill served as the locus for agricultural and social activity. In Orange County, for example, the two mills built by planter Paul Cameron on his vast estates were located at fords on the Eno River, providing convenient access for both the plantation community and the surrounding farmsteads. Clustered around each of these mills were a blacksmith shop, a distillery, a cotton gin, and a general store.[9]

Annual production of lumber at community sawmills rarely exceeded 100,000 board feet—enough to frame and cover twelve to fifteen small houses, which was more than enough lumber to meet the demands of a restricted local market. Although these mills had the capacity to produce more lumber than they did, most sawed only as much lumber as the immediate needs of neighboring farmers and craftsmen warranted. William S. Macay's sawmill in Rowan County remained idle for more than six months at a time in the 1840s and 1850s though his gristmill was almost constantly in use. In his account book for 1848, Macay recorded only half a dozen entries for sawing, chiefly to manufacture weatherboarding for nearby farmers. Himer Fox of Randolph County ran his sawmill for only nineteen days over a two-year period from 1860 to 1861 to fulfill two small jobs—sawing lumber for a waterwheel for the Cedar Falls Manufacturing Company and cutting scantling and boards used in the construction of a house for one of his relatives.[10]

Most local mills responded to specific needs by "sawing lumber to order."[11] Typically clients submitted a bill of lumber to the miller who customarily promised to fill the order within a reasonably short period of time, which may have ranged from a few days to a few weeks. Orders placed at sawmills varied from a few hundred feet of weatherboards or rough-edged sheathing for the repair of farm buildings to detailed lists of materials specified in a carpenter's bill for the construction of an entire dwelling. The lumber cut by Himer Fox for carpenter Levi Wright in December 1856 typifies a bill of sawn timber for a small frame house:

7 pieces	4 inches by	5 inches by	16 feet long
6 joists	3	6	16
25 studs	3	4	16
4 posts	4	5	16
10 sleepers	3	8	16
7 rafters	3	4	11
16 planks	1	9	14
8 planks	1	15	16
10 planks	1	10	16
8 planks	1	14	15

1,188 feet of flooring 1¼ inches by 6 inches
599 feet of ceiling plank
1,404 feet of weatherboarding[12]

The framing members missing from this bill but which occasionally appear in antebellum accounts are sills, plates, and tie beams. These massive members, like corner posts, were often too thick and too long for most early-nineteenth-century sawmills to cut. The slowness of the water-powered reciprocating sash saw also made it difficult to saw many species of hardwoods without warping, jamming, or overheating the long blade. On smaller streams there was often an insufficient volume of water to increase the speed of these cumbersome saws in order to cut thick pieces.[13] Typically, too, the carriage that held logs in place restricted the length of timbers that could be sawn. Although the carriage on one sawmill in the piedmont town of Lexington could handle logs up to 32 feet in length, few antebellum mill carriages could take logs over 25 feet long, and rarely do account books from this period record timbers sawn in lengths of more than 22 feet.[14] Because of this limitation and the difficulty of transporting heavy pieces, most principal framing members continued to be hewn or sawn by hand on or near the building site. When millwright and carpenter Berry Davidson directed the construction of a Presbyterian church in Moore County in 1851, he found that the size of the principal framing members—the sills, plates, tie beams, and posts—made them too long for any of the sawmills in the area to cut. Davidson resorted to the traditional method of hewing the pine timbers square by hand. He then put the roughed-out framing members on scaffolds where they were sawn into scantling of various dimensions by whipsaws worked by men who stood atop and below the timbers.[15] The frames of surviving antebellum structures show that Davidson's solution was not unusual; most have had at least some of their framing timbers fabricated by hand.

The supply of timber for community mills came from two sources. In rural areas where a man had access to both timberland and a team of draft animals, it was sometimes easier and cheaper for him to haul his own saw logs to the mill than to have the miller do so. When textile manufacturer E. M. Holt decided to build a frame villa from the designs of architect A. J.

Reciprocating or sash sawmill, ca. 1857. From Benjamin Butterworth, *The Growth of Industrial Art* (Washington, D.C.: Government Printing Office, 1888), 199. (Duke University Library.)

Davis in the winter of 1849, his slaves felled suitable trees on part of his Alamance County farm, loaded the logs into several wagons, and hauled them to the neighboring mill.[16] However, many without access to timber and the means of transporting it, especially those living in town, relied heavily upon the millers' timbers. A few local millers timbered their own land, an activity that often strained their finances. A large sawmill occasionally hired additional labor and equipment in order to have on hand an adequate stock of raw materials. The Moby Dick sawmill, which supplied lumber to Raleigh in the 1850s, timbered its lands located on nearby Cooper Branch. During the winter months of each year, the proprietors of the firm of Hogg and Haywood employed as many as a dozen laborers— chiefly their own slaves or slaves hired from other masters—to cut and haul logs back to the mill in anticipation of a flood of orders once the building season opened in the spring.[17]

The difficulties in getting raw materials to the mill also accompanied the delivery of the product to the customer. Throughout the state in the first half of the nineteenth century sawn lumber was always cheapest at the source of production. Customers who picked up their orders at the mill paid far less than those who had the miller deliver the lumber. The farther one transported lumber, the higher the drayage cost, which added to the price of lumber by as much as 50 percent. John Hearn of Edgecombe County charged a rate of five cents per mile per hundred board feet for lumber that he hauled with his wagon and team. Five miles east of Goldsboro, William J. Rouse advertised merchantable lumber for ten dollars per thousand feet when purchased at his mill near Hood Swamp, but the price rose to fifteen dollars per thousand feet for orders he delivered to Goldsboro.[18]

To expedite orders, reduce costs, and obtain a larger share of the local market, a number of mills near major towns opened offices and yards in them. The firm of Saurs and Long, which ran a sawmill at Oak Grove in Union County, found that orders increased when they opened an office in nearby Charlotte in the late 1850s. Miller and Porter, who had a sawmill a few miles from Charlotte, opened a permanent yard in that town under the direction of builder Jonas Rudisill.[19] Elsewhere, other mills simply authorized merchants in nearby towns to take contracts for their lumber, and some opened temporary yards there during building season. If a mill had a surplus stock of lumber, the owner sometimes hauled it into town and hawked his merchandise on the streets. This process of hauling lumber in from outlying mills survived in many areas until the last quarter of the nineteenth century. A resident of the mountain town of Lenoir recalled that as late as the 1870s plank wagons from water-powered mills located as far as eight to ten miles away "could be seen on our streets, the owners begging for purchasers of lumber."[20]

Brickmaking

Antebellum improvements in transportation systems had a less direct influence on brick production. In contrast to sawmills' dependence upon raw materials from outlying forests, brickmaking could take place almost anywhere since clay and sand, the primary ingredients, could be found in sufficient quantities in every section of the state. The manufacture of brick also required no permanent facilities but could be conducted in temporary and easily erected structures. The bulk and weight of bricks also made it more economical to make them near the building site than to transport them any long distances through the end of the century. Thus bricks were made where they were intended to be used, whether in towns, in small villages, or on isolated farmsteads.

Until the introduction of brickmaking machinery in the mid-nineteenth century, all bricks were made by hand in a process that had changed little for many centuries. Early brickmakers in North Carolina

Wood market in Asheville, late nineteenth century. (Photo, North Carolina Division of Archives and History.)

employed methods that would have been familiar to their English and European predecessors.[21] First, a brickmaker selected a place to dig clay near the building site. After the clay had been "won" from the pit, it was crushed to break up large chunks and to remove any stones. The brickmaker either employed a horse to tread the clay, or he allowed the clay to stand during the winter months so that the frost broke it up and made it more workable. After the workman screened the clay by hand for impurities, he added sand and water to temper it into a homogeneous malleable mass. Since clays varied dramatically in composition, texture, and color from one area to another, each brickmaker had to judge the amount of sand that was needed for the proper composition. In the eastern part of the state, the proportion of sand in the soil was much greater than farther west. The brickmaker tempered the clay by working a long-handled tool known as a cuckle through the clay until it no longer stuck to the blade. This process was essential, for if the clay was not broken up into a fine consistency, the finished bricks would crack apart when they were used.

The next step consisted of placing the wet clay into individual wooden or iron molds that had been sanded or oiled to prevent sticking.

Brickmaking in rural Virginia, early twentieth century. (Chappell Collection, photo, Colonial Williamsburg Foundation.)

This job required considerable skill, for the molder was also responsible for evaluating the quality of the prepared clay. As laborers brought the clay to the molder, he forced it into the mold and then scraped off the surplus from the top. A skilled molder could produce a few thousand bricks in a day. Laborers, usually small boys known as off-bearers, laid the molded bricks out in the sun on sanded beds or carried them to a storage shed called a hack where they were left to dry.

After the bricks had been taken out of the molds and dried for a few weeks, they were ready to be burned in a temporary kiln known as a clamp. Clamps could easily accommodate up to thirty thousand bricks. The brickmaker stacked the green bricks together and enclosed them by covering the outer rows with a clay daub. He set a wood or coal fire under the kiln to force the remaining water from the unbaked bricks. After a few days, he sealed the kiln tightly and raised the temperature to about 1,800° F, which he maintained for several days. He then allowed the bricks to cool a few days before he opened the kiln and sorted the bricks. Because of the difficulty of maintaining an even temperature throughout the kiln, bricks of varying quality were produced. There were many irregularly shaped bricks caused by underfiring or overfiring. In some parts of the South, brickmakers who burned bricks in temporary kilns considered the operation successful if they lost only a quarter of the total.[22]

In many rural areas the traditional process of brickmaking persisted well into the twentieth century. An account of the process in coastal Chowan County just prior to World War I illustrates the continuation of such labor-intensive methods:

> First, the prospective brick-maker picked out the least fertile spot on his place that had good accessible clay; then, with a hammer, hand-saw, axe, some nails, and a few boards and poles obtained from the near-by woods, he knocked together, within a few hours, a crude mill for grinding and mixing his material, and a shelter of similar rough character for protecting his dry bricks from the rain; next, he dug a hole in the ground near-by for water, and, finally, he made five or six molds, which completed his special equipment. It took one horse to pull the mill, and from four to six men to tend it. Thus manned, the output was from four to six thousand bricks a day, or about a thousand per man. This has reference to the actual making of the bricks and putting them on the yard; the work of hacking them and putting them under the shelter being extra. Quite often, however, one was not troubled with this latter work, for showers frequently came up and melted them down before they were dry enough to hack. On an average, one year with another, something like a third of the bricks put on the yards were lost in this way. The customary size kiln was around thirty thousand. Some seasons, when the weather was especially unfavorable, it was neces-

sary to put out twice this number in order to have the usual size kiln.

Most of the bricks were made in July and August after crops were laid by. Then in the late fall, after crops were housed, twenty-five or thirty of the neighbors would be asked to meet at the brickyard on a certain Monday morning and help "set" [kiln] them, which was an all-day job. If one had "good luck," in other words, if his bricks had been properly kilned and he had good wood and knew what he was doing, he finished burning by the following Friday or Saturday night.[23]

New Technologies

In the first half of the nineteenth century, efforts began in North Carolina to improve the efficiency and production capacity of the woodworking and brickmaking trades. Favored by abundant natural resources but hampered by chronic shortages of skilled labor, enterprising builders were quick to appreciate the potential benefits of mechanization. Technological innovations proceeded slowly along two intertwined lines of development. First, mechanics sought to replace hand labor with new machines and to improve existing machinery such as sawmills. Secondly, they attached steam engines to traditional machinery to provide a regular and, more importantly, a mobile source of power. Because these technical changes were initiated by men with practical experience in the operation of the machines rather than by engineers with scientific knowledge, innovations emerged in response to immediate problems of production. Technical progress in woodworking and brickmaking machines, as in other industries during this period, thus developed by "slow modifications of details as opposed to spectacular leaps to a new technique decisively superior from the start to its predecessors."[24]

New Saws

Invented in the late eighteenth century, but only put into use in the first quarter of the nineteenth century, the gang and circular saws displayed notable improvements over the sash or upright saw, but not so many as to immediately supersede it. In their earliest forms both new saw types had limitations that retarded their widespread adoption. Similar in principle to the sash saw, the gang saw was composed of several tensioned saw blades set closely side by side. This arrangement allowed the log to be cut into many planks in a single operation, which naturally enhanced productive capacity. But, like most of the thick-gauge saws of the period, the gang saws turned a distressing proportion of the log into sawdust. These saws also demanded a substantial amount of power for successful operation, beyond the capacity of most water-powered mills. Thus gang saws were mainly limited to mills with steam engines. One early gang saw with twenty-four blades in a Brunswick County mill in 1820 required a seventy-horsepower steam engine. Capital investment for this operation amounted to $45,000, a sum far beyond the grasp of most regional millers.[25] In North Carolina before 1850 this meant that only in the large commercial mills of Wilmington and other coastal cities could the benefit of the increased efficiency of the saw offset its high operational cost.

An important deficiency in early sash and gang saws was their slow speed. The fibrous quality of wood, unlike a crystalline material such as iron, requires a rapid cutting action; at slow speeds, wood is more likely to be torn than cut by the saw. The intermittent reciprocating movement of the sash and gang saws was inherently slow and inefficient. The desire for a saw that cut at a faster rate with an economy of motion and reduced abrasive wear led to the development of a saw that operated on a different cutting principle. The circular saw, invented in England in the late eighteenth century though not introduced into the United States until 1814, consisted of a disc with teeth on the circumference.[26] The saw's rotary motion gave a continuous cutting action and made it possible to increase operating speeds beyond those possible for reciprocating saws. Although no documentary evidence has been found to indicate that the circular saw was introduced into North Carolina before the 1830s, it may have been in use earlier in a few mills located near the coast. By midcentury, its use had spread inland to the piedmont. In 1852 a Wake County miller praised the effectiveness of his new circular saw: "I have tried it on green timber, and the saw manifests no inclination to heat whatever, and I am confident it will cut double the lumber, with one half the water, of an up and down Mill."[27] Even though millwrights readily acknowledged the superior efficiency and speed of the circular saw, it was not a clear-cut improvement over the old sash saw. Like other thick-gauge blades, it produced a broad kerf which was no less wasteful of wood. A more important limitation was its tendency to expand and wobble when it was accelerated to high velocities. Because the saw had difficulty in cutting true lines and producing a smooth quality of lumber, many millers remained skeptical of its capabilities.[28]

It took more than half a century for mechanics to correct these deficiencies and produce a reliable circular saw. In the early 1870s more than half the mills in North Carolina operated with sash saws; by 1880 the situation had changed dramatically as nearly 90 percent were now equipped with circular saws.[29] During the 1870s rapid strides were made in improving the quality of the circular saw, including small but significant contributions by mechanics in the state. In 1877, C. A. Hege of Salem, proprietor of the Salem Iron Works, patented several technical innovations to the circular saw including a head-block system which prevented the log

Miller and Laughinghouse patent friction feed sawmill, Kinston, ca. 1880. From *Historical and Descriptive Review of the State of North Carolina* 1:106. (North Carolina Collection, University of North Carolina Library, Chapel Hill.)

from sliding back and forth while it was being sawn and allowed the log to be sawn at a uniform speed that made it possible to produce a board of uniform thickness.[30]

Steam Power

The experimentation with, development of, and gradual adjustment to a more efficient saw paralleled efforts to apply steam power to woodworking. By 1800 American mechanics, most notably Oliver Evans of Philadelphia, had perfected high-pressure steam engines that increased boiler pressures and engine speeds and were successfully adapted to power various machines including the sawmill. During the next decade the first steam sawmills appeared in North Carolina in the coastal ports. Entrepreneurial merchant William Shepherd erected a steam-powered mill near the Trent River in New Bern around 1816 and placed its daily operations in the hands of an Italian mechanic, A. A. Marsaretti. A few years later, another skilled mechanic, Frederick Naested, opened the second steam-powered sawmill in that city.[31] Apparently both operators were also instrumental in establishing the first steam mills in Wilmington, the state's chief lumber-exporting city. By the spring of 1819, planter-merchant John F. Burgwin had started the Cape Fear Steam Sawmill Company with Marsaretti as his manager. Burgwin erected the steam sawmill in a warehouse near the city docks so the logs that had been floated down the Cape Fear River could be easily fed into the mill.[32] Steam sawmills soon became one of

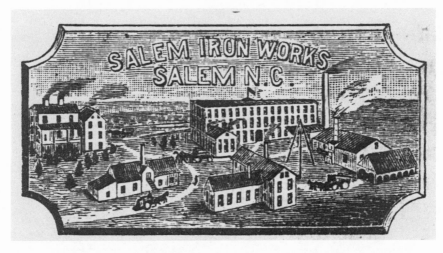

Salem Iron Works (above) and portable steam engine (opposite). After the Civil War, several iron works in North Carolina competed with northern firms in the manufacture of steam machinery. The Salem Iron Works under the direction of C. A. Hege produced portable steam engines, circular sawmills, and brickmaking machines. Salem Iron Works from Robbins, *Descriptive Sketch of Winston-Salem*, 25. (North Carolina Collection, University of North Carolina Library, Chapel Hill.) Improved Phoenix Portable Engine Class B from Raleigh *State Chronicle*, July 19, 1884. (North Carolina Division of Archives and History.)

the most successful industries in Wilmington. By 1840 the city had at least six steam-powered commercial mills, which sawed a combined total of 100,000 feet of lumber each day.[33] Wilmington was ideally suited for steam sawmills. Not only did it lie at the outlet of the Cape Fear's vast timber-lands, but as a port city, it had close ties with northern manufacturing cities. Specially manufactured engines and boilers as well as the trained mechanics to operate them were more readily available in coastal ports than in more isolated parts of the state. Steam-powered sawmills enabled commercial lumbermen to concentrate production and distribution in a single location.

Although there was a strong incentive to use steam power in the port cities, elsewhere the advantages of steam were less marked. Few of the inland commercial mills on the major rivers and practically none of the small regional mills were powered by steam before midcentury. By 1850 there were only twenty-seven steam-powered sawmills—less than 10 percent of the total number of mills in the state—and all but a handful were located near the coast.[34] The adoption of steam power depended less on technological innovations than on its relative economic benefits as compared with other available power sources.

Several factors deterred mill owners from buying steam machinery.

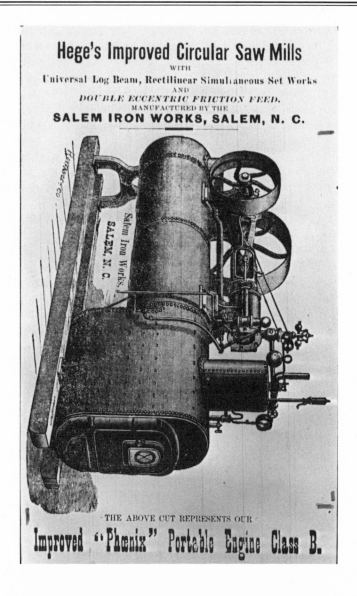

Hege's Improved Circular Saw Mills
WITH
Universal Log Beam, Rectilinear Simultaneous Set Works
AND
DOUBLE ECCENTRIC FRICTION FEED.
MANUFACTURED BY THE
SALEM IRON WORKS, SALEM, N. C.

-THE ABOVE CUT REPRESENTS OUR-

Improved "Phœnix" Portable Engine Class B.

The sheer cost of purchasing and maintaining engines and boilers offset gains in efficiency in all but the largest plants. Even though mass production had steadily lowered the cost of machinery, the price of a steam-powered circular sawmill at midcentury still averaged more than three thousand dollars.[35] The small size of local lumber markets made it risky to tie up much capital or borrow money for equipment to improve productivity, and few proprietors believed that their businesses would grow sufficiently to warrant such a substantial and permanent investment.[36]

During the antebellum period only a few North Carolina machine shops produced steam engines on a regular basis at competitive prices. The state's principal manufacturers of steam engines and sawmills were Silas Burns's Novelty Iron Works in Raleigh and the Snow Camp Machine Shop and Foundry in Alamance County, both of which began production in the late 1840s.[37] Most millers, however, relied overwhelmingly on northern manufacturers for their engines, boilers, and mill equipment and local manufacturers remained small, finding it difficult to overcome the perception that their products were inferior to those of northerners.[38]

The persistent dependence upon out-of-state manufactures made it difficult to obtain machinery and to get replacement parts. Although several northern manufacturers retained agents for their machinery in leading towns such as Wilmington, New Bern, Fayetteville, and Raleigh, many customers preferred to deal directly with the manufacturer by traveling or sending a representative to the factory to negotiate the purchase and even to supervise shipping. When the Cane Creek Manufacturing Company converted to steam power in 1855, the board of directors ignored the neighboring Snow Camp Machine Shop and Foundry and sent a mechanic to the North "to examine the engine shops and ascertain where he can obtain the best article to suit our purpose and on best terms."[39] Four years earlier, Anson County planter William Gaston Smith dispatched business associate S. W. Neal north to purchase a steam-powered circular sawmill. Neal visited shops in Philadelphia and New York before deciding to buy an engine from the Pool and Hunt foundry in Baltimore, basing his choice on a low price combined with his desire to offer his business to southern mechanics.[40]

Delays in paying the manufacturer and in arranging shipping prevented Smith from starting his lumber business for nearly a year. The saga of transporting his sawmill, steam engine, and boiler to rural North Carolina typifies the challenges involved in modernizing local mills. By June 1851 the boiler had arrived safely in Charleston where it was then loaded aboard another vessel for a trip up the Pee Dee River as far as Cheraw, but his other machinery had not arrived in the port. When low water forced boats on the Pee Dee to cease operations in midsummer, the shipping agent advised Smith to find an alternative shipment route for his steam engine and sawmill: "Should your machinery arrive in Charleston you will have to order it to Camden to get it. Should it not have left Baltimore yet, it would be best to order it to Wilmington as I believe the boats in the Cape Fear run all summer." Not until November did Smith receive all his machinery and begin sawing.[41]

Such delays were not unusual. Lacking railroads and easily navigable rivers, most of the state was cut off from convenient access to northern machinery. If the advantages of steam machinery were marginal for most small mill operations, the difficulty of purchasing and transporting machinery and parts further discouraged its use. Finally, the paucity of mechanics competent to install and repair steam machinery gave mill owners yet another reason to hesitate before investing in sophisticated machinery.

New Transportation Systems

The expansion of transportation routes and the increased use of portable steam machinery enabled the lumber industry to develop a new system for processing and marketing its products. Around midcentury, North Carolina invested heavily in the development of plank roads and railroads to spur industrial growth and help farmers get their produce to markets. These routes opened new areas for economic exploitation and expansion. They connected natural resources that were hitherto inaccessible to factories and factories to larger markets. Merchants could ship commodities greater distances at lower costs. By reducing transportation costs, railroads allowed producers to market lumber at a much lower price and to expand their markets into the backcountry. Due to access to wider markets and the promise of greater sales, owners of small mills near railroads found it economically feasible to purchase steam machinery, and railroads made acquisition and transportation of machinery easier than ever before. Invariably, the first mechanized sash and blind shops and planing mills established operations along railroads, plank roads, or rivers where the potential for a broad market made the investment in expensive equipment worthwhile.

The new plank roads and railroads of the 1850s, which inaugurated this expansion of markets, were literally built with the new woodworking machinery. Both transportation systems required machinery to process the vast volume of wood needed for construction and maintenance of roads, tracks, bridges, and buildings. Plank and railroad companies purchased sawmills for use in construction and then sold them to lumber merchants and other businessmen, thereby hastening the spread of modern steam equipment throughout the state.

Plank roads were relatively cheap and quick to build and thus appealed to many communities and investors. This speed in construction arose in part from the introduction of a portable sawmill that could produce a large volume of lumber at the construction site. An 1855 advertisement noted,

> One great point of superiority of this mill over any other now in use
> is its portability—the ease with which it can be moved from place to
> place—taking a few pieces of which the mill is composed to the logs
> instead of hauling thousands of logs, often from long distances, to
> the mill. Beside such a mill can be transferred from hand to hand,
> and is consequently a more salable property. When one has sawed
> all the lumber he wishes, he can sell his mill to go to any other
> location.[42]

Jonathan Worth, a piedmont entrepreneur and future governor, received the contract to build much of the Fayetteville and Western Plank Road in Moore and Randolph counties. Construction of the road consisted of embedding four sills into the ground over which sawn planks were laid, using timber that was cut from the right-of-way. To complete his section of the road, Worth kept four mills provided by the company running day and night. Each mill could produce forty to fifty thousand feet of plank every twenty-four hours. When each section of the road was completed, his workmen dismantled the mill and moved it to a new location.[43]

Although the directors of the Fayetteville and Western Plank Road Company had invested more than they had wanted in sawmill machinery, they acknowledged that "without [the mills] the road, in no reasonable time, could have been built."[44] Furthermore, the company recouped nearly two-thirds of the initial investment in the mills by the common practice of selling them to lumber merchants.[45]

The distinction that had existed between small local mills and coastal export mills diminished as the expansion of transportation routes and the increased use of portable steam machinery enabled the lumber industry to develop a new system for processing and marketing its products. Portable sawmills allowed lumber merchants to transfer their sawing operations to the forests. By shifting the location of sawmills from isolated waterways to railroad sites, millers expanded their market by the length of the line. In 1854 the firm of Ballenger and Cogdell informed the citizens of the growing railway junction of Goldsboro that they were prepared to take orders for lumber from their mill nearly twenty miles west of the town. The firm's steam sawmill was then situated adjacent to the newly completed section of the North Carolina Railroad and the proprietors assured the public that orders could be filled without delay on terms more favorable than those offered by any mill closer to Goldsboro.[46] In 1858 George Kittrell promised to deliver pine or oak lumber anywhere along the Raleigh and Gaston line at competitive rates.[47] Although the potential of the new supply system was evident in the 1850s, national events interrupted its growth. The system did not mature until after the Civil War, at which time the rapid growth of towns coupled with the expansion of the intrastate rail network created an unprecedented demand for lumber.

The Mechanization of Planing and Joinery

During the second quarter of the nineteenth century, the mechanical planing of lumber first appeared in North Carolina as an adjunct to commercial sawmilling in the coastal plain. In the manufacture of wood, planing generally follows the sawing operation. The principal function of a plane is to cut a smooth surface. In the eighteenth century and through much of the nineteenth century as well, this process was performed solely with an adz, jack plane, and other small planes. Builders generally limited planed or "dressed" lumber to interior woodwork such as floorboards, doors, and sheathing, where a smooth finish was desirable.

In 1828 William Woodworth of New York patented a surface-planing machine that smoothed several hundred feet of floorboards in a few hours.[48] The amount of labor saved by such a mechanical device was enormous. The machine could smooth a board of almost any size along its entire width, unlike hand planes that could smooth a width of only a few inches at a time. Two years earlier, Herman Allen of Randolph County had constructed a planing mill that could "perform the labor of about twenty men with hand planes," but apparently had limited success, for it was the Woodworth model that, under the protection of patent, dominated the national market.[49]

The number of power-driven planing machines in circulation in North Carolina at midcentury is difficult to estimate. The 1850 census listed four planing mills in the state, all attached to Wilmington's commercial export sawmills.[50] Alonzo J. Willis of New Bern had one in operation in his shop shortly after midcentury.[51] The cost of a planing mill, like other early steam-powered machinery, limited its use to commercial lumbermen with access to large markets. By the mid-1850s planing mills had been established in the principal towns of the state where there was a growing demand for dressed lumber. Typically, planing mills were added to existing shops and mills. In 1854 S. G. Buie of Fayetteville added planing machinery to his carpentry shop.[52] Thomas Hogg and Robert Haywood erected a planing mill at their Moby Dick sawmill near Raleigh in 1855.[53]

To attract new customers along the route of the North Carolina Railroad, Hogg and Haywood promised to load planed lumber aboard freight cars free of charge. In 1856 they received a large and important contract from the railroad to supply lumber for the construction of repair shops located fifty miles west in Alamance County. The mill planed more than 35,000 feet of flooring for the railroad company's carpentry shop alone. In addition, dressed lumber was shipped from the mill to other points along the line including a large amount dispatched to Goldsboro for the construction of a warehouse.[54]

Although mill-dressed lumber was a desirable material, its high cost in the 1850s probably deterred many buyers. In 1855 the Raleigh Planing Mill sold planed floorboards for $21 to $25 per thousand feet; interior sheathing for $18 to $21; and weatherboards for $16 to $21.[55] The price of the best-quality steam-sawn floorboards was roughly $12 to $15 for the same amount. Lesser-quality water-sawn floorboards sold for about half the price of dressed lumber.[56] Because of the high cost of mechanically planed lumber, in many instances it was still cheaper to have lumber planed by hand.[57]

Paralleling developments in saw and planing mills, mechanization began to transform antebellum joinery shops. To reduce the labor in-

Planing machine, 1834. From Benjamin Butterworth, *The Growth of Industrial Art* (Washington, D.C.: Government Printing Office, 1888), 198. (Duke University Library.)

volved in joinery—the precision handwork of cutting and fitting pieces of wood into paneling, doors, windows, etc.—mechanics, including joiners themselves, invented machines that would perform with power what had formerly been done by hand. This led to the development of specialized woodworking machines for planing, turning, mortising, tenoning, rabbeting, and jointing, which transformed carpenters' and joiners' shops into sash and blind factories wherever railroad expansion created sufficient markets.

Unlike rough and dressed lumber, the products of North Carolina's first antebellum sash and blind factories could not be exported to northern markets at competitive prices. Indeed with the growing market of industrial cities as a base, northern sash and blind manufacturers could transform lumber shipped from the South into finished building parts more cheaply than small southern factories. Whatever edge North Carolinians might have enjoyed because of their proximity to the forests of the Cape Fear Valley was negated by the cost of shipping. Without an export market, sash and blind factories in the state depended almost entirely on local markets, and the greatest demand for sash and blind products in the years before the Civil War came from the coastal cities and the growing railroad towns of the piedmont.

The origins of the first sash and blind factories can be traced to joiners' shops and other woodworking establishments. The practice of manufacturing a stock of building materials for sale to the public did not begin with sash and blind factories but had developed earlier in eighteenth- and nineteenth-century carpentry shops. In 1827, for example, carpenter Thomas Bragg of Warrenton advertised that he had window sash, venetian blinds, and panel doors, along with "all other kinds of shop work," on hand for his own use and for sale to clients, smaller firms, and individual craftsmen.[58]

The transformation of the joiner's shop into a sash and blind factory in most instances was a gradual process. The owner's decision to convert a shop's operation into mechanized mass production depended almost entirely on assessing the long-term benefits that might accrue with a more efficient factory system. In an early study of the use of woodworking machinery, John Richards observed in 1872 that:

> The machines are for the most part sold to men of limited means, who have not only to consider the worth of the money after investment, but have first the greater difficulty of commanding a sum sufficient to purchase the machines. To get started is the object, and the few hundred dollars that can be collected must procure a complete set of machines for joiners' work, or a planing mill. After being started the course is clear. In a few years the machines have paid for themselves; the business has grown to dimensions that warrant a larger and more permanent investment; the old machines are thrown out to be replaced with improvements.[59]

Machines for mortising, tenoning, and boring were among the first to be bought by sash and blind manufacturers since they relieved much of the labor in the production of window sash, blinds, and doors. Each of these items was secured together by mortise-and-tenon joints which, by hand, demanded long, concentrated work with chisels, but with machines, took only a matter of minutes. Panel-raising and molding machines reduced the drudgery of constant repetition of hand planes in the manufacture of doors, paneling, blinds, and linear molding. They also sped production of curvilinear moldings, an especially tedious hand process. As shops expanded, other machines were purchased to perform a variety of operations. Improved scroll saws to make brackets and mantels, along with all-purpose lathes for turning columns and balusters, became essential machines for most sash and blind factories. For shaping and finishing materials, small planing machines and circular saws soon followed in most well-stocked establishments.

Mortising machine, 1845. From Benjamin Butterworth, *The Growth of Industrial Art* (Washington, D.C.: Government Printing Office, 1888), 197. (Duke University Library.)

The first documented sash and blind factories appeared in New Bern and Wilmington, the port towns with the most extensive coastal and overseas trade with northern industrial cities and Caribbean islands. Along their riverside wharves, ships unloaded northern manufactured goods upon which many people of the state depended. Early in 1848 New Bern carpenter Alonzo J. Willis disembarked from one of these ships, and among his cargo were a few steam woodworking machines that he had purchased in a northern shop. Equipped with nearly a dozen separate

George Bishop's Steam Variety Works, New Bern, 1857. From New Bern *Union*, June 28, 1857. (North Carolina Division of Archives and History.)

machines for turning, boring, tenoning, and mortising, he set up his factory on Union Point at the foot of East Front Street and soon began manufacturing sash, blinds, and doors "in the best style, at short notice, and at New York prices."[60] Two years later, New Bern cabinetmaker George Bishop also started to manufacture building materials with the steam machinery that he used in his furniture shop on Broad Street. Bishop advertised a wide selection of window sash, blinds, and panel doors "as cheap as can be bought in the State."[61]

Willis and Bishop were probably the first mass-producers of steam-manufactured building materials in North Carolina. Both men started their careers learning the traditional methods of joinery but ended them as proponents of industrialized manufacturing. As craftsmen seeking to expand the scope and volume of their shops, Willis and Bishop recognized that the traditional labor-intensive methods were insufficient to meet the demands of any market that reached beyond the local one. Since New Bern was a port city, Willis and Bishop could ship their products to other coastal towns in the area, and such towns as Kinston, Goldsboro, and Smithfield could be reached by the Neuse River. In the mid-1850s, the extension of the North Carolina Railroad from Goldsboro to New Bern expanded the market area dramatically. An added incentive to mechanization, no doubt, was that new or replacement machinery could be acquired from northern shops without too great a delay. By the early 1850s, both

Willis and Bishop had accumulated enough capital to expand their shops without undue financial difficulties.[62] Although the cost of hiring or purchasing slave artisans might have been less than the price of many of the woodworking machines, both men apparently believed that they would benefit most in a growing market by installing machinery. Machines could do more work of a standard quality in much less time than could be done by hand.

Moreover, the two craftsmen were firmly committed to the idea of opening new markets for their products. Willis canvassed the surrounding countryside seeking patronage, actively soliciting the business of carpenters and builders. As early as 1849, agents for his products had been established upriver in Goldsboro and Smithfield.[63] The installation of new machinery allowed Willis to boast to customers in 1853 that he was ready to do "fourfold the work I have formerly done." With the motto "Sell cheap and a Heap of It," his Union Point Factory manufactured hundreds of rolling pivot blinds, plain and fancy window sash, panel doors, and shutters, as well as a stock of furniture and coffins.[64] In 1850, for example, Willis produced more than 5,500 lights of window sash and 617 feet of window blinds.[65]

Sash and blind factories spread throughout other parts of North Carolina during the 1850s. Early in 1854, S. T. Ivey established the Wilmington Sash and Blind Factory next to the depot of the Wilmington and Weldon Railroad, specializing in turning. He shipped columns, moldings, banisters, and handrails to villages all along the railroad line. Seybert and Doyle soon started a rival factory in Wilmington.[66] In the piedmont, contractor Jonas Rudisill of Charlotte installed sash and blind machinery in his planing mill about 1857.[67] At the same time Murdoch and Cairns started the manufacture of sash and blind woodwork at their mill on West Hill in Salisbury and soon won an award for one of their products at the North Carolina Agricultural Fair.[68] In the capital Briggs and Dodd, proprietors of a newly established planing mill, installed lathes, mortisers, and other sash machinery. By 1860 sash and blind factories had been started in Gates County, Asheville, Fayetteville, Goldsboro, Wilson, and Washington, North Carolina, though many remained in business for a only a few years while others were almost indistinguishable from carpentry shops.[69]

The 1860 census listed only five sash and blind factories in North Carolina that produced as much as $500 worth of materials. With a capital investment of $14,000, George Bishop's New Bern factory was the largest. His eleven employees produced over $8,000 worth of sash, blinds, doors, and moldings. A Wayne County company manufactured 3,000 feet of blinds, 300 doors, and 5,000 lights of sash that were valued at $2,900. The total product value of North Carolina's sash and blind manufacturers amounted to $56,900 in 1860.[70] Compared to other parts of the country, North Carolina and her sister southern states lagged far behind in the manufacture of building materials. Virginia, scarcely better off than her southern neighbor, had nine factories with products valued at $84,700. In contrast, the growing midwestern state of Ohio had 91 factories manufacturing nearly a million dollars worth of goods. Pennsylvania had 108 factories, and New York's 212 factories turned out over $1,500,000 worth of sash and blind materials.[71] By the time of the Civil War, sash and blind factories had revolutionized and dominated the manufacture of building materials in the North, whereas in North Carolina they only heralded the possibilities of the future.

Maturation of the Industrialized Building Process

By the 1880s, the seeds of an earlier generation of experimentation in the manufacture and distribution of building materials had matured into an industrialized building process. An 1885 pamphlet described a lumbering operation on New Bern's waterfront that was dominated by a massive steam sawmill with the "capacity equal to almost any mill on the continent." Using the latest fully mechanized systems, the mill could produce over ten million feet of pine, cypress, juniper, and oak lumber a year. "Lifted out of the sea by a powerful endless chain arrangement," logs gathered from upriver forests were "thrown on a carriage and as they are sawn up the planks are carried on revolving cylinders to where they are cut in lengths. Hardly anything is done by hand, the various vehicles of transportation by which logs are cut up and conveyed from the dock to their place on the lumber pile, being merely guided by practical hands." Nearby were wharves for loading oceangoing vessels and railroad freight cars to carry lumber overland to markets in Baltimore, Philadelphia, and New York.[72] This spectacle epitomized the coming of a new day in the production of building materials.

The Lumber Market

It was, predictably, the completion of a regional railway system that linked North Carolina to national markets, combined with construction of local lines, that provided the greatest impetus to industrial development, urban expansion, and the resultant building boom in the post–Civil War period. New sources of minerals and timber became easily accessible, as speculators and developers purchased vast tracts of virgin forests in the piedmont and mountainous west and selected promising quarry sites in the last decades of the century. Extractive and processing industries moved into these areas.

    The booming towns of the piedmont depended increasingly on lumber manufactured outside their immediate vicinity. The construction of the Raleigh and Augusta Air Line in the 1870s opened the vast pine forests of the central piedmont to large-scale timber operations. Lumber mer-

Sawmill at New Bern, ca. 1900. (Photo, North Carolina Collection, University of North Carolina Library, Chapel Hill.)

chants purchased timberland along the tracks, erected sawmills at nearly every depot, and loaded lumber aboard flatbed freight cars for shipment to finishing mills in Raleigh and Cary. In 1879 the Raleigh building firm of Ellington and Royster alone purchased nearly a million and a half feet of yellow pine lumber from Moore County.[73] By the early 1880s the villages of Hoffman, Aberdeen, Manly, Vass, and Cameron had grown into important centers for the supply of building lumber. Long trainloads of lumber departed each day from these North Carolina towns and villages for manufacturers as far away as South Carolina and Virginia.[74] In 1883 the Raleigh *State Chronicle* observed that with the construction of the Raleigh and Augusta Air Line, "It has not been many years since Moore County was considered one of the remote region's of the state. So long as it was without a railroad, it was difficult of access . . . its great natural products were not within reach of the markets. . . . Now, however, Moore County exports more dollars worth of natural products, perhaps than any other county in the state. . . . Timbered land adjacent the railroad cannot now be bought at all, and that at a reasonable distance brings a good price."[75]

The town of Cary, located where the North Carolina Railroad and the Raleigh and Augusta Air Line met eight miles west of Raleigh, was one of many born of a sawmill and a railroad. A. F. Page erected a steam sawmill there in the 1850s, and after the war, his business and that of his chief competitor William Jones flourished as they cut timber from nearby Moore County forests and shipped it by rail in all four directions.[76] In the late 1870s Page moved part of his operations to Aberdeen in the heart of the pine forests, where a visitor reported, "The company owns almost 14,000 acres of heavily timbered land a powerful logging locomotive brings great loads of saw-logs over a graded railway, reaching miles into the forests." At the sawmills, "The large circular saws almost rush through these giants of the pine forest." By the 1880s Page was credited with supplying lumber "to build more houses than any other firm in Central North Carolina."[77]

Lumber timbered in Moore, processed in Wake, and shipped to Dur-

Loading lumber at a sawmill in Wilmington, ca. 1902. (Photo, North Carolina Collection, University of North Carolina Library, Chapel Hill.)

ham, Vance, or Richmond counties, was often sold at cheaper rates and delivered much faster than lumber cut at small local mills. Although this new system of supply did not totally supersede the function of local mills, by the 1880s it dominated the growing lumber market.

Sash and Blind Factories

The same years saw unprecedented expansion of sash and blind factories. The *Manufacturers' Record*, the optimistic clarion of industrial progress in the New South, proudly announced each week the establishment of sash and blind factories across North Carolina and the South during the 1880s. One Raleigh newspaper recalled in 1884 that "a few years ago it was hard to find a sash and blind factory in North Carolina. Now no town and hard by a thriving village considers itself equipped without one or more. As a consequence, work of this kind has become much cheaper and building can be done at far less cost."[78] A town with as few as two thousand inhabitants was considered large enough to support a woodworking factory.[79] Following the path of the railroad, sash and blind manufactories spread to every region of the state, from the pine barrens in the east to the mountain valleys in the west. Despite these advances, the Raleigh paper noted that manufacturers still faced unsteady markets and suggested that

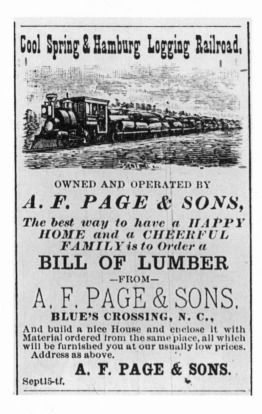

Advertisement for A. F. Page and Sons, from Raleigh *State Chronicle*, July 19, 1884. In the 1880s the Cool Spring and Hamburg Logging Railroad allowed A. F. Page and Sons to open up the forests of Moore County for timbering. (North Carolina Division of Archives and History.)

they would be overcome with the growing immigration to urban areas. With great satisfaction, it observed that "the products of our local manufactories have already about run the Yankee out of the state market in this department, and as our local demand becomes more steady this victory will be more complete."[80]

As the demand for their products increased with the rapid growth of towns in the 1880s, sash and blind factories readily replaced their old machines with improved and more specialized ones, nearly all of which were still imported from northern manufacturers. Like their predecessors a generation before, factory representatives visited the principal northern shops to inspect the latest equipment before buying. In 1882, for example, the mechanic and business manager of Ellington and Royster of Raleigh traveled to Baltimore, Philadelphia, and New York in order to find "the most improved and fast working machines in the market."[81]

The manufacture of machinery modernized rapidly. In the 1860s woodworking machines were made mostly of wood frames and usually manufactured to order, but by the 1890s they were mass-produced of iron

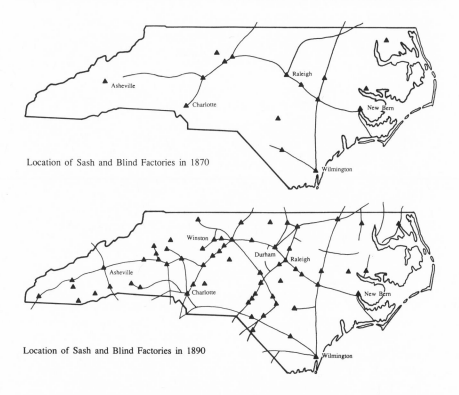

Location of Sash and Blind Factories in 1870

Location of Sash and Blind Factories in 1890

Locations of sash and blind factories in North Carolina in 1870 and 1890. The expansion of the state railway system spurred the opening of sash and blind factories. In 1870 there were less than twenty fully mechanized sash and blind factories in operation. Twenty years later, the number had increased to nearly eighty and had spread to every region of the state. (Map prepared by author, 1983.)

and steel.[82] Machines had improved in speed and precision, and several companies began to specialize in certain types of machines. H. A. Lee of Worcester, Massachusetts, concentrated on molding machines, while Goodell and Waters of Philadelphia produced a variety of general woodworking machines but made flooring machines one of their principal items.[83] Dozens of their "Keystone Flooring Machines" were installed in North Carolina factories during the 1880s, while a number of these fast-acting planing machines were employed by companies such as Spaugh, Miller, and Joyce of Winston and White Brothers of Mebane.[84] The North Carolina Car Company of Raleigh purchased a Keystone flooring machine, the speed and capacity of which amazed contemporary observers. After viewing this machine in action, a local reporter wrote: "One hun-

Located at the junction of the North Carolina Railroad and the Wilmington and Weldon Railroad, the proprietors of the Goldsboro Planing Mill and Sash and Blind Factory could market their products over a broad region served by these important rail lines. From *Historical and Descriptive Review of the State of North Carolina* 1:145. (North Carolina Collection, University of North Carolina Library, Chapel Hill.)

dred years ago, houses in North Carolina were 'planed' with a broadaze; fifty years ago the slow jack-plane did the work; but now you can see the steam plane smoothing-off an hundred feet of flooring in as many seconds."[85] In the course of a day the machine could plane and match between five and six carloads of lumber—the equivalent of 25,000 to 30,000 board feet.[86]

By the 1880s most of the larger sash and blind factories in the state had a variety of specialized machines in operation. There were blind-slot tenoners, band saws, sash tenoners, door mortisers, blind-stile boring machines, single surfacers, panel raisers, planers and matchers, dovetailers, and double spindle shapers to name but a few.

Paralleling the invention of these specialized machines was a movement to develop a machine that performed multiple functions. "Universal woodworkers" were particularly welcome in smaller shops which could neither afford nor house two dozen machines and their operatives. By changing the cutting heads and rearranging the fence and tables, some of these machines could be used to perform twenty-four different operations. They could split shingles, plane moldings, flute banisters, tongue and groove flooring, and rabbet blinds as effectively as many of the more specialized machines.[87] The appearance of these relatively inexpensive

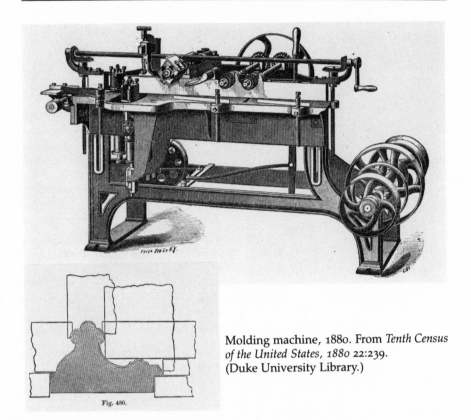

Molding machine, 1880. From *Tenth Census of the United States, 1880* 22:239. (Duke University Library.)

machines in carpentry shops in the 1880s contributed to the decline of traditional joinery in small communities and rural areas where the products of sash and blind factories had not previously appeared.

A number of manufacturing firms also designed and erected buildings. These dual functions, practiced in the 1850s by Jonas Rudisill of Charlotte and Briggs and Dodd of Raleigh, continued through the late nineteenth and early twentieth centuries in the larger firms. In the 1870s both F. W. Ahrens and Joseph Asbury operated combined factory operations with contracting firms in Charlotte. They each employed dozens of men in the shop manufacturing materials and in the field constructing buildings.[88] In the late 1870s Raleigh boasted five sash and blind manufacturers, each of which also erected buildings by contract.[89] Ellington, Royster, and Company, for example, had two dozen laborers in their factory and employed another twenty men in the field. In 1883 the firm contracted to erect thirty buildings in the capital and furnished the materials for another twenty-one. They also shipped sash and blinds to the neighboring tobacco towns of Oxford, Henderson, and Durham.[90] (The

Vance and Shaffner woodworking machinery, Salem, late nineteenth century.
(Photo, courtesy of Old Salem Restoration, Winston-Salem.)

periodic fires which devastated Durham provided ample opportunities for
Raleigh firms to supply materials or undertake contracts to rebuild the Bull
City.)[91]

Durham's tobacco rival, Winston, supported two important sash and
blind manufacturers, Miller Brothers and Fogle Brothers; in addition to
building most of Winston and Salem in the postwar decades, Fogle Brothers specialized in the construction of tobacco boxes for shipping.[92] Elsewhere, sash and blind factories concentrated on particular types of work.
In Hickory, where nearby hardwood forests supported manufacture of
furniture and wagons, the Hickory Manufacturing Company, established
in 1884, produced stairs, mantels, and paneling. By 1889 the company
employed forty laborers in its factory and concentrated on church furniture.[93] High Point and Greensboro also became important centers for the
manufacture of hardwood items, cutting timber from forests in the surrounding counties of Guilford, Randolph, and Chatham.[94] The Snow
Lumber Company of High Point, which employed thirty-five men in its
sash and blind factory and could produce 100 doors, 100 pairs of sash, and
50 pairs of blinds per day, specialized in contract work for piedmont
railroad depots and cotton factories.[95]

Universal Woodworker, 1880. From *Tenth Census of the United States, 1880* 22:242. (Duke University Library.)

Manufacture of "Knock-down" Buildings

Some woodworking firms manufactured entire buildings. Materials for a building were manufactured and fitted together according to plans and specifications in the shop, then disassembled, packed aboard freight cars, and shipped by rail to the site where the building was re-erected. Commonly referred to as "knock-down" buildings, these structures ranged from small temporary shelters for railroad construction crews to sizable warehouses. Prefabrication was not unique to postbellum sash and blind manufacturers. A certain amount of prefabrication had been employed by builders during the colonial period. Many of the heavy timber frames which supported colonial buildings were fabricated and initially pieced together away from the actual building site.[96] In the late eighteenth century, North Carolina craftsmen constructed house frames for shipment to Boston, Charleston, and the Caribbean islands.[97] Before the Civil War, the Raleigh mills of Hogg and Haywood built temporary dwellings for crews at work at the North Carolina Railroad Company Shops. The framing members were cut to size, assembled, and then disassembled and loaded onto railroad cars for their fifty-mile journey westward to the building site.[98]

Postwar completion of railway lines across the state, coupled with improved woodworking machinery, made prefabrication of buildings a big, lucrative business. Located at an important rail junction, the wood-

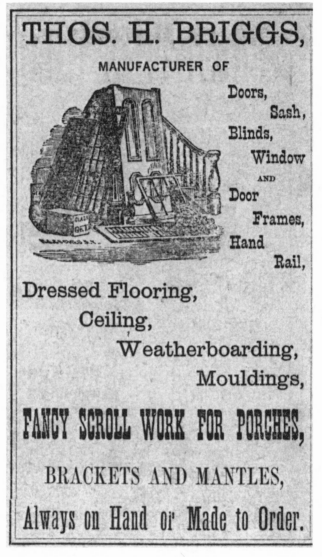

Advertisement for Thomas H. Briggs sash and blind work, Raleigh, late 1870s. (Manuscript Department, Duke University Library.)

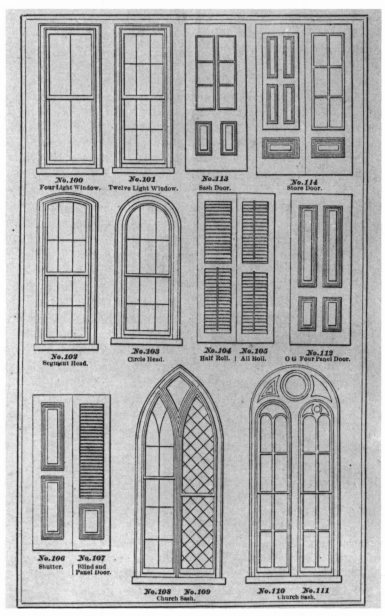

Sample of windows, doors, and blinds advertised for sale by the Toale Manufacturing Company, Charleston, South Carolina, 1877. (Manuscript Department, Duke University Library.)

working shops of Raleigh were the principal suppliers of knock-down buildings in the state in the 1870s and 1880s. By 1872 Betts, Vaughan, and Allen had a shop of forty men who made the frames, doors, windows, and flooring and assembled the buildings. During that year the company filled orders for "ready made" houses destined for Chatham, Granville, Franklin, Warren, Halifax, Edgecombe, and Bertie counties. The manufacturers boasted that "with the advantages of their machinery, [run by] steam power . . . they can in many cases sell buildings to farmers and others at less expense to them than they could be sawed and built by hand work on the farm."[99]

In the 1880s, Raleigh's North Carolina Car Company had so perfected the fabrication of knock-down buildings that it was supplying customers throughout the state and across the country. Established in 1882 to build railroad cars, the company soon branched out to manufacture sash and blinds as well as contract for buildings.[100] "House building," observed a visitor to the shops in 1885, "is and has been one of the specialties of the company, and this specialty consists in making and framing a building of any dimensions (the larger the better) and placing it aboard cars or wagons, ready for any intelligent carpenter to set it up."[101] Between 1882 and 1889 the company prefabricated a gymnasium for the University of North Carolina, a hunting lodge for a Pennsylvania resort, buildings for the State Fair, and several vacation homes for Martha's Vineyard and other summer resorts.[102] Under the supervision of English immigrant William S. Ashley, the firm actively solicited business from the industrial states of the northeast.[103] With the prefabrication of buildings and railroad cars, the company was in the vanguard of late-nineteenth-century industrialized construction, a major achievement for a southern manufacturer. "This building of ready-made houses," noted a contemporary, "has been known as the 'Chicago idea,' just now it is a North Carolina idea, and we can add that the North Carolina Car Company can and will build a frame house according to any plan—will build it in Raleigh and ship it to any point in the State, and do it for from ten to twenty percent less than local builders will undertake the same job."[104]

The spread of industrialized building methods, exemplified by the practice of the North Carolina Car Company, ensured the decline of traditional ways of making building materials. Doors, window frames, moldings, even entire houses could be conveniently purchased ready-made so that, as one agricultural journal advised farmers in 1887, it was "not profitable to make them at the bench."[105] The enticing cheapness of mill-produced building materials led most farmers and builders to abandon the reliance on old labor-intensive practices, and by the end of the century factory-made building products had found markets in the most remote areas of the state.

North Carolina Car Company, Raleigh, 1890. From William Ashley, *The City of Raleigh* (Raleigh: Edwards and Broughton, 1894), 112. (North Carolina Collection, University of North Carolina Library, Chapel Hill.)

Automation of the Brickyard

Like woodworking machinery, brickmaking machines, which came into increasing use in North Carolina in the years before the Civil War, were intended to maximize efficiency by replacing skilled labor with cheaper semiskilled or unskilled labor and to speed up the entire brickmaking operation. Technological innovations were introduced, tested, and compared with older ways of manufacturing bricks. Only when new methods proved to be useful, laborsaving, and economical were they then adopted. The mechanization of the brickyards proceeded, like many other industries, in a gradual manner.

Brickmaking machinery that replaced hand labor at each step of the process and the construction of better kilns at permanent brickyards enabled brickmakers to standardize the quality of their product to a degree previously unobtainable. Hundreds of patents for brickmaking machines had been awarded in the late eighteenth and early nineteenth centuries as tempering and molding became the first operations to be mechanized. Brickmakers began to use a cylindrical mixing chamber known as a pug mill to produce a stiffer, more homogeneous clay. Workers fed clay, sand, and water into a hopper that emptied into the cylindrical chamber in which blades radiating from a revolving control shaft at first powered by horses and later by the steam engine thoroughly pulverized and kneaded the mixture. The tempered clay was then extruded from the bottom of the chamber. Later machines combined the operation of the pug mill with the molding process. The clay was prepared and forced into a series of multiple molds that were then removed by off-bearers who took the bricks to the hacks to dry. Because these machines required less water for tempering and molding than did traditional methods, the quality of the bricks was superior because they were stronger and less porous. Also because the bricks contained less water, they had sharper corners and edges since there was less evaporation and consequently less shrinkage and unburned bricks needed less time for drying. Thus the machine expedited the entire process.

A few brickmaking machines were imported to North Carolina in the first quarter of the nineteenth century and set up in the coastal towns of the east.[106] Certainly by midcentury, brick machines, while not yet common, were incorporated into the operations of some brickmakers who had established yards near the state's more important towns. In the early 1850s, Francis H. Smith, a Baltimore brickmaker, had patented several machines which were tailored to a variety of specific needs. Widely promoted through pamphlets and newspaper advertisements, these machines proved to be popular in much of North Carolina in the half dozen years before the Civil War. For the "country gentleman intending to build," Smith manufactured "The Little Brickmaker," a hand-powered machine priced at seventy dollars that tempered and molded as many as 420 bricks per hour. With it, Smith promised that a planter could "make brick with the labor of his farm hands, and find a brick house cheaper than one of frame."

He also advertised larger machines with multiple molds that were powered either by horse or steam. Intended for the professional brickmaker, the largest of these machines had the capacity to produce as many as 25,000 bricks in ten hours. S. T. Brown of Washington, North Carolina, purchased one of Smith's four-mold machines in 1853 and soon found that it enabled him to make "more bricks by many thousand than I did last year in proportion to the hands employed. The machine worked admirably; sooner than return to the old mode, I would abandon the business." J. C. Washington of Kinston estimated that his horse-powered machine could make as many as 10,000 bricks in a day. So pleased was he with the brickmaker that he decided to purchase a steam-powered one to increase

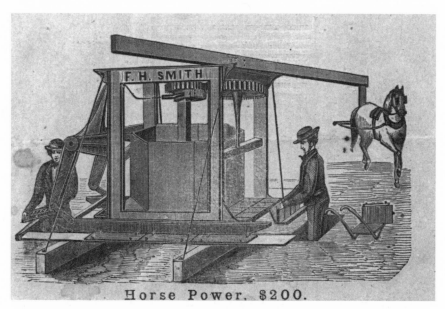

Horse Power, $200.

F. H. Smith's brickmaking machine, 1857. From Francis H. Smith, *New Brick Machine*. (Manuscript Department, Duke University Library.)

his productivity. In Wilmington, brickmaker D. E. Smith recommended brickmaking machinery for all large yards. He believed that "if I had 200,000 bricks to make, I would purchase a machine rather than make them by hand." H. J. B. Clark of New Bern manufactured as many as 22,000 bricks per day with his five-mold machine and thought that the bricks, when well burned, were "harder than New York hand-made bricks."[107] Although the number of Smith's machines in use in North Carolina remains unknown, there must have been a number of them in use among brickmakers in the larger towns; by the mid-1850s, Smith had a sales agent in New Bern who circulated advertisements for the machinery to Raleigh, Kinston, and New Bern newspapers.[108]

After the Civil War several North Carolina mechanics patented improved mechanisms for tempering and molding bricks. In 1875 George Hinshaw of Winston built a machine which produced one hundred bricks per minute. Although little is known about it, one contemporary claimed that "bricks are turned out ready for the kiln like nails out of the nail mill."[109] If the assertion was true, then Hinshaw had invented a machine which eliminated the necessity of drying the brick before firing. Less revolutionary but very efficient was the brick machine invented by Allen and Duffy of Greensboro and patented by C. A. Hege of the Salem Iron Works in 1878. Powered by a horse, the machine could grind the clay and make brick at the same time, a process not possible with the earlier Smith machines. Clay was taken directly from a bank or pit, tempered and ground in the mill, molded, pressed, re-pressed, and delivered to the kiln on a conveyor belt. Hege boasted that the machine produced eight to ten thousand "well pressed brick with perfect corners and edges" at a substantially lower cost than brick could be manufactured by hand. With the machine, he estimated that it cost "from 35 to 40¢ a thousand to prepare brick for the kiln, whereas made by hand they cost $1.25 or even more."[110] In Raleigh, mechanic William Cram invented the steam-powered "Traction Brick Machine" that reduced the time it took to temper a large pit of clay from one day to a few hours. George Cook, a prominent Raleigh brickmaker who had opened his first yard in 1855, installed one of Cram's machines and reported that the clay for twenty thousand bricks could be properly tempered in little more than two hours.[111]

In Charlotte, Daniel Asbury patented improvements on machinery to regulate the drying and burning operations. In 1884 he tested new kiln burning methods that promised to reduce the amount of firewood needed and produce even temperatures throughout the kiln.[112] The problems of accelerating the drying process and improving burning methods had attracted attention as early as the third quarter of the nineteenth century. In the 1850s Cyrus Chambers of Philadelphia experimented with a stiff clay process that allowed the clay to be tempered and molded with a low moisture content, thus avoiding the necessity of a long drying period. By the beginning of the Civil War, Chambers had invented a machine that extruded the stiff clay in a continuous bar. The bar was automatically cut into individual bricks by a knife, and the bricks were carried away on a conveyor belt.[113] A drying tunnel that forced hot air over the newly formed bricks and a tunnel kiln which baked the bricks with uniform consistency were later incorporated into this process making it the prototype for the modern continuous kiln.

Machinery allowed brickmakers greater control over the quality of their product. With machinery, fewer bricks were lost in tempering, molding, drying, and burning. Brickmakers were also at last capable of manufacturing bricks with sharp edges, smooth surfaces, and homogeneous color. A growing taste for bricks of uniform appearance in the second half of the nineteenth century led brickmakers to manufacture an extremely dense type known as a pressed or face brick. Although molded by machines like many common bricks, pressed bricks generally went through another process by which they were compressed again with considerable force to ensure regularity. Beginning in the 1850s and continuing through the early twentieth century, pressed brick became the fashionable material for the facades of commercial buildings in every town across the state.

Although common brick was seldom transported over great dis-

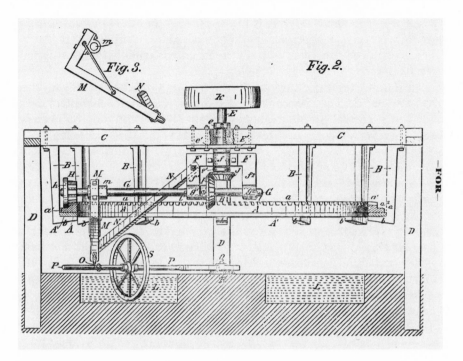

Cram's Patent Driving Machine for Clay Tempering Wheels, 1884. From *Historical and Descriptive Review of the State of North Carolina* 1:77. (North Carolina Collection, University of North Carolina Library, Chapel Hill.)

tances, pressed brick was imported into North Carolina from northern brickyards at considerable expense.[114] Philadelphia, the early center for the manufacture of pressed brick, dominated the market through the late nineteenth century.[115] As early as 1854, Joseph Keen, a contractor in Wilmington, maintained a supply of Philadelphia pressed brick for sale in the port city.[116] For the next quarter-century, native brickmakers tried to compete with out-of-state producers. Bricks manufactured at Livingston Creek in Brunswick County in 1867 were said to be "equal to the celebrated Philadelphia pressed brick, except in regard to color."[117] During the construction of the Western Insane Asylum in Morganton in 1877, forty-five laborers who were employed to make bricks produced "a substantial pressed brick," due to the "superior quality of the clay" excavated at the site.[118] But, for the most part, North Carolina offered no serious competition to northern producers of pressed brick. Brickmakers in Pennsylvania produced more than twenty times the number of pressed bricks produced by North Carolinians.[119] Thus it was typical to find bricks from outside North Carolina in commercial buildings, such as three buildings erected in Durham in the spring of 1887 that were faced with pressed brick shipped from Baltimore.[120]

In contrast to pressed brick, North Carolina produced vast quantities of common brick. The 1860 census listed fifteen major brick manufacturers with a total annual product valued at $75,000.[121] In 1880 the number of large-scale brickmakers had quadrupled while the product value doubled.[122] By 1900 there were 157 manufacturers, producing more than $600,000 worth of common brick.[123]

The rate and extent of mechanization in brickmaking depended less on the development of railroads and broader markets than on the growth of local markets. The necessity for fireproof tobacco factories and warehouses in Durham and Winston promoted the development of a sizable brickmaking industry. Led by black brickmaker R. B. Fitzgerald, Durham by 1884 had eight permanent brickyards that manufactured a total of six million bricks for local use yearly. The construction of one tobacco factory for Washington Duke and Sons required more than three million bricks.[124] The twelve brickyards operating in Winston in the spring of 1891 manufactured more than fifteen million bricks for the building season but found that even that amount was insufficient for builders' needs, and by June numerous building projects were at a standstill due to the scarcity of bricks.[125] Severe shortages of brick had also stopped building activities in Raleigh four years earlier. Businessmen had contemplated the construction of two or three tobacco prize houses but were unable to find the brick to build them. They considered purchasing brick in neighboring towns, but "the freight on them would make the cost too great."[126] Although there were strains on the local industry as these examples demonstrate, brickmakers met the rising demand for their product by acquiring more efficient machinery and by remaining in operation throughout the year.

It was new machinery that enabled brickmakers to match the pace of construction in fast-growing towns such as Durham and Winston. Cyrus Chambers, one of the fathers of mechanized brickmaking, believed the only way for a modern brickmaker to prosper in the machine age was by "carrying on his business all the year round, employing steam by hundreds of horse-power, digging his clay by steam, carrying it to the machine-house by rail, dumping it into large hoppers, and performing all the various manipulations of screening, mixing, tempering, molding, drying, and burning without being exposed to weather, and never touching the clay with hands until it issues a completely molded brick."[127]

Enterprising brickmakers in North Carolina heeded such advice as they entered the twentieth century. Yet such concern for greater consistency and capacity and lower labor costs required substantial capitalization. From 1900 until the depression North Carolina began to move into

Carolina Brick Warehouse, Henderson, 1881. Large tobacco warehouses required several million bricks. The demand for such buildings in Durham, Henderson, and other tobacco markets spurred the growth of an industrialized brickmaking industry in the Piedmont in the last quarter of the nineteenth century. From *Historical and Descriptive Review of the State of North Carolina*, vol. 1, facing p. 130. (North Carolina Collection, University of North Carolina Library, Chapel Hill.)

the forefront of brick manufacturing as state brickmakers consolidated small yards, introduced new production techniques, and aggressively sought new markets.

Craftsmanship in the Machine Age

Machine technology altered the nature and function of the building trades. As mass production and new transportation networks transformed the way in which most building materials were manufactured and distributed, woodworkers, brickmakers, and mechanics witnessed a fundamental shift in the nature of their crafts and their position within the building industry. New materials and mechanical systems required craftsmen such as gasfitters, plumbers, and tilers with skills rarely employed in antebellum North Carolina, while the increasing use of stained glass, slate, stone, and tin in the late nineteenth century provided unparalleled opportunities for glaziers, stonecutters, and tinsmiths. At the same time, in the woodworking trades the machine put an end to many familiar patterns, as mechanized production of doors and windows, for example, made the joiner redundant.

The disappearance of hand labor also reduced the usefulness of the traditional apprenticeship system. Recognizing that the unprecedented demand for building materials had necessitated the introduction of laborsaving machinery, critics of the new system, nevertheless, contended that most laborers in sash and blind factories learned little more than how to operate machinery.[128] A broad knowledge of the "art and mystery" of woodworking was disappearing as shops added more machinery and work became more specialized. The division of labor created machine operatives instead of competent and skilled craftsmen. After examining the shoddy goods produced by the laborers in a Raleigh woodworking shop, one manufacturer who had been trained in the traditional manner asserted that "there is not one in twenty of the workmen employed in our city, and the greater part of our state, who is really a skilled workman."[129]

Some critics ridiculed the quality of products manufactured by mechanized sash and blind factories. Much of this criticism, no doubt, emanated from a fear that the factory system of mass production would displace skilled workmen. Woodwork produced in the old manner, contended one artisan, was far superior to that manufactured by modern machinery since it was the result of "more thought and less machinery. . . . Hand and brain worked together then more than now."[130] Even the most ardent admirers of the new system of production sometimes questioned its consequences. The trade journal *The American Builder* praised machinery as "simply marvelous. But it can also—and here it is that the artist has occasion, now-a-days, to tremble a little—not only make bricks, and saw and plane timber, but it moulds them into 'gracious forms.' . . . But we may ask, Is this all pure gain?"[131]

Although some critics deplored the decline of the old training methods, supporters of industrialized building saw many advantages to the demise of old ways. Machinery, they pointed out, freed young laborers from much of the drudgery and laborious work traditionally associated with the woodworking trades. It allowed them the opportunity to learn a trade much more quickly since there were fewer skilled operations to master. By reducing the length of apprenticeship, boys could stay in school longer. After leaving school they would then enter "a modern shop at a mature age, [and] learn more of the business in three months than very young apprentices in former years used to learn in three years."[132]

Those who stood to lose most from the displacement of old patterns were the skilled mechanics who did not have the resources to establish their own shops. The industrialization of the building industry presented them with several alternatives: they could move to a town or city and work for a larger builder, thus suffering a certain loss of independence; they could work with machinery in sash and blind factories and specialize in the manufacture of particular building parts at the risk of losing the chance to gain a broader knowledge of joinery; or they could seek work in a setting where they could continue to operate as craftsmen had done for decades at the risk of losing jobs to more efficient and cheaper ways of building.

Christian H. Fogle (number 5) and members of Fogle Brothers sash and blind factory and building firm, Salem, 1890. A number of workmen employed by Fogle Brothers in the 1870s and 1880s had been trained in the traditional apprenticeship system in Salem in the years before the Civil War. Younger members went directly to work in the factory to learn their craft. (Photo, courtesy of Old Salem Restoration, Winston-Salem.)

Beyond a small class of skilled artisans, most North Carolinians in the late nineteenth century welcomed the new system. Machinery reduced the price of most building materials to a level that made it possible for many families to afford to install window sash, floorboards, and brick chimneys in their homes for the first time. One thousand feet of oak flooring, which cost twenty-one dollars to produce by hand labor in the decade before the Civil War, dropped to fifty-four cents when it was manufactured by machinery some forty years later.[133] Improvements in lighting, ventilation, and heating gradually appeared in all but the poorest of houses. Factory-manufactured shingles replaced rough riven boards on roofs; window glass lighted openings previously blocked by wooden shutters; fire-resistant brick for chimneys and underpinnings removed the threat of fire from wooden chimneys and the problem of decay from block foundations; sheathing planks provided tighter enclosure than had chinking; and hinges, doors, and architraves created better-fitted openings. Without the industrialized production of building supplies, housing conditions for the majority of North Carolina's poor would have been far more wretched than it was. The replacement of a few skilled craftsmen with steam machinery seemed a small price to pay.

5

The Advance in Industrial Enterprise: Building with the New Technology, 1865–1900

Manufacturing enterprises are going up all about, and the hum of machinery is heard in almost every section and suburb of the city.

—*"The City of Raleigh,"* The Manufacturer's Record, *July 15, 1892*

Introduction

NORTH CAROLINA'S recovery after the Civil War brought with it radical changes in every aspect of building. New conditions, new needs, and especially new people demanded a steady stream of building. Architects and building contractors were now joined by building component manufacturing firms and real estate developers who found more successful venues for their ventures than ever before. While these people built new types of buildings, towns, and cities, they also produced a complex and competitive climate in which both architect and contractor desired greater control of the total building process. At the same time compartmentalization of roles, whether among architects and general contractors, framing and finish carpenters, or sash and blind factory workers, conflicted directly with the ability of builders to control the building process. The industrialization of building components production changed forever the nature of building but technology did not change human nature. By 1900 the building industry was large, successful, and filled with energy and ambition, but it was also chaotic and the need to govern that chaos was beginning to be felt.

Reconstruction and Recovery

Words and numbers cannot convey the devastation of North Carolina in 1865. The defeat of the Confederacy caused the collapse of many banks, wasted the university, and paralyzed the public school system. Stores, private academies, colleges, factories, and newspapers were closed. In terms of building, everything that was not destroyed—including some roads, bridges, and railroads—needed repair. Four years of accidental fires and no painting, roofing, or new construction meant substantial wear and tear on the essentially wooden architectural fabric. Towns, homes, and farm buildings were shabby, worn, and grey. The exuberant Rip van Winkle was no more.[1]

The fabric of society was also strained as many families and communities existed in an atmosphere of hatred, anxiety, and poverty. North Carolina had entered the war reluctantly and the bitterness of defeat was compounded by acrimony and distrust between pro-war and anti-war factions. There was also white animosity toward the occupying army and white hatred and distrust of the blacks. The Freedman's Bureau, established to provide direction for the newly freed slaves, put many black carpenters and contractors to work on building projects, thus inciting the anger of white carpenters and contractors.[2] Some northern contractors and builders also appeared—carpetbaggers to be scorned and emulated.

The industrialized and despised North became a model for reconstruction of the economy.[3] The state's desire for growth and self-sufficiency after the war was a tremendous spur to efforts comparable to those of the colonies before and immediately after the American Revolution. When Henry Grady proclaimed a "New South" in 1886, North Carolina's industrialists were undoubtedly included. The growth of a transportation network, the expansion ˅f textile manufacturing, the institution of tobacco manufacturing, and the subsequent growth of towns and cities which fueled the successful introduction of industrialized building components production assured this new image for the state. Indeed North Carolinians had discovered this image in the North Carolina Exposition of 1884 which, like those fairs of the decade before the Civil War, proclaimed the values of the ambitious, progressive, and modern. And like the successes in manufacturing and transportation, the exposition was largely the creation of private enterprise.[4]

The North Carolina Exposition opened on fairgrounds outside Raleigh on October 1, 1884. A series of disappointing fairs organized by the state's Department of Agriculture prompted a group of progressive-minded gentlemen headed by W. S. Primrose, a Raleigh entrepreneur, and H. E. Fries, one of Winston's most successful manufacturers, to propose, organize, and raise funds to finance a state exposition. This exposition was to celebrate the agricultural harvest, give an overview of advances in manufacturing and other enterprises, and advertise the state and its resources. The event was magnificently successful. From its opening day, record attendance in the thousands caused the exposition's run to be extended to six weeks and glowing reports of it appeared in the national and regional presses.[5]

The main exposition hall was designed by architect Samuel Sloan with help from a local builder, William J. Hicks, and the North Carolina Car

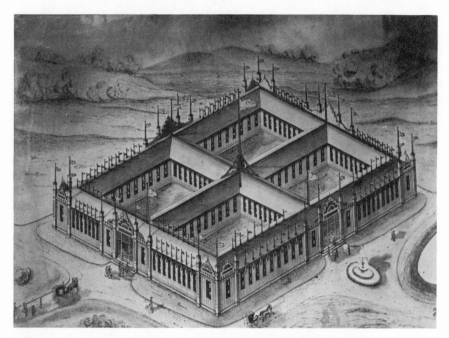

Main Exposition Hall, North Carolina Exposition, Raleigh, 1884. Samuel Sloan, William J. Hicks, and the North Carolina Car Company collaborated to produce this building. (Photo, North Carolina Division of Archives and History.)

Company, building prefabricators. It was erected with 500,000 board feet of lumber ripped and milled at the building site with machines brought from Raleigh by a rail spur from timber that had been cut in Moore County and shipped by A. F. Page from Blue's Crossing. This grand, impermanent building contained 75,000 square feet of space which housed displays from each of the counties in the state, the state Board of Agriculture, modern agricultural machinery and implements, and consumer goods.

"Today North Carolinians have discovered North Carolina," said Gov. Thomas Jarvis in his opening speech.[6] The representation of the state at the exposition was indeed quite different from the devastated state of 1865. The miraculous construction of the main building was possible because of the advances made in transportation, the development of natural resources, and the growth of a building industry and other manufacturers. But the extent of progress represented by the exposition seems to have caught many of the state's citizens by surprise. Years later U.S. senator Furnifold Simmons wrote Henry Fries his recollections of the exposition: "Until then it was not realized how rapid had been the advance in industrial enterprise and the revelation inspired hope and gave great satisfaction. . . . The exposition was of itself an illustration of progress already made, but it opened up new avenues, and stirred the people, and inspired them to go ahead. It was not only a wonderful awakening but a wonderful stimulant."[7]

This surprising self-discovery might be attributed to the end of the widespread self-doubt and pessimism that resulted from defeat in the war. The surprise, however, was also a consequence of years of severe internal political struggle. The postwar urgency for growth and self-sufficiency was constantly hampered by factional strife. The antebellum economy, which was condemned by editorial writer William Pell for its "disposition to make nothing and purchase everything," had been shaped by the white, conservative, agriculturally dependent gentry of the eastern coastal plain.[8] The former slaveholders collided repeatedly with the increasingly powerful and impatient industrialists of the piedmont and west who joined with the state's yeoman farmers to demand a more progressive and interventionist state government that would fund education and transportation networks. The lower classes of whites added their own kinds of rebellion, some supporting union with blacks to overthrow all domination; others supporting the physical and legal repression of freed blacks. There was labor unrest in the cities and conflicts between industrialists and the mill workers they hired.

Relief for these tensions, as well as federal pressure for reforms, challenged the Reconstruction legislature. The bipartisan, biracial legislature, however, was unable to sustain effective action. The stalemate produced by partisan and racial strife forced leaders of both political parties to look for means to gain control and restore party unity. Reconstruction convinced many white politicians of both parties that the road to political success was through white domination of blacks rather than through alliances between whites and blacks. This recognition brought about uneasy alliances between east and west, Republicans and Democrats.[9] By the 1880s the conservatives were willing to compromise and work with white progressives to use the greater profits that could be made from the production and sales of goods to support statewide white political control.

Although textile manufacturing did provide many new jobs and much income, the power of manufacturing was made most strikingly clear by the almost incredible success of tobacco manufacturing. The aggressive leadership of the Dukes created a financial empire by purchasing leaf tobacco at the source, placing storage and manufacturing facilities nearby, aggressively marketing the products, and rapidly expanding by re-investing profits in supplies, marketing, automation, and transportation. Success in the building industry operated on the same principles.[10]

The new roads and railroads, like manufacturing plants, brought people to towns. This movement of people—whether from out-of-state or local farms—was one of the most potent forces in sustaining the growth of the building industry. The war altered patterns of landholding and husbandry, forcing many blacks and some whites to move from farms to

View of Patton Avenue from courthouse, Asheville, ca. 1870. (Photo, North Carolina Division of Archives and History.)

towns and cities. Migration to the cities began immediately after the war and grew slowly during the remainder of the century. The general economic depression of 1873 and the agricultural depressions of the mid-1880s and mid-1890s did not encourage a return to agriculture or permit investment in new machines, fertilizers, and seeds. The railroad turned once-lonely mill sites into bustling villages, villages became towns, and towns became cities. Two towns—Winston and Durham—best exemplified this growth. Between 1870 and 1880 Winston had built nineteen factories with a total production valued at more than half a million dollars. Manufacturing also brought increased populations to older towns like Reidsville and Henderson.[11] The growing towns produced consumers, voters, and needs for city services. Roads and railroads also ameliorated old patterns of isolation. The small town habit of watching the train pass by made people aware of other towns and cities "along the line." It also fostered pride in the individuality of each town and engendered competition between communities, thus furthering civic pride and the desire for memorable and distinctive building.[12]

Postwar recovery occurred first in old towns like Wilmington, but by 1880 the recovery was general and widespread, and "boom" was a popular word in the press.[13] Moses Amis, one of Raleigh's chroniclers, later

View of South Main Street, Asheville, ca. 1895. The two views of Asheville presented in the preceding illustration and in this illustration are "before" and "after" the urban "boom" that transformed every city in the state between 1880 and 1895. (Negative, Pack Memorial Library, Asheville, photo, North Carolina Division of Archives and History.)

recalled that growth had begun in 1870 and that by 1886 the face of the city was completely changed. New suburbs and mill villages had appeared, suburban land values had increased, and the city had waterworks, a streetcar line, and electrification. These "advancements" were a source of pride and incentives to plan for even greater growth.[14]

The agricultural economy, however, did not flourish. Two depressions and the general economic downturn in 1893 did little to encourage building on farms where poverty was a threat. Some of the state's leaders recognized that the continued success of industry and manufacturing was linked to the plight of the farmer. A vital farm movement was spearheaded by Leonidas K. Polk, an energetic young journalist who founded the magazine, *Progressive Farmer*, in 1886. It was a mouthpiece for such "radical" ideas as that of farmers organizing to prevent monopolist practices by railroads and wholesalers, pooling capital for investments, and engaging in scientific farming methods. In 1884 Polk and an influential group of manufacturers, farmers, and educators formed the Watauga Club that was

Holladay Hall, North Carolina College of Agriculture and Mechanic Arts, Raleigh, 1889, Charles C. Carson, architect. (North Carolina State University Archives, photo, North Carolina Division of Archives and History.)

dedicated to the creation of a second state-supported school for agriculture and the mechanical arts that would take advantage of the federal Morrill Act (the Land Grant College Act). They were successful in their efforts. The North Carolina College of Agriculture and Mechanic Arts was chartered in 1887 and opened its doors two years later.[15] As the school catalog explained to prospective students, "It . . . [is] poor economy in a state to have to send from without its borders for skilled artisans, for architects, for builders, for superintendents of machinery, for agricultural, analytical and industrial chemists, for civil, for mechanical, for electrical engineers, when it . . . [can] educate its own sons for these useful and remunerative employments."[16]

When the state entered the new century, the North Carolina College of Agriculture and Mechanic Arts was beginning to fulfill the needs envisioned by its founders. Some architects and engineers opened successful practices to take advantage of the promise and prosperity that had brought the state into the New South era.[17] The college would significantly shape the new century through changes in building practice that were already evident in the construction and appearance of the New South.

Building in the "New South"

The postwar growth of industry and commerce must have been as phenomenal to those who experienced it as it is to those who now read about it. Manufacturing, marketing, and many consumer and retail enterprises appeared suddenly. The demand for building and for new building types was accompanied by a desire for physical evidence of progress and the material achievements associated with manufacturing and production. Antebellum words like "stylish," "permanent," "substantial," and "city-like" were once again common currency in the press and correspondence. These words described the desiderata of individuals, corporations, and the state as each commenced building projects. Even though the North Carolina penchant for economy reined in ostentation, the state's architects and contractors and their clients eagerly accepted the successive waves of architectural revivalism that swept the country. Cities, suburbs, factories, and institutional buildings were built unlike any the state had ever seen. The attitudes that fostered this building boom affected the building industry by intensifying the desire for specialized building types and stylish variety. These attitudes also encouraged the use of new materials, reinforcing changes that had already occurred in the building industry.

The prosperity that produced successive building booms in urban localities did not extend evenly to the rural areas that predominated in the state; however, rural building was influenced by the changes that were taking place in the cities. New attitudes, methods, and materials affected traditional building, by shaping and sometimes replacing older practices. An examination of some of the new buildings of the period demonstrates the capabilities of the new industry while revealing the desires and values of those who built them.

From the beginning of Reconstruction, progressive, new, modern, and stylish buildings were associated with northern forms and ideas. "What North Carolina now needs is northern people to cultivate it in a northern style and erect northern type houses," wrote Theodore Bourne of Raleigh in 1870.[18] The widespread popularity of this attitude is evidenced by many buildings constructed during this time. What is as significant, however, as the ready acceptance of Second Empire, Queen Anne, Romanesque, castellated, and neoclassical buildings was the rapid replacement of buildings and the diversification of building types and materials within towns and cities. Alfred Mullett's Federal Post Office and Courthouse built in Raleigh (1874–79) was the first of several new federal courthouses and post offices whose construction asserted the national presence in a bold and modern manner.[19]

Many county governments also displayed their authority. Between 1870 and 1900, eighteen existing courthouses were replaced, giving new strength and visibility to the conservative county political presence. The

Federal Post Office and Courthouse, Raleigh, 1874–79, Alfred E. Mullett, Office of the Supervising Architect of the Treasury. (Albert Barden Collection, photo, North Carolina Division of Archives and History.)

new brick or stone buildings incorporated many innovations—fireproof construction, gaslights, ironwork, and heating systems. These projects presented opportunities for profit and political and financial maneuvering, and they employed many hands who learned new building ideas firsthand.[20]

As important in shaping taste and technology was the ubiquitous construction of new commercial buildings and warehouses. The first important commercial buildings erected in the 1870s were confined to a few major towns where commerce and shipping had prospered before the war—Raleigh, Charlotte, Wilmington, and Greensboro. Newspapers recorded the recovery: "The busy hum of machinery is heard from early morn til night, while the chisel clink and the stroke of the hammer rings throughout the city."[21] The refrain was repeated in many newspapers because it evoked the noisy, vivid scenes of activity charged with energy, power, and material expansion that dispelled gloom and spelled prosperity. The frequent news stories about building projects and the weekly lists of new construction projects with their estimated dollar values were a source of pride and a constant reminder that building ensured more building.[22]

The first new buildings erected in a suddenly booming town like Durham or Winston were usually wood framed and plain. Few people cared what these buildings looked like—it was enough that they were being built. But the meaning of well-built buildings was not lost on the *Durham Tobacco Plant* writer who described the symbolic value of Raleigh's new stylish, pressed-brick, iron-fronted buildings of the early 1870s: "On every hand elegant buildings are being reared which ought and no doubt will perpetuate the memory of their founders, such men as Briggs, Fisher, Williamson, Upchurch and Thomas."[23] The desire for permanence became increasingly important in cities. The buildings praised by the press and visitors were the fire-resistant brick retail stores with iron trim and large windows which admitted light and displayed goods. The building materials represented physical improvements over wood-sided buildings. Iron, glass, and brick were not only symbols of permanence, but also of progress and prosperity in the city—three attributes that were frequently linked. "Many handsome residences adorn Winston, while the large three and four story brick factories and stores give it quite a city-like appearance." The *Raleigh Register* reported "scores of beautiful residences, imposing blocks of stone buildings with plate glass and with city-like fronts [in Winston]." By 1886 Fayetteville sported a business house with a solid iron front, large plate-glass windows, and a Morse elevator. A returning Wilmington resident did not recognize the 1886 city with its new buildings and dwellings as the town of the 1870s.[24]

Not every capitalist was willing to invest the time, materials, and expertise required to deal with pressed brick and plate glass. Some speculators were reluctant to spend more than was absolutely necessary and erected cheap wood-framed buildings. Durham investors in the mid-1880s, for example, continued to build in wood despite a number of devastating commercial fires. On November 16, 1886, another terrible fire swept the downtown and the December 22 *Durham Tobacco Plant* described the results. The writer noted with pleasure that the damaged buildings were being replaced but lamented the "poor class of buildings" erected by parsimonious investors. The new buildings had no "character" and were unsuited to a city that promised future greatness. The writer closed by saying empty lots would be preferable to these new buildings.[25]

By 1886 traditional wood-framed commercial buildings were considered a "poor class of buildings." Other building types that presented problems with fire were the tobacco warehouses where the bright leaf was cured and the wooden textile mills where some activities left rooms so lint filled that they were literally tinderboxes. The arsonist had many venues for his activity and sometimes was helped by competitive saboteurs. Where style had little influence, fires, the cost of fire insurance, and strengthened fire districts and ordinances combined to convince even the most tight-fisted merchant, banker, or manufacturer to invest in fire-resistant building materials.[26]

By 1890 Durham had a fire department, waterworks, electric company, telephone company, and streetcars. The *Handbook of Durham* published in 1895 described the city: "The business houses, stores and factories, are nearly all constructed of brick, none being of wood. Some of the stores, bank buildings and factories are highly ornamental in design, expensive in cost and would do credit to any large city." The construction in Durham and Winston of many huge brick tobacco warehouses and processing plants set side by side, some united by pedestrian walks and bridges, others separated and defined by firewalls and vent stacks of elaborately corbeled brick, served as corporate symbols of power and permanence.[27] The new textile manufacturing complexes of brick with their smokestacks, water towers, ranks of windows, and sawtooth roofs or high central clerestories, such as the Erwin Textile Mill in Durham and the Caraleigh Mill in Raleigh (both built in 1893), were the centers of small villages. Designed by mill architects to embody prosperity and growth, these buildings imparted a sense of endurance, security, and durability similar to the tobacco warehouses.[28]

As the cities grew, new churches, hotels, and train stations were added to the skyline. Towers, turrets, and mansards in tile, terra-cotta, and slate and pressed-brick storefronts with gleaming plate-glass windows decorated the downtown. Trolley tracks, gaslights, arc lights, sidewalks, paved streets, telephones, mail delivery, fire engines, and delivery wagons supplied visual bustle. Everywhere corporate and public institutions combined to produce a new cityscape, one of taller buildings with fireproof construction of glass and brick. Chicago buildings of the same period—Home Insurance, the first and second Leiter stores, and Monadnock—provide a notable contrast except that for both the builders of the New South in North Carolina and the builders of commercial-style buildings in Chicago, what mattered were the advantages of new materials and building methods. The towns of the New South had to create many images at one time: commerce, stability, industry, pluck, vim, and modernity. In 1889 a traveler to Greensboro reported:

> The passenger leaves his coach to find himself at once in the midst of a finished architectural effect rare in the vicinity of railroad depots. Elm Street opens north and south, a fine broad avenue, once lined with fine elms, recently cut away to bring into full view the long lines of three-story brick stores, the architecturally striking McAdoo and Barber hotels, the Federal and county courthouses and other fine public and private buildings, making North Elm Street equal in beauty to any in the State. . . . [the street from] depot to courthouse has been solidly and smoothly laid with the Belgian pavement, while it is flanked with bricks brought from Fayetteville, said to be the best for such purpose. These streets are lighted with the arc electric light and also with gas.[29]

Walker Warehouse, Durham, 1897. This was the first of eight fireproof brick buildings, the last one being finished in 1927. (Photo, Hendrik A. VanDyke, North Carolina Division of Archives and History.)

This was the image of the city: a mixture of forms and styles constructed from iron, brick, and stone. Factories rose on the fringes, streetcars clanged, and drovers' wagons lined the curbs. From Raleigh to Asheville a new variety of stores and shops attracted commerce. Business houses flourished beside old homes, and commercial areas pushed down side streets and into residential neighborhoods. The cityscape merged progress with domesticity.

Besides commercial building, speculative or purpose-built, which responded to taste, insurance requirements, local codes, and the ideologi-

Erwin Textile Mill, Durham, ca. 1910. (Photo, North Carolina Division of Archives and History.)

cal climate of the city and state, housing also continued to be a gauge of and guide to personal aspirations in North Carolina.[30] New housing was widely coveted in its many forms: residences for the wealthy, cottages for the new middle class, mill villages for the workers, and tenements for the newly arrived, poor, and unemployed. Styles were more varied and eclectic than commercial and institutional buildings, with the most expensive being unique and sometimes designed by an architect. "If you take the houses that people live in as an index of their advancement—and it is a good index—how much is our condition to be preferred to that of our fathers. The old-fashioned country house or the ancient residence in town has the huge outside chimneys, the high Corinthian pillars and the solemn goods-box shape. Now we build cottages which are more convenient much more economical of space and they look 100 percent more beautiful and generally cost no more money."[31] The great need for housing and home ownership as a measure of personal and municipal prosperity was a constant theme in the press. The combination of the need for shelter and the desire for the status afforded by ownership was met—almost at once—by the appearance of the capitalist and the general contractor who created and controlled the speculative building market. Not only did the capitalists and contractors determine the nature of the market—the appearance of what was built and bought—but they also began to create new residential patterns in the towns based on race, social status, and income. No constraints guided the speculator except those required to obtain profit and these varied from location to location. Certain patterns emerged: mill housing near factories, new tenements in already crowded neighbor-

View of South Elm Street from U.S. Post Office, Greensboro, ca. 1900. (Photo, North Carolina Division of Archives and History.)

hoods, cheap housing for the poor, better housing for the upward bound, and mansions for the wealthy. Economic reality divided the market into two major segments: property for purchase and property for rent.[32] Housing soon formed the foundation of the building business in every thriving town. The January 21, 1870 *Wilmington Star* described what became a common sight—the contrast between the fashionable, spacious residences of the wealthy and the approximately "forty [to] fifty new tenements, each separate and distinct, well adapted to the wants of people of moderate means and limited progeny." Described as small but comfortable, the town layout resembled a new settlement in the Far West. The "new village" of small houses—each probably 20 by 40 feet, with two rooms, a porch, and a rear kitchen wing, similar to those that the Cates Brothers contractors of Burlington bid on at $850 for a set of three—was almost certainly composed of rental units, possibly for mill operatives.[33] Housing was thus provided for a definite socioeconomic group and the spatial arrangement of the buildings created an identifiable neighborhood.

The location of mill villages, tenements, and new neighborhoods reinforced the growing racial and social segregation that characterized late-nineteenth-century North Carolina cities. Edward Dilworth Latta's Charlotte Consolidated Construction Company started Dilworth in 1890 as the state's first streetcar suburb on the city's southwest side. It was

Dr. Victor McBrayer House, 507 North Morgan Street, Shelby, ca. 1893. (Photo, North Carolina Division of Archives and History.)

designed to provide a neighborhood for whites outside the city, which was filled with "old hulks." Its park and streetcar line compensated for the distance from the city. Latta built a tasteful variety of house types but the key selling point was purchase on the installment plan.[34]

Installment purchase provided a bridge between rental and the outright buying of homes that few could afford. It was also a key to the development of suburbs.[35] The resourceful developers of rental or purchase housing recognized that building homes on the easily divisible former plantations and fields convenient to the existing town was the most desirable alternative to destroying existing buildings in the town. Small houses and cottages "built in a tasty style" joined handsome new mansions in suburbs like Winston's West End, far from the tobacco plants in the town; Raleigh's Oakwood, adjacent to the Governor's Mansion; and Durham's Trinity Park, near the newly opened college.[36] These neighborhoods were designed to be all white and the difference in size and scale of the houses was not as important as the fact that they all represented the ambition of home ownership. This ambition was made possible in these neighborhoods where residents rented until they could buy.

All-white neighborhoods had a direct parallel in all-black neighborhoods that appeared at the same time. In Raleigh, Winston, Charlotte, and other towns, blacks established land companies. The capital for these companies came from the government, from altruistic organizations, or

Cabarrus Cotton Mill village, Concord, begun ca. 1893. (Photo, Peter Kaplan, North Carolina Division of Archives and History.)

from whites who sought political leverage within the black community. Blacks knew the symbolic power of building and assumed control as often as possible.

In west Charlotte, blacks developed Biddleville near Biddle Institute (now Johnson C. Smith University), a college for blacks. By 1890 Raleigh had three predominantly black communities: Oberlin on the northwest side, Method on the west side between the town of Cary and the Capitol, and a large community on the southeast side which grew simultaneously with the black St. Augustine's and Shaw colleges.[37]

Many black residential neighborhoods contained other black institutions, such as churches or Masonic halls. There were few black commercial areas, however, and no black mill villages for many years. The participation of blacks in economic recovery and community growth was very limited. As separate black and white areas developed outside inner cities and towns, segregation acquired a new and more sinister meaning because both blacks and whites had heretofore lived side by side in many southern towns and cities. This change was not immediate or absolute but occurred incrementally as the towns grew and racial attitudes hardened.[38]

The vigorous, eclectic postwar buildings added glitter to the fabric of urban dwelling; as one journalist commented, "Today no city of her size is doing more to perpetuate the glory of this generation in the New South than Asheville, and I have scarcely passed a square without finding some sort of building improvements going on."[39] As in Asheville, throughout North Carolina clients, architects, builders, developers, and state and local governments saw the New South as a newly built, modern, and progressive place. The industrialization of the building process coincided

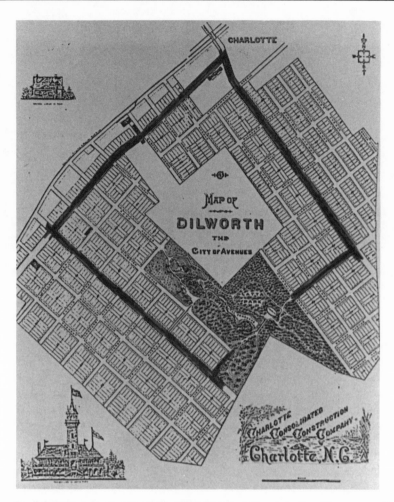

Plan for Dilworth suburb, Charlotte Consolidated Construction Company, 1891. (Charlotte-Mecklenburg Historic Properties Commission.)

with the ideological moment. The contractor or architect could offer a variety of materials, styles, and building types at costs and a speed of construction heretofore unimaginable. Commercial buildings could be built of permanent materials such as glass and iron, which made them not only stylish but progressive and modern. This created a "city-like" atmosphere of visual strength and physical density. The new residential fabric—the first great wave of speculative building and land development—ringed the older core of the towns. The popular one-story, irregular-roofed and porched cottage provided unity while the large towered, mansarded, turreted, architect-designed residences provided variety. The spatial pattern of development that ensured security from blacks, mill workers, and

Edgar Vaughn House, 1129 West 4th Street, Winston-Salem, ca. 1892, Hill C. Linthicum, architect. (Photo, North Carolina Division of Archives and History.)

the poor gave visual form to the traditional class system which emerged stronger than ever in this period of intense change.

Rural building stood in sharp contrast to urban building. Some farmhouses were expanded or remodeled and farm buildings were repaired or replaced, but the visible prosperity of the towns and cities only appeared in rural areas at the turn of the century. Increased sharecropping and tenancy necessitated the construction of more simple log and frame one- and two-room tenements. The movement of freed blacks from slave quarters to individual farms reinforced the piedmont pattern of dispersed nucleated farms, spreading them throughout the east.[40]

This almost anachronistic intensification of a small-farm rural economy was overshadowed by the constant economic growth and boom that was an essentially urban event. While the building industry and many other facets of life were transformed, much remained the same—particularly human behavior. As whites worked to regain and ensure the hegemony of the propertied class, the public and press, as it had in the past, perceived changes in terms of building and sought to remake the fabric of the state into the New South.

Masonic Temple Building, Wilmington, 1898, James F. Post, architect and general contractor. Post, one of Wilmington's most prosperous antebellum contractors, created buildings like this one whose tower, plate glass windows, and fireproof materials symbolized the progressive and "city-like" atmosphere of the New South. This is also one of the few surviving architectural drawings of the period. (Photo, North Carolina Division of Archives and History.)

The Practice of Building

Building practice in North Carolina before the Civil War underwent two significant changes. First was the emergence and more widespread use of the large-scale builder like Jacob Holt who could undertake contracts for entire projects and for more than one project at a time. The "undertaker" of antebellum years was as likely to be a wealthy entrepreneur as a builder. Builders like Jacob Holt combined both functions—builder and undertaker—to become what is now described as a general contractor. "Letting on contract" became the modern way of doing business because building continued to be a difficult and time-consuming process and because changes in the building industry required new knowledge. "Not being able to give his personal attention to it, he [the owner] will let it out on contract," read a newspaper notice in 1859.[41] A builder/contractor could control or try to control design, expenditure, component production and acquisition, and the labor force.

The second change was the increased popularity and use of the professional architect. Projects by William Nichols, William Percival, and A. J. Davis had introduced new building forms and methods of work. Like the general contractor, the professional architect was consciously sought. He was hired by people who perceived a direct relationship between architecture as practiced by the professional and the creation of a finished product with high style, a modern design, and a progressive image.

More important than a means of creating buildings, the presence of the general contractor and the professional architect initiated an evolutionary process that would finally end the traditional roles of artisan, builder, and client. The uses for which North Carolinians sought both architects and contractors were not familiar, habitual, or traditional. These people were sought because they could achieve something different— larger projects, stylish buildings, freedom for the client, a higher return on the investment. Those objectives had been achieved in antebellum North Carolina only when traditional values, methods of working, and patterns of behavior were not followed relentlessly.

The changes that had occurred before the war affected the traditional, rural, agricultural society of the state. The war and industrialization, however, changed everything by providing a new context for the practice of building—an urbanizing, consumer-oriented society. The vivid contrast of this society with the agricultural society that was still home for a vast majority of the state's people helps delineate the change. Rural society provided a stable environment for traditional building and the new towns and cities provided a fluid environment in which client, architect, and contractor found control and power expanded in some areas and diminished in others as the habits and practices of generations yielded to social, economic, and technological changes.

The Farm and the Hamlet: Self-Sufficiency and Independence

Prosperity did not extend to many farms and the user-built project continued as the traditional, indeed classical, mode of building for people of
limited or meager financial resources like sharecroppers or tenant farmers
and for persons who had no need to hire any other kind of assistance,
whether they be rich, poor, or middling.

In the post–Civil War period, both braced-frame and log construction
continued to be used for farm dwellings and outbuildings and some urban
squatter dwellings. Poor black and white tenant farmers built the ubiquitous single-story or single-story-with-loft house with stick or mud chimneys with the aid of friends, family, or co-tenants. It was possible to build
such structures without possessing particular skills but they did require
"traditional know-how," as the testimony of Jesse Lillington Jackson of Pitt
County demonstrates.[42]

In 1886 the Jackson family moved to a one-room house with a detached kitchen and dining room on a heavily timbered, fifty-acre plot of
land. Jesse Jackson's mother, father, sister, and two brothers slept there
and the four older boys slept at their grandfather's house nearby. The
family cleared the land, planted cotton, and also worked rented land one
and a half miles away. As the land was cleared, felled trees were saved for
sawlogs or fencing rails or piled for burning. The land-clearing provided
opportunities for two or three "log-rollings" and "log-tossings." When
enough logs were available, a Mr. Tripp cut them into lumber at his mill to
be used in the construction of a new house. Difficulties with Tripp made
the Jackson family alter the house plan from a two- to a one-story house.
Mr. Jackson and Buddy Bryan, possibly a local carpenter, worked on the
house while the family members continued to farm. The result was a two-
room house with a central passage, attached sheds, and an unfinished
attic.

Jesse Jackson's account of building describes the family's circumstances—a crop had to be planted, children fed, land cleared, logs cut,
fences made, and a simple house built all at the same time. His account
does not mention windows, doors, floors, or wall finishes, reminiscent of
the basic language of contractual agreements of previous centuries in
which details of traditional building were not stated explicitly but understood. Whatever Bryan's skill, it was at least no greater than that of Jackson. The process varied little from self-sufficient building in the federal
period, the only concession to technology being the sawing of planks
locally.

Changes in the building industry, however, did provide the rural
farmer who could afford it with alternatives to traditional methods. Components mass production permitted the improvement of existing structures by additions or replacements. Occasionally documented in family

letters, diaries, or daybooks, these changes are more readily discerned in the visual record of changes in fenestration, doors, floors, and mantels.

The Vestal family home in Chatham County was a late-eighteenth-century single-story-with-loft, dog-trot house that had been enlarged by the addition of a shed-roofed room before the Civil War. After the war, a parlor was added, creating an L-shaped house. Family tradition dates the milled sash, jambs, doors, and flooring to the mid-1880s or about the time of the parlor addition. "Miss Kate," who was born in 1866, claimed that her brother and his sons took out the original heart-pine floors and board-and-batten doors and replaced them with milled components because they were "old-fashioned." Thus the house was modernized by user-installed substitution of industrially fabricated components.[43]

The independent rural building project could, therefore, take advantage of the improvements and possibilities offered by prefabricated components that could be easily shipped by rail. Farmers could also order buildings shipped "knocked-down," like those produced by the North Carolina Car Company. Both these alternatives were encouraged by advertising which suggested that self-sufficient customers could use traditional skills, retain personal independence, be progressive and modern, and save money when using these kinds of aids for new construction.

The Farm, Hamlet, and City: The Artisan

The physical location of the artisan increasingly determined his role and position in his profession and in the community. North Carolina's rural society assured the continuation of the self-sufficient builder and the continuing presence of the skilled artisan. The artisan who was a farmer or owned a house and small carpentry shop retained a high degree of autonomy and a position of community importance because he was there to supply a need but he was not dependent on his particular skills for his complete livelihood.

The artisan who moved to the city, however, joined large numbers of workers with a wide range of skills. The artisan might rent a room in a cheap hotel or boardinghouse, or if married he might live with his family in one of the growing number of tenements. A surplus of framers or painters of limited ability who worked for lower wages could force him to take a job with lesser status and pay or make it impossible for him to find work. If he was willing to learn new skills, he might achieve greater independence, better pay, and higher status, but he would still work primarily as a member of a crew or for a subcontractor. In time he might become a contractor; but that was a risky business, and success was difficult to attain since there was much competition for work.

The remodeling of W. H. Worth's home in Raleigh in 1894 illustrates the fragmentation of the building process and the plight of the urban artisan who had to constantly compete, plan, and learn in order to find work. Architect A. G. Bauer furnished Worth with plans and Worth himself decided to act as his own contractor and accepted bids for each major part of the job. Some of the bidders were established general contractors who were capable of undertaking the entire job; some were job shoppers—artisans who could paint or roof or do finish work; and others were firms who specialized in plumbing, gas, lighting, painting, or papering. Elegant letterheads decorated some bids while others were submitted on cheap lined paper in barely legible handwriting. Sixteen different trades, in fact, were hired to complete this job and all who worked for the different trades, companies, and specialities were artisans of one kind or another. Each also worked other jobs which conflicted with Worth's. Each trade employed one to five people on the job and pay ranged from 50 cents per day for unskilled to $2.50 a day for skilled workers.[44]

The contrast between the town where the artisan worked amid noise and competition and the country where he worked secure in tradition was less pronounced for some artisans who lived in the small towns that dotted the rural landscape. The fact that these towns were connected to one another and the cities by the railroads made it possible for the artisan to take advantage of the industrialization of the building process. Success involved hard work in a changing environment, but the artisan was able to work with a single client or a few clients in a single building season, execute jobs from start to finish, and retain a sense of autonomy and personal worth.

The Village Building Contractor

An excellent example of the operations of the village building contractor is provided by the Cates family business. J. W. Cates was born in 1847, probably in Saxapahaw near Company Shops (now Burlington). By the mid-1880s he and his brothers William and Berry carried on a thriving small general contracting and building supply business. Their letterhead announced, "J. W. Cates and Bros. Undertakers and Dealers in shingles, lumber, doors, sash, blinds and coffins."[45] Their practice was confined to dwellings (20 by 40 feet with one or one and a half stories) and small, commercial buildings (20 by 24 feet or 20 by 15 feet with two stories). It is impossible to estimate the amount of work done by the brothers, but in 1893 they had two or possibly three buildings under construction. J. W. ran the shop in Burlington, making estimates, occasionally producing very rough drawings, ordering materials, and sending supplies to William and Berry who did the actual construction and site supervision, with the assistance of one or possibly two semiskilled laborers.

Typically J. W. and his clients worked out the design of their buildings between them, considering the budget and the eventual bid along with the floor plan. Thus William wrote to J. W. on February 13, 1893, asking him to prepare a bid on three houses to be built for a William Lloyd in

Durham. Each was to be a 600-square-foot one-story house with a central hall, four rooms, an "ell," and a porch, with a chimney and a stove flue in the ell. The house plus porch was to be built of number one lumber, "good but plain work." A later letter tells us that Berry tendered a bid of $850 for the project but William lamented, "I don't think we will get them to build as he [the client] said he could get them built for less money he thought."

In the same year, the brothers built a store in Chapel Hill for a Dr. Klutty. In a letter to J. W., William described the two-story brick building with an iron roof, iron steps on the outside, and doors inset between the large plate-glass windows on the front. For this job they hired a brick-mason.

A year later, the Cateses were furnishing a plan and estimate for two houses in Chapel Hill: "Dr. Weadon and Dr. London wants two houses built and wants us to give them a plan and estimate on them. They want a four room house and a cook room added, a hall and front and back porch. Hause [*sic*] not less than 10 ft. pitch and dont want them to coast [*sic*] over $6 or $700 each." William asked J. W. to come down to solidify the arrangements, present a plan, and discuss the bid.

The financial arrangements that the Cateses and their clients made are not clear. The houses they habitually erected were fairly small but were still not so cheap as to permit the Cateses to finance the entire project. A comparison with records from other builders suggests that the fact that J. W. was a materials broker permitted him to carry clients through several weeks or even a month but that he often got periodic payments as well as an "up-front" cash deposit against costs.[46] A project might take no more than three or four months at a cost of $800. Cates's cash flow must have been carefully balanced if he could or would not shoulder those costs over three or four months. Also, a builder's opportunity to become an independent contractor was determined in part by his ability to absorb costs (or take out loans) until a certain stage in the project was reached.

Although the Cateses were not financially independent, they could and did benefit from the changes in production and assembly of materials. The building business was completely dependent on materials suppliers for general items like lumber, nails, and roofing and more specialized ones like sash, blinds, doors, and frames. J. W. dealt with at least one hundred different suppliers between 1886 and 1907. Rarely did the Cateses fabricate components—their activities were limited to framing, siding installation, and interior finishing. Although they needed a bricklayer to construct the chimney for Klutty's store, on other projects they dispensed with the need for bricklaying by installing a cook or heating stove with manufactured flues and chimney. Similarly they did not have to rely on a joiner to make and assemble doors, windows, and frames as joiners had in the past since carpenters could install these prefabricated elements.

The Cateses did not have to command the range of skills that Luten and Bragg did in the antebellum years. No joinery, skilled planing, or shaping by hand was required. J. W. Cates was the "undertaker" and William and Berry were the artisans. This division of labor and the prefabrication of components permitted them to run a retail and contract building company. Working within a small geographical area crisscrossed by railroads and dotted with suppliers, small towns, and clients, J. W. Cates attained more than a modicum of success, evidenced by his somewhat stylish cottage in Burlington. Despite their success, the Cateses lacked the capital and the desire to expand beyond the owner-financed project, and they probably never engaged in speculative building. Like other small firms, they chose instead to build for capitalists like W. T. Blackwell, who erected two hundred speculative houses in a few years' time. In small towns all over North Carolina artisans like the Cates family flourished well into the twentieth century.

The City: Speculation and Development

The ways in which the Cateses sustained the changes in the building industry were a function of circumstances and habit. They combined traditional elements—direct client contact and building construction—with more modern elements—arranging materials supply and financing through a building supply business. This basic pattern was adopted throughout the state as artisans, builders, and manufacturers adapted to the new urbanizing environment and successive waves of building demand. These circumstances combined to introduce a new and exciting challenge—the emergence of the speculative building market.

This was a major development marking the achievement of a critical urban concentration of people, money, and need. Cities exhibit a visible record of this occurrence, evidenced in domestic housing, for example, by row houses and tenements in Boston and Philadelphia. In postwar North Carolina new suburbs of cottages and mill villages testified to the success of the entrepreneurial building contractor who was his own client, architect, and builder.

The speculative general contractor was significantly different from the Cateses. He had established credit and therefore could borrow money to hire more human resources and do a larger number of jobs in a season. This contractor undertook work to make a profit. To accomplish this he managed the entire building process with no or minimal client involvement or contact. His organization was designed to minimize interruptions or delays. Contractors of this kind diminished the distance between architects and contractors, but they did not eliminate it.

General contractors who worked in the traditional methods of the antebellum years continued to practice in locations where isolation, poor transportation, slow population growth, and poverty kept conditions much as they had been in 1840.[47] In cities like Wilmington, Winston-

404, 406, 408, and 410 Elm Street, Raleigh, ca. 1880s. These are speculative houses built in the Oakwood neighborhood. (Photo, North Carolina Division of Archives and History.)

Salem, Charlotte, and Asheville, however, firms of building contractors and building supply houses appeared, merged, collapsed, and re-emerged. As the *Charlotte Democrat* noted on September 7, 1874: "If mechanics do not get ahead in worldly affairs now they will never have a better opportunity." It was indeed a heady time and many young carpenters and masons must have had fantastic dreams in which they organized great swarms of men and materials, built wonderful buildings, and attained great wealth, power, and influence. Every building project could provide the opportunity for success.

The design of projects by speculative builders took several forms. In residential construction, the contractor became an arbiter of taste who began the design process with the banker or the pattern book and with a knowledge of components and cost. The banker sometimes shaped the form of buildings, but more regularly the contractor looked at his market and the popular publications that reproduced plans, elevations, and sources for prefabricated stylish components. The speculator chose carefully for a conservative state and produced a residential fabric that mirrored popular styles in a conservative but timely manner. Examples of contractors who undertook speculative projects include Briggs, a hard-

Henry Taylor, general contractor, Wilmington, active between 1868 and 1891. Taylor, who is said to have been a free black working in Wilmington before the Civil War, had a small but moderately successful business. (Photo, courtesy of Wright Collection, New Hanover County Museum, Wilmington.)

ware and building components supplier, and Dodd, a building contractor, who together developed Oakwood, a speculative Raleigh suburb, in the 1880s, and Fogle Brothers of Winston-Salem (who by 1885 built about one house a week) who produced speculative houses with traditional plans embellished with popular appurtenances and details.[48]

The successfully designed commercial building like Briggs Hardware Store in Raleigh came about in much the same way as the houses produced for the speculative housing market. The popular press and a desire for a progressive and modern appearance governed the choice of storefront that the builder ordered. Briggs's elegant and modern pressed-brick-and-iron-fronted three-story facade came from a catalog and was installed as the front of a typical wood-floored retail store with loft space.[49] Other establishments did the same, concentrating on plate glass, pressed brick, and cartouches on the pediment bearing dates as signs of the times. With the exception of tin ceilings which were installed as fire prevention devices, the interior space was traditional heavy wood post and beam construction because steel beams and posts were not available.

In contrast to the speculative market, the design of specialized buildings, mills, and manufacturing plants continued to demand expert knowledge and millwrights worked as before 1865. In 1890 James Allen and Sons of Wilmington advertised as "Practical Millwrights and Mill Architects," who could erect mills and place steam engine boilers and other kinds of machinery, and also specialized in hammering, retoothing, gumming, setting, and filing circular, gang, and other saws. Whether their practice was confined to lumber and planing mills is not clear. Other firms designed and erected textile mills. By the turn of the century, Lockwood Green of Greenville, South Carolina, for example, had a specialized practice that centered around Charlotte's textile establishments.[50]

The design capacity of the contractor was limited by his choice and by his particular expertise. This tendency toward specialization in design and building reinforced the current idea that a particular knowledge was required to do certain kinds of building, even though design itself was still perceived as an integral part of the building process and not yet limited to only architects.

Specialized needs could also be dealt with in other ways. Jails, fireproof vaults, and offices began to be marketed as prefabricated units, like houses, barns, sheds, and railroad cars. When the Watauga County commissioners decided to erect iron cells in 1888, the building contractor, Thomas J. Coffey, worked with Will Landrum of the Pauly Jail Company of Ohio. Landrum was the company architect who provided the detailed plans and specifications that fitted the prefabricated components to the site.[51] These patented products and many others that followed were a boon to contractors who had only to ask for plans and specifications to adapt components to meet special needs. Popular publications and eager manufacturers' representatives gave the general contractor unlimited resources for the building of his product. The product was constrained only by the market and financial feasibility.

In the antebellum years, financial responsibility for building projects meant covering the costs of materials and labor and assuming liability for mistakes, disasters, and failures of one kind or another. This did not change in any essential way in the postwar years. Jobs were still bid on a cost-plus or overhead-and-profit basis or by the piece. What did change were the ways in which financial responsibility might be assumed and liability might be shared.

The ideal situation, in terms of financial resources, is exemplified by a firm like Edward Dilworth Latta's Charlotte Consolidated Construction Company. As an offspring of Latta's larger real estate and development interests, the company could buy building materials on credit, run a yard to fabricate components, and pay workmen out of ready capital, sustaining those costs until repaid by financing homes and buildings through sales and credit. For the prospective customer the risk was in contracting a mortgage. One might lose one's job and then default on payments, losing the house and the investment. For the contractor the risk was a fluctuating market. A company like this not only had the benefit of the financial backing of the parent company but also had the capacity to work for other clients and architects independently of the speculative market, ensuring additional revenue.[52]

A more typical pattern was that of the general contractor whose resources consisted of good credit, usually based on owning and operating his own sash and blind factory, planing mill, or lumberyard, or all three. Frank Ellington and Thomas Royster owned their own building supply business in Raleigh and a lumberyard in Apex twelve miles away. The firm maintained credit at Briggs Hardware Store for materials and components only Briggs could supply. Their purchases were recorded by job and paid for monthly. Not everyone could have credit like Ellington and Royster but they were backed by their reputation and by their own sales, as well as by the income generated from lumber sales and building projects locally contracted. Nevertheless this firm went through a series of partnerships that changed almost yearly in the 1880s.[53] The market was fickle, the economy unsteady, and the building process, as always, produced delays, mistakes, and failures.

Another means of financing was that followed by tobacco magnate W. T. Blackwell. By 1884 he had entered the speculative market, planning to build about two hundred small rental houses in Durham. He hired a number of general contracting firms including two local ones, T. C. Christian and J. T. Salmon, who were also reputable independent builders. Robert Fitzgerald, a black brick manufacturer, supplied the brick. Blackwell bought supplies in quantity from local dealers and his contractors then drew on these supplies that were stored in his warehouse. In mid-1889, however, Blackwell's bank failed, and he went out of business paying only portions of his debts, causing many of his contractors, workmen, and creditors to suffer.[54]

An investor or a group of investors, with the general contractor of their choice, might agree to put up the necessary capital for a particular venture. Land was also bought and sold by use of this limited partnership. And, finally, land companies might also finance a building project.

The general contractor whose source of capital defaulted faced disaster. Bonding was not required when a firm worked for itself. If construction loans were involved, bankers were protected by lien laws and banking policies. The General Assembly's 1869 lien law gave the builder the right to take a lien on the property of an owner who did not meet the terms of his contract. Thus creditors and materials suppliers could be paid. Workers were in the least-secure position, however, since they usually had only verbal contracts. They were therefore paid last, if at all. Attempts at protective legislation for workers met resistance and only toward the end of the century did laborers gain any protection or legal recourse.[55]

Thus the speculative market had serious financial risks for the contractor but rarely for the client unless he was an investor or controlled the flow of capital into a building project as required by the contractor in some projects to purchase materials and to pay workers. Changes made it increasingly important for the general contractor to have secure financial arrangements for his projects. Some firms, like Briggs of Raleigh, began as general contracting firms but divested themselves of that role and became materials suppliers only, thus affirming the value of specialization and extending credit to selected builders.[56]

The different financial arrangements which contractors could procure for building projects opened the building industry to new forces driven by the consumer and money markets. Building had traditionally been done by only those who had or had access to the necessary funds. Now many more people could be involved in building, particularly housing, which would shape future markets and the pattern of development in towns and cities.

Once financing was arranged, the contract between builder and client or investor(s) contained the familiar elements of a certain amount of upfront money, payment by stages (usually in quarters of the total), and payment for materials and workmen by the contractor. Briggs's records show weekly and monthly tabulations of expenses by contractors for both materials and labor. Craftsmen and unskilled labor continued to be paid a daily wage tendered weekly. The workweek was still six days, dawn to dusk, and masons and skilled carpenters earned as much as $2.50 a day while an unskilled laborer might make 50 cents a day.[57] The increasing complexity of financial arrangements in building did not extend below the management level. Crews were still utterly dependent on their employers and had few means of negotiation, except the strike which was of limited usefulness at the time.

In the antebellum period, a contractor's maintenance of a lumberyard and crew ensured that he controlled materials production and component fabrication. This helped prevent shortages and delays and eliminated some middlemen. The transfer of materials production and fabrication to the mills constituted a trade-off—on the one hand less responsibility and a smaller investment in machines and crew but on the other hand less control of cost, quality, and delivery, plus the difficult problem of deciding from whom, for how much, and when to buy. For example, the contractor for the 1889 Pasquotank County Alms House asked for bids on at least three separate groups of items for the simple wood-frame single-story building: milled and manufactured materials, brick and plaster work, and carpentry. In its bid, the firm of D. S. Kramer of Elizabeth City, a major regional supplier and building firm, agreed to "furnish all material, in our line: all lumber, mouldings, sash, doors, shingles, plastering lath and weights and cords for windows" and deliver it to the site, ready for the carpenters. Brick, paint, stoves, flues, and hardware came from other sources.[58] The assembly of materials also involved logistical planning. A Winston-Salem contractor found himself constantly delayed by the failure of an Edenton firm to deliver sash and blinds. Delays were partly due to trains arriving late at the Edenton depot and partly due to the late delivery of raw materials to the manufacturer. The contractor could withhold payment but that would not speed the job—it only increased irritation and frustration.[59]

These changes in the building industry seemed to favor the absent client who no longer had the time or the knowledge to direct his own project. They also minimized the client's risk and made available more alternatives for buildings and dwellings than ever before. A client could buy or rent ready-built buildings in many styles. If he chose to work with a contractor he could minimize his role in the building process through the contractual agreement, while the variety of styles, materials, conveniences, and decorations was greater than ever. Cash was his only constraint. To acquire these materials, a general contractor, like the Cates Brothers, might deal with a hundred or more firms during a single year. The salesman who was persuasive and the manufacturer who supplied shop drawings for his products became favored suppliers.[60]

The proliferation of materials and components had only begun. It was very difficult to keep pace with the variety of components available, from gas and arc lights to brackets, cornices, pillars, screens, fireplace hoods, mantels, posts, balusters, plumbing supplies, chimney liners, and flues. The abundance became overwhelming as companies competed for attention and sales, which affected choices and cost. Suppliers, however, were still subject to the same problems—late shipments, damaged goods, or wrong color or material—which could shatter the work schedule on the building site.

Patterns of labor organization and the work schedule on the job site were not very different from the antebellum decades—despite mechanization, building construction was still labor-intensive. The division of labor by craft continued as masons, framing carpenters, finish carpenters, painters, and plasterers each performed their roles. There were, however, fewer highly skilled artisans and more semiskilled workers, and the days of slave labor were long past. Ever present were the supervisors. There were more subcontractors for specialities who therefore controlled part of the materials supply and the schedule. A general contractor frequently solicited bids from these subcontractors who performed special jobs like roofing, painting and papering, and plumbing.

Few blacks could take up the new or more specialized building trades because of lack of education and opportunity, which confined them to the unskilled or semiskilled class of workers. Many blacks worked in masonry and some black contractors manufactured brick, supplying their own crews. Other equally physical and sometimes dangerous work fell to blacks, such as roofing.[61] This pattern confirmed growing segregation even as newspapers praised black and white mechanics who worked side by side.[62] Whether segregation produced or reduced friction between blacks and whites depended on the particular situation. However, it did create one more logistical problem for the contractor whose white crews would not work with blacks.

Since building required increasing amounts of organization, the general contractor was perceived more and more as a businessman rather than a builder. His participation in labor organization and financial responsibility was essentially a management role. The site supervisor in time became the key figure involved in actual building in the field—a role many general contractors relished and relinquished reluctantly. To be on the site with the men as the building progressed from bottom up, outside to inside, was a physical and emotional event that stirred the soul. To sit in the office and write orders and send invoices was not as exciting.

The building industry became more of a business as the proliferation of general contracting firms created a climate which encouraged an efficient, organized building process. Cutting costs was essential in an increasingly competitive market. This competition led to both specialization and diversification. It also led to improvements that increased efficiency. The North Carolina Car Company, which had built the 1884 Exposition Hall, had the first electric power supply in Raleigh installed in their plant and were also instrumental in establishing the Raleigh trolley car business.[63]

The success of the building industry in North Carolina also attracted out-of-state firms. The David Getaz Company of Knoxville, a large Tennessee construction company, set up offices in Raleigh, Greensboro, and Wilmington. The company employed young men like Frank Thomson who came to Raleigh in 1897 or 1898 as a superintendent and in 1899 set up independently as an architect and David Hanna who was sent to Wilmington by the firm and by 1900 became a prominent independent contractor in that town.[64] The firm offered the client a total package from design to completion for mills, commercial establishments, and large dwellings. Design production and construction supervision were arranged vertically and an orderly hierarchy of responsibilities was contractually arranged— responsibilities for financial management, inventory and use of materials, organization and payment of labor to the completion of construction.

The creation of a system to control the complex elements involved in building became more and more important to clients and general contractors as building became more and more a business toward the end of the century. Some contractors became manufacturers and some manufacturers became brokers and builders. The traditional hierarchy of skilled craftsmen could no longer guarantee competence or success. As the Wilmington *Dispatch* complained in 1896: "The race is neither to the swift or the strong . . . but [to] the cheap contractors."[65]

Distance and Proximity: Hiring the Right Architect

Many of North Carolina's most important antebellum buildings were designed by out-of-state architects since at that time there were no professional architects from the state. All five major designers—William Nichols, David Paton, William Percival, A. J. Davis, and Samuel Sloan—visited the state, found clients, supplied their services, and left.[66] Davis and Sloan returned to their lucrative practices in the northeast, occasionally visiting projects in North Carolina, and Nichols, Paton, and Percival left to seek fortunes in other locales. The presence of these men changed the public perception of the architect and his role. The fact that these out-of-state architects had to deal with clients and contractors through correspondence and occasional site visits resulted in different methods of working for local builders, but there is no evidence that they resented the architects or that they realized that these new arrangements would affect building patterns for all time. After 1880, however, it would be difficult to find anyone involved in building who believed that building would continue as it had in the antebellum years. This widespread belief was the consequence of the great variety of projects built throughout the state that employed a professional and of the acceptance by the state of a role in creating architects and mechanics.

Unlike the antebellum years in which there was a strong figure like Davis or Percival who worked for a group of powerful clients, no architect dominated this period. Samuel Sloan might have been such a figure but he died soon after his move south in 1881. The most significant figure in the documents from this period is the contractor or building supervisor. In projects ranging from Alfred Mullett's 1874 Federal Post Office and Courthouse to Richard Morris Hunt's Biltmore House in Asheville (1890–95), with few exceptions, there is no sense of intimate engagement between the architect and the client. However, the emergence of a distinct group of North Carolinians (by birth or choice) committed to the practice of architecture in North Carolina had occurred by the end of the century, creating a new situation for everyone concerned in the building trades.

The architect's separation from the building trades is the most vital, but also the most burdensome, consequence of both professionalization and the industrialization of the building process. Mass production of new components using new materials permitted architects to design fewer elements and specify more. Better transportation and means of communication permitted architects to work at greater distances from projects. Large projects still required field supervision but the fact that architects took on more projects meant that they devoted less time to each one. Intellectual, physical, and emotional distance affected the architect's own office as well as the client and contractor. It was more difficult to develop personal relationships since each participant remained almost a stranger to the others. More time was spent on correspondence and on the production of documents that illustrate, sometimes humorously, the effects of distance from projects. Distance meant less comprehension of local circumstances and permitted misunderstandings to occur more readily. Whatever anxiety or confusion distance produced for the client, architect, or contractor, it was simply accepted as inevitable because of the speed of change.

Some of the largest and most important building projects in the state during this period were those which were initiated by the Office of the Supervising Architect of the United States Treasury, located in Washington, D.C. By the last quarter of the century it was the largest architectural office in the country and the organization of a project in that office was the most orderly, specialized, and detached. The goal of the office was to give every site chosen a stylish modern Treasury-designed building of very high quality.[67]

The site selection and design, based on estimated square footage and the budget, were decided by the client and the Treasury office through correspondence and on-site work by local agents. Once preliminary sketches and style were approved, the working drawings were executed by a number of specialized draftsmen. In the drafting division not only drawings but tracings and photographs would be prepared. In 1888 approximately twenty-five 24-by-36-inch ¼-scale drawings were required for a $150,000 building. Models of details were also sometimes prepared.

This system of producing designs, working drawings, and specifications (which in 1888 were standardized forms with blanks to be filled in) had the advantage of removing this phase of the process from the political arena—as the actual building process might not be. However, it had the already familiar disadvantage of sometimes specifying materials or techniques which were not locally available.[68]

Once working drawings were finished and tracings made for blueprinting, they were sent with the specifications to the building site to be available for local bidders. Following the awarding of contracts, a local superintendent was appointed, and if the job was large enough, he was given a clerk and a disbursing agent. The superintendent supervised the actual construction of the building. The successful bidder for the Federal Post Office and Courthouse to be built in Statesville (Iredell County) in 1890 was the firm of Demens and Harding of Asheville. A superintendent was appointed for this job and there were periodic inspectors from Washington and Atlanta.[69] Once Demens arrived in Statesville to begin the job, chaos descended. His partner Harding, a chronic alcoholic, left without notice and had failed to order materials. After lengthy correspondence with the supervising architect, Demens dissolved the partnership. There was some concern, however, over whether the performance bond that was required for a job of this size would cover the new firm, Demens Contractors.

Demens Contractors was accepted and, with the question of responsibility settled, Demens began to submit materials for approval and to actually excavate and build the foundations. Under a typical government contract the general contractor for a building was paid on a schedule designed to enable him to complete the building within a given time (one season in the South, two in the North, for a building costing $150,000). The general contractor also agreed to pay a penalty for failure to meet the schedule. Since this penalty could mean financial problems for the contractor and his bondsmen, it was a powerful incentive to staying on schedule. The work also had to pass inspection and the general contractor was held responsible. A below-standard subcontractor could not only slow the work but cost the general contractor.

Demens found himself behind schedule due to a very wet February and to slowness in approval of materials. The inspector who arrived in March 1891, E. T. Avery, wrote the supervising architect to ask for an extension or a remittance of the penalty. Avery described the extenuating circumstances and the dilemma: "You have to consider then, whether better work could be obtained resulting to the advantage of the Government, by allowing the contractor more time . . . and thus relieve them for a reasonable period from their obligations under the contract or whether to take the chances of getting bad work hurried forward to complete by a given time under contract (which is too short) make it necessary to reject

Construction site, Federal Post Office and Courthouse, Statesville, 1891, James H. Windrim, Office of the Supervising Architect of the Treasury, Peter Demens, general contractor. (Photo, National Archives, Public Building Services.)

such bad work [thereby causing more delay] and to inflict the penalty for failure to complete."[70] Demens's situation was familiar and chronic. Time was money in the building industry.

After Demens was granted an extension of time, he found he had problems with workmen and materials. Probably the four most frequent difficulties the contractor, as assembler of materials, experienced were the failure of materials or components to arrive on schedule, the inadequacy of materials or components, workmen's lack of familiarity with materials, and delays occasioned by failure of materials to pass specified tests or receive approval for substitution. The latter two problems were more typical of large state, federal, or corporate commissions. The former difficulties were universal, persistent, and, indeed, still exist.

Reports from inspectors reveal that Demens's workmen had trouble with the brick and terra-cotta work. Inspector Avery noted in March that "all is being done generally in a very good and satisfactory manner," except for sloppy mortar joints. The September inspection by Adolf Cluss was more critical. The Wadesboro red-grey sandstone of the base had been "unduly soiled and bespattered with mortar by careless mechanics working overhead." The face bricks and ornamental terra-cotta work "were inexcusably soiled by inexperienced and careless brick layers." Oil had

Federal Post Office and Courthouse, Statesville, 1892, James H. Windrim, Office of the Supervising Architect of the Treasury, Peter Demens, general contractor. (Photo, National Archives, Public Building Services.)

been improperly applied to the terra-cotta so its color varied. These defects would have to be corrected by "experienced, trained mechanics"; for the face brick "a Northern man" should be brought in.

According to an earlier report from the local supervisor for the Treasury, S. A. Sharpe, Demens had subcontracted to local workmen who were inexperienced. Sharpe claimed that Demens was coerced into hiring these particular masons by a group of local men who wanted to make money out of the project. If Sharpe's accusations were true, it is inexplicable why Demens would hire inferior workmen since correcting their errors would cost him time and money. These accusations were never proved and the work went on.[71]

Interior inspections revealed other problems. As was traditional, Demens subcontracted the plasterwork to V. T. Belote of Asheville, who sent his brother E. T. to execute the contract. E. T. refused to meet Demens's standards, claiming that "as an old hand," he knew "what was enforced in Government work." Inspector Cluss, Demens, and Belote had a final confrontation and solved the problem by "full discussions and tests of the objections to the plastering." They agreed that the plasterwork was faulty if the brown coat showed through and if the surface was uneven and marred with "cat's faces" (porous, untroweled areas). These were familiar defects that plasterers in good standing prevented. Belote accepted responsibility for his shoddy work and agreed to remedy the faults.[72] Although the problem was resolved, it had cost Demens time and had been demoralizing to him and his workmen.

The successful supervision of labor and the execution of a job was never the consequence of a simple dialogue between supervisor and mechanic but a process in which each participant's self-respect, well-being, and identity were involved. As long as commonly accepted and shared standards for work existed, critical evaluation had a clear, precise meaning. But as the traditionally shared body of knowledge was replaced or replenished with more specialized or different types of information, it became difficult for the supervisor to communicate to workmen an accurate criticism and its remedy. With regard to the treatment of the Wadesboro sandstone on the Federal Post Office and Courthouse, perhaps the masons didn't comprehend Inspector Cluss's remark that its "transparency had been lost" and therefore were unable to respond to his criticism.

In fact, Demens's knowledge and experience of standards of performance and reasonable work expectations were his reasons for choosing Asheville workmen like the Belotes as his plasterers. They failed him, while his woodwork, which came from Asheville, received very high praise. He had hired Statesville masons but their reported "bad" reputation might as easily have been a fabrication. Expectations of what constituted good work might change from location to location just as distance made a vital difference in every phase of a project. All the participants accepted these differences, however, as a logical consequence of building construction.

The Federal Post Office and Courthouse in Statesville was finally successfully completed. Demens went on to other jobs and the supervising architect of the Treasury designed many other buildings for the state. As was to be expected, not one job was problem-free.

One way in which architects during this period dealt with working at a distance from projects was by offering their services through magazines and the mail. George Barber, located in Knoxville, Tennessee, was one of the most active mail-order architects in North Carolina.[73] He published both house-plan books whose designs were available by mail and a monthly magazine, *The American Home*, that was devoted to the propagation of good design practices in home and garden. Barber's method of producing designs for a client began with his books from which one could order, ready-made, the necessary plans to scale with elevations, full-size details, blank contract forms to use with builders, color samples, and a bill of materials. Barber also encouraged clients to work out any slight changes they might desire with the builder or to request plans from his firm for greater alterations which he would provide at moderate cost: "Write to us

INFORMATION SHEET

In Writing About or Ordering Plans PLEASE MAKE ALL YOUR WANTS KNOWN AS NEAR AS POSSIBLE BY FILLING OUT THE FOLLOWING BLANKS

This will enable us to give you prompt and satisfactory service. Any of the blanks not filled will be considered as left for us to use our best judgment. SHOULD YOU NOT FIND IN OUR BOOKS any plan suitable to your location or wants, KINDLY SEND US A ROUGH SKETCH, no matter how rudely drawn, giving us your idea of a floor plan, from which we will make you a scale drawing, with such changes and improvements as we think best, FOR WHICH THERE IS NO CHARGE, the only obligation being that the drawings are not to be used and are to be returned to us. (This offer applies only to houses costing $1,500 and above.) The drawings will be sent to you for change or approval, with our price for making full working drawings, specifications, etc.

WITH OUR METHOD OF DOING BUSINESS, and our offices at your service, there is no reason why we cannot serve you just as well as if we were located in your own city. Thousands of the best people in our land, to whom we would be glad to refer you, have obtained handsome and satisfactory homes from merely rough sketches sent us.

WE INVITE YOU TO CORRESPOND WITH US FREELY

Design No._____ Floor Plan No._____ Name and Page of Book_____

1. Stone, brick, brick veneer, stucco or frame house? _____
2. Material for foundation?_____
3. Kind of stone?_____
4. Common or press brick for face walls? _____
5. Is house to be 1, 1½ or 2 stories? _____
6. Size of lot and frontage?_____
7. Nature and slope of ground?_____
8. Cellar?_____How much?_____
9. Do you want cellar floor cemented? _____
10. Laundry in cellar?_____
11. Hot water?_____ Steam?_____ Hot air heat?_____
12. Do you want coal grates or open wood fireplaces? _____
13. Do you want walls storm sheathed? _____
14. Double Floors—First story?_____ Second story?_____
15. Ceiling height for first story?_____
16. Ceiling height for second story?_____
17. Kind of Roofing material?_____
18. Do you want attic floored?_____ Otherwise finished?_____
19. Plastering finished for tinting or papering? _____

20. Do you want outside or inside blinds?_____
    Venetian?_____ Sliding?_____
21. Do you want transom over bedroom doors?_____
22. Panel Wainscoting, and where?_____
23. Beamed Ceilings, and where?_____
24. Kinds of woods rooms are to be finished in as follows:
    Hall?_____
    Parlor?_____
    Library?_____
    Living-room?_____
    Dining-room?_____
    First Story Bedroom?_____
    Second Story Bedrooms?_____
25. Hardwood Floors?_____ Where?_____
26. Have you city water supply? _____
27. Have you sewerage? _____
28. Do you want gas? _____
29. Electric Lighting?_____
30. Electric Bells?_____ Where?_____
31. About how much do you want the house to cost?_____
    (See Word of Caution below.)

A WORD OF CAUTION.—Do not try to get too much house for a certain sum, and do not require of your architect a certain size house at a certain price, for in most cases he cannot give you both. Such items as Panel Wainscoting, Beamed Ceilings, Hardwood finish, Hardwood floors, etc., are expensive.

OUR FULL WORKING DRAWINGS

Consist of foundation, roof and all floor plans, and four elevations of views of exterior, all drawn to a scale, with every dimension carefully marked. Also a complete set of SCALE AND FULL SIZE DETAILS for everything, inside and out, requiring a detail, complete specifications and contract blanks.

Your Name_____ City_____ State_____

Express Office, (if different from P. O.)_____

Date_____ No._____ Street_____

When you send a sketch write your Name and Address on it, especially if sent in separate package from your letter.

GEO. F. BARBER & CO., Architects
KNOXVILLE, TENN.

(OVER)

Information sheet for client, George F. Barber. (Courtesy of Michael Tomlin, photo, North Carolina Division of Archives and History.)

concerning any changes wanted in the plans, and keep writing till you get what you want. Don't be afraid of writing too often. We are not easily offended." To further facilitate the mail-order process, an order form questionnaire and a "handy sketch sheet" were included in his books. Barber also continued to offer the client the option of an individually designed house developed through extensive correspondence with the architect.

Barber's office was well organized. By 1900 he employed twenty secretaries and thirty draftsmen who mostly copied the designs produced by

Barber and his partners. Barber, like his competitors Palliser and Shappell, recognized the rapidly growing need for the home as a consumer product.

Barber's solution for dealing with the vagaries of the actual building process was to rely on documents: "Knowing as I do that my working drawings, when they leave the office, go out of reach of my personal supervision, I have taken especial pains to make everything plain and easily understood by mechanics generally. Every detail that goes from this office is FULL SIZE and drawn by hand (not printed)." Barber's clear drawings and other aids and the bill of materials which included nothing unexpected or unfamiliar were readily and easily used by local contractors and their framing and finish carpenters. Barber's houses were mostly frame houses with lap siding or shingles, slate roofing, brick underpinning, and stone or concrete footings. Since these materials and many of the details were traditional, the local artisans had dealt with ones like them for decades. Nevertheless the actual buildings repeatedly reveal considerable differences in craftsmanship. Uniformity was not easy to achieve since artisans all had their own habitual ways of working.

Besides architecture at a distance which was typical of the period and has also continued, there were also resident professionals in the state, for example, G. S. H. Appleget and A. G. Bauer.

G. S. H. Appleget was a carpetbagger who arrived in North Carolina from New Jersey about 1869. Appleget had no known formal training, but he did have experience, self-confidence, and ambition. He came on a wave of land development fostered by North Carolina businessmen who wanted to attract immigrants to the state. He attached himself to Jonathan M. Heck who was prominent in the group supporting land development efforts and had come to Raleigh from what is now West Virginia before the war.[74]

Appleget's estimation of himself and his role vis-à-vis the client and the building process was spelled out in one of his advertisements: "G. S. H. Appleget, Architect. Having had twenty years experience as a builder in New York, Philadelphia, and other large cities has concluded to devote his whole time to ARCHITECTURE. Designs and specifications, also Detail drawings (Fullsize) for buildings of any description, prepared at short notice . . . remodeling with French Roofs . . . WILL ALSO SUPERINTEND THE ERECTION OF BUILDINGS, WHEN DESIRED, BUT DO NOT TAKE CONTRACTS NOR EMPLOY HANDS."[75]

He could not have been more explicit. Architects design, draw, and supervise, but they do not build. In the next year Appleget wrote to the American Institute of Architects for their schedule of fees and in 1872 he applied to Mullett, unsuccessfully, for the supervisory position on the construction of the Federal Post Office and Courthouse in Wake County. Another Appleget advertisement explained that he was skilled in the use of iron and that he had five hundred drawings as examples of his work.

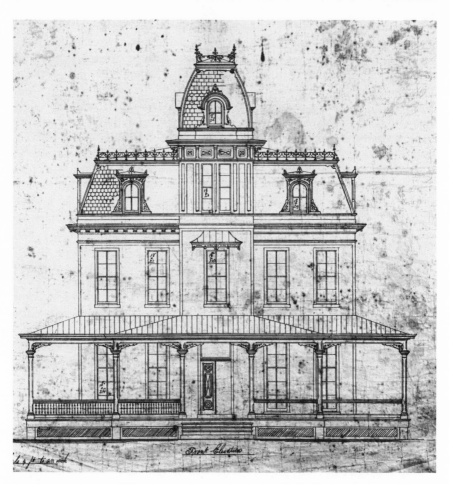

Empire-style house, Raleigh, ca. 1870, attributed to G. S. H. Appleget, architect. (W. J. Hawkins Papers, Southern Historical Collection, photo, University of North Carolina Library Photographic Service.)

He had offices in Charlotte and Raleigh and worked in Greensboro and other sites around the state in his attempts to establish his position as a practicing architect.[76]

Evidence from Appleget's work shows that he was capable of doing almost anything—residences, businesses, or courthouses. He apparently sought to free himself from the effort and responsibility required of a building contractor and was fairly successful as an architect for a time but faded from the scene in the mid-1880s.

A. G. Bauer had come to Raleigh with Samuel Sloan whose reputation had been established in North Carolina in the antebellum years. After Sloan's death Bauer established a practice, first as a draftsman. Only af-

Raleigh, N. C. Baptist University for Women.

Baptist Female University (now demolished), Raleigh, 1895–99, A. G. Bauer, architect. (North Carolina Division of Archives and History.)

ter he was better established did he call himself an architect. From the mid-1880s to the mid-1890s Bauer executed a number of large and small commissions—houses, cottages, and college, private, and public school buildings—in and around Raleigh. His flamboyant, irregular, towered, turreted, and shingled works decorated Raleigh from Capital Square to the north and south. The buildings were almost as dramatic as his life, which ended in suicide following a period of deep depression after an injury sustained on a visit to Durham.[77]

In practical terms Bauer was extremely direct, capable, and business-like. He developed working relationships with clients to produce designs that were real rather than ideal. He prepared drawings and specifications and ordered building components for doors, windows, mantels, wood-work, hardware, and other practical and decorative elements for his build-ings from catalogs. His reports to the City Council of Raleigh regarding the destruction of the old governor's mansion and the building of the Centennial School show that he was a careful, thrifty, and effective super-visor. His depression was caused in part by his belief that following his accident he was no longer capable of being a reliable practitioner.

All architects, whether at a distance or local, began work with the knowledge that they had responsibilities to the client. The design was governed by the client's budget. Once it was worked out to the satisfaction of the client, the building documents had to be produced. Drawings and specifications might be required for the purpose of borrowing money and were certainly required by the contractor for bidding, materials assembly, and scheduling.

Once bids were tendered and the contract was awarded, it was not unusual for architects to use the standard contract between client and builder in which the architect acted as the client's agent and job supervisor. The contract spelled out methods of payment, fees, rules for arbitration, and liabilities. The architect was responsible for certifying phases of construction that determined when payments were made to the contractor and might also be a disbursing agent. He was always responsible for staying within the budget, although the client and the contractor often caused cost overruns. The architect might see his plans sacrificed to budget demands if costs rose or materials had to be substituted. These documents usually did not spell out the method of payment for the architect, which from midcentury on was established as a percentage of the cost of the project. An architect usually charged 5 percent, but often negotiated to 3 percent or less. Architects' frequent complaints that they were underpaid were often well founded.

Even though contracts, like bids and budgets, drawings and specifications, supervision and certification, were means to establish controls in the building process, building was still often difficult, confusing, and chaotic. The building site, dust-filled or muddy, contained stacks of lumber, bricks, and other materials piled around the periphery and many men moved from task to task. The supervisor himself worked and then went from person to person, reassigning and reordering jobs. Bursts of hammering and sawing were interrupted by groans of frustration. The architect arrived to inspect new work but the site supervisor could not be found. The work had been done wrong and must be corrected before work could continue. The architect spent hours and sometimes days traveling from site to site. It is no wonder that the death at age 42 of Baltimore architect Charles Carson, who designed, North Carolina College of Agriculture and Mechanic Arts' first building, Holladay Hall, in 1891, was attributed to his heavy workload.[78]

It is critical to remember that the entire building process could be completely unmanageable and events could become out of control of the architect, contractor, or site workers. The inquiry into the 1891 collapse of the tower of the new Washington Duke Building at Trinity College in Durham illustrates how difficult and illusive control of the process could become. The building was designed in a Romanesque style by Samuel Leary who claimed to be an architect trained in Philadelphia. The building contractor, C. H. Norton, was thought to be very reputable. After the tower collapse, Trinity College president John F. Crowell and his building committee sought to determine what had caused the collapse and who

Washington Duke Building, Trinity College, Durham, 1890, Samuel Leary, architect, C. H. Norton, general contractor. The building was subsequently destroyed by fire and demolished 1911–12. (Photo, Duke University Archives.)

was responsible. They asked Albert L. West, a Richmond architect, to arbitrate and determine liability.

West's letter to Crowell lists three major causes of the collapse of the tower: the use of improper sand for mortar, improper methods of erection, and improper conditions for construction. West summarized by saying that it was difficult to place blame for the failure on any one person. He suggested that "whether you retain your present architect and your present contractor or not, you should by all means, employ a competent practical and reliable man to stay at the building and see that proper materials are used and that the work is properly done."[79]

West's advice exemplified the desire of every client, architect, and contractor to have a reliable person in charge at the site. Distance was not a factor in the Trinity project but proximity had not prevented the failure. The problem had resulted from inadequate control over the infinite variety of variables that are part of the building process.

The architect had now joined the contractor as a consumer of both materials and labor. Subcontractors, like varieties of brick or lumber, had to be chosen well. What product, what subcontractor was the best? What if the client wanted to use McClamrock's tiles or Snow's lumber and sash and blinds but they were out of date, expensive, or seldom delivered on time? What if the plasterer with the highest bid was the best but sometimes slow, and the low bidder met the client's budget but was unlikely to complete the work? The architect now realized that obtaining the best materials and the most skilled people as well as good planning and scheduling were as essential to his role in the building process as producing good building designs, drawings, and specifications.

"I Am Lacking . . . Rules"

Status in the building trades in antebellum North Carolina was based on skill and success. At the very top were architects, engineers, and other experts, followed by builders like Jacob Holt and Dabney Cosby, who could design and undertake substantial contracts. Highly skilled artisans —stonecutters, joiners, and brickmasons—and skilled carpenters and interior specialists came next, then the semiskilled and the unskilled workers. This hierarchy was neither precise nor absolute, however, since a man's local reputation and his connections with other people in the immediate vicinity were sometimes as important as his skill.

The position of those involved in the building trades within North Carolina's social hierarchy was ambiguous. Since the state's antebellum class structure based on landownership was essentially unchanged by the war, status was not granted to landless artisans, no matter how skilled. Status, however, might be achieved by education or wealth or by hard work, personal integrity, and association with people who had rank and position. William J. Hicks, who was involved in a succession of state building projects, was awarded the honorary title of "Colonel" by the "popular will" for his exemplary performance. Although his later financial success in the building business was important, it was his character that commended him to his fellows. It appears that Hicks's popularity was the result of his successful adaptation to the widespread changes in the building trades and the way in which he embodied traditional southern masculine values.[80] Nevertheless it was not common for men like Hicks without family, wealth, land, or reputation to achieve positions that could provide access to power.

Adaptation to changes in the building industry was very difficult since it never reached stasis. As the number of highly skilled and knowledgeable artisans declined, the contractor and his crew had to know more. There was more to know about materials and application procedures. There was more to read as the trades came to rely heavily on words—in bids, contracts, specifications, instructions on the use of materials, and advertisements. However, public education by 1900 was only beginning to make inroads into the widespread illiteracy of the state's people.

The apprentice system was also essentially discontinued. It was no longer possible to draw apprentices from the slave class, and there were few attempts to develop apprenticeships between whites and freed blacks. The new all-white state technical and mechanical college would not fill the need for skilled labor nor would the black colleges. The informal system that had always provided basic access to the skilled trades and to contracting now became the primary means of training. A young man who came from a family of builders would work as a journeyman until he felt ready to undertake work and supervise a crew himself. Then successful entry became a matter of selection of place and timing, as well as a matter of race since trades stayed within families.

The feelings of distrust of management and discontent that were common among workers in society were also common among laborers who were dependent on the building business. Pay was low and hours long. The duration of jobs was unpredictable. Strikes for better wages and attempts at forming workingmen and mechanics' organizations met with varying success. In 1873 black and white mechanics and laborers in Raleigh went on strike to procure a ten-hour day instead of the all-day— dawn to dusk—system and were successful. The next year in the northeast, mechanics agitated for an eight-hour day, but opponents in North Carolina argued that since machines made the ten-hour day acceptable, there was no need for further action in this state.[81]

Between 1868 and 1899, lien laws were sporadically written, amended, and expanded for the protection of mechanics and laborers. By 1899 protection that had once extended only to architects, contractors, and subcontractors was available to mechanics and laborers, provided they could submit an itemized statement of the amounts owed them for a job to the owner or his agents. This ensured that the owner or agent would withhold from the money due the contractor sufficient funds to pay whoever submitted bills. In short, the law permitted direct billing although in practice it did not always work. One newspaper lamented the condition of workmen: "The present plan of building in Wilmington by the cheap contractors is to take the building of houses to any price, making their living out of the workmen and laborers . . . (who they pay piecemeal) . . . Workmen! . . . You cannot go home to your dear ones when you know you cannot comfort them with messages of life. And yet you will find men who boast of how cheaply they can have their houses built."[82]

The amount of success that laborers, mechanics, and workingmen had in their attempts to organize was limited by the society in which they lived. North Carolina's powerful white gentry always interpreted attempts by workers to advance their positions as a threat to the social order. People could belong to churches but not to unions. However, the feelings of unrest were not confined to mechanics and laborers but were also experienced by the contractors and architects for whom they worked.[83]

In 1890 Charles Hartge, an architect, builder, building superintendent, and supply dealer in Tarboro, wrote J. W. Root, Chicago architect and then secretary of the American Institute of Architects:

> 1st what are the proper charges for getting up a set of plans? . . . what percent should be charged. . . . Maybe you have some printed price list, which is used by the profession. . . . I want to be paid for my work . . . as the northern and western architects are. . . .
>
> In short I would like to have something authoritative, besides my own say so, to show, what such work is worth. . . .
>
> How many plans or drawings are required to make the set ordinarily complete. Does the architect charge for his time if he must go to the site and lay off work in full size? My understanding of the business always has been that it was the architect's business to give the different sizes of materials in specifications and section drawings and the contractor or builder figures out the bill of lumber. Is the architect compelled to give a full size section through the cornice?
>
> *Now what I am lacking is some system of Rules to be governed by, that I can show and that comes from headquarters as that is what the American Institute of Architects seems to be to the profession.*[84]

Hartge's plea for rules and standards might have been written by any sensible person in the building industry at that time. The traditional ways of doing things and reliance on an implicit order and shared expectations were becoming less and less viable. Material success was no longer founded on skill, it appeared, but on money, and money was available to some people but not to others. Money too often was a consequence of reputation, age, or community status rather than success on current projects. The growing, bustling, competitive building industry that had contributed so much to the recovery of the state's financial well-being and independence had also created an economy in which architects, developers, contractors, and their crews had to compete for jobs and thus for a living.

The erosion of traditional roles combined with the competition engendered by the consumer-oriented building industry to encourage the desire for clearer social identity and position among builders and architects. A means to achieve that clarity was to organize.[85] In North Carolina, architects, contractors, and a few artisans could be members of the many different racially segregated Masonic lodges. They might also belong to church groups and civic organizations, but these provided no particular work identity.[86] Between 1865 and 1900 building contractors and building specialists began to organize, but the most visible traces of a movement toward a "professional" identity has been left by the architects.

Our understanding of the appeal of becoming known as an architect in postwar North Carolina relies on inferential presumptive evidence. No one kept a diary or wrote an account that explained why he wanted to be an architect, yet some people clearly did seek this designation. Various kinds of experience, both academic and practical, led people to call themselves architects. A few of them also sought association with a professional organization.

The American Institute of Architects (AIA), created in New York in 1857, was the logical organization to approach. Its goals of professional improvement through education, fee standardization, and the propagation of a code of ethics had gained mixed success.[87] In the 1890s the AIA attempted to recruit members in the South and a southern chapter was incorporated in Atlanta. No North Carolinians, however, were among its members. By 1894 its secretary, William P. Tinsley of Lynchburg, Virginia, indicated that there was much difficulty associated with creating an effective association over such long distances, and he doubted that this chapter would endure.[88]

Distance was not the only problem in the South. In 1896, John Carrere of Carrere and Hastings, a well-known New York firm, reported to the New York chapter about the dire situation in the "hinterlands and border states," and he chided the New York chapter for being moribund and setting a poor example. The New York chapter, he said, should be the largest and most up-to-date and set an example for others by the quality of their work and their professional standards. But, he said, there was much professional jealousy and competition in New York City. These same problems, he speculated, might be compounded by distance and poor communication between architects in widely separated cities and states.[89] He was right. Edmund G. Lind wrote from Baltimore in 1897 that the southern chapter's failure may have been caused by the AIA fee schedule which forced architects to eliminate fee competition. Architect Thomas Morgan of Bruce and Morgan in Atlanta, who did work in North Carolina, reviewed the situation two years later: "It is very difficult to work up an interest among the best men when they see that the administration of the Institute practic[ally] ignores the South. In fact they have no acquaintance among the architects generally in the south—do very little work and have no influence." Morgan added that the board had no southern members and the most important committees included no southern architects. The institute, he wrote, regarded the southern chapter "about as I would a chapter in Alaska."[90] The South was remote except to Glenn Brown, then national secretary. In 1899 he wrote to Morgan: "I myself am a southern man, having been born in Virginia. My early life was spent in North Carolina: all my people are southerners and I therefore take a special interest in the south." Over the next fifteen years Brown would work to change the situation.[91]

Certainly North Carolina was not ready for such an organization. F. K. Thomson of Raleigh wrote to Brown in 1899, inquiring about joining the AIA. Brown responded, "Looking over the list of members of the AIA there seems to be none residing in N.C. If you have any friends or acquaintances in the North who would endorse your application I would like very much to commence some members from the Old North State." Thomson replied that there were not any men in Raleigh who would "be eligible."[92]

There were, however, definite drawbacks to joining the AIA. Architects could not charge the 5 percent fee established by the AIA and still hope to get work in the state. Three percent was the norm and in some cases, such as municipal commissions, even less.[93] This was a competitive and difficult business. Although fee schedules and a code of ethics were essential to the profession, they would not work unless everyone adhered to them. In North Carolina there was nothing to encourage such a sacrifice. Personal desires for a professional organization required the addition of external pressures for architects and contractors to seek validation through organization. Those pressures would be provided in the new century by state involvement in building through licensing regulation based on the "health, safety and welfare" clauses of the state's constitution.

Conclusion

By 1900 North Carolina's appearance was radically different from that of April 1865. The state's economy and institutions had recovered from the war and had survived a series of economic reversals including the panic of 1873 and the agricultural depression of 1893. New and old cities had burst boundaries and the first waves of suburbia stood where plantations once nestled close to the towns. In the east, Wilmington and Fayetteville assumed preeminence. Among piedmont towns, Durham, Greensboro, and Winston-Salem had competed successfully with Virginia tobacco markets to acquire new and seemingly endless sources of wealth. Many new smaller textile towns were thriving along the railway lines that connected east to west and north to south. Charlotte straddled the road to the Deep South; Asheville, the gateway to the Far West, had become a famous, beautiful resort. Every city, town, and hamlet was filled with a spirit of pride, bustling energy, and success.

Growth in manufacturing and industry was the source for much of this energy. Textiles, tobacco, railroads, and the building industry flourished. Town almanacs, guides, and brochures carried advertisements of, or references to, prominent contractors, plumbers, electricians, and other new specialists who manufactured building materials. Some cities could even boast of an architect or two. Contractors and architects sought to make their own reputations on which they could build success and fortune. But many mechanics had suffered reduced wages and expectations. The artisan skilled in woodworking became a mere assembler of parts. The disappearance of apprenticeships and the glut of cheap, unskilled, or semiskilled labor created a buyer's market for the contractor who wanted to engage in speculative as well as specialized building for greater and greater profits. Role identification became increasingly important as these diversifying groups of people sought work, status, and position.

The actual physical alternatives for building forms and materials were multiplied by the use of manufactured components, transportation improvements, and reduced costs. An ever-expanding variety of ornaments and building supplies became available and affordable to many classes of clients, not just to the wealthy. Pre-cast plaster ornaments, milled tongue-and-groove ceilings, and wainscots replaced handmade and hand-carved plaster and wood decoration. Pressed brick and cast iron replaced wood, plain brick, and wrought iron, and so on in an infinite number of eccentric, eclectic varieties.

The expansion of the market met with a contraction of the roles and the amount of control held by people involved in the building process. The traditional, self-sufficient builder, the contractor, and the professional lost control of building component production to the manufacturer, the broker, and the shipper. Yet these changes made building possible on an increased scale, with greater speed of erection at reduced cost. The success of speculative building in North Carolina signaled a new era for everyone, but especially for the contractor. At the same time, the growth of specialized building types as well as the desire for the progressive and modern pointed another way to the future, which relied on the use of the architect.

North Carolina's largely rural population, however, remained half a century away from the urban prosperity that had brought the architect and the contractor success. In the rural landscape, building practice changed little, emphasizing the isolation and independence that had encouraged self-sufficiency in the first place.

The image of the independent builder in control of his project and shaping it to his needs with his tools and the help of an artisan friend contrasts sharply with the image of the architect or contractor dependent on a large, complex, and fragmented commercial world. The human desire to remain in control did not change when the architect or builder moved to town. North Carolina between 1900 and 1945 provided many locations and opportunities for the architect and contractor as both tried to consolidate, expand, and gain control of building projects within the growing state.

Charlotte V. Brown

6

The Day of the Great Cities: The Professionalization of Building, 1900–1945

Agriculture has given place to manufacture as the primary interest of North Carolina. A machine-made civilization is conditioning and supplanting the oldtime homespun, hand-made civilization of the state. The day of the great cities is at hand, and the fullness of their greatness in the coming years does not yet appear.

—E. C. Branson, News Letter 7:13, *Department of Rural Social Economics, University of North Carolina*

Introduction

THE BUILDING INDUSTRY in late-nineteenth-century North Carolina produced an architectural fabric that satisfied many needs, including self-aggrandizement and the lessening of housing shortages. The organization of the building trades that had developed to meet those needs continued apace after the turn of the century as cities, fortunes, and ambitions continued to grow. Even the countryside experienced some refurbishing as prosperity increased after the agricultural depressions of the 1880s and 1890s.

Prosperity meant that architects and builders had more opportunity to try to understand and control the building process as it was transformed by industrialization. The development of construction companies and professionalization through education and licensing marked these years with a progressive stamp. Design took two major directions as both the architect and the builder attempted to meet the needs of the conservative capitalists and urban dwellers who swelled the population and the gross national product in a society that remained conservative politically and socially.

The Day of the Cities

The individualism and independence of rural North Carolina society were not eliminated by mechanization, and divisions continued to characterize society—urban and rural, black and white, rich and poor, middle and lower classes. All were driven by first one political faction then another, as

Democrats and Republicans tried to gain control of the state's government. In the fall of 1900, Charles B. Aycock was elected as governor, and the progressive faction of the Democratic party won a great victory. Aycock had promised black disenfranchisement and universal free education for blacks and whites.[1]

Aycock's election also represented a success of the doctrine of white supremacy and he enacted Jim Crow legislation that further hardened the state's social divisions, giving the successful white Democrats a position to be maintained at all costs. The factional compromises that provided party unity that both were built on and disguised great human inequities, regional differences, and the bitter politics of racial segregation lasted for decades. This unity survived World War I and the Great Depression and was supported by the industries which had come into being after 1870.[2]

In the state's towns and cities, the energetic urban boosterism of the preceding decades continued to motivate the building industry through financial speculation, investment, and profit taking. The profits from the sales of building components and buildings also promoted the growth of the North Carolina of the New South.

The disparity among different areas of the economy also continued after 1900. Change was extremely slow to penetrate the agricultural way of life. Farm size decreased as the number of farms increased. The increase in the number of small farms meant increase in tenancy and a decrease in the value of the individual farm and its capacity to produce a cash crop.[3] E. C. Branson, a noted North Carolina rural economist, wrote in the 1920s: "Living from hand-to-mouth as most of our farmers live—both tenants and operating owners—the problems of farming as a business are well-nigh insolvable. They cannot or will not act together. . . . Furthermore, in the lonely life of isolated farms, there is developed an economic and social inertia that is stubbornly resistant to change of any sort."[4]

Resistance to changes in agricultural practices was exacerbated by racial issues. The deep hatred many poor whites felt for blacks was derived from their mutual poverty and their fear of losing their only social advantage, which was granted by the color of their skin. This deep prejudice prevented cooperation that might have helped bring about change. These conditions persisted during the Great Depression and afterward. The farm economy did not experience growth at the same rate as manufacturing, finance, building, or trade until the 1950s. The rural migration begun in the late nineteenth century continued to contribute to the growth of towns and cities.[5]

Therein lies the story of building during this period. Between 1900 and 1950, North Carolina society achieved a level of population and potential prosperity at which the building industry survived and generally prospered. The continued growth of cities, like Asheville from a population of 40,000 in 1900 to 90,000 by 1929, produced booms in the construc-

"Greetings from Charlotte, Queen City of the South," booster postcard, Charlotte, before 1930. (Charlotte-Mecklenburg Historic Properties Commission.)

tion of schools and commercial and residential buildings. Every major city added two, three, or four new suburbs between 1900 and 1940 and populations doubled or tripled. Municipal services, like public and corporate finances, were strained, contributing to the economic chaos that created the Great Depression. When the depression hit North Carolina, the results were resounding. In Greensboro, for example, the value of building permits declined 95 percent in a three-year period. Individual architects and contractors suffered, going without work, temporarily changing jobs, or even leaving the state, but just as farming never ceased, neither did building, even during the bleakest years of the Great Depression. Since building in all its facets was an integral part of society, investors, contractors, and architects were able to ride out the hard times. They survived in many different ways but they never ceased to consider the building industry as their major source of livelihood. Those who persisted through these years obtained the benefits of respect, modest wealth, and occasionally political power.

Unlike the farmer who lived in a seemingly immutable landscape, the North Carolina architect, general contractor, and components manufacturer usually lived in ever-changing towns and cities. This location with its access to money, position, and information encouraged change and growth, adaptation and adjustment.

The early-nineteenth-century builder in North Carolina had worked within the same environment as the farmer, but by 1900 this was no longer possible. The essentially urban activity of building that employs substan-

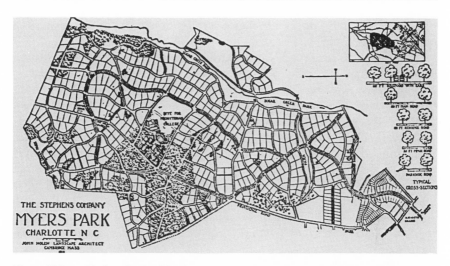

THE STEPHENS COMPANY
MYERS PARK
CHARLOTTE N C
JOHN NOLEN LANDSCAPE ARCHITECT
CAMBRIDGE MASS

Plan of Myers Park suburb, Charlotte, 1911, John Nolan, landscape architect, The Stephens Company, developers. Nolan established a standard with Myers Park that was emulated throughout the state. (Charlotte-Mecklenburg Historic Properties Commission.)

tial amounts of men and materials had finally come to North Carolina as it had previously to Georgian London or early-nineteenth-century New York City. While architects and builders gave up a certain amount of independence and control of their lives and jobs, they also assimilated the changes brought on by the industrialization of the building process into a way of working that could take advantage of the progress and prosperity the new economy and society seemed to offer.

The forty-year hegemony of conservative, white North Carolinians was a very rich period for building in spite of the vagaries of the economy. For the first time in the history of building in the state, projects were undertaken that involved erecting many buildings at once or in sequence. New building types also brought use of new materials. The state embarked on a substantial collegiate and public school building program, and, in every town and city, hospitals, churches, and commercial buildings were required. The people who commissioned these projects, like North Carolinians of the past, understood the symbolic function of buildings and the importance of appearances.

This need for building and desire for development provided local contractors and architects with opportunities and challenges that encouraged new ways to organize and control the building process. Entry into the fields of building design and construction became an area of special concern, and the state joined with architects and contractors to direct and control this process through education and licensing. By the advent of World War II, architects and general contractors were ready and able to undertake any kind of project that might be demanded by a society in a state of emergency.

World War II reshaped North Carolina, as well as affecting every other aspect of American society. The paternalism, provincialism, smugness, and insularity that characterized the secure and prosperous white American society of Sinclair Lewis's *Babbitt* had existed in North Carolina also. Through the years of World War I, the Great Depression, and the 1940s, poverty, ignorance, and racism ruled the lives of many blacks and whites, rural and urban Americans, and farm and mill workers. Political power and legal control remained in the hands of the wealthy—whether former landed gentry or the newly rich industrialists—who hired the architects and general contractors to create a fabric of building that was consonant with their values. However, the 1950s brought new attitudes, ideas, money, and people to challenge the purpose and appearance of the architecture of these years.

Buildings: Fit and Harmonious

In 1923 the nearly one-hundred-year-old state Capitol in Raleigh was cleaned and its much-used interior renovated. The building was still one of the state's most revered structures, and the newspapers followed the work closely. A *Raleigh Times* writer described the austere Greek-revival building as one "which neither Reconstruction could tear down nor populism infect."[6] The Capitol was an intact symbol of the antebellum years; it also exemplified the architectural values of the first half of the twentieth century. When Raleigh commissioned its War Memorial Auditorium in 1931, it was to be a "building of the same style of architecture as the State Capitol."[7]

The desire for buildings that used the classical vocabulary started before the turn of the century when people became newly aware of "colonial" architecture. Sketches of Tryon Palace were published in the *Manufacturers' Record* with the suggestion that it be replicated as North Carolina's pavilion at the 1893 World's Columbian Exposition because it was a "fine type of Colonial Architecture," but funds were not available for such an undertaking.[8]

By 1910 many towns and cities had built or were building a largely conservative architectural fabric that expressed the preferences and politics of white North Carolinians. There were no hard-and-fast rules—buildings could be progressive, functional, or modern. Where appropriate they might also be neoclassical, colonial, or Georgian. In the towns and small cities from the coastal plain west to Asheville, the "city-like" architecture that had been built between 1865 and 1900 was sometimes replaced by, but sometimes became the heart of, a collection of new larger and taller build-

War Memorial Auditorium, Raleigh, 1933, Atwood and Weeks, architects. (Photo, North Carolina Division of Archives and History.)

ings built between 1900 and 1945. "Hometown Illustrated" brochures and "Epitomes" published by the chambers of commerce of cities for self-promotion illustrate the cityscape—streets crisscrossed with wires and filled with horses and buggies (later cars and trucks), new buildings, neighborhoods, and parks, all of which were presented as "concrete" evidence of progress, material prosperity, and community stability.[9]

Two building types in particular were popular and could be built in any style. The first was the modern, efficient, and functional commercial building. The straightforward commercial loft with its large plate-glass windows or the simple office building with cast-iron columns between the windows and below the flat molded architrave were logical and important parts of the commercial landscape. Plain, fire-resistant, and self-effacing, standing side by side along the streets, they filled the city blocks with substance.[10]

The second was the skyscraper, which architects could design with more panache and imagination. Beginning with the seven-story Masonic Temple Building designed by Charles McMillan erected in Raleigh in 1907 and culminating with the elegant R. J. Reynolds Building in Winston-Salem, designed by New York architects Shreve and Lamb and dedicated in 1929, clients and contractors who loved the idea of the skyscraper adopted steel and concrete. Many of these buildings rose from neoclassical roots, but many, like Charles Hartmann's Jefferson Standard Life Insurance Company Building in Greensboro, combined elements of classicism with the nationally popular art deco.[11] When building resumed after the depression, another series of tall buildings based on the Shreve and

View of 100 block of East Fayetteville Street, Raleigh, 1914. The seven-story Masonic Temple Building is in the left foreground; two other "skyscrapers" are further down the street to the left. (Albert Barden Collection, photo, North Carolina Division of Archives and History.)

Lamb model appeared. The last of these, the Durham Life Insurance Company Building in Raleigh, completed in 1942, was the state's first fully air-conditioned office building.[12]

The tall office building was free to take any stylistic form that the designer gave it. Its symbolic importance as a sign of progress, permanence, and prosperity was immeasurable. Richard Spillane, a writer in the 1920s for *Commerce and Finance*, a regional booster publication, noted: "The people are proud, very proud of the great new skyscraper that towers over every other structure the whole country over." Every city wanted one, he claimed, even if it did not know what to do with it.[13]

Thus the skyscraper and the commercial building were acceptable in almost any form, but some buildings in the cityscape were required to be more than simply functional and modern. The editor of the *Wilmington Messenger* explained:

> Wilmington has some large handsome buildings. It has one
> building of fine architectural beauty that deserved special commend-
> ing. It is the city hall and opera building [Thalian Hall, built in 1858].
> . . . We judge that any one with an educated taste in architecture

Jefferson Standard Life Insurance Company Building under construction, Greensboro, 1922, Charles C. Hartmann, architect, George A. Fuller Construction Company, Washington. (Photo, courtesy Jefferson Pilot Life Insurance Company, Greensboro.)

must be impressed with the purity, simplicity and effectiveness of the massive structure . . . [whose] noble portico . . . is the most superb . . . in all North Carolina, excepting the east and west porticos of the state capitol in Raleigh. If it has a superior in North Carolina we have not heard of it. It outrivals all its fellows in this little city. It eclipses our new, costly, handsome, variegated courthouse, [built in 1884] and surpasses even the much admired new postoffice.[14]

The Wilmington writer's taste for the architecture of classicism was shared by many, locally and nationally. North Carolina and the South were not immune to the images and ideas propagated by the World's Columbian Exposition and the "City Beautiful" movement. This popular architectural style was of particular local interest because it was the style of the glorified past and eclipsed the buildings of more immediate memories.

In 1907 the taste for neoclassicism in Raleigh was explained as a natural consequence of the evolution of society. In the *News and Observer* special edition published in celebration of its new columned and porticoed fireproof building, an article called "A People Known by What They Build" explained that communities go through cyclical stages of architectural development. The first is one in which sheer necessity produces make-shift and cheap buildings. The second is a period of youthful exuberance and callowness that produces the atrocious and pretentious structure: "A grocery will boast a tower, a cottage goes upon a debauch with a frieze over its porch; a chapel aspires to be a cathedral and stops with a spire." The third phase is one of stability and confidence in which experience leads to the construction of fit, harmonious architecture. The frightful is pulled down and replaced by the appropriate. Two antebellum buildings in Raleigh exemplified the fit and harmonious: the Capitol (1833–40) and Christ Church (1856–60). The writer considered 1865 to 1900 to be the second phase of social and architectural development. By 1907 Raleigh was ready to enter a new third phase and to build buildings of grace and harmony in what the writer called a "Grecian style." Nationally it was called neoclassicism.

In addition to explicit praise for those "two early [antebellum] tri-umphs of city," the writer also noted with approval the neoclassical Eliza Pittman Battle Chapel at St. Mary's College, which he described as "hand-some . . . of permanent construction, tastefully designed," Peace Insti-tute's "colonial" design dormitory, and the neoclassical seven-story Ma-sonic Temple Building.[15]

As the years passed, numerous other buildings throughout the state, including skyscrapers, hotels, banks, churches, and office buildings, ap-peared with columns, architraves, and entablatures, but buildings of civic importance were almost always neoclassical. Perhaps the only major ex-ception was found in Asheville, the resort city that was a railroad and shipping hub and was, in fact, one of the state's most architecturally sophisticated and progressive communities. Architect Douglas Ellington, who was trained at the Ecole des Beaux Arts, designed a stunning art deco City Hall (1926–28) using the mountains and the native Indians as sources for his art deco motifs. Located at the end of Pack Square, it was soon joined by Frank Milburn's seventeen-story county courthouse, a typical temple on base. The county commissioners were too conservative to hire Ellington.[16]

County Courthouse (at left), 1930, Frank P. Milburn, architect; City Hall (at right), 1928, Douglas D. Ellington, architect; Asheville. (Photo, North Carolina Division of Archives and History.)

The growing hold of the "colonial" or neoclassical on the South was demonstrated in the building projects at the state's three major institutions of higher learning. In 1919 the University of North Carolina's consultant for long-range planning, Aberthaw of Atlanta, recommended a red-brick and white-trimmed "colonial" campus and McKim, Mead, and White of New York were hired to design it.[17] The appearance of the university buildings constructed during the subsequent ten-year campaign eventually dominated civic design in Chapel Hill, the site of the university. In the 1940s the village mandated conformity to the scale and details of the "colonial" campus.[18] At State College in Raleigh, New York architect Hobart Upjohn provided fine neoclassical buildings during the 1920s and 1930s.[19] Duke University, the private school built by tobacco money, hired Horace Trumbauer of Philadelphia to design its men's campus in English collegiate Gothic, but its women's campus was an adaptation of Jefferson's Lawn at the University of Virginia.[20]

Thus the state's urban landscape was filled with buildings that were permanent, stable, ordered, harmonious, up-to-date, modern, progressive, proud, and beautiful. Constructed of modern materials and filled with modern conveniences, these buildings boosted local self-confidence, created pride, and attested to economic health. Almost every city had stylish art deco buildings beside neoclassical ones, but those which repre-

Union and Dormitory buildings, Duke University, Durham, 1924, Horace Trumbauer, architect. (Photo, North Carolina Division of Archives and History.)

sented civic and Christian virtues were most likely to be columned, porticoed, and pedimented.

The men who built the cities and towns also shaped the suburbs. Post–Civil War eclecticism was exchanged for the heritage of the colonial and antebellum years in residential building. As Charlotte architect C. C. Hook explained, "colonial architecture" was "the most appropriate form for domestic building in the state."[21]

Between November 1903 and January 1904, Hook's architectural firm presented five "colonial" designs for houses in the *Charlotte Observer*. Hook's technique was a well-established practice that many architects and builders had used since the middle of the nineteenth century. Printed "souvenirs" or house-plan books became a method of advertising to gain new clients.[22] Hook showed four designs for single-family dwellings. The fifth was a duplex. Lot size, cost, materials, and the convenience of each particular plan was described. The text that accompanied the plans also noted that the discerning reader/potential client would be sympathetic to the designs because of the past sentiment and associations of the style. To make certain that the reader understood the connection with the past, however, Hook combined the fourth design with a history lesson that discussed residential architecture since the founding of the Republic.

In antebellum days, Hook wrote, a house of any pretension was built by a designer who was also an educated gentleman, familiar with the classics, and who relied on other colonial work for models. Following the war and "things being reversed in general we find a greater reversal in architecture . . . [because] the illiterate and unrefined, being new to wealth, desired display more than purity." The old "cultured"—whether gentleman, architect, or builder—were too busy or too poor to devote time to art. House design was turned over to "any jack-leg who could wield a hatchet." During the next twenty-five years, all colonial details and proportions were discarded as being "old-timey" and the jackleg carpenter with the voracious jigsaw "ran riot throughout the land." Even the Queen Anne, the French, and the Italian villas were brought to bad repute by the "jig-saw artist." Then he wrote:

Out of all this chaos we again have a revival of the colonial. Its symmetry, restfulness, and good proportions generally caused it to be superior to all other schools of design. Beyond doubt the colonial style in its purity expresses more real refined sentiment and is more intimately associated with our history than any of the styles mentioned, it is not only an association of English history with our own, but expresses authentic memoirs of the American people themselves.[23]

Hook avoided outright condemnation of any style but he did admit to a preference for the dignified colonial. Thus, house number four was to be of veneered brick with white quoins, portico, and an interior of white walls and imitation mahogany trim. It could be built for seven thousand dollars and it was. The symmetrical colonial box with a central entry portico and/or porch and other minor variations became a prominent suburban house type in the years before World War II.[24]

Hook, who claimed that "the Civil War marked the distinct change from good to bad architecture in the south," proposed an architecture whose sentiments are unmistakably clear—a white house with white columns based on English and colonial precedent was the architecture of the antebellum years and of a distinctive social orientation that had finally regained power and prestige. The people who espoused Hook's architectural views were those who based their wealth and power on white supremacy and the suppression of blacks, the poor, and laborers, regardless of color.[25]

Other architects across the state sold the same house types with similar techniques, as their advertising pamphlets, "souvenirs," and house-plan books show. More and more designers devoted attention to the "colonial" and then to Georgian revivals. The foursquare or rectilinear two-bay, two-story, double-pile house was popularized by publications like *Carpentry and Building*. It was eminently adaptable to either a "colonial" or a "Georgian" style. The essential differences between these two styles are academic and not significant in this context. When bungalowlike houses appeared, they too were colonialized as low-country cottages with Doric or Ionic porches or as "Dutch" colonial houses.[26]

Although it was not as significant as the form of these suburban houses, the incorporation of "modern" conveniences was also important. Such houses were built with the most convenient, modern, up-to-date materials, mechanical services, and systems and filled with the most streamlined and modern appliances available. Laundry rooms, large bathrooms, and sun and sleeping porches joined the living and dining rooms. The many Georgian revival houses designed in the 1920s and 1930s by Northup and O'Brien and Atwood and Weeks for upper and middle management at Reynolds and American Tobacco have these progressive features.[27] Along with the elevations of raised wall paneling and moldings

Cover of *Colonial Southern Homes*, Raleigh, ca. 1900, Charles W. Barrett, architect. (North Carolina Collection, University of North Carolina Library, Chapel Hill.)

L. S. Brassfield residence, Raleigh, before 1926, James A. Davidson, general contractor. It is instructive to compare this house with the photograph on the cover of *Colonial Southern Homes* in the preceding illustration. The Brassfield house perfectly exemplifies the correct Georgian revival mode that was in full flower in the 1920s and postdepression years. (James A. Davidson Scrapbook, photo, North Carolina Division of Archives and History.)

carefully copied from historic sites, there were detailed provisions for the most efficient types of heat, electrical service, plumbing, and ventilation. Since these homes were not cheap, they attracted the best building contractors who combined with the architect to build a house that was traditional in appearance and up-to-date in its construction techniques, materials, and systems. One architect expressed the design spirit of the times clearly: "If people thought they wanted a georgian house you designed a georgian house then fit in what they needed. You always had space here and there, which, if nothing else you could call a closet, but it made for a very good house."[28]

The development of the pre–World War II suburbs in North Carolina, like those of the 1880s and 1890s, was a consequence of complementary goals: the desire by many to own property, the desire of the white power structure to promote further racial and social segregation, and the desire of builders and land developers to make money. The realtors, lawyers, bankers, and merchants who controlled the development of industry and government also controlled the public services such as sidewalks, service alleys, parks, trolley lines, water, and sewer to the all-white suburbs they planned and sold. The new developments were usually located as near to the downtown as possible, with lots platted to ensure the most return on the dollar. Covenants in the deeds prevented the resale of these homes to blacks, and other covenants controlled the size and value of what was built on the property.[29]

The realtors, such as Hunter-Parker Realty Company which was responsible for Raleigh's Cameron Park suburb developed in 1914, published brochures that equated home ownership with white middle-class identification and traditional morality. A home provided a secure anchor and refuge from the difficulties of modern life and was the means to achieve social status, success, and confidence.[30] Although no two early-twentieth-century suburbs in the state are identical in plan, purpose, or realization, the architectural fabric of all the suburbs is frequently comparable, homogeneous, and, above all, architecturally conservative. The suburban neighborhoods convey a remarkable image of stability and propriety. The flashes of innovation, romanticism, or deliberate radicalism are so strikingly out of place that they confirm the intention of a majority of home owners to become a cohesive, unobtrusive part of a whole. The architectural writer for the Raleigh *News and Observer* might have been describing the desiderata of the entire state when he wrote in 1907 that "it is in the homes of Raleigh, however, that the significance of the building and architectural spirit may be best observed. . . . everywhere is a notable taste and an evident building for permanency. Whether the new houses be simple cottages or, as in many cases they are, real mansions, the note is the same, a regard for art with comfort. It is this that makes a city beautiful: that is a token, at once of its prosperity and its confidence."[31]

The suburb was a visible bastion of architectural conservativism in a politically and socially conservative society. The single-family dwelling that filled the suburbs between 1900 and 1940 contributed considerably to the appearance of every town and city and to the appearance of white prosperity. As the 1907 writer stated, it was the spirit of these homes that "makes a city beautiful." These houses meant a sound tax base, required city services, and supported schools and shops. But home ownership did not extend to a large segment of the population of any town or city. Boardinghouses, apartments, rental houses, and patterns of dwelling determined by racial segregation attest to this. Many extended families also shared one roof.[32]

During these years of urban growth, the same motives that encouraged racial segregation in the suburbs promoted it in downtown areas. Black businesses, formerly dispersed in the business districts or kept on the "ethnic" street, now clustered on a "black main street." These busi-

Drawing of V. O. Parker, partner in Hunter-Parker Realty Company, developers of Cameron Park suburb in Raleigh, begun 1914, from Adolph D. Goodwin, *Who's Who in Raleigh* (Raleigh, 1916). (North Carolina Division of Archives and History.)

Construction site, Lightner Arcade and Hotel (now demolished), Raleigh, 1921. This building was on East Hargett Street, the "black main street" of the city, two blocks east of Fayetteville Street, the main retail street. (Photo, North Carolina Division of Archives and History.)

nesses provided services that accommodated black shoppers and town visitors. In Raleigh, the Lightner Arcade and Hotel opened on East Hargett Street, where it joined the Merchants and Farmers Bank, a black movie theater, and various stores. In Durham, Pettigrew Street was the site of North Carolina Mutual Provident Association, for many years the largest black-owned insurance company in America. The buildings of the black main streets did not depart in style or materials from those erected on the white main streets of towns and cities.[33]

In this conservative building atmosphere, modernism was considered as appropriate only for commercial buildings. Architecturally modern could mean the use of conveniences, new materials, and methods just as it meant new and better ways to finance, organize, and maintain the building process. These were the factors that shaped building between 1900 and 1945.

The Practice of Building

Improved Handmade

Although the majority of building had taken place and would take place in the growing towns and cities, the society of North Carolina in 1900 was still essentially rural and agricultural. The fact that more building was done in the urban setting was a consequence of the concentration of wealth, population, and resources—both people and manufactured components. Continued improvement in the railroads and other transportation networks also served to preserve the market for buildings and materials. These factors, however, did affect the rural landscape as well. The difficulties associated with rural life in these years did not totally eliminate building from the small town and the farm. Therefore, in the first half of this century, the traditional building landscape also provided a setting in which change was especially visible. In this society with little disposable income, mass production and competition among purveyors of building components benefited many traditional and self-sufficient building projects.

The traditional self-sufficient builder was a person of some capacity and skill who relied on traditional solutions to building problems. Many living North Carolinians can still testify to this since they have the tools, knowledge, and experience required to frame up dwellings and outbuildings. The creation of a consumer market for building materials and components in the early twentieth century expanded basic skills and enlarged the construction repertoire by reducing the need for highly skilled artisans and some of the most labor-intensive work. For example, roofing shingles were replaced by tin roof sheeting, wood siding by tar paper, and brick chimneys by stovepipes. Publications, such as house-plan books, newspaper articles, and farm journals, also increased one's ability to build for oneself. The State College Agricultural Extension Service also provided information, plans, and specifications for some types of projects through its county agents. The self-sufficient project could be more self-sufficient than ever.[34]

The carpenter also maintained his presence, but the level of his skill depended on his location. When New York architect Aymar Embury II came to work in Pinehurst and its surrounding resort area in the southern piedmont, he found men whose carpentry skills were limited by circumstances.

> [The] Sand Hills, in 1911 . . . had long emerged from poverty and squalor but was still struggling hard to keep its head above water. . . . local labor could be depended upon to execute only the type of construction to which it was accustomed. Herein has been the architect's greatest handicap; good carpenters are rare; there are many who can frame well, can put on siding or shingle a roof, but when it

comes to anything outside the ordinary practice of the country careful and detailed personal explanation is necessary; even a box cornice presents difficulties to many of them. . . . The ignorance on the part of these mechanics of what seems to most of us ordinary good construction cannot be held against them. Because of the former poverty of the region all building was of the simplest and cheapest character. Until Mr. Embury began his work in the Sand Hills some contractors had never seen a blue print, or built from plans, and full sized details were unknown.[35]

Highly skilled carpenters simply were not available to work or to train apprentices in the Sandhills region, although they existed elsewhere in the state. The area could not support men with this level of ability, and even resort building used imported along with local labor.[36] Embury could hire only framing carpenters whose skills and experience were adequate to a simple house but not to a picturesque colonial mansion or country club.

The Cates Brothers' success demonstrated the fairly substantial capacity of builders who could use prefabricated components. By 1900 more farm families were able to build and the original family dwelling, perhaps a federal or antebellum house, was joined by a new larger colonial revival house, a comfortable I-house, or a large cottage. Whether in the countryside or town, these houses are a tribute to machined joinery, woodwork, and the local economy which could support a contractor who could help the farmer with his skilled labor.

The reduced costs of materials also encouraged building. According to the *Economic and Social History of Chowan County, North Carolina, 1880–1915*, written in 1917, "The two story dwelling is now all the fashion in rural sections. Almost without exception, every one in the rural districts who has put up a dwelling of more than two rooms within the past ten years has built it two stories. There seems to be a general feeling that a two story house gives a certain amount of prestige that is not conferred by a one-story house even though both cost the same."[37] Carpenters were needed to erect these houses that were symbols of the owner's personal ascendancy. Tenants and poor farmers always erected simple one-room, one- or one-and-a-half story houses.

The changes that made it possible for people to carry out a self-sufficient project also made it possible for the artisan-craftsman to retain a measure of independence and importance. In rural areas a plumber or electrician might also be a carpenter or a brickmason. One highly skilled brickmason, Edward Vestal, managed his rural Chatham County farm and commuted to Chapel Hill where he supervised construction of buildings for the T. C. Thompson Company at the University of North Carolina from 1921 until 1930. Vestal arrived on Monday morning, lived in the labor camp during the week, and went home on Friday. He then worked in the county as a mason.[38]

Changes in the building industry therefore enabled more people to have access to building components and buildings than ever before. The industry also permitted more people to live and work in surroundings that were considered modern and up-to-date, while it required fewer and fewer highly skilled artisans to be involved in the process of building.

The changes that affected artisans and self-sufficient building projects also intensified the separation between individuals involved in larger projects. The contractor no longer managed the production of components and the architect rarely was the manager of a contracting business. These changes were initially perceived as a positive consequence of industrialization and modernization. Because the changes fostered the growth of business, both the builder and the architect had more work and a greater potential for new status. However, in 1900 each was faced with alternatives in the practice of building in a market that neither could dominate. The course of these alternatives and the way in which architects, builders, and members of the trades attempted to use professionalization as a means to help gain control became important developments within the building process.

"His Personal Attention at All Times"

Sometime in the late nineteenth century, the term "general contractor" gained currency and began to replace the designation of "undertaker." The name change was significant in three respects. First, it underscored the increasingly broad range of construction projects undertaken—they were no longer just buildings, but roads, highways, lakes, reservoirs, dams, sewer systems, and parks. Second, the new label was inclusive, disguising specializations almost as they came into being. Third, it united the experienced builder with the entrepreneur who financed the construction of buildings but had never been a builder. Although capitalists were always necessary, before 1900 they were generally thought of as outside the actual building process. The shift from being a builder to supervising the building process as well as financing it probably did not occur in North Carolina firms until after the depression. When it did happen, some contractors became pure developers, leaving building to others entirely. On the other hand, some general contractors in 1900, 1925, or 1945 were little different from builders of the mid-nineteenth century whose reputations and identities were based on their shops, crews, and ability to coordinate work. A contractor might broker materials, build for speculation, and provide one client with a customized design, while working for another client on an architect-designed building.[39] There were large firms which erected a few major buildings each year and others that specialized in residential or commercial work. Eleven firms tendered bids for the construction of the Fayetteville Post Office in 1909—four were from Virginia, one each from South Carolina, Georgia, and Pennsylvania, and the remaining four from North Carolina, but not from Fayetteville. The contract went to Holladay and Crouse of Greensboro who encountered every difficulty once construction began—bad weather, labor shortages, and materials failure.[40] Problems like these, however, did not seem to deter contractors since there was always another job to be sought and a fresh start to be made.

Specialization within the building process was a result of the changes in North Carolina's population and economy. Typically firms that specialize are a response to the increased size of projects, the enlarged scope of services, and the amount of bonding required to bid on a project. By the turn of the century, out-of-state architects had been joined by several large out-of-state contractors who successfully bid on jobs and worked in the state. After 1900 there were local organizations of sufficient size to compete and the real differences between general contractors became a consequence of the size or the number of projects that they could or would undertake in a given period of time.

This issue of scale—amount of work—was not determined only by the firm's resources but was also directly related to the personal values of the general contractor and his determination to establish and maintain his control of the building process. Three firms that flourished between 1900 and 1945 illustrate how the principals responded to changes that occurred as a consequence of personal success and the success of the building industry.

Howard Satterfield of Raleigh was known primarily as a house builder. He had been a professor of mechanical engineering at State College until 1920 when he left at age 43 to run his own building firm. His house designs came from stock plans and pattern books which he personalized to suit the residential needs and desires of his clients. Sometimes alterations were superficial—wall surfaces, closets, paneling—and sometimes they were significant—stair substitutions, rearrangement of rooms, drastic changes in materials.[41]

Satterfield did not build for speculation. The approximately 150 houses and small buildings that have been identified as "Satterfield Built" ranged in cost from ten to fifty thousand dollars, twenty-five thousand dollars being the average price. Satterfield also did renovations and remodeling. His fee was usually 10 percent of the total cost of the project. His services, exclusive of design, were described in the building specifications: "The builder [Satterfield] agrees to give his personal attention at all times and his presence as often as necessary to properly carry on the work." Satterfield also agreed to obtain and pay for all required permits, to purchase materials, to pay workmen, and to carry liability insurance on

Howard Satterfield, general contractor, and his wife, Grace, Raleigh, ca. 1925. (Boynton Satterfield Scrapbook, photo, North Carolina Division of Archives and History.)

workmen at his own expense. Satterfield's other financial responsibilities were spelled out in the building proposal which he submitted to the client. It described the cost, fixed the manner of payment, and named the construction documents. Normally Satterfield received an advance of funds from the owner, which he kept in a separate bank account. Bills for materials and workmen were paid from that account. The owner received a weekly or monthly statement or was notified when another deposit was needed. The owner retained the final payment, usually a fixed percentage (10 percent) of the total cost, until the house was completed and he accepted it.[42]

Satterfield was both purchasing agent and construction manager. Although Boynton Satterfield claims that his father had his own workmen, the often incomplete records do not support that claim. Almost certainly he hired his own foreman and head bricklayer. He may have tried to retain the same teams of workmen to do footings, foundations, subflooring, fireplaces, and all interior and exterior finish carpentry, painting, papering, and hardware installation. He seems to have regularly subcontracted excavation, hauling, framing, lathing, plastering, floor finishing, concrete work, wiring, plumbing, heating, roofing, and millwork. Satterfield could keep crews constantly employed when more than one job was under construction at the same time by moving crews from job to job in the right order. For example, his exterior carpentry people might finish one job on Monday, go to a second job on Tuesday, and work there for four weeks until they were able to move on to a third job. If Satterfield maintained his own crews, he could not start up two jobs simultaneously in the same town unless he had two crews available or unless the two jobs were completely different and therefore required different types of crews. He could, however, have simultaneous starts in different towns if he hired local crews in each place. Satterfield, like Jacob Holt or the Fogle Brothers in previous eras, was limited by the size of his crew, distances between jobs, and job locations. Since he accepted work throughout eastern North Carolina, he could not expect the Raleigh crew to travel daily to Elizabeth City, Littleton, or Warrenton. Roads had been improved by the 1920s, but travel was still slow. Satterfield had to be a consummate field manager to keep five jobs going at once, and he averaged about fifteen jobs per year until 1930.

Any builder and his crew depended on the timely arrival and adequate quality of materials. Satterfield normally dealt with local suppliers whose stock he knew and who would special-order items for him. Nevertheless he was occasionally forced to use more distant sources. Among the local suppliers for the construction in 1925 of a house for George Little in Raleigh were Briggs Hardware—flue lining, nails, felt, cement, and supplies; North Carolina Hardware—lime, cement, nails, and plaster of Paris; the Raleigh Iron Company—coal shute and damper, angles, steel, lath, dump, and vents; Kramer Brothers—blinds; Isenhour and Yadkin companies—brick; and four or five other businesses for items like mortar color or acid to clean bricks, lathes, and stone. Tiles came from McClamrock's in Greensboro, five additional companies supplied light fixtures, and C. A. Nash and Son provided additional hardware.[43]

Satterfield's management of the building process was very personal and traditional. He seems to have enjoyed his clients and to have derived considerable pleasure from the building process. He tried to achieve a smooth flow of work at the site. When delays occurred because of materials suppliers, shippers, bad weather, or the vagaries of human nature, Satterfield felt confident that his clients would understand such problems. The level of trust and shared expectations was very high between Satterfield and his clients, as is borne out by parts of a poem that he submitted with the final bills on 1501 St. Mary's Street, Raleigh, a Georgian revival house built for Miss Nellie Battle:

> I am sending you this writing
> To declare that I have paid
> All the bills upon your mansion
> Both material and wage.
>
> .   .   .   .
>
> All these [bills] and many others
> I paid what was their due.
> And all the crafts were brothers
> In building this house for you.
>
> And all of us wish happiness
> To be your constant guest.
> And may we add this comment
> That we did for you our best?
>
> I declare upon my honor,
> And can back it up with proof
> That of debt there is none owing
> From its basement to its roof.[44]

When the depression came, Satterfield returned to his position at State College as a professor of engineering and worked for federal relief programs. He died in 1944.

The mutual trust and confidence between Satterfield and his clients also characterized the relationship between J. W. Coffey and his clients. Coffey, who in 1896 at the age of twenty-five came to Raleigh from Lenoir with his box of carpenter's tools, did some residential work but was primarily a contractor for commercial, industrial, and institutional buildings. He could and did work with architects, such as on the seven-story reinforced concrete and steel Masonic Temple Building, but he preferred to work directly with clients.[45]

Between 1900 and 1929, J. W. Coffey constructed a number of two-, three-, and four-story commercial buildings in Raleigh's downtown and in surrounding towns. Usually made of brick with plate-glass windows, loft or office space, and a built-up roof that sloped from front to back, these projects did not differ much in cost or execution from large residences. Building documents and financial arrangements were comparable to those used by Howard Satterfield. Coffey's son joined his father in 1929, and, when the building upturn came in the midthirties, the firm switched from commercial to residential work. The younger Coffey described the change as generally one of preference and logistics since it had become increasingly difficult to get reliable workers and foremen. In that period, the Coffeys produced some of the best houses in Raleigh's new suburbs like Budleigh and Anderson Heights. "Coffey Built" acquired the same high value that "Satterfield Built" had possessed in the 1920s.

When World War II ended, J. W. Coffey and Son, now second and third generation builders, continued to work as general contractors, building mostly residences, until the midfifties. In several recent interviews, Coffey family members implied that at this time a choice had to be made between enlarging the firm or getting out of the business. Enlarging the firm would have severely curtailed personal involvement in the building process and would have also required capitalization and reorganization of construction management. Since these circumstances would have radically changed the nature of the corporation, the Coffeys chose to retire from building.

James A. Davidson, a master carpenter who had emigrated from Scotland, began work in Raleigh about 1918. From the beginning of his career in Raleigh, Davidson had an almost legendary reputation as a good, honest, and fair general contractor. He claimed to prefer working on architect-designed projects but to be capable of undertaking almost anything which could be constructed from stock plans—whether for houses, churches, or schools.[46]

Davidson's method of work was essentially no different from Satterfield's in his early years. The only restriction on the amount of work Davidson would undertake during a season was time—he would not undertake more than he could personally supervise. The products of his firm in the years from 1919 to 1929 are a proud array of well-built homes like the S. B. Shepherd residence, churches like the First Christian Church (which is now demolished), and commercial buildings like Dworsky's Stores, all located in Raleigh.

Davidson weathered the depression by refurbishing foreclosed homes that were to be resold by the banks. During the late 1930s, he returned to the same kinds of commissions he had undertaken in the previous decade. The turning point in his history and the beginning of the transformation of Davidson's firm was in 1945 when Davidson became the partner of a young carpenter named Seby Jones who became an aggressive developer. In the post–World War II economy, risk-taking combined with careful investment soon produced the powerful regional firm—Davidson and Jones—whose profits derived from the investment of capital and expertise into designing, building, and selling shopping centers, hotels, motels, and speculative commercial buildings. Davidson ceased to work "in the field" in the 1950s. His role as an active general contractor who worked with clients, crews, and architects was transformed by age, experience, and success into that of the head of a company with hundreds of employees including architects and engineers.

The examples provided by these general contractors are instructive because each of them espoused three specific values which became inconsistent with his circumstances and each responded in a significant way. First, each of these contractors based his definition of success, as did the community, on the high quality of the workmanship in the buildings he built. Second, each attributed the high regard of the community and the high quality of his work to personal involvement in the building process through direct participation, supervision, and control. Finally, believing that quality could only be achieved by personal involvement in the building process, each carefully and personally defined his scope of work and the amount of work undertaken in a season.

As circumstances changed and the amount of work increased, each contractor learned that he would have to turn over control of the building site to foremen; the operations of purchasing and bookkeeping to agents and accountants; and the securing of permits and the arranging of contracts and insurance to persons experienced in these areas. All these people had to be paid in addition to the building crews and materials suppliers. The addition of administrative, legal, and purchasing departments to the building crews required careful planning and management. By increments, the actual building process itself, construction and site management, assumed the status of one phase in a much larger commercial enterprise.

By 1900 firm size was a measure of organizational capacity, financial stability, resources, supervisory personnel, and experience with large jobs. A general contractor with a "large firm" was able to be his own subcontractor for all aspects of a project—plumbing, heating, wiring, painting—or he used the same subcontractors so frequently that negotiations were minimized, needs were anticipated, supplies were delivered, and actual work was done when promised. Waiting for supplies, the most costly of building delays that maximized costs and losses, was decreased or eliminated altogether. Building could indeed be a big business and required an organizational structure not unlike that of any other big business where personal involvement in a project was a luxury. At the end of World War II when money and materials were again available for nonwarrelated projects, firms like Davidson and Jones were ready to play a leading role not only in building but in shaping the regional development of the state. Small firms like Satterfield's and Coffey's continued to practice on an individual "small" scale.

The general contractor who was in fact the head of a large, well-organized company for the management of building also worked in North Carolina in these years. Holladay and Crouse, Edward Dilworth Latta, and numerous other contractors had assembled the money and material to create large firms. Building by these firms provides a sharp contrast to the personal approach of men like Davidson or Coffey and the type of project they undertook. These large firms accepted commissions from institutions of higher learning—Duke, the University of North Carolina at Chapel Hill, and State College—as well as from the state of North Carolina and the federal Works Progress Administration during and following the depression. Each site provides many examples of the problems and complexities of the large project. There is little documentation, however, tracing these large projects and explaining the rationale for their implementation. Fortunately, we do have records of the project undertaken by the University of North Carolina in Chapel Hill to enlarge its campus in 1919. Because this project reveals as much about the practice of architecture on a large scale as it does about the business of general contracting, it will be discussed in more detail later in this chapter.

The Man in the Middle

By 1900 a building project that involved an architect had distinct stages: the client-architect relationship that produced a design, the work in the architect's office that produced the building documents, the negotiations between the architect and contractor, and finally, the contractual arrangements between the architect, client, and contractor. Others involved in the prebuilding phases of the project might include realtors, bankers, lawyers, insurance agents, interior designers, engineers, electricians, plumbers, building inspectors, materials suppliers, and specialists in equipment placement and installation.

New resources available for the architect and general contractor included *The Sweets Catalogue File* which appeared about 1905. Still in use today, *Sweets*, or *The Sweets File* as it is commonly known, is a compendium of building components categorized by type with information about materials, sizes, and installation procedures. It can be used to identify and specify materials and components. It was created to save time for architects and contractors by gathering and collating the information from component suppliers that had already threatened to overwhelm the architect and the builder with paper.[47]

New building documents were also introduced in this period. One, a new contract between client and architect, was probably introduced to replace a simple letter of intent to provide services or a cordial handshake. The document appeared in 1920 in *A Handbook of Architectural Practice* and was accompanied by an admonishment to architects to end the "strange timidity that Architects display in informing clients of their charges, and their willingness to go forward without any understanding whatever."[48] The *Handbook* was designed to encourage the creation of efficient, competitive, and cost-effective businesses. Architects, like building contractors, faced more and more problems of administration, supervision, liability, and control.

More important than this contract, however, was the replacement of the "Uniform Contract" that had been in use since 1888 and defined the owner-contractor-architect relationship with regard to building projects. This three-page document was no longer adequate to cover the increasing complexity of building conditions. By 1915 two documents replaced it: an agreement between the contractor and owner comparable to the earlier contract and including the architect and a substantial "General Conditions of the Contract."

The forty-five articles of the "General Conditions of the Contract" covered everything not described in the drawings and specifications, including definitions, payment, liability, arbitration, and other contingencies. These two documents, with the drawings and specifications, formed the contract documents. When these were prepared, bidding could take place.[49]

Bidding for a job was an increasingly formal procedure because of the competition between contractors and subcontractors to tender the best prices.[50] Performance bonds were required by the state and by some corporate jobs. When the bids were submitted and the contract awarded, the formal signing of the agreement between the contractor and client took place and the architect was assigned his role as supervisor. Thus, much paper work had become an integral part of every phase of the building project.

The actual building phase also had distinct components: the general contractor scheduled work, hired subcontractors, and organized materials deliveries. The client observed while the architect supervised, approved materials, inspected work, and wrote change orders when necessary to accommodate the client or solve problems. Both general contractor and architect had to arrange for legal inspections at the proper time to ensure building code conformity. This was especially important for institutional and public works. Fortunately, North Carolina had one of the nation's earliest uniform building codes, which made it easy to work from county to county and city to city. Nevertheless, interpretation could and did vary from place to place, and building inspections could halt work for days.[51]

Architects, like general contractors, experienced the same tensions between the desire to have a large and successful business and the desire to remain in control of the work that was produced by the office. Professionally architects had to be known in a community or a state in order to get commissions. They had to meet and attract clients, pay bills, and maintain an office. A 1902 article on professionalism in architecture noted: "The architectural opportunities fall to those who are preeminent for business rather than artistic ability, and thus it is they who build the architecture of the country, good, bad or indifferent. The architect must be a businessman first and an artist afterward." The writer was giving a general but accurate description of the way things were. He also encouraged architects to organize their offices as big businesses, and he questioned the ability of the one-man office to survive.[52] In North Carolina, architecture was practiced in offices with one or two principals, with few exceptions, until after World War II. This was possible for the same reasons that Satterfield, Coffey, and Davidson were successful—because most commissions were single projects for a single client. The physical size of the project no longer mattered as much because of the resources available to the designer—resources of consultants, collaborators, and components. The circumstances that taxed the one-person office were the projects that involved the construction of more than a single building and projects at a great distance. These same circumstances also taxed the general contractor and forced both architects and builders to develop new ways of project organization in North Carolina.

One Architect, One Project

Between 1900 and 1945 most architectural practice in North Carolina was done by the one-person office working directly with clients. A few architects even continued to contract and supervise construction, but most did not.[53] The design process was not very different from previous years when local traditions, buildings, shared expectations, pattern books, magazines, and budgets shaped design.

A small office building, church, local school, hospital, or simple industrial building could all be handled by the one-person office. The very factors that had multiplied the client's choices for components and conveniences also multiplied the architect's resources. Heating, ventilation, and components manufacturers could provide advice and shop drawings. An architect might have to draw more but he had to actually design and detail fewer components and fittings whether for a house or an office building.[54]

Some firms had even begun to specialize. For example, Hill C. Linthicum, a Durham architect, advertised himself as a school specialist. His basic school plan was a "T"—the wings being classrooms on each side of the corridor and the leg housing the auditorium and other ancillary services. Heating and lighting, fresh air ventilation, and fire escapes were designed specifically to meet state building code requirements as well as those specified in publications of the state's Division of School Planning of

Interior of B. H. Stephens, architect, office, Wilmington, ca. 1905. (Photo, New Hanover County Museum, Wilmington.)

the Department of Public Instruction. Built of red brick with white trim and sash or steel casement or awning windows, such schools could be built in one-, two-, three-, or four-story versions. Most were extremely functional and crisp in appearance with a faintly Jacobean flavor. They could also be built with other materials without redrawing the plans or completely reworking the specifications—documents only had to be adjusted to reflect the local conditions.[55]

Major out-of-state architects brought new men into practice in the state—national hotel architect W. L. Stoddart sent Charles Hartmann to Greensboro to supervise the construction of the O. Henry Hotel; Philadelphia's Charles Barton Keen sent Henry Wallace to oversee the building of Reynolda, the great county house Keen designed for R. J. Reynolds; and Richard Morris Hunt's New York office sent R. S. Smith to Asheville to superintend the Biltmore House; he remained in Asheville to create a very specific domestic fabric. Clients also hired work done by out-of-state firms, but the small office run by a local man was at the heart of most local work.

In the one- (or two-) principal office like that of Northup and O'Brien in Winston-Salem, the production of the building documents—working drawings, specifications, and detail drawings to scale when required—was divided into phases. The principal would produce the preliminary designs. When these were accepted, the working drawings phase would begin. Usually these drawings were produced on yellow paper and then copied by a professional draftsman in ¼ or ⅛ scale in ink onto linen or a high-quality paper that would withstand printing. Full-scale details might also be drawn at the same time. Once the drawings were finished and sized (treated with a fixative) they could be (blue)printed.

As working drawings were being readied, so too were specifications. Sometimes the principal wrote all specifications, sometimes he used a consultant, like an engineer, for help with portions. Not every drawing, detail, or specification was executed de nouveau for every project. Sections, elevations, and details from working drawings could be traced from earlier jobs. If the problem had been solved once, there was no need to spend time re-solving it. A similar rule applied for specifications. Once a format was established, similar projects could be described in almost identical terms, and most firms used printed forms as part of their "specs." Northup and O'Brien, for example, mimeographed their specifications, leaving blanks to be filled in. Both sets of documents had to be checked and rechecked for conformity with local and state building codes. To specify that these requirements would be met, it was a common practice until after World War II to state that heating, plumbing, and lighting would "meet code" or "be to code," whether for residential or industrial work.[56] This simplified things for the architects but increased the burden on local inspectors whose responsibility it was to enforce the code.

By the time working drawings and specifications were completed or in the works (frequently they were supplied as work progressed on larger projects), the architect had received up to 75 percent of his fee. The final 25 percent was due at the end of the project when the architect certified that the owner should pay the contractor his final payment and the building was turned over to the owner. The architect's fee included his general supervision of the project, including site visits, approval of changes or substitutions of materials, consideration of causes and penalties due to delays experienced by the contractor, certification of the contractor's requests for payments, and any other related chores written into the standard contract.

Within this general pattern, special circumstances could and did vary the specifics of the process in the architect's office. The most frequent causes of these variations were projects that required the principal to collaborate with another architect or with a consultant. The use of consultants, especially engineers, grew as the field became more specialized through knowledge and education and most one-person offices could not afford to have an engineer on staff. As the kinds of engineers multiplied, it was easier to hire specific consultants—mechanical (for heating, ventilation, and air conditioning), electrical, or structural engineers—for problems that such men could solve more quickly than the architect.[57]

The collaboration of architects with each other has had a long history and usually came about when a client wanted the services of a local architect but also wanted some particular expertise that that architect did not possess. Louis Asbury, a young Charlotte architect, was asked by a local congregation to design a new church and parish house in 1944. The committee told Asbury that they wanted him to work with a "specialist in gothic revival." After nearly six months, Asbury finally agreeably associated with Otto F. Langmann, formerly of Hobart Upjohn's New York firm.[58]

The most regular variation on this collaboration is the reverse of the type made by Asbury and Langmann. Both A. J. Davis of New York, who worked for the state in the nineteenth century, and Hobart Upjohn of New York, who worked for North Carolina State College of Agriculture and Engineering in the 1920s, collaborated as experts with local architects. The experts visited often, provided the designs and the building documents, and associated with a local firm for the benefit of their experience with construction and materials in the area and for site supervision. Upjohn's use of local architect James M. Kennedy placed Upjohn in a position of superiority, whereas Asbury and Langmann collaborated as equals.

Other collaborative efforts occurred when a single job required dramatically speeded-up production. When J. Allen Maxwell's one-man firm in Goldsboro was commissioned to do the Highway Building in Raleigh in 1950, he agreed to hire a larger Raleigh firm—Holloway and Reeves—which was short of work, to produce the working drawings and do the supervisory phases of the job.[59]

In these ways it was possible for many architectural offices to be run by one or two principals, a draftsman, perhaps a site supervisor, and a full- or part-time bookkeeper-secretary. None of these arrangements among architects necessarily impinged upon the general contractor. The contractor's efforts began with the actual work, and he was accountable to the supervisor sent by the architect. The compartmentalization of tasks was clear and was becoming standard operating procedure.

The architect's office, like the general contractor's organization, was geared to provide a logical organization of work on the site and relied on the ideal of a smooth, unbroken building process which moved from the ground up and from the outside in, and from unskilled, to semiskilled, to highly skilled labor. Reality seldom reached the ideal, however, as Winston-Salem architect Luther Lashmit recalled:

Brooks Hall, North Carolina State University campus, Raleigh, 1927, Hobart Upjohn, architect. (Photo, North Carolina Division of Archives and History.)

There were times when delays were due to the architect's tardiness in approving materials or in providing supplemental information necessary for the orderly progress of construction. There were delays when builders were required to remedy work due to faulty workmanship or materials. There were delays when the builder's subcontractors did not appear on the job when needed. There were delays on work for the state government due to its requirement that mechanical and electrical work be done under separate contracts, thus making the builder who was the general contractor more or less powerless to maintain tight construction schedules. Strikes in the building supply industries, abnormal seasonal weather conditions and controversies over interpretations of contract requirements were factors causing delays.[60]

Luther Lashmit's eloquent description of construction realities vividly illuminates the building process and the difficulty of exerting control over it. It emphasizes that building is not isolated in the architect's office but occurs at a specific location in an equally specific time and place. It affirms the desirability of client, architect, and contractor contact so that each can explain events to the other. Compartmentalization of the building process through industrialization and improved technology minimizes the apparent need for personal contact while increasing the real need for everyone to better understand what is happening. Compartmentalization diminishes the control of the participants. Face-to-face contact reduces client stress, maximizes the client's confidence in the architect, and provides the general contractor with a buffer from the client. Almost from the day that the architect or contractor is hired, his skill and expertise can become a source of support, comfort, or frustration for the client. With the evolution of the practice, the architect became the person who placed his client's interests first. Yet conflicts between the architect and the client are frequently over those very interests and in relation to the general contractor who can influence both by his resistance to work.

The long collaboration of the architectural firm of Hook and Rogers of Charlotte with Trinity College (the predecessor of Duke University) in Durham documents many sources of conflicts. A principal of this firm, C. C. Hook, served as architect for Trinity College from 1895 until 1925. A fire destroyed the pre-1910 correspondence between Pres. William P. Few and C. C. Hook but the remainder is copious and lively.[61] It details an involved building process on the campus which consisted of Hook providing services to the college, following a long-range plan to construct many buildings which was being realized a building at a time. By 1910 Few and Hook had reached a personal understanding built on mutual respect and tolerance. The letters between the two detail negotiation, bickering, compromise, and persistence. Hook listened to Few's advice on planning, interior work, and specifications, but Few almost never attempted to tell Hook what a building should look like except for an occasional comment on designs. Few wanted economy, durability, and safety from fire for the students. He was always concerned with the speed of production. In 1912 he complained about the length of time required to design a new dormitory, to which Hook responded, "In reference to this new Dormitory, we desire to say, that it required nearly two days work in order to get a satisfactory plan for the end sections—so that the building would not look too narrow, when placed on a line with the present North Dormitory. We trust that you understand that this kind of work requires the most careful thought and consideration."[62]

Hook's explanation of the nature of the sometimes slow design process satisfied Few, but he was not so easily satisfied on the question of site supervision. Evidently Few visited campus building sites frequently and became convinced that Hook was not there enough. He requested a schedule of visits. Hook replied, "[I] will say that we hardly know how to do this, as we have never been called upon to render such a schedule. We base our visits upon the progress and condition of the work. We make more visits to our buildings than any other architects that we know of. The custom is to visit about every two or three weeks, we visit about every week or ten days, we are told by contractors and other architects, that we visit the works more frequently than others."[63] Hook and Few never successfully resolved this problem. Visits from Charlotte, about 160 miles

Drawing by C. C. Hook of East Campus entry gates and shelters with perspective of gate showing East and West Duke buildings, Trinity College (now East Campus, Duke University), Durham, ca. 1915. East and West Duke buildings remain in use today; the new gates and the colonnade joining the two buildings were never built. (Duke University Archives.)

from Durham, required a five- or six-hour drive. Travel by train was equally arduous because the route was not direct and required a layover in Fayetteville. The mail, an important means of conveying information, could be slow and was not an ideal means of communication since it could be used to avoid issues. Hook occasionally had to send requests for overdue payment to Few, which, if not immediately honored, resulted in the need for a begging letter from the busy architect. The two also used the telephone and the telegraph for emergencies, but nothing was as acceptable and reassuring to Few as a visit by the architect to the site.[64]

Yet despite these tensions, ultimately the long relationship between Few and Hook was positive, as Few stated in a letter of reference that he wrote for the firm:

Mess. Hook and Rogers, Architects of Charlotte, N.C. have planned all but one of the buildings that have been erected at this college within the past 15 years. Mr. C. C. Hook, of this firm, years ago took charge of our buildings and we have relied pretty largely upon him ever since. He has the good taste and the imagination to plan, and the expert knowledge to execute his plans. We are now in the midst of a large building scheme, which is based entirely upon his ideas.

He has from first to last given entire satisfaction.[65]

The correspondence between Hook and Few could have been written in the nineteenth century, so personal and human is the relationship it documents. Like contractors Satterfield, Coffey, or Davidson, Hook and many other architects felt that the quality of their work was a function of their personal involvement with the client and with the contractor. This feeling was weakened and in some instances negated by the new forces that had also brought so much prosperity. Although industrialization and urbanization had created a larger market, now almost anybody could be a contractor and many devalued the importance of the architect. At the same time, the new materials, tools, and conveniences like electricity, plumbing, and central heating required specialized knowledge and more time than an untrained person might be willing or able to devote in the supervision of the erection of a building. Compartmentalization of building by trades, materials production, and labor organization also intervened to complicate questions of control and organization, so that neither the architect nor the contractor could ever adequately predict the progress of a project.

Throughout the late nineteenth century, as speculative land and building development combined to fuel the growing economy, it became very clear that if the building process could be organized vertically from excavation to completion, through the trades, the margin of profit and therefore the level of success would be greater. In building terms this translated into a large organization which could provide essentially every need and therefore control as many facets of the process as possible. One large and important building project in North Carolina between the two wars was organized vertically, and the reasons for that organization were made explicit in the press. The rationale for the project could be a model for any major twentieth-century building project.

A Team in Residence

After World War I, increased pressure for physical expansion at the University of North Carolina in Chapel Hill provoked what some architects and contractors considered a radical solution to the successful execution of a major building project. Building at the university between 1875 and 1920 had been sporadic; architects were hired as needed and no master plan guided building location or design. Montgomery Schuyler, who visited the campus in 1911, commented: "The comparative poverty of the University, compelling employment of architects of inferior inspiration who feebly followed conventional models mercifully protected the University, like others in the South, from any great intrusion of inharmonious building in

University of North Carolina Upper Quadrangle, Chapel Hill, 1907. The Upper Quadrangle, which fronts on Columbia Street, stretches to Cameron Avenue, the upper limits of the Lower Quadrangle begun in 1921. Schuyler's reference to a variety of buildings included the Davis buildings, visible to the left and right of center, and the "gothick" Memorial Hall and Gymnasium to the left of center. (Photo, North Carolina Collection, University of North Carolina Library, Chapel Hill.)

that period, so lamentable in its babel of romantic eclecticism."[66] Whether the appearance of the campus was lamentable or not, by the mid-1910s it was overcrowded. A boisterous alumni-led campaign in the press and at the General Assembly succeeded when funds were appropriated in 1919 for capital improvements on the campus. The university administration had prepared for the possibility by initiating planning studies in 1913. Boston landscape architect John Nolan, who was then designing the Myers Park suburb in Charlotte, and civil engineer Bernard Drane from Charlotte began site studies and produced an excellent series of maps of the entire campus by 1917. In 1919 Aberthaw, an Atlanta engineering firm that specialized in long-range planning for educational institutions, was hired to make recommendations for the physical development of the campus. The university administration interviewed several nationally prominent architects and chose McKim, Mead, and White of New York City as consulting architects.[67]

Aberthaw's recommendations called for a fabric of red brick with white trim, which the firm identified as "colonial" and "traditional" in North Carolina. The firm also recommended that the dormitories be stacked floors with double-loaded corridors (rooms on each side of a central corridor) rather than the entry type (with suites off each stairwell), that faculty offices be located in classroom buildings, that scholastic buildings be located in the center of the campus and dormitories at the periphery, and that all buildings be of fire resistant construction. McKim, Mead, and White began their design work with these guidelines.

The university building committee and administration then proceeded to create a team to be in residence to design and produce the buildings. Thomas C. Atwood, a nationally respected engineer who was noted for his ability to oversee monumental projects, was associated with Raymond Weeks, a Durham architect, and was working for a textile magnate there. Atwood was retained as supervising engineer. Henry P. Montgomery was sent by McKim, Mead, and White to be supervising architect but was soon replaced by Arthur Nash, a Harvard and Ecole des Beaux Arts graduate. By early 1921, after approximately six months, the office had been set up on the campus. It included an architect, waterworks engineer, draftsman, inspector, and clerks. Three classroom buildings, five dormitories, twelve faculty houses, and a railroad spur to bring in materials from the main rail line were planned for the first two-year campaign, for which $1,490,000 was available.[68]

As the drawings were started, the final step in assembling the team was taken. It was announced that bids would be taken from contractors for the work. Bids were to be based on a lump-sum fee, not a percentage of cost as was traditional. The general contractor would have to be available for work immediately and would have to show evidence of satisfactory experience in similar work elsewhere. The university also required the contractor to

> establish the job office as a going organization; . . . [set up] approved systems of accounting and cost keeping . . . supply any labor not secured locally . . . [set up] a purchasing department [for] the purchase of materials . . . subject to the approval of the [building] committee or its agent . . . prepare estimates of the cost of various structures . . . [be prepared for visits from] a traveling superintendent at least once every two weeks; . . . by an executive of the contractor at least once every month; . . . by a chief accountant at least once every two months.[69]

Local general contracting firms throughout the state accused the university of deliberately creating conditions that eliminated them from the bidding process. A reporter for the *Greensboro Daily News* wrote:

> There is not today a builder in the North Carolina [Builders Exchange] who doesn't feel that he would be a jackass if he put in a bid for this University work with no more "organization" than he has.
>
> More than that, each of the protesting contractors who discussed the case at the University feels that his bond for faithful performance of his duty would be endangered by the absence of such an "organization" as this contract emphasizes. Yet, there is not a

builder who hasn't executed contracts just as important and built dormitories and classrooms and whatnots just as good as these.[70]

The furor in the state newspapers forced university president H. W. Chase to issue a detailed rebuttal on behalf of the building committee and the Executive Committee of the Board of Trustees. Chase began by saying that the job had been open to all contractors and that it had been advertised only in the North Carolina press. Then he outlined the position of the university: "Two years are available for the work, which must be done promptly and economically. The funds are public funds and should be administered with even more care than should those of private business undertaking the same sort of operation. The locality of the operation is a small and isolated town of 1200 people, with practically no labor supply of its own."

Next he compared the two basic methods of getting work done: by accepting competitive bids on each individual job or by contracting the entire project as a whole. The major problem with the first alternative was labor—finding enough workers, using them economically, and housing them. He wrote: "It has already been demonstrated at Chapel Hill that even so few as two to three different contractors doing work on the campus, at the same time find themselves in acute difficulties . . . which slow down work, create confusion and markedly increase costs." The second alternative was the only way to avoid the problems. The university committees were unanimous in their opinion that "a firm operating on such a large contract can, in the first place, maintain a sequence of operations which will ensure the completion of work on time and lower the cost of construction. It can transfer one type of workmen from operations on one building to similar operations on another without loss of time. It can by proper planning, maintain a labor force. . . . In short, the plan is designed not to increase but to lower costs."[71]

The university, through its contractual requirements, gave both architect and contractor the ability to completely organize and coordinate the building process. The architect and contractor gladly accepted this responsibility since the pervasive business ethic that order and control produce profits prevailed.

The bidding process went forward as planned and T. C. Thompson Brothers of Charlotte was awarded the contract in 1921. This aggressive firm already had a reputation for undertaking large jobs in the region, and they had the capacity to organize and supply the needs of this contract. The rationalization of the building process by creating a single organization that could exert great control and purchasing power was successful. Materials and labor were similarly assembled and managed—both worked on the basis of a pool or inventory. The funds to create a sufficient inventory, like the funds to create the labor camp and put in the railroad, were predicated on wholesale purchase, approval and testing, rapid consumption and payment, materials standardization, use of limited component types, and reduction of overhead by standardized management. These practices usually guaranteed substantial profit.[72]

It is possible to imagine how such a project was organized, but it is impossible to imagine the organization of labor for such a job. On the one hand, excitement, anticipation, and energy are generated during the execution of such a project. The sheer magnitude of people, materials, noise, dust, dirt, and debris can only begin to be comprehended through the photographs of the project. Only in the midst of such a project can one really know how the people involved felt, thought, and worried. The stockpiling of materials and the creation of a paper schedule can be fathomed more easily than the day-to-day effort of assigning tasks and organizing the gangs of workmen in the midst of what appears as confusion. Every job, large or small, had to be assigned to one of the skilled or unskilled laborers, artisans, or subcontractors, whose hands, arms, and backs actually did the work. Some days there might be no experienced workers for a job; other days there might be too many. The workers had to be inspired as well as paid and were often, according to contractors' complaints, too few, too late, too stupid, too combative, too demanding, or too lazy. They also had to wait and be waited on during every other aspect of the building process. In this T. C. Thompson Brothers was also highly skilled and the efforts paid off.

The McKim, Mead, and White plan called for a major north/south quadrangle with the north terminus being the existing Administration Building, the first building on campus, and the south terminus being the new library, a neoclassical building like the Low Library the firm had designed at Columbia University. This major open space was to be divided in half by a less majestic east/west quadrangle which would terminate in the schools of law and business, with single scholastic buildings facing each other across the open green. Additional scholastic buildings would mirror each other and provide the flanking infill between the major and minor axes of the greens.[73]

Building proceeded rapidly: the Saunders, Murphy, and Manning buildings made up the east quadrangle, while Steele (completed in 1921, but not part of the original plan) and Bingham provided the links along the east promenade from north to south. A quadrangle of dormitories was also erected east of the South Campus, as the new complex was called. T. C. Thompson Brothers' labor camp in Carrboro, the office of the architect and engineer on the campus, and the careful administration of both produced an organization that was maintained for almost ten years under the scrutiny of university officials, state inspectors, and the legislators who funded the campaign. Altogether ten million dollars was spent on ten buildings, including the neoclassical, granite, marble-domed library.

Construction site, University of North Carolina, Chapel Hill, library, north facade, December 10, 1928, McKim, Mead, and White, architects, Arthur Nash, supervising architect, Charles Atwood, engineer. (Photo, North Carolina Collection, University of North Carolina Library, Chapel Hill.)

The depression barely slowed building as Works Progress Administration funds were available and the planning and design continued in the manner of the glorious decade of the 1920s.[74]

The project at the University of North Carolina at Chapel Hill established the precedent of vertical control of the building project, and the creation and implementation of a master plan for the university shaped subsequent projects on each of the state-owned campuses. However, no single architect or contractor would ever again dominate a state-funded project of such scale as had Nash, Atwood, and T. C. Thompson Brothers.

The form of the campus also satisfied its creators. The South Campus emerged as a kind of small "city beautiful" and its conservative and functional classicism was as ideologically sound as its fabric.

The collaborative effort that produced the new buildings at the university was being taken up by more architects and builders by the 1930s. The large Works Progress Administration projects and then the desire to qualify for defense contracts simply required larger offices with greater capacity. Architect Henry I. Gaines recalled:

Crew setting library dome, University of North Carolina, Chapel Hill, after December 1928. (Photo, North Carolina Collection, University of North Carolina Library, Chapel Hill.)

> The other architects and engineers in our area were facing the same problem and receiving the same answer so the thought occurred to us, "why not pool our organizations?" So six of us—Earl Stillwell, Charles Waddell, Tony Lord, Bill Dodge, Stewart Rogers and I—had lunch together at the S&W Cafeteria and agreed to pool our operations and make a united effort to obtain some defense work. This combination produced an organization of about forty people, and since there were six of us we thought "Six Associates" would be an appropriate name.[75]

The merger that produced Six Associates was very successful and brought the large contracts they sought. But their approach was quite different from that taken by J. N. Pease's firm in Charlotte. Colonel Pease, an engineer who had worked for Lockwood-Green of South Carolina, opened his own office in the 1930s. Pease's experiences as an engineer and his work in larger offices convinced him that his firm should offer not only engineering but also architectural services. Pease hired in-house structural, electrical, and mechanical engineers, which many other architectural firms soon would supply, and he hired engineers who specialized in the new types of services that were required by the growing cities in the state and region, such as sanitary facilities, water, and waste treatment. It was this range of services that prompted the government to hire Pease for the rebuilding of Fort Bragg, the large military base near Fayetteville.

Lower (south) campus, University of North Carolina, Chapel Hill, 1929, McKim, Mead, and White, architects, Arthur Nash, supervising architect, Charles Atwood, engineer. (Photo, North Carolina Collection, University of North Carolina Library, Chapel Hill.)

Pease's office would provide all the essential documents and services and supervision of contractors on the vast project, which was to be built on a short schedule.[76]

The internal organization of these two firms was radically different.[77] Pease's firm had a hierarchical structure. The main principals sought and assigned work to job captains—architects or engineers—for design. These job captains created a team of specialists from each department. The project head might not ever meet clients and did not supervise construction work. Interior designers; heating, air conditioning, and ventilation engineers; and other specialists would all perform roles in designing the building.[78] By contrast Six Associates remained much more wedded to a "principal philosophy" in which a principal did the job from beginning to end: meeting clients, traveling, designing, consulting with other designers and engineers, and supervising the construction.[79]

These two organizational models have been in use for many years. Architects say that each reflects a different philosophy of architecture: the first, that architecture is a business; the second, that it is an art. Both, however, permit the architect to function within the building industry. The effectiveness of each model is a matter of the personal preference of the architectural firm.

"The Architect Is in the Middle"

Between 1900 and 1945, pressures of time and distance, combined with an ever more complicated scope of work, steadily eroded the control the architect exerted over a building project. The level of erosion intensified as the major elements of the building process became more and more separate. This compartmentalization was accepted by architects, contractors, clients, and artisans. Although some doubted that the separation was advantageous, many perceived this evolution as progress that was to be expected in the modern world. The building industry permitted more people to do more work, producing more buildings, requiring more materials, components, and laborers, and perhaps yielding more profits.

Changes in the building industry affected the architect and the building contractor in different but related ways. Much of what the architect did in the way of design was affected by component manufacturing and by what could be done by a general contractor. The contractor's schedule of work and the progress of the building were also dependent on components, but weather and labor added other variables. The fees of both architect and contractor were affected by the cost of labor and materials which in turn was dependent on the manufacturers and on supply and demand of raw materials and finished products. Building had become part of the elaborate economic structure of the country and the implications of these numerous linkages were unavoidable.

Even as the industry compartmentalized, many general contractors did the opposite and created a vertical structure that controlled the process from beginning to end, thus exerting controls of a different kind on the economy. A general contractor that was his own developer, designer, and purchasing agent could compete far more successfully in and help create a speculative market.

The architect organized his office to provide services with speed and dispatch. New specialists saved costs by being available in-house, thereby increasing the capacity of the firm to acquire different kinds of jobs. Some firms specialized, providing design and supervision built on a reputation of experience earned over time and widely, though quietly, touted to potential clients. For the most part, however, the architect did not create the kind of organization that would give him control over the capital as well as the process. As architect Luther Lashmit eloquently and simply stated, "The problem has always been to assure the owner received full value for his expenditure while the builder must receive a reasonable profit. The architect is in the middle."[80] And there the architect remained in 1945, marketing a professional service to the sectors of society that most frequently required these services—corporations, hospitals, schools, churches, public institutions, and the wealthy.

Social Role and Position: Anonymity, Identification, and Access

The rise of professionalism and the institution of state regulation of entry into design and building represented a combination that provided architects and contractors with the means to gain more control and power in the building industry. The regulation of access to the fields of architecture and general contracting through licensing and education legitimized the practitioners and made them essential components of the industry. Professionalism, however, meant more than entry control. It also provided architects and contractors with a means to gain access to the people with the capital to build or to provide backing for building by giving power to their jobs through association and enhanced community identification.

In the North Carolina of 1900 and 1945, community position for many families was still based on landownership and remnants of wealth that remained after the Civil War. Many of the old gentry joined with the newly wealthy of industry through marriage or social contact to control the emerging white middle-class society and to make its traditional values those of the state. The burgeoning towns and cities provided a more fluid structure, however, and many individuals achieved considerable rank and power through the accumulation of wealth. Among these were some architects and building contractors. They represented the apex of a group in North Carolina society that had begun several centuries earlier as respected artisans and mechanics and were granted social position for their skill, knowledge, and expertise.

The artisans and mechanics who had formed the basis of mid-nineteenth century society had been reduced to a large and shifting population of people in the building trades with varying degrees of skill. A sample from the daybooks of the supervising architect of the Treasury or from the daily reports filed by the building supervisors at Duke University reveal that these people had become subject to an extensive anonymity that included the unskilled with the skilled laborers and artisans. Certainly supervisors could not list by name everyone on a job, but carpenters, electricians, and plumbers were as nameless as the laborers who dug the trenches or carried the stone.[81]

The reason for the anonymity of the reports is clarified by a realization of the numbers of workers involved. Contractors like Satterfield or Coffey listed their workers, skilled and unskilled, in their account books by name and trade. Each contractor might deal with a total of fifty men on a job costing between $10,000 and $25,000. However, L. A. Simon, who kept the daybook for the construction of the Federal Post Office at Fayetteville in 1910–11, dealt with a total of 150 to 200 men over the season. He might deal with as few as fifteen or as many as fifty men a day for the post office which cost $45,000. Therefore, he listed workers by types: two carpenters, six laborers, one electrician.[82] E. H. Clements, who supervised stone

Commercial National Bank site, Raleigh, 1912. Atlanta architect P. Thorton Marye designed this Gothic revival fourteen-story skyscraper, shown here with its crew of roughly fifty-two craftsmen, with blacks grouped left, right, and in the background and whites in the center and on the steel. (Photo, North Carolina Division of Archives and History.)

masonry at Duke University, only observed the two to three hundred workers under his supervision each day.[83] The only way to keep track of assignments, pay, and sick time was through foremen and accountants who might or might not get to know workers by their names. Certainly Clements and Simon, like Coffey, knew particular men on their projects, but it's doubtful that they knew the average artisan or laborer. If a worker's name was not known, how could his work be recognized?

The organization and compartmentalization of the building industry therefore eroded the power and esteem attached to a position, job, or skill. Certain artisans remained highly ranked because of their skills, but others, like the newly required steelworkers or the gas and electrical workers, might or might not be reliable. A foreman was frequently the judge of the skill and therefore the pay of the less skilled. Supervisors might be more strict when measuring work done by a person they did not know or respect or whose work they had had to correct, and they could be prejudiced, biased, or unfair, but their word affected the pay. Who you knew could determine where you worked, for whom, and when. Trades that had organized in the nineteenth century had some influence, but it was limited. Skilled artisans and laborers had organized into associations and unions to get wage and hour concessions and protection from unscrupulous general contractors and builders, but this process occurred very slowly in North Carolina. Throughout the building boom years, trades did organize but their influence was limited by size, the economy, and the absence of a strong apprenticeship system which would have controlled the labor supply.[84]

In many small communities, the skilled artisan retained a respected position as did the general contractor. William Tucker, who had been a general contractor in Laurinburg since the turn of the century, was eulogized in 1948: "He was a master workman and was intolerant of anything short of that in others. When he built a house people knew it was built right and that it would endure. . . . His execution of any and all jobs, his integrity, and the rule by which he lived are worthy of emulation of all those who would become good workmen and masterbuilders."[85]

This eulogy summarized those attributes which gave Tucker his reputation and helped him achieve financial and political success (he had also served as mayor of the town). Tucker's esteem in the community also gave him access to a position with some power and influence, which enabled him to get work, financial credit, and the respect of the laborers, the artisans, and the many other people with whom he dealt. Without land, the traditional base of power and influence in North Carolina, Tucker was dependent upon the power that could be derived from his name alone, and his name was made powerful by its association with the quality of his work.

This example was common in North Carolina between 1900 and 1945 and this type of success heightened consciousness of the importance of individual position in a social hierarchy within and without the industry. Position affected the ability to get commissions and execute work, which further strengthened role identification and status within the community. Hard times showed that reputation could be as valuable as work itself, and when times improved, connections once again had the power to provide prosperity. The erosion of traditional values and positions had encouraged general contractors to organize, but like the architects in North Carolina there seems to have been no strong impetus to organize until about 1900, when work, commissions, self-esteem, and financial security became more clearly associated with social position and identity in the community. Although this phenomenon was not new in America, it was new in North Carolina.

The desire for a professional identity originated in the broad middle class that developed in the urban economy of mid-nineteenth-century America. Groups within this middle class sought status, identity, and power by associating their work with jobs historically granted professional status. This association also sought to foster the belief that certain jobs could only be done by specialists. Organizations were formed to define roles and responsibilities, to guard access to professional knowledge, and to encourage clients to use trained professionals. These organizations created codes of ethics and standards of behavior for their members. The organizational process was further enhanced by removing job training from the traditional apprenticeship or shop system and placing it into the collegiate setting. The final step was the establishment of state requirements of certification (licensing acts) for performing certain tasks.[86] North Carolina's architects and general contractors began this process shortly after 1900.

The American Institute of Architects (AIA) could not organize a North Carolina chapter until there was a sufficient number of architects who wanted to organize and could agree on how to organize.[87] The first successful attempt came in 1906 when a few architects in Charlotte founded the North Carolina Architectural Association (NCAA). By 1909 the organization set two goals: association with the AIA and the passage of a practice act which was being considered by the General Assembly. The organization was very active, meeting in Wrightsville Beach near Wilmington in June 1909 and in Raleigh in December 1910.[88] The following year, AIA executive secretary Glenn Brown started a national membership recruitment campaign and North Carolina was one of the targets. Hill C. Linthicum, an energetic, ambitious architect located in Durham who had become point man for the NCAA's efforts to affiliate with the AIA, invited Brown to the December 1911 NCAA meeting in Winston-Salem and Brown attended. By May 1912 Linthicum sent Brown a proposed constitution and by-laws which met Brown's approval. He also agreed to endorse the NCAA architects that he knew for AIA membership, a crucial prerequisite for acceptance.[89]

Four months later Linthicum wrote happily to Brown, "I am getting the boys applications, drawings, specifications and fees, all in shape, and in a few days I will forward them to you." He enclosed a copy of the Practice Act Bill being introduced in the state legislature for the third time. (Although this bill failed too, the failure did not slow down Linthicum.)[90]

At Brown's invitation, Linthicum attended the December AIA convention in Washington and returned directly to the semiannual meeting of the NCAA in Charlotte. Linthicum wrote triumphantly to Brown that the major result of the Charlotte meeting was the expressed desire of many members of the NCAA to become a chapter of the AIA. He outlined a strategy that he hoped would prevent any conflict about the affiliation.[91] In the interim, Linthicum and four other North Carolinians were elected to membership in the AIA.[92] With this election, North Carolina had a core of five AIA members who formally organized the North Carolina chapter of the AIA, which was incorporated August 8, 1913.[93] The chapter met in Greensboro on September 16, elected officers under their state charter, and made official application to the AIA. Linthicum explained to Knicker-bocker Boyd, AIA secretary: "We have only 5 institute members and 7 chapter members. Total 12. We are a baby chapter." The baby chapter was chartered by the AIA on September 25, 1913.[94]

The establishment of the chapter did not take place without some dissatisfaction. Some of the Charlotte architects associated with the NCAA did not join the AIA—including the important practitioners C. C. Hook, O. D. Wheeler, J. M. McMichael, and Franklin Gordon. Two reasons that have been suggested for this are that the split reflected regional differences between the more rural, traditional east and the more urban, industrialized west and that the men who did not join objected to the membership requirements and ethical code of the AIA which tried to eliminate competition through a standard fee schedule.[95]

The new AIA chapter grew slowly. It added only one new member in 1913, three in 1916, one in 1917, and five in 1920. By 1929 its membership included approximately 39 of the 100 North Carolinians registered as architects in the state. In 1940 the NCAA combined with the North Carolina AIA (NCAIA).[96]

Following close on the heels of the successful chartering of the NCAIA came the passage of the Practice Act Bill in 1915. This was the fourth attempt to pass the bill, which had first been introduced in 1909. Many of the same people who had sought AIA membership were involved in the campaign for the practice act. Whatever differences there were among individuals about organizational affiliation, members of both the NCAA and the NCAIA agreed on the necessity of a legislative act which provided for a board of registration and a licensing procedure. The five members of the first North Carolina Board of Architectural Registration and Examination established by the 1915 act were a mix of NCAA and NCAIA members: J. E. Leitner, Wilmington (NCAA); C. C. Hook, Charlotte (NCAA); C. E. Hartge, Raleigh (joined NCAIA in 1916); R. S. Smith, Asheville (NCAIA); and Hill C. Linthicum, Durham (NCAIA). The regis-

Opposite:
Nineteenth Annual Meeting of the North Carolina Chapter of the American Institute of Architects, Charlotte, January 25–26, 1929. Barbecue held at Ornamental Stone Company. Identification taken from a tissue overlay made by Louise M. Hall when she incorporated this photograph in the NCAIA Chapter Archives. She noted that some initials, names, and origins were missing. Fred McCanless (in middle of tables). *Left to right, around table:* E. Stillwell (Asheville); J. Lynch, C. C. Hook, Simmons, and F. Gordon (Charlotte); L. Northup (left of Gordon, Winston-Salem); 3 unidentified; G. Berryman (Greensboro); H. E. White, Louis Asbury, Sr., Skinner, and M. Boyer (Charlotte); 3 unidentified; H. Hunter; 4 unidentified, Walter Hook (Charlotte); 1 unidentified; G. N. Rhodes, Buffington, M. Helms, J. D. Beacham (Asheville and Charlotte); H. I. Thrower (Greensboro), H. Peeps (Charlotte); L. Ellis; 1 unidentified. (Photo, North Carolina Division of Archives and History.)

4th Annual Meeting of the Men's Chapter of the A.I.C.
Charlotte, N.C. Jan. 29 & 1922
Barbecue at Ornamental Stone Co.

tration board also included members who did not belong to either the NCAIA or the NCAA.[97]

"An Act to Regulate the Practice of Architecture and Creating a Board of Examiners and Registration of Same" was ratified on March 9, 1915. It was one of the earliest in the nation and placed North Carolina among the first dozen states to license architects.[98] The act defined architecture as "the art of designing for safe and sanitary construction for public and private use, as taught by various colleges of architecture recognized by the AIA." Other sections provided for the creation of the board, the examining apparatus, the certified seal, and the refusal of a certificate (license). Certificates could be refused to anyone convicted of a felony or anyone who, in the opinion of the board, was "guilty of gross unprofessional conduct or who [was] addicted to habits that render him unfit to practice." The act included a grandfather clause that permitted established architects to be licensed without examination. People who practiced without a certificate were guilty of a misdemeanor and could be fined up to fifty dollars.[99] The act also permitted nonresident architects to apply for certification in the state on the basis of licensing in other states or association with a firm registered in the state.

The board's goals complemented those of the NCAIA, which sought to encourage "artistic, scientific and practical efficiency" through education and self-study, lectures, and the creation of a library. The NCAIA chose to admit only those individuals licensed by the state.[100]

The AIA code of ethics also coincided with the goals of the board, but the AIA went further by establishing a fee standard to eliminate unfair competition and by creating guidelines for the performance of work. The code of ethics provided for disciplining members, but it is unclear how this was carried out since it was not documented. The board assumed even greater responsibility for punishing infractions of professional standards, although it did not define activities for which an architect could be disciplined under state civil statutes until after World War II.[101]

The degree to which the board and the AIA continued to be mutually supportive and reinforcing after 1915 is not clear. Since the license was required to practice, many more architects were licensed than joined the NCAIA.[102] The slow growth of the chapter and the persistence of the NCAA suggest that licensing was the primary desideratum, not professional association. But the activities of the NCAIA encouraged other groups to seek or require state certification.

The roots of the Associated General Contractors (AGC) were in World War I.[103] The war effort demanded the centralization of many tasks, including building. Rapid construction of large army camps could only be accomplished by carefully structured methods of materials procurement and organization, deployment, and supervision of workmen and laborers. Although there were numerous organizations of construction workers,

"Industry leaders gathered January 4, 1923 outside of the Charlotte Chamber of Commerce," from Moorhead, *Construction in the Carolinas.* Identification taken from Moorhead. *Left to right:* C. P. Ballenger (Greenville), 2 unidentified, Nello L. Teer (Durham), Conrad Jamison (High Point), 1 unidentified, John Phipps (Greensboro), E. C. Derby (Charlotte), 1 unidentified, O. Max Gardner (Raleigh), 2 unidentified, Norman Underwood (Durham), 1 unidentified, R. C. Marshall, Jr. (for the national AGC), John Boyd (Charlotte), W. A. Crary (Columbia, S.C.), John M. Porter (Charlotte), Brown, Brown-Harry (Gastonia), E. H. Clements (Charlotte), Mark Reed (Asheville), 1 unidentified, Earle Whitton (Charlotte), E. W. Terrell (resident engineer for roads and streets, Grove Park Inn, Asheville).

no one organization reached general contractors as a single identifiable group.

These difficulties prompted Pres. Woodrow Wilson to encourage the formation of a national organization of general contractors. Wilson chose Daniel A. Garber, a New York contractor with a branch office in Winston-Salem, to chair a committee to create such an organization. Garber's rationale for the organization was more overtly political than that of the AIA.[104] Contractors needed influence to shape laws covering mortgages, loans, workmen's pay and compensation for injuries, labor unions and relations, liability, and the bidding procedures for state and local governments.

On November 20, 1918, the Associated General Contractors of America was formed and Garber was elected president. A significant decision was made to establish local chapters of the organization. Garber immediately sought to organize in North and South Carolina because of his ties there. The February meeting at the Selwyn Hotel in Charlotte in 1920 is considered the first meeting of the AGC in the state. Within two years, the AGC granted a charter to a North Carolina chapter (NCAGC).[105]

The external impetus for organization surely enhanced local awareness of the potential value of identification and recognition. C. P. Street, president of the NCAGC in 1944, described the contractor's situation when he finished school in 1919: "Contractors were not highly regarded in those days. Builders were thought of as black sheep of the business complex. Well, black sheep is probably not quite correct. Bankers, merchants, professional people simply did not know how to judge us. Other businesses were owned and managed by white collar men. We wore working clothes. Other businesses minimized financial risk, seldom took chances. We gambled on most every job: that was a natural part of construction."[106]

The contractor, like the architect, had to know construction from inside out, but he also had to be a credible businessman. Thus the desire for power and a better image helped produce the general contractors' licensing act. Impetus also came from the fact that in 1921 engineers and land surveyors had organized and obtained a licensing act.[107] It was therefore natural that general contractors sought and obtained their licensing act in 1925. By 1926 there was a five-member board, three of whom were charter members of the NCAGC.[108]

As with the architects, the contractors gained their licensing act almost simultaneously with association with a national organization. The "Act to Regulate the Practice of General Contracting" became Chapter 318 of the Public Laws of North Carolina in March 1925. Shorter and less complex than the architects' licensing act, it recalled the role of the contractor in building for nearly a century. It defined a general contractor as one who "for a fixed price or fee undertakes construction of plans by an architect or engineer where cost is in excess of $10,000." The licensing board, appointed by the governor, was to have at least one person knowledgeable in each of the three specialities: public utilities, highways, and buildings. Application for a certificate cost twenty dollars, and it was renewable each January. The board might revoke the license of anyone guilty of fraud or deceit in obtaining the license or "gross negligence, incompetency or negligency."

A contractor qualified for a license by submitting a résumé and recommendations from clients and architects. Initially anyone who was qualified for the license was eligible for any job. By 1931 the act was amended to provide a system of classification based on the cost of the job—therefore defining the capacity of firms to provide services and accountability and meet bonding requirements.[109] As leading Raleigh contractor James A. Davidson so succinctly put it: "We had to have the act to keep the jack-legs out. They were a danger to all of us."[110] He did not specify if the danger was due to competition or lack of skill.

The ongoing relation between the licensing and professional organization of general contractors was not immediately clear nor was it automatic. Thirty-five firms were charter members of the NCAGC, yet hundreds were licensed to practice.[111] Like architects, general contractors were still free to choose their associates and their associations. Like the AIA, the AGC was still an untested organization in the state. Also, until after 1954, both organizations were limited to white members only.

Licensing of architects and general contractors in North Carolina was based on the constitutional duty of the state to assure the health, safety, and welfare of its citizens through regulation of those activities that affected them. Licensing, like professional organization, seemed to serve the public good by identifying the competent and eliminating the incompetent. This link between professionalism and licensing also forged another link between the professional and the state. North Carolina State College, dedicated to teaching the engineering and mechanical arts, responded to licensing in its curriculum. Thus the chain was forged—organization, licensing, education—to identify and create the professional.

The education of a building contractor or an architect in 1900 might or might not include collegiate training, and collegiate training varied widely from school to school. In North Carolina, State College was the only white school offering training in engineering and for many years architectural training consisted of engineering courses and mechanical drawing. The black schools in the state were oriented to the building trades, not toward producing general contractors.[112] A survey of the *State College Alumni Association Directory* in 1927 shows that of the twenty-four graduates who were listed as employed in the building industry, three were architects, one was a mill engineer and architect, and the rest were contractors, building materials suppliers, or engineers in a variety of specializations. Two of the earliest graduates, Leslie Boney, Sr., and James M. Kennedy, who practiced in the state and were licensed as architects, had received bachelor of engineering degrees in textiles because there was no degree program in architecture in the School of Engineering when they graduated in 1905.[113]

The situation changed in 1920 when State College altered its curriculum specifically to include architectural engineering as part of a four-year degree program. The 1920–21 *Catalogue of North Carolina State College* explained that the General Assembly of North Carolina had passed an act to regulate architecture by licensing. "The purpose of this law is to protect the builder as well as the bona fide architect from the practice of inexperienced or poorly trained men. To meet this demand, a new course in Architectural Engineering has been added to the curriculum." The bachelor of architecture would be awarded to those who completed the course.[114]

This new program was developed by Ross Shumaker, an architect-educator who had joined the faculty in 1920. Shumaker had a bachelor's degree in architecture from Ohio State and had done graduate work at Pennsylvania State and Harvard. The new curriculum was somewhat comparable to that offered at older institutions like Carnegie-Mellon or Pennsylvania State, which had courses or degree programs in architecture. Most schools formed before 1900 had curricula dominated by courses in engineering and the pure sciences. State College's courses in architectural history, composition, and watercolor reflected the beaux-arts ideal of combining the aesthetic and cultural with the practical and theoretical of which there was plenty.[115]

Shumaker remains an ambiguous figure who is spoken of gingerly by those who remember him. He was a teacher and was deeply and sometimes controversially involved in the NCAIA, the licensing board, and his own practice.[116] Whatever conflicts he personally generated, he was tenacious in his efforts to free architecture from identification with civil engineering. Shumaker's first step came in 1927 with the creation of the Department of Architectural Engineering. The curriculum still relied on engineering for a portion of its program, but the formation of a separate department encouraged a heightened sense of professional identity.[117]

Although the first graduates of the architectural program were faced with the depression job market, Shumaker focused on the future and increased the intensity with which he pursued his ideal of excellence in architectural education. By 1940 he had laid the groundwork for the establishment of a five-year "professional" degree program in architecture. With this program providing access to the profession, architectural education entered a new era.[118]

A similar and parallel process began for general contractors. In 1927–28 the engineering curriculum at State College expanded to include construction engineering, "in order to educate men for the profession of Engineering particularly as it related to construction." The course preamble explained how the school saw the role and status of the building contractor in the state:

> North Carolina's progress indicates great increase in building and general construction. Construction needs more and better trained men to meet the immediate demands as well as to anticipate the greatly increased demands of the future. Builders, as few others, need to know at all times exactly where they stand on the projects they undertake. The contractor, to be successful must conduct his business systematically and economically. Therefore, he must learn not only general engineering technique but also something of Architecture and business methods and practices; he must delve further into construction and learn the principles involved, the methods, practices and successful policies in use.[119]

The curriculum description that followed mentioned courses in architecture, business, engineering, and the theory of construction, including estimating, management, and inspection, both theoretical and real. It ends with these words: "This curriculum is designed to prepare the student to enter the work of actual construction of modern structures and to lay a foundation for future work as owners, managers or executives in the construction industry."[120]

The curriculum for construction engineering combined elements from many programs. It continued to be revised through the 1930s and 1940s. In 1948 a four-year college program in construction engineering leading to a bachelor of science in construction was offered in the School of Engineering. A curriculum report noted: "The emphasis in this program, as compared with traditional studies in civil engineering, is in planning and management aspects of all types of construction activities rather than on design . . . [and] it has enjoyed the strong support and encouragement of the construction industry, particularly . . . the North Carolinas Branch of the AGC and the North Carolina Road Builders Association."[121]

The separation between architecture and building was made complete and formalized in the educational apparatus of the state.

Conclusion

North Carolina's prompt response in developing licensing procedures for architects and general contractors seems, in retrospect, almost too good to be true. But in the decades from 1900 to 1945, urbanization and industrialization achieved a momentum that neither wars nor the depression could completely stifle. Leaders in business and education recognized that North Carolina urban society was reaching new levels of affluence and influence, and the building industry experienced rapid growth and change within this context of momentous economic and social reorganization. It was an unusual time for architects and contractors who found themselves associated with the forces of progress and modernity. In this fluid environment, licensing and organization were means for gaining social recognition, sufficient compensation, and positive control of access to the building industry.

For architects in North Carolina, licensing and professional organization was the formal acknowledgment of role definition. Neither licensing nor membership in the NCAIA had little immediate effect on the performance of work. Rather, both offered legal and social recognition of a service that required skills acquired through education and experience. Some architects believe that neither the North Carolina Board of Architectural Registration nor the North Carolina chapter of the American Institute of Architects played a role of any importance in the profession until after World War II when architects felt threatened by the building industry itself. These threats—prefabricated buildings, expansion of the right to provide design services, issues of liability—raised new and concrete fears that architects had achieved redundancy, and the need for political action and influence to affect these issues made the license and NCAIA membership important. Others felt that the licensing board should not do anything but grant licenses and that the purpose of the NCAIA was to pro-

INSURANCE BUILDING, HOME OFFICE OF THE DURHAM LIFE INSURANCE COMPANY
RALEIGH, NORTH CAROLINA

NORTHUP AND O'BRIEN, ARCHITECTS

GENERAL CONTRACTOR — GEORGE W. KANE
Concrete, Ready Mixed — Southern Equipment Corporation
Steel & Miscellaneous Iron — Salem Steel Co.
Miscellaneous Iron — Mitchell & Becker Co.
Flooring, Clear Quarter Sawed White Oak Herringbone, Laid in
    Mastic — R. L. Dresser
Terrazzo & Tile Work — Atlantic Marble & Tile Co., Inc.
Plumbing — Robb Plumbing & Heating Co.
Heating — Robb Plumbing & Heating Co.
Pressed Steel Door Frames — J. B. Wilkins, Inc.
Steel Windows — Carolina Steel & Iron Co.
Flashing Blocks — Pine Hall Brick & Pipe Co.
Rubber Tile — David G. Allen
Steel Stairs — Mitchell & Becker Co.
Plastering — C. W. Kirkland

SAWED FLAGSTONE TERRACE LAID IN CEMENT
MR. AND MRS. EARL N. PHILLIPS RESIDENCE

SUPPLIED BY CAROLINA FLAGSTONE COMPANY
HIGH POINT, NORTH CAROLINA

GENERAL CONTRACTOR — R. K. STEWART & SON
Interior Decoration — Morrison-Neese, Inc.
Sawed random rectangular Carolina Bluestone for porches, terrace,
    steps, walks, buttress caps, etc. — Caroline Flagstone Co.
Steel & Miscellaneous Iron — Salem Steel Co.
Plumbing — Robb Plumbing & Heating Co.
Heating — Robb Plumbing & Heating Co.
Paint (Pittsburgh) — Brewer Paint & Wall Paper Co.
Tile & Marble — The McClamroch Company
Linoleum — The McClamroch Company
Linwall — The McClamroch Company
Slate Flagging — The McClamroch Company
Painting — Brewer Paint & Wall Paper Co.

RESIDENCE OF MR AND MRS EARL N PHILLIPS, HIGH POINT, NORTH CAROLINA

54

mote social interaction and camaraderie and that it had served that purpose admirably.

The effect of the AGC seems equally unclear. There were doubts that a professional organization for general contractors within a large and heterogeneous industry had any value except a social one. Licensing, on the other hand, reinforced specialities through classification by fiscal worth and through licensing by speciality. Contractors on the whole, however, felt that an active political role was important and necessary because of the significance of building in the state's economy.

Far more important than organization or licensing in its impact on building between 1900 and 1945 was the increase in the volume of work and in the number of architects and builders in practice. Firms grew in manpower, created organizational structures to support this growth, and added in-house components—engineers in architectural firms, architects in general contracting firms. In architecture the small one- or two-person office still dominated practice in 1945 but the pattern was changing. Similarly, the small general contractor persisted along with the firms that became major developers organized vertically to control the entire process from land acquisition, to design by in-house architects, to the erection and marketing of the product.

By 1945 in North Carolina, the building process had been transformed into a component of a massive industry. In this context, the role of every participant—architect, builder, client, artisan, laborer—was eroded by changes even as each experienced an increase in his or her potential to design, build, and participate in the industry. More people than ever were able to own more homes and buildings and more architects and builders were available to fill those needs. But as the right to participate as client or builder was extended to more and more people, the economic disparities that prevented some groups of people from owning and building were emphasized. These people experienced the social control that could be exerted by those who built for and rented to them, affecting their social positions through location and type of building. In North Carolina, as in other places and times, architects, builders, developers, community leaders, and others recognized the power that the ability to build confers on the people who can do it. The self-sufficient project is the personal macrocosm that confers power; the vertical organization of the general contract-

Opposite:

Recent work by Northup and O'Brien, Architects, Winston-Salem, ca. 1938–40, in *Carolina Architecture and Allied Arts*, 1942. This publication appeared annually in the late 1930s and early 1940s. It is a version of a "souvenir" without being considered advertising by architects because it is paid for by the advertisements of many materials producers, components and furniture manufacturers, and general contractors. The contrast between the two projects illustrated is a wonderful example of the design range of architectural firms in the postdepression years. (Photo, North Carolina Division of Archives and History.)

ing firm is its logical extension into the social cosmos. The architect who works on his or her own outside this organization plays a very complex role as interpreter and guide to those who have, on their own, the power to build. It is possible, therefore, to understand the magic and mystery of building and to understand why people involved in the process want to be able to control it. Building is power. In North Carolina the power building confers joined it irrevocably to the desire for independence, self-sufficiency, control, progress, and conservativism that characterized the white upper-middle-class society of the late 1940s. The duality of architecture and building, like the conflicts between elitism and idealism, are part of the story of the new New South of post–World War II years.

Ernest H. Wood III

7

The Opportunities Are Unlimited: Architects and Builders since 1945

Prologue: Building Races toward the Future

IN THE nineteenth century, the North Carolina State Fair was a showcase of agriculture and the mechanical arts, where the accomplishments of the building industry were on exhibit alongside the accomplishments of agriculture. Despite war and depression, fairs symbolized both progress already made and hopes for the future. A hundred years later, North Carolina remained a largely rural state, though its towns and cities had grown dramatically. As the nation emerged from World War II, there was again great optimism for the future.

It is appropriate, then, that the building that should emerge as a symbol of this new era would be on the State Fairgrounds in Raleigh. Designed by Matthew Nowicki, a young Polish architect who arrived in the capital city in 1948 as acting head of the architecture department at the new School of Design at North Carolina State College, the J. S. Dorton Arena was both a challenge and a triumph for the state officials who commissioned it, the architects and engineers who designed it, and the contractors who erected it. It was a key not only to the vision of the fair but also of agriculture, for in the postwar period, rural North Carolina made rapid economic and architectural strides in its efforts to catch up with development in the rest of the state. The arena brought the cutting edge of architecture into the public view at a time when architects zealously believed that their work could change the world. Clients, contractors, workmen, and architects each had their own niche in building, but in the early 1950s they shared a common goal—to find the future.

At first known simply as the State Fair Arena, the building also had a simple function: it was a place for judging livestock. Yet looming over the fairgrounds, which were then and are now populated by thrill rides, hot dog stands, midway games, and souvenir shops, the building had a majestic presence. It was used for the first time in 1952, even though it was incomplete. Reported the *News and Observer*: "They took the wraps off the 85th edition of the N.C. State Fair yesterday morning at 10 o'clock, and the eyes of the early fairgoers popped right out. Every fair boasts of some new fashioned addition to its facilities, but this year's has been an unusual innovation. The parabolic arches of that architectural wonder, the state fair arena, catch the spectator's eyes immediately, no matter where he alights from his car."[1]

If the general citizenry greeted the building with the same amazement they felt for the midway shows, the architectural community displayed a level of excitement that would greet a pioneering scientific discovery. Nowicki had created a design based on a revolutionary use of the forces of tension and compression. Two parabolic arches interlocked at their bases and leaned away from each other, supported at the top by a network of cables and on the sides by only a few vertical columns. The arena received wide publicity in the architectural press, and the American Institute of Architects gave the building an honor award of 1954. As the *Student Publication of the School of Design* noted in its first issue, which was dedicated to Nowicki: "The clients wanted a fair facility that would advertise North Carolina as a progressive state and they wanted no copy of anything done before."[2]

Attention to the arena—and its architect—was heightened by Nowicki's death in an airplane crash in 1950. The design as it now stands, slightly altered with added vertical supports, was completed by associate architect William Henley Deitrick of Raleigh and engineers Severud, Elstad, and Kreuger of New York. The arena was erected by the William Muirhead Construction Company of Durham. Nowicki remained, however, a powerful symbol of the modernist period in the state for both the public and the architectural profession. Among the young architects in school at the time and those who would follow shortly—the generation that would establish modernism in the state—the gifted young architect who was killed in his prime became nearly a cult figure.

The construction of the arena, in reality, resulted from an extraordinary mating of architectural talent with ambition from both the architectural and agricultural communities. J. S. Dorton, the fair manager whose ambition was "to make the N.C. State Fair the most modern plant in the world,"[3] first approached Henry Kamphoefner, dean of the new School of Design, within a year of the school's founding, saying that he wanted some special buildings constructed on the fairgrounds. Kamphoefner, who wanted to build the reputation of the school and secure work for its

Matthew Nowicki, Raleigh, ca. 1948. The brilliant young Polish architect had a profound and lingering influence on postwar North Carolina architects despite his premature death. (Photo, North Carolina State University Archives.)

faculty, suggested Nowicki. "I had no trouble persuading him about the abilities of Matthew Nowicki," Kamphoefner recalled in an interview in 1980. He described Nowicki as "a very charming person." Throughout the project, in fact, Nowicki's charm played a major role. Dorton "didn't have any idea of what he was going to get," recalled Kamphoefner, "but

Dr. J. S. Dorton and the State Fair Arena, Raleigh, ca. 1953. Dorton's vision was for a modern fair that would symbolize agriculture in the state. (Photo, North Carolina State Fair.)

Nowicki and Deitrick were very good salesmen" and had no trouble getting the $1.5 million building approved and funded, though it was considered very expensive for the day.[4]

Again and again, those who knew the young Polish architect commented not only on his extraordinary talent but on his unassuming yet powerful personality, which meshed well with the state's populist traditions. The result was immense popularity. As architecture critic Lewis Mumford, a visiting lecturer at the School of Design who had suggested Nowicki for the university position, wrote after Nowicki's death: "Nowicki's dictum that the client makes an important contribution to the building and deserves part of the credit stemmed from his profound respect for ordinary men and their ways, and this was fully rewarded by the popular response his personality and his work evoked."[5] Thirty years later, Thomas T. Hayes of Southern Pines, who had been a young architect in Deitrick's office during the arena project, remembered Nowicki's approach vividly: "As he developed these projects, he had a way of making people think that they had done it." Whether it was the governor, an official of the Department of Agriculture, or another architect, Nowicki would ask his opinion. "But there was no question that he had directed your opinion to what he wanted you to say," Hayes recalled. The technique worked. Noted Hayes, "These were tobacco chewing, cigar smoking country boys, who were powerful, and they loved Nowicki and he loved them, and it was that kind of relationship. These were powerful men who knew their power and they didn't worry about what people said."[6]

Like state architect William Nichols, who in the early nineteenth century had prodded his clients into redesigning the State House to accommodate the Canova statue of George Washington, Nowicki met criticism for the cost and ambition of the arena. Critics dubbed the building the "Cow Palace." But like Nichols's State House renovation, Nowicki's arena did exactly what it set out to do—elevate the level of North Carolina's public architecture and draw attention to the state. Reporting on the October 20, 1953 dedication of the arena, the *News and Observer* called the building "a great architectural wonder that seems to lasso the sky." The politicians' oratory also soared. Gov. William B. Umstead called the building a great tribute to the vision and foresight of the builders and the people of North Carolina. Kerr Scott, who had been governor when the building was approved and built and who at the dedication was a candidate for the U.S. Senate, called complaints about the arena's cost and design "opposition where there should have been no opposition." Said the former governor: "This [building] is the mirror of the Agriculture Department."[7]

The arena mirrored more than one government department, however. It was a symbol of what architecture and building could do and what postwar North Carolina wanted—even if it was not a symbol of general construction in the state. Like the Capitol a hundred years earlier, its direct effect on everyday building was negligible. Yet it was part of a widespread spirit of experimentation. Like the Capitol, it was to become a symbol of the city, and many people viewed it with both affection and pride. In the late 1970s, an auto dealer used it in his advertisements. The arena was a familiar spot for special events such as the circus and concerts. A local sporting-goods store sponsored a ten-kilometer run that coincidentally linked these two important buildings, the Capitol and the arena. Said the run's organizer: "Every time I go by the building, I say to myself, 'Gee, that's really something.' "[8]

An Era of Growth and Specialization

If the Dorton Arena was the standard-bearer of North Carolina's postwar architectural ambitions, it also held some ironies. The revolutionary structure's placement amid the honky-tonk of the fairgrounds is the obvious one. But an even greater irony—and one with more significance for the building industry—appears when the arena is considered with another of its builder's projects. Even as it was erecting this pioneering structure, the

William Muirhead Construction Company was working on the most traditional project of the decade, the reconstruction and restoration of Tryon Palace in New Bern.

The fact that these two projects were going up simultaneously (work on Tryon Palace began in 1952, about a year before the arena was completed, and finished in 1959) may not be as odd as it seems, however, for in the late 1940s and early 1950s, North Carolina stood on the brink of a transformation. Buildings and builders alike were caught between the urge to change and the search for traditional roots.

Across the country, the 1950s heralded a new era of technology, epitomized by structures such as the Dorton Arena that radically altered the perception, if not the reality, of building. In North Carolina, the transformation had an added dimension—the shift from a rural to an urban state. Ever since the 1830 census, the state's cities had been growing at a faster rate than the rural areas. By the 1930 census one hundred years later, cities for the first time showed a larger gain in numbers of persons than rural areas, though the state still was only 25.5 percent urban. Cities continued to grow at a steady rate, however. The first census after the war, taken in 1950, placed the state's urban population at 30.5 percent. Thirty years later, in 1980, it stood at 48 percent. The same 2.5 percent urban growth rate that North Carolina experienced between 1970 and 1980 would make the state more than half urban for the first time in 1990.[9]

Conditions on the farm had improved over the years, thanks to such innovations as rural electrification. From the establishment of the North Carolina Rural Electrification Authority in 1935, the number of farms served by electricity grew rapidly—from only about 3 percent to 20 percent in the first ten years, to nearly 97 percent by 1954. With agricultural mechanization requiring fewer workers and urban industrialization offering new jobs, however, the cities held great attraction. Twenty-two counties had fewer residents in 1954 than in 1940.[10]

As a result of the farm exodus, the agricultural labor force dropped from 34 percent of the state's total workers in 1940 to 25 percent in 1950 to 20 percent in 1955. Many left the farm for North Carolina's cities. Many, especially blacks, left the state seeking urban employment elsewhere. In addition to manufacturing, cities offered opportunities in such fields as education, research, retailing, and public service. While farm employment dropped by more than half—from 590,000 in 1950 to 241,000 in 1970—the state's nonagricultural employment continued to grow, totaling 1,745,900 in 1970, seven times the number of farm workers.[11]

The low percentage of agricultural workers in a still-rural state reflects another phenomenon, as many others remained in rural areas but were employed in work other than farming. In 1960, only 17.8 percent of the state's residents were classified as "rural farm," whereas 42.7 percent were classified as "rural non-farm," and 39.5 percent were "urban." Many of those who remained in rural areas found new work in industry, like those who moved to the cities, for after World War II many businesses began to decentralize and add to their traditional base in the Piedmont. The state gained 5,000 manufacturing plants—more than any other southern state —between 1939 and 1967 for a 250 percent increase.[12] The growth of industry in rural areas helped boost the economy, prompting construction of new homes and businesses and improvement of existing ones.

Construction is not normally listed as one of the state's top industries, perhaps because of its fragmented nature and perhaps because, unlike textiles, tobacco, or furniture manufacturing, it is no more characteristic of North Carolina than elsewhere. But it nonetheless employed a large portion of the state's growing number of nonfarm workers—both those who resided in the cities and in the country. By 1980, some 119,134 North Carolinians were engaged in construction trades. Professionals (architects numbered 1,909 and engineers, 22,310) and people in other aspects of construction (truck drivers and other transportation workers numbered 12,910, clerical workers, 8,257, and sales and administrative support, 11,388, for example) added another 162,467[13] for a total of 281,601. However, even the lower number—those employed directly in building trades —ranked construction second among North Carolina employers, behind only textiles, which employed 266,778 in 1980. Building ranked ahead of agriculture, forestry, and fishing (89,430); apparel and other finished textiles (82,920); and food and kindred products (36,638).[14]

The construction industry, which had been nearly at a standstill during World War II, began to grow immediately after the cessation of hostilities in 1945. In May, the month Germany surrendered to the Allies, the state's 26 largest cities issued 77 building permits. That number continued to rise during the summer, and in August, when Japan surrendered, the same cities issued 183 permits. A year later in August, they issued 474. Two years later, they issued 1,367.[15] The immediate postwar boom was only the beginning. In 1980, August building permits numbered 39,876 for 45 cities; in 1985 they numbered 57,171 for the same month.[16]

In such a climate of change, a certain plurality was inevitable. Style is a case in point. The postwar emphasis on progress was fertile ground for modernist architecture, which promised a more uniform quality and style of building. The movement was most successful in institutional and governmental building, including schools, which showed a marked growth due to the high postwar "baby boom" birthrate. Housing meanwhile remained staunchly traditional. The immediate postwar emphasis on architectural theory, however, did lay the groundwork for an issue-oriented period in construction, when academic, ethical, and social concerns such as energy consciousness, history, the natural environment, accessibility for the handicapped, and housing for the poor became nearly as important as the long-standing questions of finance, technology, and division of labor.

Architecture and building's new roles were sometimes sources of conflict, but in an age of growing specialization, they more often simply coexisted. This was a period that simultaneously could support the mobile home industry and historic preservation, university training for architects and giant retail chains that sold building materials for do-it-yourselfers. In what could at times appear to be chaos in building, companies such as Muirhead, which handled projects as different as the "Cow Palace" and the royal governor's palace, illustrate how well the industry could accommodate the state's needs and desires.

Muirhead Construction obtained each of these jobs in the same time-honored way—by submitting the low bid. Yet as different as they were, each was a job for which the company was well suited. Its experience in highways, heavy construction, utilities, and large buildings—nearly all aspects of the industry except residential building—provided an appropriate background for the arena. William Muirhead's personal background suited the palace equally well. A native of Scotland, he had emigrated to New York as a young man to work for a steel company. While working on a job in North Carolina, he decided Durham was a pleasant and promising community, and in 1925 he founded his company there. During reconstruction of the palace (which had burned in 1798), he made several trips back to England and Scotland to purchase materials and to consult architect John Hawks's original drawings, which were still on record in London. "The arena was a whole lot of fun for him, it was something new," recalled Muirhead's son Alastair, who succeeded his father as head of the company. "He probably had a good time two or three times during his 50 years [in the business]. This was one and Tryon Palace in New Bern was another."[17]

The company also approached each job in surprisingly ordinary ways. For the arena, Muirhead generally used its own crews. "Very little of it was subbed," recalled Alastair Muirhead, who as a twenty-four-year-old was in charge of the ready-mix concrete plant the company set up at the site. "We normally did all the concrete on any building. We used all our own men. The only boy we did bring in was an engineer from Chapel Hill. We brought him in to do the survey engineering."[18] At Tryon Palace, the company sent a thirty-four-year-old former carpenter named Tommy Lampley to oversee the work. Lampley, who lived in a house on the palace grounds for the seventeen months he was on the job, hired local workmen, preferring those with experience working on New Bern's old homes. He normally had between eighteen and twenty-five men—mostly masons and carpenters—on the job. Most were between forty and sixty-nine. The sixty-nine-year-old, recalled Lampley, was a former boat builder. Work-

Reinforced concrete crew at work, Muirhead Construction Company, State Fair Arena, Raleigh, 1952. The pioneering structure was erected with conventional techniques. (Photo, North Carolina Division of Archives and History.)

men at both the palace and the arena were not organized any differently than they would have been on any other job, according to both Muirhead and Lampley. "As far as a carpenter, if he could follow orders and knew what he was doing, then he was all right," said Lampley. "It boiled down to: a mechanic is a mechanic. If he can do one job, he can do any job. All you have to do is stop and think about it."[19]

Such common-sense building characterized not only Muirhead's workmen but the way the company itself approached each job. It meant working closely with the architects and engineers, especially on the arena. "I think they learned along with us," recalled Muirhead. The builders were undaunted. "We had done similar things with bridges," he said. "As far as the seats went, we had done that with Kenan Stadium in Chapel Hill. So you put the pieces together. It wasn't that unusual. The roof was the main [unusual] thing."[20] The restoration architect for the palace, William Perry of Boston, had more experience with his project, having worked at Colonial Williamsburg in Virginia and on other preservation projects. When problems or questions arose, he flew to New Bern.

Carpenters framing dormers, Muirhead Construction Company, Tryon Palace restoration, New Bern, 1956. The contractors employed local workmen with traditional skills. (Photo, Tryon Palace Restoration Complex.)

Lampley was as confident as Muirhead about his men's ability to do the job, however. "It doesn't take you long to learn if you want to," he said. That confidence continued on other jobs as well. After working on the palace, Lampley went to work on a women's dormitory on the East Campus of Duke University. "It was from old to modern," he recalled. "No problem."[21]

But other segments of the building industry and much of the public did have problems accommodating both the traditional and the modern— at least when it came to style. Most chose one or the other, and in the public debates over architectural styles that ensued, the tug-of-war within building became highly visible. For whereas the cause of modernism before 1945 was represented only by a few architects and their buildings, it reached a new intensity in the postwar era, now that it had an organized voice in the School of Design at North Carolina State College. Architects, through both the school and the new buildings they designed, strongly promoted modernism as the "correct" style. In the state's new prosperity, they saw the opportunity for a new beginning. The resistance they met,

like the opposition that greeted architectural writer A. J. Downing's revolutionary ideas a century before, however, indicated how deeply embedded tradition was in the state.

In 1948, a professor of architecture from the University of Oklahoma
named Henry Leveke Kamphoefner arrived in Raleigh as the first dean of
the School of Design. One of North Carolina's attractions for Kamphoefner was the state's progressive reputation in both the arts and politics. A
few months after arriving, he wrote to Josef Albers, the Bauhaus painter
working at the experimental Black Mountain College outside Asheville:
"When my colleagues and I decided to come to North Carolina, being near
Black Mountain College was considered by all of us to be one of the
advantages."[22] Later in the same academic year, Kamphoefner wrote to
North Carolina's U.S. Senator Frank Porter Graham: "One of the major
factors in my final decision to come to North Carolina was the fact that you
are here. I thought that any university where Frank Graham had been
President for so many years would be liberal, progressive and fair."[23] And
in a 1949 statement for the State College yearbook, *The Agromeck*, Kamphoefner referred to North Carolina as "the most progressive state in the
South." In such a state, he wrote, "the opportunities are unlimited for the
school's graduates to contribute to the solution of problems in building
design, planning and general construction."[24]

The School of Design turned the architectural community on its ear.
Nowicki's arena was the largest project to come from the school in the
earliest days, but there was a steady stream of smaller innovative works
from other faculty members. In 1954 Argentine architect Eduardo Cata-
lano built a revolutionary house for himself in Raleigh with a thin-shell
hyperbolic paraboloid roof that was widely published. George Matsu-
moto, who had come with Kamphoefner from Oklahoma, quickly built a
name for himself as a designer of modern residences and won a number of
local commissions and design awards. Visiting lecturers, such as Frank
Lloyd Wright, who spoke to four thousand people in Reynolds Coliseum
on the campus in 1950, Walter Gropius, Mies van der Rohe, and dozens
more who visited for short times, contributed to the school's reputation
for experimentation and excellence. R. Buckminster Fuller, who spent
longer periods on the campus over several years as a visiting professor in
the 1950s, did seminal work on his geodesic dome design while in Raleigh.

During this period, Kamphoefner was busy promoting the cause of
modernism in whatever ways he could. A 1954 invitation to speak to the
Kiwanis Club in Elkin came from a member who had heard a similar talk
in Wilkesboro. "I was impressed with the new house designs that included air movement and solar heat," he wrote.[25] Kamphoefner visited
new buildings, such as a school in Hickory designed by architect Robert L.
Clemmer, and complimented the clients on the result. "The building is a
progressive departure from the dark and depressing buildings that were

Henry Kamphoefner (right) with Frank Lloyd Wright, North Carolina State College, Raleigh, 1950. Like Wright, Kamphoefner was an untiring and outspoken advocate of modern architecture. (Photo, School of Design, North Carolina State University.)

built a generation ago and called schools," he wrote the superintendent of the Hickory schools after his visit.[26] He also counseled clients to follow through with their architect's recommendations. When the Concordia Evangelical Lutheran Church balked at installing the copper roof that architect A. G. Odell, Jr., of Charlotte had designed, Kamphoefner wrote to assure them that "the material is and must be an integral part of the design." Himself the son of a Methodist clergyman, Kamphoefner ended his letter to the pastor with a bit of evangelizing on the behalf of modernism: "I congratulate you and your committee again on bringing to one of the smaller North Carolina communities an outstanding example of first-rate contemporary architecture."[27] The church was built as designed.

Kamphoefner was not alone, of course. In Charlotte, architect Odell was the strongest supporter of modernism. A member of a wealthy Concord textile family who in 1950 achieved architectural prominence with his domed design for the Charlotte Coliseum, he also served as president of both the NCAIA (1953–55) and the national AIA (1964–65) and until his retirement in 1982 headed one of the most successful firms in Charlotte.[28] In the early 1950s, Odell wrote to another church client that his office was "only interested in the design of contemporary church architecture." He added, "We have had many inquiries with respect to our willingness to execute church design, and we have refused commissions due to the owners' insistence upon the execution of cheap copies of the great church architecture of the past."[29] The press also championed modern architecture. In a 1955 editorial titled "Goodby to Gothic and Williamsburg," the *Charlotte News* wrote: "North Carolina architecture is slowly being revitalized. Someday fadism and eclecticism will disappear and the devitalized and sterile forces will be defeated. That is the challenge for Tar Heel architecture today."[30]

The newspaper's "someday" never really came, however. For though modern architecture could do nearly anything technologically, it could not always make itself popular. The movement won over many institutional buildings, but architecture's "challenge" also turned into pitched battles. Tradition won the largest battle—the debate over the new campus for Wake Forest University in Winston-Salem. Arguments flew back and forth following the Z. Smith Reynolds Foundation's 1946 offer that prompted the move from Wake Forest, but by the 1951 ground breaking, the university had settled on the Georgian style, the same that had been used on its old campus.

Most architects apparently supported a modernist approach for the new campus. A questionnaire sent by the Winston-Salem *Journal and Sentinel* in 1948 to 160 architects yielded twenty responses, only one of which favored the traditional design.[31] But the architects held little sway over the building committee. The chairman of the college's board of trustees, who also served on the committee, wrote to Kamphoefner after he had criti-

Left to right: R. J. Reynolds, Jr., head of the Reynolds Foundation; Jens Frederick Larson, architect of the new Wake Forest University campus; and Charles H. Babcock, donor of land for the campus; Winston-Salem, 1956. The traditional design raised a furor in the architectural community, but not among the public. (Photo, Hank Walker, Life Magazine © Time Inc.)

cized the Georgian design: "My chief difference with you is that I can see something valid and beautiful in various types of design other than that taught and advocated by you . . . I see no valid objection to having different schools of thought and conception in the field of architecture. For this reason, I take vigorous exception to the remark you made recently in Winston-Salem that if Wake Forest College used the Georgian type architecture, it would be headed for the educational graveyard. Such remarks as that coming from a responsible person as you are, make it all the more difficult for us who are now going through the travail of trying to raise the money for the buildings here in Winston-Salem."[32] Kamphoefner replied in a letter the next day that he had said "architectural" not "educational" graveyard, but he stood by his views on the design.[33]

The debate became acrimonious. Jens F. Larson, the New York architect commissioned to design the new, traditional campus, chastised his critics—especially the academics—for having "adopted a dangerous practice of attempting to dictate to the profession without creating through actual building. This in turn is causing fallacious teaching of students who are being led hypnotically into argument instead of into creative effort."[34] After Larson spoke at the NCAIA's annual meeting at Atlantic Beach in 1948, Kamphoefner referred to the New Yorker in a letter to a colleague as "architecture's No. 1 four-flusher."[35]

Elsewhere the traditional also had its adherents, and those architects and builders who designed and built in a more historicist mode, such as architect Archie Royal Davis of Durham, were as popular and busy as ever. Davis was the architect who designed most of the "Williamsburg" buildings for downtown Chapel Hill during the town's 1940s campaign to create a village with a homogeneous and unified style. In 1951, a woman's club in Raleigh asked Davis to speak on "Preserving the Traditional." The topic was chosen, wrote the chairwoman of the committee that invited him, "because the present trend toward 'off with the old and on with the new' has become so evident and I might say reckless, that a warning should be sounded."[36]

One more serious incident, however, pointed out the gap between the state's intellectual community, desirous of change, and its conservative population. In the fall of 1951, W. E. Debnam, a commentator for WPTF Radio, Raleigh's most powerful station, attacked visiting lecturer Lewis Mumford as a socialist, perhaps even a communist.[37] Debnam based his attacks, aired statewide over a fifteen-station network during his show "Debnam Views the News," on Mumford's book *Technics and Civilization*, which was being used as a text at State College in a contemporary civilization class,[38] but much of the controversy that ensued was centered on the School of Design because of Mumford's guest lectures there. For the rest of the academic year, Mumford's fourth at the college, the attacks continued. At one point, Debnam sent a pamphlet to the members of the General Assembly and to the university system's board of trustees summarizing his attacks. Its cover was pink.

Before the academic year was over, Mumford had been offered and had accepted a professorship at the University of Pennsylvania and had decided not to return to Raleigh for the coming year,[39] but when Debnam heard that Mumford was not returning, he took credit for having the critic dismissed. "We are happy to report," Debnam broadcast on June 19, 1952, "that as a result of our report on this situation at North Carolina State College, basic communist—and that's his own phrase—Lewis Mumford is to appear no more as a visiting professor at North Carolina State."[40] College chancellor J. W. Harrelson wrote to Debnam in support of Mumford, and the board of the NCAIA voted to issue a statement supporting the School of Design against Debnam's attacks,[41] but Mumford left the college bitter.

In the Mumford incident, the state's architectural and university communities were drawn into a drama that had its origins elsewhere—principally the anticommunist crusade of U.S. Senator Joseph McCarthy—and was not aimed directly at building. For the most part, it was over in a year. There may have been a connection, however, between "The Affair Mumford," as Debnam called it, and the distrust of modern architecture among much of the public, a reaction against outsiders such as Mumford, or a growing tendency of North Carolinians to be influenced by events elsewhere.

The debates over modern versus traditional architecture certainly were an attack on architecture's self-assuredness, and as such, they concerned a great deal more than style. They were about control, for they raised the very basic question: Who is in charge? To the architect, and any other professional, the responsibilities and benefits of professionalism included an expertise and a resultant authority that no other group could—or should—possess. Clients and builders, recalling earlier traditions, sometimes resisted the architects' attempts to place themselves at the head of the industry.

This was an old story. One sore spot was the North Carolina client's traditionally parsimonious nature, which continued to be a major influence on building and continued to cause friction and frustration. Twenty-five years later, in a discussion of regionalism for *North Carolina Architect* magazine, Fayetteville architect Daniel MacMillan would decry that nature as a characteristic strong enough to distinguish the state from its neighbors: "That is this sort of austere, no nonsense approach that we've always had. But it doesn't really allow much in the way of frills or even quality."[42] Local architects chafed at the state's lingering tendency to import architects for major commissions, such as the state Legislative Building (1962) and the North Carolina Museum of Art (1983), both designed by Edward Durell Stone of New York. Though Stone associated with a local firm (Holloway and Reeves of Raleigh) for construction drawings and site supervision, as was the common practice, it was the New Yorker who handled the buildings' designs and who received recognition for the projects. There also remained a long-standing friction between architects and builders. Even when relations within the industry were good, architects and contractors retained a reputation for mutual distrust and animosity. After returning from the 1961 Associated General Contractors convention, where he apparently had found the contractors most cordial to architects, Raleigh architect Albert Haskins commented on the widespread perception that the two professions did not get along. "I can't understand," he wrote, "why the remark is constantly made that some of the contractors flare up every time the word 'architect' is mentioned."[43] Perhaps the remark was made because it often was true. In 1957, for example, Raleigh City Councilman John Coffey, a general contractor, had cautioned his fellow councilmen in a debate over the proposed new municipal building not to build a monument to the architect, saying he knew architects who would "crucify you."[44]

As each participant in the building process sought to enforce his identity and wishes and to protect his position against encroachment by other groups, there arose an increasing institutionalization in building. Institutionalization, however, was due to more than individual controversies. Its leading cause probably was the sheer number of people now involved in building. In the four decades from 1940 to 1980, the number of tradesmen employed in construction increased two and a half times from 47,246[45] to 119,134,[46] prompting more involvement from the government and from professional, trade, and marketing associations. Building was becoming so complex and its scale so large that many architects and builders needed help to wend their way through the process. Some needed monitoring to assure they designed or built with proper care. State and local regulations such as building codes and professional organizations such as the Associated General Contractors and the American Institute of Architects had existed for years, but their attempts at influencing construction were growing. Just as in the years following the Civil War, everyone in construction seemed to acknowledge the industry would be changing rapidly in the coming decades. Better organized now, they all set out to protect themselves and influence the industry's direction.

Architects, engineers, general contractors, plumbing and heating contractors, and electrical contractors all had licensing requirements before World War II. In the postwar period, the state passed licensing acts governing refrigeration contractors (1955), water well contractors (1961), and landscape architects (1969). By the 1980s, interior designers were discussing the need for a licensing act.

Each act was constitutionally based on the need to protect public health and welfare, though a certain degree of exclusivity was inherent in any licensing. One effect was to automatically divide up much of the work. A project's size and the architectural practice act's requirements, or the project's complexity, ambition, and sophistication, often dictated who would perform which tasks in the building process. In 1961, for example, Wilbur Hardee of Rocky Mount sketched the first plan for a Hardee's hamburger restaurant on the back of an envelope. But before he built, he had a local architect, Russell Sorrell, design the final version. As Hardee's became a successful restaurant chain, all subsequent designs also were created by architects or professional design firms.[47] Sometimes exclusivity went too far, however. In 1957 the state supreme court ruled unconstitutional a thirty-year-old statute requiring registration of tile contractors, saying that "the statute can not be upheld as an exercise of police power, since its provisions have no substantial relation to the public health, safety or welfare but tend to create a monopoly."[48]

The Southern Building Code Congress, which had organized in 1940, published its first code in 1945, intended for use in rural areas and small towns where codes were not already in force.[49] Over the ensuing decades, codes regulating structure and "life safety" issues such as fire protection not only evolved and were refined, but government programs of all kinds increased, especially during the 1960s, 1970s, and 1980s. They ranged from a federal requirement that certain contracts on government buildings be set aside for small contractors, to state regulations mandating access to buildings for the handicapped or limiting the amount of runoff and erosion at a construction site.

Education for the building trades and professions also was institutionalized, with the founding of the School of Design at North Carolina State College (1948) and the College of Architecture at the University of North Carolina-Charlotte (1970), building options in the civil engineering program at North Carolina State (prewar and postwar programs reorganized and merged in 1953), new programs for construction education in the state's community colleges and technical institutes, and apprenticeship and training programs for tradesmen through the state departments of labor and education.

In the building business, however, which traditionally was composed of individuals, such programs met with mixed success. The North Carolina Home Builders Association (founded 1962) had little trouble with its goal to help members with building technology and marketing. Likewise, the North Carolina chapter of the American Institute of Architects successfully aided architectural education and helped its members in their practices. But the NCAIA fell short in its attempts to make architects the leaders of the entire construction industry. Education for the trades never reached the numbers it sought either, for further industrialized building lessened the skills that were required to get a job, and a booming economy meant young people could find work before they finished their studies—if they chose to enter construction at all.

For large, complex buildings designed and constructed entirely by professionals, the general contractor's role as an organizer of construction had been well established before the war. The postwar period, however, saw a tremendous increase in the number of small contractors—especially homebuilders. Ironically, the technology they used remained little changed since the 1930s. Standardized parts may have been on the increase, but builders continued to put them together by hand. Homebuilders' newfound prominence was the result instead of a tremendous need for housing and of changes in financing, which allowed them to meet that need through a new, broader scale of building. At the same time, real estate developers, bankers, and others who greased the wheels of construction also grew in numbers and importance, as did interests from out-of-state.

These changes led to the further development of the speculative building industry and the increased perception of building as a business rather than a trade or a profession. Prefabricated, pre-engineered, and factory-built buildings were the ultimate in this approach to off-the-shelf buildings. Prefabs usually were small structures, but pre-engineered buildings, which were designed elsewhere and assembled on the local site with materials supplied by national fabricators, could be quite large. Though they filled a definite need for clients and eventually won acceptance from the architectural profession, they were sources of friction in the building industry for years. The state building inspector required the designing architect's or engineer's seal on the building plans, but if the designer did not have reciprocity with North Carolina, out-of-state firms sometimes built without his seal. Architects bristled at attempts to obtain seals from local architects or engineers. "The architectural board has been concerned about the large number of owners, particularly interstate chain operations, which are in the market to 'buy a seal' for the sole purpose of obtaining building permits," noted Raleigh attorney R. Mayne Albright, counsel for the NCAIA and the North Carolina Board of Architecture, in 1970.[50]

Prefabricated construction had been practiced in the state since the colonial period, when house frames were shipped to Boston, Charleston, and the Caribbean. In the 1880s, the North Carolina Car Company of Raleigh shipped barns, houses, and railroad cars across the country. The technique reached new heights after World War II, however, in the manufactured housing industry. Commonly known as mobile homes but seldom truly mobile after they were delivered from the factory, manufactured housing grew steadily in popularity, especially in rural areas and on the fringes of towns and cities. By the late 1970s, North Carolina ranked fifth nationally in both units manufactured and sold.[51] Ten years later, the state ranked third (behind Georgia and Indiana) in manufacture, with 22,786 units, and second (behind Florida) in sales, with 22,699 units.[52] Some 705,665 North Carolinians lived in the state's 320,757 manufactured homes.[53] Compared to conventional homes, these provided low-cost housing. The average price of a single-section home in 1988 was $19,733 for 942 square feet; the average multisection home was $37,276 for 1,446 square feet.[54] The average site-built home cost two to three times the price of even the largest mobile home.

Because a manufactured home could be shipped only about three hundred miles, factories usually were located near their markets. In the early 1970s, the state had as many as forty-nine factories (seven locally owned) turning out homes on an assembly-line basis, using mostly unskilled labor trained on the job. Each factory employed between seventy-five and one hundred persons. The homes generally were designed by engineers or architects hired by the companies.[55] By the late 1980s, the

Assembly line, Sterling Manufactured Homes, Albemarle, 1985. North Carolina is one of the national leaders in the manufacture and sale of mobile homes. (Photo, North Carolina Manufactured Housing Institute, Raleigh.)

number of plants had declined to thirty (five locally owned), but the plants were larger, employing an average of about two hundred persons each.[56] The number of units produced also increased, from about 18,000 a year in the late 1970s[57] to more than 22,000 in 1988.[58] So did the number of retail centers, from 500[59] to 650.[60]

Like architects and builders, persons in the manufactured housing industry found the need for a professional association. Founded in 1968 from the two-state Mobile Home Association of the Carolinas, the North Carolina Manufactured Housing Institute included by the late 1980s about 1,300 members, ranging from those who were involved with manufacturers and sales centers to those who towed, financed, insured, and furnished mobile homes. Its concerns centered on such issues as mobile home park zoning, sizes of homes that were allowed to be shipped on highways, and building codes for manufactured housing. The code, which was developed first in North Carolina (a voluntary code in 1969, mandatory in 1971) and helped lead to federal Department of Housing and Urban Development standards (1976), produced a marked improvement in the quality of manufactured housing.[61]

At the other end of the spectrum from the completed, manufactured building were the parts of buildings, and in materials supply North Carolina also saw significant changes in the postwar period. Chief among these was the phenomenal success of Lowe's stores, a discount building products chain that in the mid-1940s consisted of one store. By the mid-1980s, it had grown to three hundred and had become the largest building supply company in the nation.[62]

The company traces its origins to 1921 when L. S. Lowe incorporated North Wilkesboro Hardware. Upon his death in 1940, the business passed to his daughter, Ruth, who apparently had little interest in hardware, for in that same year she sold her share of the business to her brother James L. Lowe and married H. Carl Buchan, an employee of Commercial Credit in Charlotte. Buchan, however, saw more opportunity in the hardware business than his wife had. Three years later, he bought back a half-interest in the store for $12,500 and assumed management. Located in two 50-by-140-foot buildings in downtown North Wilkesboro, the business had an inventory that included notions, dry goods, horse collars, harnesses, snuff, produce, groceries, small miscellaneous hardware, and building materials. Buchan immediately sold all the stock except the heavy hardware and building materials.[63]

Buchan's timing could not have been better, for the end of World War II produced a tremendous demand for building products. His concept of retailing could not have been better, either. For in a time when building materials were sold through a controlled distribution system involving manufacturer, wholesaler, and retailer, which also limited sales territories, Buchan sought to eliminate steps by buying directly from the manufacturer whenever possible and selling "in volume at a lower cost because you would have a lower operating expense."[64]

Many manufacturers resisted the idea and refused to supply materials to Buchan. But enough agreed to work with him that he could implement his plan. Builders, naturally, jumped at the chance to save money on materials, and Lowe's fame spread, even without advertising. At first builders drove in from western North Carolina, southwestern Virginia, and eastern Tennessee to pick up supplies. Soon they came from as far away as South Carolina, Kentucky, West Virginia, Ohio, and Illinois. Recalled Petro Kulynych, who began work as a bookkeeper and later became vice-president in change of purchasing: "We'd get in a carload of doors, and the word would spread so fast we wouldn't even have time to unload them. We'd go down to the rail siding with a cigar box, for making change, and sell them right off the boxcar to lines of builders that would stretch for a block or more. All sales were cash and all were final. There were many afternoons when I'd go to the bank to deposit four or five thousand dollars in cash, most of it in hundred dollar bills."[65]

Lowe and Buchan soon began their expansion. First, they purchased a feed mill in Sparta forty miles away, which they converted to a store to serve their customers across the mountains. The success of that store

Carl Buchan and the original North Wilkesboro Hardware, North Wilkesboro, ca. 1959. A single store grew to be the nation's largest chain of retail building suppliers. (Photo, Lowe's Companies.)

enabled them to expand even more, and they acquired an automobile dealership and a cattle farm. In 1952, Buchan traded his interest in these nonbuilding ventures for Lowe's interest in the building supply stores and assumed total control of the company. Ninety days later, he opened a third store in Asheville.[66] In that year sales reached $4.1 million. The next, $6.4 million. The following year, a fourth store opened and the total sales were $9 million. In 1955, two more stores opened and sales hit $11.9 million, nearly three times the amount of only three years earlier. By 1959, with fifteen stores, Lowe's emphasized the professional builder as its primary customer. The company expanded its fleet of trucks and began delivery to job sites and in 1960 also began selling lumber. Annual sales had reached $30.7 million.[67]

On October 22, 1960, at age 44, Carl Buchan suffered a heart attack and died in his sleep. He already had taken steps to pass the ownership of the company to the employees, however, and his successors continued his policies of growth and change. In 1964, for example, the company put computers on the retail sales floors to track inventory, compute sales, and save money. In 1968, the company recognized the growing market of home owners as well as builders and began specially training sales people to service each market. In 1970, it adopted a standard design for all its stores and emphasized highway sites in smaller cities and in the suburbs of major cities.[68] Capitalizing on a growing market in the do-it-yourself business that was fueled by inflation in the 1970s, Lowe's by the mid-1980s defined itself as "a specialty retailer, an upscale discounter of building materials and related products for the do-it-yourself (DIY) home improvement and home construction markets."[69] With three hundred stores in twenty-one states across the South Atlantic and South Central regions, Lowe's employed 14,783 persons. The average store in 1986 had 125,000 customers and did $7.8 million in sales, 55 percent of which was to nonprofessionals and 45 percent to professional builders. Most contractors who bought from Lowe's built single-family houses. The company also had identified a group it called "buy-it-yourselfers," home owners who purchased materials themselves but contracted the labor to professionals.[70]

Prefabricated building and materials marketing were long-standing segments of the building industry. What changed in the postwar period was the scale. Size alone did not mean control in such a diversified business as building, however. From 1977 to 1987, Lowe's doubled its percentage of the national do-it-yourself market and sold $1.26 billion in products, but that still amounted to only 1.5 percent of the national total.[71] Clearly, there was room for entrepreneurs in building. Many builders and professionals found their niche through the opposite of comprehensiveness and size—specialization. Sometimes they narrowed the focus of traditional practice. Sometimes they found work created by the emergence of new concerns.

In Raleigh beginning in the 1970s, for example, architect Ron Mace, who used a wheelchair himself, ran a firm that specialized in design for the handicapped.[72] By the late 1980s, fifteen persons—including architects, interior designers, builders, and businessmen—had qualified for the designation "Certified Kitchen Designer" given by the National Kitchen and Bath Association in recognition of the need for specialists in designing this technically oriented part of the house.[73] Interior designers had expanded beyond their roots in decorating and were increasingly designing residential additions and remodelings and other small-scale architecture. Numbering some five hundred in the state by the late 1980s,[74] they also were joining architectural firms to design commercial interiors or were planning interior spaces of large speculative buildings that architects left unfinished for clients. Perhaps the two most widespread and characteristic specialist groups, however, were those involved with historic preservation and energy efficiency. Each sprang from a combination of grass-roots and professional concerns, and each evolved in different ways.

Historic preservation existed on only a small scale before World War

II. The state's first large-scale preservation projects occurred shortly afterward, however, with the restoration of Old Salem in Winston-Salem, begun in the late 1940s, and the reconstruction of Tryon Palace in New Bern in the 1950s. Until the late 1960s and early 1970s, however, historic preservation was almost entirely the province of old families and patriotic and historical societies. Though architects showed a slightly more wide-ranging interest, their involvement was often limited to academic and professional concerns of structure and style. Greater public involvement in historic preservation began in the early 1970s with the revitalization of inner-city neighborhoods. Home owners often did much of their own labor, usually because they wanted to save money or because they could not find tradesmen who knew traditional building techniques—or both. Older carpenters, especially, were highly prized in these neighborhoods. To meet the new demand, some schools, such as Durham Technical Institute, offered programs in restoration for carpenters, masons, and others who wanted to specialize in preservation work. Many of the new preservation specialists, however, were simply those who had taken the time to learn from the buildings they had worked on and who cared about old buildings. Many architects received their first exposure to preservation during the recession of 1974 and 1975 when they took on renovation projects after new construction slowed.[75] Though some architects were involved in residential restoration, a larger number found preservation work in adaptive reuse. Much of this work was prompted by federal tax incentives for rehabilitating commercial structures. By the 1980s, turning warehouses into offices and condominiums or turning storefronts and old houses into restaurants had become a major part of many architectural firms' work.

Like historic preservation, the concern for energy-efficient design was shared by the public and professionals. With roots in the counterculture movement of the 1960s, the concern quickly came to a head in the mid-1970s, when energy costs skyrocketed. Both builders and architects opened offices specializing in this field. However, it just as quickly lost much of its appeal in the late 1970s and early 1980s, as costs subsided. But energy consciousness never totally disappeared. Construction techniques such as better insulation and double-glazed glass became common practice. Like preservation, energy consciousness was a field that not only attracted young architects and builders, it directly involved building owners. Especially in residences, owners concerned with energy savings often made modifications themselves. As in preservation, owners and professionals alike often approached their subject with a missionary zeal. In 1974, a young magazine publisher named John Shuttleworth located his fledgling alternative life-style magazine *Mother Earth News* and its related research divisions in Hendersonville. By 1980, the magazine had a circulation of 1.2 million nationwide, employed 120 persons, and spent a half million dollars annually on research in the Hendersonville area. Projects ranged from building technology to alternative fuels and motors. On mountain land they owned, the researchers revived such vernacular housing forms as the Mongolian yurt. Though only a very few builders or owners used such esoteric techniques from the magazine as rammed-earth construction, *Mother Earth News'* philosophy was indicative of a great deal more. It was evidence that many people still believed in building for themselves—though probably with the help of a plumber or an electrician. This grass-roots involvement in building and reaction against specialization, professionalism, and institutionalization was anything but a new phenomenon. It was the historical backbone of building. It was an approach well expressed by a spokesman for the magazine: "Part of our job," he said, "really is to de-mystify technology. . . . It's been our experience that a lot of people can hang things that work together with 2 × 4s and spit."[76]

A Different Modernism Rebuilds the Farm

With the efforts to win the state over to modernist architecture and the success of many institutional buildings such as the Dorton Arena built in that style, the post–World War II era is generally regarded as the "modern" period of architecture and building in the state. Both styles and technology raced toward the future. While modern architecture may have been a symbol of what the state wanted, however, it was far from what it had. For many North Carolinians, especially those in rural areas, housing and other buildings often were primitive and substandard.

Until the 1950s, most of the state's architectural progress and prosperity had been centered in the cities; the farm remained as it always had been—an isolated outpost where change was slow to come. It also remained the home of most North Carolinians, accounting for nearly 70 percent of the state's 1950 population.[77] This was, nonetheless, a period in which giant strides were taken in rural building, especially housing. The state's increasing affluence and the postwar building boom spread new construction to all parts of the state. Builders could make their living in the country as well as the city. The growth of Lowe's stores helped those who did their own construction obtain building products to improve their homes and farm buildings, and the mobile home industry provided low-cost completed housing.

The postwar interest in improving rural construction appeared even as the war was ending. In its 1945 annual report, the Agricultural Extension Service at North Carolina State College reported that 2,498 families in 97 of the state's 100 counties had assisted in constructing dwellings and 4,516 had participated in remodeling. By far the largest number were involved in a simple but basic task—in 88 counties, 8,406 farm families participated in "screening or using other recommended methods of controlling flies or insects."[78] The numbers may seem small, given the fact that there were more than 200,000 farms in the state, but any construction at all in a wartime economy is noteworthy. The interest in improving housing foreshadowed more sweeping changes to come.

The 1946 report noted that "during the war, normal construction was retarded and the built-up demand coupled with the higher prices which farmers received for their products has created a desire for new construction, repairs, and remodeling." This postwar surge in building also brought some changes. The scarcity and poor quality of lumber stimulated new interest in concrete masonry. This interest, in turn, brought unskilled people and poorly equipped plants into the concrete block business.[79] The year 1947 followed a similar pattern, with shortages of lumber, galvanized metal, and brick.[80]

Since the 1930s, the Agricultural Extension Service at North Carolina State College had operated a building plan service, through which it distributed free of charge both its own building plans and plans created by the United States Department of Agriculture. The plans were for all types of farm buildings, but in the late 1940s, the greatest emphasis was on farm buildings other than homes. In 1948, the extension service mailed out 8,430 plans, only 847 of which were for houses. The greatest demand was for a flue tobacco barn crop drier, with 5,000 plans distributed.[81] The execution of a farm building—whether a home or a tobacco barn—remained up to the farmer, however, and in spite of the plan service and assistance offered through county agents, many rural residents relied on their own resources when it came time to build.

A study of 266 farm families who built new homes between 1948 and 1950 found some uniquely rural conditions in farm building. Like the Moravian settlers in the 1750s or farmer Jesse Jackson in the 1880s who stopped building to tend to planting, building fences, clearing land, and other chores, the mid-twentieth century farmer in North Carolina had to place the needs of agriculture first. Although anyone who builds a house is likely to make some sacrifices to achieve his goal, farmers made sacrifices that were particular to rural life. "Twice as many sacrificed family needs as did farm needs," reported the study. Farmers also were influenced by the season of the year more than their urban counterparts.[82]

When they did get around to building, most farmers continued to work in a self-reliant manner, obtaining their design ideas, for example, from seeing other houses or talking to neighbors, relatives, and friends but seldom consulting professionals other than builders. Although standard plan books were popular, more than a third used no written plans at all, again relying on themselves or their builders for any necessary drafting. Most farmers let only two contracts—usually for utilities, masonry, plastering, or floor finishing—and in contrast to urban practice, more than half obtained only one bid. Sometimes this was feasible because the farmer knew the contractor personally, but it also could be necessary where there were not enough bidders available. Most who did not contract an entire house said they wanted to save money by doing some of the work themselves. The study went on to note, however: "Perhaps the most unique phase of farmhouse building, as compared to urban residential construction, is the use of labor. Since most farmers contract for only limited numbers of jobs in building their houses, much of the construction must be done by them with the assistance of others."[83]

Most farmers were assisted by five or six people in building their homes. Of those who had help, four out of five were aided by relatives, but 90 percent required help from "other" workers at some point in the project. Twice as many skilled workmen—mostly carpenters—were used as unskilled, and the "other" workers generally were experienced in their jobs. But 40 percent of the family members and friends worked at tasks that were new to them. Among relatives, farmers most commonly had help from sons, followed by brothers, brothers-in-law, wives, and fathers.[84]

Almost a third of all workers and four-fifths of the relatives were not paid. The "other" workers were the highest paid, but the mean rate for all workers of $1.06 per hour was much less than the average of $1.88 per hour earned by construction workers nationwide. A third of the farmers expected to build for less than $1,950, and among all farmers, only a quarter of the funds were borrowed—another sharp contrast to urban practices. Most used funds from inheritances or insurance policies. When they had to borrow, most borrowed from individuals.[85]

Despite such improvements as rural electrification and despite the Agricultural Extension Service's efforts, the quality of rural building in North Carolina remained modest at best. The mean size of new homes in the 1948–50 study was 1,000 square feet with five to six rooms. More than three-fourths had one living room, two to three bedrooms, and one to two porches. When it came to plumbing and heating, however, measures that are commonly used to gauge the quality of homes, even the new houses seemed deficient. Some 46 percent had no bathrooms at all. In addition, stoves were used to heat most houses; even among those of highest quality, 62 percent were heated this way. Less than 9 percent had any type of central heating. Electric lights usually were installed, but "a kitchen sink and drain were installed in less than one half of the houses."[86] Such deficiencies would prove to be a persistent problem. As late as 1970, some 20.4 percent of rural houses contained no flush toilet, as compared to 1.7 percent of urban houses; 14.8 percent of rural houses had no complete kitchen, compared to 2.9 percent of urban houses.[87]

The need for better education and increased assistance was clear. In 1951, the extension report on existing rural housing noted, "There is

Demonstration house, Nash County, 1956. The Agricultural Extension Service built model homes to show rural North Carolinians that they could improve outdated and substandard homes like the one behind this new house. (Photo, L. S. Bennett, Agricultural Communications, North Carolina State University.)

reason to believe that progress in farm housing in North Carolina is not keeping pace with the overall progress of the state. For instance: It is estimated that only 10 percent of farm homes have sanitary sewage disposal; only 30 percent have running water; only 25 percent have bathtubs; and only 45 percent have screens."[88] As a result, the Agricultural Extension Service in 1950 inaugurated a demonstration housing program through which it helped selected farmers plan and build homes. The houses then were open for public tours. By 1954, there were thirty-two demonstration houses in various stages of completion.

Perhaps the most successful of the demonstration houses was built in Waxhaw by a dairy farmer named Brown Howey. The department assisted in planning the three-bedroom house for Howey, his wife, and their two teenage children. Like farmers and builders of a century before, Howey cut the timber on his farm and did most of the construction himself. He hired out only $435.75 worth of labor. The materials came to $3,020.75, making the total cost about $3,500 for a house that had been estimated at $8,000. When *Better Farm*, a national farm magazine, publicized the house, the extension service received more than two thousand requests for plans from all forty-eight states, Puerto Rico, and Canada.[89]

The number of residential plans distributed by the service was on the rise. By 1952, only 322 of the 12,055 plans sent out were for homes. By 1954, the number of house plans distributed had tripled, while the total remained about the same. For those other farm buildings, the service noted:

A majority of our farmers are still satisfied with the type of buildings that have been in use for generations, but the more progressive farmers are following the recent developments as publicized through the Extension Service, newspapers, magazines, radio, and commercial literature, and many of them are even ahead of what the college has to offer in their demands for information on building design. During 1954, the Extension Service has been particularly active in promoting interest in better silos, tobacco barns, sweet potato storage houses, and grain drying and storage facilities.[90]

For the next several years, the number of house plans distributed remained constant at slightly more than one thousand until 1961, when the service reported an increased interest in home improvement due to the Federal Housing Act of 1961, which made borrowing easier for new homes or for remodeling. The same act authorized the Farmers Home Administration to make loans to rural nonfarm families and allowed the Federal Housing Administration to insure mortgages with smaller down payments or longer terms. Noted the extension report: "There is need for educational work on housing to protect home buyers as well as to promote interest in good housing. Extension agents appear at the present to be more keenly interested in housing in North Carolina than ever before."[91] In addition, 1961 was the first year that the extension service distributed more plans for residences—2,614—than for any other category of major buildings. (The largest category remained miscellaneous equipment buildings.) Over the following years, the residential plan service continued to rise steadily. In 1966, the residential service distributed 8,775, or 41.6 percent, of the 21,093 plans of all types sent out.[92]

Clearly, the Agricultural Extension Service—along with other programs of the federal government—played a major role in reshaping the architecture of rural North Carolina. For the first half of 1962, the extension service recorded 1,200 rural homes built through Farmers Home Administration financing—double the number for the entire previous fiscal year. More than half of the homes built with Farmers Home Administration loans used extension plans—"greater than in any other state" said the service.[93] In 1963, the extension service reported: "Easy credit for rural housing has contributed as much as any one thing to rural home improvement. The Farmers Home Administration housing loans have been a cardinal example."[94]

The Agricultural Extension Service was, of course, made up of individuals, and from the number of plans distributed, it is obvious that these individuals had an impact on building in the state far greater than any architect. Matthew Nowicki designed a one-of-a-kind structure in the Dorton Arena. The extension service's chief designer spawned thousands of buildings. Like many of their forerunners throughout North Carolina's history, these were unpretentious buildings, and their very existence and the manner in which they were designed were well in keeping with the populist traditions of the state.

In the fall of 1945, a twenty-eight-year-old army veteran from Princeton, North Carolina, named Woodley C. Warrick went to work for the Agricultural Extension Service. As a student at North Carolina State College in the late 1930s, Warrick had worked in the service's plan office. With the degree in agricultural engineering he had received in 1941, Warrick's first assignment after military service in the war was to help a dairy farmer in Wilson County rebuild a barn that had burned. The plans that Warrick and the farmer used were from the extension service's plan book. This was the period in which most farm building still involved structures other than housing. With the exception of a period in the late 1940s when he ran his own bulldozing and earth-moving business in Johnston County, Warrick's career was to follow the service's growth and influence on rural home-building.

It was Woodley Warrick who in 1954 worked with dairy farmer Brown Howey on the service's successful demonstration house. Fifteen years later, he designed the most popular of the extension service's home plans, a 1,044-square-foot ranch-style home known simply as "Number 90."

The times were ripe for improving rural housing. In a 1981 interview, Warrick recalled the demonstration housing program: "Sometimes we'd have three or four hundred people. They'd be parked down the street like a funeral. People were hungry for better housing." As for the extension service's home plans in general, he said, "You know, they're just little mansions to these people. Brick veneer. Controlled heat. Hardwood floors."[95]

Despite his background in engineering, Warrick was largely self-taught when it came to housing. He did not know how to draw plans when he first came on the job, but he felt that "if you have the basics in structures, you can adapt it to housing." He worked closely with home economists on the extension service staff to develop kitchen designs. He used data from the United States Department of Agriculture that documented farmers' preferences for such design features as single-story homes over two-story homes. (This was a shift from the previous generation's preference for two-story homes, revealed in a 1917 economic study of Chowan County.) He took information from building codes on such items as standard door sizes and plumbing. He worked with the limitations imposed by lenders such as the Farmers Home Administration, whose specifications included a 1,200-square-foot limit and prohibition of air conditioning. He also worked closely with the county agents and the farmers. Whenever he visited a family, Warrick tried to take the agent with him and to ask the family—even the children—what they wanted in a house.

The extension service's most popular plan, Number 90, was devel-

Woodley C. Warrick, Raleigh, 1981. Thousands of North Carolinians built homes from plans by Warrick, the chief designer of the Agricultural Extension Service. (Photo, Ernest H. Wood.)

oped in the late 1960s in the same manner, with an agent and a black family in Nash County. The basic requirement was for a three-bedroom house with a living room, bathroom, and kitchen. The key to its success was the creation of an area in the kitchen where the family could eat and the children could play away from the living room. "Most rural people," Warrick recalled, "if they work with their hands, they're going to get dirty . . . and the women would want one place [the living room] they can keep neat." The carport, which could double as a porch, had storage to supplement other farm buildings, and there was an entry directly from the carport into the family area. The brick veneer meant easy maintenance, and the ranch-house styling was conservative, though several elevations were offered. "It looked like a simple house to build, and it had attributes to make people comfortable," Warrick explained. And it caught on. Lowe's printed and distributed the plans throughout its chain of stores. One subdivision in Wilson County was built with about two hundred of the homes. A contractor built one at the State Fair in 1968 for ten thousand dollars. The home had forty thousand visitors, six thousand of whom picked up copies of the plans. Warrick recalled that the home was even more popular at the fair the following year, when it was furnished with old, everyday furnishings rather than new furniture.

Part of Number 90's popularity may have derived from the period in which it was developed, for it was about at this time, in the late 1960s, that credit became easier for farmers to obtain. Most of the state's new rural housing has been built since that time. "I can recognize the houses I've done just riding along," mused Warrick, who retired in 1981. "It's somewhat gratifying to drive along and be able to say, 'This is Number 90, and this is Number 73.' "[96]

Throughout, the Agricultural Extension Service's primary mission remained education, which to the housing division meant educating people about houses. Repeating the ideals invoked by A. J. Downing who in the 1840s sought to improve all of rural life, not just building, through cottage designs, Glenda Herman, an extension service housing specialist, later described the extension service's goal: "Instead of just letting the builder always make the decision, to educate the family so they can make a better consumer choice."[97]

The extension service's role was directed at convincing farmers to improve their homes and helping them achieve that goal. The service worked less with actual construction, which it might have been more involved in during the late 1940s when many farmers built their own homes. The Farmers Home Administration policies of the 1950s and 1960s, in fact, prevented owners from building their own homes, for it required general contractors for projects it financed. The requirement gave work to many small contractors—some operating out of their homes and their trucks—and to many minority contractors. But it signaled the end of many owner-built homes. It is ironic that while the extension service's self-help policies encouraged farmers to improve their standard of living, they were simultaneously discouraged from making the improvements themselves.

The design goals, however, remained the same throughout the extension service's postwar work. Explained Warrick: "So it has a lot to do with social norms and mores. . . . People don't change that fast. And I think

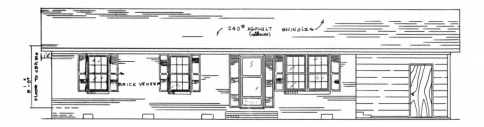

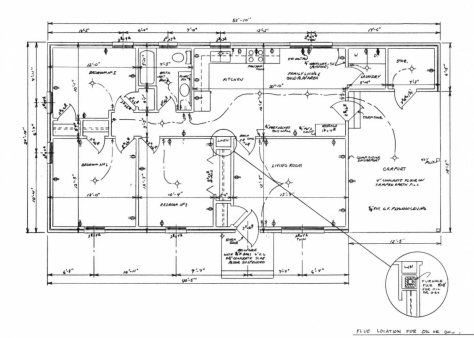

Plan number 90, Agricultural Extension Service, Raleigh, ca. 1968. The service's most popular plan owed much of its success to its simplicity and to the family area that adjoined the kitchen. (Courtesy of North Carolina Agricultural Extension Service.)

that's where I was successful as a housing specialist. I worked with the people to give them what they wanted and with the Farmers Home Administration to give them what they wanted."[98]

Tradesmen: Up by Their Bootstraps

Carpenter John Watts and tile-setter Wayne McArthur never met. Nearly everything about them and their work was different—their generations, cities, trades, and the scale of the buildings they helped build. As construction tradesmen, they were members of the largest and most diverse professional group in building. They were two of thousands who dug the foundations, raised the walls, ran the wiring, connected the plumbing, tiled, painted, and roofed the buildings of North Carolina's post–World War II building boom.

Yet despite their diversity, Watts, McArthur, and North Carolina's other tradesmen were heirs to a common history and tradition. They also were faced with the same task: to blend new tools and technology with those traditional roles and standards.

Building in the late twentieth century was in need of men (and a few women) to fill both the traditional and emerging jobs that the construction of the era's huge number of new, more complex buildings required. Just like their job specialties, these tradesmen were a mixed lot. Some gained experience in rigorous apprenticeships before the war, and some learned trades in the military. The greatest number learned from family members, friends, and coworkers. Those who entered the trades after the 1950s might also have had technical school training. Eventually, some tradesmen were promoted to managers. Others broke away to form their own businesses, becoming entrepreneurs.

Given North Carolina's rural heritage, it should be no surprise that both Watts and McArthur came from farms. Watts, born in 1934, grew up with cotton and corn in Catawba County.[99] McArthur, born in 1960, was from a tobacco farm in Robeson County.[100] Like generations before, they discovered that building was an integral part of the farmer's life. "That's where the construction starts," recalled Watts, "because you're always building things, doing something around the farm."[101] Like so many other North Carolinians in the postwar period, however, both Watts and McArthur saw and pursued opportunities in the cities.

John Watts's parents were separated, his mother on the farm and his father working as an itinerant carpenter. "Construction work at the time wasn't something you'd get in one place," recalled Watts of the still-rural North Carolina of the 1940s. "You'd have to travel around from job to job." Watts left high school at age seventeen without graduating (he later earned a high school equivalency diploma in 1976) and spent four years as a military policeman in the Air Force before joining his father as a carpenter. Tiring of the travel within a year, however, he signed on with Hickory Construction Company on Labor Day 1956 and remained with the company the rest of his career.[102]

Watts's work with his father and his early employment at Hickory Construction constituted an informal apprenticeship. For five years, however, he sought additional education beyond work, driving twenty miles from his home to Catawba County Technical Institute to study such subjects as lumber grading, blueprint reading, hardware, surveying, and concrete. Watts could have been a carpenter without this training, but he regretted passing up opportunities for schooling earlier. With the technical courses, he said, "I better understood what I was doing." The combination of his carpentry skills and knowledge of construction apparently also pleased his employers, for by the mid-1960s, he was made a job superintendent. That promotion made him responsible for work on projects as diverse as manufacturing plants, schools, churches, and housing and for supervising as many as seventy men. Despite his original desire to stay close to home, Watts worked in such cities as Brevard, Hendersonville, Asheville, Boone, Blowing Rock, and North Wilkesboro, in addition to Hickory. The work's concentration in western North Carolina and improved highways meant, however, that he usually could return home on weekends. "They schedule it out so one man doesn't have to be out all the time," Watts explained. "But it's been quite a good bit I've been out of town."[103]

The carpenter's need to travel to sometimes distant job sites has not changed over the years, although with larger cities travel is less frequent and improved transportation makes it less of a hardship. In much the same way, other aspects of the trade have both changed and stayed the same. Although it is not always a structured apprenticeship, for example, much of the carpenter's training still takes place on the job. "We try to take young people who are eager to learn and work them along with someone who's weathered in with what he's doing," explained Watts. The young carpenters usually learned quickly. "I've known older carpenters who couldn't read at all, but they could do the job," he recalled. "Now, most of the younger people are a bit better educated, and they understand building better." That education may be necessary, for although power tools have made work easier and faster, their use has required carpenters to perform a greater variety of tasks. Meanwhile, buildings continue to grow more complex. As for himself, Watts planned a traditional retirement—he wanted to continue working on the job site as long as he was fit. "I could have had a job inside as an estimator, but I'm an outdoors kind of person," he said. "I've been trained to work outdoors and do what I do, so I think I'll try to retire from out there."[104]

Wayne McArthur was a member of the next generation of tradesmen. Like Watts, he first encountered building on the farm among members of his family. As early as age ten, he helped cousins during the summers who were building houses in Wilmington by performing simple tasks such as nailing down plywood subflooring. He discovered tile-setting after he graduated from high school. "I kind of got into it by accident," McArthur recalled. "I was working with a man on some home improvement work, and I was a pretty fair jack-of-all-trades. I was tearing out tubs and another man would come in and set tiles, and I started watching him, and one day, I said, 'Well, if he can do it, I can do it.'"[105]

Gradually learning more and more, McArthur went to work for a commercial tile company, setting tile in schools, supermarkets, condominiums, office buildings, and other large projects from Georgia to Virginia. He soon tired of commercial work, however, and settled in Raleigh during the city's early 1980s housing boom to specialize in residential tile-setting. "Cuts weren't so important on the commercial jobs—it wasn't necessary to have everything perfect," he explained. "But when people live in a house, they notice everything." After his first employer went out of business, McArthur and a friend, Eddie Strickland, started their own business and laid not only ceramic tile but quarry tile, slate, and marble "in everything from three-quarters of a million dollar houses to regular spec homes."[106]

McArthur trusted that the quality of his work would carry him through the economic peaks and valleys of the building industry, but it ironically was his high standards that posed the greatest problem for his company's future growth. "I don't know that I'll ever give up tile," he said at age twenty-eight. "Me and this boy I'm partners with, we're looking ahead to the future. We're doing basically residential, but it's so hard to find help to do residential work because it's so tedious. . . . I can go out and find a couple of jacklegs that call themselves tile-setters, and they'd take a handful of tile and stick it on the wall, but it wouldn't look like nothing." McArthur was afraid that too many tile-setters wanted only the same big, easy jobs that he already had rejected. But he was optimistic about the future. "We're going to change, and hopefully grow bigger," he said.[107] All he needed was the workmen.

The number of people employed in building has always fluctuated with the economy. Building companies and architectural offices traditionally have hired help when they had work and laid off workers when times were lean, leaving the individual tradesman, draftsman, or clerk to fend for himself. As in earlier periods, postwar North Carolina often experienced a steady increase in employment for a period of years, followed by a corresponding slowdown or decrease. Overall, however, the number of tradesmen shows a steady growth at a rate faster than that of the general population. From 1940 to 1980, the number of tradesmen increased from 47,246[108] to 119,134,[109] or 154 percent. By contrast, the state's total population rose from 3,572,000 in 1940 to 5,882,000 in 1980, a 64-percent increase.[110]

The building industry continued to employ both blacks and whites, as it had since its earliest days, but the postwar period showed a dramatic increase in the number of blacks in some trades. In North Carolina cities in 1950, only one skilled trade classification—plasterers and cement finishers—employed more blacks than whites, with 72 percent, though blacks also accounted for 52 percent of unskilled laborers. In the traditionally black trowel trades—masons, tile-setters, and stonecutters—39 percent of the workers were black. The number in other trades was even less: 11.7 percent of plumbers, 9.5 percent of carpenters, 3.6 percent of construction managers, 1.8 percent of electricians, and a minuscule 0.6 percent—two out of 318—of architects.[111]

Three decades later, each of these trades either retained the same black-white ratio or increased the number of blacks. The greatest gains for blacks, however, came in the upper echelons of construction—management, trades requiring licensing, and the professions. The increased percentages were still small, but they represented a significant change and reflected better education and improved professional opportunities for blacks in a better-integrated society. Black supervisors now numbered 7.7 percent, black electricians 7.6 percent, and black architects 3.5 percent. (Plumbers, the other licensed trade, retained the same 11.7 percent as in 1950.) The one major loss for blacks occurred in plastering, which almost disappeared as a trade in the postwar period. The black-white ratio of the remaining plasterers in 1980 was identical to that in 1950, but among drywall installers, who had taken their place in the building process, only 10 percent were black.[112]

Women, who had barely been represented at all in building in 1950, showed a greater increase, though their numbers still remained small compared to those of men. The wartime influx of women into the general labor force hardly affected building, since construction nearly stopped from 1942 to 1945. Though women counted for 44 percent of wage earners in North Carolina industry by the end of 1944,[113] there were ample men who were young, old, or deferred from military service to fill the slim needs of the building industry. North Carolina Department of Labor statistics do not even list a category of construction employment for women, but the low demand is illustrated by the fact that of the 55,718 sixteen- and seventeen-year-olds (both male and female) working in 1943, only 1 percent were in construction.[114] There was no "Rosie the Riveter" in the construction industry. By 1950, as a result, women counted for more than 1 percent of workers in only two trades or professions—2 percent of architects and 1.1 percent of painters. In nearly every category recorded by the 1950 census, the percentage of women in construction at least doubled between 1940 and 1950, but the increase was probably due more to opportunities presented by the postwar boom than the need for women workers during the war, for the prewar numbers of women builders were tiny. In 1940, carpentry employed 29 women, more than any other trade—but there were 15,876 male carpenters in the state, making women only 0.18 percent of the total.[115] The following decades did see growth in the number of women in construction. By 1980, women accounted for at least 1 percent of the workers in each of the groups recorded in 1950 except one—masons, where they were 0.9 percent. The greatest percentage of women were in the two extremes of construction—in the growing profession of architecture, where they numbered 4 percent, and in the dying trade of plastering, where they numbered 10 percent. Women numbered 2.9 per-

Drywall finisher, Raleigh, 1988. The new material almost entirely replaced plaster, eliminating one trade and spawning another. (Photo, Steve Wilson, Spectator Magazine, Raleigh.)

cent of electricians, 2.3 percent of supervisors, and 1.4 percent of plumbers. As in 1950, carpentry employed more women than any other trade—706. But with men numbering 37,660, women still were only 1.8 percent of the total.[116]

Though blacks always had been an integral and widely accepted part of building, the entrance of women into the trades was new and met with resistance from some employers. As late as 1980, a contractor in West Jefferson was quoted as saying, "Why, I wouldn't hire a woman unless she was a master carpenter, ugly as a dog, and would work for two dollars an hour." Women reported harassment on the job, such as being given less desirable work, being sent on meaningless errands, or being the object of tricks, "like one time I used the porto-John and they [the men] tried to turn it over," as one female plumber working on a nuclear power plant reported.[117] Women in construction received a great deal of media attention, particularly during the 1970s as the movement for women's equality in all fields grew. Women's involvement in building may have been a passing phenomenon, however. A Chapel Hill builder who had employed both men and women in the past said in 1985, "I haven't had a woman apply in five years."[118]

Although workmen employed by general contractors comprised the largest group, the postwar period also saw an increase in the number of building contractors dealing in specialties. Subcontractors had been around for a century or more, but trades evolving from the new complexity of construction meant that work was parceled out to them more and more often. A comparison of wages paid to tradesmen shows both the importance of the new trades and the strength of the traditional skills. But not all traditional skills were equally rewarded. By the postwar period, carpenters, who in the nineteenth century had been among the best paid of building artisans, were near the bottom of the economic ladder. Figures compiled by the North Carolina Employment Security Commission in 1960 for twenty-two trades in eleven cities, for example, rank them fifteenth. The trowel trades—tile-setters, terrazzo workers, and bricklayers—were the best paid, followed by plumbers, steamfitters, structural ironworkers, and electricians. The lowest paid in the skilled trades were roofers. The unskilled, laborers and mason tenders, were the lowest paid of all. From city to city, both the unskilled and those in the traditional skilled trades were paid at fairly uniform rates. In other trades, however, especially the newer skilled ones, there was variation between cities, with the larger cities paying better than the smaller ones.[119]

The increase in the number of trades and the number of individual jobs provided nearly unlimited opportunities for persons wishing to enter the construction business. If they were tradesmen, they could pick from a growing list of jobs, and even though employment remained seasonal and fluctuated with the economy, there was usually plenty of work to go around. The number of workmen involved in a single house could run more than one hundred: graders, footing contractors, mason subcontractors, backfill crew, framing crew, siding and boxing crew, concrete crew, interior trim crew, cabinet crew, painters, landscapers, and more.[120] There also was increased opportunity for entrepreneurs who wished to run the business side of the construction industry. The contractor as a coordinator of workers and the worker as an assembler of parts were roles well established before World War II. Now, those roles became even more firmly entrenched.

With the chain of organization, licensing, and education established, some professions and skilled trades had assured themselves of not only professional and social identity but also adequate training for their work. It was nearly impossible, for example, to become an architect without completing a university-level architectural program. For all the licensed professions and trades, from architects to electricians, the licensing examination assured that an applicant possessed a certain level of knowledge and skill. For the other trades, however, training programs often did not fit either the industry's or the individual's needs. Apprenticeship as a means of taking care of indigent or orphaned children had begun to fade out after the Civil War and had virtually disappeared by the turn of the century. While other forms of apprenticeship continued, in which parents apprenticed a child or an individual apprenticed himself to a craftsman to learn a trade, the advent of machine-made parts and processes diminished the need for traditionally trained workers. Instead, workers often learned their trades simply by joining a company and learning on the job, much as would the clerk who worked in the construction company's front office. They might also attend trade schools or take specialized courses in conventional schools.

The result was a widespread—and widely lamented—loss of skilled workers, even as the total number of workers was increasing. When *North Carolina Architect* magazine assembled six architects and an architectural historian in 1977 for a roundtable discussion on regionalism, the talk turned to building materials and the local labor force as influences on design. Brian Shawcroft of Raleigh bemoaned the use of plywood sprayed with a sand mixture to resemble concrete. "Well," noted Daniel MacMillan of Fayetteville, "you can go down to the employment office and hire these guys off the street to do this kind of thing. This is what we see so much of. Where we used to have these 60-year-old carpenters to do these things, now they take kids and people off the street and they can do Sheetrock work and all these other things. We're doing a courthouse that's about a six and a half million dollar building and it has $8,000 worth of carpentry work. There are no carpenters." Added Milton Small of Raleigh: "I'll tell you what the problem is. That is, that every time that we have a little recession—or a big recession, like 72–73—you can just take a great big layer of semi-skilled and skilled people out of the construction field. They find out, 'Well, gee, I'm not doing too bad here working in a filling station, and I work every day and I get paid, and why should I go out and get back in the construction business?' "[121]

Ever since the nineteenth-century advent of machine-made building components, there had been complaints about the superiority of old-fashioned building techniques and training and about the inferiority of the current work force. It may have been especially common for members of one segment of the construction industry to complain about members of another, just as these architects in the late 1970s complained about workmen. The workmen probably complained about the architects, too. But whatever the validity of the complaints and whatever the reason for the disappearance of skilled workmen, it was clear that the supply in the post–World War II period was sorely inadequate for the booming construction industry. One factor that made the attrition of older workers so disastrous was the small number of younger workers entering training programs for the construction trades. Gone were the days when many young boys entered the trades as apprentices whether they wanted to or not. In 1962, general contractor H. S. Crain, president of Crain and Denbo of Durham, analyzed the problem in a speech announcing an Associated General Contractors program aimed at encouraging young people to enter construction. At recent "Career-O-Rama" days in Winston-Salem and Charlotte, he said, less than .5 percent of the thirty thousand high school students attending "showed any interest in the selection of a career in construction." Similarly, at a Career Day in nearby Iredell County, only three out of four hundred tenth graders attending chose construction as their first choice of a career. Crain placed part of the blame on the glorification of the college degree and the low esteem given to the trades. Those who do enter construction simply "drift" into the industry "and somehow pick up a smattering of knowledge and skill regarding a certain trade to do some kind of job, maybe a pretty sorry job, but enough of a job to just get by," according to Crain. He added, "Simple mathematics will lead me to conclude that in another decade or so, after all of the older, really good mechanics have died off or retired, about 90 percent of our work requiring skill will have to be performed by these drifters, by these poorly trained mechanics." Crain expressed special concern that this decline in skilled workmanship was occurring precisely at the time that buildings were becoming more complex and technologically sophisticated.[122]

There were, however, programs in existence to train workers for the construction industry. At the urging of labor unions, the U.S. Congress in 1937 had established an apprenticeship training program through the federal Department of Labor. The following year, North Carolina also passed an apprenticeship act to be administered by the state Department of Labor. The program peaked at fifteen thousand apprentices training for a variety of trades—not just in building—following World War II, when large numbers of returning servicemen enrolled. Many did so solely to receive veterans' benefits and were apprentices only on paper.[123] By the late 1970s and early 1980s, however, when requirements for apprenticeships were better regulated and programs should have been able to attract

Roofer, Raleigh, 1988. New tools such as the nail gun required less skill, but workmen often were asked to perform more duties as a result. (Photo, Steve Wilson, Spectator Magazine, Raleigh.)

more candidates, they still were far from meeting the industry's needs. In 1981, for example, only 1,478 apprentices were enrolled in the thirty-eight building industry programs, and only 191 completed their training and attained journeyman status. The most popular program was for electricians, with 525 enrolled and 48 new journeymen completing the program. The next most popular was carpentry, with 264 enrolled and 20 new journeymen. Attrition in the programs was fairly high, however, with the electrical program losing 279 the previous year and carpentry losing 96. Also, some trades had very few apprentices enrolled. Architectural drafters, structural drafters, stained-glass glaziers, building inspectors, construction superintendents, ripsaw operators, sawmill workers, and house movers registered only one apprentice each, and several other trades had none. The sole apprentice learning how to cut stone with a circular saw completed training, and no new apprentices signed up. The only apprentice in the mobile home repair program dropped out.[124] The small numbers in the program are even more dramatic when compared to the total in the construction industry. For while there were not quite 1,500 enrolled in construction apprenticeships in the early 1980s, the Employment Security

Commission was projecting some 3,500 new construction workers would be needed annually. For the period 1976 to 1982, it predicted the state would need 436 new electricians each year, a number that even that most popular apprenticeship program, with its 48 new journeymen—only 11 percent of the need—was far from realizing.[125]

The apprenticeship programs, which the state Department of Labor coordinated through local employers, offered prescribed training procedures designed to meet national standards. Most programs in the construction industry required three years or more to complete, at which time the apprentice received a certificate and the designation of journeyman. The program for drywall mechanics, for example, involved four thousand hours of on-the-job training. Cement masons, bricklayers, and roofers required six thousand hours. Plasterers, draftsmen, carpenters, electricians, and heating and air conditioning mechanics required eight thousand hours. Plumbers required ten thousand hours. The carpenter's training included rough forming and form building, outside and inside finishing, hardware fitting, layout, and care and use of tools and woodworking machinery. The electrician's included not only instruction in tools and equipment, materials, installation of motors and controls, hazardous conditions, grounding, and maintenance, but also 160 hours of customer relations.[126]

Such comprehensive programs would seem to be an ideal way to train journeymen, and there was an abundance of applicants. The program was kept small, however, by the number of employers willing to participate. Many were reluctant to join the state program because they thought only large firms could take on apprentices (when, in fact, the average program involved a small company with two apprentices), because they feared unionization would follow (though less than 2 percent of apprentices were in union programs), because they were wary of state regulation, or because they did not want to guarantee the progressive wage scale for apprentices that the state required.[127]

One alternative lay in programs that were independent of private employers. The state's network of community colleges and technical institutes grew rapidly in the 1960s and 1970s, and it was through these schools that many workers obtained their training. By 1974, nine schools offered two-year programs in architectural technology or drafting, which prepared students to work in the offices of architects, engineers, contractors, government, or industry.[128] In addition, the community college system offered one-year vocational programs in fields such as heating and air conditioning. Because their purpose was education, not construction or profit making, the schools were better able to provide training for the large numbers of people needed in construction and other technical fields than was the apprenticeship program. In 1980, approximately 100,000 students were enrolled in certificate and degree programs of all kinds at the state's fifty-eight two-year public institutions. Still more were enrolled for only a

Apprentice bricklayers, North Carolina State Fair, Raleigh, 1988. The annual contest was a showcase for the state apprenticeship program. (Photo, North Carolina Department of Labor.)

course or two. (At the same time, apprenticeship programs accounted for only about 3,000.) Some 15,000 of these were in programs with applications to construction, ranging from welding (3,510) and masonry (541) to architectural technology (868). Other areas such as business administration and data processing were training students who also might find work in construction. But while the community college system helped train the large numbers needed by the construction industry, it, too, had limitations. Students who were offered jobs often left school without completing their programs. Even for those who finished, on-the-job training usually was necessary to complete their educations.[129] As the head of the state Department of Labor's apprenticeship program said, "The truth is that all jobs that require manual dexterity require on-the-job training."[130]

Many tradesmen still felt that experience was all that was necessary, however. In a 1988 letter to the *News and Observer*, a carpenter named Joe Panichelli from Winterville protested the suggestion that builders need more education:

> I learned my trade as a carpenter by working for two contractors, neither of whom could read or write. Both were well respected and very successful businessmen. They taught me well, for I have been in this business 15 years and knew nothing when I began.
> Formal Education does not always mean success. Some things are best learned by doing.[131]

Contract Builders: Taking Care of Business on the Home Front

The growth of the contract builder shows one of the most distinct evolutions of all groups in the building industry. Three hundred years ago, he did not exist. "Undertakers" of the eighteenth century evolved into the first generation of true contractors in the mid-nineteenth century. Today, there is a contractor for every size and type of project.

The contractors' recent evolution has been marked, as have many developments in the post–World War II boom, by a tremendous increase in the scale of building and its related business. For while some prewar builders, such as the Coffey family in Raleigh, left the business rather than allow their companies to grow to a size they felt was too large, others became the giants of the industry, ranking among the largest in the country. Their metamorphosis, in turn, opened opportunities for smaller builders. Most rose from the ranks of the tradesmen, for the boom created a fluid business in which an individual could readily percolate up through building. In recent years, a growing number entering the business have been college graduates or have come to building through experience in business management elsewhere. No matter what route they took, however, there always has been room for the entrepreneur in building.

The very largest firms achieved their size in part because they predated the war. Those that survived the depression found work in government contracts during World War II. McDevitt and Street Company of Charlotte, founded in 1917, for example, built the wartime Camp Davis near Wilmington and Camp Picket in Virginia.[132] Another Charlotte firm, J. A. Jones Company, founded in 1890, built military camps in the United States and South America, ships in Panama City, Florida, and the atomic bomb research facility at Oak Ridge, Tennessee.[133] When the war was over, each was in a position to begin civilian work immediately. In 1945 McDevitt and Street, in a joint venture with F. N. Thompson, another large Charlotte contractor, built a twenty-million-dollar automobile assembly plant in Atlanta, Georgia. That was followed in 1946 by a ten-million-dollar naval hospital in Beaufort, South Carolina. Recalls Emmett Sebrell, who joined the company immediately after his discharge from the navy and rose to vice-chairman of the board, "Then we just went on from there, up to today, just building buildings. We were not in heavy construction, we were not in utilities, we were just building buildings."[134] By 1988 McDevitt and Street was ranked as the seventh largest general builder in the nation, with $740,600,000 in contracts during the previous year. J. A. Jones Company, which had changed its name to The Jones Group to encompass various divisions that handled road construction, utilities, and other types of work, was ranked fifth in building, with $1,015,600,000 in contracts. (The Jones Group's contracts were even greater when divisions such as highway construction were included, making it the fifteenth largest builder of any kind. Other North Carolina building contractors ranking among the largest in the nation were Davidson and Jones of Raleigh, with $131,400,000; Barnhill Contracting of Tarboro, with $114,100,000; George W. Kane of Durham, with $53,500,000; T. A. Loving of Goldsboro, with $52,600,000; and Miller Building Corporation of Wilmington, with $50,600,000.)[135]

Both The Jones Group and McDevitt and Street achieved their size by taking work and establishing branch offices all over the country. Each company handled the details of its growth differently, however. By the late 1980s, only about 10 percent of The Jones Group's work was in North Carolina. McDevitt and Street did more local work, with the majority of its work in-state, according to Sebrell. The Jones Group was purchased in 1978 by a German contracting company. McDevitt and Street remained locally owned by the heirs of the Street family. It was the largest privately held company in North Carolina. The Jones Group was a microcosm of the construction industry, employing some ten thousand people, ranging from tradesmen to architects and engineers to management and marketing personnel. McDevitt and Street employed only about two thousand, principally management (most of them engineers), supervisors, foremen, and the like. It had a nucleus of tradesmen who moved from job to job, but the company preferred to subcontract most of its specialty work to local contractors.[136]

Neither actively pursued development, though Jones had a small development division. Instead, they prospered by efficiently building other people's projects. Even this seemingly straightforward way of doing business evolved in the postwar period, however. "In the past," recalled Sebrell in 1988, "an owner hired an architect who drew plans and you bid on it, and at that time, the low bidder and the architect assumed almost an adversarial role. The low bidder tried to give as little as he could, and the architect tried to get as much as he could, and the owner was stuck in the middle wondering when he was going to get his building." By the 1980s, however, fewer buildings—except government work—were built on contracts awarded purely on the basis of open bidding. Owners might invite a small number of contractors to bid or they might invite contractors simply to interview for the job. "Now, owners pick their contractors like they pick their architects," explained Sebrell. "It's a team approach to building."[137] That approach kept contractors' marketing divisions as busy as their building divisions. It was a development that paralleled changes in other segments of the building industry, particularly among homebuilders and architects.

Though neither McDevitt and Street nor The Jones Group were developers, many builders in North Carolina saw in the state's postwar boom the opportunity to create their own work. In the late 1940s, J. W. "Willie" York of Raleigh took advantage of a large tract of fields and woodlands

McDevitt and Street's Charlotte Plaza under construction, 1981. Coordination by one of the nation's largest contractors resulted in completion of the building three and one-half months ahead of the owner's nineteen-month schedule. (Photo, Rick Alexander and Associates.)

only a few miles from downtown to fill the need for housing and retail establishments by opening Cameron Village, a development of housing, offices, and shops that was to become the Southeast's first regional-scale shopping center. From three stores, a restaurant, and a nursery, the development grew to 70 stores, a string of offices, and 556 apartments.[138]

Heir to the York Construction Company founded in 1904, York had his first experience in the industry as a water boy. After graduating from North Carolina State College, he worked for the United States Parks Service before joining the family business in 1937. He did not, however, limit himself to building, though he later characterized construction as his "real love." York developed office parks and other shopping centers and built schools, motels, and housing, mostly in Raleigh and Durham. He also was active in politics and public service, from the local school board and airport commission to gubernatorial campaigns, which led to his appointment as secretary of conservation and development by Gov. Dan K. Moore. His daughters made their bows at debutante balls. He took hunting trips to Europe. His son, Smedes, who also joined the family business, was elected mayor of Raleigh. Since York's interests were diversified, when a sluggish economy slowed construction in 1974, he closed down the York Construction Company to concentrate on property management, planning, development, and property ownership. Two years later, when the economy picked up, he resumed the construction business.[139]

With the role of the general contractor and developer well established by midcentury, contract builders found a natural place in the huge numbers of buildings that were needed by the growing state. The large, well-established firms handled development and construction of the largest buildings. Individual tradesmen handled the smallest projects. However, there was a size of building in the middle—including houses—that was ripe for the picking. After World War II, tradesmen who recognized this opportunity began moving up en masse to manage their own contracting firms. This new generation of builders grew so large and so successful that homebuilding for the first time became identified as an industry unto itself.

The sheer volume of work in the post–World War II period not only allowed but encouraged entrepreneurs to strike out on their own. The large number of builders needed, the increased dollar value of building, and the complexity of construction made the coordinator more and more important and powerful. By 1980, when there were more than one hundred thousand employed in construction trades and nearly three hundred thousand in the entire industry, there seemed to be a contractor for every type and scale of building. Pulte Homes of Detroit, Michigan, the nation's fifth largest homebuilder, topped the new home sales list in Raleigh in 1988, for example, after only one and a half years in the market. Meanwhile, in Durham the top homeseller was local builder Bryant B. Roberts, who had been in the business since 1975 and still visited sites himself to supervise construction. Like Roberts, most contracting firms were small, however. In Wake and Durham counties, six hundred builders each completed fewer than thirty homes a year. Noted one contractor: "The builder who drives a pickup truck is alive and well in the Triangle."[140] The builder's effect on the community also went beyond the house he built. Due to the ripple effect involving workmen, contractors, and products suppliers and manufacturers, each new home in the mid-1980s was said to bring the state $425,000 in income tax revenues. In the mid-1980s, the 50,000 new homes projected for one year would require 92,500 man-years of work and use 535 million board feet of lumber, 250 million bricks, 11 million gallons of cement, and 10 million squares of roofing.[141]

Despite the wide-ranging effect of the industry, most tradesmen never had to sit for a licensing exam as long as they confined their work to small-scale construction and did not undertake electrical or plumbing work or other crafts regulated by the state. If they aspired to large-scale building (in 1980 defined as any work costing $30,000 or more), however, they had to be licensed as a general contractor.

From its establishment in 1925 to the close of World War II twenty years later, the North Carolina Licensing Board for General Contractors licensed 1,030 contractors. Thirty years later, the number had grown to 18,386. Much of that growth came in the late 1970s and early 1980s. Applications in the mid-1970s averaged about 225 to 250 a year. By the end of the decade, however, some 1,200 annually were sitting for the exam. That number doubled by the mid-1980s.[142] The sudden increase was due to both a general building boom and stricter enforcements of building codes. Many contractors who had been operating for years without licenses were now refused building permits unless they became licensed.[143] The North Carolina Home Builders Association had urged builders since its inception in 1962 to improve their credibility through licensing. Many new builders—some from out of state, some native North Carolinians— also were setting up shop.

At a typical examination, one or two applicants had only a year's experience and a few had been contracting for twenty-five years or more. Most, however, had between five and eight years of experience. A majority had worked in one of the trades, such as carpentry, and were attempting to become managers. Occasionally, architects and engineers took the exam. A few with university business degrees, who generally were employed with very large construction firms, also applied. The contractors faced an average failure rate on the licensing examination of 40 to 43 percent, most falling victim to lack of professional experience or, according to the North Carolina Licensing Board for General Contractors, of "freezing up" in an examination whose format by necessity resembled an academic exam as much as a practical one. In addition to passing the written test, applicants were required to furnish financial background to assure that they had the capital to see their jobs through. Based on that data, those who passed were placed in one of three categories—limited, which allowed them to undertake projects up to $175,000; intermediate, which allowed projects up to $500,000; and unlimited, which had no cost ceiling. Contractors further were divided into five more categories, according to the type of construction they intended to undertake—building contractor (which included all types of buildings), residential contractor, highway contractor, public utilities contractor, and specialty contractor (for such trades as roofing and insulation).[144]

By the 1980s, the largest and fastest-growing category of contractors was for residential construction, which allowed builders to erect single-family and two-family dwellings. Some 60 to 70 percent of all registered contractors were in this category. It is difficult to know whether this was a long-standing trend, as the designation for residential builders was created only in 1979,[145] but it is likely that it was. Many builders who specialized in homes and other small projects had begun as tradesmen themselves, had been born into families of builders, or both, thus swelling the ranks from the bottom up.

Eugene Gulledge was a prime example. In 1946, after discharge from his World War II service in the navy, Gulledge went to work for a general contractor in Greensboro as a laborer. He was paid eighty-five cents an hour, and after six months he quit to open an auto body shop with his wife's older brother. The business needed a building, so Gulledge and his brother-in-law built one. It measured 35 by 70 feet, with a 12-foot ceiling. Gulledge never opened the shop, however, for as soon as the building was finished, another businessman, who also needed space, offered to buy it. Here, in the postwar economy of shortages, was an opportunity. Gulledge approached another brother-in-law, a carpenter who had helped him obtain his laborer's position, and suggested they go into business together building houses. For the next 7½ years, Eugene Gulledge worked as a carpenter on his own jobs. Then, in 1953, he laid down his tools and became a businessman.

Gulledge obtained a general contractor's license in the unlimited category, and his company grew to build not only houses—95 percent of which the company originated itself—but shopping centers, hotels, schools, warehouses, and other large buildings. He became one of the organizers in 1962 of the North Carolina Home Builders Association and in 1969 became president of the National Association of Home Builders. Also in 1969, Gulledge was named assistant secretary of the federal Department of Housing and a commissioner of the Federal Housing Administration. He left Greensboro for Washington, D.C., and when his term with the federal government was over, stayed in Alexandria, Virginia, where he entered real estate development and syndication.

For businessmen such as Eugene Gulledge, there was no formal path to becoming a builder. But by the early 1950s, he had learned that he needed to be more than a carpenter. "Coming out of the navy, I sure wasn't qualified to build houses or run a business—but you learn as you go," Gulledge recalled in a 1985 interview. Many of the builder's subsequent decisions were based on simple pragmatism. Gulledge's company, for example, did most of its business within two hundred miles of Greensboro, in an area roughly bounded by Wilmington; Rock Hill, South Carolina; and Richmond, Virginia. "We figured if a man couldn't get there in a half a day, he wasn't going to go," Gulledge explained.[146]

Such decisions apparently were the right ones, for the company grew to include as many as fifty people. By the late 1950s, the company did not only its own carpentry, but also its own painting, tiling, landscaping, cabinetry—everything except work such as electrical, plumbing, and heating, ventilation, and air conditioning that required separate state licenses. Gulledge had his own custom panel factory to produce his own interior and exterior panels. He employed draftsmen, and from 1958 through 1965 he had his own in-house architect, a Czechoslovakian refugee named Yaraslav Kabatnik, though for houses and other small projects, Gulledge said, "I considered myself to be an excellent designer for this kind of thing."[147]

Employing his own workmen for the various trades was one end of the contract builder's spectrum. The other was to subcontract as much work as possible and remain entirely a coordinator. Gulledge entered several joint venture projects with a Greensboro builder named Clyde Elrod who handled business that way. Elrod had one employee and worked out of an office in his basement. Said Gulledge: "You can sub out everything or try to control as much as you can. I don't think there's any answer to which is better. It's just your own management style."[148]

Whichever method of management the contractor adopted, the age-old problem of finding and coordinating workers persisted. Like others in the building industry, Gulledge believed that the ability of workmen had declined over the years. He put part of the blame on the depression, which had decimated the labor supply, and on World War II, which had halted civilian construction. Although he found a bright spot in two programs from these periods that taught men how to build, the Civilian Conservation Corps and the Seabees, he felt that they had not produced nearly enough workmen to fill the postwar demand. In other parts of the country, labor unions ran training programs for new workmen. However, because there were few unions in North Carolina and other southern states, these states had to rely on workmen who learned their trades on the job.[149]

Gulledge's solution was to make sure that his company attracted good people and kept them. He tried not to hire a lot of workers when times were good and then let them go when business slowed down. The panel plant helped provide work in slack times and let the company get ahead on its work. Profit sharing and bonuses added enticements that led some employees to stay as long as thirty years. A reliable work force allowed a builder to maintain control over the quality of his work, and Gulledge had enough confidence in his employees that he used the same crews on all his homes, no matter what the budget. The variables were the site, size of the house, and quality of finishes and fixtures such as appliances—not the work force. As for subcontractors, Gulledge tried to find reliable ones and use them again and again: "I knew what standard they could produce and they knew what standard I wanted."[150]

Besides being a coordinator of workmen, however, a builder also was a coordinator of materials and marketing. All were interrelated, especially when projects were developed on speculation to be sold after they were completed. The introduction of thinset tile shows the process. The material was not itself a response to unskilled labor, but without the traditional thick mortar base, it could be laid by less-skilled workmen—and with less material in less time. Gypsum wallboard, precut studs, PVC (polyvinyl chloride) pipe, prehung windows and doors, and prefabricated roof trusses grew in popularity the same way. Price and expediency—always a concern but now tied to marketing—were growing influences on the work force and the quality of construction.[151]

Public acceptance of these materials was gradual, but it eventually came. Gypsum wallboard is a case in point. The material had been marketed as early as 1917,[152] though plaster was almost universally preferred. By the late 1940s and early 1950s, wallboard was still considered "fit for the henhouse and nowhere else."[153] But by 1962, when Eugene Gulledge and Greensboro architect Edward Lowenstein used wallboard in one of an annual series of demonstration houses they designed and built with the schools of economics and art at The Woman's College of the University of North Carolina, no one who toured the house responded negatively to the material on a questionnaire about the house.[154] Within only a few years, gypsum wallboard virtually eliminated the use of plaster.

Though such construction materials were mass-produced, they generally were assembled by hand at the job site, giving buildings—especially when they were custom designed by an architect or builder—the aura of a one-of-a-kind structure. Components such as trusses or wall framing that did not show in the final product could be manufactured off-site. Other materials, however, were too extreme a change to gain acceptance. Though used in commercial buildings, entire prefabricated walls never caught on for residences, and homebuilding remained largely stick built, as it was before World War II. Builders say the cause was the public's reluctance to accept new materials. "Housing," according to builder C. L. Reavis of Wilmington, "has followed the line of what people will accept."[155]

Certainly, home styles followed the public's wishes. "Styles have changed but they haven't changed that much," noted Reavis, a builder who began as a masonry contractor in 1950, was licensed as a general contractor in 1958, and became a licensed real estate agent in 1966.[156]

Except for a brief flirtation with modernism in the 1950s, most house styles remained conservative. Eugene Gulledge built only two flat-roofed houses —one for himself and one for a dentist—out of the two thousand or more homes he built in North Carolina.[157] Mel Daughtridge, a builder in Rocky Mount, has observed, "Every little idea in the world, like windows in the corners of the house—anything that was different, people tried it. But people got out of that because they found their houses were dated."[158] Most builders either designed their own homes or bought designs from a plan service. Architects seldom had a hand in merchant-built homes. Many homes were built entirely on speculation and completed before they were sold.

In the custom-built house, tradition extended beyond style, and the result could be surprisingly like homebuilding of the past. When Lee and Ann Davis, a young couple in Raleigh, built their first home in 1987, builder Ken Rose took care of not only the construction but also the design. No architect was involved here, either. Like clients a century or two earlier, the Davises patterned their house after others they had seen. Said Lee Davis: "From all of the people we had talked to we found out that the simplest way to build was to go straight up and keep the shape rectangular. . . . I didn't know any of this; I was being tutored on the way."[159] In a time-honored manner, Davis had entrusted the entire project to the person who would construct his house. For the larger merchant builders, however, tradition generally ended with style. Traditional style meant a secure and predictable business—essential elements when an increased volume of building meant increased risk. To further secure their position, however, builders turned to aggressive modern business techniques such as marketing and professional organization.

Mel Daughtridge grew up with his father's building business and began work at age seven snapping chalk lines on subflooring so carpenters would know where to drive their nails. His always had been a family business, involving various uncles, brothers, and sons-in-law, and it had always been small. Once it employed between fifteen and twenty men, mostly carpenters and carpenters' helpers. By the mid-1980s, however, the company employed only four men and subbed out all work. The Daughtridge family built mostly in Nash and Edgecombe counties. Like many builders, they designed the houses they built themselves. Limiting a geographical area and producing designs that sold there provided two ways to market homes successfully. But relying on such basic techniques was becoming less effective, especially when large companies from other cities came into a builder's area and increased the competition. "It takes marketing expertise that the plain old country builder doesn't have," explained Daughtridge.[160]

Because of competition, the economy, and the increasing complexity of building, builders who had buyers waiting for homes to be completed in the late 1940s and early 1950s found by the 1960s that they needed help with their businesses. That help came in the form of the North Carolina Home Builders Association. Some builders had been attending national homebuilders' meetings since the late 1940s; subsequently builders in several cities, led by those in Charlotte (1945) and Greensboro (1957), founded local organizations. The awareness that builders "knew more collectively than we did individually"[161] was growing; but there also was some reluctance to share knowledge. Mel Daughtridge, who was president of the North Carolina Home Builders Association in 1968–69, compared the attitude to that held by many of the builders' professional forebears, the tradesmen and artisans. A carpenter who worked for Daughtridge for twenty-five years refused to teach his skills to young men. "His idea was that if he taught a man something, then the man would know his own knowledge plus the carpenter's knowledge," Daughtridge explained. The carpenter had worked through the depression, was afraid for his job, and did not want extra competition.[162] Contractors tended to be the same way—cordial toward their colleagues but not overly friendly or helpful. But gradually, said Daughtridge, "they decided that if we put our collective ideas together, we could have a better product." The Home Builders Association did sponsor seminars and other practical programs for its members; but builders count the fellowship, the intangible benefits of belonging to a group with a common purpose, to be just as important to their success.[163]

The timing of the homebuilders' association was fortuitous. In the late nineteenth century, selling houses on the installment plan was an innovation that was a key to suburban development. In the early 1960s, the financial and marketing aspects of building became more sophisticated and allowed many builders to enter a new scale of construction. "Financing," noted builder and realtor Reavis of Wilmington, "had more of an influence on housing than any other one item. It [success in building] had nothing to do with the influence or availability of products or technology."[164]

Before the late 1950s, most homes were financed by Savings and Loan Associations, which required a down payment of 25 percent and financed the remaining 75 percent for fifteen years. A builder would simply borrow the money to build a house and sign the loan over to the buyer when construction was complete. In the late 1950s, builders who wanted to build more than fifteen or twenty homes a year, however, met resistance from lending institutions that did not want to finance such large numbers of projects with this type of mortgage. So builders and lenders turned to the financing technique of construction loans. The builder would borrow money only for the period of construction and pay the loan off when he sold the house. The buyer then originated a new loan, usually for thirty years, with 10 percent down on a conventional mortgage, 5 percent down

Eugene Gulledge (third from left) and other officers of the National Association of Home Builders with President Lyndon Johnson in the White House, 1967. Professional associations both protected their members' interests and influenced public policy. (Photo, courtesy Eugene Gulledge.)

on a Federal Housing Administration loan, and even no money down with a Veterans Administration loan.[165] The low down payments created a new demand for housing, and the bankers' policies allowed builders to construct homes in the volume necessary and at attractive prices to meet that demand.

By the 1980s, homebuilders were working on a scale never before imagined. The John Crosland Company of Charlotte, for example, did more than $100 million in business in 1985. Like many builders, John Crosland, Jr., grew up in a construction business family. His father, John Crosland, Sr., was president of Central Lumber Company in Charlotte and began building homes before the depression. By the late 1930s, he bought several hundred-acre tracts in Charlotte and started developing subdivisions. Aside from summer jobs during his years at Davidson College, however, John Crosland, Jr., did not work on actual construction sites.[166] Like the eighteenth-century planters and merchants who became "undertakers," he was never a tradesman.

Immediately upon receiving his bachelor of arts degree in business administration in 1951, Crosland started a homebuilding company and planned to erect a five hundred-unit subdivision in Charlotte. Interrupted by his army service during the Korean War, the project was only partially completed. Upon discharge in 1953, Crosland joined his father as a vice president in what was by then the Crosland Company, supervising the construction of new subdivisions, handling sales, "really everything there was except to handle the books," he recalled in an interview. The homes were modest, 1,000- to 1,400-square-foot structures, in the Charlotte area.[167]

The demand for housing through the mid-1950s kept the Croslands and other builders going. But later in the decade, their business began to change, characterized by the addition of sales managers and the elimination of more traditional positions. Though in the early years the company had its own workmen, Crosland had determined by the 1980s that a business could be more stable and predictable if all the actual construction was subcontracted. The company, nonetheless, had about four hundred employees, from the business managers in the Charlotte office to apartment complex managers and maintenance men spread from Charlotte to Raleigh and Wilmington and to Charleston, Myrtle Beach, and Columbia, South Carolina. Like earlier builders who had not been afraid to import designs from Philadelphia, Baltimore, or other more stylish cities, the Crosland Company employed architects from Florida, Pennsylvania, Texas, and California. The intent, said John Crosland, was to find "new ideas and to work with people who have been successful in developing a good product."[168]

The 1980s were the period of the company's greatest growth outside Mecklenburg County. Marketing, however, demanded a regional touch. Local architects and draftsmen often changed home and apartment elevations for each city. The company applied sophisticated marketing techniques, including annual market surveys and in-house interviews with buyers. "Now," said Crosland, "it's more of a thought-out plan and a controlled process, and one in which we have done a great deal of research before we put a step forward."[169]

The approach worked. In 1986, *Professional Builder* magazine named John Crosland, Jr., "Homebuilder of the Year," noting he "set an example for other builders by his ability to manage growth rather than react to it." The emphasis on marketing and large-scale development turned homebuilding from an artisan-wrought project into a merchandised product. In *Professional Builder*, Crosland explained his company's sudden growth in the 1980s this way: "We were production driven and we wanted to be market driven."[170] In 1987, the company changed yet again, selling its homebuilding interests to Centex Real Estate Corporation of Dallas, Texas, to concentrate instead on commercial and multi-family development.[171]

By the last quarter of the century, marketing concerns were influencing builders on every scale. Even smaller builders were increasingly aware of their role as businessmen. Typical of many was R. B. Fitch of Chapel Hill who like Crosland came from a construction business family. His

In 1938 it was considered one of the best built homes in Charlotte.

It still is.

The skill and care with which we built our first home fifty years ago still makes it a prime place to live today.

The skill and care with which we're building homes now will make them prime places to live many years in the future.

We thought you'd like to know that. Especially if you're looking for a home.

Because in fifty years, we've faced a lot of challenges. We've passed a lot of tests. Including the ultimate test of any home builder: The test of time.

John Crosland Company
A DIVISION OF CENTEX HOMES

Charlotte, Raleigh, Myrtle Beach, Wilmington, Charleston, Atlanta

Corporate Headquarters: 145 Scaleybark Road, Charlotte, NC 28209-2608, (704) 523-8111

Advertisement for John Crosland Company, Charlotte, 1988. Marketing became crucial as the scale of homebuilding grew. (Courtesy of John Crosland Company.)

father and grandfather had run a retail lumber company, which Fitch expanded to include renovations and additions in the 1960s. In 1974 he began Fearrington, a planned community in northern Chatham County, where he built forty to fifty houses a year. "I'm a small business person and I'm an entrepreneur," he explained. "I'm a merchant who happens to be in the building business."[172]

Those building on Fitch's scale could not afford elaborate marketing schemes and usually relied instead on local real estate agents. Fitch handled his own marketing, counting on his knowledge of Chapel Hill and his ability to produce a superior product. His summary, nonetheless, stands for all builders in the twentieth century's age of speculative building: "There's one thing that can flat put you out—if you don't sell your product. You can cope with about anything else."[173]

Professionals Strive to Uphold Standards

On February 18, 1955, Greensboro physician, Dr. Maurice LeBauer, wrote to Durham architect Archie Royal Davis to inquire about designing a house. A friend, also a client of Davis, had suggested the architect to LeBauer and his wife, Carolyn, as they wanted a "colonial"-style home, and Davis was one of the most popular architects in the state still working in traditional styles. The relationship that developed between architect and client could have existed at any time, for Davis apparently was given to traditional values as well as traditional design. He was apt, for example, to send presents of duck or geese to a client after a hunting trip. Letters addressed "Dear Mr. Davis" soon gave way to ones that opened with a simpler "Dear Archie." A few were from Dr. LeBauer, but the bulk of the correspondence was handled by his wife. Letters show a friendly, open, and honest relationship tinged with both excitement and disenchantment—building design in its purest form, a service to a client through what always has been a difficult and frustrating process.

In mid-May 1955, three months after the LeBauers' initial inquiry, a two-sentence letter from Mrs. LeBauer to Davis stated simply: "You gave me permission to 'needle' you, so here goes: how are the plans coming?"

May 30, 1955, Mrs. LeBauer to Davis: "After pouring [sic] over the last plans that you brought me, I have arrived at the conclusion that I'm going to have to give up the idea of the James River type of house that we had hoped to have. We just can't afford a house at $15 or $16 a foot, and since you can't have one frill without all the others, I think I had better make up my mind to have just a house. . . . I'm pretty much convinced that it will have to be a box, but maybe you can give me a nice door, or dress it up with a New Orleans type porch on the second floor. . . . Anyway, you know what I want, just see what you can come up with that won't cost so much, but will give me better size rooms."

June 21, 1955, Davis to Mrs. LeBauer: "We are sending you under separate cover a revised scheme. I do not feel that we have increased the cost appreciably, if any, in making these changes, and I feel that it will not be 'just a house' but will be an attractive house with a true tradition."

June 30, 1955, Mrs. LeBauer to Davis: "I'm getting embarrassed! I don't like those last plans you sent, and I'm wondering if you aren't getting tired of hearing me say that everything you have sent is wrong."

September 26, 1955, Mrs. LeBauer to Davis: "So sorry I missed you yesterday, but I was certainly pleased when I saw the plans sticking in the mail box when I got home. I like what you have done, and am anxious to see you and discuss them with you. If you aren't coming here, and would rather have me come down there I will be glad to make the trip. The important thing is that I want to 'get the show on the road.' "

January 4, 1956, Mrs. LeBauer to Davis: "Many thanks for your lovely Christmas card. . . . I am anxious to wind up the finishing touches on the house so that we can get started on building it in the early spring, and hope that you will have time to work on it in the near future. . . . Also, don't forget to try to turn the kitchen around, giving me an outside window in it, also making the maid's room a more respectable size."

August 24, 1956, Mrs. LeBauer to Davis: "Thank you for sending your friends to call on us about the heating arrangements for the house. We are about to settle the whole issue, and will end up with a York furnace and two ulcers. We can't put in the air conditioning unit, but have made provisions to do so at a later date, when the ship comes in."

September 13, 1956, Mrs. LeBauer to Davis: "The time has come, we have to know something about those screens to those doors in the living room. I know the hunting season has started, and I'm sorry to have to bother you now, but we are about to get around to making drapes, and ordering rods for curtains. So, my friend, get off your ———— you know what and do something about this mess for me. We have started plastering, and I'm getting quite excited. I do hope you drew good plans, I'm afraid I'm no judge at this point, all I'm interested in is seeing the job finished. We have been picking out hardware, and what a nuisance! I thought houses were born with such uninteresting stuff as that."

October 1, 1956, Mrs. LeBauer to Davis: "Thanks for sending the material from Mr. Rockmore [a lighting dealer in New York City]. I must admit to you that none of the catalogues that he enclosed interested me in the least. Also, after trying to figure out what the discount was on light fixtures, I was just as confused as the little boy who dropped his chewing gum in the chicken lot. . . . At this point, I'm beginning to wonder why I ever started building a house, but I guess we'll live through it. I hope it isn't going to be tacky, but I'm getting nervous."

October 16, 1956, Mrs. LeBauer to Davis: "The house is really coming along, the carpenters will be out next week, and we start the paint job. It's

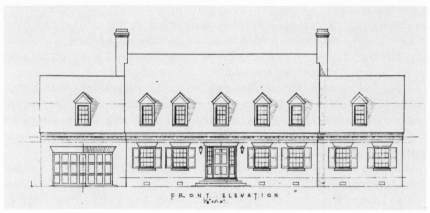

Plans for LeBauer residence, Greensboro, 1955–56, Archie Royal Davis, architect. Plans by the Durham architect evolved through several versions before he reached the design that was built. (Southern Historical Collection, University of North Carolina Library, Chapel Hill.)

all very exciting, and I still love all the people on the job, which is something. I understand some ladies are ready to flip their lids during house-building time, but I've loved it all."[174]

Archie Davis's work with the LeBauers embodied a fundamentally traditional approach to the practice of architecture. With only the architectural style or the scale changed, it was the type of relationship that even the most modernist of architects of the period probably encountered on individual projects. It was a type of building that most architects soon were to abandon, however. For while there always would be some architects who designed custom homes, the profession found itself during the

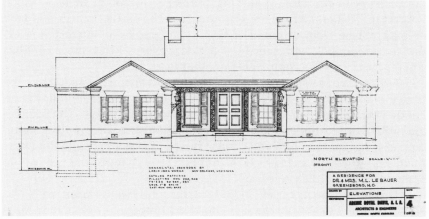

post–World War II building boom swept into designing ever larger and ever more complex buildings.

Following World War II, the number of larger, more profitable buildings became so great that most architects did not have to bother with houses. Their interest in merchant-built houses was even less, and as homebuilders grew increasingly aggressive and became marketers of homes as a product rather than builders of shelter, most architects abdicated what little share of the housing market they had. One exception was Charlotte architect R. Emory Holroyd who in the mid-1950s employed five to six designers to serve twenty-five to thirty builders with floor plans, elevations, and land planning. Designing for builders was a different line of work for most architects, he admitted. In a committee report to the NCAIA, he wrote that "the architect must bear in mind that he is designing a product to be sold to the general public in a highly competitive field." Architects must constantly research new products and be prepared to produce plans quickly, he explained. And because of the volume of work and repetition of plans, Holroyd's fees were as low as 0.75 percent but no higher than 3 percent of construction costs. Despite these departures from traditional practice, he urged more architects to enter the field.[175]

Holroyd's urgings fell on deaf ears, however. The NCAIA had difficulty finding architects to serve on its Committee on Relations with the Homebuilding Industry,[176] and in 1961, Goldsboro architect Conrad Wessell, chairman of that committee, reported that he had "come to the obvious conclusion that the Chapter members are not interested in having 'Relations with the Home Building Industry.' Although there is much interest in Residential Design, it is entirely in the smaller offices and may or may not be from economic reasons. No particular interest was expressed in working with merchant builders even when fees or royalties could produce profits comparable to other work."[177]

Architects had sought to set themselves and their work apart from the trades and building for a long time. The disdain for homebuilding was yet another sign that architecture was becoming more exclusive. The postwar attempt to dictate modernism as an architectural style was another. Architects also sought to define and control their profession by regulating how their colleagues ran their practices. But first they changed the way young architects entered the profession.

The most effective way to control the profession—from who was admitted into it to how it would be practiced—was to control architectural education. Even before his arrival in Raleigh as new dean of the School of Design, Henry Kamphoefner was suggesting changes, including the replacement of five nontenured instructors and one full professor.[178] Kamphoefner's new staff that began work in the summer of 1948 included Matthew Nowicki and eight other faculty members of the new dean's own choosing. Four of the new faculty came with Kamphoefner from Oklahoma, as did eighteen students handpicked from more than one hundred applicants.[179]

For Kamphoefner, the faculty was the key to the school. (Certainly, the facilities were not so crucial. In its early years, the school was housed in campus barracks left over from World War II. Later, the school moved into more adequate space in the old university library.) In 1953, Kamphoefner wrote to Harwell Hamilton Harris, dean of the School of Architecture at the University of Texas, who a decade later would join the faculty at the School of Design and become one of its most respected teachers: "The way I believe I increased the effectiveness of teaching at North Carolina

Architecture students, School of Design, North Carolina State College, ca. 1949. In the early years of the school, classes met in old army barracks on campus. (Photo, North Carolina State University Archives.)

State College was to appoint a competent and talented staff. First, of course, I had to eliminate the incompetent deadwood. . . . I have been gradually eliminating the others during the past five years, and by 1955, all of the staff with the exception of one will have been appointed by me. The effectiveness of teaching in that way seems to be taking care of itself."[180]

Kamphoefner also spent considerable energy on upgrading the student body. Architectural engineering, which Kamphoefner felt "was being used by the weaker students in the department [of engineering] as a short cut into the profession,"[181] had graduated about fifty students between 1936 and 1948. In 1942, a five-year program in architecture had been established, but it granted only one degree before 1948. With the establishment of the School of Design, that program was phased out and the last students were graduated in 1950.[182]

The 1948–49 academic year began with 332 students in architecture, but by the spring term, enrollment had dropped to 239. Already, the process of elevating the school's academic standards and weeding out the weaker students had begun. It was a process that the faculty expected would take five years to complete.[183] During those five years, enrollment figures also began a pattern of attrition by which fewer and fewer students reached the successive levels of the program. Of the 51 who entered the five-year architectural program in 1948, some 48 returned for their second year, 33 for their third, 40 for their fourth, and 19 for their fifth, a loss of 63 percent from the starting class.[184]

Though the immediate effect was to make the school smaller, Kamp-hoefner achieved his ultimate goal—a stronger, more rigorous academic community. By 1970 the School of Design granted ninety degrees for its three departments of architecture, landscape architecture, and product design (which had opened in 1958), compared to thirty-three in 1963, and a higher percentage of students were graduating. In 1967, Kamphoefner reported: "Less than 150 new students were selected for admission in the fall of 1967 from more than 700 applicants. The quality of the student, because of more and more careful selection, has changed the mortality rate so that it is now less than half what it was five years ago, so that fewer and fewer students are being admitted while more and more are being graduated."[185]

Nonetheless, there was some opposition and bitterness to the newly elevated standards at the school, especially in the early years. A delegation of mothers called on the governor to complain, and some of the state's older architects complained that the school was training elitist architects. Recalled Kamphoefner: "They wanted to tone it down to accommodate the country boys who were coming in."[186] There was some animosity, naturally, from students who did not make the grade in architecture. In 1961, an unsuccessful member of the class of 1953 wrote Kamphoefner criticizing the dean for not running a school "which would encourage rather than discourage so many students."[187] Kamphoefner's contention, however, was that few actually flunked out. Instead, they realized they would not be able to complete the program at the School of Design and transferred to other divisions of North Carolina State College or to the University of North Carolina at Chapel Hill, usually graduating success-fully.[188]

Those who remained often met with outstanding academic success. During Kamphoefner's tenure as dean from 1948 to 1972, five of the school's students won architecture's most prestigious academic award, the Paris Prize. Three architecture and landscape architecture students won fellowships to the American Academy in Rome. Faculty and gradu-ates won three Guggenheim Fellowships and nineteen Fulbright Scholar-ships (the latter among only twenty-one in the entire university for the period).[189]

Just as Kamphoefner had predicted when he came to the school, graduates also found unprecedented opportunities for practice once they completed their studies. In the summer of 1956, when architect Beemer Harrell of Hickory wrote to Kamphoefner seeking recent graduates to work in his office, the dean replied that he had none to offer: "By com-mencement day, I think all of our graduates had at least a dozen offers each, and almost everyone was committed by that time. Although we graduated only twenty-five, I feel quite certain that we could have placed two hundred in the offices of North Carolina, which is enjoying one of the most tremendous building booms in the history of the state."[190] Most did stay in North Carolina. A half-year after graduation, for example, seventeen of the twenty-three architecture graduates in the class of 1959 were working in the state, two were working out of state, three were in the armed services, and one was in graduate school out of state.[191]

The building boom of the 1950s and 1960s meant not only work for architects but the opportunity to run their own practices. In addition to demand for housing, public projects that had been postponed during the war were desperately needed, as were schools for the education of the postwar baby boom. As a result, the last graduates of the North Carolina State College Department of Architectural Engineering and the first graduates of the School of Design were a tight-knit group who became an almost instant "old boy" network within the profession. Architects such as J. Bertram King of Asheville were able to open offices as soon as they were licensed. King, who would go on to win several design awards from the NCAIA, kept his firm small, principally because a city the size of Asheville could not support more large firms than the already-established Six Associates.[192] Others, however, such as King's classmate, F. Scott Ferebee of Charlotte, established major firms in large cities. Another classmate, Thomas T. Hayes of Southern Pines, established a smaller firm, but one no less influential for his locale. Norman Pease, Jr., joined his father's architecture and engineering firm about the time it was making its greatest strides toward the principal practice of architecture, strides that were to make it by the 1970s the largest such firm in the state. All became presidents of the NCAIA, and Ferebee in 1973 served as president of the national AIA.

Architecture traditionally had been a white, male profession. In 1950, only 7 of the state's 325 architects were women (all white) and only 2 were black.[193] By 1980, however, there were 68 white women, 20 black women, and 45 black men among the state's 1,909 architects. (There also were 10 Asian and Hispanic architects in the state.)[194] Most of the increase of female and black architects came in the 1970s, though there had been a slower, gradual growth among these groups earlier.

When William A. Streat, a black architect who taught in North Carolina Agricultural and Technical State University's architectural engineering program, applied for membership in the NCAIA in 1961, the chapter required a special interview before he was admitted.[195] With the admission of Streat, one white architect inquired about transferring his membership to a nonintegrated chapter.[196] However, North Carolina A&T, which had operated a program in architectural engineering since 1924 on its predominantly black campus in Greensboro, increased its enrollment by

80 percent to 170 during the 1970s. The largest group of students in the program were black American males, though enrollees also included black American females, white American males, and foreign students, mostly from the Middle East and Africa. Most graduates went to work for engineers or for firms that built as well as designed buildings. Only one or two of a typical class of ten to fifteen became registered architects.[197] The state's most well-known black architect, Harvey Gantt, who was elected mayor of Charlotte in 1983, was a graduate of Clemson University in South Carolina and the Massachusetts Institute of Technology.[198]

The School of Design graduated its first woman, Elizabeth B. Lee, in 1952. She practiced in her hometown of Lumberton and in 1979 was elected president of the NCAIA. But it was not until the early 1960s that the school graduated its next woman—and it was four years more before it graduated the next.[199] Women graduates were few and far between until the 1970s. Then, they generally were white, just as were their male counterparts. As they set up their practices, however, some began to achieve distinction. Norma DeCamp Burns, for example, practicing under the name Burnstudio in Raleigh, designed a social services office building in Pittsboro that *Time* magazine picked as one of the nation's best buildings of 1984.[200]

By controlling the education of those entering the profession and influencing the style of the state's buildings, the School of Design went a long way toward controlling architecture in the state. But while architecture was an exciting, futuristic field in the 1950s intellectually, many in the profession took a business-as-usual approach when it came to practice. Work was easy to come by, and instead of aggressively seeking new markets as builders were doing, architects sought to ensure that they would have work by protecting their traditional positions.

Schedules of minimum fees, for example, which had been maintained for years by both the architectural profession and clients, were a long-held practice that architects clung to tenaciously. The NCAIA, in fact, was held up as a national model for the profession in 1953 after members signed an agreement refusing to do state government work after the state's Budget Bureau proposed a fee schedule that the architects felt was too low. The NCAIA newsletter referred to one meeting on the subject as "probably the most significant meeting that the North Carolina Chapter has ever had."[201] A compromise later returned relations between the state and the profession to normal.[202]

In 1954, Raleigh architect Carter Williams, as vice president of the NCAIA, explained some reasons for fee schedules in a letter to a Durham architect whom he was trying to convince to adhere to the plan: "As you know, the whole purpose of adopting a minimum service schedule is to assure that the public obtains complete and proper services from the profession at a minimum fee. We also know that where the element of competition on the basis of fee enters in, it will eventually lead to improper services or incomplete services to the detriment of our own and our client's interest."[203]

The architects, who had been complaining for more than a century that they were underpaid, also justified the fee for their own protection, as they often were cutting their profit to the bone already. The architect's fee could not sink too low, it was reasoned, since the 4 to 7 percent of construction costs he received (depending on the type of building and the cost of the project) was his total gross pay, before expenses. Of that fee, one-third usually went for salaries, one-third for overhead such as holidays, sick pay, Social Security, supplies, clerical assistance, rent, electricity, taxes and insurance, and one-third covered capital expenditures, working reserves, and profit. The fee generally was figured as three times the applicable payroll, plus reimbursement of direct expenses such as transportation and consultants, when approved by the owner.[204]

The cases of those architects who did not adhere to the fee schedule offer some interesting insights into the difficulties of architectural practice. In 1954, when the chapter was trying to establish a 6 percent basic fee for government work, an architect in Statesville named Thomas Hutchins was accepting school projects at 5 percent. W. R. James of Winston-Salem, chairman of the chapter's committee on school buildings, wrote to NCAIA president A. G. Odell after meeting with the offender: "Hutchins justified himself with the old argument that every time he tries to get a fee based on our schedule he is informed that cheaper service is available and he gets nowhere. This, of course, is tough on a young architect. . . . I got the impression that Hutchins, as a fairly new and not too well established architect, feels that he must get work in any way he can."[205] In a similar case, involving an architect named Charles W. Connelly from Charlotte, Odell explained why the chapter members were so interested in convincing their colleagues to adhere to the fee schedule or in disciplining them if they did not: "If we are not in a position to enforce compliance of the fee schedule by our own members, our hard work on behalf of our new fee schedule and arrangements with the Budget Bureau and Department of Public Instruction will certainly be nullified."[206] The NCAIA clearly felt that even a few errant members could erode the financial security of the entire profession.

The architects, who had put so much effort into fee schedules, soon were left without that technique for sustaining their practices, however. In 1971, the Antitrust Division of the federal Department of Justice threatened to sue the AIA on the grounds that its fee schedules were an illegal restraint of trade. Rather than enter a court battle, the Justice Department and the AIA in 1972 entered into a consent decree, which directed architects to set their own fees for professional services, rather than following fees established by the institute. The decree allowed, but did not require, clients to request competitive bidding on projects. Likewise, it remained legal for clients, including governmental bodies such as the state Board of Education or the university system, to establish their own fee schedules.[207]

While the fee schedules were a means of guaranteeing the architects' incomes, other provisions of the AIA code of ethics controlled the architect's professional behavior. They were forbidden, for example, to compete for work with builders, contractors, and each other on the basis of fees and to advertise their services. The chapter policed transgressions doggedly, and at least one architect resigned from the NCAIA after being reprimanded for advertising.[208] In Greensboro, an associate AIA member was criticized for printing the letters "AIA" larger than the word "associate" on a job-site sign. Following the reprimand, he stated his intention to continue in the AIA, but he wondered: "There seem to be many flagrant violators of the architectural laws of the state of North Carolina, as well as violators of the Standards of Professional Practice of the AIA. It appears to me that many of the members are misusing the AIA, using it like a stick to fight among the registered architects rather than against the non-registered law violators and plan factories. In light of this activity, however, the AIA finds time to be picayunish to a fault about the size of the letters on a sign."[209]

Perhaps the answer to this concern can be found in a letter from Carter Williams in Raleigh to a Winston-Salem firm concerning an advertisement. Williams wrote in part: "We do not want our professional standard lowered to that of a strictly commercial enterprise."[210]

Such exclusivity, in fact, seemed to be a major goal of the profession. Architects often sought out opportunities to plead the case that their work was somehow different from commercial enterprises or "mere building." The use of the initials AIA after an institute member's name became common in the early and mid-1950s, expressly as a means to distinguish themselves not only from designers and engineers, but also from architects who did not subscribe to the AIA's code of ethics.[211] In 1954, the NCAIA began publishing *Southern Architect* (which ten years later became *North Carolina Architect* and still later *North Carolina Architecture*), a bimonthly magazine that was distributed without charge to both the state's architects and such influential persons as legislators, bankers, and school superintendents. Favorable publicity surrounding the heady, early days of the School of Design certainly promoted the idea that architecture was something special. The profession's efforts to inform the public about architecture usually were limited to custom design, however. In 1951, for example, Henry Kamphoefner wrote to Dean J. B. Kirkland of North Carolina State College's School of Education asking that the Industrial Arts Department discontinue its course "How To Plan a House." "In our experience," wrote Kamphoefner, "we have found the house to be the most difficult problem in architecture, and I believe giving students too little information is much worse than giving them none at all."[212]

Some architects, however, saw a problem with the profession's growing exclusivity. In 1947, when the NCAIA had balked at designing stock plans for a Brick and Tile Service plan book, William Henley Deitrick of Raleigh, collaborating architect on the Dorton Arena, noted: "It is well known that this is a very busy and profitable time for the profession, and any contributions of plans to this project represent a distinct effort and sacrifice of time and money, but if the profession in the future fails to maintain a proper place in our fast changing and growing society, it will undoubtedly be because of a lack of 'human' qualities rather than of technical abilities."[213]

The refusal to enter the commercial world of building and the withholding of information to those who might build on their own were two tools that the profession used to set itself apart. A third—and more effective—tool lay in the General Statutes of North Carolina, which had established the state Board of Architectural Registration and Examination in 1915 (later known as the Board of Architecture) to license the profession. Legislation defined the profession in a legal manner that distinguished it from other aspects of building. Practicing architecture without being a licensed architect was in turn declared unlawful, though several exceptions existed. Engineers could perform architectural work that was "incidental" to engineering projects. Any person could design a residence or a building of any type within a specified dollar limit and could make "plans or data for a building for himself."[214] The "building for himself" provision, which did not exist in any other state, proved to be controversial, for it applied to all building types and did not prohibit the lease or sale of a building once it was completed.[215] Architects continually complained about this provision, though in fact it was a continuation of the state's traditional, self-sufficient building practices.

There were numerous cases of individuals or corporations stepping over the line that architects had drawn around themselves, but the State Board of Architecture seldom used its authority to take offenders to court. Despite a few celebrated cases, such as a 1953 restraining order issued to prohibit Mayor Harrelson Yancey of Gastonia from acting as an architect or preparing plans and specifications,[216] most cases were settled out of court, often with a letter from the Board of Architecture or with the cooperation of another state agency such as the Department of Labor or the Department of Public Instruction. In 1961, for example, only one board action reached the courts, though there had been twenty-two inquiries or complaints alleging illegal practice.[217]

Dealing with individuals who violated the architectural practice act was an ongoing and time-consuming battle, which the architects fought on legislative and legal fronts with mixed success. When the state's architectural practice act first became law in 1915, it defined the practice of architecture, but it did not require architects for any specific types of buildings. As late as the 1940s, contractors were allowed to execute designs (without extra compensation, the law said) for buildings or renovations they had been commissioned to execute, a practice akin to today's design-build techniques in which architects also act as contractors. The 1951 General Assembly, however, amended the act to require an architect for any nonresidential structure costing more than twenty thousand dollars. Due to inflation, that amount was gradually raised over the years, and by 1985 it had reached ninety thousand dollars. The 1985 act also required an architect for any nonresidential structure of 2,500 square feet. However, the legislature also allowed anyone to erect as many as eight attached residential units, and it amended the engineers' practice act to allow design beyond what was incidental to engineering, a change that further blurred the definition of architecture and caused conflicts between architects and those engineers who designed buildings.[218]

Another ultimately more serious battle emerged on the economic fronts of practice, however. For the architects' greatest dilemma was not based on direct competition. It came instead from the complexity of building technology, which added new players to the scenario, in turn making financing a building and paying design fees even more difficult. In 1962, Charlotte architect James Stenhouse prepared a summary of the changing technology as it affected architects' and engineers' fees. "The change has been drastic within the past forty years," he wrote, "and it has brought financial inequity in professional fees along with it."[219]

In the past, wrote Stenhouse, buildings had been simple, and the architect had been solely in charge. He had little overhead, spent most of his time drawing plans, and could design the mechanical and electrical engineering himself or leave it up to the contractor. The standard architectural fee for any type of building was 6 percent, on which the architect "could make a comfortable living, or even better if he got many large jobs."[220]

The increased complexity of buildings spawned new specialists, however. By 1950, for example, consulting engineers, who had barely existed only a few years before, were so numerous that they formed a professional organization. In 1960, they established their own fee schedule. Complicating matters even further was the change in design theory and materials. "When the 6 percent fee was established," wrote Stenhouse, "traditional styles with their standardized detail were used over and over, with little time being required for study sketches. Building methods were standardized also, and there was little choice of materials." The division of labor added even more costs: "Another quite considerable factor that is often overlooked is the fact that contractors no longer take complete charge of the construction as they once did. Today, they are hardly more than material and labor brokers and much of the job of coordinating and expediting falls on the shoulders of the architect and his consultants."[221]

Stenhouse did not seek to deny engineers, contractors, and others adequate compensation for their work. Rather, he sought to increase the compensation for architects, based on the new complexity of building and the addition of engineers to the building team. To support his case, he compared costs of designing a hypothetical building during the thirty-five-year period from 1926 to 1961. During that period, the cost of a $200,000 building would have risen to $620,000. The architectural fee would have dropped from 6 percent to 5.5 percent (under the state government fee schedule), and the dollar amount the architect received would have risen from $12,000 to $34,000. However, the architectural and engineering costs, based on draftsmen's salaries, Social Security, unemployment insurance, and other overhead, had risen considerably, from $7,680 to $36,960. This was based not only on increased pay, which would have risen from $60 per week to $130 per week for the average architectural employee, but on the increased man-weeks required for the job, which rose from 80 to 140. The result was that in 1926, the architect would have made a $4,320 profit on the building; in 1961, he would have lost $2,960.[222]

Both the new complexity of buildings and the accompanying financial problems of practice made it increasingly difficult for an architect to practice by himself. In 1954, Kenneth C. Diehl, an architect on his own in Rocky Mount, wrote to the NCAIA that the outlook for firms such as his was bleak. "For some months," he wrote, "I have considered closing up the office and getting out of the profession. It has come to a point where there is not much future in the profession in the Eastern part of the state and looking over the state as a whole, there is not much anywhere else. This contemplated action may be unusual since it appears everybody else is busy, though I am not sure of this. As I see it, the day of the individual architect is rapidly running out. The three and four man organizations seem to be getting all the work and they run all over the state getting work to keep their organizations going." A few months later, according to NCAIA records, the financially strapped Diehl was dropped from membership in the institute for nonpayment of dues.[223]

Other ultimately more successful architects took the opposite approach, however, increasing the size of their firms and adding other professions to meet the competition. In the same year that Diehl considered closing his office, Charlotte's A. G. Odell, one of the state's most successful practitioners, noted: "For the past fifteen years, it seems that quite a few architectural firms here in North Carolina have either incorporated or affected a joint title of 'Architects and Engineers' in order to compete with engineering firms in the state who also are practicing architecture."[224] Debates also involved whether the definition of an architect was as an individual or an incorporated body, and whether an engineering firm or other concern could include only one architect and legally practice architecture. In 1955, architect Lucian J. Dale of Charlotte, cochairman of the NCAIA committee on collaboration of the design professions, wrote chapter president Carter Williams of Raleigh concerning a new firm with three engineers and one architect: "That corporation must be *knocked out of the box now*, while it is aborning, and so must all future corporations dipping into architecture. It must be done before it has done work and started its inroads on our profession."[225]

The growth of the combined architectural and engineering firms, however, was part of a trend toward offering a complete package of design services in-house. Architects had always seen the growth of prefabricated and pre-engineered buildings as illegal competition. This type of firm delivered a completed building, a service the architects could not claim, since until 1978 the AIA ethics forbade members from acting as contractors. The institute felt such a service would create a conflict of interest. There was growing recognition, however, that the problems may have been of the architects' own making. The Package Deal Committee of the AIA, which studied manufacture of prefabricated and pre-engineered buildings and companies that provided both design and construction services, reported in 1957: "The committee feels that the architect himself has created a vacuum which the 'package dealer' fills, and that what many architects now consider to be a normal architectural service is, or will soon be sub-normal. The architects, in short, must do a more comprehensive job."[226]

As buildings became more complicated and expensive, many firms were to take on not only engineers but landscape architects, interior designers, urban planners, and other specialists in an attempt to convince the client that they could most effectively handle a project. Meanwhile, architects increasingly realized that they must be businessmen as well as designers—and that they were not always particularly good businessmen, even when times were good. In 1955, a recent graduate of the School of Design had written to Henry Kamphoefner, "You can report to the boys that the business of architecture is booming now, but is still not the most lucrative profession."[227]

A 1969 study titled "The Economics of Architectural Practice in North Carolina, South Carolina, and Georgia," commissioned by the South Atlantic Region of the AIA as part of an effort by the national institute to help architects run their own practices better, was more specific. According to the report, architects in North Carolina averaged an 8 percent pretax profit, less than the national average of 8.3 percent and the regional average of 8.5 percent. By contrast, most principals in architectural firms regarded 16 to 25 percent as a fair profit. In the three South Atlantic states, architects lost money on almost one out of every three projects. The

A. G. Odell, Charlotte, 1982. The Charlotte architect was a strong advocate of modernism and professionalism. (Photo, © 1982 The Charlotte Observer/Fred Wilson.)

national average was one out of four. Work for individuals, private institutions, and corporations was most profitable; work for the state was least profitable. Midsize firms also proved more profitable than small or large ones.[228]

A year earlier, the NCAIA had sponsored a planning seminar for architects "designed to help architects in private practice cope with the ever increasing 'profit squeeze' in which they find themselves."[229] The NCAIA's 1975 convention, with the theme "This Business of Architecture," also focused on this topic. Noted one speaker: "The economic aspects of our practice are the most neglected items in our educational training both in the schools and in our apprenticeship practice."[230]

The following year, at the NCAIA convention, which focused on the dichotomy of business and design, an architectural management consultant reminded the architects that the 1950s had been a decade in which technology had flourished and the quantity of construction had been most important; that the 1960s had been the "quality decade," when technology held its own but when design reigned, encouraged by a booming economy; and that the 1970s were another decade influenced by economics, but with a new emphasis on management. Clients were demanding more efficiency and better organization. Said one speaker, "Quality is not enough—it must be fast, it must be versatile, and it must be affordable."[231]

Like builders, architects increasingly had to consider not only a building's budget but how economics influenced actual construction. "Because of inflation," noted Winston-Salem architect Lloyd G. Walter in 1980, "we're going to have a faster response time to delivery of the finished building. Money and interest on money are very real issues." In 1978, the AIA had changed its ethical standards to allow architects to engage in contracting on buildings they also designed. Walter predicted that such "design-build" projects and other cooperative ways of working with developers and contractors would become more important, adding that architects would more often confer with contractors during design "to adjust your design not so much as to the aesthetic you're after, but how you get there."[232] Even A. G. Odell, so well known for his modern designs and his AIA leadership, characterized architecture as 90 percent business and 10 percent art.[233]

Granting the go-ahead to design-build was not the only change in ethics that the AIA made in 1978. It also lifted its ban on advertising. Few architects took advantage of either of these changes, preferring instead to maintain traditional practices, but together the new standards represented a more wide-ranging approach to architectural practice. Already such changes were appearing in the schools. When Henry Kamphoefner retired as dean of the School of Design in 1972, he was replaced by Claude McKinney, who was neither an architect, landscape architect, nor product designer but had been trained as a painter. Coming from a city planning group called the Center for Urban Policy Research in Columbia, Maryland, McKinney, who served as dean until 1988 when he was made an assistant to the chancellor of the university in charge of developing a new portion of the campus, announced his intention to create a community of disciplines and designers to meet the needs of a more diverse society.[234] At the College of Architecture at the University of North Carolina at Charlotte, architecture graduates increasingly were branching out into nontraditional fields. The college had been founded to help meet the state's established architectural firms' demand for young architects. In the 1960s, Henry Kamphoefner had predicted that he could place an entire graduating class from the School of Design in offices in Charlotte alone. By the early 1980s, however, the economy, the number of architects already in practice, and the concerns of students had changed. Dean Charles Hight estimated that out of a typical graduating class of forty, only half would remain in architecture. The rest would go into construction, work for utility companies, or enter other segments of the building industry. The larger construction companies were searching for employees with knowledge of the construction field rather than those who simply drifted in. A few would join businesses such as IBM.[235]

By the late 1970s and the 1980s, architects were learning that they had to adjust to the changing world of building if they wanted successful practices. This was a hard-learned lesson for some of the doctrinaire modernists. But it did have its precedents in earlier generations and among those architects whose careers spanned both prewar beaux arts design and postwar modernism. A notable example was William Henley Deitrick of Raleigh. Though remembered by architectural history principally as Nowicki's collaborator on the Dorton Arena, Deitrick in fact maintained a practice that was just as willing to produce the traditional as the cutting edge. Deitrick's career took off rapidly when he won a competition for the design of Raleigh's Needham B. Broughton High School in 1927, three years after he arrived in Raleigh from his native Virginia to work for the state architect and only one year after he opened his own practice. Like most of the schools, offices, and homes that would follow, the Lombardy Gothic-style high school was traditional. But in the mid-1930s, Deitrick designed the modernist Raleigh Little Theatre for the Works Progress Administration and in 1940 produced a nurses' residence for Rex Hospital that featured a flat roof and casement windows. Following the war, Deitrick designed the Carolina Country Club (1947), said to be the first country club in the nation in the modern style, and continued his well-established practice specializing in schools—by then all contemporary. Deitrick's designs were a tempered modernism, however. Noted Guy Crampton, the architect who took over the practice after Deitrick retired: "[Deitrick] was very sensitive to people, their feelings and thoughts, which I think is a very important thing to the practice of architecture. In fact, in the early 1950s, when everything in architecture seemed to get awfully cold, he wanted that changed. He thought architecture should have warmth and beauty."[236]

Deitrick also was sensitive to the concerns of the profession, both as a group and as individual practitioners. He served as president of the NCAIA in 1947 and in 1963 donated his office building, the old city water tower, to the chapter as its headquarters. His office was one of the primary training grounds for young architects in Raleigh, a role that prominent firms—Odell in Charlotte, for example—often assumed. "The tower also became a professional training laboratory for young architects, a function I believe, to which all good architects should subscribe," Deitrick once said.[237] Upon his death in 1974, several of those young architects who had worked for him eulogized Deitrick for his "open-mindedness" and willingness to accept "the new ideas of new designers."[238]

It was about that time, however, that an entirely new breed of young architects was emerging. This new generation was influenced by changing attitudes toward both design and practice—especially those attitudes that affected the business of architecture.

The Charlotte firm of Clark, Tribble, Harris, and Li probably best represented the ways in which design and business blended in the late 1970s and 1980s. Though small firms continued to handle residential and light commercial work, those with fifty or more employees were best suited to the needs of developers and dominated economically.[239]

Begun on a shoestring ("Including college art work and all our possessions, the four of us together were probably worth one tenth of what we needed," recalled founding principal Joe Harris),[240] the firm successfully weathered the following year's recession and experienced slow but steady growth. Revenues of $100,000 in 1977[241] grew to $1.3 million in 1981—and then skyrocketed. By 1985, billings were $15 million and the firm had opened offices in New York and Washington, D.C., to supplement its Charlotte base. Over the three locations, the firm had 200 employees.[242] In 1986, it issued stock worth $5.8 million on the London exchange to raise capital necessary to continue its growth[243] and in 1987 made a move toward what it termed "an international consortium of design firms" by acquiring not only a Florida firm but one in London.[244]

Clark, Tribble, Harris, and Li's phenomenal success was due to more than architectural talent, though design was a definite part of their appeal. Since 1975, the firm had been a consistent winner in design competitions sponsored by the AIA, the North Carolina Home Builders Association, other associations, and magazines. In addition to the quality of their work, changes in design theory undoubtedly aided their success. In the 1970s and 1980s, modernism had given way to postmodernism, which promoted designing buildings that used historical forms that appealed to users. The architects, therefore, were free to design a modernist office building for a corporate client or Cape Cod-style condominiums for middle-income homebuyers, rather than forcing a single-minded approach. The architects estimated, however, that though design attracted clients, the speed and accuracy of the firm's work kept them.[245] Said one real estate executive: "The strength of Clark, Tribble, Harris, and Li is that they have the ability to design a sexy building that's very marketable and do it for reasonable numbers—it's not an architect's pipe dream that can't be built."[246]

One dream the architects did fulfill was the typical young architect's wish to have his own firm. But after that, Clark, Tribble, Harris, and Li's approach was all business. From the beginning, they assembled the best design talents possible as consultants to supplement their staff. That approach worked well on Charlotte's Discovery Place museum, a 1980 South Atlantic Regional AIA award winner that foreshadowed the firm's "consortium" approach to architecture. Following the AIA's change in ethics rules, they also used advertising, client endorsements, and videos to promote the firm—an approach that one observer called "uncharacteristic marketing chutzpah" for a profession generally so loathe to promote itself.[247] Gerald Li stressed the importance of marketing in a roundtable discussion conducted by *Architectural Record* magazine in 1985: "It is absolutely imperative that a promotional effort be made; it will make you more

Cover of office brochure, Clark, Tribble, Harris, and Li, Charlotte, 1980. Aggressive marketing helped this firm grow from four young architects to a huge operation with offices in several states and overseas. (Photo, Clark, Tribble, Harris, and Li Architects, P.A.)

valuable at the next fee negotiation." Another of Li's comments at the same meeting hit closer to home and explained why many architects consistently have had a difficult time as businessmen. "Architects have failed to remedy the compensation problem," Li said, "because of a strange self-perception I call the 'privilege syndrome.' The very act of practicing—the simple fact that we are heirs to an art that has a tradition and history—is seen as an end in itself, a reward of its own. The privilege syndrome causes architects to undervalue their own worth. We are in this way our worst enemy."[248]

With design awards still coming in, Clark, Tribble, Harris, and Li have not left architecture. However, because about 85 percent of their work is for developers and 10 to 20 percent is for "high-design projects such as museums and federal jobs," they have most successfully penetrated the business world. It is difficult to know whether a developer or an architect is speaking when Gerald Li says, "We had to make long-range plans and become market driven. We planned for growth but it has involved a lot of luck also. Our firm is very entrepreneurial and aggressive."[249] Certainly it is not a traditional architect.

Conclusion

In the years following World War II, building in North Carolina boomed in every conceivable way—in the size, complexity, numbers, and cost of buildings; the numbers of people; and the variety of construction skills. Changes came faster and more often as improved transportation and communication made local conditions less of a constraint. The population became better educated and more sophisticated, and large numbers of North Carolinians moved from the farm to the city where opportunities abounded. But despite its newfound prosperity and its reputation as a progressive southern state, North Carolina kept its traditional reserve. Even the flamboyant architectural symbol of the new postwar era, the Dorton Arena on the State Fairgrounds, was not an ostentatious building. The state was not showing off. It was flexing its muscles and stretching the limits of building in ways that were more practical than pretentious. More important, the arena had resulted from a coming together of talented and ambitious architects, builders, and clients who shared a vision of the future.

In contrast to the modernist, urban architecture of the day, the state's traditional rural buildings began the postwar period with less of a bang. Many farmers still erected their own homes, and many buildings still lacked the basic necessities. With the help of government loan programs and the Agricultural Extension Service's home design and improvement programs, however, rural building in North Carolina was transformed during the postwar period. These programs produced modest structures, which nevertheless met the need for improved housing, and when the number of people these buildings affected is considered, their importance is far greater than any single architectural wonder. Continuing the state's strong tradition of building for one's self, Lowe's Companies showed phenomenal growth after the war, beginning as a hardware store in North Wilkesboro and becoming the largest building supply retailer in the nation. By the late 1960s and 1970s, two grass-roots movements, historic preservation and energy consciousness, had captured the attention of both building owners and professionals. Though the interest in conserving energy mostly came and went with the rise and fall of fuel prices, historic preservation continued to grow and transform individual buildings, neighborhoods, and downtowns alike.

With the huge numbers of tradesmen needed for the building industry came the age-old issues of training and skill. The common wisdom held that workmanship had seriously deteriorated as the older generations, trained by traditional methods, retired. It was true that more tradesmen were learning their skills informally on the job. Though the state Department of Labor sponsored apprenticeship programs and the new community colleges and technical institutes founded after the war offered training in building skills, neither could keep up with the demand for tradesmen. In an era of increased industrialization, the role of the tradesman as an assembler of parts became more and more the rule. Apprenticeship and college programs did provide a core of skilled workmen and did train those who were to work in the more technical trades, however. There always remained, too, a number of tradesmen whose own high standards would not permit them to perform "jackleg" work.

Another large number of workmen, however, saw in the postwar boom an opportunity to go into business for themselves. Large contracting firms who bid on other peoples' projects continued the role they had established before the war. Some added development to their building interests. But the growth of the homebuilder was a new phenomenon. Most were former tradesmen—carpenters, masons, and the like—who wanted to move up to management. Most also built only a small number of houses a year. As the great entrepreneurs of the building industry, they also created a new concept of building, however. Though custom work still was available, most house building was no longer a service for a particular client. It was a commercial enterprise that produced a product to be sold on the speculative market. Just as architects and general contractors had before them, homebuilders created a professional association to help share ideas and techniques. With the explosive growth in the number of builders, construction saw a radical change. By the 1980s, homebuilding was attracting businessmen who had never known a trade.

Many were college graduates or had experience in other businesses. They brought with them a marketing expertise that continued to foster the importance of business and sales.

Though they had left the fast-growing homebuilding industry to its own devices, architects captured plenty of work and attention in the postwar period. The baby boom generation needed schools, and the growing economy needed factories, stores, and office buildings. The School of Design at North Carolina State University earned an international reputation for innovation, and its graduates reshaped not only buildings but the practice of architecture in the state. In the 1950s, there was a strong emphasis on professionalism. Architects may have preached the revolutionary gospel of modernism, but they relied on traditional techniques of finding work, shunning advertising and adhering strictly to a fee schedule. Although professionalism and the building boom together with the architectural practice act guaranteed enough work for architects through the 1960s, they almost boxed the architects into a corner in the 1970s, however, as competition for work increased. The architects' subsequent recognition that they must be more aggressive and must expand their services produced multitalented firms offering a variety of in-house services. In this period, also, the specialist roles of the architect began to grow. Architects realized they need not concentrate solely on modernist office buildings. Now they could concentrate on historic preservation, energy efficiency, or such super-specialties as design for the handicapped. The profession also began to give more attention to the business needs of practitioners. With the loosening of the AIA's ethical standards in the 1970s to allow advertising and contracting (fee schedules had already been dropped under threat of an antitrust suit by the Justice Department), architects were free to enter the business world on its own terms. Those who did found the same wide-open entrepreneurial atmosphere that builders had already discovered. Entrepreneurship fulfilled the period's promise of unlimited opportunities.

Postscript

MORE THAN three hundred years have passed since carpenter Robert Bodnam built a twenty-foot-square house on North Carolina's Albemarle Sound for Indian trader Nathaniel Batts. In that time, the "crudely worked buildings" and "dear and scarce" workmen of the early colony have evolved in ways no settler could have imagined. A North Carolinian today can buy a fully furnished mobile home right off the lot or purchase the parts necessary to build his own home from the giant building products supplier, Lowe's. Subdivisions offer homes built for the speculative market by merchant builders—with market research assuring that each one includes all the latest gadgets the buyer is likely to want. If high style is the goal, a prospective owner can commission a large, multinational architectural firm or any number of smaller offices, each with its own speciality and design philosophy.

The change is obvious. Building in North Carolina takes place in a different world today than it did when the state was a frontier settlement. We have traced the evolution of building from the wilderness, through the antebellum emergence of architects and contractors and the late-nineteenth-century industrialization of building, to the twentieth-century emphasis on professionalism and big business.

Across this history, attitudes about building and buildings have also changed regularly. In every period the "old" buildings have been viewed with skepticism, and many buildings have been replaced by the new and more "up-to-date." Indeed, few buildings have been praised consistently from decade to decade. These changing attitudes toward what is appropriate—and necessary, desirable, or functional—are essential to understanding the history of building, and they have provided a backdrop for this narrative. Identifying, describing, and trying to understand these changes over time and across a broad spectrum of building has given us a profound respect for *all* that is built and all who *would* build.

Building technology has been another obvious source of change that affected both builders and their buildings. In the mid-nineteenth century, technology redefined the role of artisans, turning them from fabricators into assemblers of parts. Early worries over obtaining nails or glass have

429

evaporated in an era when doors come pre-hung in their frames and studs are made of metal.

But has building itself changed? Once we look beyond the PVC pipe and the gypsum wallboard, the computer-aided design and the power nailers, and consider instead the ambitions, the failures, the training, the division of labor, and the simple fact that building is plain hard work—all the elements, in other words, that contribute to why people build and how they do it together—is the process different for today's builders than it was for their predecessors? The answer, we have been surprised to discover, is that very little has in fact changed.

The process of building remains what it always was—a site-specific, labor-intensive, fragmented, unpredictable event, economically driven, utterly dependent on materials suppliers, hired labor, transportation, and the weather. The human relationships central to the process do not change.

Early in our research we outlined the basic premise and structure of this study: that there are four modes of building that have continued throughout North Carolina's history. The most basic buildings were erected by their owners. Others were built by artisans, skilled in craft in the Old World tradition. Still more were built by teams of artisans organized by contractors. Finally, some were designed by architects. In each of these modes—and in the interaction between them—lie threads that tie today's building and builders together with their predecessors. What to each author first appeared to be isolated anecdotes in the history of building soon wove themselves into patterns. It is from such common threads of history that our discoveries and conclusions about the nature of building have emerged.

Building is seldom a solitary venture; it involves a team. That team begins with the client, who is as important an influence as the builders themselves. The union initiated by the client—whether with an architect, builder, artisan, or all three—is not just a mechanical, contractual one. It is a potent, human one. It is a relationship charged with tension that both draws the participants together and drives them apart. Every building grows from this tension. Tension links past and present, it is inevitable, and it affects the role of each participant. It is a part of the job of all who enter the building process.

In this matrix of people and energies, all the participants have roles and responsibilities and a place in the organization of work, from producing the drawings to working on the site. And everyone involved has a desire to control the process. We have seen this concern throughout history, regardless of the style of the building, the materials, or the era. Who decides what a building will look like? Who takes responsibility for obtaining materials? Who puts the parts together? Who organizes the workmen? How do craftsmen and professionals learn their jobs? No single person or institution can control all these factors. It is the partnership and negotiations among individuals, who today include developers, bankers, planners, and inspectors, that allow the building to come into being. The ways of managing this creative tension are myriad, and builders have responded to it in much the same way they have dealt with the other uncertainties of their lot. Kindness, toughness, humor, gentle persuasion, patience, pleading, and threats all have had their places, as have laws, building codes, organizations, and politics.

Because our history covers the entire spectrum of building in North Carolina, it opens a world filled with builders—all builders, not just the famous. This approach, which sets the study apart from most histories of architecture, grew from the knowledge that buildings represent the consequence of a vast range of needs and dreams and that their builders therefore represent the broad spectrum of society in North Carolina.

Our study has shown the dogged persistence with which successful builders pursue their trade. Risks are inherent throughout the process. Bankruptcy, structural and material failure, the dissatisfaction of clients, and liability for death and injuries on the job site are risks implicit in every project. In the face of such difficulties builders have revealed themselves as a hardy, combative group, willing to fight vigorously for the positions they deem theirs. Whether artisans, architects, or contractors, whether nationally famous or isolated in the rural, conservative, agricultural society of North Carolina, they are a tenacious, assertive, even contentious group, who have met and dealt with change with all the varieties of response available to human nature.

Just as tenacious, however, is the extraordinary constancy of the circumstances that shape building, including the fact that while changes do occur, they do not always signal progress or increase the likelihood that people today will approve of the buildings of yesterday. For building is not merely a reflection of society. It is an integral part of society. Building in North Carolina has played a role in the state's history from settlement in the forests and the evolution of an agrarian, slave society to the wrenching changes of the Great Depression and the striking innovations of the post–World War II boom. The growth of railroads, factories, highways, and government has affected building and in turn been affected by it. The number of players has increased dramatically during the history of the state. So have the opportunities and complexities. Throughout the centuries, North Carolina's architects and builders have had as many common experiences as unique ones. They came to building seeking jobs or were born into their trades, made or lost fortunes, died leaving monumental buildings or only a few tools. Their struggles to survive, to control their own destinies, or to exert control over others are universal experiences, not just part of a job.

Notes

Abbreviations

Frequently cited books, journals, and repositories have been identified by the following abbreviations in notes.

Publications

ACNC James H. Craig. *The Arts and Crafts in North Carolina, 1699–1840*. Winston-Salem: Museum of Early Southern Decorative Arts, 1965.

CRNC William L. Saunders, ed. *The Colonial Records of North Carolina*. 10 vols. Raleigh: State of North Carolina, 1886–90.

DAB Allen Johnson, Dumas Malone, et al., eds. *Dictionary of American Biography*. 20 vols. New York: Charles Scribner's Sons, 1928–36.

DNCB William S. Powell, ed. *Dictionary of North Carolina Biography*. 3 vols. to date. Chapel Hill: University of North Carolina Press, 1979– .

EANC Frances Benjamin Johnston and Thomas Tileston Waterman. *The Early Architecture of North Carolina*. Chapel Hill: University of North Carolina Press, 1947.

MR *Manufacturers' Record*.

RM Adelaide L. Fries, Douglas LeTell Rights, Minnie J. Smith, and Kenneth G. Hamilton, eds. *Records of the Moravians in North Carolina*. 11 vols. Raleigh: North Carolina Historical Commission, 1922–69.

SRNC Walter Clark, ed. *The State Records of North Carolina*. 16 vols. numbered 11–26. Winston and Goldsboro: State of North Carolina, 1895–1906.

Archival Repositories

A&H North Carolina Division of Archives and History, Raleigh.

AIAA American Institute of Architects Archives, Washington, D.C.

Avery Avery Architectural and Fine Arts Library, Columbia University, New York.

DUA Duke University Archives, Perkins Library, Durham.

Duke Duke Manuscript Department, Perkins Library, Durham.

MMA Metropolitan Museum of Art, New York.

NA National Archives, Washington, D.C.

NCC North Carolina Collection, Wilson Library, University of North Carolina, Chapel Hill.

NCSUA North Carolina State University Archives, Raleigh.

NYPL New York Public Library, New York.

SHC Southern Historical Collection, Wilson Library, University of North Carolina, Chapel Hill.

SS Secretary of State Papers, Archives and History, Raleigh.

VHS Virginia Historical Society, Richmond.

VSL Virginia State Library, Richmond.

433

Introduction

1. Other related English works include Summerson, *Georgian London*; Salzman, *Building in England Down to 1540*; Colvin, *Biographical Dictionary of English Architects*; Kaye, *Architectural Profession in Britain*; and Chalkin, *Provincial Towns of Georgian England*.

2. On colonial and early national period building, see also Whiffen, *Eighteenth-Century Houses of Williamsburg*; Quimby, *Craftsman in Early America*; and Herman, *Architecture and Rural Life*.

3. Other recent studies include Hounshell, *From the American System to Mass Production*; Salinger, "Artisans, Journeymen, and the Transformation of Labor"; and Skemer, "David Alling's Chair Manufactory."

4. United States, *Seventh Census*, 317. (There were also 498 brick and stonemasons and more than a thousand others listed in trades such as painters, sawyers, millwrights, and joiners that were often tied to construction work. Moreover, the large but unknown number of slaves working in construction may well have doubled these figures for the total population.) United States, *1980 Census of Population*, vol. 1, *Characteristics of the Population*, Occupations by Industry, 503–4. Jacquelyn Dowd Hall et al., *Like a Family*, is an excellent recent study of textile mill workers, standing in a long tradition of textile mill literature.

Chapter 1

1. For a discussion of the settlement of the Albemarle, see Butler, "Early Settlement of Carolina"; and Powell, *Ye Countie of Albemarle*.

2. In 1664 the proprietors divided their new colony into three counties. The northeastern part of their territory was named Albemarle County after George Monck, Duke of Albemarle, one of the Lords Proprietors.

3. Powell, *Ye Countie of Albemarle*, xxvii–xxix.

4. Parramore, "Tuscarora Ascendancy," 307–26.

5. See, for example, the opinion of Quaker leader George Fox who visited the Albemarle in the 1670s in Penny, *Journal of George Fox* 2:234. Gov. Thomas Culpeper of Virginia also had a very low opinion of early Carolina settlers as can be seen in his statement quoted in Morgan, *American Slavery, American Freedom*, 239.

6. Records of the Proceedings of the Vestry of St. Paul's Church, Edenton, Mar. 2, 1714, 26, A&H.

7. Inventory of the Estate of George Branch, Feb. 2, 1696, SS, Council Minutes, Wills, and Inventories, 1677–1701, 108.

8. Boyd, *William Byrd's Histories*, 305.

9. Carr and Menard, "Immigration and Opportunity," 216–27.

10. *CRNC* 2:419.

11. Virginia, *Statutes at Large* 2:445.

12. Boyd, *William Byrd's Histories*, 52.

13. Wolf, "Patents and Tithables," 274.

14. Ibid., 272.

15. Price, *Higher-Court Records, 1709–1723*, 340.

16. Boyd, *William Byrd's Histories*, 54.

17. Ibid., 110.

18. *CRNC* 1:712.

19. For Massachusetts, see Cummings, *Framed Houses of Massachusetts Bay*; for southeastern Pennsylvania, see Michael, "Manner and Fashion."

20. The Cupola House was built in the mid-1720s by Richard Sanderson, a wealthy tobacco planter. For a study of the house, see Cheeseman, "Cupola House of Edenton."

21. Carson et al., "Impermanent Architecture," 136. For an analysis of English impermanent timber-framing techniques, see Charles, "Post-Construction and the Rafter Roof," 3–19;

Rahtz et al., "Architectural Reconstruction of Timber Buildings," 39–47; Bettey, "Seventeenth Century Squatters' Dwellings," 28–30; and Beresford and Hurst, *Deserted Medieval Villages*, 89–117.

22. For the development of the "Virginia house," see Carson et al., "Impermanent Architecture," 158–60; Carson, " 'Virginia House' in Maryland," 185–86; and Upton, "Early Vernacular Architecture."

23. Late-seventeenth-century records clearly distinguish a range of construction techniques. For reference to an English framed house, see, for example, Westmoreland Co., Va., Court Order Book, 1705–1721, Mar. 28, 1707, 49, VSL.

24. Davis, *William Fitzhugh*, 202–3.

25. Quoted in Carson et al., "Impermanent Architecture," 160.

26. Ibid., 155; *CRNC* 1:300.

27. Lawson, *New Voyage to Carolina*, 223–24; Parker, *Higher-Court Records, 1670–1696*, 312.

28. Boyd, *William Byrd's Histories*, 94; Powell, *History of Caswell County*, 32.

29. Norfolk Co., Va., Will and Deed Book C, 1651–56, Nov. 15, 1655, 180, VSL.

30. Peter Carteret, Report to the Lords Proprietors about Plantation on Colleton Island, Dec. 3, 1674, Thurmond Chatham Papers, Box 1, Folio 27, A&H.

31. Ludwell, "Boundary Line Proceedings, 1710," 7.

32. Boyd, *William Byrd's Histories*, 313–14.

33. Parker, *Higher-Court Records, 1670–1696*, 191.

34. See, for example, "Agreement between Capt. Nicholas James of Bath County and William Tomson of Bath County, bricklayer," Nov. 28, 1701, Beaufort Co. Deed Book I, 12, A&H.

35. Price, *Higher-Court Records, 1709–1723*, 106.

36. Inventory of the Estate of Francis Godfrey, probated Mar. 5, 1676, Mar. 1680, and May 19, 1680, SS, Council Minutes, Wills, and Inventories, 1677–1701, 17. The "porch" was not the familiar open porch or piazza typical of later eighteenth-century farmhouses but an enclosed one- or two-story projection that may have contained a stair to the upper floor. Other houses of the period featured porches with chambers overhead on the second floor that were used for sleeping. In 1709 Francis Tomes's house in Perquimans Precinct contained a porch chamber. A few enclosed porches survive in Virginia houses such as Bacon's Castle and Criss Cross. Will of Francis Tomes, Oct. 10, 1709, SS, Wills, 1712–1722, 55. For a discussion of the enclosed porch in Virginia, see Upton, "Vernacular Domestic Architecture," 104–6.

37. Inventory of the Estate of Isaac Ottwell, SS, General Assembly Laws, 1715, Inventories of Estates, 1728–1741, 19.

38. Will of George Durant, May 25, 1730, SS, Wills.

39. Will of Patrick Maule, Apr. 19, 1736, SS, Wills, 1738–1752, 238.

40. Inventory of the Estate of Francis Godfrey, probated Mar. 5, 1676, Mar. 1680, and May 19, 1680, SS, Council Minutes, Wills, and Inventories, 1677–1701, 17.

41. Financial Accounts of Peter Carteret in Carolina, 1672–73, Thurmond Chatham Papers, Box 1, Folio 24, A&H.

42. Price, *Higher-Court Records, 1709–1723*, 333.

43. Boyd, *William Byrd's Histories*, 96.

44. For the social significance of brick chimneys, see Neiman, "Architecture at the Clifts Plantation," 3126.

45. Brickell, *Natural History of North Carolina*, 37.

46. All three houses had the major part of their woodwork removed earlier in this century.

47. Around the turn of the century, the General Assembly passed an act for building Anglican churches. By 1703 one Anglican church had been constructed and two more were proposed for immediate construction. Francis Nicholson, governor of Virginia, generously

supported the effort of the North Carolina Anglicans by contributing ten pounds for each structure. Henderson Walker to the Bishop of London, Oct. 21, 1703, Society for the Propagation of the Gospel, London, Letter Book A, I. Sometime before 1706 the General Assembly proposed the construction of a provincial courthouse "60 feet long, 20 feet wide" in Chowan Precinct. The building was to have "two roomes and an entry to the Secretary's office and one to the office of the Clerk of the Assembly." It was apparently never built. Olds, *Counties of North Carolina*, 22.

48. *CRNC* 4:604–5.

49. Boyd, *William Byrd's Histories*, 68, 96.

50. Schoepf, *Travels in the Confederation*, 33.

51. "Extract of a Letter from Rev. John Urmstone to the Secretary of the Society for Propagating the Gospel, London, July 7, 1711," quoted in Hawks, *History of North Carolina* 2:216.

52. Norfolk Co., Va., Will and Deed Book C, 1651–56, Nov. 15, 1655, 180, VSL. This practice first occurred in the Chesapeake where builders were dispatched by English emigrants or Chesapeake planters to ready plantations for settlers. See Carson et al., "Impermanent Architecture," 144–46.

53. Parker, *Higher-Court Records, 1697–1701*, 503; Perquimans Co. Deed Book A, 380, A&H.

54. Ship captain John Whitty had both a carpenter and a cooper working for him in 1666. Thomas Harris, one of the first settlers on the north shore of the Albemarle Sound, probably had a carpenter or someone skilled in building in his household as early as 1665. John Colleton to Peter Carteret, Mar. 7, 1666, Thurmond Chatham Papers, Box 1, Folio 5; Will of Thomas Harris, Aug. 1, 1665, Colonial Court Records, Land Papers, and Wills, 1665–1746; Inventory of the Estate of Thomas Harris, Apr. 3, 1680, SS, Council Minutes, Wills, and Inventories, 1677–1701, II, A&H.

55. Neve, *Purchaser's and Builder's Dictionary*.

56. Moxon, *Mechanick Exercises*, 63.

57. Parker, *Higher-Court Records, 1670–1696*, 312; Lawson, *New Voyage to Carolina*, 223–24.

58. Parker, *Higher-Court Records, 1697–1701*, 263, 301.

59. Inventory of the Estate of Patrick Ogleby, Mar. 1727, SS, Wills, 1722–1735, 109–12.

60. Cummings, *Framed Houses of Massachusetts Bay*, 40. Compulsory indentures recorded in court order books in Tidewater counties of Virginia between 1701 and 1730 totaled 60 joiner apprenticeships compared to 354 carpenter apprenticeships. See court order books for Elizabeth City Co., 1715–1723; Essex Co., 1703–1729; Henrico Co., 1707–1724; Isle of Wight Co., 1715–1726; Middlesex Co., 1705–1726; Norfolk Co., 1719–1734; Prince George Co., 1714–1720; Princess Anne Co., 1691–1728; and Surry Co., 1691–1718, VSL.

61. Inventory of the Estate of Francis Beasley, July 1, 1719, SS, Wills, 1712–1722, 206–7.

62. Inventory of the Estate of Thomas Robinson, Apr. 19, 1719, SS, Wills, 1712–1722, 208–11.

63. Lawson, *New Voyage to Carolina*, 90, 98–100.

64. The specifications for the new courthouse in Currituck Precinct in 1723 called for cypress shingles. Cain, *Higher-Court Minutes, 1724–1730*, 174.

65. Parker, *Higher-Court Records, 1697–1701*, 410.

66. Will of Thomas Pollock, Sr., Aug. 8, 1721, Wills, SS; Cummings, *Framed Houses of Massachusetts Bay*, 50. See also Moody, "Massachusetts Trade with Carolina," 43–53.

67. Todd and Goebel, *Christoph Von Graffenried's Account*, 188.

68. Perquimans Co. Court Minutes, 1698–1707, Jan. 1700, A&H; Price, *Higher-Court Records, 1709–1723*, 348, 502–4; Will of Thomas Lee, Mar. 14, 1717, SS, Wills, 1712–1722, 161.

69. Treasurer's and Comptroller's Papers, Port of Roanoke, Customs House Papers, 1682–1760, vol. 13 passim, A&H. Colonial officials considered the port of Roanoke to consist of all the landings along the streams that emptied into the Albemarle Sound.

70. In 1719 Edward Moseley, the undertaker of the Chowan Precinct courthouse, purchased shingles for the building from Chowan planter John Marks. Chowan Co. Deed Book W-1, 93; Deed Book B-1, 518; Chowan Co. Misc. Records, Bill of Materials for the First Chowan Co. Courthouse, 1719, A&H.

71. Neve, *Purchaser's and Builder's Dictionary*.

72. Parker, *Higher-Court Records, 1697–1701*, 405, 410, 436, 491.

73. Codicil to the Will of Thomas Pollock, Sr., July 20, 1722, SS, Wills.

74. *SRNC* 23:70.

75. Craven Co. Court Minutes, 1712–1715, 100, A&H.

76. Perquimans Co. Court Minutes, 1698–1707, Mar. 1703, A&H.

77. Chowan Co. Deed Book W-1, 107–8, A&H.

78. Perquimans Co. Deed Book A, 104, A&H; Price, *Higher-Court Records, 1702–1709*, 61.

79. Pasquotank Co. Misc. Deeds, 1700–1747, Oct. 1, 1700, 1, A&H; *CRNC* 1:591.

80. Information on Thomas Robinson's origins provided by Raymond A. Winslow, Jr., Perquimans Co. historian, letter to author, Mar. 24, 1981. See also *CRNC* 2:42.

81. In Virginia, a number of apprentices complained that their masters were "imployinge them to worke in the ground contrary" to their apprenticeship indentures. See Norfolk Co., Va., Will and Deed Book D, 1656–1666, 381a, VSL.

82. *CRNC* 2:171, 241, 262.

83. Will of Lemuel Taylor, Nov. 3, 1719, SS, Wills, 1722–1735, 29; Inventory of the Estate of Lemuel Taylor, Sept. 13, 1720, SS, Wills, 1712–1722, 260–61; Perquimans Co. Deed Book B, 189, A&H. Robert Herman, a neighboring joiner, probably trained his son Robert in his profession as well. Will of Robert Herman, Jan. 20, 1715, SS, Wills, 1712–1722, 102.

84. Carteret Co. Court Minutes, 1723–1747, Sept. 1725, A&H; Will of John Dicks, Feb. 10, 1706, SS, Wills.

85. Price, *Higher-Court Records, 1702–1709*, 61.

86. Although no detailed building contracts from the seventeenth century have survived in North Carolina, a sample contract from Virginia illustrates the responsibilities of builder and client. On January 28, 1657 carpenter James Hugate contracted to build for planter Thomas Swann of Surry County, Virginia, a framed servants' house and other buildings. Hugate agreed

> to build & Finish . . . one small quarteringe house of twentye five, or thertye foote Longe & Soe much other out houses as will make up the same ninetye Foote of houseing, the Bredth of them not to be under fiveteene nor above twentye Foote, all to be done as the sd Swann Shall contrive & give directions; & the sd Hugate is to finde, & Diett himselfe at his own Charges. In consideration whereof the sd Th: Swann is to allowe the sd Hugate 125 pounds tob: & Caske, for Every Length of Boards . . . also to finde him a Couple of hands to assist him in the Woodes to Sawe timber, & bring it in place, as alsoe to helpe him to reare & one to hand Boards to him for Coveringe, And all manner of nayles, & other things as shall be necessarye . . . From wch the sd Hugate is not to depart nor any wayes neglect the same, by intermedlinge with any other worke belonginge to any other person . . . untill the sd Housinge be Compleated, & Finished . . . Moreover the sd Hugate is to have the house next to the water side to live in, & to have the benifitt thereof for him and his wife . . . Like wise the sd Hugate is to have ground within the field for the plantings of Corne, hee . . . helpinge to mend the Fence, & secure the same, and alsoe the grounds about the houseing by the waterside to plant tob: on & what else hee pleaseth. (Surry Co., Va., Order, Deed, and Will Book, 1652–1672, 96, 260, VSL)

Seven years after James Hugate signed the building contract with Thomas Swann, he was murdered.

87. *CRNC* 1:416, 437.

88. Price, *Higher-Court Records, 1709–1723*, 448.

89. Peter Carteret to Sir George Carteret, Dec. 1674, Thurmond Chatham Papers, Box 1, Folio XXVI, A&H.

90. Boyd, *William Byrd's Histories*, 305.

91. Parker, *Higher-Court Records, 1670–1696*, 346, 433.

92. Thomas Pollock Letter Book, 21, A&H; Moody, "Massachusetts Trade with Carolina," 51–53.

93. Will of Edward Moseley, Mar. 20, 1745, SS, Wills; Parker, *Higher-Court Records, 1670–1696*, 221; Perquimans Co. Deed Book A, 145, A&H.

94. Parker, *Higher-Court Records, 1670–1696*, 118.

95. For a study of the public building process in early Virginia, see Upton, *Holy Things and Profane*, 11–34.

96. Cain, *Higher-Court Minutes, 1724–1730*, 174.

97. Bill of Materials for the First Chowan Co. Courthouse, 1719, Chowan County Courthouse, Edenton. William Davis apparently also worked on the Chowan courthouse in some capacity independent of Edward Moseley's supervision. In September 1722, Davis was paid twenty pounds "for building the Court House." By comparison carpenter Charles Fortee who worked under Moseley received eighty pounds for working on the courthouse. *North Carolina Historical and Genealogical Register* 1 (July 1900): 444.

98. Carteret Co. Court Minutes, 1723–1747, Mar. 4, 1729, 12, A&H. Another craftsman who may have operated as an undertaker in the late seventeenth century was Thomas Davis. An English bond from 1682 transcribed in Latin referred to Davis, who was living in Kingston upon Thames in the county of Surrey, as "architectis" or master builder. Within two years of this bond, Davis had emigrated to the Albemarle where he may have continued his trade as a building contractor. Parker, *Higher-Court Records, 1670–1696*, 435. For a description of the role of an "architect" in seventeenth-century English building, see Colvin, *Biographical Dictionary of British Architects*, 22–23.

99. Records of the Proceedings of the Vestry of St. Paul's Church, Edenton, Dec. 15, 1701, 1, A&H; *EANC*, 246.

100. *North Carolina Historical and Genealogical Register* 1 (Oct. 1900): 613 and 3 (Apr. 1903): 250; Parker, *Higher-Court Records, 1697–1701*, 453; Price, *Higher-Court Records, 1709–1723*, 500; Records of the Proceedings of the Vestry of St. Paul's Church, Edenton, Oct. 13, 1702, 4, A&H.

101. Records of the Proceedings of the Vestry of St. Paul's Church, Edenton, Oct. 14, 1702, 5, A&H.

102. Ibid., Oct. 6, 1703, Mar. 4, 1704, Jan. 3, 1706, May 11, 1708, July 25, 1708, 9, 10, 13, 17, 19, 80, 85; *CRNC* 1:711–12, 769. The church that was begun in the late 1730s is the present brick structure.

103. Thomas Pollock Letter Book, 254, A&H.

104. Hartwell, Blair, and Chilton, *Present State of Virginia*, 9–10.

105. Will of Thomas Robinson, Mar. 24, 1719, 169–70 and Inventory of the Estate of Thomas Robinson, Apr. 19, 1719, 208–11, SS, Wills, 1712–1722; Raymond A. Winslow, Jr., to author, Mar. 24, 1981.

106. Will of Lemuel Taylor, Nov. 3, 1719, SS, Wills, 1722–1735, 29; Inventory of the Estate of Lemuel Taylor, Sept. 13, 1720, SS, Wills, 1712–1722, 260–61.

107. Will of John Brothers, Nov. 28, 1733, SS, Wills; Inventory of the Estate of John Brothers, Apr. 21, 1735, SS, General Assembly Laws of 1715, Inventories of Estates, 1728–1741, 27.

108. *CRNC* 1:764.

109. In 1723 Anglican minister Thomas Newnam observed that Edenton was "beginning to grow very populous. All the Publick Officers being oblig'd by an Act of Assembly to reside there. . . . I hope to see here a large and beautiful Brick Church go forward. At present

indeed all things seem to stand in status quo with relation to church Buildings. . . . by reason the Publick Buildings are now in hand such as ye Courthouse ye Council Room Prison etc." (Society for the Propagation of the Gospel, London, Letter Book B, IV, May 9, 1723). For the presence of resident craftsmen in Edenton, see Chowan Co. Deed Book B-1, 164, 534, 624, 659, A&H.

110. Tomson died before he could earn enough money to establish his own household. Before his death, he did some work in his trade, plastering a house for a Mr. Barrow. His impoverished estate was valued at a little more than eighteen pounds. Beaufort Co. Deed Book I, 15, 17, 33, A&H.

111. Under the pressure of growing debts, Lyon "claindestinely Departed the Government," leaving Mrs. Durant bereft of several pounds. Parker, *Higher-Court Records, 1697–1701*, 456, 463–64.

112. Inventory of the Estate of Samuel Ashton, Feb. 20, 1736, General Assembly Laws 1715, Inventories of Estates, 1728–1741, 49 and Inventory of the Estate of Uriah Cannon, Beaufort Co. Deed Book I, 23, A&H.

113. Due to the uneven nature of these early records, this discrepancy in the average values of inventories of the two groups should be approached with some caution. The estates of carpenters also differed from planters in holdings of livestock and slaves. Although 75 percent of the inventories of each group listed some amount of livestock, animals accounted for a greater percentage of a farmer's estate. More than a third of the value of a farmer's personal property was in livestock compared to less than a quarter of the value of a craftsman's estate. Stock raising proved to be one of the most important sources of income for a farmer because, unlike tobacco, livestock required little labor. By contrast, only 17 percent of small planters owned slaves, whereas over 50 percent of the identified carpenters held one or more slaves, some of them skilled or unskilled building laborers. Substantial tobacco planters in contrast to these two groups left estates valued between £350 and £1,000, with labor accounting for a larger proportion of their value. SS, Wills, 1712–1722 and SS, Wills, 1722–1735 passim.

114. Inventory of the Estate of Francis Beasley, July 1719, SS, Wills, 1712–1722, 206–7.

115. Inventory of the Estate of William Davis, Dec. 7, 1728, SS, Wills, 1722–1735, 188.

116. Price, *Higher-Court Records, 1702–1709*, 224; Perquimans Co. Court Minutes, 1698–1707, Feb. 1703, A&H.

117. Price, *Higher-Court Records, 1709–1723*, 158.

118. Perquimans Precinct court, for example, frequently used carpenters James Coles and Francis Beasley to make inventories of the goods and chattels of deceased artisans in their part of the precinct during the first decade of the eighteenth century. Price, *Higher-Court Records, 1702–1709*, 272, 340, 355.

119. Price, *Higher-Court Records, 1709–1723*, 106.

120. Ibid., 415, 448.

121. Dorchester Co., Md., Land Records No. 1, 1669–1683, Dec. 6, 1686, 148–49.

122. Jane Baldwin Cotton, *Maryland Calendar of Wills* 1:216; Parker, *Higher-Court Records, 1670–1696*, 14, 191, 272, 391–93; Dorchester Co., Md., Land Records No. 1, 1669–1683, Dec. 6, 1686, 148–49; *North Carolina Historical and Genealogical Register* 1 (Jan. 1900): 140; Perquimans Co. Court Minutes, 1688–1693 and Perquimans Co. Deed Book A, 61, 104, A&H; Parker, *Higher-Court Records, 1697–1701*, 196–97; Nelson, *Calender of New Jersey Wills*, 128, 230, 233, 317, 342.

123. For a study of the class and occupations of those who held office in local and provincial government, see Lowry, "Class, Politics, Rebellion."

124. Thomas Pollock Letter Book, 254, A&H.

Chapter 2

1. William Dickson to Thomas Henderson, Nov. 24, 1810, Thomas Henderson Papers, A&H, reproduced in Newsome, "Twelve North Carolina Counties," *North Carolina Historical Review* 5, no. 4 (Oct. 1928): 440.

2. On the colonial period, see Ekirch, *"Poor Carolina"*; Merrens, *Colonial North Carolina*; and Ramsey, *Carolina Cradle*.

3. Cullen Pollock to Nathaniel Duckinfield, Dec. 20, 1741, as cited in Ekirch, *"Poor Carolina,"* 15; John MacDowell to Secretary of the Society for the Propagation of the Gospel, Apr. 17, 1760, *CRNC* 6:236, 238; Scotus Americanus, "Informations Concerning the Province of North Carolina . . . ," in Boyd, *Some Eighteenth Century Tracts*, 448; "French Traveler in America," 738.

4. Lefler and Newsome, *North Carolina*, 715, 321, 315.

5. Ekirch, *"Poor Carolina,"* esp. 3–47; Johnson, *Ante-Bellum North Carolina*, 55–56. The percentage of slaveholders decreased from 31 in 1790 to 27 in 1860.

6. William Byrd, in Wright, *Byrd Prose Works*, 207, quoted in Ekirch, *"Poor Carolina,"* 32. See also Henry Eustace McCulloh to James Iredell, Sept. 5, 1768, in Higginbotham, *Papers of James Iredell* 1:19.

7. Escott and Crow, "Social Order and Violent Disorder," 375. See also Escott, *Many Excellent People*, 3–31, and Ekirch, *"Poor Carolina,"* 19–40.

8. On the federal period in North Carolina, see Lefler and Newsome, *North Carolina*, 254–326; Johnston, *Ante-Bellum North Carolina*; and Harry Watson, *An Independent People*.

9. Hoyt, *Papers of Archibald D. Murphey* 2:105; Murray, *Wake*, 204–10.

10. In 1790, according to one estimate, the free population of 292,554 occupied 40,018 dwellings. By 1850 there were an estimated 104,996 dwellings for free residents. These figures do not include slaves' dwellings, nor do they account for replacement of buildings. Johnson, *Ante-Bellum North Carolina*, 227. Quote from Gowans, *Images of American Living*, 14. On the stages of homesteading from hovel to house, see Carson et al., "Impermanent Architecture," 140–41. See also "William Logan's Journal," 14.

11. "William Logan's Journal," 9. Bishop Reichel in Virginia, 1780, quoted in Marzio, "Carpentry in the Southern Colonies," 237. See also Charles Woodmason's 1756 account of backcountry Carolina: "All new settlers, extremely poor, live in Logg Cabbins like Hoggs." The description was of South Carolina, which Woodmason believed slightly superior to North Carolina (Hooker, *Carolina Backcountry*, 7, 80–81). Similar houses were described in Virginia between Williamsburg and Richmond in Smyth, *Tour of the United States* 1:30. On log buildings and clay and wood chimneys elsewhere, see Terry Jordan, *Texas Log Buildings* (Austin: University of Texas Press, 1978), 95–99.

12. For the 1730 Craven County wooden courthouse that was replaced by a brick one set on pillars over a market, see Herzog, "Early Architecture of New Bern," 55–56, and Dill, "Public Buildings in Craven County," 301–26. Joseph P. Brown, *Commonwealth of Onslow* (New Bern: Privately printed, 1960), 9, 15, 17; Wynette Parks Haun, *Johnston County, North Carolina Court Minutes 1759 thru 1766* (Durham: Privately printed, 1974), 3, 7; Jo White Linn, *Abstracts of the Minutes of the Court of Pleas and Quarter Sessions, Rowan County, North Carolina, 1753–1762* (Salisbury: Privately printed, 1977), 5, 53, 62, 81 (on 1756 courthouse); *SRNC* 24:149; Orange Co. Court Minutes (Pleas and Quarter Sessions), folio 45, 90; *SRNC* 24:177, 461, 692, 844, 942; courtesy of Mary Claire Engstrom. See also *SRNC* 23:680, 747, and Marzio, "Carpentry in the Southern Colonies," 235–37.

13. Compare data in *ACNC* with settlement chronology map in James W. Clay et al., *North Carolina Atlas*, 15. See also Tilley, "Industries of Colonial Granville County," 273–89, and Rowan Co. Deed Book 1, 103–8, and Book 7, 14, 15, A&H, for men identified as carpenters and joiners buying and selling real estate in the 1750s and 1760s. Alan Gowans found a similar lag between settlement and permanent, substantial architecture in Salem

County, New Jersey (and elsewhere). See Alan Gowans, "The Mansions of Alloways Creek," in Upton and Vlach, *Common Places*, 375.

14. Newsome, "Twelve North Carolina Counties," *North Carolina Historical Review* 6, no. 3 (July 1929): 299; 6, no. 2 (Apr. 1929): 6, no. 1 (Jan. 1929): 82; 6, no. 2 (Apr. 1929): 184; 6, no. 3 (July 1929): 285. Also see such contemporary travelers' accounts as Francis Hall, *Travels in Canada and the United States in 1816 and 1817* (London: Longman, Hurst, 1818), 241; and Elkanah Watson, *Men and Times of the Revolution*, 38, Francis Asbury, *Journal* 3:51, and Adam Hodgson, *Letters from North America* 1:35, quoted in Johnson, *Ante-Bellum North Carolina*, 120–21.

15. *SRNC* 23:143; *Virginia Gazette*, Oct. 15, 1736; Robert B. Drane Papers, SHC; *CRNC* 6:237, and 7:515; *SRNC* 25:391–92. See also *CRNC* 4:1292 on problems in completing public buildings.

16. *RM* 2:618, Apr. 20, 1771.

17. Dill, *Governor Tryon and His Palace*; Newsome, "Twelve North Carolina Counties," *North Carolina Historical Review* 6, no. 3 (July 1929): 300.

18. Andrews, *Journal of a Lady*, 160, 185; Jacob Hyatt Papers, Rutherford, Apr. 5, 1825, A&H; *Diary of a Geological Tour by Dr. Elisha Mitchell in 1827 and 1828*, James Sprunt Historical Monograph No. 6 (Chapel Hill: University of North Carolina, 1905), 54; Newsome, "Twelve North Carolina Counties," *North Carolina Historical Review* 6, no. 2 (Apr. 1929): 184.

19. Ekirch, "Poor Carolina," 193; "Atticus" to William Tryon, [1771], in Powell, *Correspondence of William Tryon* 2:835. "Atticus" also complained of another aspect of what he believed to be Tryon's inappropriately pretentious behavior, citing "the arrogant Reception you gave to a respectable Company at an Entertainment of your own Making, seated with your Lady by your Side on Elbow Chairs, in the Middle of the Ball Room [which bespeaks] a Littleness of mind, which, believe me, Sir, when blended with the Dignity and Importance of your Office, renders you truly ridiculous." "Atticus" has been variously identified as Maurice Moore of Brunswick and Samuel Johnston of Edenton. Powell, *Correspondence of William Tryon* 2:841; Marvin L. Michael Kay, "The North Carolina Regulation, 1766–1776: A Class Conflict," in *The American Revolution: Explorations in the History of American Radicalism*, ed. Alfred F. Young (DeKalb: Northern Illinois University Press, 1976), 122 n. 102; and author's conversation with William S. Price, 1986.

20. James C. Johnston to Joseph Blount, July 15, 1817, Hayes Collection, SHC.

21. William R. Davie to John Steele, Aug. 3, 1801, Steele Papers, SHC, reproduced in Hood, *Architecture of Rowan County*, 365. Davie himself lost popularity in North Carolina because of his aristocratic tendencies, which gives his remark special piquancy.

22. Nathaniel Macon, *Speech to the Senate*, Jan. 20, 1820, quoted in Butler and Watson, *North Carolina Experience*, 184–85.

23. Wilmington *Cape Fear Herald*, Nov. 2, 1803; Wilmington *Cape-Fear Recorder*, May 27, 1816; Fayetteville *Carolina Observer*, Aug. 13, 1818. See also John Winslow of Fayetteville's description of William Nichols's plan for a penitentiary as "elegant," in Johnson, *Ante-Bellum North Carolina*, 666; the description of a large elegant new house in Windsor, in the Edenton *State Gazette*, July 24, 1789; and the reference to a "beautiful and elegant villa" near Warrenton, in the *Warrenton Reporter*, Oct. 4, 1825.

24. Raleigh *Star*, May 31, 1810. "Vandalism" here carries a meaning of primitiveness. Raleigh *Star*, Nov. 15, 1810, and *Raleigh Register*, Dec. 2, 1805, Murray files; Robert Bolling to Calvin Jones, Apr. 1, 1816, Calvin Jones Papers, SHC; Bishir and Bullock, "Mr. Jones Goes to Richmond."

25. William Tryon to Sewallis Shirley, July 26, 1765, in Powell, *Correspondence of William Tryon* 1:139; Patricia Booth, native of Nash Co., N.C., to author, Apr. 1981. For carpenters' tools in planters' estate inventories, see, for example, Grimes, *Wills and Inventories*, 69, 132, 308, 475, 477, 483, 489, 498–99, 500–501, 504, 508, 513, 514–22, 534, 541, 542, 543, 544–45. See also Dobbs to Board of Trade, Aug. 24, 1755, in *CRNC* 5:362. See Clarence Ford and Mabel R.

Blume, *Historic Rocky River Church Buildings and Burying Grounds* (privately printed, 1958), 4, for a typical church sequence of a 1754 log church, a 1776 log church, an 1807 frame building, and an 1860 brick church. For an account of a 1758 pioneer family hiring local men to erect its buildings before moving to North Carolina, see "Autobiography of Col. William Few of Georgia," *The Magazine of American History* 7 (1881): 343. On building for oneself and community building efforts, see Glassie, "Vernacular Architecture and Society," 10; Martin, *Hollybush*; and Boyce, *History of Chowan County*, 41.

26. On the traditional design process, see Rapoport, *House Form and Culture*, 4; Deetz, *In Small Things Forgotten*, 38–43, 92–117; Glassie, *Folk Housing in Middle Virginia*; and Upton, "Vernacular Domestic Architecture."

27. New Bern *Federal Republican*, Mar. 8, 1817; *ACNC*, 2–3; J. H. Smith to Duncan Cameron, Mar. 10, 1829, Cameron Family Papers, SHC.

28. Architect John Hawks and carpenter Benjamin Soane, both of Craven County, each possessed eleven architectural books at their deaths. Craven Co. Estates Papers, A&H. More typical was carpenter-joiner Gilbert Leigh of Perquimans County whose estate inventory in 1793 included "1 Architecters Book," 2 chests of carpenter's tools, 1 whip saw, 1 cross-cut saw, a quantity of 2-foot shingles, and 160 six-penny nails. In the same county, carpenter-joiner Henry Pointer's estate in 1800 comprised several books, including "1 Carpenters Book," a *Spectator*, some sermons, and a dictionary. Perquimans Co. Estates Papers, A&H, quoted in Haley and Winslow, *Historic Architecture of Perquimans County*, 28. He owned more than 200 tools as well. Haley and Winslow, *Historic Architecture of Perquimans County*, 256–60.

29. Estate Inventory, Arthur Dobbs Papers, SHC. This is the only colonial period inventory found that included titles of architectural books. These volumes were evidently Colin Campbell's *Vitruvius Britannicus* (London, 1715–71) and Sebastien Le Clerc's *Traite d'architecture; A treatise of architecture* (Paris, 1714 and London, 1723–24). There is no indication of which editions Dobbs possessed of the works of Italian architects Andrea Palladio and Vincenzo Scamozzi. Neither Schimmelman nor Park lists other American colonists in possession of Scamozzi's work. See Schimmelman, *Architectural Treatises and Building Handbooks*; Park, *List of Architectural Books*; and Hitchcock, *Architecture Books*.

30. Governor and planter David Stone's library of 1,499 volumes included Abraham Swan's *British Architect* and William Pain's *Practical House Carpenter*. Reynolds, " 'Hope.' " In 1811 planter Ebenezer Pettigrew's book order from New York included "Adams Roman Antiquities" for three dollars and "Pains Architect Quarto" for seven dollars; he found that "Nicholsons Architecture was not to be had in New York." Pettigrew Papers, A&H. In 1818 an Asheville storekeeper bought from a Philadelphia supplier 2 "Nicholson's Carpenter's Guide" ($7.50), 1 "Nicholson's Student Instructor" ($4.50), and 3 "Carpenters Book of Prices" ($2.25) but found his supplier out of "Town and Country Builder's Assistant" and "Builders Easy Guide." Epistolary Correspondence, vol. 3, Nov. 23, 1818, David L. Swain Papers, A&H. See also the following advertisements: Fayetteville *North Carolina Chronicle*, Sept. 17, 1790, "Price's British carpentry" and "Langley's builder's jewel"; *Raleigh Register*, May 27, 1800, William Pain's "Carpenter's Repository and Pocket Dictionary" and Nicholson's "Carpenter's and Joiner's Assistant"; *Edenton Gazette*, Mar. 2, 1808, Langley's "Builder's Jewel." A simple stair bracket commonly used in New Bern's finer houses of the early nineteenth century appears to come from Pain's *Practical House Carpenter*, and other elements of New Bern carpentry probably also drew upon Pain's works. See Sandbeck, *Historic Architecture of New Bern*, 57, 67–68, 91–92. Stairs and mantels from Biddle's *Young Carpenter's Assistant* appear frequently in North Carolina, and a copy owned by builders John Faucett and John Berry exists at the Rare Book Room, University of North Carolina Library, Chapel Hill; photocopy in possession of author, courtesy of Mary Claire Engstrom.

31. Sketch of barn framing, undated probably by Ebenezer Pettigrew, in Pettigrew Papers, A&H; Ebenezer Pettigrew to James Iredell, Jr., Dec. 13, 1804, "I have superintended the building of a large barn and threshing machine" (Lemmon, *Pettigrew Papers* 1:356). Also see

correspondence between Pettigrew and James C. Johnson about building projects under their direction in Lemmon, *Pettigrew Papers* 1:567, 587, 590, 621, 648, 654. Duncan Cameron, bills and contracts, for Fairntosh and figures for timber for farm buildings, Cameron Family Papers, folder 133, SHC, courtesy of Jean Anderson. Richard Dobbs Speight to John Haywood, July 2, 1802, and James McKinlay to John Haywood, June 15, 1808, Ernest Haywood Papers, SHC. (McKinlay sent Haywood an elaborate recipe for painting brickwork to prevent the penetration of moisture. He even painted imported Philadelphia brick, of which his own house was built: mix 50 lbs. red lead with 30 lbs. Venetian red or Spanish brown, add 2 lbs. rosin, mix with oil to proper thickness, add turpentine, paint when wall is dry; paint joints with white lead ground with oil with brush.)

32. Lenoir Family Papers, SHC; York, "Many Faces of Fort Defiance."

33. "Berry Davidson Autobiography."

34. Stevens Gray and Gilbert Leigh, May 1, 1786, Gray Family Papers, SHC. Spanish dollars were a common medium of exchange in the period before the national currency became settled. Henry King Burgwyn Diary, Mar. 24, 1841, A&H.

35. English examples of traditional building contracts appear in Salzman, *Building in England Down to 1540*, 413–584. With the exception of Moravian examples and John Hawks's work cited later, I have found no examples of colonial drawings for North Carolina buildings. However, there are later examples of simple drawings for traditional buildings. A few examples include drawings for Burke Co. Jail, 1819, Burke Co. Misc. Records; Caswell Co. Poor and Work House, 1826, Caswell Co. Misc. Records; Pasquotank Co. Jail, 1809–1810, Pasquotank Co. Accounts, 1752–1896; and Wayne Co. Jail, 1813, Wayne Co. Accounts and Court Orders, A&H. See also Taylor, *From Frontier to Factory*, 17; Powell, *First State University*, 13, 16.

36. Agreement between Macon Whitfield and Richard Gill and Benjamin Ward, Carpenters, Feb. 14, 1774, Bertie Co. Land Papers, 1736–1819, A&H, courtesy of George Stevenson. One of many similarly brief examples is an 1813 agreement between Samuel Savage and Samuel Lemley in Rowan County. For three hundred dollars Lemley was to build a house "28 feet long & 16 feet wide with a shed of 22 feet & 12 feet wide, a passage of 8 feet to be taken off one end of the house for the Stairs to run up in with one partition up Stairs, with the necessary number of Windows & doors, the work to be done in a plain neat workmanlike manner, and by the directions of the said Sam. S. Savage, the windows to be finished glazed neatly, any deviation from the above plan to be at the incresed expense of the said S. Savage" (Rowan Co. Misc. Papers, A&H). For an example of failure to meet "good and sufficient" standards, see William Nichols to Samuel B. Ash, agent for deceased brickmaker, Aug. 6, 1821, Legislative Papers, Box 369, A&H.

37. Stevens Gray to Gilbert Leigh, May 1, 1786, Gray Family Papers, SHC. It is believed that the Gray house, Rosefield, which is still standing in Bertie County, includes this section and a 1790s expansion that is also probably Leigh's work. Marshall Bullock, National Register Nomination for Rosefield, 1982, A&H.

38. Agreement, Thomas Fields and William Lenoir, Mar. 18, 1788, Lenoir Family Papers, SHC and York, "Many Faces of Fort Defiance." Commas added for clarity.

39. Agreement, Maxwell Chambers on behalf of John Steele and Elam Sharpe, Mar. 18, 1799, Steele Papers, SHC in Hood, *Architecture of Rowan County*, 358.

40. Maxwell Chambers to John Steele, Nov. 5, 1799, Steele Papers, SHC in Hood, *Architecture of Rowan County*, 358–59.

41. John Steele to Mary Steele, Feb. 27, 1801, Steele Papers, SHC in Hood, *Architecture of Rowan County*, 361.

42. Wren to Bishop of Oxford, 1681, in Jenkins, *Architect and Patron*, 128–29, and on English payment methods, see 124–25.

43. Measuring is discussed in many architectural handbooks, which supplied formulae for figuring costs. Each trade had its own peculiar ways of measuring. A practical "Arithmetic

book" written by a Virginian in 1761 noted, for example, that joiners measured by the square yard, but "they have a custom & say, We ought to measure where our plane touches, and in taking the Height of a Room, where there is a Cornice about, and Swelling Pannels and Mouldings they with a string, begin at the Top, girt over all the Moulding; which may well make the Room to measure much higher than it is; then for measuring about the Room, they only take it as it is upon the floor." When joiners "measured" work done on both sides— paneling, for example—they figured for "work & ½ work," not twice as much. William Ellett Arithmetic Book, Duke, courtesy of William Erwin.

44. Mary Harrell Account with William Freeman, 1768, Bertie Co. Estates Papers, A&H, courtesy of George Stevenson. There are many such examples. See account of Burrell Bell with William Lakey, 1755, Bertie Co. Court Records, Pleas and Quarter Sessions, New Actions, Jan. 1756, A&H, courtesy of George Stevenson. The 1755 carpenter's account listed such work as casing 5 doors and 5 windows, making dormer sashes, making and hanging cellar doors, laying lower floor, making 1 large chimney facing and 1 small chimney facing, making 2 "shells over doors," making stairs and putting them up, making 1 cradle, and so on. In the same bill, he also charged by the day (at 2 shillings 6 pence a day) and by the measure (155 feet of chair and wash boards). See also the account of work by Ambrose Knox for John Sutton, Perquimans County, 1824, which itemizes raising and covering a house, building sheds and piazzas, building a smokehouse, making and hanging a gate, in Perquimans Co. Estates Records, 1824, A&H, and quoted in Haley and Winslow, *Historic Architecture of Perquimans County*, 29.

45. See Schlotterbeck, " 'Social Economy,' " 3–28. Countless examples in North Carolina estates papers and accounts repeat the pattern described by Schlotterbeck (" 'Social Economy,' " 17–18) and indicate that this "social economy" was an essential element of the economy.

46. William Lenoir, Agreements with Thomas Fields, Mar. 18, 1788, Lenoir Family Papers, SHC. The "fort field" was probably the site of the former fort that gave the plantation its name and also contained an orchard, from which Lenoir reserved the apples and half the cherries. Receipt of Olivo Roberts, Mar. 22, 1790, Lenoir Family Papers, SHC, and York, "Many Faces of Fort Defiance," 14–15. This system of exchange lasted for a long time, especially in many rural communities.

47. William Jones, Proposal to Jones and Henderson, Raleigh, July 11, 1810, Calvin Jones Papers, A&H; William Lenoir, Agreement with Thomas Fields, Mar. 18, 1788, Lenoir Family Papers, SHC; carpenter Zachariah Sneed's suit against Peter Perkins for work and materials, Stokes Co. Civil Action Papers, 1797, A&H, courtesy of George Stevenson. See Cameron Family Papers, Hayes Collection, and Lenoir Family Papers, SHC, and Pettigrew Papers, A&H, for additional examples.

48. Richard Bennehan, Account for Building Store, 1787, Cameron Family Papers, vol. 18, SHC. See also John Haywood to Eliza Haywood, Apr. 10, 1799, Ernest Haywood Papers, SHC.

49. William Ellett Arithmetic Book, Duke. See also Buchanan, "Eighteenth-Century Frame Houses," 54–73.

50. Although hand cutting of wood predominated throughout the colonial and federal periods, a few sawmills were erected near the coast and along inland streams. Dobbs to Board of Trade, Mar. 29, 1764, *CRNC* 6:1030, and Tryon to Board of Trade, Jan. 30 and Feb. 22, 1767, *CRNC* 7:430, 440. See account of sawmill development in Chapter 4.

51. See Tom Darlet, Windsor, to James C. Johnston, Apr. 19, 1814, on purchase of pine timber; W. W. Wilkins to James C. Johnston, Apr. 10, 1814, sending Moses and his partner Stephen and Gilbert and his partner Randal to saw Johnston's 50,000 feet of lumber. "My usual price is 5/Va.money per hundred for common plank and scantling, for wide plank 6/, but when the quantity is as large as yours," he would charge 4 shillings 6 pence per hundred feet. Notes on workmen sawing in Plantation Notebooks, James C. Johnston, 1810–1818, Hayes Collection, SHC.

52. Maxwell Chambers to John Steele, Nov. 1799, and Jan. 9 and Apr. 28, 1800, and accounts with Houcks, 1799–1800, Steele Papers, SHC.

53. Typescript copy, Estimate of Expense of House [1799], Steele Papers, SHC.

54. *CRNC* 7:241; South, "Russellborough"; and Bishir, "Philadelphia Bricks."

55. *RM* 1:45.

56. Stuart Schwartz, interview with author on freshwater shells in mortar of Hezekiah Alexander House, Charlotte, Nov. 1984.

57. On the ordering of colonial period glass, see Vestry Minutes, St. Paul's Church Records, May 23, 1767, A&H. Indenture, John Taylor et al. and John Linch, Oct. 2, 1771, Francis Lister Hawks Collection, A&H. For early national period sources of manufactured goods, see William Nichols to James C. Johnston, May 1, 1817, 1814–1817, Hayes Collection, SHC; John Donnell Account Book, Sept. 5, 1818, Bryan Family Papers, SHC. Receipt and bill, Zane Chapman Wellford, Mar. 17, 1800, Steele Papers, SHC. See also William Poyntell and Co., Philadelphia, American Manufactory of Composition Ornaments, which advertised ornaments to be furnished "to any part of the continent," in Halifax *North Carolina Journal*, June 29, 1795, and "Two American Mantelpieces," *Bulletin of the Metropolitan Museum of Art*, Feb. 1919, 36–37. See also Norfolk merchant's advertisement for chimney pieces of composition upon wood from Philadelphia that are "more elegant than those in general made use of here" in *Norfolk Herald*, Aug. 8, 1795.

58. See *Edenton Gazette*, Dec. 17, 1811, and *Fayetteville Intelligencer*, Mar. 22, 1811, on local nail manufacturing, and Fayetteville *Gazette*, May 21, 1793, on English nails for sale, and Aug. 6, 1793, on sale of "Swedish and Country [local] Iron," nails, and glass. Receipt of Maxwell Chambers, May 1799, from Rich and Trotter, for nails; receipt of Andrew Caldcleugh, Mar. 8, 1800, Philadelphia, for hardware; and receipts for shipping, June 30, 1800, Steele Papers, SHC.

59. Donaldson & Macmillan to John Haywood, Aug. 12, 1805, Ernest Haywood Papers, SHC.

60. Account of John Steele with Henry, George, and William Hauck, 1799–1800, Steele Papers, SHC.

61. Josiah Collins, "Account of Work Done by Sundries on the Academy," 1800, Cupola House Papers, SHC. See Bishir, "Black Builders," 459–61, for extracts from Collins's account.

62. Clement Blount to Ebenezer Pettigrew, June 6, 1837, Pettigrew Papers, A&H. See also James C. Johnston Correspondence, 1813–1815, Hayes Collection, SHC; *RM* 5:2045, and 6:2573.

63. Marshall Park to James C. Johnston, Oct. 5, 1815, Hayes Collection, SHC.

64. Maxwell Chambers to John Steele, Nov. 5, 1799, in Wagstaff, *Papers of John Steele*, 181–82; Maxwell Chambers to John Steele, Apr. 28, 1800, Steele Papers, SHC.

65. James C. Johnston Plantation Expense Books, 1813–1818, Hayes Collection, SHC. See also Johnston to David Clark, June 2, 1814, Hayes Collection, SHC.

66. Ebenezer Pettigrew to James C. Johnston, May 19, 1817, in Lemmon, *Pettigrew Papers*, 568.

67. Perquimans Co. Court Minutes, July 1755, 23, A&H, quoted in Haley and Winslow, *Historic Architecture of Perquimans County*, 15. The Archives and History county records contain a wealth of such material, as do records of state building projects in the Treasurer's and Comptroller's Papers. Compare essentially identical committee duties in Virginia colonial churches in Upton, *Holy Things and Profane*, 11–22, and Marcus Whiffen, "The Early County Courthouses of Virginia," *Journal of the Society of Architectural Historians* 18, no. 1, 2–10.

68. Person Co. Misc. Records, 1824, A&H. The contract went to John Berry, Samuel Hancock, and John A. Faucett of Hillsborough.

69. See notice for plans and bids for Episcopal Church, New Bern, in *Raleigh Register*, Dec. 1, 1820.

70. Charles Shuler was paid 2 pounds 8 shillings for drawing a plan and making up a bill

of timber for a district jail in Edenton in 1786. Cupola House Papers, SHC. Lewis Leroy and William Ross were thanked for a "Handsome Drawing and plan" for a jail in 1813 in Beaufort Co. Court Minutes, 1809–1814, 463, A&H.

71. Report of Committee to Erect Clerk's Office, 1831, Northampton Co. Building Records, A&H.

72. Report of Committee to Build Jail, 1828, Northampton Co. Building Records, A&H.

73. William L. Sherrill, *Annals of Lincoln County, North Carolina* (Charlotte: privately printed, 1937), 89; Charles L. Coon, *North Carolina Schools and Academies* (Raleigh: Edwards & Broughton, 1915), 201–8. (The Lincolnton committee agreed unanimously to build a two-story brick house, 40 by 25 feet, with a portico, but subsequently omitted the portico because of cost.)

74. Onslow Co. Court Minutes, Oct. 1755, 217, and Edgecombe Co. Court Minutes, May 26, 1772, 29, A&H.

75. Richmond Co. Jail, 1813, Richmond Co. Misc. Records, A&H.

76. On medieval and later use of reference to existing buildings in England, see Colvin, *Biographical Dictionary of British Architects*, 6; Jenkins, *Architect and Patron*, 23; Whiffen, *Public Buildings of Williamsburg*, 75–76; and Catherine W. Bishir, " 'Good and Sufficient' Language for Building," paper given at Annual Meeting, Society of Architectural Historians, 1986.

77. See two-story Wake County Jail of wood, 56 by 24 feet, "not inferior to the Jail in Hillsborough," in Raleigh *Minerva*, Sept. 15, 1806; Brunswick County Courthouse to have roof and finish "at least equal to the Court-House in Wilmington" as well as other similar features, in Wilmington *True Republican*, Jan. 1, 1809; and cupola on new Stokes County Courthouse to be "not inferior to that on the Courthouse in Salisbury," in Stokes Co. Misc. Records, 1819, A&H.

78. Edenton Academy (Edenton *Encyclopedian Instructor*, May 21, 1800); Brunswick County Courthouse (Wilmington *True Republican*, Jan. 1, 1809); Warren County Jail (*Raleigh Register*, Sept. 5, 1817); Cape Hatteras Lighthouse (Richmond *Virginia Gazette*, July 8, 1795, and Baltimore *Federal Intelligencer*, May 5, 1795).

79. Richmond *Virginia Gazette*, Feb. 4, 1768.

80. See Governor's House in Raleigh, "Commissioners will communicate, on personal application, the plan of the buildings, and the period for their completion," Raleigh *Star*, May 27, 1814; Franklin County Courthouse description given in advertisement but plan to be seen by application to commissioners, Raleigh *Star*, July 19, 1811; plan for market house in Edenton to be seen "on application" to the town clerk or any of the commissioners, *Edenton Gazette*, July 1, 1808; and Wake County Jail, Raleigh *Minerva*, Sept. 15, 1806.

81. Richmond *Virginia Gazette*, June 4, 1767. The Edenton Courthouse design may have come from John Hawks, architect of Tryon Palace in New Bern (see below). Washington *American Recorder*, Jan. 29, 1819. On plans to be given at time of bidding, see Northampton County Courthouse (Raleigh *Minerva*, Mar. 29, 1816); Wilkes County Jail (Raleigh *Star*, May 27, 1814); and Cabarrus County Jail (Raleigh *Star*, June 14, 1810).

82. Haun, *Johnston County*, 3. Similar interaction between the explicit and the unstated as part of the reliance on local standards continued well into the nineteenth century. Thus the Northampton County commissioners of 1828 said merely that a jailer's house should be built "in the common way of good framed buildings"—wainscoted, plastered, whitewashed, covered with "good nine inch featheredg plank nicely drest," and roofed with cypress shingles—while to assure security of the jail they defined precisely the thickness of massive floor and ceiling planks and walls of 18-inch-thick heart-pine logs, "well dove tailed and dowelled and pinned at the corners or dovetail lap." Northampton Co. Jail, 1828, Northampton Co. Building Records, A&H.

83. Indenture, John Taylor et al. and John Linch, Oct. 2, 1771, Francis Lister Hawks Collection, A&H. See Upton, *Holy Things and Profane*, 233–34, for a comparable contract for a simpler 1747 church in Virginia, and 23–46 for builders' roles in Anglican church construction in colonial Virginia.

84. "Money disbursed on Acct. of the Church," 1736, Robert B. Drane Papers, SHC.

85. Jail Records, 1821–1825, Craven Co. Public Building Accounts, A&H; Bishir, "Philadelphia Bricks." See also Lincoln Co. Jail, 1816–1817, Lincoln Co. Accounts and Claims, A&H, and Lincolnton Female Academy, 1824–1825, in Sherrill, *Annals of Lincoln County*, 88–89.

86. See, for example, Onslow Co. Court Minutes, vol. 2, 1749–1765, 217, 245, A&H, and advertisements for undertakers for the courthouse in Edenton and for a church in Hillsborough, in Williamsburg *Virginia Gazette*, June 4, 1767, and Feb. 4, 1768.

87. Person Co. Courthouse, lump-sum contract, Person Co. Misc. Records, 1824, A&H. For First Presbyterian Church in Raleigh, materials and workmanship of various trades to be divided into five or six contracts, see *Raleigh Register*, Feb. 16, 1816.

88. Governor's office, Raleigh *Minerva* and Raleigh *Star*, June 23, 1815; brick academy building at Oxford, *Raleigh Register*, July 15, 1816.

89. Stark Holeday, estimates, probably 1817, Benjamin Huske Papers, SHC.

90. Haun, *Johnston County*, 22, 23; Linn, *Abstracts of the Minutes*, 5, 28, 62, 81.

91. The vestry in Hillsborough in 1768 expected to pay the undertaker for their new church fifty pounds "in hand," half of the total cost at "the raising of the house," and the remainder when it was complete. Richmond *Virginia Gazette*, Feb. 4, 1768. When Virginia carpenter John Linch contracted to build Nutbush Church in 1771, the parish vestry agreed to pay him in three annual installments of 255 pounds, 12 shillings, 3½ pence each, provided that the building was raised, covered, and glazed by December 25, 1772, and "ready to be delivered up" the following Christmas. Indenture, John Taylor et al. and John Linch, Oct. 2, 1771, Francis Lister Hawks Collection, A&H.

92. Day Book of Ebenezer Pettigrew, 1821, Pettigrew Papers, A&H.

93. See Contract, James Patterson, George Lucas & Patrick St. Lawrence, July 19, 1793, University Papers, University Archives, Chapel Hill, with specifications that the building was to be 96'7" by 40'1½". Of note in the specifications is the requirement that the roof be "such as is called by builders a principal Roof, framed in the strongest and best manner," meaning a principal rafter roof of large main rafters and smaller secondary ones, a type sometimes used for large buildings.

94. William R. Davie to John Haywood, Mar. 7, 1796, Ernest Haywood Papers, SHC. Main Building was mocked by Davie's anti-Federalist enemies as a "useless Palace" and a "Temple of Folly," spawned by the "demi-god Davie" and his grand ideas. It stood unfinished for years until funds were found for completing it in 1814. Henderson, *The Campus of the First State University*, 74; Powell, *First State University*, 38.

95. Samuel Hopkins to John Haywood, Nov. 11, 1799, Ernest Haywood Papers, SHC.

96. Legislative Papers, 1792–1795, 110–23, A&H; Capital Buildings Papers, Treasurer's and Comptroller's Papers, 1792, A&H, copies in Murray files.

97. Halifax *North Carolina Journal*, Aug. 7, 1793.

98. Legislative Papers, Nov. 29, 1792, A&H, copies in Murray files; Capital Buildings Papers, Treasurer's and Comptroller's Papers, 1792–1795, A&H. The political aspect is suggested by scattered circumstantial evidence: Willie Jones, anti-Federalist leader, defended Atkins's work in a report intended to "undeceive the public, and do justice to Mr. ATKINS," which was printed in various papers (Halifax *North Carolina Journal*, Aug. 7, 1793; Fayetteville *Gazette*, Aug. 6, 1793). Later, Atkins was the object of condemnation by Federalist William R. Davie. Davie to John Haywood, May 27, 1799, Ernest Haywood Collection, SHC. Although Davie and Jones were close neighbors in Halifax, they were intense political rivals.

99. *Raleigh Register*, June 26, 1812; Raleigh *Star*, Aug. 25 and Sept. 1, 1815.

100. Hirsch, *Roots of the American Working Class*, 8.

101. Records of 1820 U.S. Census of Manufactures, Wake Co., A&H. Totals for Raleigh and Wake County reproduced in Murray, *Wake*, 137. None of the other towns provided such comprehensive figures in the census. It is not indicated whether these figures include only free workers or also slaves. Murray, *Wake*, 672.

102. Estate inventory, Benjamin So[a]mes, Craven Co. Records, A&H.

103. These included carpenters and joiners Joseph Palmer, John Dewey, Martin Stevenson, John Oliver, Asa King, Benjamin Good, Uriah Sandy, and Hardy B. Lane and brickmasons Bennett Flanner, Wallace Moore, Joshua Mitchell, and Donum Montfort, a free black. See Herzog, "Early Architecture of New Bern," and Sandbeck, *Historic Architecture of New Bern*.

104. Herzog, "Early Architecture of New Bern," 302–6, 318, 329–35; Sandbeck, *Historic Architecture of New Bern*, 89–94, 248–49.

105. See Public Building Records, Craven Co., 1790s–1830s, A&H; Bishir, "Philadelphia Bricks"; Herzog, "Early Architecture of New Bern"; and Sandbeck, *Historic Architecture of New Bern*, 43–73, 89–90. John M. Roberts, New Bern, to Duncan Cameron, Feb. 20, 1833, attributing to Asa King the Smallwood and Donnell houses and State Bank, Cameron Family Papers, SHC, courtesy of Ford Peatross; John Donnell Account Book, Apr. 19, 1819, Bryan Family Papers, SHC.

106. New Bern *Carolina Centinel*, July 14, 1821. See Herzog, "Early Architecture of New Bern," on individual artisans' economic status and work.

107. The principal codification of apprenticeship came in 1760, when one of many laws enacted by the assembly to improve order in the fast-growing colony was an "Act for better care of orphans." This law codified customary apprenticeship practices, affirmed the authority of the court to bind out poor or potentially poor children (orphans without estates and illegitimate children, especially mulattoes) as apprentices, regularized the keeping of apprenticeship bonds by county courts, and added to the old 1715 orphan law a requirement that the master actually teach an apprentice a trade and reading and writing as well as supplying food and clothing; failure to teach the apprentice "the trade, profession or Employment, to which he or she was bound" was made sufficient cause for terminating the indenture. Finally, again restating custom, at the expiration of the apprenticeship—for which no specific length of time was set by law—the master was to pay the apprentice a sum of money "as is by Law appointed for servants by indenture or Custom." While this law probably increased the number of apprenticeship bonds being kept after the mid-eighteenth century, neither it nor later laws dealt with the content of apprenticeship. *SRNC* 23:581. Similar situations obtained even in large cities, as described in Quimby, *Apprenticeship in Colonial Philadelphia*, 32–44. On apprenticeship in other southern colonies, see Marzio, "Carpentry in the Southern Colonies," 240–41; Whiffen, *Eighteenth-Century Houses of Williamsburg*, 18–21; and Bridenbaugh, *Colonial Craftsman*, 30–31. On English and other European apprenticeship terms, see Colvin, *Biographical Dictionary of British Architects*, 2, and Harvey, *Mediaeval Architect*, 70–71, 90–92, 99. For examples of North Carolina apprenticeship bonds and lengths of terms of apprenticeship, see *ACNC*. See also North Carolina, *Revised Statutes*, 67–69. On artisan regulation in cities, see Bridenbaugh, *Colonial Craftsman*, 144–46; Moss, "Master Builders," and "Origins of the Carpenters' Company"; and Louise M. Hall, "Artificer to Architect."

108. A New Bern builder advertised for fifteen to twenty journeymen, *Norfolk Herald*, Feb. 4, 1796. Warrenton carpenter Thomas Bragg sought two or three journeymen, *Warrenton Reporter*, July 8, 1825. See also Powell and Faux advertisement, Fayetteville *Gazette*, Feb. 1, 1790. Wilmington carpenter John Allen sought one or two white journeymen who understood framing, *Wilmington Chronicle*, Sept. 24, 1795. Allen's preference for whites here is noteworthy since he was the first signer of local mechanics' objections to slaves operating as free agents, which is discussed below.

109. See Henry Jocelin, cabinetmaker, who "served a regular apprenticeship with an eminent master," *Wilmington Gazette*, May 15, 1804, and Garret Barry, Irish carpenter and "Master Builder . . . regularly bred to his business," *Milton Intelligencer*, Apr. 2, 1819. "A Tradesman," Raleigh *Minerva*, Apr. 21, 1815.

110. Warren Co. Deeds, 1810–18, Deed Book 19, 16, 18, 164, 205; Deed Book 20, 178, 265,

266; Deed Book 27, 185–87, 401–4, 432, A&H, summary courtesy of Mary Hinton Kerr, Warrenton; Northampton Co. Building Records, 1831, for Clerk's Office, A&H; Raleigh *Star*, Nov. 15, 1810.

111. See Morris, *Government and Labor*, 38–39, on workdays; Maxwell Chambers account with Houcks, 1799–1800, Steele Papers, SHC; Moravians' decision to stop the distribution of drams of brandy to workmen, *RM* 5:2015; Rock, *Artisans of the New Republic*, 296–301, on alcohol as part of the "premodern" work pattern; and complaints on drunkards in William R. Davie to John Haywood, Apr. 25, 1799, Ernest Haywood Papers, SHC, Clement H. Blount to Ebenezer Pettigrew, June 6, 1837, Pettigrew Papers, A&H, and Bragg advertisement, *Warrenton Reporter*, July 8, 1825.

112. Pasquotank Co. Records, Apr. 12, 1752, John Allen and William Luten Account Books, and Chowan Co. Misc. Records, A&H.

113. Dobbs to Board of Trade, Mar. 29, 1764, *CRNC* 6:1026; Main, *Social Structure*, 74–81, 115–20; "William Logan's Journal," 12. Morris, in *Government and Labor*, 45, suggests that the colonial workman's real wages exceeded those of English workers by 30 to 100 percent.

114. Records of the remodeling of the State House in July 1821 note the following payment of masons and bricklayers: 2 paid at $2.25 a day, 3 at $2.00, 7 at $1.75, 1 at $1.62½, 2 at $1.50, 1 at $1.25, and 1 at 90 cents. Of 20 carpenters, 1 was paid at $2.25 a day, 5 at $1.30 to $1.50, and several slaves earned for their owners from $10 to $20 a month. Twenty laborers that month were paid 25 to 75 cents a day or their owners received $10 to $15 a month. Master builder-architect William Nichols received $400 per quarter. Capital Buildings Papers, 1821, Treasurer's and Comptroller's Papers, A&H.

115. Carpenter Jesse Carraway of Tyrrell County was paid $2.00 a day in 1817 and $2.50 in 1821, Pettigrew Papers, A&H. Martin Stevenson was paid $1.25 a day, Contract, James Bryan and Martin Stevenson, Sept. 25, 1803, copy in Bryan House file, Survey and Planning Branch, A&H; and later he was paid $2.50 a day, Account, Martin Stevenson and Hardy Whitford, Apr. 1827, Public Building Accounts, Craven Co. Misc. Records, A&H.

116. *CRNC* 1:764; Brickell, *Natural History of North Carolina*, 275–76; *RM* 2:780; Charles Fisher to North Carolina House of Commons, reported in *American Farmer*, 9 (Jan. 1828): 353. See Crow, *Black Experience*, esp. 6–12; Peter H. Wood, *Black Majority*, 106–10; Stavisky, "Origins of Negro Craftsmanship"; and Bishir, "Black Builders."

117. *Norfolk Herald*, July 1, 1814; *Raleigh Register*, July 23, 1819; *Wilmington Gazette*, Apr. 18, 1803; *Raleigh Register*, Sept. 15, 1815; *Wilmington Centinel and General Advertiser*, Feb. 26, 1789; and Raleigh *Minerva*, Mar. 24, 1801, Murray files.

118. *Wilmington Centinel and General Advertiser*, July 9, 1788. Benjamin Smith was a Brunswick County planter who served as governor and owned vast property along the Cape Fear River, including Smith (Baldhead) Island. Raleigh *Minerva*, Dec. 16, 1814; Raleigh *Star*, Sept. 2, 1814; *Raleigh Register*, Aug. 4, 1815; Raleigh *Star*, July 28, 1815; Raleigh *Minerva*, July 28, 1815; Raleigh *Star*, Dec. 6, 1810.

119. Planter John Burgwin advertised for a carpenter to direct the work of six to eight Negro carpenters, in Halifax *North Carolina Journal*, Oct. 1, 1798. Robert Strange of Fayetteville advertised for hire by the month three carpenters, two of them "excellent," in Fayetteville *Gazette*, May 29, 1822. The Hill family of Wilmington offered three good house carpenters by the week or the month, in *Wilmington Centinel*, Dec. 3, 1788. A New Bern merchant sought to hire out Jim, the town's best house mover, for a year, in John Daves to John Haywood, Jan. 21, 1800, Ernest Haywood Papers, SHC.

120. Schoepf, *Travels in the Confederation* 2:148. See also *SRNC* 24:725–30.

121. Receipt, Ebenezer Pettigrew to Josiah Collins, Oct. 4, 1816, Pettigrew Papers, A&H; James C. Johnston Plantation Notebooks, 1814–1817, Hayes Collection, SHC; Receipts, 1819–1824, Capital Buildings Papers, Treasurer's and Comptroller's Papers, A&H.

122. Thomas Bragg paid between $400 and $1,100 for slaves, some of whom were doubtless artisans. Deed summary, courtesy of Mary Hinton Kerr, Warrenton: Warren Co.

Deed Book 19, 16, 18, 164, 205; Book 20, 178, 265, 266; Book 22, 38; and Book 27, 185–87, 401–4, 432, A&H. See Bishir, "Black Builders," 437. See planter Ebenezer Pettigrew's estimate of subsistence costs for a slave in 1817 in Lemmon, *Pettigrew Papers*, 540.

123. John Donnell Account Book, 1823–1824, Bryan Family Papers, SHC.

124. Brewer, "Legislation Designed to Control Slavery."

125. *Petersburg Intelligencer*, Oct. 4, 1816.

126. Browning, "James D. Sampson." It should be noted that it was the status (slave or free) of the mother that determined the status of a child. Thus the child of a slave mother and a free black or a white father was a slave. Manumission became increasingly difficult in the early nineteenth century. For an excellent discussion of free blacks, including artisans, see Franklin, *Free Negro in North Carolina*.

127. Donum Montfort Estate Papers, Craven Co. Records, A&H; Herzog, "Early Architecture of New Bern," 342; Robinson et al., "Thomas Day and His Family"; and Barfield, *Thomas Day, Cabinetmaker*.

128. Hardy B. Lane to David Paton, July 14, 1839, Capital Buildings Papers, Treasurer's and Comptroller's Papers, A&H. Asa King went to Alabama, Bennett Flanner became a merchant in Wilmington, and Martin Stevenson left building for the funeral trade. Herzog, "Early Architecture of New Bern," and Sandbeck, *Historic Architecture of New Bern*, on individuals cited.

129. See Young Dortch's Bill, Mar. 24, 1807, and John Mayfield, bill for building house at Fish Dam Ford, 1808, Cameron Family Papers, SHC, reproduced in Anderson, "Fairntosh"; Ebenezer Pettigrew to Ann S. Pettigrew, Nov. 21, 1815, in Lemmon, *Pettigrew Papers*, 498; Josiah Collins, notes on Edenton Academy, 1800, Cupola House Papers, SHC; Bishir, "Black Builders," 459–61; and Robert Warren, advertisement, Murfreesboro *Hornet's Nest*, Feb. 25, 1813. See also Peter Newton and Edward McGrath's notice of a partnership in plastering, bricklaying, and painting, in Charlotte *Catawba Journal*, Dec. 23, 1828, and receipts for "repairs for Government House," 1800, H. Gorman paid for glazing, plastering, burning a shell kiln, and "Rumfordizing" fireplaces, Ernest Haywood Papers, SHC.

130. Lemmon, *Pettigrew Papers*, 429.

131. Raleigh *Minerva*, Dec. 23, 1805. See similar advertisements in *ACNC*. Even more itinerant were John Baptiste Gabriel Doyen, new arrival in Wilmington as carpenter and millwright, in *Wilmington Gazette*, Apr. 17, 1804, and Scotch stonemason Francis Graham, boarding in Rowan County, in Salisbury *Western Carolinian*, Mar. 22, 1825. Linear moves combined with subsequent circular moves in the career of John J. Briggs, in Carroll, *They Lived in Raleigh* 1:12–13. On mobility and scarcity of skilled workmen, see Morris, *Government and Labor*, 28–33.

132. Dobbs to Board of Trade, Mar. 29, 1764, *CRNC* 6:1026; Lemmon, *Pettigrew Papers*, 563. On the combination of farming and artisanry in general, see Rapoport, *House Form and Culture*, 4; Marzio, "Carpentry in the Southern Colonies," 230–31; Michael Smith, *North Carolina Furniture*, 1. Bivins, *Furniture of Coastal North Carolina*, 60–62, discusses farming among early cabinetmakers. He finds that "in rural areas, it was a rare tradesman of any sort who did not engage in some farming" (60). See Boyce, *History of Chowan County*, 41, on the continuing combination of farming and trades through the nineteenth century. On property qualifications for voting, see Lefler and Newsome, *North Carolina*, 222, 379. For a graphic depiction of the farmer-craftsman's annual work cycle and an analysis of such workers' lives elsewhere, see St. George, "Fathers, Sons and Identity," 102.

133. In the eighteenth century, a good number of artisans were also landowners and planters active in community affairs. Although evidence of change is insufficient to be conclusive, examples suggest that this situation began to change in the nineteenth century as wealth and power became more concentrated and class differences more pronounced. The distance between the planter elite and the middling farmer and artisan class grew greater, especially in the slaveholding eastern region; in counties where subsistence farming contin-

ued and wealth was less concentrated, the change was less marked, and farmer-artisans continued to be prominent. This observation of change is impressionistic at this point. For the period before 1850, data on trade identities is insufficient to make meaningful quantitative statements about landownership among artisans. However, the United States Census of 1850 gives data on both occupations and property ownership, and, as is noted in the next chapter, there is considerable difference in landholding among artisans from region to region, with landholding greater among white artisans in regions where slaveownership was less and yeoman farming greater. On social classes, see Johnson, *Ante-Bellum North Carolina*, 52–79.

134. John Allen Account Book, 1774–1798, and Estate Inventory, John Allen Papers, A&H. On the Allen family, see Watson, *An Independent People*, 17–24. Allen's accounts, like those of William Luten, typify the continual economic and social interaction described in Schlotterbeck, " 'Social Economy.' "

135. Thomas and William Luten Estate Papers and Wills, Chowan Co. Records, A&H. William had moved in with his son before his death and may have disposed of other property. William Luten Account Book, 1764–1787, A&H.

136. William Luten Account Book, A&H. Subsequent references to Luten are all from this source. On Luten's furniture making, see Bivins, *Furniture of Coastal North Carolina*, 63.

137. As late as the 1880s, one longtime resident recalled, it was rare to find a finished interior in a Chowan County house: "Not more than four per cent of [the dwellings] in the Country, nor twenty-five per cent in town were either ceiled or plastered" (Boyce, *History of Chowan County*, 219).

138. Bridenbaugh, *Colonial Craftsman*, 9.

139. Tarboro *Free Press*, Nov. 28, 1826; *Warrenton Reporter*, Oct. 7, 1825; Halifax *Roanoke Advocate*, Sept. 6, 1831; *Raleigh Register*, Nov. 21, 1817, advertising a cabinetmaking shop in Louisburg and workers from Petersburg and New York; Fayetteville *Gazette*, Feb. 1, 1790.

140. *Edenton Intelligencer*, June 4, 1788; Washington *American Recorder*, Sept. 5, 1823; Salisbury *Western Carolinian*, May 13, 1828; Rutherfordton *North Carolina Spectator and Western Advertiser*, Oct. 15, 1830; Charlotte *Miners' and Farmers' Journal*, Mar. 10, 1831. For other itinerant examples, see Malcolm and Palmer painting houses, doors, etc., in New York style in New Bern in 1829, in *New Bern Spectator*, Mar. 21, 1829, and N. Wilson of Philadelphia, in New Bern *Carolina Centinel*, Sept. 23, 1826, in Herzog, "Early Architecture of New Bern," 356, 357, and J. Johnson, who advertised that he would do house and sign painting and gilding, "during his stay" in Raleigh and that clients were to leave orders at "Mr. Parlaska's Picture shop," *Raleigh Register*, Nov. 22, 1808, Murray files. In Salem, F. W. Marshall noted, cabinet-makers did painting and glazing, in *RM* 5:2148.

141. Tinner Benjamin Churchill, New Bern *Carolina Centinel*, May 22, 1819; E. M. Bronson, Charlotte *Catawba Journal*, Nov. 2, 1824; *Raleigh Minerva*, Sept. 27, 1810; slaters for jail, 1821–1823, Public Building Accounts, Craven Co. Misc. Records, A&H; and Bishir, "Philadelphia Bricks," 65.

142. Agreement, John Steele and John Langdon, Mar. 13, 1800, in Wagstaff, *Papers of John Steele*, 785–86; Hood, *Architecture of Rowan County*, 324–25, 360–61; Anderson, "Fairntosh," 30–37; Bills of Elias and John Fort (1813, 1814), Elhannon Nutt (1811), H. Gorman (1812), John J. Briggs (1821) etc., Cameron Family Papers, SHC, reproduced in Anderson, "Fairntosh."

143. Draft agreement, John Steele and John Langdon, Mar. 9, 1800, and John Steele to Mrs. Steele, Apr. 11, 1801, Steele Papers, SHC. See also *The Rules of Work of the Carpenters' Company of the City and County of Philadelphia, 1786*, annotation and introduction by Charles E. Peterson (Philadelphia: Bell Publishing Co., [1978]) for full list of rates and explanation of books of rates. Langdon's draft agreement is the only example found of the use of these rates in North Carolina.

144. For examples of localized work in this period, see Haley and Winslow, *Historic*

Architecture of Perquimans County; Hood, *Architecture of Rowan County*; Little-Stokes, *Historic Architecture: Caswell County*; Bishir, "Montmorenci-Prospect Hill School"; and Pearce, *Early Architecture of Franklin County*.

145. William R. Davie to John Haywood, Mar. 7, 1796, Ernest Haywood Papers, SHC; Bishir and Bullock, "Mr. Jones Goes to Richmond."

146. Raleigh *Star*, Oct. 11 and Oct. 25, 1816, courtesy of Mary Claire Engstrom. On Elias Fort, see Anderson, *Piedmont Plantation*. On other efforts to set rates, see *Richmond Enquirer*, May 30, 1820, "The Richmond and Alexandria Builders' Price Book"; Upton, "Pattern Books," 111, rural Massachusetts in 1814; and *RM* 2:764, 899 and 5:2034, 2042.

147. "A Tradesman," Raleigh *Minerva*, Apr. 21, 1815.

148. Petition to General Assembly, by the Incorporated Mechanical Society and Other Inhabitants of the Town of Wilmington, General Assembly Records, 1802, Petitions, Box 4, A&H. Twenty-one persons signed the petition, and at least two of them—John Allen and Benjamin Jacobs—are known to have been among the town's leading builders. The Wilmington organization continued to meet in the 1810s, as did other local mechanics' groups established across the state and nation, to discuss artisans' common interests and promote mutual benefits. Wilmington *Cape-Fear Recorder*, Dec. 7, 1816. See also Louise M. Hall, "Artificer to Architect"; Charleston *City Gazette*, Oct. 20, 1789; and *Charleston Courier*, Oct. 17, 1809. For other white artisans' actions and protests against slaves and free blacks in New York, Philadelphia, Charleston, and elsewhere, see Morris, *Government and Labor*, 182–88.

149. For similar problems elsewhere, see Commons et al., *History of Labour*, 12, 68–73; Moss, "Master Builders," 14–20, 181–86; and Morris, *Government and Labor*, 136–207.

150. *RM* 2:883.

151. Francis Griffin, "The Moravians," in Bivins, *Moravian Potters in North Carolina*, xi–xii. On Moravian architecture and practice, see Murtagh, *Moravian Architecture and Town Planning*; Campbell, "Buildings of Salem"; Taylor, *From Frontier to Factory*; and Paula Welshimer Locklair, "The Moravian Craftsman in Eighteenth-Century North Carolina," in Quimby, *Craftsman in Early America*, 273–98. The account presented herein only skims the surface of information on building practices that can be found in Fries et al., *Records of the Moravians in North Carolina* (*RM*). In turn, those volumes represent only a fraction of the original material located in the Provincial Archives of the Moravian Church, Winston-Salem. For the sake of accessibility, I have restricted documentary references to published sources. I am especially indebted to John Larson, former director of restoration, Old Salem, Inc., for his generosity in sharing his knowledge and insights on the Moravians.

152. *RM* 1:73–80. Those with particular expertise in construction included Erich Inge-bretson, Norwegian millwright and carpenter, and Henrich Feldhausen, Holstein shoe-maker, millwright, carpenter, turner, and farmer. Names and trades of the initial fifteen settlers (eleven of whom stayed at Bethabara) appear in *RM* 1:73–74. The house where the men settled had been built the year before by a German, Hans Wagner, who had moved toward the Yadkin River. *RM* 1:78.

153. Ibid., 90–91.

154. Ibid., 90–106.

155. Ibid., 112, 129, 156. Ibid., 130–31 describes ceremonies for the congregation house and lists the men who worked on it and 484–94 lists arrivals of 1754 immigrants.

156. Ibid. 2:604; Campbell, "Buildings of Salem," 53–56. Many German settlers in America used fachwerk in their first substantial buildings. See Tishler, "Fachwerk Construc-tion," and Edward A. Chappell, "Germans and Swiss," and William H. Tishler, "Midwestern Germans," in Upton, *America's Architectural Roots*, 68–73, 142–48. Frederic William Marshall, administrator of Wachovia, wrote in his personal notebook the following description (in English) of clay-filled fachwerk: "Then laths ¾ of an Inch thick are nailed from post to post about five feet distant and the Laths five inches distant. These are wrapped around with a

straw clay and thus the Plaistering may be added with a thin Coat of Mortar, and all Vacancies are filled up. The Coat of Clay at that rate will be about 3 Inches thick" (*RM* 2:604).

157. *RM* 1:147–61. *RM* 1:156 lists accomplishments by the end of 1756, including buildings completed. *RM* 1:173, 161.

158. Ibid., 253–55, 489; 2:605–6.

159. Ibid., 1:313–448 and much of volume 2 deals with the building of Salem. See also Campbell, "Buildings of Salem," and Murtagh, *Moravian Architecture and Town Planning*.

160. *RM* 2:589.

161. Ibid., 1:477–83. In 1759, Reuter reviewed a grandiose city plan for Salem that had been presented in 1750 by Herrnhut leader Count Zinzendorf, pointed out its impracticality in the North Carolina piedmont, and made suggestions for a plan that could accommodate local topography and needs. When planning began for Salem in the early 1760s, Reuter incorporated some of Zinzendorf's ideas into a grid plan that, with some amendments, became the basis of the new town. Thorp, "City That Never Was," 51–52.

162. *RM* 1:313–15, 324–25, 372, and passim. See also *RM* 6:2956–57. Late in his life, it was said, the leader's eyes "often filled with tears as he thought of all that the Lord had brought to pass in Wachovia through his efforts" (6:2956).

163. See ibid. 2:605–6, for labor shortages that necessitated hiring outside labor and payment of a florin to a reichsthaler per day or more; 1:442 and 2:617–19, for references to Regulators; and 1:323–28, for the beginning of the construction of Salem in 1766 and daily accounts of work that follow.

164. Ibid. 1:383, 390–91. For other building accidents, see ibid. 1:323, 398 and 2:777.

165. Ibid. 2:660, 693–96. "Br. Bressing is not unwilling to buy the joiner's tools, belonging to the building account, which is approved, except that Br. Enerson may wish to keep a few. . . . Br. Rasp will take over the mason's and stone-breaker's implements from the building account to his own" (2:706).

166. See Horton, " 'Guild' System in Salem," and Bivins, *Moravian Potters in North Carolina*, 45–53, on trade roles and apprenticeship practices in Wachovia.

167. See apprentice bond of 1769, in *RM* 2:608–9.

168. Ibid., 768.

169. Horton, " 'Guild' System in Salem," 13. See also Bivins, *Moravian Potters in North Carolina*, 45–53.

170. *RM* 2:724. See also Horton, " 'Guild' System in Salem," and Bivins, *Moravian Potters in North Carolina*, 45–53, on trade roles.

171. *RM* 5:2043, 2045, 2233; John Larson, typescript biography of Johann Gottlob Krause in possession of author, and Contract for Boys' School, Feb. 25, 1794, displayed at Boys' School, Old Salem.

172. See Campbell, "Buildings of Salem," 308–20, and *RM* 5:2213, 2237. See also *RM* 5:2228–29, 2238, 2243, 2277, 2278; 7:3142, 3150, for rulings on buildings in Salem.

173. *RM* 5:2030, 2034, 2041–42, 2045.

174. Ibid. 2:899 and 5:2041.

175. Morris, *Government and Labor*, 146; *RM* 3:1211–12, 1226, 1259; Horton, " 'Guild' System in Salem," 11.

176. *RM* 5:2045.

177. Ibid., 2041–42, 2031. Home Church Contract, July 13, 1799, Old Salem, Inc.

178. *RM* 7:3544 cites "a rule adopted long ago, studied and readopted in 1803" stating that "in general" no one is to keep in the congregation town slaves owned by them, but granting certain exceptions.

179. Ibid., 3446. See also Taylor, *From Frontier to Factory*, 18–20, and *RM* 5:2231, 2276, 2334.

180. Collegium Minutes, Jan. 24, 1820, quoted in Horton, " 'Guild' System in Salem," 14.

181. *RM* 9:4821–24. It should be noted that the Moravians' argument against the training of slave artisans made no complaint against the quality of their work but acknowledged the attractions of using such workmen.

182. Horton, " 'Guild' System in Salem," 14; Taylor, *From Frontier to Factory*, 17–20.

183. *RM* 1:477–83; M. H. D. Kerr, "William Christmas," *DNCB* 1:369–70; Mary Claire Engstrom, "William Churton," *DNCB* 1:370–71; William P. Cumming, "John Abraham Collet (Collett)," *DNCB* 1:402–4; and William P. Cumming, Claude Joseph Sauthier, *DNCB*, forthcoming.

184. Colvin, *Biographical Dictionary of British Architects*, 14–18. See also Jenkins, *Architect and Patron*, 91–159; Whiffen, *Public Buildings of Williamsburg*, 16, 40–52; Upton, "Pattern Books," 111–14; and Catherine Wilkinson, "The New Professionalism in the Renaissance," and John Wilton-Ely, "The Rise of the Professional Architect in England," in Kostof, *The Architect*, 125–59, 180–208.

185. See Dill, "Tryon's Palace," and *Governor Tryon and His Palace*; Herzog, "Early Architecture of New Bern," 68–114, 308–15; and *EANC*, 32–33. Kimball and Carraway cite Hawks as "the first professional architect to remain in this country" ("Tryon's Palace," 20–21). See also Hugh Morrison, *Early American Architecture*, 289–90; Pierson, *American Buildings*, 141–42; and Rasmussen, "Designers, Builders, and Architectural Traditions," 198–212. Powell, *Correspondence of William Tryon* 2:533 and 1:140, 423.

186. John Hawks File, 1790, Craven Co. Estates Papers, A&H.

187. Powell, *Correspondence of William Tryon* 1:399–401; *EANC*, 84; *SRNC* 23:664–65. The salary must have been a bit slim for Hawks, for Tryon got him a post as port inspector to eke out expenses. *CRNC* 7:535.

188. Dill, "Tryon's Palace," explains the chronology of the drawings. Final drawings were sent to London for Crown approval on February 23, 1767. See also *EANC*, 82–86, and Herzog, "Early Architecture of New Bern," 69–74. Hawks's 1773 drawing of a jail which has color washes to denote materials survives, but the surviving palace drawings at the New-York Historical Society do not have color washes. John Hawks Papers, SHC, and Audrey Michie, Curator, Tryon Palace, to author, Feb. 6, 1987. John Hawks to Joseph Hewes, Sept. 29, 1773, John Hawks Papers, SHC, cites full-size detail drawings. On drawing conventions in this era, see David Gebhard, "Drawings and Intent in American Architecture," in Gebhard and Nevins, *200 Years of American Architectural Drawings*, 27.

189. Powell, *Correspondence of William Tryon* 1:423, 412. On local manufacture of brick, see Herzog, "Early Architecture of New Bern," 76, and Dill, "Tryon's Palace," 136.

190. *CRNC* 7:542–43; Powell, *Correspondence of William Tryon* 1:610–11; *SRNC* 23:711.

191. Dill, "Tryon's Palace," 133–34; Powell, *Correspondence of William Tryon* 2:533, 539.

192. Unlike Tryon, who soon left North Carolina for New York, Hawks spent the rest of his life in New Bern, where he became prominent in political activities and in the Patriot cause. Whether he continued to pursue his profession actively after the Revolution is uncertain. A few New Bern buildings have been attributed to him on stylistic grounds, but the only documentation of his professional activities concerns public buildings in Edenton—a drawing for a church steeple, plans and specifications for a prison, and a letter concerning an unidentified building, probably the Chowan County Courthouse, all dating from before the Revolution. John Hawks Papers, 1769–1773, SHC.

193. Benjamin Henry Latrobe to Christian Ignatius Latrobe, Nov. 4, 1804, Latrobe Letterbooks, Papers of Benjamin Henry Latrobe, Maryland Historical Society, quoted in Edward C. Carter, II, *Benjamin Henry Latrobe*, 7; Merritt, *Engineering in American Society*, 3–8. See also Upton, "Pattern Books," 109–15.

194. Salisbury *Western Carolinian*, Aug. 3, 1824, Feb. 8, 1825, and Oct. 11, 1825; Salisbury *Carolina Watchman*, Dec. 14, 1844, on death of Ithiel Town Lemly, Brawley files.

195. The committee offered to pay Latrobe $3,000 a year. They agreed that he "stood at the head of the Civil Engineers in the United States" and believed that he was an honest man

because so much public money had passed through his hands without enriching him personally. The committee expected that "he would be highly useful and valuable; provided his extravagant taste or turn for expending Money, was properly checked." Latrobe regretfully refused and recommended that the committee seek candidates in France or England. Hoyt, *Papers of Archibald D. Murphey* 1:103–15, 148–50 and 2:111–23.

196. George Stevenson, "Robert H. B. Brazier," *DNCB* 1:215–17.

197. [Joseph Caldwell], *The Numbers of Carlton* (New York: G. Lang, 1828), 5. Caldwell's complaint about starting work with low, intentionally misleading estimates repeated one of "Atticus"'s complaints about William Tryon. Powell, *Correspondence of William Tryon* 2:835.

198. Peatross, *William Nichols, Architect*; William Nichols, Naturalization Papers, 1813, Chowan Co. Records, A&H; Receipt, Jan. 3, 1822, for "William Nichols, esq., state architect," paid £400 for the quarter, Capital Buildings Papers, Treasurer's and Comptroller's Papers, A&H.

199. Ellen Mordecai to Solomon Mordecai, Apr. 15, 1825, Jacob Mordecai et al. Papers, Duke. Payments to Nichols appear in May 1825–Dec. 1826, vol. 17, Mordecai Family Papers, SHC, courtesy of John Sanders and Elizabeth Reid Murray. See also Nichols paid £475 for "building [Baptist] Meeting House, as per contract," in Edenton ca. 1810–12, reproduced in *The Wake Forest Student* 26, no. 1 (Sept. 1906): 49–50.

200. William Nichols to James C. Johnston, May 1, 1817, Hayes Collection, SHC.

201. "Specification of Carpenter's and Joiner's Work to be done in repairing and compleating the Church in the town of Edenton"; Statement of restoration expenses, Dec. 12, 1805–Jan. 6, 1807; Payments made to William Nichols, Aug. 22, 1806–Feb. 11, 1809; Report of the restoration committee, July 9, 1805; Josiah Collins to William Nichols, Jan. 18, 1806; Nichols to Collins, Feb. 29, 1806; Collins to Nichols, Apr. 4, 1806; Restoration committee to Nichols, May 12, 1806; and Nichols to Collins, May 28, 1806, St. Paul's Church Records, Edenton, transcribed and provided to author by Elizabeth V. Moore.

202. William Nichols to "The Committee appointed to confer with the superintendent of public buildings as to the disposal of the Statue of Washington," undated, Capital Buildings Papers, Treasurer's and Comptroller's Papers, A&H.

203. Report of Committee on public buildings, 1819, Capital Buildings Papers, A&H.

204. *Raleigh Register*, June 22, Oct. 19, and Dec. 28, 1821; Holmes to Assembly, Nov. 18, 1822, published in *Raleigh Register*, Nov. 22, 1822, quoted in Peatross, *William Nichols, Architect*, 12, and Murray, *Wake*, 210–11. See also Murray, *Wake*, 210, for visitors' detailed accounts of the revamped State House and its fittings.

205. Raleigh *North Carolina Standard*, Feb. 8, 1854, shortly after Nichols's death in Mississippi; David L. Swain, *Early Times in Raleigh* (Raleigh: Walters, Hughes, & Co., 1867), 8, quoted in Peatross, *William Nichols, Architect*, 15.

Chapter 3

1. On the antebellum period, see Clayton, *Close to the Land*; Johnson, *Ante-Bellum North Carolina*; Lefler and Newsome, *North Carolina*, 327–440; Elgiva D. Watson, "Pursuit of Pride"; and Harry Watson, "Squire Oldway," and " 'Old Rip.' " I thank James Brawley, Salisbury; Elizabeth Reid Murray, Raleigh; and William Reaves, Wilmington, for the use of their files of local newspaper data.

2. Raleigh *North Carolina Standard*, Jan. 2, 1835, quoted in Watson, "Squire Oldway."

3. Tarboro *Free Press*, June 21, 1831.

4. Lefler and Newsome, *North Carolina*, 359–415.

5. Murray, *Wake*, 226–33, with quote from *Raleigh Register*, June 23, 1831.

6. *Raleigh Register*, Apr. 29, 1834, quoted in Johnson, *Ante-Bellum North Carolina*, 39; *Compendium of the Enumeration*, 185. Only Tennessee had a lower per capita investment in houses than North Carolina. States listed as having housing built in that year valued at one to two million dollars included newly settled areas such as Mississippi, Louisiana, Kentucky,

Ohio, Indiana, Illinois, and Missouri, and also older states including South Carolina, Massachusetts, Connecticut, and Pennsylvania. The average per capita investment (the total amount of housing construction value divided by the total population of the state) was as high as $3.75 in Massachusetts, $2.92 in New Jersey, and $2.54 in South Carolina. Few states had an average of under $1.00, and Tennessee at 51 cents and North Carolina at 54 cents were the lowest. The accuracy of these figures is uncertain.

7. Lefler and Newsome, *North Carolina*, 353–58.

8. *Raleigh Register*, June 19, 26, 12, and 16, 1840.

9. Lefler and Newsome, *North Carolina*, 362–67, 381–84.

10. Johnson, *Ante-Bellum North Carolina*, 117; Salisbury *Carolina Watchman*, June 12, 1851; *Fayetteville Observer*, Aug. 17, 1857. See also Raleigh *Weekly Post*, Nov. 13, 1852; *Greensboro Times*, Jan. 31, 1856; Elgiva D. Watson, "Pursuit of Pride," 85; and Cecil Kenneth Brown, *State Movement in Railroad Development*.

11. Lefler and Newsome, *North Carolina*, 391. One report attributed the "abundant" money to rising cotton prices and gold from California. Raleigh *North Carolina Standard*, June 12, 1850.

12. Lefler and Newsome, *North Carolina*, 403–28, 715; Johnson, *Ante-Bellum North Carolina*, 151–90, 259–467, 644–831; Murray, *Wake*, 300–387.

13. "Although *Rip Van* would appear to be *waking up* yet I fear he will gasp and stretch a while; then fall asleep again" (William A. Lenoir to William W. Gant, Mar. 31, 1834, Lenoir Family Papers, SHC, quoted in York, "Many Faces of Fort Defiance," 88).

14. James W. Osborne in De Bow, *Industrial Resources*, 183. See also, for example, Cameron, *An Address*.

15. See Butts, "Challenge to Planter Rule," and " 'Irrepressible Conflict' "; Jeffrey, "Progressive Paradigm"; and Harry Watson, " 'Old Rip.' "

16. David A. Barnes, *Address Delivered to the Students of the Warrenton Male Academy, June, 1850*, NCC, 11. For similar ideas and rhetoric in North Carolina and the nation, see Elgiva D. Watson, "Pursuit of Pride," 96, and Marx, *Machine in the Garden*, 119.

17. Raleigh *Southern Weekly Post*, Oct. 1 and 15, 1853; Raleigh *Weekly Post*, Dec. 13, 1851; Richard S. Mason to Richard Upjohn, Nov. 27, 1847, Richard Upjohn Collection, NYPL; Report of Committee to Draw Plans for Caswell Co. Courthouse, 1831, Caswell Co. Misc. Records, A&H; *Greensboro Patriot*, Oct. 15, 1858. For other praise of the rising public spirit in architecture and new buildings, see, for example, *Raleigh Register*, Mar. 14, 1845, and Raleigh *North Carolina Standard*, June 29, 1853, Murray files; Raleigh *Weekly Post*, Jan. 24 (on better construction of smokehouses), and Feb. 14 (on rural architecture), 1852.

18. Thomas Jefferson was one of many who linked classic virtues with classic architecture (Roth, *Concise History of American Architecture*, 84). Nineteenth-century English writers including William Morris and John Ruskin and A. C. Pugin's linkage of architectural and moral values influenced American thinkers as well. For a recent discussion of morality and American architecture, see Clifford Edward Clark, Jr., *American Family Home*, especially chapter 1, "Reforming the Foundations of Society."

19. Grand Jury Presentment, 1831, Pasquotank Co. Accounts, Buildings, and Correspondence, A&H; Raleigh *Southern Weekly Post*, Oct. 1 and 15, 1853; Raleigh *Weekly Post*, Dec. 13, 1851. See also *Raleigh Register*, Mar. 14, 1845 (on public spirit and taste in building); Raleigh *North Carolina Standard*, June 29, 1853 (on new buildings in the city); and Raleigh *Weekly Post*, Jan. 24 (on better construction of smokehouses), and Feb. 14 (on improving rural architecture), 1852.

20. See advertisements for construction bids on new courthouses in Salisbury *Carolina Watchman*, Jan. 19, 1833 (Burke Co.), Mar. 29, 1833 (Rutherford Co.), Mar. 4, 1837 (Davie Co.), Apr. 30, 1842 (Stanly Co.), June 28, 1845 (Catawba Co.), and Jan. 13, 1848 (Alexander Co.); *Wilmington Herald*, Mar. 12, 1853 (Brunswick Co.); and *Wilmington Herald*, July 19, 1855 (Harnett Co.). On rebuilding commercial districts in masonry after fires, with frequent

emphasis on fireproof construction, see, for example, on Wilmington: *Wilmington Weekly Chronicle*, Sept. 2, 1840, Mar. 31, 1841, Sept. 28, 1842, and May 17, 1843, and *Wilmington Chronicle*, Nov. 5, 1845; on Raleigh: Murray, *Wake*, 265–66, *Raleigh Register*, Jan. 21, 1839, and Jan. 8, 1853, and Raleigh *North Carolina Standard*, June 12, 1850; on Fayetteville: *Wilmington Chronicle*, Sept. 9, 1846; on Salisbury: Salisbury *Carolina Watchman*, Oct. 2, 1855. Newspaper references concerning antebellum building trends come mostly from the files of James Brawley, Elizabeth Reid Murray, and William Reaves, whose assistance I acknowledge with thanks. See Herman, *Architecture and Rural Life*, 12, on 1820–70 as an era of replacing and remodeling.

21. For examples of specifications for simple or traditional buildings, see Richmond Co. Poor House and House for Lunatics, 1853, Richmond Co. Misc. Records, Stokes Co. Poor House, 1852, Stokes Co. Misc. Records, and Wayne Co. Poor House, 1836, Wayne Co. Accounts, A&H; Meeting House near Kinston, Kinston *American Advocate*, May 27, 1858; Specifications for School House No. 4, Aug. 4, 1842, John L. Clifton Papers, Duke. On wooden chimneys in town, see Salisbury *Carolina Watchman*, Apr. 26, 1845. See also Lounsbury, "Building Process," 435–37, and Olmsted, *Journey in the Seaboard States*, 348.

22. Although many authorities assert that balloon frame construction had "almost completely replaced the hewn frame for domestic construction by the time of the Civil War" (Roth, *Concise History of American Architecture*, 122), in North Carolina field surveys demonstrate the prevalence of heavy mortised-and-tenoned house frames until the Civil War and in some cases for several years thereafter. See also specifications for Heck House, Raleigh, 1869, Jonathan M. Heck Papers, A&H.

23. See, for example, William Eaton House, ca. 1843, Warrenton; First Baptist Church, 1848, New Bern; and Dongola (facades in different bonds), 1835–1838, Yanceyville, Survey files, Survey and Planning Branch, A&H.

24. Mortimer DeMott, "Sojourn in Wilmington and the Lower Cape Fear, 1837," *Lower Cape Fear Historical Society, Inc., Bulletin* 22, no. 3 (May 1979); *Wilmington Chronicle*, Aug. 26, 1846, quoting extract from Providence, R.I., *Journal*; *Harper's New Monthly Magazine* 14, no. 84 (May 1857): 751. See also *Farmer's Register* 8, no. 4 (Apr. 30, 1840): 243, and *Wilmington Herald*, Nov. 17, 1857. On reinvigoration in other towns, see Montgomery, *Sketches of Old Warrenton*, 197; Tarboro *Southerner*, May 23, 1857; Murray, *Wake*, 265–99; and Salisbury *Carolina Watchman*, Dec. 18, 1855, Nov. 2, 1858, and July 12, 1859.

25. John M. Morehead to A. J. Davis, Dec. 16, 1849, A. J. Davis Collection, NYPL; Greiff, *John Notman, Architect*, 103–8 (on hospital plans); Murray, *Wake*, 372; Salisbury *Carolina Watchman*, Dec. 28, 1858 (on "modern principles" in design of local Boyden House Hotel).

26. Murray, *Wake*, 265–66; *Raleigh Register*, Jan. 21, 1839; *Wilmington Herald*, Nov. 17, 1857.

27. On brick buildings under construction after fires, see *Raleigh Register*, Aug. 6, 1833; *Wilmington Weekly Chronicle*, Mar. 31, 1841; Wilmington *Daily Journal*, Oct. 2, 1851; Salisbury *Carolina Watchman*, Dec. 18, 1855; and *Salisbury Herald*, Mar. 11, 1857. On the use of Philadelphia bricks, see *Wilmington Journal*, July 4, 1851. On the use of New York bricks, see Wilmington *Tri-Weekly Commercial*, June 9, 1853. On the use of Baltimore brick in New Bern, see Sandbeck, *Historic Architecture of New Bern*, 112. On decorative brickwork as improvement over stuccoed work, see Salisbury *Carolina Watchman*, Nov. 2, 1858. On rough-cast stucco over soft brick, scored to resemble ashlar, see Bullock, "Enterprising Contractor," 13, and Bushong, "William Percival," 314.

28. *Raleigh Register*, July 16 and Oct. 15 and 24, 1833, and May 6, 1834; Murray, *Wake*, 268; *Wilmington Herald*, Aug. 23, 1851; Charlotte *Western Democrat*, Sept. 15, 1857; "Murphy's Granite Row," in Salisbury *Carolina Watchman*, Apr. 20, 1858; Hamlin, *Greek Revival Architecture*, 103–8 (on national use of granite rows).

29. Raleigh *North Carolina Standard*, Nov. 16, 1859 (on architect William Percival using brownstone in various buildings); *Fayetteville North Carolinian*, Nov. 13, 1858, quoting *Rich-*

mond Enquirer; Salisbury *Carolina Watchman*, Nov. 9, 1858, quoting *Weldon Patriot* (on Orange and Wake counties' brown sandstone); *Raleigh Register*, Nov. 10, 1858 (on N.C. sandstone at State Fair); *Wilmington Chronicle*, Apr. 8, 1846 (on Wilmington importing brown "free-stone" for commercial buildings), and Aug. 20, 1845 (on red sandstone for Custom House); Wrenn, *Wilmington*, 206–7 (on marble); Sandbeck, *Historic Architecture of New Bern*, 112 (on brownstone in New Bern).

30. *Wilmington Herald*, Aug. 23, 1851 (on a four-story iron-front building under construction on Market St.); *Raleigh Register*, Feb. 20 and Apr. 12, 1856; Charlotte *North Carolina Whig*, Sept. 18, 1860; Wrenn, *Wilmington*, 87–89, 94–95, 143–44; Condit, *American Building*, 76–86.

31. See descriptions of iron doors and window shutters at Custom House, *Wilmington Chronicle*, Aug. 30, 1845; cast-iron pillars and galvanized iron roof at Market House, *Wilmington Chronicle*, Aug. 18, 1847; and iron roof and columns at engine house, 170 feet in diameter, Wilmington *Daily Journal*, Aug. 11, 1860. See also advertisement of Philadelphia maker of ornamental and architectural ironwork, *Raleigh Register*, Jan. 4, 1854.

32. Salisbury *Carolina Watchman*, Mar. 29, 1859; North Carolina, *Public Laws*, 1854–55, 434, and 1858–59, on gaslight companies in New Bern, Salisbury, Raleigh, and Washington.

33. For the national context, see Roth, *Concise History of American Architecture*, 85–125; Gowans, *Images of American Living*, 243–328.

34. Fayetteville *Carolina Observer*, July 3, 1832. See Bishir, "Asher Benjamin's *Practical House Carpenter*."

35. See Malone, "Levi Silliman Ives," esp. 184–85, and Patrick, "Ecclesiological Gothic."

36. For Wilmington examples, see Wrenn, *Wilmington*, and Bishir, "Jacob W. Holt."

37. Fayetteville *Carolina Observer*, July 3, 1832; Raleigh *North Carolina Standard*, Dec. 25, Aug. 28, and July 12, 1850, and Sept. 26, 1860. See also Tarboro *Southerner*, May 23, 1857.

38. Hitchcock, *Architecture Books*, iii; Upton, "Pattern Books"; Clifford Edward Clark, Jr., *American Family Home*, 16–25. Dozens of advertisements for such books appeared in North Carolina newspapers. See, for example, *Raleigh Register*, Apr. 21, 1849, for Turner's North Carolina Bookstore's ad including Minard Lafever's *Beauties of Modern Architecture*, Elliott's *Cottages and Cottage Life*, R. G. Hatfield's *American House Carpenter*, and Downing's *Cottage Residences*. Wilmington papers regularly carried similar advertisements.

39. *Farmers Journal* 1, no. 1 (Apr. 1852): 31; no. 3 (June 1852): 93–94; and no. 4 (July 1852): 117; *Carolina Cultivator*, May 1855; Raleigh *Southern Weekly Post*, Oct. 1, 1853.

40. Cameron, *An Address*, 40; Barringer, *Address*, 13.

41. See Lounsbury, "Building Process," 447, citing Solon Robinson in *American Agriculturalist* 5, no. 2 (Feb. 1845): 57–58, on elitism of Downing's ideas.

42. Downing, *Cottage Residences*, 213, 211, 214–15. See also Upton, "Pattern Books."

43. *Carolina Cultivator*, Dec. 1855, and Raleigh *Southern Weekly Post*, Nov. 3, 1855, both quoting from "The Plough, the Loom and the Anvil," Oct. 1855, an article by L. Durand of Connecticut.

44. Agreement for Meeting House, Anson Co., Nov. 1842, William Alexander Smith Papers, Duke. See Rutherford *Carolina Gazette*, May 18, 1837, cited in Lounsbury, "Building Process," 439; and Rev. Samuel Rothrock Diary, 1830s and 1840s, on community house and stable raisings, and Henry King Burgwyn Diaries, 1840s, on planter's direct involvement in building projects, A&H.

45. Massenburg Farm Journal, 1838, Massenburg Family Papers, SHC. There are many other examples of the continuity of traditional arrangements in building. Among the best documented are Northampton County planter Henry Burgwyn's plantation buildings of the 1840s and 1850s. See Henry King Burgwyn Diaries, A&H, and Anna Greenough Burgwyn Series, Burgwyn Family Papers, SHC.

46. *Fayetteville Observer*, June 27, 1859.

47. On the emergence of contracting in London and New York, see Summerson, *Georgian London*, 70–72; *A History of Architecture and the Building Trades of Greater New York* (New

York: Union History Co., 1899), 388–90, quoting *Longworth's Trade Directory* of 1805–6; and Rock, *Artisans of the New Republic*, 151–52.

48. Downing, *Cottage Residences*, 212–13.

49. By comparison, in 1850 South Carolina listed 12 "builders" and 9 contractors; Georgia listed 38 builders and 54 contractors; and Indiana listed 363 builders and 140 contractors. United States, *Seventh Census*, 317, 344, 376, 789, and *Population*, 362–63.

50. George Dudley was "prepared to take contracts for building . . . in a master-like manner and in the shortest time possible" and sell lumber (Goldsboro *North Carolina Telegraph*, July 13, 1854). William Ashley was "contractor for public and private buildings of every style of architecture" in Wayne and surrounding counties (Kinston *American Advocate*, Apr. 3, 1856). Dudley and Ashley subsequently built the elaborate classical revival–style Davidson County Courthouse in Lexington, North Carolina. Murdoch and Darby of Salisbury were prepared to "take contracts in any part of the state" (Charlotte *Western Democrat*, Aug. 3, 1858). G. B. Lipscombe and others were "prepared to take jobs either by contract for the whole or by the day" in Edgecombe and adjoining counties (Tarboro *Southerner*, Sept. 23, 1854).

51. On the careers of these builders, see Bullock, "Enterprising Contractor"; Ruth Little-Stokes, "Dabney Cosby," *DNCB* 1:435–36; Bishir, "Jacob W. Holt"; and Seapker, "James F. Post." See also James F. Post Ledger, A&H; Wrenn, *Wilmington*; and Mary Claire Engstrom, "John Berry," *DNCB* 1:146–47.

52. William Ashley in Kinston *American Advocate*, Apr. 3, 1858; William Murdoch in *Greensboro Patriot*, June 1, 1858, and Salisbury *Carolina Watchman*, Apr. 20, 1858. See also *Raleigh Register*, Mar. 7 and Apr. 25, 1837, praising the "taste, judgment and fidelity" of the builder of the new courthouse in Raleigh, and Apr. 3, 1840, citing Cosby's "acknowledged skill and taste"; *Mecklenburg Herald* (Virginia), Apr. 26, 1871, praising Holt's "architectural taste" as well as his faithfulness in executing contracts; Bullock, "Enterprising Contractor," 72–73; and Bishir, "Jacob W. Holt," 22–27.

53. John Berry to Thomas Ruffin, June 16, 1831, in Hamilton, *Papers of Thomas Ruffin* 1:35. See also Berry's obituary, Raleigh *Daily Sentinel*, Jan. 18, 1870.

54. Gatling, "John Berry."

55. Bullock, "Enterprising Contractor."

56. Downing, *Architecture of Country Houses*, 131; Seapker, "James F. Post"; Wrenn, *Wilmington*, 87–89, 94, 132–35, 142–44, 214.

57. Bishir, "Jacob W. Holt."

58. Bullock, "Enterprising Contractor."

59. Journal of Rufus Bunnell, Bunnell Family Papers, Yale University Manuscripts and Archives, typescript copy, pp. 1, 3, 5, 11, provided by Janet K. Seapker, New Hanover County Museum, Wilmington, to whom I am greatly indebted for sharing this recently located material.

60. Contract between J. W. Holt and R. D. Baskerville, Oct. 6, 1857, Baskervill(e) Family Papers, private collection, courtesy of William R. Baskerville, Jr.; Ranlett, *The Architect*, vol. 2, plates 19–20. The use of a separate structure for a kitchen was perceived at the time as a southern practice. See E. M. Holt to A. J. Davis, Mar. 2, 1849, A. J. Davis Collection, NYPL.

61. Mr. P. G. Alston's bill, undated, unsigned, in Henry G. Williams Papers, SHC, was possibly a preliminary contract for Cherry Hill, Warren County, pictured in Bishir, "Jacob W. Holt," 16. See also Andrew Murphy House, Salisbury, to be built with eaves to "project over at least two feet or more and to have bracketts and be finished off something like Robert Murphy's house," Articles of Agreement between Michael Davis and Andrew Murphy, Dec. 14, 1852, typescript copy, courtesy of James Brawley, Salisbury; and Temperance Hall, Building Specifications, Hertford, 1851, with roofline to be "finished like the ends of the house built by Dr. Skinner," Caleb Winslow Family Papers, A&H, reproduced in Haley and Winslow, *Historic Architecture of Perquimans County*, 260.

62. Bill for Extra Work, undated, Baskervill(e) Family Papers, private collection. The extra work totaled $996.40. Sloan, *The Model Architect*, reprinted as *Sloan's Victorian Buildings*, facing p. 32.

63. Contract between J. W. Holt and R. D. Baskerville, Oct. 6, 1857, Baskervill(e) Family Papers, private collection.

64. See Memorandum of an Agreement between Dabney Cosby and Mrs. R. J. Williams, Jan. 9, 1840, Wake Co. Misc. Records, A&H, reproduced in Bullock, "Enterprising Contractor." Specifications of the Carpenter's Work for a Brick House to be Built for Mrs. A. W. Mordecai, Sept. 14, 1840, Mordecai Family Papers, SHC; and Articles of Agreement between Michael Davis and Andrew Murphy, Dec. 14, 1852, typescript copy, courtesy of James Brawley.

65. James F. Post Ledger, 1848, A&H; Panthea Twitty, Warren Co., to author, June 17, 1974. "Jno. E. Boyd to J. W. Holt, Jan. 8, 1858, extra costs" for Sylva Sonora, Warren Co., photocopy in possession of author, courtesy of Miriam Boyd, Warrenton, is an account balancing Holt's work against Boyd's list of workmen, boarding costs, and a line for "trap door steps to garrett." See also 1855–56 accounts for Waverly, Mecklenburg Co., Va., in William R. Baskervill(e) Papers, VHS. For the remodeling job costing $1,805.09, the planter client supplied goods and labor worth $1,499.20.

66. See J. C. and R. B. Wood, "contractors & builders," advertising lime, brick, etc., for sale in *Wilmington Journal*, Mar. 28, 1851; Montgomery, *Sketches of Old Warrenton*, 332. See also Joseph L. Keen, Wilmington "contractor & builder" and supplier of Philadelphia brick, in *Wilmington Journal*, July 4, 1851, and Thomas Coates, granite supplier and building contractor, in *Raleigh Register*, Jan. 11, 1860.

67. New Bern *Republican*, June 14, 1848; *Goldsboro Telegraph*, Jan. 31, 1850; Raleigh *North Carolina Standard*, June 9, 1858; Briggs Hardware Account Book, 1847–1856, and Seventh (1850) and Eighth (1860) Censuses of the United States, N.C. Industrial Schedules, manuscript returns and microfilm, A&H. See also *Fayetteville Observer*, Oct. 1, 1860; *Wilmington Journal*, Apr. 19, 1852; Goldsboro *North Carolina Telegraph*, June 10, 1854; Tarboro *Southerner*, Sept. 5, 1857; Charlotte *North Carolina Whig*, Jan. 19, 1858; Charlotte *Western Democrat*, Feb. 22, 1859. See Lounsbury, "Building Process," esp. chap. 4.

68. See Bullock, "Enterprising Contractor," 66, 72, on Cosby subcontracting for carpentry work in Raleigh in 1840 and purchasing manufactured carpentry items from Thomas Briggs in 1849–53.

69. Daniel S. Hill to Ellis Malone, Aug. 19, 1854, Ellis Malone Papers, Duke, courtesy of Joe Elmore.

70. J. W. Holt to R. B. Baskerville, Aug. 9, 1859, Baskervill(e) Family Papers, private collection. See also Bullock, "Enterprising Contractor," 19.

71. See Lucy Martin Battle to William H. Battle, Oct. 14, 1851, Battle Family Papers, SHC, reporting that two white men and two black men of Berry's were at work on their house in Chapel Hill and that "the Capt. [Berry] stays with them a good part of the time too." Mrs. Robert B. Street (granddaughter of John Berry) to Mary Claire Engstrom, June 25 and July 8, 1964, copy in possession of author, courtesy of Mary Claire Engstrom. Also see Lucy Martin Battle to William H. Battle, Oct. 13 and Nov. 11, 1851, Battle Family Papers, SHC.

72. Agreement, George Shackleford and Ephraim Clayton, Jan. 21, 1853, George Shackleford File, Buncombe Co. Estates Papers, A&H. Also see partnerships established and dissolved by G. B. Lipscombe in Edgecombe Co., Tarboro *Southerner*, July 20 and Oct. 21, 1854, Aug. 2, 1856, Feb. 14, 1857, and Mar. 13, 1858.

73. Dabney Cosby to David L. Swain, May 11, 1846, University Papers, University Archives, Chapel Hill.

74. Dabney Cosby to Dabney Cosby, Jr., Nov. 28, 1850, Dabney Cosby Papers, SHC; Bullock, "Enterprising Contractor," 14–18, 44, 55, 69; Dabney Cosby to David L. Swain, May

11, 1846, University Papers, University Archives, Chapel Hill.

75. "Old Time Warren Negro: A Tribute to a 98-Years-old Darkey Who is Highly Esteemed," Raleigh *News and Observer*, Oct. 3, 1909, courtesy of Frank Ainsley. "Under Mr. Holt," the writer recalled, Boyd "had built the chimneys in a great majority of the best houses of ante-bellum days."

76. Bishir, "Jacob W. Holt"; Seventh (1850) and Eighth (1860) Censuses of the United States, Warren Co., N.C., Population and Slave Schedules, manuscript returns, Warren Co. tax lists, A&H; Accounts in Baskervill(e) Family Papers, private collection, and William R. Baskervill(e) Papers, VHS; *Proceedings of the Grand Lodge of the Ancient York Masons of North Carolina* (Raleigh: Various printers, 1855–57); Montgomery, *Sketches of Old Warrenton*, 89; Accounts, Warren Co. Courthouse, 1850s, Warren Co. Records, and Vine Hill subcontract, J. W. Holt with Francis O'Day for masonry work, 1856, Archibald Davis Williams Account Book, A&H.

77. James F. Post Ledger, 1847–61, and Seventh (1850) and Eighth (1860) Censuses of the United States, Wilmington, New Hanover Co., N.C., Population and Slave Schedules, manuscript returns, A&H.

78. Journal of Rufus Bunnell, Mar. 8 and Jan. 2, 1860, Bunnell Family Papers, Yale University Manuscripts and Archives. Bunnell remembered that one day "I told Jim to go to the Post house (he was hired of his master by Mr. P. for both house and office use) and bring me some old bread, (for I wanted to use it for cleaning off some drawings on the boards.) Jim, grinning all over while supposing I wanted the bread *to eat*, started up the street for it on a trot. And he was yet more astonished when I used it in that way" (Journal of Rufus Bunnell, July 5, 1859).

79. Journal of Rufus Bunnell, Feb. 11, 1860, Sept. 28, 1859.

80. Dabney Cosby to Dabney Cosby, Jr., undated (judged by Bullock to be between Feb. 21 and Mar. 10, 1845), Dabney Cosby Papers, SHC; see also Bullock, "Enterprising Contractor," 44. The Chapel Hill buildings were Old East and Old West, remodeled from designs by A. J. Davis.

81. Dabney Cosby to Dabney Cosby, Jr., Jan. 26, 1843, Dabney Cosby Papers, SHC, quoted in Bullock, "Enterprising Contractor," 18.

82. Edward Jennings Carter, "A History of Mars Hill College" (Master's thesis, University of North Carolina, 1940), 10.

83. [Mrs. L. R. Ligon], *Oxford Orphanage: A Pictorial History* (Oxford: Privately printed, [1973]), 9; *Proceedings of the Grand Lodge*, 1857, 11.

84. A. G. Jones to Ellis Malone, Ellis Malone Papers, Duke; Warren Co. Deed Book 31, May 2, 1855, 359, A&H. It is noteworthy that Jones, a builder, wanted not only builders but a farmer—representative of common community values—to judge the worth of his work.

85. Tarboro *Southerner*, May 5, 1857, and Jan. 9, 1858. See also Edgecombe Co. Deed Book 26, 400; Book 27, 51, 174, 408, 565, 824; and Book 28, 224, 266, 494, 686, 687, A&H.

86. Dabney Cosby to Dabney Cosby, Jr., Nov. 28, 1850, Dabney Cosby Papers, SHC; Bullock, "Enterprising Contractor," 73–75.

87. On the problems and goals of the profession nationally in the mid-nineteenth century, see Bernard Michael Boyle, "Architectural Practice in America, 1865–1965—Ideal and Reality," in Kostof, *The Architect*, 309–10; Paul R. Baker, *Richard Morris Hunt* (Cambridge: MIT Press, 1980), 108; Hamlin, *Greek Revival Architecture*, 22–24, 60–61, 90–92, 140; and Upton, "Pattern Books," 111–15. I especially wish to acknowledge with thanks Upton's suggestions on this topic.

88. The 1850 census listed 181 architects in the state of New York, 89 in Pennsylvania, 81 in Massachusetts, 31 in Missouri, 25 in New Jersey, 24 in Ohio, and from 1 to 20 in other states. United States, *Seventh Census*, lxvii. A good account of the beginnings of the AIA appears in Baker, *Richard Morris Hunt*, 108–17. A. J. Davis was chairman and Thomas U.

Walter secretary of the group that first met in 1836 and then organized formally in 1837 with William Strickland as president. Richard Upjohn took the lead in organizing the 1857 AIA, and Walter and Davis were among the first members.

89. Joseph W. Murphy, Scuppernong, N.C., to John H. Hopkins, Jr., Aug. 2, 1859, Richard Upjohn Collection, NYPL.

90. *Raleigh Register*, July 16, 1833. This discussion of the Capitol draws upon the research of John L. Sanders, whose unpublished research report, "The North Carolina State House and Capitol, 1792–1872," I acknowledge with thanks. See also Sanders, "North Carolina State Capitol," "The State Capitol: A Tourguide," and "This Political Temple." See also Cecil Elliott, "North Carolina State Capitol." Primary sources include North Carolina, *Reports of the Commissioners*, and documents collected in the State Capitol File, Capital Buildings Papers, Treasurer's and Comptroller's Papers, A&H, cited herein as State Capitol Papers, including references supplied by Elizabeth Reid Murray, Raleigh. On the views of the commissioners as work proceeded, see North Carolina, *Reports of the Commissioners* 1835, 4; 1838, 3; 1836; and 1840, 1–2; Elliot, "North Carolina State Capitol," May 1958, 21; and Sanders, "The State Capitol: A Tourguide," 46.

91. "If any further architectural skill be necessary, Mr. Nichols, or his father, on being requested to do so, will pay occasional visits to Raleigh during the progress of the work" (*Fayetteville Observer*, Apr. 16, 1833). Elliot, "North Carolina State Capitol," May 1958, 20, and June 1958, 23; Sanders, "The State Capitol: A Tourguide," 5–6; North Carolina, *Report of the Commissioners*, 1834, 5. On the younger Nichols's unwilling departure from the project, see W. Nichols to David L. Swain, Dec. 22, 1833, Epistolary Correspondence, David L. Swain Papers, SHC.

92. *Fayetteville Observer*, Apr. 16, 1833; North Carolina, *Report of the Commissioners*, 1834, 5.

93. Hamlin, *Greek Revival Architecture*, 140; North Carolina, *Report of the Commissioners*, 1834, 5, on Town, noting his fee of $550. Elliot, "North Carolina State Capitol," June 1958, 23–24. Town was acquainted with John Cameron (brother of building commission chairman Duncan Cameron), Robert Donaldson (Town's New York client and a native of Fayetteville), and William Gaston (Town's lawyer and Donaldson's father-in-law and a revered and persistent proponent of internal improvements and fine architecture). Allcott, "Robert Donaldson," 345–55.

94. Elliot, "North Carolina State Capitol," June 1958, 23.

95. Ithiel Town to David Paton, Nov. 15, 1834, David Paton Papers, A&H; Elliot, "North Carolina State Capitol," 24; Sanders, "The State Capitol: A Tourguide," 6–8, and "David Paton," *DNCB*, forthcoming; typescript in possession of author.

96. Ithiel Town to David Paton, Mar. 2, 1835, David Paton Papers, A&H; Elliot, "North Carolina State Capitol," June 1958, 24.

97. On Edinburgh neoclassicism in Paton's work, see Mary Jane Scott, "David Paton: Scottish 'Athenian' in America," *The Architectural Heritage Society of Scotland: The Journal and Annual Report*, no. 13 (1986): 16–36. Sanders, "North Carolina State Capitol," 481, 483.

98. John J. Briggs to Commissioners, July 9, 1839, State Capitol Papers, and John Steele to David Paton, Nov. 9, 1838, David Paton Papers (on Paton's relations with artisans), A&H; Raleigh *News and Observer*, Aug. 11, 1924.

99. North Carolina, *Report of the Commissioners*, 1836, 7. Beverly Daniel to William Strickland, Oct. 30, 1837, William Strickland to Beverly Daniel, Nov. 10, 1837, and William Strickland to David Paton, Nov. 4, 1836, David Paton Papers, A&H. Strickland suggested a fret or honeysuckle as more properly Grecian.

100. Elliot, "North Carolina State Capitol," June 1958, 24–25. Clipping from unidentified Raleigh newspaper, [June], 1840 cites Paton's departure on May 23. *Memorial of David Paton*, David Paton to Col. S. Birdsall, Apr. 22, 1840, and David Paton to D. Beckwith, June 6, 1840,

David Paton Papers, A&H. See also Elliot, "North Carolina State Capitol," June 1958, 25–26, and Sanders, "The State Capitol: A Tourguide," 9.

101. See Gilchrist, *William Strickland*, 89–91; William Bell to David Paton, Aug. 17, 1835, and Mar. 5, 1837, David Paton Papers, A&H; T. H. Ashe to Secretary of the Treasury, June 24, July 20, and Aug. 20, 1858, Public Buildings Service, General Correspondence, Letters Received, RG 121, NA (Custom House, Marine Hospital). Norris won the Custom House job through local connections made while overseeing construction of St. James Church in 1839 from designs by Philadelphian Thomas U. Walter.

102. A committee from Wilmington traveled north in 1858 to choose an architect—Samuel Sloan—to design the Baptist Church. Wrenn, *Wilmington*, 211. A church member from New Bern sailed to New York to employ T. Thomas and son for a New Bern Baptist church. John D. Whitford, "The Home Story of a Walking Stick," 270, undated typescript (ca. 1900), John D. Whitford Papers, A&H; Herzog, "Early Architecture of New Bern," 271–72.

103. Richard Upjohn Collection, NYPL.

104. On Davis's career in North Carolina, I would like to acknowledge the scholarship of John V. Allcott. See his "Architect A. J. Davis in North Carolina," "Robert Donaldson, the First North Carolinian to Become Prominent in the Arts," "Scholarly Books and Frolicsome Blades," and "Architectural Developments at 'Montrose' in the 1850s." See also Lane, *Architecture of the Old South*, 235–57.

105. *Raleigh Register*, Feb. 23, 1844, in Murray files. The Macon allusion is probably to conservative political leader Nathaniel Macon. See also Raleigh *North Carolina Standard*, June 12, 1850, for an objection to employing northern mechanics to build the Insane Asylum.

106. *Fayetteville Observer*, Jan. 2, 1857; William H. Battle to William A. Graham, Aug. 25, 1859, W. A. Graham Papers, SHC, quoted in Bushong, "Montfort Hall," 87.

107. John England to William Gaston, June 28, 1839, courtesy of Stephen C. Worsley; see also Worsley, "Catholicism in Antebellum North Carolina," 415–18. England commented, "I am an advocate for fine building, [but] money sunk in prematurely paying to make a fine building . . . would overwhelm me with perplexity if not with ruin."

108. William A. Graham to A. J. Davis, May 11, 1853, W. A. Graham Papers, SHC, quoted in Allcott, "Architectural Developments at 'Montrose,' " 92.

109. A. A. Martin to R. Upjohn, July 10, 1857, Richard Upjohn Collection, NYPL. See also Raleigh *North Carolina Standard*, Nov. 16, 1859. The Babel story reportedly originated in an English legal case in 1817 in which an architect testified that his profession was "totally different" from that of a builder. Colvin, *Biographical Dictionary of English Architects*, 23.

110. See State Capitol File, Capital Buildings Papers; A. J. Davis Collections, MMA and NYPL; and Richard Upjohn Collection, NYPL.

111. Bishir, "Jacob W. Holt"; Bogart in Kinston *American Advocate*, Oct. 14, 1856, and Goldsboro *Daily Rough Notes*, Feb. 25, 1861; Seapker, "James F. Post."

112. Raleigh *North Carolina Standard*, Nov. 6, 1859; *Raleigh Register*, Sept. 29, 1858; Bushong, "William Percival." See also Percival's advertisement in *Greensboro Patriot*, Aug. 6, 1858, citing his "Educational Training for his Profession and practical experience."

113. For examples of specifications for North Carolina buildings, see William Strickland's specifications for U.S. Mint, Charlotte, 1835, in Stautzenberger, *Establishment of the Charlotte Branch Mint*, 107–9; specifications (unsigned) for Northampton Co. Courthouse, 1858, Northampton Co. Records, A&H; G. J. F. Bryant, specifications (23 pages) for Thornbury plantation house, Northampton Co., probably 1840s, Burgwyn Family Papers, SHC.

114. Richard Upjohn to Richard Sharp Mason, Oct. 14, 1846, and Memorandum of Agreement between James Puttick, Robert Findlater, and Justin Martindale and Vestry of Christ Church, Raleigh, June 7, 1848, Christ Church Records, A&H. See also *Raleigh Register*, Nov. 13, 1846, Mar. 22, 1848, and Jan. 7, 1854, in Murray files.

115. Baker, *Richard Morris Hunt*, 109–10.

116. A. J. Davis 2:189, A. J. Davis Collection, MMA; Hamlin, *Greek Revival Architecture*, 143–44. See Davis drawings in Avery, MMA, NYPL, and University Papers, University Archives, Chapel Hill. For the Presbyterian Church in Chapel Hill in 1847, he charged thirty dollars for four drawings, thirty dollars for working drawings, and ten dollars for detail drawings and explanations in response to inquiries. A. J. Davis Collection, Avery. As work on his massive Davidson College proceeded, he received inquiries from the builder, J. N. Scofield, and in response, he noted, he "Answered with drawings . . . $10.00." Scofield to Davis, Feb. 22, 1859, and Davis notation, Mar. 2, 1859, A. J. Davis Collection, MMA.

117. John M. Morehead to Davis, Dec. 16, 1849, Davis Day Book, 1850, A. J. Davis Collection, NYPL.

118. "Specifications of the Materials and Works Required for Building . . . N.C. State Hospital," A. J. Davis Collection, NYPL; Cord, "A. J. Davis," 354–59. Jane Davies to author, Jan. 26, 1981, gives 1845 as date of Davis's first use of printed specifications.

119. Hutton in *Wilmington Herald*, Dec. 19, 1859, in Reaves files; Walker in Wrenn, *Wilmington*, 92; James F. Post contract, Nov. 1, 1855, Lower Cape Fear Historical Society Archives, reproduced in Isabel M. Williams, "Thalian Hall"; Seapker, "James F. Post," 4.

120. Alamance County industrialist E. M. Holt had already hired a local carpenter and begun to get materials for his house when he asked Davis for a design in 1849. E. M. Holt to A. J. Davis, Mar. 2, 1849, A. J. Davis Collection, NYPL; Occasional Diary of Edwin Michael Holt, E. M. Holt Papers, SHC; Lounsbury, *Alamance County*, 33–34. Francis Fries, an industrialist determined to modernize Salem, went to New York to get plans from Davis for Salem College, and upon his return he contracted for the project and superintended the work himself. Francis Fries Diary, Oct. 29, 1853, Archives of the Moravian Church in America, Southern Province, Winston-Salem, courtesy of Gwynne S. Taylor. For the construction of Davidson College, a contract was let for the entire job to a South Carolina building firm. Charlotte *Western Democrat*, May 5, 1857. For the Insane Asylum, the state let contracts in various trades. Raleigh *North Carolina Standard*, Feb. 6 and June 12, 1850.

121. John M. Morehead to A. J. Davis, Dec. 16, 1849, A. J. Davis Collection, NYPL.

122. Robert Donaldson to A. J. Davis, Jan. 14, 1844, A. J. Davis Collection, NYPL.

123. Joseph W. Murphy to Richard Upjohn & Co., Oct. 4, 1859, Richard Upjohn Collection, NYPL.

124. T. A. Ashe to Secretary of the Treasury, Apr. 22, June 24, and Aug. 22, 1858, Public Buildings Service, General Correspondence, Letters Received, RG 121, NA.

125. A. J. Davis Day Book, 1844, A. J. Davis Collection, NYPL; Davis to Swain, Oct. 22, 1851, A. J. Davis Collection, Avery; Swain to Davis, Apr. 12, 1851, and John Berry to Davis, June 26, 1851, A. J. Davis Collection, MMA.

126. Powell Family Papers, private collection; photocopies in possession of author.

127. Aldert Smedes to Richard Upjohn & Co., May 15, 1856, and Joseph W. Murphy to Upjohn, Oct. 4, 1859, Richard Upjohn Collection, NYPL. See also Donaldson to Davis, Jan. 14, 1844, A. J. Davis Collection, NYPL, on giving explicit instructions for workmen.

128. R. S. Tucker to Thomas Briggs and James Dodd, Aug. 2, 1859, Briggs Family Papers, private collection, quoted in Wodehouse, "Elusive William Percival," 9–10, courtesy of Marie Moore and Lawrence Wodehouse.

129. Dabney Cosby to Collier and Waitt and Swain, Feb. 25, 1845, University Papers, University Archives, Chapel Hill, quoted in Allcott, "Architect A. J. Davis," 12 (also see for further discussion of Cosby's problems with Davis's plans); John Berry to Davis, June 26, 1851, A. J. Davis Collection, MMA.

130. Charles Phillips to Davis, Mar. 3, 1848, A. J. Davis Collection, Avery. Lilacs bloom in the piedmont of North Carolina in early April.

131. Specifications, Wayne Co. Courthouse, 1848, and John E. Becton and others, Bond, Nov. 23, 1848, for Wayne Co. Courthouse and Jail, Wayne Co. Accounts, A&H.

132. Civil Actions Concerning Courthouse, Pitt Co. Misc. Records, A&H. Subsequent

references to this project are from this source. Mr. Holt was probably Thomas J. Holt. He had assumed the role of architect by the late 1850s. Earlier in the decade he had been delegated by his brother Jacob to build a Gothic-detailed, towered college building in Oxford designed by a Virginia architect, which may have inspired him to give the Pitt County Courthouse a Gothic flair.

133. The Seventh Census of the United States in 1850 was the first to give occupations of all free residents, in addition to race, place of birth, age, literacy, and value of real estate owned.

134. Some critics complained that Carolina artisans were inadequate because their training was too short. Raleigh *North Carolina Standard*, June 12, 1850.

135. United States, *Seventh Census*, 317. There were, as noted above, 5 architects and 13 contractors. Other workers connected with building trades included 10 brickmakers, 6 civil engineers, 54 joiners, 737 mechanics, 354 millwrights, 211 painters and glaziers, and 49 sawyers.

136. Franklin, *Free Negro in North Carolina*, 18, 134–35. In later years, the predominance of blacks in the trowel trades was frequently noted. Antebellum census figures show that there were more carpenters of both races, but that a higher proportion of blacks were bricklayers and plasterers.

137. On decorative painting, see the following advertisements: William A. Bassett and Benjamin A. Richardson, partners as practical painters, and gilding, glazing, graining, and fresco work, Tarboro *Southerner*, Feb. 14, 1857, and partnership dissolved, Tarboro *Southerner*, May 23, 1857; B. A. Richardson, house, sign, and ornamental painter, *Warrenton Reporter*, Feb. 26, 1858, and practical house painter, *Warrenton Reporter*, Aug. 24, 1860; Edward Zoeller, house, sign, ornamental, and fresco painters and gilders, bronzers, and imitators of wood and marble, Tarboro *Southerner*, Dec. 17, 1857; C. & S. Frazier, house, sign, and flag painting, imitations of every variety of marble and all kinds of wood, wall painting, paper hanging, and glazing, *Raleigh Register*, Oct. 18, 1841. Laura Phillips of Winston-Salem is conducting a study of ornamental painting of this type, as presented in her paper, "Grand Illusions," Vernacular Architecture Forum Annual Meeting, 1988.

138. Tarboro *Southerner*, Dec. 17, 1857; *Warrenton News*, Mar. 24, 1853; Washington *North State Whig*, Feb. 6, 1850; *Washington Dispatch*, Dec. 23, 1857. See Seventh Census of the United States, 1850, Lincoln Co. and Rowan Co., N.C., Industrial Schedules, A&H, on operation of house carpenters' shops. Jeremiah Brown, Rowan County house carpenter, for example, employed six workers, used 40,000 feet of lumber, and produced five houses a year. In 1858 N. R. Wood from Kinston advertised his large shop of ten, twelve, or more hands. Kinston *American Advocate*, Jan. 7, 1858.

139. Abraham Spencer, Oxford, to Duncan Cameron, Feb. 16, 1832, Cameron Family Papers, SHC.

140. Johnson, *Ante-Bellum North Carolina*, 70; C. L. Hinton to David L. Swain, Sept. 5, 1839, David L. Swain Papers, A&H, noting charge of three dollars per square for roofing; Henry H. Ryder, bill of prices for making and laying brick, 1850, James Webb Papers, SHC, courtesy of Mary Claire Engstrom.

141. Seventh (1850) and Eighth (1860) Censuses of the United States, N.C. Population Schedules, A&H.

142. Seventh (1850) and Eighth (1860) Censuses of the United States, Warren Co., N.C., Population Schedules, A&H. When Waddell's fiancée's father sought to end their courtship, Waddell's crew built a ladder to her window and the couple eloped. They returned to Chapel Hill, where they met the father on the street and announced their marriage. Waddell may have gone to Chapel Hill to superintend construction of a Holt house there and maintained a connection with Holt after his return to Warren County. In the late 1850s he built two houses in southern Warren County, Cherry Hill and the John Buxton Williams house (Buxton Place), perhaps in association with Holt since both houses were very much in the Holt shop style.

After the Civil War he and John M. Wilson operated the large Wilson and Waddell construction and lumber business at Wilson's Mills in Johnston County. John Buxton Waddell, Jr., interview with author, Mar. 1985.

143. John D. Whitford, "The Home Story of a Walking Stick," 329, undated typescript (ca. 1900), John D. Whitford Papers, A&H. See similar views expressed toward Thomas Bragg of Warrenton in Grady McWhiney, *Braxton Bragg and Confederate Defeat* (New York: Columbia University Press, 1969) 1:3.

144. Tarboro *Southerner*, May 22, 1858; *Fayetteville North Carolinian*, Jan. 30, 1854. See also bricklayer and plasterer James Morris of Kinston, advertising in the *Goldsboro Patriot*, July 28, 1849, for work in Lenoir, Green, Jones, Duplin, and Wayne counties, and millwright Robert L. Moore of Troublesome Creek, Rockingham, advertising in the Greensboro *Patriot and Flag*, Jan. 8, 1858, for building and repair work on mills in Rockingham and adjoining counties.

145. Murray, *Wake*, 252–55; Seventh (1850) and Eighth (1860) Censuses of the United States, Wake, Caswell, Edgecombe Co., N.C., Population Schedules, A&H. Christ Church Parish Register, 1830s, Raleigh, A&H, notes several strangers as stonecutters, and Raleigh's City Cemetery contains several graves of immigrants identified as stonecutters who died during the project.

146. John Campbell Letter, Sept. 31, 1833, A&H.

147. Free Wilmington Building Artisans by Place of Birth

	1850	1860
North Carolina: whites	60	97
North Carolina: blacks	34	41
From other states (all white)	21	23
Canadians	1	0
Germans	1	1
British	3	7
Scandinavians	0	2
Total	120	171

(These figures include carpenters who were employed primarily in railroad construction rather than building. Source: Seventh [1850] and Eighth [1860] Censuses of the United States, New Hanover Co., N.C., Population Schedules, A&H.)

148. See *Wilmington Chronicle*, Jan. 28, 1846, Jan. 23, 1850, noting departure of builder James Milmore for California, Aug. 29, 1849, on men leaving "in pursuit of golden fortune," and Feb. 13, 1850, on payment of twelve to sixteen dollars a day for carpenters and masons in California gold rush towns. See also: James Morris of Philadelphia announcing availability, *Wilmington Advertiser*, Mar. 8, 1839; death of C. H. Dahl, carpenter, formerly of New York, *Wilmington Weekly Chronicle*, July 28, 1841; death of stonecutter David Jenkins, formerly of New York City, *Wilmington Chronicle*, Feb. 6, 1850; death of head bricklayer for Presbyterian Church, George Wilson of Baltimore, Wilmington *Daily Journal*, July 6, 1860. On the mobility of Wilmington slaves, see Dick, a bricklayer, about 26 years old, who had "worked in most of the Counties of the State," *Wilmington Advertiser*, June 30, 1837, and Cornelius, a carpenter, owned by a New Bern master but working for James F. Post of Wilmington in 1854, Wilmington *Daily Herald*, July 12, 1855.

149. James Brawley, "Outstanding Builders Had Rowan Roles," *Salisbury Post*, Apr. 25, 1971, in Brawley files; Hood, *Architecture of Rowan County*, 318; Franklin, "James Boon"; Elizabeth Reid Murray, "Stewart Ellison," in *DNCB* 2:152–53.

150. The whites were Joseph C. Deal, George Barr, and Nicholas Dugan; the slaves were Ben Berry and Ephraim Bettencourt; and the free black carpenter was Solomon Nash, "a very respectable man of his class," who was fatally injured. *Wilmington Chronicle*, July 1, 1846.

151. Berlin and Gutman, "Natives and Immigrants," 1192. Berlin and Gutman base their argument in part on the assumption that the number of slave artisans can be determined

from the number of slaves who belonged to artisans. In North Carolina's building industry, such a method of estimating the number of slave artisans is not reliable. From available records it is evident that ownership of slave artisans was by no means restricted to, or even highly concentrated among, artisans. Rather, ownership of slave artisans was distributed among all classes of slaveowners, such as lawyers, planters, widows, children, and merchants, as well as artisans. Thus to assert a decline in the number of slave artisans based on the decline in the number of slaves owned by artisans is not valid. If anything, the rising cost of slaves meant that more and more artisans had to hire rather than purchase workmen and this tendency increased with the growing number of large building projects requiring many workmen. However, records of nearly every antebellum building project for which documentation of workmen is available show a continued reliance on slaves throughout the slave-owning areas of the state.

152. George P. Rawick, ed., *The American Slave: A Composite Autobiography*, ser. 2 (Westport, Conn.: Greenwood Press, 1972–77) 15:329. See Bishir, "Black Builders," for other examples of slave artisans' activities in this era.

153. Bishir, "Black Builders"; *Acts Passed by the General Assembly of the State of North Carolina, 1830–1831* (Raleigh: Lawrence and Lemay, 1831), 12–14. The 1830–31 session of the assembly passed a number of laws repressing slaves and free blacks, including the provision forbidding freemen or slaves from teaching slaves to read and write. These measures came in the wake of various abolitionist efforts and threats of slave rebellion.

154. Salisbury *Carolina Watchman*, Jan. 4, 1859, stated that slaves were selling for at least 25 percent more than in the previous year, but hiring rates were lower. Moses A. Bledsoe in *Ad Valorem Taxation* (Raleigh: Holden and Wilson, 1859), 8–9, claimed that a slave mechanic was worth about two thousand dollars, while a field hand was worth five hundred dollars.

155. Rawick, *American Slave*, 2. Several members of the Artis family were listed as free blacks in the manuscript population schedules of the U.S. Census for antebellum Wilmington, but Price and the Fineys were not and therefore may have been slaves. Elvin Artis—who may have been related to or identical with "Jim" Artis—was the free black contractor on the Bellamy Mansion. Price and the Fineys did appear in *Smaw's Wilmington Directory . . .* (Wilmington: Frank D. Smaw, Jr., 1867) immediately after the war. See also Isabel M. Williams, "Thalian Hall."

156. See Butts, " 'Irrepressible Conflict,' " and "Challenge to Planter Rule," 51–98; and Berlin and Gutman, "Natives and Immigrants."

157. Stonecutters' and quarry hands', carpenters', and laborers' time books, 1833–1840, State Capitol Papers; *Raleigh Register*, July 8, 1834, and Aug. 6, 1833. See also *Raleigh Register*, Aug. 6, 1833, on 120 men working at the Capitol, and Feb. 23, 1850, on Capitol workmen promoting internal improvements.

158. North Carolina, *Laws of the State of North-Carolina*, 123–24; Murray, *Wake*, 277–78, listing officers including a sign painter, a printer, a tin and coppersmith, and, from the Capitol workmen, carpenters Anderson Nicholson and James Dodd, stonemason James Puttick, and blacksmith Silas Burns. Quote in *Raleigh Rasp*, July 16, 1842. See also *Raleigh Register*, Oct. 30, 1840, and *Raleigh Rasp*, July 17, 1841. See other mechanics' associations in North Carolina (New Bern), *Laws of North Carolina, 1844–1845*, 158, and North Carolina (Granville County), *Laws of North Carolina, 1848–1849*, 324–25. All included locally prominent builders.

159. *Lecture Read Before the Raleigh Mechanics' Association by William W. Holden, Esq., on their 4th Anniversary, July 12, 1842* (Raleigh: Raleigh Star, 1842), 17–18.

160. Raleigh *North Carolina Standard*, June 12, 1850; *Arator* 1, no. 1 (Apr. 2, 1855); *Greensboro Patriot*, Aug. 6, 1858, on patronage of local mechanics.

161. Franklin, *Free Negro in North Carolina*, 137–39. Salisbury meeting is described in Salisbury *Carolina Watchman*, Dec. 19, 1850. North Carolina, *Public Laws*, 1860–61, 69; Franklin, *Free Negro in North Carolina*, 156–62.

162. *Wilmington Herald*, Aug. 6, 1857.

163. Petitions from citizens of Beaufort Co. (a location substituted for New Hanover Co. on a printed petition form), undated, but probably 1854, and bills and committee reports, Legislative Papers, 1854–1855, A&H, courtesy of Steve Massengill. The original bill was introduced for only a few counties, including New Hanover, Pitt, Cumberland, Robeson, Warren, and Sampson, and evidently originated as a bill for New Hanover County. The senate referred the matter to a committee to study the idea of adopting such a law for the whole state. The committee returned a negative report. Raleigh *North Carolina Standard*, Oct. 20 and Dec. 16, 1854, and Feb. 17, 1855. And see printed version of bill in North Carolina, *Legislative Documents 1854–55*, 253–54. For an example of an account and suit filed under the Mechanics' Lien Law, see W. J. Smith account, Mar. 21, 1879, Davie Co. Misc. Records, A&H. On mechanics' lien laws elsewhere around 1830, see Commons et al., *History of Labour*, 220–21, 279–80, 297. Architects and builders considered mechanics' lien laws so important that at least one builder's guide, Edward Shaw's *Modern Architect* (Boston: Dayton & Wentworth, 1855), carried the entire text of the 1851 Massachusetts lien law and amendments, plus a list of the amendments of the law in force in other states: Maine, New Hampshire, Connecticut, New York, Pennsylvania, Missouri, New Jersey, Ohio, Indiana, Illinois, Michigan, Wisconsin, Maryland, and California. No state south of Maryland was listed. An explanation of the reasons for southern states' resistance to lien laws requires further study.

164. A tax on income of some classes had been on the books as early as 1848–49, when a tax of three dollars was levied on five hundred dollars or more annual income of such professionals as dentists, physicians, lawyers, and some judges (North Carolina, *Public Laws*, 1848–49, 131; 1854–55, 80; 1856–57, 39). In the late 1850s, however, the amount of tax was increased to 1 percent and the law was extended to "every person in the employment of incorporated or private companies, societies, institutions or individuals, and every other person" whose practice, salary, or *wages* amounted to five hundred dollars or more (North Carolina, *Public Laws*, 1858–59, 36). It was the expansion of coverage plus the increase in rate that set off the workmen and mechanics. See Butts, "Challenge to Planter Rule," 28–30. The 1860–61 revenue law did repeal the taxation of salaries of mechanics and artisans. Butt, "Challenge to Planter Rule," 128; North Carolina, *Public Laws*, 1860–61, 64.

165. Raleigh *Spirit of the Age* and *North Carolina Standard*, Oct. 19 and Oct. 26, 1859; Salisbury *Carolina Watchman*, Oct. 25, 1859; Greensboro *Patriot*, Oct. 28, 1859, with an editorial comment on similarities with the Regulator movement. See also Butts, "Challenge to Planter Rule," 60–63, which identifies the membership of the group as including 1 "skilled craftsman," 1 carpenter, 1 marblecutter, 2 painters, 1 merchant, several printers, 1 railroad agent, 1 lawyer, 1 educator, and 1 machinist. Some members also belonged to the Raleigh Mechanics Association, including metalworker W. J. Lougee. On "agrarianism," see Commons et al., *History of Labour*, 234–40.

166. Raleigh *North Carolina Standard*, Dec. 10, 1859, and Feb. 15, 1860; Murray, *Wake*, 277–78; Butts, " 'Irrepressible Conflict,' " esp. 54–55; Lefler and Newsome, *North Carolina*, 388–89; Butts, "Challenge to Planter Rule." Murray, *Wake*, 277–78, notes that the group resumed activities after the Civil War, as cited in the Raleigh *Telegram*, May 6, 1871.

167. Raleigh and other newspapers contain detailed accounts of events and displays. *Spirit of the Age*, Oct. 27 and Nov. 3, 1858; *Raleigh Register*, Oct. 26, 1859, Oct. 24, 1860; *North Carolina Standard*, Oct. 22, Oct. 26, and Oct. 29, 1859.

168. *Carolina Cultivator* 3, no. 8 (Oct. 1857): 181; Raleigh *Spirit of the Age*, Oct. 27 and Nov. 3, 1858; *Greensboro Times*, Oct. 30, 1858; *Raleigh Register*, Oct. 26, 1859; Salisbury *Carolina Watchman*, Nov. 8, 1859; *Raleigh Register*, Oct. 24, 1860.

169. Raleigh *North Carolina Standard*, Oct. 26, 1859. Davis client E. M. Holt wins prize, *Raleigh Register*, Oct. 24, 1860; Davis patron John Motley Morehead speaks at fair, *Raleigh Register*, Oct. 26, 1859; Percival member of committee on premiums for fair, *Greensboro Patriot*, Aug. 26, 1859; Lind client Mrs. J. A. Engelhard judge in fine arts category, *Raleigh*

Register, Oct. 26, 1859; Downing proponent D. M. Barringer judge in fine arts category and speaker at fair, *Raleigh Register*, Oct. 26, 1859.

170. *Greensboro Times*, Oct. 30, 1858.

171. Raleigh *North Carolina Standard*, Oct. 29, 1859.

Chapter 4

1. Greeley et al., *Great Industries*, 40–41.

2. The notion that demand promoted experimentation in production methods was current at the time. See, for example, the 1871 publication, *One Hundred Years' Progress of the United States*, 356–57.

3. See Cochran, *Frontiers of Change*, 78.

4. Peterson, "Early Lumbering," 68. Lacking an organized body of sawyers to oppose power sawing and an abundance of cheap labor, the colonial government encouraged settlers to build sawmills. In 1736, for example, the government offered 640 acres of timberland to anyone who would erect a sawmill on the Cape Fear River. *CRNC* 4:220.

5. Fourth Census of the United States, 1820, Brunswick Co., N.C., Manufacturing Schedule, manuscript returns, A&H. For an account of commercial sawmilling in the colonial and antebellum periods, see Lounsbury, "From Craft to Industry," 156–66.

6. Seventh Census of the United States, 1850, Rowan Co., Alamance Co., N.C., Industry Schedule, manuscript returns, A&H.

7. The 1840 census was the first to record information on manufacturing in any detail. Unfortunately, that census failed to distinguish sawmills from other lumbering activities such as the production of shingles, the manufacture of window sash and blinds in small shops, and the planing of lumber. As a result, the census recorded 1,056 sawmills in the state, which is probably three times the actual number of establishments that sawed lumber. Scrutiny of the Industry Schedule for each county in the 1850 census reveals 261 manufacturers who actually produced sawn lumber. However, this figure does not include many of the smaller operations whose output was less than five hundred dollars annually. The figure of 261 is also slightly less than the number printed in the statistical compendium to the 1850 census. See United States, *Sixth Census*, 189; Seventh Census of the United States, 1850, N.C. Industry Schedule, manuscript returns, A&H; and United States, *Abstracts of the Statistics of Manufactures*, 73.

8. Seventh Census of the United States, 1850, Alamance Co., N.C., Industry Schedule, manuscript returns, A&H.

9. Anderson, "Preliminary Report on Stagville Plantation," 41.

10. William S. Macay Account Book, 1845–1855, vol. 7, Macay-McNeely Papers, SHC; Himer Fox Account Book, 1844–1875, Duke.

11. Charlotte *Western Democrat*, May 19, 1857. See also, for example, *Newbernian*, Sept. 2, 1851; Goldsboro *North Carolina Telegraph*, July 13, 1854; *Fayetteville Observer*, July 30, 1855; and *Greensboro Patriot*, July 2, 1858.

12. John A. Craven Ledger, 1855–1880, Dec. 1856, Duke.

13. See, for example, Defebaugh, *History of the Lumber Industry* 2:442; Richards, *Operation of Woodworking Machines*, 141; Kinston *American Advocate*, Sept. 28, 1855; and *Semi-Weekly Raleigh Register*, Jan. 1, 1853.

14. *Greensboro Patriot*, July 2, 1858.

15. "Berry Davidson Autobiography."

16. Occasional Diary of E. M. Holt, 1844–1854, 1849, E. M. Holt Papers, SHC.

17. Hogg and Haywood Account Book, 1855–1856, vol. 18, T. D. Hogg Papers, SHC. The amount of timber consumed by a sawmill in a given year naturally varied according to the output of sawn lumber and the size and quality of the logs. Small mills which produced no more than 100,000 board feet usually needed no more than 500 saw logs. In 1850 Samuel Cotters of Caswell County turned out 20,000 feet of lumber with 100 logs. Moses Evans's

sawmill in Forsyth County consumed 300 pine and oak logs in the manufacture of 60,000 feet of boards and scantling. Commercial mills used several thousand logs yearly. Dwight Mc-Keithan of Cumberland County needed 3,000 logs to produce 600,000 board feet. Much of the timber used in these early mills was unfortunately turned into sawdust rather than lumber. The thick blades of the sash and circular saws produced a broad kerf which wasted a sizable portion of the saw log. For the problems of wasteful saw blades, see Winston *Union Republican*, Dec. 14, 1882 and Richards, *Operation of Woodworking Machines*, 141.

18. Tarboro *Southerner*, June 20, 1857. In Salisbury, William Locke assessed a surcharge of 25 percent over his standard rates for all lumber that he carted. Salisbury *Rowan Whig and Western Advocate*, Oct. 17, 1855; Goldsboro *New Era*, Oct. 27, 1853.

19. Charlotte *North Carolina Whig*, Dec. 3, 1859 and Jan. 12, 1858.

20. *Raleigh Register*, Mar. 5, 1884.

21. For the English background in brickmaking and the use of bricks, see Wight, *Brick Building in England*, and Brunskill and Clifton-Taylor, *English Brickwork*. For a study of traditional methods of brickmaking, see McKee, *Introduction to Early American Masonry*, 41–44, and McGrath, "Manufacture of Hand-Made Bricks," 88–94.

22. See *Scientific American* 9 (Oct. 1, 1853): 24.

23. Boyce, *History of Chowan County*, 113–14.

24. Habakkuk, *American and British Technology*, 19.

25. Fourth Census of the United States, 1820, Brunswick Co., N.C., Manufacturing Schedule, manuscript returns, A&H.

26. Condit, *American Building Art*, 16. For a study of the origins of the circular saw, see Ball, "Circular Saws," 79–80.

27. *Raleigh Register*, Jan. 1, 1853.

28. Winston *Union Republican*, Dec. 14, 1882. Another problem with the circular saw was the development of an uneven cutting edge after short use. The wearing away of the teeth reduced the circumference of the saw and thus the length of the cutting surface that came in contact with the wood. See Ball, "Circular Saws," 81–85.

29. Although the 1870 census does not list the type of saw used in every mill in the state, the partial list is overwhelmingly composed of sash saws. Ninth Census of the United States, 1870, N.C. Industry Schedule, manuscript returns, A&H. The 1880 census makes the first detailed list of saw types. Nearly 90 percent of the mills enumerated were equipped with circular saws. Tenth Census of the United States, 1880, N.C. Schedule of Manufactures, Lumber Mills and Saw Mills, manuscript returns, A&H.

30. Constantine A. Hege, "Improvement in Head-Blocks for Saw-Mills," Patent Number 196,577, Oct. 30, 1877, United States Patent Office, Washington, D.C.

31. Herzog, "Early Architecture of New Bern," 35; New Bern *Carolina Federal Republican*, Dec. 21, 1816; New Bern *Carolina Centinel*, May 30, 1818; Lemmon, *Pettigrew Papers*, 607–8, 629.

32. Wilmington, *Cape-Fear Recorder*, May 15, 1819 and Nov. 4, 1820.

33. *Farmers' Register* 7 (Apr. 30, 1840): 243.

34. Seventh Census of the United States, 1850, N.C. Industry Schedule, manuscript returns, A&H.

35. Bishop, *History of American Manufacturies*, 557; *Second and Third Annual Reports*, 5; *Fayetteville Observer*, Apr. 3, 1854; Cane Creek Manufacturing Company Minute Book, 1836–1857, Sept. 3, 1855, 113, Duke.

36. To pay for their new machinery, many of the early steam sawmills in Wilmington priced their lumber at a higher rate than that of the water-powered mills. In 1823, for example, pine boards and scantling sold for twelve to thirteen dollars per thousand feet at the steam mills while "river" lumber sawn at water mills sold for six to eight dollars per thousand feet. By producing lumber for export rather than for a local market, the steam mills

were able to sell their lumber profitably. See Wilmington *Cape-Fear Recorder*, Sept. 6, 1823. For differences in prices a quarter-century later, see *Goldsboro Patriot*, July 28, 1849.

37. Raleigh *North Carolina Star*, May 15, 1850; Raleigh *Spirit of the Age*, Aug. 29, 1855; *Fayetteville Observer*, July 23, 1853; *Arator* 1 (Feb. 1856): 352. Burns won several awards at the North Carolina State Fair during the 1850s for his machinery. See Raleigh *North Carolina Standard*, Oct. 28, 1857; Salisbury *Carolina Watchman*, Nov. 2, 1858; and *MR*, May 17, 1884. Another early manufacturer of circular sawmills was the Eagle Foundry and Machine Shop located in Tyro in Davidson County. *Greensboro Patriot*, July 2, 1858.

38. See, for example, *Arator* 1 (Apr. 1855): 14. In an unsigned editorial, the writer claimed that North Carolina had "only tolerable mechanics with few of superior quality and those so scattered that they were scarcely known to exist among us."

39. Cane Creek Manufacturing Company Minute Book, 1836–1857, Mar. 5, 1855, 109–10, Duke.

40. S. W. Neal to W. G. Smith, Jan. 30, 1851, William Alexander Smith Papers, Duke. Neal told the Pool and Hunt Shop foreman that "we belong to the South and wanted to patronize the South." Such feelings, characteristic in part of the growing sectional antagonisms fostered by the acrimonious debate surrounding the Missouri Compromise of 1850, aided the efforts of many southern mechanics to overcome local prejudices. S. W. Neal to W. G. Smith, Jan. 25, 1851, William Alexander Smith Papers, Duke.

41. J. W. Amory to W. G. Smith, June 24, 1851, ibid. See W. G. Smith and E. D. Ingram Steam Mill Ledger, 1851–1857, III, 16, ibid.

42. Starling, "Plank Road Movement," 37; Kinston *American Advocate*, Sept. 28, 1855.

43. *Second and Third Annual Reports*, 5.

44. Ibid.

45. Similarly, the Greenville and Raleigh Plank Road Company offered for sale three of its portable circular saws. Perceptive lumbermen, well aware of the advantages of such machinery, eagerly purchased the low-priced saws. Washington *North State Whig*, Mar. 30, 1853.

46. Goldsboro *North Carolina Telegraph*, July 13, 1854.

47. *Warrenton News*, Feb. 26, 1858.

48. Butterworth, *Growth of Industrial Art*, 198.

49. *Greensboro Patriot*, Aug. 9, 1826.

50. Seventh Census of the United States, 1850, New Hanover Co., N.C., Industry Schedule, manuscript returns, A&H.

51. *Newbernian*, Nov. 1, 1852.

52. *Fayetteville Observer*, Jan. 1, 1855.

53. Hogg and Haywood Account Book, 1855–1856, T. D. Hogg Papers, SHC; Amis, *Historical Raleigh*, 122.

54. *Semi-Weekly Raleigh Register*, Feb. 20, 1856; Hogg and Haywood Account Book, 1856, T. D. Hogg Papers, SHC.

55. *Semi-Weekly Raleigh Register*, Feb. 20, 1856.

56. See, for example, price lists in the Goldsboro *New Era*, Oct. 27, 1853; Salisbury *Rowan Whig and Western Advocate*, Oct. 17, 1855; Tarboro *Southerner*, June 20, 1857; Greensboro *Patriot and Flag*, Jan. 8, 1858; *Greensboro Patriot*, June 11, 1858; and *Wilson Ledger*, July 11, 1858.

57. By 1860 only four planing mills in operation outside of Wilmington produced more than five hundred dollars worth of materials. Eighth Census of the United States, 1860, N.C. Industry Schedule, manuscript returns, A&H.

58. *Warrenton Reporter*, Mar. 2, 1827.

59. Richards, *Operation of Woodworking Machines*, 51.

60. *Newbernian*, Nov. 1, 1852; New Bern *Republican*, June 11, 1848; Sandbeck, *Historic Architecture of New Bern*, 96.

61. *Newbernian*, Mar. 5, 1850; New Bern *Atlantic*, June 14, 1854.

62. The 1850 census listed Alonzo Willis in possession of $3,500 in real property, a considerable amount for a member of New Bern's artisan class. George Bishop operated both a factory and separate showroom. See Seventh Census of the United States, 1850, Craven Co., N.C., Population Schedule, manuscript returns, A&H; New Bern *Union*, Feb. 9, 1857.

63. *Goldsboro Telegraph*, Jan. 31, 1850.

64. New Bern *Atlantic*, Feb. 21, 1854.

65. *Newbernian*, Mar. 5, 1850.

66. *Wilmington Journal*, Jan. 13, 1854 and Apr. 7, 1854; *Fayetteville Observer*, Jan. 15, 1855.

67. Charlotte *North Carolina Whig*, Jan. 5, 1858.

68. Raleigh *North Carolina Standard*, Oct. 28, 1857; Salisbury *Carolina Watchman*, Apr. 20, 1858; Raleigh *Spirit of the Age*, Oct. 27, 1858.

69. See *Fayetteville Observer*, Jan. 15, 1855; Washington *North Carolina Times*, Oct. 8, 1856; *Fayetteville Observer*, Oct. 17, 1859; *Wilson Ledger*, Nov. 13, 1860; and Eighth Census of the United States, 1860, N.C. Industry Schedule, manuscript returns, A&H.

70. Eighth Census of the United States, 1860, N.C. Industry Schedule, manuscript returns, A&H.

71. United States, *Eighth Census*, vol. 3, *Manufactures*, passim.

72. *Historical and Descriptive Review* 2:81.

73. Raleigh *Hale's Weekly*, Dec. 16, 1879.

74. Raleigh *Daily News*, Aug. 2, 1878.

75. Raleigh *State Chronicle*, Sept. 23, 1883.

76. Raleigh *Daily News*, July 2, 1875 and Jan. 12, 1876.

77. Raleigh *State Chronicle*, Mar. 24, 1887 and Sept. 23, 1883.

78. Raleigh *Visitor* quoted in *Fayetteville Observer*, Feb. 13, 1884.

79. Butterworth, *Growth of Industrial Art*, 198.

80. *Fayetteville Observer*, Feb. 13, 1884. Although the newspaper reporter thought that northern goods had ceased to be important competitors of North Carolina sash and blind factories, other contemporaries were less sure. In November 1884, Charles Wells, a correspondent for *Manufacturers' Record*, wrote from Asheville, "I was standing in the Swannanoa hotel office, calculating the value of the vast outlying timber regions about there, when a carpenter came in to put up a new door. It was of white pine, neatly finished but stamped on the edge was the name of a well-known Boston firm of lumber dealers! A Yankee door in the heart of the greatest lumber country in the whole South!" (*MR*, Nov. 22, 1884).

81. Raleigh *News and Observer*, Aug. 2, 1882.

82. *MR*, Mar. 26, 1892.

83. *The Manufacturer and Builder* 6 (July 1874): 149.

84. See, for example, *MR*, Apr. 4, 1885; *Greensboro Patriot*, Jan. 18, 1889; *Wilmington Star*, Feb. 28, 1888; and *MR*, Apr. 4, 1885.

85. Raleigh *Farmer and Mechanic*, May 30, 1883.

86. Raleigh *News and Observer*, May 30, 1882.

87. F. R. Hutton, "Machine Tools and Wood-Working Machinery," in United States, *Tenth Census*, vol. 22, *Power Machinery*, 241–44; *The Manufacturer and Builder* 6 (Aug. 1874): 177.

88. *Beasley and Emerson's Charlotte Directory*, 145; *MR*, Aug. 21, 1886.

89. The five were Thomas Briggs & Sons, established in 1858; Jacob S. Allen, successor to Betts, Vaughan, and Allen, a large firm which was begun in the late 1860s; Kingsley and Ashley, established in 1875; Ruffin Roles, established in 1877; and Ellington, Royster, and Company, established in 1878. For a detailed description of their activities, see Raleigh *Hale's Weekly*, Dec. 16 and 23, 1879. Tenth Census of the United States, 1880, Wake Co., N.C., Schedule of Manufactures, manuscript returns, A&H.

90. Raleigh *Hale's Weekly*, Dec. 16, 1879; Raleigh *State Chronicle*, Jan. 12, 1884; *Historical and Descriptive Review* 1:91–92.

91. Raleigh *State Chronicle*, Nov. 24, 1887. After fire destroyed a sizable portion of the Wilmington business district in February 1886, a number of Raleigh craftsmen poured into the port city looking for work. Jacob Allen, a prominent contractor from Raleigh, may have settled there permanently following the fire. See Raleigh *State Chronicle*, Apr. 6, 1888.

92. See Robbins, *Descriptive Sketch of Winston-Salem*; Salem *People's Press*, Feb. 26, 1880; Winston *Union Republican*, Oct. 19, 1882 and Dec. 18, 1884; and H. A. Pfohl, "Fifty Years of Woodworking," Fogle Brothers Company Archives, Winston-Salem.

93. *MR*, Aug. 7, 1886; Raleigh *State Chronicle*, June 7, 1889.

94. See *Kernersville News*, June 15, 1883; *MR*, June 8, 1889; Raleigh *State Chronicle*, July 5, 1889; James W. Albright, *Greensboro, 1808–1904*, 96–98.

95. Raleigh *State Chronicle*, July 5, 1889.

96. Cummings, *Framed Houses of Massachusetts Bay*, 60.

97. Between July 1785 and October 1787, for example, fourteen house frames were listed in manifests of ships that cleared the port of Brunswick (Wilmington). The destination of all of these frames was Charleston. Treasurer's and Comptroller's Papers, Port of Brunswick, Box 10, Vessels Cleared, 1785–1790, A&H.

98. Hogg and Haywood Account Book, Aug. 1856, T. D. Hogg Papers, SHC.

99. Raleigh *Daily News*, Mar. 21 and Oct. 4, 1872. William Jones of Cary also manufactured "ready Built" houses. Raleigh *Daily News*, July 2, 1875.

100. See *Proceedings of the Stockholders*, 10; Raleigh *News and Observer*, May 30, 1882.

101. *Durham Recorder*, July 29, 1885.

102. Ibid.; University of North Carolina, *The Alumni Quarterly* 1 (Jan. 1895): 57; Raleigh *News and Observer*, Aug. 20, 1887; *MR*, May 11, 1889.

103. Tenth Census of the United States, 1880, Wake Co., N.C., Population Schedule, manuscript returns, A&H.

104. *Durham Recorder*, July 29, 1885.

105. *American Agriculturist* 46 (May 1887): 214.

106. See, for example, *Scientific American* 9 (Oct. 1, 1853): 24.

107. Francis Smith, *New Brick Machine*, 10–15.

108. Kinston *American Advocate*, Sept. 28, 1855; Raleigh *Spirit of the Age*, Oct. 3, 1855.

109. Raleigh *Daily News*, Jan. 11, 1876.

110. Salem *People's Press*, July 18, 1879; *Winston Leader*, Apr. 1, 1879. In Goldsboro in 1879, the brick used in the construction of the Bonitz House was manufactured by an Allen brick machine. *Wilmington Star*, Aug. 30, 1879.

111. Raleigh *News and Observer*, July 11, 1884.

112. Ibid., July 19, 1884.

113. *MR*, Feb. 3, 1893.

114. Pressed brick often cost from three to five times as much as common stock brick. See *American Architect and Building News* 2 (Sept. 8, 1877): 289–90 and Raleigh *Farmer and Mechanic*, Aug. 15, 1883.

115. *The Manufacturer and Builder* 1 (Feb. 1869): 35; *MR*, July 18, 1891.

116. *Wilmington Journal*, May 20, 1854. A few months later, M. W. Jarvis advertised in New Bern that he had just received 24,000 northern pressed bricks that had arrived aboard the schooner *Francis* from New York. *Newbern Journal*, Sept. 28, 1854.

117. Wilmington *Daily Journal*, Aug. 4, 1867.

118. Salem *People's Press*, July 19, 1877.

119. United States, *Tenth Census*, vol. 2, *Report on Manufactures*, 449.

120. *Durham Tobacco Plant*, Apr. 13, 1887.

121. United States, *Eighth Census*, vol. 3, *Manufactures*, 437–38.

122. United States, *Tenth Census*, vol. 2, *Report on Manufactures*, 449.

123. United States, *Twelfth Census*, vol. 8, *Manufactures*, 928.

124. Paul, *History of the Town of Durham*; *Raleigh Register*, Apr. 23, 1884; *MR*, Feb. 23, 1884.

125. *MR,* June 13, 1891.

126. Raleigh *News and Observer,* Apr. 9, 1887.

127. *MR,* Feb. 3, 1891.

128. See *American Architect and Building News* 2 (May 5, 1877): 143–44.

129. Raleigh *State Chronicle,* May 3, 1884.

130. *American Architect and Building News* 12 (Aug. 19, 1882): 84–85.

131. *The American Builder* 10 (Dec. 1874): 269.

132. *The Manufacturer and Builder* 11 (Mar. 1879): 56 and 11 (May 1879): 99.

133. Doucet and Weaver, "Material Culture," 571.

Chapter 5

1. Lefler and Newsome, *North Carolina,* 477–78.

2. Ibid., 80–81, 485.

3. Newspaper and journal references to the North as exemplary were frequent. See, for example, Charlotte *Daily Carolina Times,* July 30 and June 22, 1869; Raleigh *Farmer and Mechanic,* Jan. 17, 1883; and *MR,* Mar. 15, 1884. *MR* advertised the South as a place for industrialization like the North.

4. Henry E. Fries Papers, A&H. All subsequent references to the North Carolina Exposition of 1884, unless otherwise noted, are based on material included in the Henry E. Fries Papers. See also Raleigh *News and Observer,* Apr. 3, 18, 24, June 22, and Aug. 6, 1884.

5. *MR,* Nov. 8, 1884.

6. Raleigh *Daily Chronicle,* Oct. 1, 1884.

7. Furnifold Simmons to Henry E. Fries, Dec. 3, 1912. Fries apparently wrote to a number of prominent North Carolinians in 1912 asking them about the effect of the exposition. The respondents were Simmons, H. A. London, and W. J. Peele of Raleigh, all attorneys.

8. Raleigh *Daily Telegram,* Apr. 16, 1871.

9. Escott, *Many Excellent People,* 137–95.

10. Mansell, "American Tobacco Company," 3–15; Lounsbury, "From Craft to Industry," 127–40, 203–33, 272–94.

11. For accounts of growth, see Paul, *History of the Town of Durham,* xvi–xvii; *Durham Tobacco Plant,* Sept. 6, 1879; Charlotte *Southern Home,* Nov. 7, 1871; Raleigh *Daily News,* Oct. 2, 1874; Raleigh *News and Observer,* Sept. 9, 1881; Raleigh *Daily Constitution,* Aug. 11, 1875; *Oxford Torchlight,* May 25, 1886; Raleigh *State Chronicle,* Oct. 27, 1883.

12. Amis, *Historical Sketches;* Greensboro *New North State,* Dec. 7, 1871.

13. Raleigh *State Chronicle,* Sept. 27, 1883; *Raleigh Register,* Apr. 2 and 9, 1884.

14. Amis, *Historical Raleigh,* 67–68; *MR,* July 22, 1892.

15. Lefler and Newsome, *North Carolina,* 523–29, 533.

16. *Announcement of the A&M College,* 1889, 15, NCSUA.

17. *North Carolina A&M, Seventh Catalogue,* 1895; *Alumni Directory,* N.C. State College of Agriculture and Engineering, Raleigh, 1927, "Graduates Employed as Architects and Contractors in 1927," NCSUA.

18. Charlotte *Southern Home,* quoting Theodore Bourne of Raleigh to the *Christian Intelligencer,* Mar. 17, 1870.

19. Public Buildings Services, General Correspondence, Letters Received 1843–1910, Wake Co. Post Office and Courthouse, 1857–74, RG 121, NA.

20. Burns, *100 Courthouses* 2:74–79, 153–55, 366–72, 133–38, 354 (demolished, 1972), 447.

21. Raleigh *Daily News,* May 19, 1873.

22. Ibid., May 29, 1873.

23. Ibid., Oct. 7, 1874, quoting from *Durham Tobacco Plant.*

24. Pittsboro *Chatham Record,* Nov. 11, 1879, quoting from Raleigh *Hale's Weekly; Raleigh Register,* Feb. 27, 1884; Raleigh *News and Observer,* Sept. 23, 1886.

25. *Durham Tobacco Plant*, Dec. 22, 1886.

26. Mansell, "American Tobacco Company," 16–30.

27. Flowers, *Bull Durham*, 6, 41; Lounsbury, "From Craft to Industry," 31–33; *Handbook of Durham*, 10; Mansell, "American Tobacco Company," 58–60.

28. C. V. Brown, "Caraleigh Mill," Raleigh, 1981, National Register Nomination, A&H.

29. *MR*, Nov. 16, 1889.

30. Raleigh *State Chronicle*, Dec. 3, 1885. In Bishir and Earley, *Early Twentieth-Century Suburbs*, 31–76, five cities—Raleigh, Durham, Greensboro, Winston-Salem, and Charlotte—are presented and the patterns of post-1870s growth that affected suburban development in each city are well summarized and documented.

31. *Durham Tobacco Plant*, July 13, 1887; Raleigh *State Agricultural Journal*, July 31, 1875; Raleigh *Daily News*, Mar. 23, 1878; Raleigh *State Chronicle*, Aug. 30, 1884.

32. Swaim, *Cabins and Castles*, 38–42, 77–95; Brown, "Moore Square," in Harris, *Early Raleigh Neighborhoods*, 43–47; Little-Stokes, *Inventory of Historic Architecture, Greensboro*, 3–15; "The New South Neighborhoods: Biddlesville, Fourth Ward, and Myers Park," Charlotte-Mecklenburg Historic Properties Commission, Charlotte, 1981.

33. J. W. Cates Papers, Wake Forest University Archives, Winston-Salem.

34. Morrill, "Edward Dilworth Latta"; *MR*, May 16, 1891; Thomas Hanchett, "Historical Architecture of Charlotte," unpublished paper and notes supplied by author. See Raleigh *News and Observer*, Mar. 31 and Apr. 28, 1887, for further references to "old hulks."

35. *Raleigh Register*, Jan. 7, 1885, quoting from Durham *Chronicle* on Blackwell's property; *Durham Tobacco Plant*, July 13, 1887.

36. Bishir and Earley, *Early Twentieth-Century Suburbs*, 31–48, 59–67.

37. Charlotte-Mecklenburg, "Biddlesville"; Harris, *Early Raleigh Neighborhoods*, 25–30; Taylor, *From Frontier to Factory*, 55–67, esp. 57.

38. Woodward, *Strange Career of Jim Crow*, 11–49; Wilmoth Carter, *Urban Negro in the South*, 27–39, 142–48; Edmonds, *The Negro and Fusion Politics*, 20–23, 29–38.

39. Raleigh *News and Observer*, Apr. 12, 1887, quoting from article by C. T. Logan in Atlanta *Constitution*.

40. Lefler and Newsome, *North Carolina*, 523–29, 576–80.

41. *Fayetteville Observer*, June 27, 1859.

42. Jesse L. Jackson (b. 1874), typescript of autobiography, Pitt Co. Records, A&H.

43. Grady Vestal, interview with author, Dec. 1982, also noted in Vestal family Bible, in possession of Grady Vestal, Siler City, N.C.

44. William H. Worth Papers, A&H.

45. J. W. Cates Papers, Wake Forest University Archives, Winston-Salem, for this and all subsequent references.

46. W. S. Chaffin Collection, Duke, includes statements from the construction of Chaffin's house near Jonesboro in 1888. These records of the operations of a different building supply company provide a contrast to what one would expect of a builder like Cates. W. A. Sloan & Co. also supplied building materials and paid the artisans and laborers on Chaffin's project and billed Chaffin monthly. The total cost was $1,119.95 and was carried from August 8, 1888 to January 23, 1889. Chaffin paid $600 on December 29 and another $300 on January 23. Sloan, like Briggs of Raleigh, had other sources of income and could afford to carry Chaffin's project.

47. County Buildings and Township, Watauga Co. Records, A&H, for this and subsequent references to the county courthouse to be erected in Boone, contract executed June 3, 1873.

48. Lounsbury, "From Craft to Industry," 135–44, 284–85.

49. For an example of another building identical to Briggs Hardware, see Taylor, *From Frontier to Factory*, 36.

50. Col. J. N. Pease, interview with author, July 1981. As a young professional before

and during the depression, Pease worked for Lockwood Green.

51. County Buildings and Township, Watauga Co. Records, A&H.

52. Morrill, "Edward Dilworth Latta."

53. Briggs Hardware Account Books, A&H.

54. Lounsbury, "From Craft to Industry," 280–84.

55. North Carolina, *Public Laws*, 1868–69, chap. 117, *Public Laws*, 1869–70, chap. 206, *Laws and Resolutions*, 1887, chap. 67, *Laws and Resolutions*, 1891, chap. 203, and *Laws and Resolutions*, 1899, chap. 335.

56. James Briggs, "Briggs Family History," 1963. Copy in files of author.

57. Ibid. See also Briggs Hardware Account Books, A&H.

58. Public Building Records, Pasquotank Co. Records, A&H.

59. James H. Mitchell Papers, copies in author's files.

60. The Van Dorn Iron Works advertisements stressed the large number of counties and cities they had supplied. They installed a jail in Elizabeth City in 1889 which was bid by the Pauly Jail Co., which was equally busy installing jails in Beaufort County in 1893 and Watauga County in 1895.

61. Wilmoth Carter, Dec. 1980; Boynton Satterfield, Feb. 1981; James C. Stenhouse and Col. J. N. Pease, July 1981, interviews with author.

62. Raleigh *Sentinel*, Apr. 19, 1869 is an early postwar account of blacks working along-side whites on the North Carolina Standard Building in Raleigh, but these accounts are rare. Artisan-laborer, black-white enmity continued and was not discouraged. Edmonds, *The Negro and Fusion Politics*, 158–63.

63. Amis, *Historical Sketches*, 127; Lounsbury, "From Craft to Industry," 237–39.

64. Raleigh *News and Observer*, Aug. 24, 1899; *Wilmington Star*, Mar. 4, 1899. For subsequent accounts of Hanna's success covering the period 1900–1906, see William Reaves files, Wilmington.

65. Wilmington *Dispatch*, July 28, 1896.

66. "Death of Samuel Sloan," *American Architect and Building News*, Aug. 2, 1884, 49; Cooledge, *Samuel Sloan*. See also Bushong, "A. G. Bauer," 304–31.

67. Percy Clark, "New Federal Buildings," 365–68, for this and all subsequent references to the supervising architect of the Treasury.

68. Public Buildings Service, General Correspondence, Letters Received, 1843–1910, Wake Co. Post Office and Courthouse, RG 121, NA.

69. Federal Post Office and Courthouse, Statesville, N.C., ibid.

70. E. T. Avery to James H. Windrim, SA, Mar. 26, 1891, Adolf Cluss to Windrim, Sept. 23, 1891, S. A. Sharpe to Windrim, July 2, 1890, ibid.

71. Cluss to Windrim, Sept. 23, 1891, ibid.

72. Avery to Windrim, Mar. 26, 1892 and Cluss to Windrim, Sept. 23, 1891, ibid.

73. Tomlan, "Toward the Growth of an Artistic Taste." All subsequent references to Barber are from this source and from notes supplied to the author by Tomlan.

74. Specifications of J. M. Heck House, July 22, 1869, Jonathan M. Heck Papers, A&H; Harris and Lee, *Raleigh Architectural Inventory*, 79.

75. Raleigh *Daily Sentinel*, Jan. 18, 1870.

76. G. S. H. Appleget to A. B. Mullett, Sept. 12, 1872, Public Buildings Service, RG 121, NA; G. S. H. Appleget to American Institute of Architects, Scrapbook, 1857–74, RG 801, SR1.2, AIAA.

77. "Death of Samuel Sloan," *American Architect and Building News*, Aug. 2, 1884, 49; Bushong, "A. G. Bauer," 304–9.

78. "Death of Architect Charles Carson," *American Architect and Building News* 34, no. 835 (Dec. 1891): 190.

79. A. L. West to the Building Committee, Trinity College Building, Aug. 28, 1891, Trinity College, DUA.

80. William Bushong, "A. G. Bauer," 310. See also Ashe et al., *Biographical History of North Carolina*, 167–73.

81. Raleigh *Daily News*, May 21, 1873; "Black Bricklayers Strike for Higher Wages," Raleigh *State Chronicle*, Apr. 21 and 28, 1887. See also "The Prospects of Labor," *The Manufacturer and Builder*, May 1874, 98–99.

82. Wilmington *Dispatch*, July 28, 1896.

83. See Raleigh *Weekly Progressive*, Oct. 4, 1866; Raleigh *Daily Standard*, May 26, 1869; and Raleigh *Daily Telegram*, May 18, 1871 for accounts of various attempts by mechanics and workingmen to organize. The files of William Reaves of Wilmington contain many references to both workingmen's organizations and union activities. See, for example, from *Wilmington Star*, "Mechanics Aid and Protective Association," Jan. 8, 1869; Feb. 2, 1869; "Labor Union Association" (an organization for blacks and whites), Mar. 24, 1869; June 2, 1869; "Wilmington Mechanics and Blacks Union," Nov. 23, 1873; "Farmers, Mechanics, and Laborers Union and Association of New Hanover Co.," Mar. 8, 1874; and "Knights of Labor, White and Colored," Mar. 20 and May 1, 1886; and "Wilmington White Labor Union," Wilmington *Dispatch*, Oct. 28 and Nov. 21, 1898; *Wilmington Messenger*, Feb. 2, 1899. Following the Wilmington riots of 1898, which some historians attribute to the success and power of that city's black community, there was a marked preference for white labor in construction work. See, for example, *Wilmington Star*, Jan. 21, 1899; Edmonds, *The Negro and Fusion Politics*, 158–63.

84. Charles Hartge to John W. Root, May 6, 1890, RG 801, SR1, Box 4, AIAA.

85. Louise M. Hall, "Artificer to Architect," 19–39.

86. Based on biographical sketches to appear in a companion volume to this study; typescripts in author's files.

87. *Handbook of Architectural Practice*.

88. Dankmar Adler to W. P. Tinsley, Mar. 8 and June 26, 1892. Tinsley, of Lynchburg, Virginia, was secretary of the southern chapter, A. C. Bruce of Atlanta was the first president, and E. G. Lind was vice-president. The chapter was chartered in June 1892 and included members from Louisiana, Tennessee, South Carolina, Georgia, Kentucky, Alabama, Texas, Virginia, and Mississippi (RG 801, SR1, Box 6, Folder 1, AIAA). Alfred Stone, AIA secretary, wrote Tinsley on September 14, 1893 that "an increase in the membership . . . from the Southern states would . . . be a gain as it would help to extend its influence and to foster a more professional feeling . . . provided that the personal character and professional conduct of the man applying for membership is, however, of the proper standard" (RG 801, SR1.1, Box 3, vol. 8, AIAA). The correspondence between Stone and Tinsley continued in 1894 and 1895, and a central issue was whether southern chapter members were associate members of the institute and eligible to be Fellows (then equivalent to full membership). By 1894 the chapter had 61 members and M. J. Dimmock of Richmond was president, Thomas Morgan of Atlanta was vice-president, and Tinsley was secretary/treasurer. Thirteen members of the southern chapter were listed as members of the AIA (W. P. Tinsley to Alfred Stone, Sept. 29, 1894, RG 801, SR3, Box 1, Folder 24, AIAA). The southern chapter adopted the schedule of minimum charges established by the AIA in 1884. The fee was 5 percent for full professional service. Virtually no other references are made to the southern chapter. E. G. Lind wrote to Alfred Stone, February 13, 1897: "It was the percentage business closed up the last chapter." Whether this is in reference to a Baltimore chapter or the southern chapter is not clear (RG 801, SR1, Box 13, Folder 8, AIAA).

89. John M. Carrere to Alfred Stone, Dec. 10, 1896, RG 801, SR1, Box 11, Folder 5, AIAA.

90. Thomas Morgan to Glenn Brown, Feb. 18, 1899, RG 801, SR1, Box 5, Folder 12, AIAA.

91. Glenn Brown to Thomas Morgan, Jan. 18 and 23, 1899; Glenn Brown to Thomas Morgan, Feb. 2 and 19, 1899; RG 801, SR1, Box 5, vol. 12, AIAA.

92. F. K. Thomson to Glenn Brown, Feb. 9 and Mar. 1, 1899, RG 801, SR1, Box 16, Folder

7, AIAA; Glenn Brown to F. K. Thomson, Feb. 20, 1899, RG 801, SR1.1, Box 5, vol. 12, AIAA.

93. E. G. Lind to Alfred Stone, Feb. 13, 1897, RG 801, SR1, Box 13, Folder 8, AIAA.

Chapter 6

1. Lefler and Newsome, *North Carolina*, 550–63.

2. Ibid., 563–629; Hobbs, *North Carolina: Economic and Social*; Terrill and Hirsch, *Such as Us*.

3. Lefler and Newsome, *North Carolina*, 520–29, 580.

4. Ibid., 579.

5. Ibid., 620–29, 644–54.

6. *Raleigh Times*, Aug. 17, 1923.

7. Ibid., Aug. 12, 1931. See also *Raleigh Times*, Apr. 9, 1931, architects interviewed for commission; *Raleigh Times*, July 9 and 10, 1931, concerning commission and Atwood and Weeks; and Raleigh *News and Observer*, July 9 and 22, 1931, mentioning that the city had wanted to use stone like that used for the Capitol but it was too expensive.

8. *MR*, May 13, 1892.

9. See, for example, *Raleigh: Epitome of the City's Progress; Raleigh Illustrated*; Olds, *Annual Report*.

10. "A People Known by What They Build," Raleigh *News and Observer*, June 6, 1907. The writer is not identified. This special edition was published to celebrate the newspaper's new building.

11. Ibid.; Little-Stokes, *Inventory of Historic Architecture, Greensboro*, 16, 36, 37. See also Taylor, *From Frontier to Factory*, 55–65; and Marley Carroll, AIA, project architect for the restoration of the Reynolds building, interview with author, Feb. 1981.

12. Durham Life Insurance Company Building designed by Northup and O'Brien, Winston-Salem, Northup and O'Brien Papers, SHC.

13. Spillane, "Men and Mills of Greensboro," 2117.

14. *Wilmington Messenger*, Mar. 12, 1899.

15. "A People Known by What They Build," Raleigh *News and Observer*, June 6, 1907.

16. "New City Hall," Asheville *Citizen*, Mar. 18, 1928; Brendel, "Urban Asheville," 10–15; Swaim, *Cabins and Castles*, 30; Brendel, "Urban Asheville," 11. Photographs and notes in the files of the author.

17. Aberthaw Co. Report to University President, Apr. 28, 1921, cited in Wilson, *University of North Carolina*, 361–74.

18. Diane Lea and Ernest Wood, "Williamsburg Style Creates a Village Atmosphere," *North Carolina Architect* 26, no. 1 (Jan./Feb. 1979): 14–19.

19. Chancellor's Office, Presidents, 1889–1923, Box 1, Buildings, Chancellor's Office, Pres. E. C. Brooks, Chancellors' Reports, 1923–24, 1924–25, 1925–26, 1926–27; see also Board of Trustees, Executive Committee Meeting, Jan. 27, 1925, Chancellor's Office, Buildings, 1922–23, Box 1, 1926–27, Box 3, NCSUA. Hobart Upjohn's long-range plan was considered in 1923.

20. DUA has extensive correspondence and records on the design development and working drawings phases of the Gothic West Campus.

21. *Charlotte Observer*, Nov. 29, 1903.

22. The use of house-plan books and "souvenirs" as a form of advertising is beginning to be documented. Mary N. Woods of Cornell is doing a major study of this development in the nineteenth and early twentieth centuries. "By the 1920's," she writes, "there were at least three . . . publishing houses exclusively devoted to souvenir sketchbook production" (Woods to author, July 23, 1984). These books are an excellent guide to change in taste and style. In North Carolina, books from the first decade of the twentieth century show an ambivalence about what constitutes classical, colonial, or Georgian style. North Carolina architect W. P. Rose's *That House*, published in 1900, opens with an essay that reviews the

history of building in the state. It's not clear from the essay which style Rose favors, but the designs show a conscious eclecticism that relies heavily on antebellum architecture. The same is true of Barrett's *Southern Colonial Homes* from 1903 but they seem to be consciously moving from eclecticism toward a more academic classicism that can be seen in designs for work in Southern Pines. Copies of both books are in the NCC, along with several by Hook and Sawyer and Milburn.

23. *Charlotte Observer*, Dec. 20, 1903.

24. C. V. Brown, "Raleigh's Early Twentieth-Century Suburban Neighborhoods," National Register Nomination, 1981, A&H.

25. David R. Goldfield, "North Carolina's Early Twentieth Century Suburbs and the Urbanizing South," in Bishir and Earley, *Early Twentieth-Century Suburbs*, 9–19; C. V. Brown, "Raleigh's Early Twentieth-Century Suburban Neighborhoods," National Register Nomination, 1981, A&H; Hanchett, "Architectural Resources of Charlotte"; Taylor, *From Frontier to Factory*, 55–65; Little-Stokes, *Inventory of Historic Architecture, Greensboro*, 16–19.

26. Hook and Sawyer, *Some Designs*; Hanchett, "Foursquare Housetype."

27. Luther Lashmit, interview with author, Feb. 1981. See also Plans and Specifications for the Lindsay Holcomb Residence, Mt. Airy, Job File #1128, Northup and O'Brien Papers, SHC.

28. Lashmit interview.

29. Thomas Hanchett, "Charlotte," in Bishir and Earley, *Early Twentieth-Century Suburbs*, 68–75; Morrill, "Edward Dilworth Latta," 301–50; C. V. Brown, "The Glenwood Neighborhood," in Harris, *Early Raleigh Neighborhoods*, 31–34.

30. C. V. Brown, "The Cameron Park Neighborhood," in Harris, *Early Raleigh Neighborhoods*, 39–42.

31. "A People Known by What They Build," Raleigh *News and Observer*, June 6, 1907.

32. C. V. Brown and William Bushong, "Boylan Heights," in Harris, *Early Raleigh Neighborhoods*, 34–39.

33. Wilmoth Carter, *Urban Negro in the South*, 27–82, 85–141; C. V. Brown, "Moore Square Area," in Harris, *Early Raleigh Neighborhoods*, 43–47.

34. Boyce, *History of Chowan County*, 119.

35. Whitehead, "Work of Aymar Embury," 506.

36. For example, William Bass Shelton, a skilled carpenter from Mt. Airy in Surry County, near the Virginia line, was hired to work on the Carolina Hotel in Pinehurst and regularly took the train to Pinehurst to work during the week and then returned home by train on weekends. Frances L. Shelton, interview with author, Apr. 1987.

37. Boyce, *History of Chowan County*, 119.

38. Mary V. Vestal, interview with author, Dec. 1983.

39. J. E. Holland Papers, Elizabeth Reid Murray files, Raleigh; Jesse M. Page, interview with author and William Bushong, Feb. 1981; James C. Stenhouse, Col. J. N. Pease, and Norman Pease, Jr., interviews with author and Ernest Wood, July 1981. See, for example, notes on W. D. Tucker, Herman Moore, S. Beaman, Valentine Rackley, Stewart Ellison, Howard Satterfield in author's files. Peter Demens, contractor for the Statesville Courthouse and Post Office (1890–91), was not only a builder but also a land speculator whose involvement in railroad building gave him the experience to become a general contractor in Asheville. Michael Southern, "Peter Demens," author's files.

40. Public Buildings Service, General Correspondence and Related Records, 1910–1939, Fayetteville, N.C., Post Office, RG 121, NA.

41. These and all subsequent references to Howard Satterfield, unless otherwise noted, are based on copies of notes in author's files, a family history generously loaned to author by Boynton Satterfield, and an interview with him in Feb. 1981.

42. Specifications for the M. W. Ranson House, Littleton, generously loaned to author by the owners; copy in author's files.

43. George C. Little Papers, A&H.

44. Poem for Miss Nell Battle, on the completion of 1501 St. Mary's Street, Raleigh, generously loaned to author by the owners, William and Jane Myatt; copy in author's files.

45. These and all subsequent references to J. W. Coffey and Sons, unless otherwise noted, are based on interviews with Mr. and Mrs. J. N. Coffey, Jr., Mrs. Frances Coffey Green, sister of J. N., Jr., and daughter of J. W., by author and Marilyn Dutton, Feb. 1982, and on records generously loaned to author by the Coffey family.

46. These and all subsequent references to James A. Davidson, unless otherwise noted, are based on an interview with Davidson by author and William Bushong, March 1981, and on records generously loaned to author; copies in author's files.

47. *The Sweets Catalogue File* (New York: McGraw-Hill Information Systems Co., 1980). *Sweets* is published annually and is a multivolume resource of approximately 12 to 17 volumes.

48. *Handbook of Architectural Practice*, 15, Appendix E.

49. *Handbook of Architectural Practice*, 58–62, Appendixes J and K. Dundin, "AIA Standard Documents."

50. Repositories for plans and specifications called plan rooms were first provided by the Associated General Contractors for general contractors in Charlotte in 1922. This practice was encouraged because contractors could survey work and determine if they wanted to bid on it before having to pay for a set of plans and specifications, as required for most large jobs, particularly for the state (Moorhead, *Construction in the Carolinas*, 25). It has also been suggested that plan rooms encourage bid-rigging because they give contractors the opportunity to discuss work under consideration. Some architectural and engineering firms now have plan rooms in their offices. Pease interviews with author, July 1981.

51. Philip Green, Jr., "North Carolina's Comprehensive Building Regulation System," *Popular Government* 45, no. 4 (Spring 1980): 26–31. North Carolina enacted a building law in 1905 that governed construction in all towns with populations over one thousand, thus permitting great mobility for members of the building trades.

52. Bernard M. Boyle, "Architectural Practice in America, 1865–1965," in Kostof, *The Architect*, 317.

53. Contract loaned to author by James Bonitz; copy in author's files.

54. Lashmit, Page, and Stenhouse interviews.

55. Marvin Johnson, AIA, interview with author, July 1982. Johnson was a staff member of the Division of School Planning, North Carolina Department of Public Instruction. He described school planning prior to 1950 from his knowledge of documents and his association with former staff members who are now deceased. He described the "Linthicum plan."

56. Lashmit, Pease, Page, and Stenhouse interviews.

57. Lashmit, Stenhouse, and Page interviews; Northup and O'Brien Papers (practice opened in Winston-Salem, 1907) and Louis (Lewis) Asbury Papers (practice opened in Charlotte, ca. 1925), SHC. See also *Handbook of Architectural Practice*.

58. Lewis H. Asbury to E. C. Griffin, Sept. 5 and 28, 1944; Asbury to AIA, Oct. 30, 1944; Asbury to Payne-Spiers Studios and to Pittsburgh Stained Glass Studios, Nov. 6, 1944; Asbury to F. L. S. Mayer and others, Nov. 14, 1944; and Asbury Office Files, Christ Church, Charlotte, Louis (Lewis) Asbury Papers, SHC.

59. Conrad Wessel, AIA, Goldsboro, successor to J. Allen Maxwell, interview with author, July 1982.

60. Luther Lashmit to author, Sept. 1981.

61. William King, Duke University archivist, interview with author, Feb. and Mar. 1981.

62. C. C. Hook to W. P. Few, Nov. 11, 1912, William C. Few, Trinity College, DUA.

63. Hook to Few, Mar. 2, 1911, ibid.

64. Hook to Few, Oct. 6 and Feb. 25, 1911, ibid.

65. William P. Few to persons unnamed, copy sent to Hook, Apr. 1, 1911, ibid.

66. Montgomery Schuyler, "The Architecture of American Colleges. VIII: The Southern Colleges," *Architectural Record* 30 (July 1911): 62–64.

67. Wilson, *University of North Carolina*, 361–74.

68. Ibid., 368–69; *Greensboro Daily News*, Apr. 22, 1921; *Durham Herald*, Apr. 22, 1921; Raleigh *News and Observer*, Apr. 22, 1921.

69. *Greensboro Daily News*, May 22, 1921; Winston-Salem *Journal*, May 22, 1921. See also Trustee Minutes, 1917–24, 306–7, 315–16, cited in Wilson, *University of North Carolina*, 368–69.

70. *Greensboro Daily News*, May 22, 1921.

71. *Durham Herald*, May 25, 1921. See also Brent S. Drane to the Editor, *Charlotte Observer*, June 1, 1921, in support of single contractor and method of work.

72. Earl Hartsell, "Expending a Million and a Half for a Greater University," *The Carolina Magazine* 52, no. 7 (Apr. 1922): 22–24.

73. McKim, Mead, and White, *Buildings Designed for Educational Institutions*.

74. Henderson, *First State University*, Appendix C, University Buildings, 363–69.

75. Gaines, *King's Maelum*, 79–82.

76. Pease interviews and notes on the work of the firm in author's files.

77. Anthony Lord, interview with author, Sept. 1981; Gaines, *King's Maelum*, 79–82.

78. Pease interviews.

79. Lord interview.

80. Luther Lashmit to author, Sept. 1981.

81. Duke University Building Accounts, 1925–40, DUA.

82. "The Diary of the Post Office, Fayetteville, N.C.," Francis Brooke Stein Library, Fayetteville; Public Buildings Service, General Correspondence, 1910–1939, Box 339, RG 121, NA.

83. E. H. Clement (masonry supervisor) to Horace Trumbauer, Aug. 2, 1937, Building Accounts, Daybooks and Ledgers, DUA.

84. Wilmington *Dispatch*, Oct. 6, 1902 described attempts by the American Federation of Labor to organize there; Nov. 24, 1902 reported on a Central Federation of Labor which was to include representatives from Carpenters and Engineers and Electrical Wire Workers, along with railroad employees of all kinds. *Wilmington Star*, June 9, 1907 announced that "the building trades of Wilmington have now been thoroughly organized . . . [and] more satisfactory conditions are promised for the building men of the city." The evidence tells us, however, that nothing changed. On Aug. 26, 1917, the *Dispatch* reported that the Carpenters and Joiners adopted a minimum wage of fifty cents per hour for a nine-hour day with time and a half for overtime and double time for holidays and an eight-hour day beginning November 1, 1917. North Carolina, *32nd Report of the Department of Labor and Printing* reported, however, a very limited membership in building trade unions and that the workday remained between nine and ten hours. (31–33). This continued to be true until after World War II.

85. *Laurinburg Exchange*, Apr. 1, 5, 1949; Butchko, *Inventory of Historic Architecture*.

86. Burton Bledstein, *The Culture of Professionalism*, 80–128; Dell Upton, "Pattern Books," 107–50.

87. Attempts at some kind of organization occurred before 1906. Charles Pearson, a Raleigh architect, wrote Glenn Brown on December 20, 1900 telling him of a meeting held in Raleigh on October 25, 1900 by a group of men who agreed to try to organize a North Carolina chapter of the AIA. He asked Brown to send copies of the AIA constitution and by-laws and requirements for membership. Pearson also said that he would include a copy of the minutes of the Raleigh meeting, which would presumably list those people present and give increased credibility to Pearson's ambitions. Unfortunately he either failed to send the minutes or they were lost. What connections, if any, this meeting had to later ones is unclear because Pearson soon left North Carolina and there is no way of knowing who else was involved in this effort (RG 801, SR1, Box 18, Folder 2; and see also RG 801, SR1, 1901P, Box 20, Folder 7, AIAA).

88. See Franklin Gordon (Charlotte architect) to Glenn Brown, June 19, 1906, telling of an association "taking shape in the state" and asking for the AIA constitution and by-laws (RG 801, SR1, Box 31, Folder 9, AIAA). There are similar requests from H. E. Bonitz, Wilmington (RG 801, SR11, Box 10, vol. 35) and from Barrett and Thomson, Raleigh (RG 801, SR11, Box 5, vol. 12 and RG 801, SR1, Box 33, Folder 1). Frank Thomson to Glenn Brown, Feb. 10, 1909, describes a licensing act being prepared and a bill considered in the General Assembly (RG 801, SR1, Box 40, Folder 4, AIAA), and Franklin Gordon to Glenn Brown, Jan. 11, 1909, contained a copy of the proposed act (RG 801, SR1, Box 40, Folder 4). See also *Wilmington Star*, July 9, 1907 and Wilmington *Dispatch*, June 28, 1909 for accounts of meetings of the North Carolina Architectural Association.

89. Glenn Brown to Hill C. Linthicum, Oct. 18 and 30, Nov. 1 and 20, 1911, and May 27, 1912; Hill C. Linthicum to Glenn Brown, Sept. 23, 1912, with draft of licensing act to be introduced to the North Carolina General Assembly; RG 801, SR4, Box 3, Folder 1, AIAA.

90. Hill C. Linthicum to Glenn Brown, Sept. 23, 1912. The "boys" were R. S. Smith, Asheville; W. C. Northup, Winston-Salem; G. R. Rose, Durham, and Linthicum. Linthicum to Brown, Nov. 13, 1912, ibid.

91. Brown to Linthicum, Nov. 16, 1912; Linthicum to Brown, Dec. 17, 1912, ibid.

92. Brown to Linthicum, Jan. 22, 1913, ibid.

93. Linthicum to Brown, Aug. 8 and 12, 1913; Brown to Linthicum, Sept. 6, 1913; Linthicum to Brown, Sept. 18, 1913, ibid.

94. Linthicum to D. Knickerbocker Boyd, AIA secretary, Sept. 17, 1913, RG 801, SR5, Boyd, Box 14, Folder 1, AIAA. Brown to Linthicum, Sept. 25, 1913, RG 801, SR4, Box 3, AIAA.

95. Louise M. Hall, AIA, *N.C. Chapter Centennial Observance AIA 1857–1957*, 13.

96. AIA Membership Lists and Louise Hall, "Founding Fathers, NCAIA," N.C. Chapter, AIA, A&H.

97. Wilmington *Dispatch*, Mar. 19 and 26, 1915. See also N.C. Board of Architectural Registration, microfilm, A&H. A tragic automobile accident in 1933 killed W. H. Lord of Asheville who had served as NCAIA president from 1917 to 1920 and as president of the National Council of Architectural Registration Boards. Records of the board and the AIA were destroyed in the accident. Thus, there is little archival material on the board. Hall, "Founding Fathers, NCAIA," N.C. Chapter AIA, A&H; Lord interview.

98. Turpin C. Bannister, *The Architect at Mid-Century: Evolution and Achievement* (New York, 1954) = *Report of the Commission for the Survey of Education and Registration of the American Institute of Architects*, 1:357. Bannister gives the following list: Illinois first licensed architects in 1897, Arkansas and California in 1901, New Jersey in 1902, Colorado in 1909, Utah in 1910, and North Carolina, *incorrectly*, in 1913. He may have confused the date of the chartering of the NCAIA with the date for the passage of the practice act.

99. North Carolina, *Public Laws*, 1915, chap. 270.

100. N.C. Chapter AIA, "Requirements for Membership," copy in author's files.

101. To be discussed in Chapter 7.

102. N.C. Board of Architectural Registration, microfilm, A&H.

103. Davidson interview; Moorhead, *Construction in the Carolinas*, 7–8.

104. Moorhead, *Construction in the Carolinas*, 9.

105. Ibid.

106. Ibid., 14.

107. North Carolina, *Public Laws*, 1921, chap. 1. Montgomery Spier (executive director, N.C. Board of Licensing for Engineers and Land Surveyors), interview with author, July 1981.

108. Moorhead, *Construction in the Carolinas*, 14–15.

109. North Carolina, *Public Laws*, 1920, chap. 318, 1931, chap. 62. The licensing board for general contractors only keeps files of general contractors who have kept their licenses active for the past five years. All other records of licenses have been destroyed. A list of some older

and current licenses is available on microfilm but the records are poor (A&H).

110. Davidson interview.

111. N.C. Board of Registration for General Contractors, microfilm, A&H.

112. Survey of North Carolina, *Catalogue[s] of the North Carolina State College*, 1889–1920; Lefler and Newsome, *North Carolina*, 589–97.

113. *Alumni Directory*, N.C. State College of Agriculture and Engineering, 1927.

114. North Carolina, *Catalogue of the North Carolina State College*, 1920–21, 92–93.

115. Ibid., 93–94; Joan Draper, "The Ecole des Beaux-Arts and the Architectural Profession in the U.S.: The Case of John Howard Galen," in Kostof, *The Architect*, 209–35.

116. Raleigh *News and Observer*, obituary, Apr. 9, 1960. See also Shumaker, Membership File, Inactive, N.C. Chapter, AIA, A&H.

117. Ross Shumaker, "Brief on the Department of Architectural Engineering," School of Engineering, Annual Reports, 1932–33, NCSUA.

118. Lashmit, Pease, Page, and Stenhouse interviews; Ross Shumaker, "Brief on the Department of Architectural Engineering," School of Engineering, Annual Reports, 1940–41, NCSUA.

119. North Carolina, *Catalogue of the North Carolina State College*, 1927–28, 98.

120. Ibid.

121. "The Construction Program at NCSC," School of Engineering Committees, Curricula 1940–41, NCSUA.

Chapter 7

1. "85th Fair Proves an Eye Popper," Raleigh *News and Observer*, Oct. 15, 1952.

2. William Henley Deitrick, "Matthew at the Fair," in *Student Publication of the School of Design*, 1:22.

3. "Eight-Million Dollar State Fair Plant Planned," Raleigh *News and Observer*, Oct. 13, 1950.

4. Henry Kamphoefner, interview with author, Feb. 1982.

5. Lewis Mumford, "Skyline," in *The New Yorker*, Nov. 18, 1950.

6. Ernest Wood, "A Radical Settles Down in Raleigh," 54.

7. "State Fair Begins Five Day Run; Governor Leads Dedication Rites," Raleigh *News and Observer*, Oct. 21, 1953.

8. Ernest Wood, "A Radical Settles Down in Raleigh."

9. United States, *1980 Census of Population, Number of Inhabitants*, 7.

10. Lefler and Newsome, *North Carolina*, 649, 644.

11. Ibid., 642.

12. Ibid., 630.

13. United States, *1980 Census of Population, Number of Inhabitants*, 5.

14. United States, *1980 Census of the Population*, vol. 1, *Characteristics of the Population, Occupations by Industry*, 503.

15. North Carolina, "Labor and Industry," July, Aug., Sept., and Oct. 1945, Oct. 1946, Oct. 1948.

16. United States, "Construction Authorized in North Carolina by City, by Month, 1980 and 1985," computer printouts provided by N.C. Department of Labor, in author's files.

17. Alastair Muirhead, interview with author, Dec. 1987.

18. Ibid.

19. Tommy Lampley, interview with author, Feb. 1988.

20. Muirhead interview.

21. Lampley interview.

22. Henry Kamphoefner to Josef Albers, Dec. 14, 1948, N.C. Chapter, AIA, A&H.

23. Henry Kamphoefner to Frank Graham, May 6, 1949, School of Design Papers, NCSUA.

24. Henry Kamphoefner, *The Agromeck* manuscript, 1949, ibid.

25. Hubert M. Willis to Henry Kamphoefner, Mar. 13, 1954, ibid.

26. Henry Kamphoefner to W. S. Hamilton, Nov. 13, 1952, ibid.

27. Henry Kamphoefner to the Rev. R. F. Lineberger, Jan. 18, 1957, ibid.

28. "A Designing Man: Looking Back on the Career A. G. Odell Built," *Charlotte Observer*, Aug. 15, 1982.

29. A. G. Odell to Prof. C. G. Brennecke, Oct. 1, 1953, N.C. Chapter, AIA, A&H.

30. "Goodby to Gothic and Williamsburg," *Charlotte News*, Jan. 10, 1955.

31. Chester Davis to Henry Kamphoefner, July 19, 1948, School of Design Papers, NCSUA.

32. Irving C. Carlyle to Henry Kamphoefner, Mar. 29, 1949, "C" Misc. 34–53 File, ibid.

33. Henry Kamphoefner to Irving C. Carlyle, Mar. 30, 1949, "W" Misc. 40–64 File, ibid.

34. "Wake Forest Architect Hits 'Do Nothing' of Modernists," undated newspaper clipping, "W" Misc. 40–64 File, ibid.

35. Henry Kamphoefner to John Allcott, July 30, 1948, UNC Art Dept. File, ibid.

36. Vivian H. Schreffler to Archie Royal Davis, Mar. 21, 1951, McIver Residence/Chapel Hill Planning Board File, Archie Royal Davis Papers, SHC.

37. Henry Kamphoefner to Lewis Mumford, Oct. 5, 1951, School of Design Papers, NCSUA.

38. Henry Kamphoefner to Lewis Mumford, Oct. 5, 1951 (different letter), ibid.

39. Lewis Mumford to Henry Kamphoefner, July 1, 1952, ibid.

40. WPTF Broadcast Transcript, June 19, 1952, ibid.

41. Board Minutes, Architectural Foundation 1952 File, N.C. Chapter, AIA, A&H.

42. "Roundtable: Regionalism Present," *North Carolina Architect*, Jan.–Feb. 1978, 18.

43. Albert Haskins to James Hempill, Nov. 10, 1961, N.C. Chapter, AIA, A&H.

44. "Not a Monument for an Architect," Raleigh *News and Observer*, Aug. 12, 1957.

45. United States, *Census of Population: 1950*, 260.

46. United States, *1980 Census of Population*, vol. 1, *Characteristics of the Population*, 504.

47. "Sign of the Times: Hamburger Architecture," Raleigh *News and Observer*, Jan. 25, 1976.

48. North Carolina, "Report on the Licensing Board for Tile Contractors."

49. Stephanie M. Stubbs, "The Widening Webb of Codes and Standards," in *Architecture*, Dec. 1987, 128.

50. R. Mayne Albright to John D. Watson, Dec. 2, 1970, N.C. Chapter, AIA, A&H.

51. Becky Griffin, North Carolina Manufactured Housing Institute, interview with author, Aug. 1981.

52. "Production of Mobile/Manufactured Homes by State, January–December 1988" and "Shipments of Mobile/Manufactured Homes by State, January–December 1988," typescript statistics, Manufactured Housing Institute, Arlington, Va.

53. Goodpasture Communications, Charlotte, public relations counsel for the North Carolina Manufactured Housing Institute, to author, Jan. 16, 1989; letter in possession of author.

54. "Average Multi-Section now $37,276, Monthly Payment Averages $397," *North Carolina Manufactured Housing News*, N.C. Manufactured Housing Institute, Nov. 1988.

55. Griffin interview.

56. Goodpasture Communications to author.

57. Griffin interview.

58. "Production of Mobile/Manufactured Homes by State."

59. Griffin interview.

60. Goodpasture Communications to author.

61. *North Carolina Manufactured Housing News*, articles on association's twentieth anniversary, Jan. 1988, cover, 2, 7.

62. Lowe's, *1986 Annual Report*, 23.

63. Lowe's Corporate History, 1.

64. Ibid., 1–2.

65. Ibid., 2–3.

66. Ibid., 3–4.

67. Ibid., 4, 7.

68. Ibid., 7, 9, 10.

69. Lowe's, *1986 Annual Report*, 1.

70. Ibid., 24–25, 18, 1, 22, 21.

71. Ibid., 18.

72. "Breaking Down Barriers, Stubbornly, by Design," Raleigh *News and Observer*, Aug. 7, 1988.

73. Society of Certified Kitchen Designers, *Directory of Certified Kitchen Designers, 1986–87*.

74. Gwen Taylor, administrative assistant to North Carolina Chapter, American Society of Interior Designers, Charlotte, interview with author, Apr. 1988.

75. Ernest H. Wood, "As the Decade Turns . . . Architecture Changes Directions," *North Carolina Architect*, Jan.–Feb. 1980, 11, 12.

76. John Vogel, spokesman for *Mother Earth News*, interview with author, Aug. 6, 1981, notes in possession of author.

77. Lefler and Newsome, *North Carolina*, 715.

78. N.C. Agricultural Extension Service, *1945 Annual Report*, 1.

79. N.C. Agricultural Extension Service, *1946 Annual Report*, 1.

80. N.C. Agricultural Extension Service, *1947 Annual Report*, 1.

81. N.C. Agricultural Extension Service, *1948 Annual Report*, 3.

82. Green, *House Building by Farm Owners*, 35–37, 44.

83. Ibid., 46, 47, 48, 56, 60, 61, 70.

84. Ibid., 70, 77, 71.

85. Ibid., 80, 87, 93.

86. Ibid., 15, 21, 22, 25, 26.

87. United States, *Census of Housing: 1970*, 35–94.

88. N.C. Agricultural Extension Service, *1951 Annual Report*, 7.

89. N.C. Agricultural Extension Service, *1954 Annual Report*, 13–14.

90. Ibid., 17.

91. N.C. Agricultural Extension Service, *1960 Annual Report*, 12.

92. N.C. Agricultural Extension Service, *1961 Annual Report*, 26.

93. N.C. Agricultural Extension Service, *1962 Annual Report*, 12.

94. Ibid., 15.

95. Woodley C. Warrick, interview with author, Sept. 1981.

96. Ibid.

97. Glenda Herman, interview with author, Sept. 1981.

98. Warrick interview.

99. John Watts, interview with author, Apr. 1988.

100. Wayne McArthur, interview with author, Apr. 1988.

101. Watts interview.

102. Ibid.

103. Ibid.

104. Ibid.

105. McArthur interview.

106. Ibid.

107. Ibid.

108. United States, *Census of Population: 1950*, 260.

109. United States, *1980 Census of Population*, vol. 1, *Characteristics of the Population*, 503.

110. United States, *Historical Statistics*, 32.

111. United States, *Census of Population: 1950*, 241–52.

112. United States, *1980 Census of Population*, vol. 1, *Characteristics of the Population*, 266, 271.

113. North Carolina, "Labor and Industry," Feb. 1945.

114. Ibid., Aug. 1943.

115. United States, *Census of Population: 1950*, 226.

116. United States, *1980 Census of Population*, vol. 1, *Characteristics of the Population*, 271.

117. Ramsbotham and Farmer, "Women Working."

118. R. B. Fitch, interview with author, Nov. 1985.

119. N.C. Employment Security Commission, "Prevailing Wage Rates in the Construction Industry, Eleven North Carolina Cities," typescript, Chapter Publications File, N.C. Chapter, AIA, A&H.

120. "Who Does What: A Team Effort," Raleigh *Spectator*, Feb. 11, 1988, S7.

121. "Roundtable: Regionalism Present," typescript of Nov. 4, 1977 roundtable discussion in possession of author.

122. H. S. Crain, "Construction Education—A Responsibility of Management," typescript of speech, July 1962, Summer Meeting 62 File, N.C. Chapter, AIA, A&H.

123. John M. Crumpton, Jr., N.C. Department of Labor, interview with author, July 1981.

124. N.C. Department of Labor computer printouts, provided by John M. Crumpton, 1981, in possession of author.

125. North Carolina, "Projections to 1982."

126. N.C. Department of Labor, typescript descriptions of apprenticeship requirements, 1981.

127. Crumpton interview.

128. Listing and description of community college and technical institute programs, *North Carolina Architect*, May–June 1974, 16–20.

129. H. James Owen, Department of Public Instruction, Division of Community Colleges, interview with author, June 1981.

130. Crumpton interview.

131. Letter to the Editor, Raleigh *News and Observer*, Jan. 16, 1988.

132. Emmett Sebrell, executive vice-president and vice-chairman of the board, McDevitt and Street Company, interview with author, Apr. 1988.

133. Ede Graves, public relations director, The Jones Group, interview with author, Apr. 1988.

134. Sebrell interview.

135. "The Top 400 Contractors," *Engineering News Record*, Apr. 14, 1988, 38, 40, 46, 47, 50, 53.

136. Sebrell and Graves interviews.

137. Sebrell interview.

138. "The Village That Willie Built," Raleigh *News and Observer*, Dec. 15, 1974, IV-1.

139. Edmisten, *J. W. Willie York*, 132–33.

140. "Companies Use Different Styles to Get to the Top," Raleigh *News and Observer*, Feb. 14, 1988, F1.

141. "Home Builders Cite Lucrative Ripple Effect," Raleigh *News and Observer*, Nov. 18, 1984, F1.

142. Henry McGowan, N.C. Licensing Board for General Contractors, interview with author, Apr. 1988.

143. Henry McGowan, interview with author, Nov. 1985.

144. Henry McGowan, interview with author, May 1981.

145. McGowan interview, 1985.

146. Eugene Gulledge, interview with author, Nov. 1985.

147. Ibid.

148. Ibid.

149. Ibid.

150. Ibid.

151. Ibid.

152. Forrest Wilson, "A Time of Relentless Technological Change," in *Architecture*, Dec. 1987, 116.

153. Gulledge interview.

154. Ibid.

155. C. L. Reavis, interview with author, Oct. 1985.

156. Ibid.

157. Gulledge interview.

158. Mel Daughtridge, interview with author, Oct. 1985.

159. "Brick by Brick: The Diary of a First-Time Home Builder," Raleigh *Spectator*, Feb. 11, 1988, S5.

160. Daughtridge interview.

161. Gulledge interview.

162. Daughtridge interview.

163. Ibid.

164. Reavis interview.

165. Ibid.

166. John Crosland, Jr., interview with author, Oct. 1985.

167. Ibid.

168. Ibid.

169. Ibid.

170. "John Crosland, Jr."

171. Paul Leonard, vice president of John Crosland Company, interview with author, Feb. 1989.

172. Fitch interview.

173. Ibid.

174. Carolyn LeBauer to Archie Royal Davis and Davis to LeBauer, various letters, File #4259, Archie Royal Davis Papers, SHC.

175. R. Emory Holroyd, Report on the Home Building Industry, Feb. 1, 1956, N.C. Chapter, AIA, A&H.

176. A. G. Odell, memo, Jan. 31, 1955, Misc. Jan. 55–57 File, ibid.

177. Conrad Wessell, 1961 Report, NCAIA Committee on Relations with the Home Building Industry, ibid.

178. Henry Kamphoefner to Chancellor J. W. Harrelson, Nov. 25, 1947, School of Design Papers, NCSUA.

179. Henry Kamphoefner to M. Luke Lietzke, Akron Art Institute, Oct. 1, 1948, "A" Misc. 35–52 File, ibid.

180. Henry Kamphoefner to Harwell Hamilton Harris, "H" Misc. 42–53 File, ibid.

181. Henry Kamphoefner to Ossian P. Ward, Secretary of the Western Kentucky Chapter, AIA, AIA 54–57 File, ibid.

182. School of Design History, typescript, National Architectural Accrediting Board File, ibid.

183. School of Design Annual Report, July 30, 1949, Harrelson 47–50 File, ibid.

184. Enrollment statistics, 1948–1959, ibid.

185. Henry Kamphoefner, School of Design Annual Report, Dean of Faculty 65–67 File, ibid.

186. Kamphoefner interview.

187. Jefferson D. Brooks III to Henry Kamphoefner, June 18, 1961, Misc. 64–66 File, School of Design Papers, NCSUA.

188. Kamphoefner interview.

189. Henry Kamphoefner, "The School's Beginnings," in *North Carolina Architect*, Sept.–Oct. 1978, 11.

190. Henry Kamphoefner to Beemer Harrell, July 14, 1956, Architects, State, 56–58 File, School of Design Papers, NCSUA.

191. Henry Kamphoefner, School of Design Annual Report, 1960, ibid.

192. J. Bertram King, interview with author, Aug. 1981.

193. United States, *Census of Population: 1950*, 226, 241.

194. United States, *1980 Census of Population*, vol. 1, *Characteristics of the Population*, 266.

195. Various letters concerning membership, 1961, Membership File, N.C. Chapter, AIA, A&H.

196. J. Burton Wilder to Albert Haskins, July 28, 1961, Membership File, ibid.

197. Wood, "As the Decade Turns," 14.

198. "Architect/Planner Discusses New Role as Charlotte's Mayor," *Architecture*, Feb. 1984, 30.

199. Wood, "As the Decade Turns," 13.

200. "Ten Best Designs of 1984," *Time*, Jan. 7, 1985.

201. NCAIA newsletter, Judiciary Committee 52–54 File, N.C. Chapter, AIA, A&H.

202. "Peers and Chapter Solidarity," *Journal of the AIA*, Oct. 1953, 177–79.

203. Carter Williams to Marion A. Ham, May 5, 1954, Judiciary Committee 52–54 File, N.C. Chapter, AIA, A&H.

204. Odell Associates, statement, Old Business 1962 File, ibid.

205. W. R. James to A. G. Odell, Architect-State Fee Committee 1953 File, ibid.

206. A. G. Odell to Ross Schumaker, Sept. 28, 1953, ibid.

207. Scott William Braley, Georgia State University, "Oh, Sherman, You've Done it Again," typescript, Mar. 13, 1975, AIAA.

208. Charles C. Hartman to NCAIA, Mar. 24, 1959, Executive Committee 58–61 File, N.C. Chapter, AIA, A&H.

209. Thomas P. Heritage to NCAIA, Aug. 17, 1959, ibid.

210. Carter Williams to McMinn, Norfleet, and Wicker, Jan. 20, 1955, Judiciary Committee 52–54 File, ibid.

211. AIA Press Release, 1954, ibid.

212. Henry Kamphoefner to J. B. Kirkland, May 28, 1951, School of Education 51–58 File, School of Design Papers, NCSUA.

213. William Henley Deitrick to George Hackney, Nov. 26, 1947, N.C. Chapter, AIA, A&H.

214. R. Mayne Albright and Haskins, *Handbook of North Carolina Building Laws*, 90, 92–93.

215. Ibid., editor's note, 93.

216. R. Mayne Albright, memo to NCAIA membership, Sept. 26, 1953, Chapter Business and Meetings, 1953 File, N.C. Chapter, AIA, A&H.

217. R. Mayne Albright, Summary of Unauthorized Practice in 1961, N.C. Chapter, AIA, A&H.

218. Cynthia Skidmore, North Carolina Board of Architecture, interview with author, Apr. 1988.

219. James Stenhouse to North Carolina Division of Property Control, Apr. 24, 1962, Office Practice File, N.C. Chapter, AIA, A&H.

220. Ibid.

221. Ibid.

222. Ibid.

223. Treasurer's Records, 1954, ibid.

224. A. G. Odell to William Stanley Parker, Boston, Mass., July 14, 1954, AIA Personal 53–54 File, ibid.

225. Lucian J. Dale to F. Carter Williams, Oct. 2, 1955, Design Professions, Collaboration With, Jan. 55–Jan. 57 File, ibid.

226. Package Deal Committee, AIA, 1957 Report, Institute 57 File, ibid.

227. Charles Wheatley to Henry Kamphoefner, Apr. 20, 1955, NCAIA 54–55 File, School of Design Papers, NCSUA.

228. *The Economics of Architectural Practice in North Carolina, South Carolina, and Georgia*, Apr. 1969, I-1, IV-7.

229. Seminar program, Profit Planning Seminar File, Apr. 1968, N.C. Chapter, AIA, A&H.

230. Jack D. Train, "Know Your Costs," in *North Carolina Architect*, Jan.–Feb. 1975, 9.

231. "Seminars Focus on Design, Creativity, Energy and Change," Raleigh *News and Observer*, Feb. 29, 1976, 10-V.

232. Wood, "As the Decade Turns," 15.

233. "A Designing Man."

234. "Dean Has Designs on a New Community Development," Raleigh *News and Observer*, Feb. 4, 1973.

235. Charles Hight, interview with author, July 1981.

236. "Deitrick Paralleled—and Made—Architecture History," Raleigh *News and Observer*, July 21, 1974.

237. Elizabeth Culbertson Waugh, "Firm in an Ivied Tower," in *North Carolina Architect*, Jan.–Feb. 1971, 14.

238. "Deitrick Paralleled—and Made—Architecture History."

239. Gutman, *Architectural Practice*, 50.

240. Clark, Tribble, Harris, and Li, "Retrospective," *Architects*, office brochure, 1980, 4.

241. "Charlotte Architectural Firm Sells Shares on London Market," *Charlotte Observer*, Dec. 9, 1986.

242. "Structuring a Firm for Success," *Building Design and Construction*, May 1986.

243. "Charlotte Architectural Firm Sells Shares on London Market."

244. "Tribble Harris Li Buys London Architect Firm," *Charlotte Observer*, Oct. 7, 1987.

245. "Managing Growth," *North Carolina Architect*, Sept.–Oct. 1984.

246. "A Remarkable Return on Design Investment," *Real Estate Forum*, Sept. 1987.

247. "Giving Design the Business," *Venture*, Dec. 1987, 25–26.

248. "Practice: Why Are Architects on the Defensive?" *Architectural Record*, Apr. 1985, 42.

249. "Structuring a Firm for Success."

Bibliography

Manuscripts and Archival Material

Annapolis, Maryland
  Hall of Records
    Dorchester County Land Records

Chapel Hill, North Carolina
  Southern Historical Collection, Wilson Library, University of North Carolina
    Louis (Lewis) Asbury Papers
    Daniel M. Barringer Papers
    Battle Family Papers
    Henry E. Bonitz Papers
    Willis Briggs Collection
    Bryan Family Papers
    Burgwyn Family Papers
    Cameron Family Papers
    Dabney Cosby Papers
    Cupola House Papers, microfilm
    Archie Royal Davis Papers
    Arthur Dobbs Papers, microfilm
    Robert B. Drane Papers
    W. A. Graham Papers
    Gray Family Papers
    Peter W. Hairston Papers
    W. J. Hawkins Papers
    John Hawks Papers
    Hayes Collection
    Ernest Haywood Papers
    T. D. Hogg Papers
    William H. Holleman Papers
    E. M. Holt Papers
    Benjamin Huske Papers
    Calvin Jones Papers
    Lenoir Family Papers
    Macay-McNeely Papers
    Massenburg Family Papers

Mordecai Family Papers
Northup and O'Brien Papers
John Steele Papers
David L. Swain Papers
James Webb Papers
Henry G. Williams Papers
University Archives, Wilson Library, University of North Carolina
University Papers

Durham, North Carolina
Duke Manuscript Department, Perkins Library, Duke University
William Thomas Blackwell Journal
Cane Creek Manufacturing Company Minute Book
W. S. Chaffin Collection
John L. Clifton Papers
Dabney Cosby, Jr., Papers
John A. Craven Ledger
William Ellett Arithmetic Book
Himer Fox Account Book
Ellis Malone Papers
Jacob Mordecai et al. Papers
William Alexander Smith Papers
Duke University Archives, Perkins Library
Building Accounts, Daybooks, Ledgers
President Crowell, Trinity College, Correspondence
William C. Few, Trinity College, Correspondence Received

London, England
Society for the Propagation of the Gospel in Foreign Parts
Letter Books

New Haven, Connecticut
Yale University Manuscripts and Archives, Sterling Library
Journal of Rufus Bunnell, Bunnell Family Papers

New York, New York
Avery Architectural and Fine Arts Library, Columbia University
A. J. Davis Collection
Richard Upjohn Collection
Metropolitan Museum of Art
A. J. Davis Collection
New York Public Library
Alexander Jackson Davis Collection, Rare Books and Manuscripts Division
McKim, Mead, and White Collection
Richard Upjohn and Richard Michell Upjohn Papers

Raleigh, North Carolina
  North Carolina Division of Archives and History, Department of Cultural
    Resources
    Archaeology and Historic Preservation Section
      National Register of Historic Places Nominations
      Research reports, Restoration Branch
      Survey files of historic properties, Survey and Planning Branch
    Archives and Records Section
      Church Records
        Christ Church, Raleigh
        St. Paul's Church, Edenton
      County Records, original and microfilm
      Loyalist Claims, photocopies of originals at Public Record Office, London
      North Carolina State Government Records
        Capital Buildings Papers
        General Assembly Records: Petitions
        Legislative Papers
        North Carolina Board of Architectural Registration
        North Carolina Board of Registration for General Contractors
        North Carolina Chapter, American Institute of Architects
        North Carolina Regulatory Agencies
        Port Records
        Prison Department Papers, Central Prison, Box 42
        Public Instruction, Negro Education, Box 8 (Rosenwald Fund)
        Secretary of State Papers
        Treasurer's and Comptroller's Papers
        United States Censuses, First through Twelfth Censuses, 1790–1900;
          manuscript returns and microfilm
        United States Census of Manufacturing, 1820, microfilm
    Private Collections
      John Allen Papers, microfilm
      James Boon Papers
      Thomas H. Briggs Papers
      Briggs Hardware Account Books, originals and microfilm
      Henry King Burgwyn Diaries
      John Campbell Letters
      Thurmond Chatham Papers
      Beverly Daniel Papers
      Francis L. Fries Papers
      Henry E. Fries Papers
      Marmaduke James Hawkins Papers
      Francis Lister Hawks Collection, microfilm
      Jonathan M. Heck Papers
      Thomas Henderson Papers
      William J. Hicks Papers
      Jacob Hyatt Papers
      Calvin Jones Papers
      George C. Little Papers

William Luten Account Book
Fred A. Olds Papers
David Paton Papers
Pettigrew Papers
Thomas Pollock Letter Book
James F. Post Ledger, microfilm copy
Rev. Samuel Rothrock Diary, microfilm copy
William Laurence Saunders Papers
David L. Swain Papers
John Walker Papers
John D. Whitford Papers
Archibald Davis Williams Account Book, microfilm
Caleb Winslow Family Papers
Jonathan Worth Papers
William H. Worth Papers
North Carolina State University Archives
Chancellors' Reports
School of Design Papers
School of Engineering, Curriculum

Richmond, Virginia
Virginia Historical Society
William R. Baskervill(e) Papers
Virginia State Library, Richmond
County Records

Washington, D.C.
American Institute of Architects Archives
AIA Scrapbook, 1857–74
Baldwin Biograpical Archive
Members' Surveys, 1917, 1940, 1946
National Archives
General Correspondence, 1910–39
Letters Received, Public Buildings Services, 1843–1939, RG 121
Letters Received Relating to the Construction of Customhouses and Other
Structures, RG 56, K Series
United States Patent Office
Description of Patents, 1877

Wilmington, Delaware
Joseph Downs Manuscript Collection, Henry du Pont Winterthur Museum
W. M. Green Letter

Winston-Salem, North Carolina
Museum of Early Southern Decorative Arts
Research files
Old Salem, Incorporated
Research files

Wake Forest University Archives
    J. W. Cates Papers, Baptist Collection

Private Collections
    Baskervill(e) Family Papers, Mecklenburg County, Virginia
    James Brawley research files, Salisbury
    Dixon Family Papers, Wendell
    Fogle Brothers Company Archives, Winston-Salem
    Dr. Beverly Jones Papers, Bethania
    Elizabeth Reid Murray research files, Raleigh
    Powell Family Papers, Tarboro
    William Reaves research files, Wilmington
    St. Paul's Church Records, Edenton, transcribed by Elizabeth V. Moore

Newspapers and Periodicals

All towns of publication listed below are in North Carolina, except Norfolk, Richmond, and Williamsburg, which are in Virginia.

AIA Journal
American Agriculturist
American Architect and Building News
The American Builder
Arator
Architectural Record
Architecture
Asheville Citizen Times
Asheville Democrat
Carolina Cultivator
Charlotte *Catawba Journal*
Charlotte *Miners' and Farmers' Journal*
Charlotte News
Charlotte *North Carolina Whig*
Charlotte Observer
Charlotte *Southern Home*
Charlotte *Western Democrat*
Country Gentlemen
Durham Herald
Durham Recorder
Durham Sun
Durham Tobacco Plant
Edenton *Encyclopedian Instructor*
Edenton Gazette
Edenton *State Gazette*
Engineering News Record
Farmers Journal
Farmers' Register
Fayetteville *Carolina Observer*
Fayetteville *Gazette*

Fayetteville North Carolinian
Fayetteville Observer
Goldsboro *New Era*
Goldsboro *North Carolina Telegraph*
Goldsboro Patriot
Goldsboro Telegraph
Greensboro Daily News
Greensboro *New North State*
Greensboro Patriot
Greensboro *Patriot and Flag*
Greensboro Times
Halifax *Roanoke Advocate*
Journal of the AIA
Kinston *American Advocate*
The Manufacturer and Builder
Manufacturers' Record
Milton Intelligencer
Milton Spectator
New Bern *Atlantic*
New Bern *Carolina Centinel*
New Bern *Carolina Federal Republican*
New Bern *Federal Republican*
Newbernian
Newbern Journal
New Bern *North-Carolina Gazette*
New Bern *Republican*
New Bern Spectator
New Bern *Union*
Norfolk *American Beacon and Commercial Diary*
Norfolk Herald
North Carolina Architect
Oxford Torchlight
Pittsboro *Chatham Record*
Raleigh *Daily News*
Raleigh *Daily Sentinel*
Raleigh *Farmer and Mechanic*
Raleigh *Hale's Weekly*
Raleigh *Minerva*
Raleigh *News and Observer*
Raleigh *North Carolina Standard*
Raleigh *North Carolina Star*
Raleigh Register
Raleigh *Southern Weekly Post*
Raleigh *Spirit of the Age*
Raleigh *Star*
Raleigh *State Chronicle*
Raleigh Times
Raleigh *Visitor*

Raleigh *Weekly Post*
Richmond *Virginia Gazette*
Rutherford *Carolina Gazette*
Rutherfordton *North Carolina Spectator and Western Advertiser*
Salem *People's Press*
Salisbury *Carolina Watchman*
Salisbury *Rowan Whig and Western Advocate*
Salisbury *Western Carolinian*
Scientific American
Semi-Weekly Raleigh Register
Statesville *Iredell Express*
Student Publications of the School of Design [North Carolina State University]
Tarboro *Free Press*
Tarboro *Southerner*
Warrenton News
Warrenton Reporter
Washington *American Recorder*
Washington *North Carolina Times*
Washington *North State Whig*
Williamsburg *Virginia Gazette*
Wilmington *Cape Fear Herald*
Wilmington *Cape-Fear Recorder*
Wilmington Chronicle
Wilmington *Daily Journal*
Wilmington *Dispatch*
Wilmington Gazette
Wilmington Herald
Wilmington Journal
Wilmington Messenger
Wilmington Star
Wilmington *Tri-Weekly Commercial*
Wilmington *True Republican or American Whig*
Wilmington Weekly Chronicle
Wilson Ledger
Winston Leader
Winston-Salem *Journal and Sentinel*
Winston *Union Republican*

Government Documents

North Carolina. *Catalogue[s] of the North Carolina State College of Agriculture and Mechanic Arts* (and similar titles). Various printers for the state, 1889–1940.
———. *Laws of the State of North-Carolina, 1840–41*. Raleigh: W. R. Gales, 1841.
———. *Legislative Documents 1854–1855*. Raleigh: W. W. Holden, 1855.
———. *Public Laws*. Various printers for the state, 1849–1932.
———. *Report[s] of the Commissioners for Rebuilding the Capitol* (and similar titles). Various printers for the state, 1833–40.
———. *Report[s] to the Board of Trustees of the North Carolina College of Agriculture and Mechanic Arts* (and similar titles). Various printers for the state, 1889–1940.

———. *Revised Statutes of the State of North Carolina.* Raleigh: Turner and Hughes, 1837.

———. *The 32nd Report of the Department of Labor and Printing of the State of North Carolina, 1919–20.* Raleigh: Department of Labor and Printing, 1921.

North Carolina. Department of Labor. "North Carolina Labor and Industry." Newsletter. Raleigh, 1943–48.

North Carolina. Employment Security Commission. "Projections to 1982: Employment and Job Needs by Occupations." Typescript. Raleigh, 1979.

North Carolina. Governmental Evaluation Commission. "Report on the Licensing Board for Tile Contractors." Typescript. Raleigh, 1979.

North Carolina State University. Agricultural Extension Service. *Annual Reports.* Raleigh: N.p., 1945–62.

United States. *Abstracts of the Statistics of Manufactures, Seventh Census, 1850.* Washington, D.C.: Robert Armstrong, 1859.

———. *Census of Population: 1950.* Vol. 2, *Characteristics of the Population*, Part 33, *North Carolina.* Washington, D.C.: Government Printing Office, 1952.

———. *Census of Housing: 1970.* Vol. 1, *Housing Characteristics for States, Cities, and Counties*, Part 35, *North Carolina.* Washington, D.C.: Government Printing Office, 1972.

———. *Compendium of the Enumeration of the Inhabitants and Statistics of the United States, as Obtained from the Returns of the Sixth Census.* Washington, D.C.: Blair and Rives, 1841.

———. *Eighth Census of the United States, 1860.* Vol. 3, *Manufactures.* Washington, D.C.: Government Printing Office, 1865.

———. *Historical Statistics of the United States from Colonial Times to 1970.* Washington, D.C.: Government Printing Office, 1976.

———. *1980 Census of Population, Number of Inhabitants*, Part 35, *North Carolina.* Washington, D.C.: Government Printing Office, 1982.

———. *1980 Census of Population.* Vol. 1, *Characteristics of the Population*, Chapter D, *Detailed Population Characteristics*, Part 35, *North Carolina.* Washington, D.C.: Department of Commerce, 1983.

———. *Population of the United States in 1860.* Washington, D.C.: Government Printing Office, 1864.

———. *Seventh Census of the United States.* Washington, D.C.: Robert Armstrong, Public Printer, 1853.

———. *Sixth Census of the United States, 1840: Compendium of the Inhabitants and Statistics of the United States.* Washington, D.C.: Thomas Allen, 1841.

———. *Tenth Census of the United States, 1880.* Vol. 2, *Report on Manufactures of the United States*, and vol. 22, *Power and Machinery Employed in Manufactures.* Washington, D.C.: Government Printing Office, 1884 and 1888.

———. *Twelfth Census of the United States, 1900.* Vol. 8, *Manufactures.* Washington, D.C.: Government Printing Office, 1902.

United States Department of Labor, Research and Statistics Division. "Construction Authorized in North Carolina by City, by Month, 1980." Typescript. Washington, D.C., 1980.

———. "Construction Authorized in North Carolina by City, by Month, 1985." Typescript. Washington, D.C., 1985.

Virginia. *The Statutes at Large; Being a Collection of all the Laws of Virginia.* Edited by Hening, William Waller. Various printers for the editor, 1819–23.

Interviews

Notes or tapes are in the possession of interviewers.

Catherine W. Bishir
John Buxton Waddell, Jr., March 1985
Charlotte V. Brown
Mayne Albright, September 1981
Leslie N. Boney, Jr., September 1981
J. N. Coffey, Jr., February 1982
Mrs. J. N. Coffey, Jr., February 1982
James A. Davidson, March 1981
William Waldo Dodge, Jr., March 1981
Mrs. Frances Coffey Green, February 1982
Luther Lashmit, February 1981
Anthony Lord, September 1981
Jesse M. Page, March 1981
Col. J. N. Pease, July 1981
Norman Pease, Jr., July 1981
Boynton Satterfield, February 1981
Frances Lee Shelton, December 1987
Montgomery Spier, July 1981
James C. Stenhouse, July 1981
Grady Vestal, December 1982
Mary V. Vestal, December 1983
Conrad Wessel, July 1982
Ernest H. Wood
John Crosland, Jr., October 1985
John M. Crumpton, Jr., July 1981
Mel Daughtridge, October 1985
R. B. Fitch, November 1985
Ede Graves, April 1988
Becky Griffin, August 1981
Eugene Gulledge, November 1985
Glenda Herman, September 1981
Henry Kamphoefner, February 1982
Tommy Lampley, February 1988
Wayne McArthur, April 1988
Henry McGowan, April 1988
Alastair Muirhead, December 1987
H. James Owen, June 1981
C. L. Reavis, October 1985
Emmett Sebrell, April 1988
Cynthia Skidmore, April 1988
Gwen Taylor, April 1988
Woodley C. Warrick, September 1981
John Watts, April 1988

Books, Articles, and Unpublished Sources

Abbott, F. C. *Fifty Years in Charlotte Real Estate*. Charlotte: Privately printed, 1947.

Albright, James W. *Greensboro, 1808–1904*. Greensboro: Joseph J. Stone Co., 1904.

Albright, R. Mayne, and A. L. Haskins. *Handbook of North Carolina Building Laws*. Charlottesville, Va.: The Michie Co., 1966.

Alexander, Ann C. *Perspective on a Resort Community: Historic Buildings Inventory, Southern Pines, North Carolina*. Raleigh: Archives and History, 1981.

Allcott, John V. "Architect A. J. Davis in North Carolina . . . His Launching at the University." *North Carolina Architect*, Nov./Dec. 1973, 10–15.

_____. "Architectural Developments at 'Montrose' in the 1850s." *North Carolina Historical Review* 42, no. 1 (Jan. 1965): 85–95.

_____. *The Campus at Chapel Hill: Two Hundred Years of Architecture*. Chapel Hill: Chapel Hill Historical Society, 1986.

_____. *Colonial Homes in North Carolina*. Raleigh: Carolina Tercentenary Commission, 1963. Reprint. Raleigh: Archives and History, 1975.

_____. "Robert Donaldson, the First North Carolinian to Become Prominent in the Arts." *North Carolina Historical Review* 52, no. 4 (Oct. 1975): 333–66.

_____. "Scholarly Books and Frolicsome Blades: A. J. Davis Designs a Library-Ballroom." *Journal of the Society of Architectural Historians* 33, no. 2 (May 1974): 145–54.

Amis, Moses. *Historical Raleigh*. Raleigh: Commercial Printing Co., 1913.

_____. *Historical Sketches of the City of Raleigh*. Raleigh: Edwards and Broughton, 1887.

Anderson, Jean B. "Fairntosh Plantation and the Camerons." Research report, 1978, copy in Historic Sites Section, Archives and History, Raleigh.

_____. *Piedmont Plantation: The Bennehan-Cameron Family and Lands in North Carolina*. Durham: Historic Preservation Society of Durham, 1985.

_____. "A Preliminary Report on Stagville Plantation." Research report, 1977, copy in Historic Sites Section, Archives and History, Raleigh.

Andrews, Evangeline Walker, ed. *Journal of a Lady of Quality*. New Haven: Yale University Press, 1922.

Ashe, Samuel A. *David Paton, Architect of the State Capitol, An Address by Samuel A. Ashe*. Raleigh: North Carolina Historical Commission, 1909.

Ashe, Samuel A., et al. *Biographical History of North Carolina*. Greensboro: Charles L. Van Noppen, 1907.

Bailyn, Jonathan. "An Historical Study of Residential Development in Greensboro, 1808–1965." Master's thesis, University of North Carolina, 1968.

Ball, Norman. "Circular Saws and the History of Technology." *Association for Preservation Technology* 7, no. 3 (1975): 79–89.

Barbee, Jennie M. *Historical Sketches of the Raleigh Public Schools, 1876–1941/42*. Raleigh: Edwards and Broughton, 1945.

Barfield, Rodney. *Thomas Day, Cabinetmaker*. Raleigh: North Carolina Museum of History, 1975.

Barrett, Charles W. *Colonial Southern Homes*. Raleigh: Edwards and Broughton, 1903.

Barrett, Charles W., and Frank Thomson. *Photographs: Barrett and Thomson*. Raleigh: N.p., 1900.

————. *Plans for Public School Houses, 1901*. Raleigh: Edwards and Broughton, 1903.

Barringer, Daniel M. *Address Delivered Before the Mecklenburg Agricultural Society at Charlotte, Oct. 27, 1859*. Charlotte: Western Democrat, 1860.

Beard, Geoffrey. *Craftsmen and Interior Decoration in England, 1660–1820*. New York: Holmes and Meier, 1981.

Beasley and Emerson's Charlotte Directory. Charlotte: Beasley and Emerson, 1875.

Benjamin, Asher. *The Practical House Carpenter*. Boston: R. P. and C. Williams, Annin and Smith, 1830.

Beresford, Maurice, and John G. Hurst. *Deserted Medieval Villages*. New York: St. Martin's Press, 1972.

Berlin, Ira, and Herbert G. Gutman. "Natives and Immigrants, Free Men and Slaves: Urban Workingmen in the Antebellum American South." *American Historical Review* 88, no. 5 (Dec. 1983): 1175–1200.

"Berry Davidson Autobiography." Typescript copy, undated, source unknown, from Alamance County Planning Department files. Copy in files of Carl R. Lounsbury.

Bertelson, David. *The Lazy South*. New York: Oxford University Press, 1967.

Bettey, J. H. "Seventeenth Century Squatters' Dwellings: Some Documentary Evidence." *Vernacular Architecture* 13 (1982): 28–30.

Billings, Dwight B., Jr. *Planters and the Making of a "New South": Class, Politics, and Development in North Carolina, 1865–1900*. Chapel Hill: University of North Carolina Press, 1979.

Bishir, Catherine W. "Asher Benjamin's *Practical House Carpenter* in North Carolina." *Carolina Comments* 27, no. 3 (May 1979): 66–74.

————. "Black Builders in Antebellum North Carolina." *North Carolina Historical Review* 61, no. 4 (Oct. 1984): 423–61.

————. "Jacob W. Holt, an American Builder." *Winterthur Portfolio* 16, no. 1 (Spring 1981): 1–32. Reprinted in *Common Places: Readings in American Vernacular Architecture*, edited by Dell Upton and John Vlach. Athens: University of Georgia Press, 1986.

————. "The Montmorenci-Prospect Hill School: A Study of High-Style Vernacular Architecture in the Roanoke Valley." In *Carolina Dwelling*, edited by Doug Swaim, 84–103. Raleigh: North Carolina State University School of Design Student Publication, 1978.

————. "Philadelphia Bricks and the New Bern Jail." *Association for Preservation Technology* 9, no. 4 (1977): 62–66.

Bishir, Catherine W., and Marshall Bullock. "Mr. Jones Goes to Richmond: A Note on the Influence of Alexander Parris' Wickham House." *Journal of the Society of Architectural Historians*, 43, no. 1 (Mar. 1984): 71–74.

Bishir, Catherine W., and Lawrence S. Earley, eds. *Early Twentieth-Century Suburbs in North Carolina*. Raleigh: Archives and History, 1985.

Bishop, J. Leander. *A History of American Manufactures, 1607–1830*. 3 vols. Reprint. New York: A. M. Kelly, 1966.

Bivins, John, Jr. *The Furniture of Coastal North Carolina*. Winston-Salem and Chapel Hill: Published by the Museum of Early Southern Decorative Arts and distributed by the University of North Carolina Press, 1988.

————. *The Moravian Potters in North Carolina*. Chapel Hill: University of North

Carolina Press, 1972.

Black, Allison Harris. *An Architectural History of Burlington, North Carolina*. Burlington: City of Burlington, 1987.

Black, David. *Historic Architectural Resources of Downtown Asheville, North Carolina*. Asheville: City of Asheville, 1979.

Bledstein, Burton J. *The Culture of Professionalism*. New York: W. W. Norton, 1976.

Bonner, James C., ed. "Plantation Experiences of a New York Woman." *North Carolina Historical Review* 33, no. 3 (July 1956): 384–412, and 33, no. 4 (Oct. 1956): 529–46.

Boyce, W. Scott. *Economic and Social History of Chowan County, North Carolina, 1880–1915*. New York: Columbia University, 1917.

Boyd, William K., ed. *Some Eighteenth Century Tracts Concerning North Carolina*. 1923. Reprint. Spartanburg: The Reprint Co., 1973.

―――. *William Byrd's Histories of the Dividing Line Betwixt Virginia and North Carolina*. 1929. Reprint. New York: Dover Publications, 1967.

Branson, Levi. *Branson's North Carolina Almanac and Directory of Raleigh, 1891*. Raleigh: L. Branson, 1891.

Brendel, Susanne. "Urban Asheville." *North Carolina Architect*, July/Aug. 1978, 10–15.

Brewer, James Howard. "Legislation Designed to Control Slavery in Wilmington and Fayetteville." *North Carolina Historical Review* 30, no. 2 (Apr. 1953): 155–66.

Brickell, John. *The Natural History of North Carolina*. 1737. Reprint. Murfreesboro, N.C.: Johnson Publishing Co., 1968.

Bridenbaugh, Carl. *The Colonial Craftsman*. Chicago: University of Chicago Press, 1961.

Briggs, M. S. *The Architect in History*. Oxford: Oxford University Press, 1927.

Brown, Cecil Kenneth. *A State Movement in Railroad Development*. Chapel Hill: University of North Carolina Press, 1928.

Brown, Claudia, Diane Lea, and Robert M. Leary. *The Durham Architectural and Historic Inventory*. Durham: City of Durham, 1981.

Brown, Marvin A. *Our Enduring Past: A Survey of 235 Years of Life and Architecture in Lincoln County, North Carolina*. Lincolnton, N.C.: Lincoln County Historic Properties Commission, 1986.

Brownell, Blaine A., and David R. Goldfield. *The City in Southern History*. Port Washington, N.Y., and London: National University Publications, 1977.

Browning, James B. "James D. Sampson." *Negro History Bulletin* 3 (Jan. 1940): 56.

Brunskill, R. W. *Illustrated Handbook of Vernacular Architecture*. 2d ed. London: Faber and Faber, 1978.

Brunskill, R. W., and Alec Clifton-Taylor. *English Brickwork*. London: Ward Lock, 1977.

Buchanan, Paul E. "The Eighteenth-Century Frame Houses of Tidewater Virginia." In *Building Early America*, edited by Charles E. Peterson, 54–73. Radnor, Pa.: Chilton Book Co. for the Carpenter's Co. of Pennsylvania, 1976.

Bullock, James Marshall. "The Enterprising Contractor, Mr. Cosby." Master's thesis, University of North Carolina, 1982.

Burnham, Alan. "Biltmore Estate." *North Carolina Architect*, July/Aug. 1978, 16–18.

Burns, Robert, ed. *100 Courthouses: A Report on North Carolina Judicial Facilities*. 2 vols. Raleigh: Administrative Office of the Courts, 1978.

Burton, Orville Vernon, and Robert C. McMath, Jr. *Class, Conflict, and Consensus: Antebellum Southern Community Studies.* Westport, Conn.: Greenwood Press, 1982.

Bushong, William B. "A. G. Bauer, Architect for the State of North Carolina, 1883–1893." *North Carolina Historical Review* 60, no. 3 (July 1983): 304–31.

———. "Montfort Hall and Its Architect, William Percival." Master's thesis, Appalachian State University, 1979.

———. "William Percival, an English Architect in the Old North State, 1857–1860." *North Carolina Historical Review* 57, no. 3 (July 1980): 310–39.

Butchko, Tom. *An Inventory of Historic Architecture, Sampson County, North Carolina.* Clinton, N.C.: City of Clinton, [1981].

Butler, Lindley S. "The Early Settlement of Carolina: Virginia's Southern Frontier." *The Virginia Magazine of History and Biography* 79 (Jan. 1971): 20–28.

Butler, Lindley S., and Alan D. Watson. *The North Carolina Experience: An Interpretive and Documentary History.* Chapel Hill: University of North Carolina Press, 1984.

Butterworth, Benjamin, ed. *The Growth of Industrial Art.* Washington, D.C.: Government Printing Office, 1888.

Butts, Donald. "A Challenge to Planter Rule: The Controversy over the Ad Valorem Taxation of Slaves in North Carolina: 1858–1862." Ph.D. dissertation, Duke University, 1978.

———. "The 'Irrepressible Conflict': Slave Taxation and North Carolina's Gubernatorial Election of 1860." *North Carolina Historical Review* 58, no. 1 (Jan. 1981): 44–66.

Cain, Robert J., ed. *North Carolina Higher-Court Minutes, 1724–1730.* Vol. 6 of *Colonial Records of North Carolina*, 2d ser. Raleigh: Archives and History, 1981.

Cameron, Paul Carrington. *An Address Before the Orange County Society for the Promotion of Agriculture, the Mechanic Arts and Manufactures . . . 1854.* Hillsboro, N. C.: D. Heartt and Son, 1855.

Campbell, Betty Jean. "The Buildings of Salem, North Carolina, 1766–1856." Ph.D. dissertation, Florida State University, 1975.

Carolina Homes: A Plan Book of Small Homes. Greensboro: Carolina Brick and Tile Service, 1948.

Carr, Lois G., and Menard, Russell R. "Immigration and Opportunity: The Freeman in Early Colonial Maryland." In *The Chesapeake in the Seventeenth Century*, edited by Thad W. Tate and David Ammerman, 206–42. New York: W. W. Norton, 1979.

Carroll, Grady Lee Ernest. *They Lived in Raleigh: Some Leading Personalities from 1792 to 1892.* 2 vols. Raleigh: Privately printed, 1977.

Carson, Cary. "The 'Virginia House' in Maryland." *Maryland Historical Magazine* 69, no. 2 (Summer 1974): 185–96.

Carson, Cary, Norman F. Barker, William M. Kelso, Garry Wheeler Stone, and Dell Upton. "Impermanent Architecture in the Southern American Colonies." *Winterthur Portfolio* 16, nos. 2/3 (Summer/Autumn 1981): 135–96.

Carter, Edward C., II. *Benjamin Henry Latrobe and Public Works: Professionalism, Private Interest, and Public Policy in the Age of Jefferson.* Essays in Public Works, no. 3. Washington, D.C.: Public Works Historical Society, 1976.

Carter, Wilmoth. *The Urban Negro in the South.* New York: Vantage Press, 1962.

Chalkin, C. W. *The Provincial Towns of Georgian England: A Study of the Building Process, 1740–1820*. Montreal: McGill-Queen's University Press, 1974.

Chamber of Commerce. *Annual Report, 1888*. Greensboro: Chamber of Commerce, 1888.

Chamber of Commerce. *Greensboro, City of Progress*. Greensboro: Various printers, 1907, 1911, 1915, and 1921.

Chappell, Edward A. "Acculturation in the Shenandoah Valley." *Proceedings of the American Philosophical Society* 124, no. 1 (1980): 55–89.

Charles, F. W. B. "Post-Construction and the Rafter Roof." *Vernacular Architecture* 12 (1981): 3–19.

Charlotte City Directory 1889. Charlotte: Hirst Publishing and Printing Co., 1889.

Cheeseman, Bruce S. "The Cupola House of Edenton, Chowan County." Research report, 1980, copy in Restoration Branch, Archives and History, Raleigh.

———. "The Survival of the Cupola House: 'A Venerable Old Mansion.' " *North Carolina Historical Review* 63, no. 1 (Jan. 1986): 40–73.

Chiaramonte, Louis J. *Craftsman-Client Contracts: Interpersonal Relations in a New-foundland Fishing Community*. Newfoundland Social and Economic Studies, no. 10. St. Johns: Memorial University of Newfoundland, 1970.

Clark, Clifford Edward, Jr. *The American Family Home, 1800–1960*. Chapel Hill: University of North Carolina Press, 1986.

Clark, Percy. "New Federal Buildings." *Harper's Weekly* 32 (May 19, 1888): 367–68.

Clark, Walter, ed. *The State Records of North Carolina*. 16 vols. numbered 11–26. Winston and Goldsboro: State of North Carolina, 1895–1906.

Clayton, Thomas H. *Close to the Land: The Way We Lived in North Carolina, 1820–1870*. Series edited by Sydney Nathans. Chapel Hill: University of North Carolina Press, 1983.

Cochran, Thomas. *Frontiers of Change: Early Industrialism in America*. New York: Oxford University Press, 1981.

Coffey, J. W. and Son. *Houses by Coffey*. Raleigh: Edwards and Broughton, 1945.

Colvin, H. M. *A Biographical Dictionary of British Architects, 1600–1840*. New York: Facts on File, Inc., 1978.

Commons, John R., et al. *History of Labour in the United States*. Vol. 1. New York: Macmillan, 1918.

Condit, Carl W. *American Building*. Chicago: University of Chicago Press, 1968.

———. *American Building Art: The Nineteenth Century*. New York: Oxford University Press, 1960.

Cooledge, Harold N., Jr. *Samuel Sloan: Architect of Philadelphia, 1815-1884*. Philadelphia: University of Pennsylvania Press, 1986.

———. "A Sloan Check List, 1849–1884." *Journal of the Society of Architectural Historians* 19, no. 1 (Mar. 1960): 34–38.

Cord, Marion. "A. J. Davis and the Printed Specification." *College Art Journal* 12 (Summer 1953): 354–59.

Cotton, Jane Baldwin, ed. *Maryland Calendar of Wills*. 8 vols. to date. Baltimore: Genealogical Publishing Co., 1968– .

Cotton, J. Randall. *Historic Burke: An Architectural Inventory of Burke County, North Carolina*. Morganton, N.C.: Historic Burke Foundation, 1987.

Craig, James H. *The Arts and Crafts in North Carolina, 1699–1840*. Winston-Salem: Museum of Early Southern Decorative Arts, 1965.

Crittenden, Charles Christopher. *The Commerce of North Carolina, 1763–1789*. New Haven: Yale University Press, 1936.

Crow, Jeffrey J. *The Black Experience in Revolutionary North Carolina*. Raleigh: Archives and History, 1977.

Cummings, Abbott Lowell. *The Framed Houses of Massachusetts Bay, 1625–1725*. Cambridge: Harvard University Press, 1979.

Darroch, A. Gordon. "Migrants in the Nineteenth Century: Fugitives or Families in Motion?" *Journal of Family History*, Fall 1981, 257–77.

Dauphine, Durand de. *A Huguenot Exile in Virginia 1687*. Translated and edited by Gilbert Chenard. New York: Press of the Pioneers, 1934.

Davidson, Robert L. "Progress in Prefabrication." *Journal of the American Institute of Architects* 1 (May 1944): 234–42.

Davies, Jane. "Blandwood and the Italian Villa Style in America." *Nineteenth Century* 1, no. 3 (Sept. 1975): 11–14.

Davis, Richard Beale, ed. *William Fitzhugh and His Chesapeake World*. Chapel Hill: University of North Carolina Press, 1963.

De Bow, J. D. B. *The Industrial Resources of the Southern and Western States*. New York: De Bow's Review, 1853.

Deetz, James. *In Small Things Forgotten: The Archeology of Early American Life*. Garden City: Anchor Press/Doubleday, 1977.

Defebaugh, James E. *History of the Lumber Industry in America*. 2 vols. Chicago: American University, 1906.

Denny, James M. "Vernacular Building Process in Missouri: Nathaniel Leonard's Activities, 1825–1870." *Missouri Historical Review* 78, no. 1 (Oct. 1983): 23–50.

Dill, Alonzo Thomas, Jr. *Governor Tryon and His Palace*. Chapel Hill: University of North Carolina Press, 1955.

———. "Public Buildings in Craven County." *North Carolina Historical Review* 20, no. 4 (Oct. 1943): 301–26.

———. "Tryon's Palace: A Neglected Niche of North Carolina History." *North Carolina Historical Review* 19, no. 2 (Apr. 1942): 119–67.

Directory of Certified Kitchen Designers, 1986–87. Hackettstown, N.J.: Society of Certified Kitchen Designers, 1986.

Directory of Charlotte, North Carolina, 1893–94. Charlotte: J. S. Drakeford, 1895.

Directory of the City of Charlotte, 1896–97. Charlotte: Charlotte Directory Co., 1896.

Dorson, Richard M. *Folklore and Folklife, an Introduction*. Chicago: University of Chicago Press, 1972.

Doucet, Michael J., and John C. Weaver. "Material Culture and the North American House: The Era of the Common Man, 1870–1920." *The Journal of American History* 72, no. 3 (Dec. 1985): 560–87.

Downing, Andrew Jackson. *Architecture of Country Houses*. 1850. Reprint. New York: Dover Publications, 1969.

———. *Cottage Residences*. New York: John Wiley, 1853.

Dundin, Joseph. "A Hundred Years (Or So) of AIA Standard Documents." *Architecture*, Oct. 1988, 119-22.

Durden, Robert F. *The Dukes of Durham: 1865–1929*. Durham: Duke University Press, 1975.

Earle, Carville V. "Environment, Disease, and Mortality in Early Virginia." In *The Chesapeake in the Seventeenth Century*, edited by Thad W. Tate and David

Ammerman, 96–125. New York: W. W. Norton, 1979.

The Economics of Architectural Practice in North Carolina, South Carolina, and Georgia. San Francisco: Case and Co., 1969.

Edmisten, Linda Harris. *J. W. Willie York: His First Seventy-Five Years in Raleigh.* Raleigh: Privately printed, 1987.

Edmonds, Helen. *The Negro and Fusion Politics in North Carolina, 1894–1901.* Chapel Hill: University of North Carolina Press, 1951.

Edmunds, Mary Lewis Rucker. *Governor Morehead's Blandwood and the Family Who Lived There.* Greensboro: Privately printed, 1976.

Ekirch, A. Roger. *"Poor Carolina": Politics and Society in Colonial North Carolina, 1729–1776.* Chapel Hill: University of North Carolina Press, 1981.

Elliot, Cecil D. "The North Carolina State Capitol." *The Southern Architect* 5, no. 5 (May 1958): 19–22; 5, no. 6 (June 1958): 23–26; and 5, no. 7 (July 1958): 24–27.

Erlich, Mark. *With Our Hands: The Story of Carpenters in Massachusetts.* Philadelphia: Temple University Press, 1986.

Escott, Paul D. *Many Excellent People: Power and Privilege in North Carolina, 1850–1900.* Chapel Hill: University of North Carolina Press, 1985.

Escott, Paul D., and Jeffrey J. Crow. "The Social Order and Violent Disorder: An Analysis of North Carolina in the Revolution and Civil War." *The Journal of Southern History* 52, no. 3 (Aug. 1986): 373–402.

Ezell, John S., and Judson P. Wood. *The New Democracy in America: Travels of Francisco Miranda in the United States, 1783–84.* Norman: University of Oklahoma Press, 1963.

Fenn, Elizabeth A., and Peter H. Wood. *Natives and Newcomers: The Way We Lived in North Carolina before 1770.* Series edited by Sydney Nathans. Chapel Hill: University of North Carolina Press, 1983.

Field, Walker. "A Re-examination into the Invention of the Balloon Frame." *Journal of the Society of Architectural Historians* 2, no. 4 (Oct. 1942): 3–29.

Fitch, James Marston. "The Profession of Architecture." In *The Professions of America,* edited by Kenneth S. Lynn and the editors of *Daedalus.* Boston: Beacon Press, 1967.

Flowers, John. *Bull Durham and Beyond.* Durham: Bicentennial Commission, 1976.

Franklin, John Hope. *The Free Negro in North Carolina, 1790–1860.* Chapel Hill: University of North Carolina Press, 1943.

———. "James Boon, Free Negro Artisan." *Journal of Negro History* 30 (Apr. 1945): 150–80.

"A French Traveler in America." *American Historical Review* 26, no. 4 (1920–21): 726–47.

Fries, Adelaide L., Douglas LeTell Rights, Minnie J. Smith, and Kenneth G. Hamilton, eds. *Records of the Moravians in North Carolina.* 11 vols. Raleigh: North Carolina Historical Commission, 1922–69.

Gaines, Henry I. *King's Maelum.* New York: Vantage Press, 1972.

Gatling, Eva Ingersoll. "John Berry of Hillsboro, North Carolina." *Journal of the Society of Architectural Historians* 10, no. 1 (Mar. 1951): 18–22.

Gebhard, David, and Deborah Nevins. *200 Years of American Architectural Drawings.* New York: Whitney Library of Design, 1977.

Giedion, Siegfried. *Space, Time and Architecture.* Cambridge: Harvard University Press, 1941.

Gilchrist, Agnes Addison. *William Strickland, Architect and Engineer, 1788–1854*. Philadelphia: University of Pennsylvania Press, 1950.

Glass, Brent. "Southern Mill Hills: Design in a 'Public' Place." In *Carolina Dwelling*, edited by Doug Swaim, 138–49. Raleigh: North Carolina State University School of Design Student Publication, 1978.

Glassie, Henry. "Eighteenth-Century Cultural Process in Delaware Valley Folk Building." *Winterthur Portfolio* 7 (1972): 29–57.

_____. *Folk Housing in Middle Virginia: A Structural Analysis of Historic Artifacts*. Knoxville: University of Tennessee Press, 1975.

_____. "Vernacular Architecture and Society." *Material Culture* 16, no. 1 (Spring 1984): 5–24.

Goldthwaite, Richard. *The Building of Renaissance Florence: An Economic and Social History*. Baltimore: Johns Hopkins University Press, 1980.

Gowans, Alan. *Images of American Living*. Philadelphia: J. P. Lippincott Co., 1964.

Greeley, Horace, et al., eds. *The Great Industries of the United States*. Hartford, Conn.: J. B. Burr and Hyde, 1872.

Green, James W. *House Building by Farm Owners in North Carolina*. Raleigh: North Carolina State College, 1950.

Greiff, Constance M. *John Notman, Architect*. Philadelphia: The Atheneum of Philadelphia, 1979.

Griggs, Linda Mackie. "Haywood Hall." Research report, 1984, copy in Restoration Branch, Archives and History, Raleigh.

Grimes, J. Bryan. *North Carolina Wills and Inventories*. Raleigh: Edwards and Broughton for the Trustees of the Public Libraries, 1912.

Gunter, S. Carol. *Carolina Heights, Wilmington*. Wilmington, N.C.: City of Wilmington Planning Department, 1982.

Gutman, Robert. *Architectural Practice: A Critical View*. Princeton: Princeton University Press, 1988.

Habakkuk, H. J. *American and British Technology in the Nineteenth Century*. Cambridge: Cambridge University Press, 1962.

Haley, Dru Gatewood, and Raymond A. Winslow, Jr. *The Historic Architecture of Perquimans County, North Carolina*. Hertford, N.C.: Town of Hertford, 1982.

Hall, Jacquelyn Dowd, James Leloudis, Robert Korstad, Mary Murphy, Lu Ann Jones, and Christopher B. Daly. *Like a Family: The Making of a Southern Cotton Mill World*. Chapel Hill: University of North Carolina Press, 1987.

Hall, Louise M. "Artificer to Architect in America." Ph.D. dissertation, Radcliffe College, 1954.

Hamilton, J. G. de Roulhac, ed. *The Papers of Thomas Ruffin*. 4 vols. Raleigh: Edwards and Broughton, 1914–18.

Hamlin, Talbot. *Benjamin Henry Latrobe*. New York: Oxford University Press, 1955.

_____. *Greek Revival Architecture in America*. 1940. Reprint. New York: Dover Publications, 1964.

Hanchett, Thomas W. "Architectural Resources of Charlotte, North Carolina." Unpublished research report, Charlotte Historic Properties Commission, n.d.

_____. "The Four Square House in the United States." Master's thesis, University of Chicago, 1986.

A Handbook of Architectural Practice. Washington, D.C.: American Institute of Architects, Inc., 1920.

Handbook of Durham. Durham: Chamber of Commerce, 1895.

Harris, Linda L., ed. *Early Raleigh Neighborhoods and Buildings*. Raleigh: [City of Raleigh Planning Department, 1983].

Harris, Linda L., and Mary Ann Lee. *Raleigh Architectural Inventory*. Raleigh: City of Raleigh Planning Department and Archives and History, 1978.

Hartwell, Henry, James Blair, and Edward Chilton. *The Present State of Virginia and the College*. Edited by Hunter D. Farish. Williamsburg: Colonial Williamsburg, 1940.

Harvey, John. *The Mediaeval Architect*. New York: St. Martin's Press, 1972.

Hawks, Francis L. *History of North Carolina*. 2 vols. Fayetteville: E. J. Hale and Son, 1858.

Henderson, Archibald. *The Campus of the First State University*. Chapel Hill: University of North Carolina Press, 1949.

Herman, Bernard L. *Architecture and Rural Life in Central Delaware, 1700–1900*. Knoxville: University of Tennessee Press, 1987.

Herzog, Lynda Vestal. "The Early Architecture of New Bern, North Carolina, 1750–1850." Ph.D. dissertation, University of California at Los Angeles, 1977.

Higginbotham, Don, ed. *The Papers of James Iredell*. 2 vols. Raleigh: Archives and History, 1976.

Hirsch, Susan E. *Roots of the American Working Class: The Industrialization of Crafts in Newark, 1800–1860*. Philadelphia: University of Pennsylvania Press, 1978.

Historical and Descriptive Review of the State of North Carolina. 2 vols. Charleston: Empire Publishing Co., 1885.

Hitchcock, Henry-Russell. *Architecture Books: A List of Books, Portfolios, and Pamphlets on Architecture and Related Subjects Published in America before 1895*. Enl. ed. New York: DaCapo Press, 1976.

Hobbs, S. H. *North Carolina: Economic and Social*. Chapel Hill: University of North Carolina Press, 1930.

Holden, William W. *Lecture Read Before the Raleigh Mechanics' Association . . . July 12, 1842*. Raleigh: Raleigh Star, 1842.

Hood, Davyd Foard. *The Architecture of Rowan County*. Salisbury, N.C.: Rowan County Historic Properties Commission, 1983.

Hook, C. C., and F. M. Sawyer. *Some Designs by Hook and Sawyer*. Charlotte: Queen City Printing & Paper Co., 1902.

Hooker, Richard J., ed. *The Carolina Backcountry on the Eve of the Revolution: The Journal and Other Writings of Charles Woodmason, Anglican Itinerant*. Chapel Hill: University of North Carolina Press, 1953.

Horton, Frank. "The 'Guild' System in Salem." Typescript, 1967, copy at Old Salem, Inc., Winston-Salem, N.C.

Hounshell, David A. *From the American System to Mass Production: The Development of Manufacturing Technology in the United States*. Baltimore: Johns Hopkins University Press, 1984.

Hoyt, William Henry, ed. *The Papers of Archibald D. Murphey*. 2 vols. Raleigh: North Carolina Historical Commission, 1914.

Jackson, Robert Max. *The Formation of Craft Labor Markets*. Studies in Social Discontinuity. Orlando, Fla.: Academic Press, 1984.

Jeffrey, Thomas E. "The Progressive Paradigm of Antebellum North Carolina Politics." *Carolina Comments* 30, no. 3 (May 1982): 66–75.

Jenkins, Frank. *Architect and Patron*. London: Oxford University Press, 1961.

"John Crosland, Jr.: The Builder of the Year." *Professional Builder*, Jan. 1986, 273.

Johnson, Allen, Dumas Malone, et al., eds. *Dictionary of American Biography*. 20 vols. New York: Charles Scribner's Sons, 1928–36.

Johnson, Guion Griffis. *Ante-Bellum North Carolina: A Social History*. Chapel Hill: University of North Carolina Press, 1937.

Johnston, Frances Benjamin, and Thomas Tileston Waterman. *The Early Architecture of North Carolina*. Chapel Hill: University of North Carolina Press, 1947.

Johnston, Hugh Buckner. "The Journal of Ebenezer Hazard in North Carolina, 1777 and 1778." *North Carolina Historical Review* 36, no. 3 (July 1959): 358–81.

Jones, H. G. *North Carolina Illustrated, 1524–1984*. Chapel Hill: University of North Carolina Press, 1983.

Jones, Steven. "Afro-American Architecture and Spirit of Thomas Day." Term paper, 1973, copy in Museum of History, Archives and History, Raleigh.

Kaplan, Peter R. *The Historic Architecture of Cabarrus County, North Carolina*. Concord, N.C.: Historic Cabarrus, 1981.

Kaye, Barrington. *The Development of the Architectural Profession in Britain: A Sociological Study*. London: George Allen and Unwin, 1960.

Keister, A. S. "A City in Depression, Greensboro, North Carolina." *Social Forces* 13 (Oct. 1934): 91–99.

Kelly, Kevin. " 'In Dispers'd Country Plantations': Settlement Patterns in Seventeenth-Century Surry County, Virginia." In *The Chesapeake in the Seventeenth Century*, edited by Thad W. Tate and David Ammerman, 183–205. New York: W. W. Norton, 1979.

Kimball, Fiske, and Gertrude Carraway. "Tryon's Palace." *New-York Historical Society Quarterly Bulletin* 24, no. 1 (Jan. 1940): 20–21.

Kostof, Spiro, ed. *The Architect: Chapters in the History of the Profession*. New York: Oxford University Press, 1977.

Lane, Mills. *Architecture of the Old South: North Carolina*. Savannah: Beehive Press, 1985.

Lawson, John. *A New Voyage to Carolina*. 1709. Reprint. Edited by Hugh Talmage Lefler. Chapel Hill: University of North Carolina Press, 1967.

Lea, Diane. "Williamsburg Style Creates a Village Atmosphere." *North Carolina Architect* 26, no. 1 (Jan./Feb. 1979): 14–19.

Lefler, Hugh Talmage, and Albert Ray Newsome. *North Carolina: The History of a Southern State*. Chapel Hill: University of North Carolina Press, 1963.

Lemmon, Sarah McCulloh, ed. *The Pettigrew Papers*. Vol. 1. Raleigh: Archives and History, 1971.

Lennon, Donald R., and Ida Brooks Kellam. *The Wilmington Town Book, 1743–1778*. Raleigh: Archives and History, 1973.

Lethaby, W. R. *Architecture*. London: Home Library Series, 1911.

Little-Stokes, Ruth. *An Inventory of Historic Architecture: Caswell County, North Carolina*. Yanceyville, N.C.: Caswell County Historical Association and Archives and History, 1979.

———. *An Inventory of Historic Architecture, Greensboro*. Greensboro: City of Greensboro and Archives and History, 1976.

———. *An Inventory of Historic Architecture: Iredell County, North Carolina*. Statesville, N.C.: City of Statesville, Town of Mooresville, Iredell County, and Archives and History, 1978.

———. "The North Carolina Porch: A Climatic and Cultural Buffer." In *Carolina Dwelling*, edited by Doug Swaim, 104–11. Raleigh: North Carolina State University School of Design Student Publication, 1978.

Lockmiller, David A. *History of North Carolina State College, 1889–1939.* Raleigh: Edwards and Broughton, 1939.

Logan, Frenise A. *The Negro in North Carolina, 1876–1894.* Chapel Hill: University of North Carolina Press, 1964.

Lounsbury, Carl R. *Alamance County Architectural Heritage.* Graham, N.C.: Alamance County Historical Properties Commission, 1980.

———. "The Building Process in Antebellum North Carolina." *North Carolina Historical Review* 60, no. 4 (Oct. 1983): 431–56.

———. "The Development of Domestic Architecture in the Albemarle Region." *North Carolina Historical Review* 54, no. 1 (Jan. 1977): 17–48.

———. "From Craft to Industry: The Building Process in North Carolina in the Nineteenth Century." Ph.D. dissertation, George Washington University, 1983.

Lowe's Companies. *1986 Annual Report*, North Wilkesboro, 1986.

Lowe's Corporate History, undated, unpublished typescript, Public Relations Department, Lowe's Companies. Copy in files of Ernest H. Wood III.

Lowry, Charles B. "Class, Politics, Rebellion, and Regional Development in North Carolina in the Nineteenth Century." Ph.D. dissertation, University of Florida, 1979.

Ludwell, Philip. "Journal of the Boundary Line Proceedings, 1710." *The Virginia Magazine of History and Biography* 5, no. 1 (July 1897): 1–21.

Main, Jackson Turner. *The Social Structure of Revolutionary America.* Princeton: Princeton University Press, 1965.

Malone, Michael Taylor. "Levi Silliman Ives: Priest, Bishop, Tractarian, and Roman Catholic Convert." Ph.D. dissertation, Duke University, 1970.

Maloney's Charlotte City Directories. Atlanta: Maloney Directory Co., 1897–1900.

Mansell, Elizabeth. "American Tobacco Company Brick Storage Warehouses in Durham, North Carolina: 1897–1906." Master's thesis, University of North Carolina, 1980.

Manufactured Housing Institute. "Production of Mobile/Manufactured Homes by State, Jan.–Dec. 1988." Typescript. Arlington, Va., 1989.

———. "Shipment of Mobile/Manufactured Homes by State, Jan.–Dec. 1988." Typescript. Arlington, Va., 1989.

Martin, Charles E. *Hollybush: Folk Building and Social Change in an Appalachian Community.* Knoxville: University of Tennessee Press, 1984.

Marx, Leo. *The Machine in the Garden: Technology and the Pastoral Ideal in America.* New York: Oxford University Press, 1964.

Marzio, Peter C. "Carpentry in the Southern Colonies during the Eighteenth Century with Emphasis on Maryland and Virginia." *Winterthur Portfolio* 7 (1972): 230–50.

Mathews, Alice Elaine. *Society in Revolutionary North Carolina.* Raleigh: Archives and History, 1976.

Mattson, Richard L. *The History and Architecture of Nash County, North Carolina.* Nashville, N.C.: Nash County Planning Department, 1987.

McDonald, Forrest, and Grady McWhiney. "The South from Self-Sufficiency to Peonage: An Interpretation." *American Historical Review* 135, no. 5 (Dec. 1980): 1095–1111.

McGrath, Thomas. "Notes on the Manufacture of Hand-Made Bricks." *Association for Preservation Technology* 11, no. 3 (1979): 88–94.

McKee, Harley J. *Introduction to Early American Masonry.* Washington, D.C.: National Trust for Historic Preservation, 1973.

McKim, Mead, and White. *Recent Buildings Designed for Educational Institutions.* New York: Beck Engineering Co., 1936.

McLaurin, Melton A. "The Nineteenth Century North Carolina State Fair as a Social Institution." *North Carolina Historical Review* 59, no. 3 (July 1982): 213–29.

Merrens, H. Roy. *Colonial North Carolina in the Eighteenth Century: A Study in Historical Geography.* Chapel Hill: University of North Carolina Press, 1964.

Merritt, Raymond H. *Engineering in American Society 1850–1875.* Lexington: University of Kentucky, 1969.

Michael, Jack. "In a Manner and Fashion Suitable to Their Degree: Preliminary Investigation of the Material Culture of Early Rural Pennsylvania." *Working Papers from the Regional and Economic Research Center* 5 (1981): 1–83.

Milburn, Frank P. *Designs from the Work of Frank P. Milburn.* Columbia, S.C.: State Co., 1901.

———. *Designs from the Work of Frank P. Milburn.* Columbia, S.C.: State Co., 1903.

Milburn, Frank P., and Michael Heister. *Selections from the Work of Milburn, Heister & Co.* Columbia, S.C.: State Co., 1907.

Mohney, Kirk Franklin. *The Historic Architecture of Davie County, North Carolina.* Mocksville, N.C.: Davie County Historical Society, 1986.

Montgomery, Lizzie Wilson. *Sketches of Old Warrenton, North Carolina.* Raleigh: Edwards and Broughton, 1924. Reprint. Spartanburg, S.C.: The Reprint Co., 1984.

Moody, Robert. "Massachusetts Trade with Carolina, 1698–1709." *North Carolina Historical Review* 20, no. 1 (Jan. 1943): 43–53.

Moorhead, John L. *Construction in the Carolinas, 1920–1970.* Charlotte: Association of General Contractors, Carolinas Branch, 1970.

Morgan, Edmund. *American Slavery, American Freedom: The Ordeal of Colonial Virginia.* New York: W. W. Norton, 1975.

Morrill, Dan. "Edward Dilworth Latta: The Charlotte Consolidated Construction (1890–1925): Builders of a New South City." *North Carolina Historical Review* 62, no. 3 (July 1985): 293–316.

Morris, Richard B. *Government and Labor in Early America.* New York: Columbia University Press, 1946. Reprint. New York: Harper and Row, 1965.

Morrison, Hugh. *Early American Architecture.* New York: Oxford University Press, 1952.

Morrison, Mary Lane. *John S. Norris, Architect in Savannah, 1846–1860.* Savannah: Beehive Press, 1980.

Moss, Roger William, Jr. "Master Builders: A History of the Colonial Philadelphia Building Trades." Ph.D. dissertation, University of Delaware, 1972.

———. "The Origins of the Carpenters' Company of Philadelphia." In *Building Early America,* edited by Charles E. Peterson, 35–53. Radnor, Pa.: Chilton Book

Co. for the Carpenters' Co. of Philadelphia, 1976.

Moxon, Joseph. *Mechanick Exercises: Or the Doctrine of Handy-Work.* 3d ed. London: N.p., 1703.

Mullin, Gerald. *Flight and Rebellion: Slave Resistance in Eighteenth-Century Virginia.* New York: Oxford University Press, 1972.

Murray, Elizabeth Reid. *Wake: Capital County of North Carolina.* Vol. 1. Raleigh: Capital County Publishing Co., 1983.

Murtagh, William J. *Moravian Architecture and Town Planning.* Chapel Hill: University of North Carolina Press, 1967.

Nash, Gary B. *The Urban Crucible.* Cambridge: Harvard University Press, 1979.

Nathans, Sydney. *The Quest for Progress: The Way We Lived in North Carolina, 1870-1920.* Series edited by Sydney Nathans. Chapel Hill: University of North Carolina Press, 1983.

Neiman, Fraser. "Domestic Architecture at the Clifts Plantation: The Social Context of Early Building." *Northern Neck Historical Magazine* 28 (Dec. 1978): 3096–3128.

Nelson, William, ed. *Calendar of New Jersey Wills, 1670–1730.* Vol. 23 of *Documents Relating to the Colonial History of the State of New Jersey.* 1st ser. Paterson, N.J.: Press Printing and Publishing Co., 1901.

Neve, Richard. *The City and Country Purchaser's and Builder's Dictionary: Or the Complete Builder's Guide.* 3d ed. London: B. Sprint etc., 1736.

Newsome, Albert Ray. "Twelve North Carolina Counties in 1810–1811." *North Carolina Historical Review* 5, no. 4 (Oct. 1928): 413–46; 6, no. 1 (Jan. 1929): 67–99; 6, no. 2 (Apr. 1979): 171–89; 6, no. 3 (July 1929): 281–309.

Newton, Roger Hale. *Town & Davis, Architects.* New York: Columbia University Press, 1942.

Oates, John A. *The Story of Fayetteville.* 2d ed. Fayetteville: Fayetteville Woman's Club, 1972.

Olds, Fred. *Annual Report of the Chamber of Commerce and Industry.* Raleigh: Edwards and Broughton, 1910.

————. *Story of the Counties of North Carolina with Other Data.* Oxford, N.C.: Oxford Orphanage Press, 1921.

Olmsted, Frederick Law. *A Journey in the Seaboard States in the Years 1853–1854.* New York: Dix and Edwards, 1856.

Olton, Charles S. *Artisans for Independence, Philadelphia Mechanics and the American Revolution.* Syracuse, N.Y.: Syracuse University Press, 1975.

One Hundred Years' Progress of the United States. Hartford: L. Stebbins, 1871.

Outlaw, Alain C. "Governor's Land Archaeological Excavations: The 1976 Season." Research report, 1976, copy in Virginia Research Center for Archaeology, Yorktown.

Owsley, Frank Lawrence. *Plain Folk of the Old South.* Baton Rouge: Louisiana State University Press, 1982.

Park, Helen. *A List of Architectural Books Available in America before the Revolution.* Los Angeles: Hennessey and Ingalls, 1973.

Parker, Mattie Erma Edwards, ed. *North Carolina Higher-Court Records, 1670–1696.* Vol. 2 of *Colonial Records of North Carolina,* 2d ser. Raleigh: Archives and History, 1968.

_____. *North Carolina Higher-Court Records, 1697–1701*. Vol. 3 of *Colonial Records of North Carolina*, 2d ser. Raleigh: Archives and History, 1971.

Parramore, Thomas. *Cradle of the Colony: The History of Chowan County and Edenton, North Carolina*. Edenton: Chamber of Commerce, 1967.

_____. *Express Lanes and Country Roads: The Way We Lived in North Carolina, 1920–1970*. Series edited by Sydney Nathans. Chapel Hill: University of North Carolina Press, 1983.

_____. "The Tuscarora Ascendancy." *North Carolina Historical Review* 59, no. 4 (Oct. 1982): 307–86.

Patrick, James. *Architecture in Tennessee, 1768–1897*. Knoxville: University of Tennessee Press, 1981.

_____. "Ecclesiological Gothic in the Antebellum South." *Winterthur Portfolio* 15, no. 2 (Summer 1980): 117–38.

Paul, Hiram. *History of the Town of Durham, N.C.* Raleigh: Edwards and Broughton, 1884.

Pearce, Thilbert H. *Early Architecture of Franklin County*. Freeman, S.D.: Privately printed, 1977.

Peatross, C. Ford. *William Nichols, Architect*. Birmingham: University of Alabama Art Gallery, 1979.

Penny, Norman, ed. *The Journal of George Fox*. 2 vols. New York: Octagon Books, 1973.

Peterson, Charles E. "Early Lumbering." In *Material Culture of the Wooden Age*, edited by Brooke Hindle, 63–84. Tarrytown, N.Y.: Sleepy Hollow Press, 1981.

_____, ed. *Building Early America: Contributions toward the History of a Great Industry*. Radnor, Pa.: Chilton Book Co., 1976.

_____. *The Rules of Work of the Carpenters' Company of the City and County of Philadelphia, 1786*. Philadelphia: Bell Publishing Co., 1978.

Phillips, Laura A. W. *Simple Treasures: The Architectural Legacy of Surry County*. Winston-Salem: Surry County Historical Society, 1987.

Pierce, Donald C., and Hope Alswang. *American Interiors: New England and the South, Period Rooms at the Brooklyn Museum*. New York: Brooklyn Museum, 1983.

Pierson, William H., Jr. *American Buildings and Their Architects: The Colonial and Neoclassical Styles*. Garden City: Anchor Press, Doubleday, 1976.

_____. "Richard Upjohn and the American Rundbogenstil." *Winterthur Portfolio* 21, no. 4 (Winter 1986): 223–42.

Powell, William S., ed. *The Correspondence of William Tryon and Other Selected Papers*. 2 vols. Raleigh: Archives and History, 1980.

_____. *Dictionary of North Carolina Biography*. 3 vols. to date. Chapel Hill: University of North Carolina Press, 1979– .

_____. *The First State University: A Pictorial History of the University of North Carolina*. Chapel Hill: University of North Carolina Press, 1972.

_____. *A History of Caswell County, 1777–1977*. Durham: Moore Publishing Co., 1977.

_____. *Ye Countie of Albemarle in Carolina*. Raleigh: Archives and History, 1958.

Price, William S., Jr., ed. *North Carolina Higher-Court Records, 1702–1709*. Vol. 4 of *Colonial Records of North Carolina*, 2d ser. Raleigh: Archives and History, 1974.

_____. *North Carolina Higher-Court Records, 1709–1723*. Vol. 5 of *Colonial Records of*

North Carolina, 2d ser. Raleigh: Archives and History, 1977.

Proceedings of the Stockholders of the Raleigh and Gaston Railroad. Raleigh: Edwards and Broughton, 1882.

Quimby, Ian M. G. *Apprenticeship in Colonial Philadelphia*. New York: Garland Publishing Co., 1985.

———, ed. *The Craftsman in Early America*. New York: W. W. Norton, 1984.

Rahtz, P. A., J. T. Smith, Guy Beresford, and P. A. Barker. "Architectural Reconstruction of Timber Buildings from Archaeological Evidence." *Vernacular Architecture* 13 (1982): 39–47.

Raleigh Directory, 1880–81. Raleigh: Edwards and Broughton, 1879.

Raleigh: Epitome of the City's Growth and Progress and Industries. Raleigh: Edwards and Broughton, 1907.

Raleigh Illustrated. Raleigh: Edwards and Broughton, 1910.

Ramsbotham, Ann, and Pam Farmer. "Women Working: The Building Trades Begin to Open Up." *Southern Exposure*, Spring 1980, 37–39.

Ramsey, Robert W. *Carolina Cradle: Settlement of the Northwest Carolina Frontier, 1747–1762*. Chapel Hill: University of North Carolina Press, 1964.

Ranlett, William. *The Architect*. 2 vols. New York: DeWitt and Davenport, 1849.

Rapoport, Amos. *House Form and Culture*. Englewood Cliffs, N.J.: Prentice-Hall, 1969.

Rasmussen, William M. S. "Designers, Builders, and Architectural Traditions in Colonial Virginia." *The Virginia Magazine of History and Biography* 90, no. 2 (Apr. 1982): 198–212.

Reynolds, Gregory T. " 'Hope,' the House that David Stone Built." Research paper, 1976, copy in Survey and Planning Branch, Archives and History, Raleigh.

Richards, John. *A Treatise on the Construction and Operation of Woodworking Machines*. London: E. and F. N. Spon, 1872.

Riley, Jack. *Carolina Power and Light Company: A Corporate Biography*. Raleigh: Edwards and Broughton, 1958.

Robbins, D. P. *Descriptive Sketch of Winston-Salem*. Salem: Sentinel Job Printing, 1888.

Robinson, W. A., et al. "Thomas Day and His Family." *Negro History Bulletin* 13 (Mar. 1950): 123–26, 140.

Rock, Howard. *Artisans of the New Republic: The Tradesmen of New York City in the Age of Jefferson*. New York: New York University Press, 1979.

Rose, W. P. *That House*. Raleigh: Edwards and Broughton, 1900.

Roth, Leland M. *A Concise History of American Architecture*. New York: Harper and Row, 1979.

Rouse, J. K. *Historical Shadows of Cabarrus County, North Carolina*. Charlotte: Crabtree Press, 1970.

Rutman, Darrett B., and Anita H. Rutman. *A Place in Time: Middlesex County, Virginia, 1650–1750*. New York: W. W. Norton, 1984.

Salinger, Sharon V. "Artisans, Journeymen, and the Transformation of Labor in Late Eighteenth-Century Philadelphia." *The William and Mary Quarterly*, 3d ser., 40, no. 1 (Jan. 1983): 62–84.

Salzman, L. F. *Building in England Down to 1540: A Documentary History*. Oxford: Clarendon Press, 1952.

Sandbeck, Peter B. *The Historic Architecture of New Bern and Craven County, North Carolina.* New Bern: Tryon Palace Commission, 1988.

Sanders, John L. "The North Carolina State Capitol of 1840." *The Magazine Antiques,* Sept. 1985, 474–84.

———. "The North Carolina State House and Capitol, 1792–1872." Research report, 1972, copy in Restoration Branch, Archives and History, Raleigh.

———. "The State Capitol: A Tourguide." Typescript, 1977, State Capitol/Visitor Services Section, Archives and History, Raleigh.

———. " 'This Political Temple, the Capitol of North Carolina.' " *Popular Government* 43, no. 2 (Fall 1977): 1–10.

Saunders, William L., ed. *The Colonial Records of North Carolina.* 10 vols. Raleigh: State of North Carolina, 1886–90.

Schimmelman, Janice G. *Architectural Treatises and Building Handbooks Available in American Libraries and Bookstores through 1800.* Worcester: American Antiquarian Society, 1986.

Schlotterbeck, John T. "The 'Social Economy' of an Upper South Community: Orange and Greene Counties, Virginia, 1815–1860." In *Class, Conflict, and Consensus: Antebellum Southern Community Studies,* edited by Orville Burton and Robert C. McMath, Jr., 3–28. Westport, Conn.: Greenwood Press, 1982.

Schoepf, Johann David. *Travels in the Confederation, 1783–1784.* 2 vols. New York: Burt Franklin, 1968.

Seapker, Janet K. "James F. Post, Builder-Architect: The Legend and the Ledger." *Lower Cape Fear Historical Society, Inc., Bulletin* 30, no. 3 (May 1987): 1–7.

Second and Third Annual Reports of the President and Directors of the Fayetteville and Western Plank Road Company. Fayetteville: E. J. Hale and Son, 1852.

Sims, Anastatia. "The King House of Bertie County." Research report, 1976, Research Branch, Archives and History, Raleigh.

Skemer, Don C. "David Alling's Chair Manufactory: Craft Industrialization in Newark, New Jersey, 1801–1854." *Winterthur Portfolio* 22, no. 1 (Spring 1987): 1–21.

Sloan, Samuel. *The Model Architect.* Philadelphia: E. S. Jones and Co., 1852. Reprinted as *Sloan's Victorian Buildings,* introduction by Harold Cooledge. New York: Dover Publications, 1980.

Smith, Darrell Hevenor. *The Office of the Supervising Architect of the Treasury.* Baltimore: Johns Hopkins University Press, 1923.

Smith, Francis. *New Brick Machine.* Baltimore: N.p., 1857.

Smith, H. McKelden. *Architectural Resources: An Inventory of Historic Architecture. High Point, Jamestown, Gibsonville, Guilford County.* Raleigh: Archives and History, 1979.

Smith, Michael. *North Carolina Furniture, 1700–1900.* Raleigh: North Carolina Museum of History, 1977.

Smyth, J. F. D. *A Tour of the United States of America.* 2 vols. Dublin, 1784. Reprint. New York: Arno Press, Inc., 1968.

South, Stanley A. "Russellborough: Two Royal Governors' Mansion at Brunswick Town." *North Carolina Historical Review* 44, no. 4 (Oct. 1967): 367.

Southern, Michael T. "The I-House as a Carrier of Style." In *Carolina Dwelling,* edited by Doug Swaim, 72–83. Raleigh: North Carolina State University School of Design Student Publication, 1978.

Spillane, R. "Men and Mills of Greensboro." *Commerce and Finance*, Nov. 1923, 2112–22.

Sprague, Paul. "The Origins of Balloon Framing." *Journal of the Society of Architectural Historians* 40, no. 4 (Dec. 1981): 311–19.

Starling, Robert. "The Plank Road Movement in North Carolina." Master's thesis, University of North Carolina, 1938.

Stautzenberger, Anthony Joseph. *The Establishment of the Charlotte Branch Mint: A Documented History*. Austin: Privately printed, 1976.

Stavisky, Leonard. "The Origins of Negro Craftsmanship in Colonial America." *The Journal of Negro History* 32 (July 1947): 417–29. Reprinted in *The Other Slaves: Mechanics, Artisans and Craftsmen*, edited by James E. Newton and Ronald L. Lewis, 183–91. Boston: G. K. Hall and Co., 1978.

St. George, Robert Blair. "Fathers, Sons and Identity: Woodworking Artisans in Southeastern New England, 1620–1700." In *The Craftsman in Early America*, edited by Ian M. G. Quimby. New York: W. W. Norton, 1984.

Stilgoe, John R. *Common Landscape of America, 1580 to 1845*. New Haven: Yale University Press, 1982.

Summerson, John. *Architecture in Britain, 1530 to 1830*. 6th ed., rev. New York: Penguin Books, 1977.

_____. *Georgian London*. Cambridge: MIT Press, 1978.

Surratt, Jerry L. "The Role of Dissent in Community Evolution among Moravians in Salem, 1772–1860." *North Carolina Historical Review* 52, no. 3 (July 1975): 235–55.

Swaim, Douglas, ed. *Cabins and Castles: The History and Architecture of Buncombe County, North Carolina*. Asheville: City of Asheville, County of Buncombe, Archives and History, 1981.

_____, ed. *Carolina Dwelling*. Raleigh: North Carolina State University School of Design Student Publication, 1978.

Sweeney, Kevin M. "Mansion People: Kinship, Class, and Architecture in Western Massachusetts in the Mid-Eighteenth Century." *Winterthur Portfolio* 19, no. 4 (Winter 1984): 231–56.

Taylor, Gwynne Stephens. *From Frontier to Factory: An Architectural History of Forsyth County*. Winston-Salem: Winston-Salem/Forsyth County Historic Properties Commission and Archives and History, 1981.

Terrill, Tom, and Jerrold Hirsch. *Such as Us: Southern Voices of the Thirties*. Chapel Hill: University of North Carolina Press, 1978.

Thorp, Daniel B. "Assimilation in North Carolina's Moravian Community." *Journal of Southern History* 52, no. 1 (Feb. 1986): 19–42.

_____. "The City That Never Was." *North Carolina Historical Review* 61, no. 1 (Jan. 1984): 36–58.

Tiffany, Nina Moore, ed. *Letters of James Murray, Loyalist*. Boston: Gregg Press, 1972.

Tilley, Nannie May. *The Bright-Tobacco Industry 1860–1929*. Chapel Hill: University of North Carolina Press, 1948.

_____. "Industries of Colonial Granville County." *North Carolina Historical Review* 13, no. 4 (Oct. 1936): 273–89.

Tindall, George Brown. *The Emergence of the New South, 1913–1945.* Baton Rouge: Louisiana State University, 1967.

Tishler, William H. "Fachwerk Construction in the German Settlements of Wisconsin." *Winterthur Portfolio* 21, no. 4 (Winter 1986): 275–92.

Todd, V. H., and J. Goebel, eds. *Christoph Von Graffenried's Account of the Founding of New Bern.* Raleigh: North Carolina Historical Commission, 1920.

Tomlan, Michael A. "Toward the Growth of an Artistic Taste." Introduction to George F. Barber, *Cottage Souvenir #2.* Watkins Glen, N.Y.: American Life Foundation and Study Institute, 1982.

Touart, Paul Baker. "The Acculturation of German-American Building Practices of Davidson County, North Carolina." In *Perspectives in Vernacular Architecture, II,* edited by Camille Wells, 72–80. Columbia: University of Missouri Press for the Vernacular Architecture Forum, 1986.

_____. *Building the Back Country: An Architectural History of Davidson County, North Carolina.* Lexington, N.C.: Davidson County Historical Society, 1987.

Upton, Dell. "Early Vernacular Architecture in Southeastern Virginia." Ph.D. dissertation, Brown University, 1980.

_____. *Holy Things and Profane: Anglican Parish Churches in Colonial Virginia.* Cambridge: MIT Press, 1986.

_____. "Pattern Books and Professionalism: Aspects of the Transformation of Domestic Architecture in America, 1800–1860." *Winterthur Portfolio* 19, nos. 2/3 (Summer/Autumn 1984): 107–50.

_____. "Traditional Timber Framing." In *Material Culture of the Wooden Age,* edited by Brooke Hindle, 35–93. Tarrytown, N.Y.: Sleepy Hollow Press, 1981.

_____. "Vernacular Domestic Architecture in Eighteenth-Century Virginia." *Winterthur Portfolio* 17, nos. 2/3 (Summer/Autumn 1982): 95–119.

_____, ed. *America's Architectural Roots: Ethnic Groups That Built America.* Washington, D.C.: Preservation Press, 1986.

Upton, Dell, and John Michael Vlach, eds. *Common Places: Readings in American Vernacular Architecture.* Athens: University of Georgia Press, 1986.

Wagstaff, H. M., ed. *The Papers of John Steele.* Vol. 1. Raleigh: North Carolina Historical Commission, 1924.

Wallace, Wesley H. "North Carolina's Agricultural Journals 1838–1862: A Crusading Press." *North Carolina Historical Review* 36, no. 3 (July 1959): 275–306.

Walsh, Lorena, and Russell R. Menard. "Death in the Chesapeake: Two Life Tables for Men in Early Colonial Maryland." *Maryland Historical Magazine* 69, no. 2 (Summer 1974): 169–84.

Walsh, Richard. *Charleston's Sons of Liberty: A Study of the Artisans, 1763–1789.* Columbia: University of South Carolina Press, 1959.

Warren, James Robert. "History in Towns, Wilmington, North Carolina." *The Magazine Antiques,* Dec. 1980, 1251–66.

Watson, Alan D. *Money and Monetary Problems in Early North Carolina.* Raleigh: Archives and History, 1980.

_____. *Society in Colonial North Carolina.* Raleigh: Archives and History, 1975.

Watson, Elgiva D. "The Pursuit of Pride: Cultural Attitudes in North Carolina, 1830–1861." Ph.D. dissertation, University of North Carolina, 1972.

Watson, Harry. *An Independent People: The Way We Lived in North Carolina, 1770–*

1820. Series edited by Sydney Nathans. Chapel Hill: University of North Carolina Press, 1983.

————. *Jacksonian Politics and Community Conflict: The Emergence of the Second American Party System in Cumberland County, North Carolina.* Baton Rouge: Louisiana State University Press, 1981.

————. "'Old Rip' and a New Era." In *The North Carolina Experience*, edited by Lindley S. Butler and Alan D. Watson, 217–40. Chapel Hill: University of North Carolina Press, 1984.

————. "Squire Oldway and His Friends: Opposition to Internal Improvements in Antebellum North Carolina." *North Carolina Historical Review* 54, no. 2 (Apr. 1977): 105–20.

Waugh, Elizabeth Culbertson. "Firm in an Ivied Tower." *North Carolina Architect*, Jan./Feb. 1971, 10–28.

————. *North Carolina's Capital, Raleigh.* Chapel Hill: University of North Carolina Press, 1967.

Weaver, William Woys. "The Pennsylvania German House: European Antecedents and New World Forms." *Winterthur Portfolio* 21, no. 4 (Winter 1986): 243–65.

Wells, Camille. *Canton: The Architecture of Our Home Town.* Canton, N.C.: Canton Historical Commission, 1985.

————, ed. *Perspectives in Vernacular Architecture, I.* Annapolis, Md.: Vernacular Architecture Forum, 1982.

————. *Perspectives in Vernacular Architecture, II.* Columbia: University of Missouri Press for the Vernacular Architecture Forum, 1986.

Whiffen, Marcus. *The Eighteenth-Century Houses of Williamsburg.* Williamsburg: The Colonial Williamsburg Foundation, 1960.

————. *The Public Buildings of Williamsburg.* Williamsburg: The Colonial Williamsburg Foundation, 1958.

Whitehead, Russell F. "Some Work of Aymar Embury, II in the Sandhills of North Carolina." *Architectural Record* 55 (June 1924): 505–68.

Whitworth, Henry P., ed. *Carolina Architecture and Allied Arts.* Miami: Frederick Findiesen, 1939.

————. *Carolina Architecture and Allied Arts.* Miami: Frederick Findiesen, 1940.

————. *Carolina Architecture and Allied Arts.* Miami: Frederick Findiesen, 1942.

Who's Who in the South. Washington, D.C.: Mayflower Publishing Co., 1927.

Wight, Jane. *Brick Building in England from the Middle Ages to 1550.* London: Humanities Press, 1972.

Wilentz, Sean. *Chants Democratic: New York and the Rise of the American Working Class, 1788–1850.* New York: Oxford University Press, 1984.

"William Logan's Journal of a Journey to Georgia, 1745." *Pennsylvania Magazine of History and Biography* 36 (1912): 1–16, 162–86.

Williams, Isabel M. "Thalian Hall." Research report, copy in Restoration Branch, Archives and History, Raleigh, n.d.

Williams, Michael Ann. *Marble and Log: The History and Architecture of Cherokee County, North Carolina.* Murphy, N.C.: Cherokee County Historical Museum, 1984.

Wilson, Louis R. *The University of North Carolina, 1900–1930.* Chapel Hill: University of North Carolina Press, 1957.

Wodehouse, Lawrence. "Architecture in North Carolina." *North Carolina Architect*,

Nov./Dec. 1969, and Jan./Feb. 1970.

_____. "The Elusive William Percival, Architect." Typescript, copy in Historical Publications Section, Archives and History, Raleigh, n.d.

_____. "Frank Pierce Milburn (1868–1926), a Major Southern Architect." *North Carolina Historical Review* 50, no. 3 (July 1973): 289–303.

Wolf, Jacquelyn H. "Patents and Tithables in Proprietary North Carolina." *North Carolina Historical Review* 56, no. 3 (July 1979): 263–77.

Wood, Ernest, III. "A Radical Settles Down in Raleigh, N.C." *AIA Journal*, Sept. 1980, 54–61.

Wood, Peter H. *Black Majority*. New York: Alfred A. Knopf, 1974.

Woodward, C. Vann. *The Strange Career of Jim Crow*. 3d rev. ed. New York: Oxford University Press, 1974.

Worsley, Stephen C. "Catholicism in Antebellum North Carolina." *North Carolina Historical Review* 60, no. 4 (Oct. 1983): 399–430.

Wrenn, Tony P. *Wilmington, North Carolina: An Architectural and Historical Portrait*. Charlottesville: University Press of Virginia, 1984.

York, Maurice C. "The Many Faces of Fort Defiance." Research report, 1979, copy in Research Branch, Archives and History, Raleigh.

Index